The

AUDACITY
OF HOPS

The History of America's Craft Beer Revolution

REVISED AND EXPANDED EDITION

TOM ACITELLI

CHICAGO
REVIEW
PRESS

Copyright © 2017 by Tom Acitelli
All rights reserved
Second edition
Published by Chicago Review Press, Incorporated
814 North Franklin Street
Chicago, Illinois 60610
ISBN 978-1-51373-708-8

Cover design: Jonathan Hahn
Cover photographs: Michael Halberstadt
Typesetting: Nord Compo

Library of Congress has cataloged the previous edition as follows
Library of Congress Cataloging-in-Publication Data
Acitelli, Tom.
The audacity of hops: the history of America's craft beer revolution / Tom
Acitelli.
—First edition. pages cm
Summary: "Charting the birth and growth of craft beer across the United
States, Tom Acitelli offers an epic, story-driven account of one of the
most inspiring and surprising American grassroots movements. In 1975,
there was a single craft brewery in the United States; today there are more
than 2,000. Now this once-fledgling movement has become ubiquitous
nationwide—there's even a honey ale brewed at the White House. This
book not only tells the stories of the major figures and businesses within
the movement, but it also ties in the movement with larger American
culinary developments. It also charts the explosion of the mass-market
craft beer culture, including magazines, festivals, home brewing, and
more. This entertaining and informative history brims with charming,
remarkable stories, which together weave a very American business tale of
formidable odds and refreshing success"—Provided by publisher.
Includes bibliographical references and index. ISBN 978-1-61374-388-1 (pbk.)
1. Beer—United States. I. Title.
TP573.U5A25 2013 641.2'3—dc23
2013002264

Printed in the United States of America
5 4 3 2 1

"A book for the craft beer nerd who thinks he or she already knows the st
—*Los Angeles Times*

"This book is a delightful read, painstakingly researched, often humorous, and filled with stories that breathe life into the birth of our industry."
—David L. Geary, president of D. L. Geary Brewing Company

"Journalist and beer-lover Acitelli's exceptional document of this remarkable growth profiles the brewers, breweries, and brewhounds that have played a part in today's booming craft beer industry... It's an ingenious means of telling a story with so many influential characters, and Acitelli pulls it off, with an eye for detail and a nose for drama."
—*Publishers Weekly*

"*The Audacity of Hops* chronicles the rich history of America's craft brewing revolution with deft portraits of the resourceful pioneers, the innovative brewers, and the intrepid entrepreneurs who are changing the way the world thinks about beer."
—Steve Hindy, cofounder of Brooklyn Brewery
and coauthor of *Beer School*

"Excellent history."

—*Slate*

"Tom's narrative threads moments of insider anecdote with a historian's vision of what makes growing, outsider movements so dynamic, meaning-ful, and, in our case, delicious. An important achievement."
—Jeremy Cowan, author of *Craft Beer Bar Mitzvah*
and proprietor of Shmaltz Brewing

Once again, to my parents

CONTENTS

PART III

PART IV

FOREWORD

Everything Comes from Somewhere
by Tony Magee

I magine that you're sitting at the bar in an ale hall on a crowded street and you're sipping your favorite beer, maybe it's a stout or a brown ale or an IPA or possibly a richer style of pilsner—there are more than a few styles to choose from. The beers aren't brewed with corn or rice and the alcohol content is meaningful.

Imagine that there are about twelve thousand Americans for every brewery and that the average size of those breweries is pretty small, say about fifteen thousand barrels . . . Maybe you'd call them microbreweries or, worse yet, maybe you'd call them craft breweries, but, either way, you'd be way, way ahead of your time. The symmetries are somewhat calming. What year do you think it is? 2016?

Maybe, but it could also be 1870, which is what year it was when it was like that.

We all think of the "small brewing" of big beers to be a revolution in the world of beer and it is, in the sense that in revolution there is eternal recurrence, a wheel that revolves, goes around and around and the history of which will always repeat itself, albeit with small oscillations in the orbit of the thing in motion.

We American small brewers have brought our own oscillation in the form of community, but also in flavor via the endless research of a couple of folks in Yakima, Washington, working in relative obscurity developing hops whose flavors and aromas are new under the sun. These flavors have been exploited by us small brewers in ways that were not originally anticipated by their creator, yet those aspects of their creation have changed the palate of, first, US beer lovers and, more recently, beer lovers in the other twenty-one time zones in circuit around the planet.

So there is revolution, symmetry, orbit, procession, and eternal recurrence; all of which are arcs creating cycles over time, populated by events, or points, on a curve. Every moment in life and every moment in small brewing since Fritz Maytag rescued Anchor Brewing from its terminal chapter in brewing history are points on a curve.

It's complicated business, points on a curve are. It involves a thing called calculus. Since points on a curve only exist in time, they are fleeting things to calculate precisely and so it takes an approximation to describe them accurately with respect to their locus and rate of change in velocity, which takes into account their speed and direction, a thing distinct from their description. But what's it all got to do with beer? Everything. Am I wrong? I say no.

One good brewer out of Washington, itself on a point on the curve of small brewing, made a delicious pale ale during the early 1990s that sported a nearly cherrywood hue. It was delicious and I drank a lot of it at my brother's 1990 wedding in PDX. So did a lot of other Portlanders. The beer was a popular one locally. It seemed for all the world that that cherrywood was the new color of a pale ale and who was to say that it wasn't?

Historically, the textbooks said that *antiquitous* pale ales could easily be that dark due to the inaccuracies of thermometers way back when. There were other brewers making pale ales and the colors varied like the textbooks said they might. However, the future is a curve and never a straight line from any one point forward.

These straight lines are called tangents and you know what it means to go off on a tangent; it means to become irrelevant. Honest brewers find something special they can brew and they then proceed straight ahead from their point on the curve (following a tangent), and the curve bears away from the line they are pursuing. So it was for the cherrywood version of a pale ale because another contemporary brewer would become dominant in the world of pale ales and, as it rose in popularity, its own lighter straw-colored brew would become what was expected of a pale ale. There are thousands of stories like that one. Darwin is anything but nostalgic.

Thus is the tyranny of life on a curve. The difference between relevance and irrelevance isn't so much about doing one thing well as it is about being connected to the environmental rate of change and aligning your own rate of change with that of your environment.

It's a tall order. They say that a fish doesn't really know what water is. The fish knows what NOT water is, but the water of its world is invisible. For us brewers, being connected to the changing water of our environment is job No. 1. The founder of a great brewery in Newport, Oregon, once said it concisely: "We are in the change business."

Change requires steering, and steering a company, even a smallish one, is difficult. Steering an organization, a brewery, means fighting inertia to create change. That force must come from somewhere. Will; plain-old willpower. The will of the person at the helm of that organization, combined with the willingness of the organization to follow. That is the source of that force and one has to hold the attention and imagination of an organization to stay on the curve.

Momentum is the goal of every business and it is also the enemy of change. Momentum is usually thought of as a resource, but it can work against you—the perils of benefactors and the blessings of parasites. In any case, summoning that amount of will year after year is exhausting.

Maybe even impossible. Better to cheat the system and tap the possibilities within the change environment and be wrong and irrelevant in the present in exchange for the possibility of being right and relevant in a larger future, once the curve of the future catches up with you, if only for a short time. So it's interesting that in a parabolic environment, the inevitability of tangential trajectories present opportunities as well. Such is the slippery world my brewery has experienced and such is the elusive history addressed in this book. It's dizzying.

Tom Acitelli's first edition of this book charted, as accurately as was possible, the shape-shifting five-dimensional hyperbolic topology of small brewing better than any before. His approach was almost forensic, in a good way. He sliced through the press releases and company statements and revealed the inside baseball/backstage version of the story of American small brewing.

Everyone knows Bob Dylan and Eric Clapton, while their inspirations— Maybelle Carter and Sonny Boy Williamson, for instance—remain more obscure. Everything comes from somewhere. With this update, Tom explores the recent period of shape-shifting, five-dimensional hyperbolic-ness, bringing it into the context of history, and, in doing so, helps make sense of it all.

He does this by combining the steely eyed focus of a journalist with the thinly veiled enthusiasm of a beer-geek's recalcitrance. The less-than-visible threads and interactions that were and are the neural pathways of learning, inspiration, and action in US small brewing are revealed through Tom's research.

When I think of our experience over the last twenty-five years it all seems chaotic, desperate, clutching—you know . . . anything but orderly. Reading a book like this one makes it all seem noble and pioneering and even worthy . . .

I will lobby for Bill Murray to play me in the movie version of this book, or Tim Roth. I dunno. Maybe Paul Rubens. Definitely not DiCaprio.

Tony Magee
Founder and chairman of the Lagunitas Brewing Company
November 2016

AUTHOR'S NOTE

When I finished the first edition of *The Audacity of Hops* in late 2012, there were approximately twenty-four hundred breweries in the United States. The vast majority were smaller craft breweries making beer from more traditional ingredients with more traditional methods. At the end of 2015, the number of breweries crested forty-one hundred—more than at any time in the nation's history and a nearly 60 percent increase from just three years before. Like in 2012, most were craft breweries. In 2012, five states had more than one hundred craft breweries each. Three years later, fifteen did.

What's more, statistics that the Brewers Association trade group released as this book was going to press showed that the number of American breweries had leaped once more in 2016, tipping to more than five thousand before December of that year. Again, nearly all were craft breweries, and sixteen states now had more than one hundred such operations each.

At the same time as the number of craft breweries dramatically increased, so did their market share. In 2012, craft breweries hauled in perhaps 6.5 percent of the dollars spent on beer in the United States. In 2015, the latest figures showed that that share had more than doubled. By the end of 2015, craft beer claimed more than one-fifth of the $105.9 billion domestic beer market, with its growth in dollar volume outpacing that of the macrobreweries that produce brands such as Budweiser and Miller Lite. Simply put, craft breweries were gaining, slowly but steadily, on their much bigger rivals. (The largest craft breweries might produce a few million barrels of beer annually, while macrobreweries turn out tens of millions just in the United States.)

Hard numbers aside, there has been ample anecdotal evidence of the growth of craft beer recently. To name just a few examples since 2012: the rise of the beer-sharing social media app Untappd; the debut of the TV show *Brew Dogs*;

the legalization of homebrewing in all fifty states, Mississippi and Alabama having been the last holdouts; the minting of three craft brewers as bona fide billionaires; the billion-dollar sale of at least one craft brewery (and the multi-million-dollar sales of several others); the Smithsonian's announcement of a permanent exhibit dedicated to brewing, particularly craft brewing; and the opening in Europe of US-based craft breweries that had once struggled to stay in business locally.

In short, craft beer has arrived. It has attained in just the past few years a cultural and economic presence that would have been unthinkable a short while ago. Even in 2012 and 2013, when I was doing publicity for the first edition of *The Audacity of Hops*, the questions from media as disparate as the BBC and Fox News were understandably basic: what is craft beer, why is it popular, who drinks it, etc. (When I did publicity for a fine wine history a couple of years later, no one ever asked me to explain Merlot—the popularity of it and other wine varieties was a given.) Craft beer itself and the people behind it were still largely seen as curiosities measured against the larger beer monoculture that Anheuser-Busch and other Big Beer operations had established shortly after World War II. Or craft beer was seen as the playground of a few better-known brands such as Sierra Nevada or Samuel Adams.

Not anymore. The sheer number of breweries now, their market share, and the media coverage that has attended this growth ensures that more Americans than ever realize just how big this thing has gotten. When President Barack Obama drank a honey ale, homebrewed at the White House, on national television in February 2015, most who commented noted the novelty of a president drinking alcohol on TV, not the beer he drank—such a thing didn't seem so exotic anymore.

This book is the most complete telling yet of how America and its craft beer got to this point. It covers all the major personalities and pivots, the triumphs and the tribulations. It includes fresh research on major turning points during the past fifty-plus years and the many goings-on since 2012. Indeed, the statistics and the anecdotes above are from just the past few years. Delve back to 2000 or 1980 or 1960, and the story of American craft beer's success becomes even more dramatic and improbable. There were perhaps five craft breweries by 1980 and fewer than twenty-five years later, all concentrated at either time in a handful of states and each holding on precariously in a rapidly consolidating industry where it seemed only the strong—and the bland—would survive. After all, analysts by the mid-1980s were predicting one or two American breweries total by the twenty-first century.

That did not happen. Not by a long shot. And here's why.

Prologue

AMERICA, KING OF BEER

Turin, Italy; Paris; Washington, DC | 2009–2010

It was the last week in October 2010, cloudy and cool, and hundreds of thousands of people were streaming toward the Olympic Village in Turin, a united Italy's first capital in the 1860s and the ancestral home of the nation's royal family until after World War II. History had everything and nothing to do with the reason the crowds were gathering: Salone del Gusto, the biannual trade show and tribal gathering of Slow Food, the international movement that grew out of a 1986 protest in Rome over Italy's first McDonald's. Slow Food's show, like the movement itself, was a middle finger to homogenization and mass production. It meant to highlight locally produced, communally enjoyed foodstuffs: cheeses, fish, jams, oils, meats, nuts, legumes, wine, honey, bread—and beer.

The last one was a bit of a surprise to me. The surprise was not that there was beer at the show, but that most of the beer came from Italy, a nation known more in the same breath as France for its varied wines. These included the drier Barolo and Barbera of the north; the heavier, lusher central Italian wines like the Montepulciano in Abruzzo; and the sweeter Nero d'Avola and Marsala of Sicily. Italian beer, though? Whoever heard of the porters of Florence? Or the pale ales of Bologna? The pilsners of Reggio di Calabria? Wrong part of Europe, *signore*, surely—it was supposed to be all blandly industrial Peroni and Moretti. But there they were: Italian-made craft beers, tasting in their complexity and depth very much like the American-made ones I could find back home then in Brooklyn.

I would learn that those American craft beers had had a profound influence on the nascent Italian craft beer movement in the 1990s and 2000s, as had American beer figures at that 2010 Salone del Gusto like Sam Calagione, a brewer whom I recognized from an epically detailed *New Yorker* profile published two years before, and Charlie Papazian, an author whom I had just seen at the Great American Beer Festival (GABF) in Denver the previous month. They were on a panel together about American influences on Italian beer, where their observations prattled through several near-instantaneous translations into dozens of earphones in a college classroom–like setting.

It was a curious thing: American influence on another country's beer. I knew enough about the topic already to know that that was not a small thing: America had never been anyone's influence on beer . . . unless it was to mimic the engineering behind the watery lagers of what I'll call Big Beer: Budweiser, Coors, Miller, and others. These were admirable engineering triumphs, with millions of bottles and cans tasting the same no matter where they were made or how far they were shipped. But these beers did not influence the ones at Slow Food. Those beers were American craft beers—and American craft beers had never been bigger. Nor had the beer culture that had grown up around them.

That same European trip, I discovered what's considered the best beer store in Paris. Here, in the capital of another traditional wine country, the store's owner told me in frank English that he would be willing to trade bottle for bottle his European beers for any American ones I might be able to bring over on subsequent visits. He knew plenty about American craft beer, including the popular styles and the brewers themselves, but couldn't readily get them in France. He motioned resignedly to a far corner of the store where, in and around wooden crates, rested several bottles of only one American craft brand. There was, he explained, demand for so many more.

The year before my trip, all of America was enveloped in a heated debate surrounding beer: the White House Beer Summit. It sprang from the arrest of Harvard historian Henry Louis Gates Jr. in his home by Cambridge, Massachusetts, police sergeant James Crowley. President Obama had commented on the arrest in Gates's favor, and the commentariat demanded a sit-down between the parties, plus vice president Joe Biden. The president chose to hold the meeting over that most sacred of national drinks, beer, and the debate soon pivoted to not only what the parties would say when they sat down at the White House but also what they would drink. They had so many choices.

It is impossible to overstate how far beer in America has come in just the last two generations. The nation's five biggest breweries by 1970 together produced nearly half of all of America's commercially available beer. That number would crest 85 percent by the 1990s, though the number of breweries in the market share would actually shrink. Big Beer's brew was deliberately insipid and inoffensive, what one craft brewer explained as "alcoholic soda pop." It was engineered, to wallop and not to wow, in gigantic factories: Anheuser-Busch's headquarters in St. Louis grew to cover the equivalent of sixty city blocks, or roughly 125 acres. It was also phenomenally popular. By the middle of the twentieth century, Americans were drinking an average of twenty-one gallons of beer per person per year, up from around eighteen gallons before Prohibition. A sizable part of this success was not only the engineering but other technological advances such as the Interstate Highway System, the aluminum can, and the television. It was also due to a largely no-fault divorce between consumers and foodstuffs. Beer had once been an intensely local thing: hundreds of breweries in dozens of cities dotting the landscape before Prohibition in 1920, shipping their fare not that far from where it was brewed. These regional breweries, and even smaller local ones, died off one by one as beer, like other American industries after World War II (accounting, snack foods, media, computer manufacturing, soda, you name it), experienced a convulsion of consolidation.

By 1965, there was one craft brewery in the entire United States: the Anchor Brewing Company in San Francisco. The reach of its beers, though, did not extend beyond California. It would have no company, either, for years—a veritable culinary freak show in an increasingly homogenized American food landscape. Then, within thirty years, the number of American craft breweries increased more than 500 percent. Not only that, but these breweries were widely acknowledged—even by the Northern Europeans, who were the heirs to just about every beer style we know—as the most innovative, if not the best, in the world. Simply put, within two generations, America came to dominate the way we think, talk, and write about beer, never mind drink it.

This book will explain how that happened. It will not only tell the history of the American craft beer movement from 1965 to the present; it will also place the movement within larger social and business contexts, including ones that it took a lead in developing. It will show the very development of the term "craft beer," which is the product of a "craft brewery." (This type of brewery includes any small, independently owned brewery that adheres to traditional brewing practices and ingredients. Craft breweries are distinct from larger regional and national breweries, which often use nontraditional ingredients and brew on a much vaster scale.)

This book is not a tasting or style guide nor a guide to breweries (there were more than five thousand in the United States by June 2017, more than at any time ever), and it is not a history of American beer before the craft beer movement arose. Instead, it is a book on how this movement, with the odds stacked against it, survived and thrived to dominate the world's conception of beer and to change the American palate forever.

It is a story populated by quintessential American characters: heroes and villains, hippies and yuppies, oenophiles and teetotalers, gangsters and G-men, men in kilts and men in suits. It is a story of advances and retreats, long nights of the soul and giddy moments of triumph. Further, the story's scope demands that each chapter be delineated by geography. America's a big place, and its craft brewers have done big things.

Note: The reader does not have to be intimately familiar with the brewing process. Here it is in a nutshell: cracked grains that have been roasted (or, in brewing lingo, "malted") are boiled to bring out their sugars; during the boil, other ingredients, including hops and spices, are added; then, after the product of this boiling (called "wort") has cooled, yeast is added, which essentially eats through the sugars during fermentation, converting them to ethyl alcohol, the intoxicating element of beer. There are perhaps thousands of brewing yeast strains, and they, along with hops and malted grains, give beers most of their flavors. Yeast strains also, more often than not, dictate a beer's style. There are dozens of styles, though the reader does not have to be familiar with those, either. The book explains them when necessary.

PART I

THE LAST SHALL BE FIRST

San Francisco | 1965

On a breezy, warm day in August 1965, Fritz Maytag walked into the Old Spaghetti Factory on Green Street in San Francisco's trendy North Beach neighborhood and ordered his usual beer: an Anchor Steam. Fred Kuh, the restaurant's owner, ambled over.

Kuh was a bit of a local eccentric in a city increasingly full of them amid the trippy 1960s counterculture. He was a Chicago stockbroker's son and World War II veteran whom legendary San Francisco newspaper columnist Herb Caen would label "the father of funk." Kuh rented a small flat in the Telegraph Hill neighborhood, crammed with Victorian baubles and knick-knacks, and called himself "a bohemian businessman." The Old Spaghetti Factory Cafe and Excelsior Coffee House was his greatest triumph. He opened it in 1956, converting a defunct pasta factory into what the *San Francisco Chronicle* described as the city's "first camp-decor cabaret restaurant," complete with chairs hanging from the ceiling, beaded lampshades, and second-hand furniture from brothels. Kuh plucked a fortuitous moment: his factory became among the few venues in town that San Francisco's beatniks—and later hippies—would frequent, a reliable lefty redoubt that even became the unofficial local headquarters of Adlai Stevenson's doomed 1956 presidential campaign against the staid Dwight Eisenhower.

Fritz Maytag was no beatnik, though it was difficult to pin a label on him just yet. A trim Midwestern transplant with wire-rimmed glasses, close-cropped brown hair, and pointed eyebrows that gave him the appearance of either perpetual bemusement or skepticism, he had come westward originally to attend Stanford, where he earned an American literature degree. He then spent a few years doing graduate work in Japanese through the university, even living a year in the Far East. After president John F. Kennedy's

3

assassination in November 1963, he told himself he had to move on, that what he was doing in grad school "was very minor." He dropped out and moved to San Francisco to collect his thoughts. Twenty-five, married, and the father of two children, Maytag found himself in the midst of what would one day be called a quarter-life crisis. He knew only that whatever path his life was supposed to take ran through the West rather than through any place on the Rockies' other side. He was just in San Francisco to figure it all out.

And he was just in the Spaghetti Factory for what had become his favorite beer—he tasted his first Anchor Steam five years before in the Oasis bar near campus in Palo Alto. It was the only beer Kuh ever had on draft. He loved the idea of a local brewery.

"Fritz, have you ever been to the brewery?" Kuh asked, nodding to the beer that was the color of dried honey and that spawned a head like lightly packed snow. Kuh was a fan of the beer; he liked to patronize local goods made by other San Franciscans.

"No."

"You ought to see it," Kuh said. "It's closing in a day or two, and you ought to see it. You'd like it."

The next day, Maytag walked the mile and a half from his apartment to the brewery at Eighth and Brannan Streets and, after about an hour of poking around, bought a 51 percent stake. When the deal closed on September 24, he controlled what was about to become America's last craft brewery. It was a risky business move, but Maytag could make it. His great-grandfather and namesake, Frederick Louis Maytag, the eldest of ten children born to German immigrants in central Iowa, had founded the Maytag Washing Machine Company more than sixty years before. Frederick Louis's son E. H., moreover, had bought a herd of Holstein cows to raise on the family farm in Newton, about thirty-five miles east of Des Moines. *His* son, Frederick Louis II, used those Holsteins—and some help from the dairy science department at Iowa State—to churn out a notable blue cheese brand modeled after the Roquefort style in France. And, like the French, Frederick Louis II aged the blue cheese in caves: two 110-foot-deep ones dug into the family farm in 1941. His eldest son, Fritz, grew up surrounded by the cheese business; in fact, he would inherit it in 1962, when Frederick Louis II died. Before that, he'd been sent east, to the elite Deerfield Academy in rural Massachusetts, for boarding school and then west to Stanford. The blue cheese of his father, though, would play a pivotal role not only in Maytag's life but in the culinary life of the United States. It was one of those seemingly uniquely American intersections of moxie and chance.

Maytag bought control of the Anchor Brewing Company for what he later described as "less than the price of a used car" in 1965. Like many a used car, it was in sad shape: cramped, the equipment run down, only one employee with not all that much to do. Maytag could cover the purchase and early operating costs with his inheritance. What of his business acumen, though? What would a literature degree and three years of Japanese studies cover? More important, while Maytag was an unabashed fan of Anchor's signature steam beer, he himself knew nothing about brewing, much less *craft* brewing—a term that had all but disappeared from the national lexicon.

The signature beer that Maytag made his own was perhaps unique in the world. Steam beer has no one agreed-upon genesis, no creation story (or even myth), though just about all who've looked into it, including Maytag, agree it was developed in California. After that, take your pick. The brewery itself has said, "Anchor Steam derives its unusual name from the nineteenth century, when 'steam' seems to have been a nickname for beer brewed on the West Coast of America under primitive conditions and without ice." The *Journal of Gastronomy* said the "steam" referred to the "volatile, foamy" behavior of beer from San Francisco when it was warm. Some said it was the additional yeast called for in original steam beer recipes—thus more foam from more fermentation. Others said the inventor was named Pete Steam; others contended steam actually used to rise from a freshly popped bottle top; still others dismissed it all as a mere marketing ploy because of the nineteenth century's fascination with newfangled steam power or as an incongruous byproduct of the Gold Rush (Anchor was originally founded in 1896 and had gone through several owners before Maytag). What was definitively known was that Anchor Steam was amber colored and produced a thick, creamy head when poured properly. Its alcohol content ran to nearly 5 percent per volume. The beer had a slightly bitter taste and a smooth, almost citrusy finish. And, despite its heavier ale-like mouthfeel, it was a lager.

That was important. Maytag's brewery was part of a centuries-old continuum that had found its place in America only a few generations before. Lager yeast, which sank to the bottom of vats during fermentation, birthed a lighter, clearer type of beer that did not spoil as easily as what had become by the early 1800s the world's most popular type: ale. Ale, its yeasts hearty and virtually invulnerable to temperature, could be brewed and fermented just about anywhere. Lager, on the other hand, derived from the German verb meaning "to store," could be brewed only at cooler temperatures—thus its development at the tail end of the Middle Ages in the Bavarian Alps. Lager did not take hold in America until the late 1800s, with the advent of industrial refrigeration, pasteurization to goose its shelf life, and faster ships to transport its mercurial yeast across the Atlantic before spoilage. Once it did, lager, lighter on the palate and less complex in taste than ale, was off to the entrepreneurial and dynastic races. American beer production, driven by lighter and longer-lasting lagers, particularly a Czech-born style called pilsner, spiked.

Competition was fierce, financial reward relatively fast and immense. Brewing became a feature of the landscape of big business in the same baronial age as Andrew Carnegie, Henry Ford, and J. D. Rockefeller. From the end of the Civil War to the beginning of the First World War forty-nine years later, America's domestic commercial production of beer increased sixteenfold, from 3.7 million barrels annually to 59.8 million (one barrel equals thirty-one gallons, or roughly 320 twelve-ounce bottles). More revealing, even though the nation's population grew during this half-century, the per-person rate of beer consumption grew as well. Beer became the de facto national drink, displacing whiskey, rum, and other spirits atop the tippling totem poll—thanks again in no small part to the central European immigrants, who not only eschewed the heavier ales born in Britain, Ireland, and especially Belgium, but who also incorporated lagers into their daily lives, oftentimes drinking on the job without taboo. By 1915, the average American adult was consuming 18.7 gallons of beer a year, up from barely 3 gallons in 1865.

And the beer they drank was a local thing. Breweries and the beers they brewed were delineated by geography. What you got in Cleveland, you couldn't get in Brooklyn; the brands in Pittsburgh would seem unusual to someone from San Diego. The nature of beer was a big part of this: it was a foodstuff that tasted best fresh and could spoil after a few weeks in the bottle or barrel. It was best, then, to have it produced nearby. Every big city—and several smaller ones—had at least a couple of breweries, and some had a lot more than that. St. Louis and Milwaukee were each home to dozens; Brooklyn, New York City's most populous borough, by the 1870s had forty-eight breweries, most clustered in German immigrant neighborhoods (a stretch of North Eleventh Street in Williamsburg today boasts street signs harking back to when it really was a "Brewers' Row"). Philadelphia had about one hundred at one point. From 1865 to 1915, the average American brewery went from producing 1,643 barrels a year to 44,461, and the number of breweries nationwide rose to as high as 2,783. Beer seeped into the national consciousness—president Teddy Roosevelt was known to hoist a cold one and took more than five hundred gallons of beer on safari in 1909—and it became a cultural fulcrum on which so much of the nation's collective memory turned. Indeed, most beer during this time was consumed in public houses—bars, taverns, locals, pubs—and served from barrels and kegs tapped with colorful tabs; the technology of packaging beer, especially in aluminum cans, had not yet caught up to the demand.

Not that it mattered. On January 29, 1919, came the Eighteenth Amendment: Prohibition. Producing any commercial beverage with over one-half of 1 percent of alcohol became illegal. Following repeal at the federal level in December 1933, American brewing reemerged into a new business environment that size rather than geography quickly defined. Breweries wanted to get as big as they could as fast as they could, and they did this as would most any industry: through mergers and acquisitions. The number of American breweries shrank to 684 by 1940. From 1935 to 1940 alone, with the backdrop of the Great Depression and its grinding unemployment, the number of breweries nationwide fell by 10 percent. Some cities, such as New York, never really recovered their pre-Prohibition status as brewing hubs. There, the number of breweries dropped steadily, through consolidation and simple economic stress, until by the early 1960s there would be only a few left. The same was true three thousand miles away.

At 2:31 in the afternoon on December 5, 1933, word reached San Francisco that the Twenty-First Amendment repealing Prohibition had been ratified. The siren on the city's Ferry Building facing the mainland United States sounded, and fourteen trucks trundled up Market Street to City Hall to present mayor Angelo Rossi with cases of spirits and wine.

While some of San Francisco's windy, wending streets literally ran with booze over the next few days, the actual situation for retailers and for manufacturers was a different matter entirely. Not only had Prohibition wiped out, through neglect and police action, much of the infrastructure for commercially producing alcohol, but San Francisco also emerged from the dry years into a business climate stultified by what was being called the Great Depression. Until the 1930s, Americans had applied that term to the economic downturn of the early 1870s; but this more recent one was something else entirely, with over one-fourth of the eligible American population out of work and no social safety net to catch them and their families. In San Francisco, the number of unemployed jumped an estimated 47 percent from 1930 to 1931. Such statistics got worse and worse for months, and then years, until a cruel reality seemed to settle over the City by the Bay like so much fog.

Into this fog stepped Joseph Kraus. A German immigrant steeped in brewing, Kraus was part of a trio of owners who had kept Anchor going after its original owners, Ernst Baruth and his son-in-law Otto Schinkel Jr., died more than a decade before Prohibition (Schinkel was killed in 1907 in a fall from a San Francisco cable car just as a fresh version of the brewery was going up at Eighteenth and Hampshire Streets). In the spring of 1933, eight months before repeal and with the state's OK, Kraus reopened Anchor a few blocks north, at Thirteenth and Harrison, only to have the brewery burn down the following February (a fire, spawned by the Great Earthquake of 1906, had also destroyed a previous location). Tragedy of a more bromidic kind struck Anchor after Kraus and a partner, brewmaster Joe Allen, reopened yet again at another spot: demand waned so much that Allen, by then the sole owner following Kraus's death, closed the brewery in 1959.

And why not? American tastes in beer were homogenizing, and breweries were consolidating, the Big Beer ones such as Schlitz, Anheuser-Busch, and Pabst either gobbling up smaller competitors directly or rendering their market shares to a trifle. By the start of 1959, the five largest breweries produced over 28 percent of the beer Americans consumed, a jump of 10 percentage points since the end of World War II. That market share would grow to nearly half within a decade, and most of the beer would be a distinctly watery interpretation of the lager style called pilsner. At the same time, new technologies were revolutionizing the way brewers distributed their beers and how Americans drank them. In January 1959, Bill Coors, a Princeton-trained chemical engineer who would later chair the brewery that his grandfather founded, introduced the seven-ounce aluminum beer can; by 1963, with the introduction of the pull-tab opening, aluminum had supplanted tin as the preferred metal for canning beer, as tin sometimes dissolved into the beer. (Despite his pivotal role in this reverberating technology, Bill Coors, asked in 2008 by a Colorado newspaper to name the biggest change during his seventy years in brewing, replied, "That so many breweries have gone out of business. . . . When an industry starts to consolidate, you either get consolidated or you consolidate.")

As much as it was once a local product, beer was also something that Americans consumed largely communally: in bars, taverns, pubs, and restaurants; at ballgames, political rallies, and celebrations such as weddings or graduations. Such technology as the aluminum can—and the proliferation of home refrigeration and the development of the Interstate Highway System starting in the mid-1950s—ensured that such communality was doomed. Throughout the 1950s, breweries packaged more and more beer for wider distribution, hundreds of cases at once rumbling over America's new highways, to be shelved in freshly built supermarkets (a word that itself entered the national vocabulary during that decade) and to be drunk in dens and living rooms just beyond the flickering penumbras of thousands, then millions, of rabbit-eared television sets. By the end of the decade, breweries sold well over eight in ten of their beers in packaging—aluminum cans in a six-pack, glass bottles along the beverage aisle. Various state and local governments abetted the trend away from communal to private consumption. Crime associated with Prohibition-era speakeasies having spooked them, legislatures made it more difficult for new watering holes to open. At the same time, a three-tier distribution system was emerging that ran from producers to distributors (or wholesalers) to retailers, ensuring that the bigger the producer the more influence in the distribution system.*

Producers such as Anchor never stood a chance. They did not bottle their product—and certainly did not can it—and they had neither the means nor, at first, the inclination to distribute it beyond the usual customers: local bars and restaurants. They would never be big enough to hold the attention of distributors. With distributors increasingly uninterested, and demand slackening at local bars and restaurants as more consumers drank at home, the game was truly up. Smaller breweries across the nation closed or were absorbed by Big Beer at a fantastic rate. Joe Allen's Anchor Brewing Company at Seventeenth and Kansas in San Francisco was no different.

Still, the brewery that Maytag bought control of had been given one last shot in 1960, under the ownership of Lawrence Steese, who historian Maureen Ogle described as "a laid-back, pipe-smoking dreamer," and Bill Buck, who came from a wealthy family in nearby Marin County. Neither knew much about brewing, and the beer suffered. Tipplers from the time remembered "a truly terrible beer" and a "foul" one, "kept alive more by the enthusiasm for the idea than for the beer," as Maytag himself recalled. Buck soon sold his 51 percent stake to two overconfident ad men, who, in turn, after trying to save Anchor through more aggressive marketing, sold their stake to Maytag. Steese remained as a minority partner until Maytag bought him out, too, in 1969; and the brewery remained as essentially the ward of a few local clients, especially Frank Kuh. "We were doing a hundred kegs a month," Maytag said, "and if the Old Spaghetti Factory weren't taking ten each week, we'd have been in trouble. I always say Frank Kuh was the one who really saved Anchor Steam."

Maytag did his part, to say the least, leaving Steese in the early months as de facto brewmaster while he schlepped about San Francisco's hilly streetscapes as head salesman, going door to door to convince more bar and restaurant

---

* Some states, such as Pennsylvania, even inserted themselves into the three-tier system as retailers.

owners to carry a beer thoroughly down on its luck. So far down, in fact, that some owners refused to believe Anchor was even still brewing. They thought Maytag was some kind of weirdo—an oddity even in the counterculture's capital city, babbling about how he owned a brewery that wasn't named Miller or Pabst. He did not savor much success. But that left him time to ponder Anchor's marketing, distribution, and, especially, production. Where to take it? What to do to get it there? Maytag's decisions throughout the late 1960s, though he could not have realized it, set the ground rules for the craft beer movement to come and were collectively a milestone in American cuisine.

First, size: Maytag kept Anchor small. Part of that was the beer market-place—there was not much demand beyond Kuh and a few other locals for a beer that had become a pale shadow of its pre-Prohibition self. Part of it was an almost preternatural desire not to grow. That was a foreign concept to entrepreneurs, to capitalism itself, but perhaps an approach that only an heir to a family fortune could take. "I want to make all our beer in this build-ing—hands on," Maytag would say. "I mean this: we do not—emphatically do not—want to get too big." Anchor in the early years of his ownership brewed a hundred kegs a month among five workers, including Maytag. Forty years after Maytag bought control of Anchor, the Brewers Association, the nation's leading trade group for craft brewers, chose a definition for "craft brewer." The first of three adjectives that the group used in its definition? "Small."

The second was "independent." For Maytag's Anchor, this was easy early on: the brewery was a money loser for years and persisted in producing a product strange to most consumers—who would ever want to buy him out? Besides, its independence was part of Anchor's marketable charm. It was the plucky, back-from-the-dead (many times), little brewery in what one journal-ist described as "a dump of a building," a local curiosity crafted deliberately by hand. The hands increased at only a glacial pace—the number of employees would barely rise above fifty even three decades later—and Anchor splashed "Made in San Francisco since 1896" prominently across each bottle in block-black letters, trading on local lore and enticing consumers to think about their beer in terms then increasingly uncommon: as the carefully created product of a certain time and a certain place. Made only in X since Y—it was the antithesis of mass production, where history matters little and place even less.

Finally, the Brewers Association in 2005 defined a craft brewer as "tra-ditional." Here, Maytag's influence in setting the movement's ground rules was unmistakable. When he bought control of Anchor in 1965, the brewery was occasionally resorting to corn syrup in its recipe, a cheaper way to goose the alcohol content and to play with the flavor. Maytag returned the steam-beer recipe to all barley malt, reaching back through the decades to Anchor's nineteenth-century roots; it was a pricier approach that introduced greater uncertainty into the brewing. A few degrees the wrong way in the boiling part of the brewing, a mismatch of malts, or a wrong measurement of the same, and the batch was ruined; its ruination, in fact, likely only to be discovered after weeks of fermentation, the unusable rotted fruits of many hours of labor the money-losing operation could never get back. To Maytag, though, that was the point. He set up a little place in the Eighth Street building that he called "the lab," and it was exactly that: a place to tweak Anchor's recipes, to find what ingredients worked and in what proportions. It was also where the beer was made more palatable for distribution; one of the first triumphs of Maytag's team was preventing the draft beer from souring before it made it to local restaurants and bars. Another was finding a way to bottle the beer for shipment without loading it with preservatives. By the start of the 1970s, Anchor would accomplish both.

Still, the brewery failed to turn a profit, despite literally no competition from other craft breweries. And yet the barely thirty-year-old Maytag kept at it—small, independent, and traditional. He had grave doubts, but he was genetically hardwired to be stubborn when it came to starting a new business. Plus, he absolutely loved the idea of making a product locally for local consumption—what would one day be labeled "locavore." It was a love he got from his father, who had crafted the famous blue cheese. "I saw the pride with which my father reacted when people would ask him, 'Have you anything to do with that blue cheese?' I saw that, and I saw I had a chance of developing a food product that could do the same." He had a sense that the demand was out there, beyond San Francisco, a sort of commercial Manifest Destiny in reverse, a movement rolling eastward, back toward his native Iowa, all the way to the Massachusetts where he was schooled, back to a time when geography mattered in food and when people took the time to care about what they ate and drank. "We had a feeling that we had a better mousetrap and the world would lead a path to its door."

Maytag had no idea how many Americans would want him to be right.

DO IT YOURSELF

Dunoon, Scotland; Fairfax County, VA | 1964–1968

The tugboat dragged the nuclear submarine alongside Jack McAuliffe and his fellow technicians aboard the navy's first nuclear submarine tender, the USS *Simon Lake*. They were in Holy Loch, an inlet of the River Clyde on the Scottish coast, about thirty-five miles northwest of Glasgow. The technicians had had their breakfast chow, shaken off their hangovers from tippling in pubs in the nearby town of Dunoon, and were setting about another workday amid a typically damp, foggy morning in the mid-1960s, repairing the tubular champions of US Cold War policy in action: the Polaris subs.

Launched in 1960 and eventually numbering forty-five, the subs were each equipped with sixteen nuclear missiles and the capacity to cruise underwater for up to three years, though the typical deployment was a still-onerous sixty days beneath the surface. Usually that surface bobbed within twelve hundred miles of major cities in the Soviet Union, the Polaris having been designed as a fast-strike force, each capable of unloading the nuclear-arsenal equivalent of either Britain or France in quick rounds. It was within this Cold War bubble, with its daily shadow of Armageddon, where McAuliffe, then barely out of his teens, plied his skillful trade. For, while the one-hundred-man Polaris crews were among the most trained and disciplined of the navy's sailors, the maintenance crews aboard the *Simon Lake* were arguably the branch's most technically blessed. The submarines' "effectiveness will depend on precise maintenance," according to a *Time* magazine profile of the launch of the first two Polaris subs, the *George Washington* and the *Patrick Henry*, the week of Thanksgiving 1960.

Heady responsibilities for a kid from Fairfax County, Virginia. But McAuliffe knew his stuff. The navy had trained him for thirty-eight weeks on Treasure Island in San Francisco Bay. There McAuliffe finished second in his electronics class, and the navy let him pick what he wanted to do. He chose what he called the antennae shop at Holy Loch, repairing and refitting

Polaris subs for those sixty-day deployments with fresh crews. He and his fellow mechanics were not necessarily sure how the subs ran, but they knew how to fix them.

Before the navy, McAuliffe had led a bit of a peripatetic life, thanks to a father in the federal government and a boyhood fascination with how things got put together. He was born in 1945, two years after his father, John, was drafted into the FBI because he had just completed a master's degree in German and the United States was two years into World War II. Also fluent in Spanish, John McAuliffe was first stationed in the Venezuelan capital of Caracas, where Jack was born, serving as an interpreter at the American embassy at a time before the CIA existed, when the FBI engaged in international espionage. The McAuliffe family moved after the end of the war, when Jack was six months old, to another South American assignment, this one with the State Department in Medellín, Colombia, where John ran a State Department center that advised Colombians who wanted to study in the United States. It was while doing this that the elder McAuliffe began to help develop the textbooks and the methodology that would become the English as a Second Language programs, opening further career opportunities. He moved his family once more, to Fairfax County, Virginia, for an ESL-related job through American University in Washington, DC, when his oldest child was in the third grade.

By the time the McAuliffes moved in, Fairfax was much more country than city—barely one hundred thousand people spread over 395 square miles, its population set to quadruple between 1950 and 1970. It was there young Jack developed an avocation that would reverberate down through the next quarter-century, into every homebrewer's kitchen and craft brewer's bottling line, into the very cuisine of the country: he started tinkering with things.

Perhaps this love of tinkering began when his mother taught him to sew when he was only three years old—in part to keep him busy—though wherever it came from, it was in full bloom by his teen years. McAuliffe was particularly fascinated with the joining of metals. So in the tenth grade, he apprenticed himself to a local welder. He would jump off the school bus in the late afternoons and tool around the shop for no pay, doing the grunt work, absorbing systematically how welding happened, and sometimes getting to go out on jobs. It was Jack's responsibility to get everything set up while the welder, Clay, chatted with the customer. Perhaps most important, this included coaxing forth the acetylene pressure from torpedo-shaped tanks—he had his own oxygen acetylene kit—and when everything was set, calling out, "Clay, we're ready to go!" Then the razor-like spit of red-blue flame would work its magic before the apprentice's goggled eyes. Chemistry, physics, mathematics—it was all there, joining together some things to make *something*.

After high school, McAuliffe tried college for a year, didn't like it, and, in 1964, followed his father into the service, volunteering for the navy. After the thirty-eight weeks of technical training on Treasure Island, he was assigned to the USS *Simon Lake*, which, after loading up on weapons during a six-month docking in Charleston, South Carolina, headed across the Atlantic to Holy Loch and the Polaris subs. It took eleven days at fifteen knots.

We do not know—and McAuliffe does not remember—whether he, while in training in San Francisco, ever visited the pre–Fritz Maytag Anchor Brewery at Eighth and Brannan Streets, or tasted any of its drafts in local haunts such as Fred Kuh's Old Spaghetti Factory. We shouldn't be surprised if he didn't. Though it wasn't bad by the standards of the time, Anchor's steam beer in 1964 was still American-made beer, and American-made beer was by and large still very much haunted by Prohibition, the ghosts of its storied past disquieting smaller breweries across the land as the likes of Anheuser-Busch and Miller got bigger and bigger and developments such as the pull-tab for aluminum cans (first introduced by Pittsburgh's Iron City Brewing Company in 1963) and the Interstate Highway System drove consumers farther and farther from where the beer they drank was produced. So neither San Francisco transplant—not the restless heir of the home-appliance empire nor the precocious child of the trilingual G-man—would have had cause, really, to care about locally produced beer in that last full year before the American craft beer movement began. Their paths would finally cross a few years later, in the same city, though under much different circumstances and with far-echoing effects on that very movement.

In the four years between his departure from and return to San Francisco, in the free time he had away from repairing the Polaris subs, inside a little gray stone cottage in the town of Dunoon, in a move both prosaic in that men had been doing what he did for millennia and profound in that what he did would alter the American palate, Jack McAuliffe began to brew his own beer. He did it more from necessity than anything else, and he was confident from the get-go that he could do it. The confidence sprang from a young life working with his hands as dictated by his brains, whether toward the joining of metals or the repairing of nuclear armaments. It also sprang from a legal sea change in Great Britain around the time McAuliffe sailed into Holy Loch.

In April 1963, Reginald Maudling, the chancellor of the exchequer (the British equivalent of treasury secretary), did away with an eighty-three-year-old law that required a license—and a concomitant small fee—for homebrewing any amount of beer. Suddenly, the English, the Welsh, (some of) the Irish, and the Scots could brew what they wanted and however much they wanted. Not surprisingly, as would happen in the United States twenty years later, a retail industry arose to service them. At first, the enthusiasm for homebrewing far outweighed the quality of the end results. Not that it mattered too much. It's unlikely anyone was ever prosecuted for not paying the shillings, and homebrewing was rare in a Britain still feeling the effects of wartime austerity. Sugar was rationed from 1940, after the start of World War II, until 1954, and other homebrewing ingredients were supremely difficult to come by. Hops were usually sold at wine-making stores in large, open-topped buckets, and they were unnamed, dry, and flavorless. Malt extracts came in tins. Nobody really knew what they were doing: any how-to books were highly technical, and institutional knowledge barely existed. Britain, after all, had no old-timers who could tell you about the bathtub beer they had made during Prohibition. Instead, homebrewing on the isles often made a mockery of the kingdom's grand tradition of fine ales and lagers. "Many times I added lemonade to improve the taste of a thin, high-alcohol beer due to high rates of granulated sugar," Bill Lowe remembered. He was in the Royal Navy then, serving mostly on submarines. Decades later he would be a judge at beer festivals and a founder of the Northern Craft Brewers Craft Brewing Association in England. "It was impossible to obtain named varieties of hops, grains, and yeasts until around 1980."

McAuliffe got the idea to homebrew while running errands in a Boots drug store in Glasgow in late 1966. It had occurred to him that once he returned to the States, the beer he'd discovered in Scotland would be almost wholly unavailable. Oh, man, what am I going to do? he thought. His eyes surveyed the store's shelves and settled upon another echo of Maudling's legal change: *The Big Book of Brewing* by Dave Line. Line was an electrical engineer and one of the first to explain homebrewing in plain English. While most books that touched on homebrewing were heavy on mechanical jargon, aimed more at commercial brewers than amateurs, Line wrote simple, step-by-step instructions for creating clones of classic English styles right in your kitchen. The equipment would seem dated today and many of the recipes laughingly basic—no grains, just malted barley and hop syrups, with dry, somewhat listless yeast—but in the early 1960s they were revelatory.*

---

* Line's book would not be published in the United States until 1974, and it may not have been published commercially in the United Kingdom until around that time. But both McAuliffe and others in the craft beer movement recall seeing copies of the book before then. Line died in 1979.

Bang!, McAuliffe thought. That's how I'm going to do it—I'm going to make my own beer like the beer I have here! He bought Line's book and a homebrewing kit for a pale ale from a display underneath it. He also bought a plastic trash can.

Back at the cottage in Dunoon, McAuliffe stoked the kitchen's coal-burning fireplace (gas or electric heat were not options) and got to work boiling the admixture of water and syrups to create what brewers call "wort," or unfermented beer. He then let the wort cool, tossed in the yeast, wiggled the pot to aerate it, and cleaned out the trash can. Able to hold five gallons, it would serve as the fermentation vessel for this first new batch of the American craft beer movement. McAuliffe at first left the can open at the top (what brewers call "open fermentation"). For the later stages, he capped it with a plastic airlock to let out carbon dioxide, a by-product of fermentation, and to keep out oxygen, which could doom the wort to bacterial infection. The brewing took a few hours. After a couple of weeks of fermentation, McAuliffe bottled what could now be called beer in used swing-top bottles and aged it a further two weeks.

The beer disappeared, as did subsequent batches—McAuliffe remembers no complaints. In fact, not only were his fellow American servicemen delighted by the reproduction of the ales they'd enjoyed in Dunoon's pubs, but the Scots themselves also liked McAuliffe's kit-driven concoction; the neighbors put it away as thirstily as the compatriots. It was likely the first time since Prohibition that American-crafted beer had so impressed foreigners. An old trajectory had begun to reverse itself.

BEER FOR ITS OWN SAKE

Okinawa, Japan; Portland, OR | 1970

Fred Eckhardt loved the book, of course—he just didn't care for the title, *A Treatise on Lager Beers*. Something about the highfalutin word "treatise," with its thirteenth-century etymological roots and its academic pretensions, rankled him. The compact, fifty-eight-page paperback, after all, was meant to be an accessible guide to homebrewing the most popular type of beer on the planet; it was not meant to turn off would-be hobbyists with superfluous jargon. That was the last thing Eckhardt, the book's author, wanted to do. At forty-three, with a compact, muscular frame born of years in the US Marines and a handlebar moustache that would become a trademark, he saw himself as an evangelist of good beer—the sorts of flavorful, robust ones he had had amid overseas deployments, including during the Korean War in the early 1950s. It was then, as a flight radio operator stationed in what is now Osaka International Airport in Japan, that Eckhardt tasted the mildly bitter pale lager Tuborg, out of Denmark, the first good beer he ever had.

Though Tuborg was—and remains—more akin to the likes of Budweiser than to what would be called craft beer, it was for Eckhardt a far cry from the beer his father had made in Everett, Oregon, twenty years before. That was standard Prohibition hooch: one can hops, ten gallons of water, several pounds of sugar, translating into roughly ten gallons of very strong—and very not good—beer. At age six, with Prohibition the law of the land, Eckhardt and a friend, at their fathers' prodding, had a glass of the beer; the aftertaste lingered through the decades and colored his perception of what beer could be. He took that perception with him, out of Oregon and to the Pacific Theater during the waning days of World War II in 1945, when Eckhardt was part of the American occupation of a vanquished Japan and stationed on the southern island of Okinawa.

To him, the Japanese beer at the war's end was pathetic, though it came in interesting packaging to mark the interesting times. He and his fellow marines at the Yokosuka Air Base were allowed a ration of six beers weekly in cans—a new technology vis-à-vis beer, one so nascent then that the cans Eckhardt and his comrades drank from might seem exotic today. Their tops were conically shaped, with metal caps, the same kind used for bottles, sealing the opening—a sort of hybrid of today's cans and bottles. The Allies welcomed beer on Okinawa, however terrible in retrospect; rations of tomato juice or what servicemen remembered as an "Aussie can of chocolate milk of some sort" were substituted when beer supplies didn't arrive. "Wretched stuff," thought the Oregon-raised San Francisco native barely out of his teens.

Eckhardt stayed in the US Marine Reserves after 1945 and was called up in October 1950 for service again as a flight radio operator, this time throughout the Pacific, including back in Japan, where he encountered that Danish Tuborg. During this period he also earned a degree at the University of Washington in Seattle, joining tens of thousands of veterans on a GI Bill–infused march that would transform so many existing industries, including the increasingly homogenized brewing industry, and invent so many others. For his part, Eckhardt left the Marine Reserves in 1958, the same year he finished college in Seattle, and moved from there back to Oregon as a partner in a Portland photography studio. He had dabbled in photography in the marines and then had worked with a studio that did child photography door-to-door; the studio was hoping to branch out to Portland, and Eckhardt went with it.

His new city had a population of just over 372,000, sitting in the temperate valley of the Willamette River, which bisected it. By 1965, the year after Eckhardt arrived, Portland had 316 barber shops, 30 movie theaters, 24 funeral homes, and—important for him—76 photography studios. But it had only one brewery—as was often the case in the cities that had any at all. In Portland's case, it had the Blitz-Weinhard Brewery, a brick amalgam spanning four blocks on the edge of the industrial Pearl District and employing up to 220 people brewing as many as thirty-one different beers.

Blitz-Weinhard's history—and its ubiquity in the Portland area at the time—offers a good example of America's regional breweries. Founded in 1856 by Henry Weinhard, a twenty-six-year-old immigrant from the Württemberg region of present-day Germany, it was still run by the family—Henry's great-grandsons Frederic and William—but was on its way, like other regional breweries in that era of industrial consolidation, toward being acquired by Big Beer (which happened via Pabst in 1979). For the time being, though, the brewery was a point of civic pride, the nexus of Oregon's bestselling beer and a link to its more rugged past. Indeed, Henry Weinhard had made his way westward ninety years before from Cincinnati, which was itself developing a busy brewing scene powered by like-minded German immigrants, to Portland because there were no breweries to slake the thirst of the dockworkers and lumberjacks.

Still, Blitz-Weinhard, particularly its flagship lager, was, like Tuborg, more akin in flavor and production to Big Beer than to what we would now call craft beer. Olympia beer, brewed in Tumwater, Washington, was big in Portland, too, and Portlanders considered Coors out of Colorado positively exotic. For a budding beer snob like Eckhardt, these beers weren't going to cut it; something had to be done. Like navy nuclear mechanic Jack McAuliffe, with his plastic trash can half a world away around the same time, the former marine radio operator turned to homebrewing. It was, as it was for McAuliffe in Scotland, a rather daunting task: supplies, particularly grains and especially yeast strains, were difficult to come by (homebrewers often substituted bread yeasts and batches made entirely with grains were rare, with syrups as the main substitutes); instructions were often arcane, if not also archaic, highly technical in their explanations, and, Eckhardt figured, more useful to commercial brewers than to homebrewers. But he plunged forward, and by 1968 he was not only producing passable batches of lager but also teaching homebrewing and wine making at Wine Art of Oregon, a supply shop near I-84 that served as a meeting place and clearinghouse for Portland homebrewers. There were fifteen to twenty students per class, and they worked off instructions that sprang from books that themselves sprang from overseas or from the Prohibition era: books like Englishman C. J. J. Berry's *Home Brewed Beers and Stouts* (1963) and the second edition of Carl Nowak's *Modern Brewing* (1934).

Eckhardt eventually found himself with an ace up his sleeve, though. He had been self-publishing a journal titled *Amateur Brewer*, which sought to teach and connect homebrewers with techniques and each other. For an article in the spring of 1968, he visited the only craft brewery in America: Fritz Maytag's Anchor. The brewery was then on Eighth Street, between Brannan and Bryant Streets in San Francisco's South of Market (SoMa) neighborhood. It was the same location Maytag had walked to from his apartment three years before to buy 51 percent of the failing brewery for the price of a used car. And, like Maytag, Eckhardt had been introduced to Anchor years earlier at Fred Kuh's Old Spaghetti Factory. "You should try it," a friend had suggested. "It tastes like homebrew." It couldn't possibly, Eckhardt thought. The American beer he had encountered after the marines was all so bland, so homogenous—it didn't even approach that Tuborg he tasted a decade before in Japan. But why not? Eckhardt ordered the only beer on tap at Kuh's place and was impressed. I could brew beer like this at home, he thought.

And there he was, a few years later, at the source. Maytag and Eckhardt struck up a rapport, with the brewer sharing his time and expertise generously and his visitor shooting photos of the equipment: the brew kettle; the mash kettle; the primary fermenter, which to Eckhardt looked like "a small swimming pool," its surface yellowy white and alive with the churning yeast, devouring the sugars unleashed by the earlier boiling soak of the cracked grains. This type of brewing had been done for centuries, but it was rarely done on this scale anymore—not in the United States, at least. We do not know the exact thoughts passing through the minds of Maytag and Eckhardt as they toured Anchor's brewhouse, with its worn wood floors, copper kettles, and walls of red and white brick; neither man, after all, thought to record them, as they were not aware of the specialness of their meeting. How could they have been? It had been years since Maytag's acquisition now, and no other craft brewers had come after. There was nothing to indicate to either man that they were at the start of something—if anything, it felt like the end.

Eckhardt did take it upon himself soon after the visit to try to induct at least one more person into the movement. Charles McCabe, who wrote an oftentimes acerbic column for the *San Francisco Chronicle* called "The Fearless Spectator," had complained about the quality of American beers. Eckhardt wrote in to set McCabe straight on the tradition right in his own backyard. From then on, McCabe became a champion of Maytag's little outfit, a cheerleader in what was then one of America's largest and most influential newspapers. Here was one rhapsody on April 20, 1970:

> If you happen to feel patriotic, Steam is the ONLY American beer. Other beers in this country have been named after the middle-European cities where they gained their fame . . . .
> Yet Steam had as much to do with the building of San Francisco and Northern California as the Christian virtues, good stout Levi's, shovels, and the saving presence of whores. When people really drank Steam, there were 27 breweries in San Francisco alone. Hundreds dotted the Mother Lode Country. Now, as stated, it is made in but one place here.

Eckhardt returned to Portland with his Anchor photos and his feedback from Maytag, and he spun the two together into a slideshow for his home-brewing students. One slide would show how a brewing step—say, mashing the grains—was done at home; the next would show how it was done in a small brewery (Anchor); and so on, alternating slides to give an idea of how efforts in the kitchen might translate into the commercial realm. It was an extra mile Eckhardt went for his students. Jack McCallum, Wine Art's owner, thought he could go even further.

"Why don't you write a book?" McCallum asked his friend one day. Eckhardt was known to be good with recipes, with the sort of organization needed to build something from some things.

"Geez, write a book?" Eckhardt replied. "Who am I to write a book?" McCallum dropped the idea, only to bring it up again later. This time, Eckhardt reconsidered. Why not? he thought. Eckhardt bought a gallon of rose wine and drank it as he hammered out on a new typewriter what the book's subtitle plainly called "A Handbook for Americans and Canadians on Lager Beer." But it was more than that; it was a manifesto. The last paragraph of the introduction reads more like a palatal call to arms than a jumping-off point for a collection of recipes:

After Prohibition, it remained illegal to make homebrew (it still is) and so even then there was no light to be shed on the subject. Now more than 35 years after the end of Prohibition we are just beginning to explore the possibilities of home brewing. Beermaking began in the home long before it became commercial, and now we can take it back to the home. The commercial brewers in this country have tailored their product to the lowest common denominator. There are almost no quality beers made in this country, so if you want good, old-country style beer you must make it yourself. Even the German beers imported into this country are being made to the so-called American taste. Pabulum and pap for babies. You actually can make beer just as good as the great European master brews in your own home. This book is only a start.

In the following forty-eight pages, in conversational prose that would not be unfamiliar to a twenty-first-century blog reader, Eckhardt spelled out the vocabulary of lager beer; the equipment and ingredients needed for brewing its various styles at home; the steps involved, including troubleshooting; and the care in aging and serving it postfermentation (there was even a short section on making your own bottle labels). The recipes he recounted sprang from a recipe that Wine Art had been giving to customers. It was a Canadian one, highly technical, and, to Eckhardt, poorly organized. He broke it apart and put it back together around several different lager styles—light, Bohemian pilsner, Vienna, Bavarian, and more—along the way writing of beer in personal and personable terms, a rather novel approach in a period when the nation's five biggest breweries produced nearly half its beer. Here was Eckhardt on the illegality of homebrewing: "We should all work to have the law changed so that there is no doubt about the home brewer's rights alongside his winemaking brother." Here he was on alcohol per volume:

There are those who think that a beer should be relatively high in alcohol. This is not reasonable, after all, why do you drink beer? If all you want is inebriation, drink hard liquor. Beer is a convivial beverage between friends, to be drunk for its own sake, as a friendly thing, not a *drunking* thing. Five to six percent is plenty of alcohol, your friends won't laugh if your beer clobbers them.

Published through McCallum's Wine Art in April 1970, *A Treatise on Lager Beers* was an earnest salvo, one that steered future craft-brewing pioneers, who decades later would be able to still recall its influence on them. But it was also a fifty-eight-page paperback sold locally in a midsize city with a single brewery unknowingly on its way into the perpetually parched maw of Big Beer. Plus there was that title with the word "treatise" that so bothered the author but that enamored McCallum, who suggested it as a way of lending gravitas to a subject many would not believe worth the weight. The word did not seem to hurt the book, though. It sold enough to warrant second through fifth printings by July 1972 (it would over the next forty years warrant two more printings and sell over one hundred thousand copies), and Eckhardt earned pennies on each. It was never much, and he would remember it mostly as just a lot of fun. Like Fritz Maytag and the Anchor brewery he had visited and photographed, Eckhardt's book seemed terminally anachronistic—the isolated whimsy of an American who liked good beer and who was discovering it was increasingly hard to find.

EDEN, CALIFORNIA
Davis, CA | 1970

Michael Lewis was abundantly aware that, in 1970, he was one of a kind in the United States: its sole full professor of brewing science. And he was further aware that the four-year degree program in brewing that he was helping craft at the University of California, Davis would be unique as well. The decade before had been a fortuitous one for the English transplant, one of happy accidents and potential realized. And it all started with a terrible time in Buffalo, New York.

Lewis, a witty Brit with a ready grin, fresh from finishing his PhD in microbiology and biochemistry at the University of Birmingham in central England, arrived in Buffalo in 1960 to discover not only for the first time in his life apocalyptic winters, but also that the facility where he was to work had burned down. It set the tone for an unfulfilling couple of years, punctuated by feelers to potential employers. He wrote, for instance, to Herman J. Phaff, a food sciences professor at UC-Davis and a world-renowned pioneer in wine yeasts. At that time, Phaff replied that he had nothing for the twenty-something researcher. But before he was to leave Buffalo for England, Lewis wrote him one more time, and Phaff replied in March 1962 that he had just gotten a grant from the brewing industry and Lewis's background was perfect for it; he should come to California and do a postdoctorate. The next month, Lewis and his wife piled their belongings (including a cat they had rescued) into their Simca, the French compact he had bought brand-new for twelve hundred dollars, and drove into New Jersey; then they turned westward along what would become Interstate 80 but which was then Route 40. The car broke down twice, including an unplanned three-day sojourn in Wyoming during inhospitably cold weather, before the couple reached the Rockies and began to crest toward a California that was itself rapidly changing.

The state had grown steadily since the turn of the century, but its population really began to boom during the Great Depression as downtrodden Americans, like those depicted in John Steinbeck's *The Grapes of Wrath*, headed westward in search of work, California as much an idea of opportunity as a reality. Then manufacturing jobs spiked during World War II, with factories for munitions and other wartime necessities like aircraft swelling the population even more; from 1940 through 1960, California added more than nine million residents and in 1963 displaced New York as America's most populous state. With the new residents arrived a stereotype of an entire California lifestyle, one of leisure buoyed by stable jobs in growing industries, rapid housing development, perpetually sunny beaches, Disneyland, fast cars on clean new highways, and a feeling of boundary-pushing that one could not expect on the older East Coast, certainly not in Buffalo, New York. The very symbol of soaring twentieth-century commerce, the airplane found its perfect environment in California; the state's wide-open vistas and benign weather made it the perfect place to build and test them. By 1935, Seattle-based Boeing was the only airplane manufacturer on earth without a California address.

For California's newest resident, the descent through the Sierra Nevada Mountains into the central valley was like entering Eden. Lewis saw palm and grapefruit trees, and the job under Phaff at UC-Davis promised research opportunities that he knew could not be had elsewhere in the United States. He turned out to be right. In 1964, he developed the university's first brewing classes and research program. By 1970, Lewis, then barely out of his twenties, and a faculty colleague, wine-chemistry expert Vernon Singleton, were charged by Chancellor James Meyer to craft what would become the nation's first bachelor's degree in fermentation science, with concentrations in wine making and brewing—and he would become America's only professor of brewing sciences for the next two decades. Lewis and other faculty culled the beer-concentration curriculum from existing courses on oenology and food microbiology. They added to these classes standard-fare scientific vertebrae such as physics, chemistry, engineering, and mathematics, which, along with courses in business, formed a strong but flexible backbone for what would become a phalanx of American brewers over the next forty years. Before the UC-Davis program, if an American brewer (as opposed to, say, a Belgian or a German one imported for his expertise) said he went to brewing school in the States, it invariably meant he had taken classes at the venerable Siebel Institute of Technology in Chicago. Now, with the first BS degrees in fermentation science offered in 1971, American brewing expertise was beginning to be redefined. UC-Davis alumni set out for jobs in Big Beer—the only game in town, save for Anchor, seventy-five miles to the southwest on I-80. And, more important for our story, the university's brewing research served as a beacon for entrepreneurs. In fact, in 1974 Michael Lewis would sit down with a navy veteran in his late twenties who told him he planned to open his own brewery in an old warehouse nearby. Could Lewis direct him to some research on the subject?

Before Jack McAuliffe paid that visit, though, a chance order at a dinner in Munich on the other side of the world would profoundly alter the beer world's chemistry and make efforts such as his and those of Fritz Maytag all the more difficult. Craft beer as a movement in America remained, for the time, largely academic.

TV DINNER LAND
San Francisco | 1970–1971

Mark Carpenter needed a change—or at least a place to work where he could figure out what that change should be. A tall, lanky native San Franciscan in his early twenties with a heavy beard, he knew the telephone company, where he was working, was not such a place. What about that brewery on Eighth Street? He and some friends had toured it earlier in 1971—almost entirely for the free beer at the end—and Carpenter thought that might be just the spot, and an interesting one at that. He went there one day in September and told the office manager he was looking for a job. She found Fritz Maytag, who happened to be there that day and not out on sales calls or traveling for research. He and Maytag talked; Maytag introduced him to Gordon MacDermott, a 1968 Anchor hire who then ran the brewery's day-to-day operations. Carpenter, a restless soul when he entered the brewery that day, left with a positive feeling. He knew he had nailed it; he knew he had the job. He did. The brewery called him, and he started work on September 30.

The Anchor that Carpenter stepped into was in transition. By February 1969, Maytag had bought out the "pipe-smoking dreamer" Lawrence Steese and was the brewery's sole owner. It seemed to be perpetually stuck in start-up mode, however, producing with a crew of five or fewer employees, including Maytag, about a thousand barrels of draft beer a year via a fifty-seven-barrel system (keep in mind that in 1970, Anheuser-Busch, the nation's biggest brewer, opened in Merrimack, New Hampshire, what was the state's first brewery since 1950, with an annual capacity of 1.8 million barrels). One thousand barrels per year meant actually brewing only about once a month; the other days were spent on other chores such as cleaning and repairing the brew-house. With its one pump, copper kettles, and nearly constant need of maintenance, Anchor resembled a nineteenth-century operation more than the sleeker engineering triumphs of Big Beer embodied in that Merrimack plant (in fact, it had no refrigeration or stainless-steel pipes or tanks when

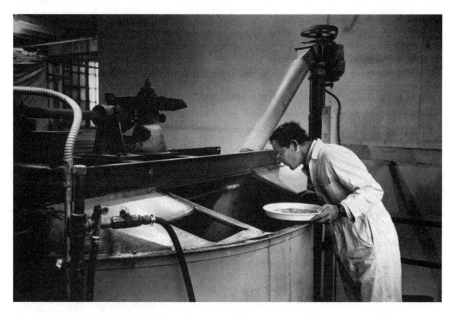

Fritz Maytag inspects a kettle at the old Anchor brewery on Eighth Street in San Francisco. Courtesy of Anchor Brewing Company

Maytag first bought it). It was, according to one visitor on the tours that Maytag would personally lead, "a crude and primitive, old brewery."

Another big chore was distribution, which the brewery handled entirely by itself, Maytag and his crew schlepping kegs to enthusiastic—also often simply sympathetic—local establishments. It was a great place, Carpenter thought, for a brewing novice to learn every aspect of the trade. But it did not make for a stable business model. Six years after Maytag's purchase, Anchor was still just getting by and not turning a profit, a pioneer in unwelcoming lands. Decisions had to be made.

The first decision came in early 1971: Anchor would become the first craft brewery since Prohibition to bottle its beer for sale. In retrospect it was an inevitable move. Unlike today, when bars in cities the size of San Francisco might sport dozens of tap handles, most bars then had one or two taps apiece. It was precious real estate, and not given over readily to some micro-brand out of SoMa; indeed, most of Anchor's local accounts were in counterculture redoubts such as the Old Spaghetti Factory and Perry's restaurant, places that, like the brewery, swam against the dominant stream, or in smaller eateries such as the deli Tommy's Joynt. Had Maytag not decided then to bottle, Anchor may never have emerged beyond a curiosity; as it went, the decision proved another pioneering move, allowing the nation's only craft brewery to enter the ebb and flow of the beer industry's regnant distribution trend, however at a trickle. Big Beer, as we've noted, had embraced packaging so fervently following the repeal of Prohibition in 1933 that by 1970 more than 85 percent of beer in the United States was sold through bottles and cans at retailers. This was partly due to the myriad legislative roadblocks that cities, counties, and states threw up post-Prohibition to discourage communal drinking (obtaining liquor licenses in large cities such as Los Angeles and New York would for decades remain a laborious process full of public hearings and form filling). It was also partly due to the unrolling Interstate Highway System, which sped up the transportation of beer that could now be sealed completely thanks to the growth of aluminum cans.

And it was due to the expanded productivity capabilities of Big Beer, buoyed as they were by cheaper ingredients like rice and corn, and the economies of scale that were increasingly possible as consolidation gobbled up more small players. That new Anheuser-Busch brewery in Merrimack, for instance, would be able to produce eight million twelve-ounce bottles in twenty-four hours in a one million-square-foot facility spread over 294 acres. The same year the Merrimack brewery opened, Schlitz, the second-biggest US beer producer, unveiled a plant in Winston-Salem, North Carolina, that covered thirty-four acres *under one roof*—about thirty-one football fields, the largest ground-up brewery in history, capable of four million barrels annually (or roughly 1.3 billion bottles). It worked so efficiently that by 1973 Schlitz could close its Brooklyn plant; it was cheaper just to brew in Winston-Salem, even for distribution up North.

Finally, American consumption habits were changing along with the American home and landscape. New-home construction was on its way to a postwar peak in the early 1970s as suburban developments spilled across the map, whole communities springing up in isolation from city centers, the distance to commercial and retail destinations covered with ever more automobiles as Americans ambled to favorite spots less and less. In 1973, American factories turned out 9.6 million new cars, the most ever. Once home from their car trips, Americans were gathering not as much around the dinner table but around something else: the television. In 1969, a record 13.3 million television sets were sold in the United States; more than sixty million households (out of sixty-three million total) owned at least one. Other appliances became more ubiquitous as well; sales of the countertop microwave, born of World War II radar research and introduced by Raytheon in 1967, would outpace those of the gas range stovetop by 1975. It had epochal company: Swanson introduced the first "TV dinners" in 1954. The plastic-wrapped meals-in-minutes could be consumed in front of the small screen's inviting glow, perhaps a can of Schlitz beside them, both picked up at the same store during the car commute home. And, no matter the living room's location, be it in Buffalo or San Francisco or thousands of points in between, the tastes of the food and the beer would be identical.

It was into this America that the first two hundred cases of Anchor rolled on April 23, 1971. The bottles clattered off a line, set up just off the first-floor taproom, that could turn out seventy-four bottles per minute if everything went right. It turned out 256,080 bottles that first year, or 10,670 cases. And the bottles went largely to the same local accounts as the kegs of draft beer—though one account was as far afield as the No Name Bar in Sausalito, nine miles away. The bottles were originally loaded and delivered by Maytag and his crew. It just made economic sense. "I need the markup for myself," Maytag told Don Saccani, a Sacramento native turned distributor out of San Rafael, just north of San Francisco, who had been asking him for Anchor's business. "I've calculated it over and over, and I have to have that markup. We're very small, and we're going to have to continue to deliver our beer ourselves." Then Maytag's driver quit in the summer of 1971, only months after the pivotal bottling decision. He found himself behind the wheel of the delivery truck in San Francisco one afternoon not long after with dozens of things on his mind—and dozens of bottles of beer to deliver. Maytag called Saccani.

"Why don't you take over San Jose for us?"

"I'll do it," Saccani quickly replied. "I'll be there tomorrow."

He would get all of Anchor's accounts and eventually began carting the beer out of California in refrigerated trucks over freshly paved highways. The first shipment left the state in 1975, and rumors of the beer began traveling as far as the East Coast around the same time, though it was liable to be lumped in with Coors, also a western creation. Oddly enough, one of Anchor's first extra-California destinations was Coors's home state; Maytag's reasoning was that Coors had been "bringing a little of Colorado to California for so long that we thought we'd reciprocate." Regardless of the wider distribution, Maytag still refused to advertise, and he set the price for his product in line with the prices of European imports, or about twice what a consumer would pay for Big Beer six-packs.

Turning the distribution over to Saccani meant Maytag and his crew could focus on brewing. The beer they were making now was getting better

The Anchor brewery team in the 1970s, led by Fritz Maytag,
in tie in the middle. Mark Carpenter is standing immediately
to Maytag's right. Courtesy of Anchor Brewing Company

and better, more uniform in its taste and appearance. This was partly a consequence of the lab that Maytag had set up shortly after his stake purchase in 1965. There, with his microscope and his books on microbiology and chemistry (Louis Pasteur's *Studies on Fermentation: The Diseases of Beer, Their Causes and the Means of Preventing Them* was a particularly trusted reference), Maytag worked through the transition of Anchor's steam recipe back to its nineteenth-century roots. He also sought and got help from chemists such as John Borger, a field rep for a chemical company, and Joseph Owades, who would play a pivotal role in several other breweries, big and small.

Maytag likened such brewing advice to getting input on cooking from Julia Child, another pioneer changing the American palate. Uniformity in the beer was also a prerequisite for bottling—it had to taste the same wherever it went, just like the Big Beer brands did. And, unlike kegged beer, it had to retain that taste should it sit on a supermarket shelf or in a bar's cooler. If there were too many sour-tasting—or "skunked"—bottles circulating, Anchor's reputation would suffer. There were a few such bottles in the early going, but they were caught before they left the brewery and Anchor disposed of the entire batch they were a part of. By 1973, in Maytag's estimation, Anchor was producing "consistently marvelous stuff." Ironically, and unbeknownst to him and his crew, that was the same year that the dinner in Munich loosed an idea that would transform American brewing.

LITE UP AHEAD
Munich; Brooklyn | 1970–1973

George Weissman, chairman of Philip Morris International, was on a diet. That presented a challenge, as his dinner guest for the evening was John Murphy, the new president of Miller Brewing, which Philip Morris had finished acquiring in 1972 from the descendants of its eponymous founder, Frederick Miller, after a battle for control with rival suitor PepsiCo.

Murphy, a six-foot-three-inch, 250-pound Bronx-born backslapper with an accounting degree from Villanova and a JD from Columbia, enjoyed a stiff drink and a good joke. He once declared that running a brewery was any good Irishman's dream come true, though he freely admitted to knowing next to nothing about brewing. He suggested he and his calorie-conscious boss have beers with dinner. Why not? Milwaukee-based Miller was, after all, one of the ten largest breweries in the United States, with a history stretching back to before the Civil War. The brewery had been among those early pioneers of American pilsner—the pale, uncomplicated cousin of the Czech original and the lager style that had found such massive favor in the marketplace. Weissman, also a Bronx native, worked in small-town newspapers after getting a business degree from City College, and later did PR in Hollywood; Murphy had been a lawyer with Philip Morris since 1962. By the time the pair sat down to dinner during a business trip, Miller, along with nine other household names like Anheuser-Busch, Schlitz, Pabst, and Coors, was producing over two-thirds of all beer sold in the United States, and that market share was growing. It was only fitting then and perhaps no accident that Miller's pilsner, baldly called "The Champagne of Beers" in marketing materials and advertisements, was the color of gold.

Still, Murphy had not been appointed merely to be a caretaker. Miller's new corporate parent planned to aggressively expand in a bid to belt Anheuser-Busch from the top spot among American brewers (Frederick Miller himself competed in the mid-1800s with Anheuser-Busch cofounders Adolphus Busch and his father-in-law, Eberhard Anheuser—America's beer scene, in some ways, had not changed for a century). Miller had already expanded its Fort Worth brewery and bought land in Delaware for another one; it had also recently acquired Canadian brewery Formosa Springs and was hunting for others. Miller would also be moving away from the chichi in its marketing and advertising, darkening its collar a deeper shade of blue in a common ploy of Big Beer, then and now: changing the image rather than the recipe. Murphy planned to banish the "Champagne of Beers" tag in favor of something more everyday, less exclusive. Size and perception—Miller was changing both by the time of the Munich trip.

But would that be enough to best a brand that had been calling itself "The King of Beers" since the nineteenth century? For every beer Miller produced in the early 1970s, Anheuser-Busch produced three—and sold much more. Powered by Budweiser, the St. Louis–based brewery's signature red-and-white-and-drank-all-over brand, Anheuser-Busch seemed almost effortlessly ubiquitous, accounting for nearly one-fourth of the beer sold in the United States annually; in 1973, for instance, Americans would buy more than 9.6 billion cans and bottles of Anheuser-Busch beers, which along with Budweiser included brands like Michelob and Busch. Weissman and Murphy knew what Miller was up against. The last twenty years of competition had left only a handful of big American brewers standing. And the ones that were left were still thirsty. Schlitz had been the number-one brewer in 1950. It was number two now, and fading fast behind Adolphus Busch's heirs. What to do?

A waiter offered Weissman a German beer called Diat pilsner (or Diat pils), a low-sugar lager targeted toward diabetics. It was fermented longer than most beers, thereby burning off more sugar and more carbohydrates. The thorough fermentation, however, produced a greater alcohol content—some Diat pilsners reached 6 percent alcohol per volume, nearly 2 percentage points stronger than a typical Miller or Budweiser—and that greater alcohol content amped up the calorie count. So while in fact it did not have fewer calories than regularly fermented beers, Diat pilsner quickly gained a reputation in Europe as beer for the weight-conscious. It didn't have as much sugar or carbohydrates—that had to be good, right? Weissman took the waiter up on his suggestion. Murphy joined him. The two titans hoisted to their lips the unfamiliar pilsner with the pale complexion and the effervescent texture.

"There's room for something like this in America," Murphy said.

Modern light beer was born. What's more, the repercussions of Murphy's chance dinner encounter with Diat pilsner not only sparked the launch of Miller Lite in February 1975, but it also reverberated through America's cuisine. Even the bastardized word itself—which Philip Morris and its hired ad agency, McCann Erickson Worldwide, popularized, though its usage might go back to the nineteenth century—weaved its way inextricably into the lexicon, becoming both an adjective and a verb in many ways. "Lite" meant action on the part of the consumer, a verbal shorthand for healthier living. "The word skittered across hundreds of new-product labels (more than 350 in the first half of the eighties)," wrote business reporter Rob Walker in a *New York Times* obituary for Murphy, who died in 2002 at age seventy-two. "Light became lite, and took on a life of its own." Businesses fell in line with the trend, whether they produced pie fillings or barbecue sauces or . . . beer. Schlitz introduced its own light beer by 1976 (Miller sued unsuccessfully to prevent Schlitz from using "Light" in its marketing); Anheuser-Busch introduced Natural Light a year later. Both beers were priced more cheaply than most other brands.

The lower-alcohol imitation of the Diat pilsner that Murphy tasted in 1972 was the latest major innovation recipe-wise by Big Beer. It was a smash hit. Within a generation, almost half the beer sold in the United States would be light. Two-thirds of that would be Miller Lite. As Walker noted, "Murphy was right beyond anything he could imagine." His triumph had so little to do with taste. Miller Lite and all of Big Beer's light concoctions to date owe their straw-yellow appearances, alkaline aftertastes, and mild buzzes to a simple business move: buying the rights to a formula for lower-calorie brew. What then sold the public on light beer was the selling of light beer itself.

First, Murphy's people didn't market it as a diet beer despite the 96 calories per bottle. There had been one such stab already: Gablinger's Diet Beer, which biochemist Joseph Owades developed at Rheingold Brewing in Brooklyn. Owades found a way to isolate an enzyme that could break down higher-calorie starches and make them easier for yeast to gobble up. It notoriously flopped after its 1967 debut; the clunky name didn't stick and the advertising was corny. One early commercial showed an obese man shoveling spaghetti with one hand and drinking a Gablinger's with another, as if the beer would do little to add to his weight. "Not only did no one want to try the beer," Owades remembered, "they couldn't even stand to look at this guy!" And Miller had already tried the diet beer approach and failed, too. Miller had acquired Meister Brau, a bankrupt Chicago brewery, around the time of Murphy's Munich revelation. Meister Brau had been brewing its own diet beer, using Owades's recipe after acquiring it from Rheingold. When Miller took over, it followed the failed Gablinger's lead and marketed its newly acquired Meister Brau Light as a diet beer to "people with a weight problem or to women," remembered one Murphy protege. "There was a woman on the can even." It flopped.

Diet, then, was out as a marketing scheme—beer drinkers just weren't the sort to count calories, and alcohol was not exactly regarded as a curative. What then? Change the perception of the beer. Tell American consumers what they want, and then give it to them, an inversion of sorts of one of capitalism's sacred tenets: the supply would not only precede the demand but create it as well. For Big Beer in the early 1970s, new was never really new; and besides, who but the ruling breweries had the resources to develop a new product and mass-market it? It was an approach that Fritz Maytag's Anchor could not imagine, with its two-hundred-case bottling runs and self-distribution.

So Murphy retired the longtime, gilded Miller tag, "The Champagne of Beers," and birthed the earthier "Great Taste, Less Filling" and "Everything You Always Wanted in a Beer. And Less" as well as the simple "It's Miller Time." With an advertising budget that would swell to nearly a quarter of a billion dollars in Miller Lite's first seven years, the brewery bought the exclusive beer spots on *Monday Night Football* and the *College Football Game of the Week*, where its ads relentlessly flogged the point that Miller was a beer for every occasion, every day (this was, of course, a pre-web era of three networks and only nascent cable television). This Everyman pitch was cemented when Rodney Dangerfield, Mister "I Don't Get No Respect," began appearing in Miller commercials in the 1980s along with retired pro athletes. In well under ten years, Miller had, through the aggressive marketing of an acquired product, elbowed its way into the number-two spot behind Anheuser-Busch, leapfrogging five other breweries. Its annual sales crested $4.6 billion. Weissman's chance order in Munich had worked; all it took was some titanic marketing. The brewing was the easy part.

"BREWED THROUGH A HORSE"
Los Angeles; Chicago | 1973–1978

In January 1978, Merlin Elhardt, who had for years been homebrewing the delicate German lagers he had encountered while a US soldier in Europe, pecked out the following as part of a newsletter for his fellow enthusiasts:

> Have you ever made a keg of beer and then couldn't figure out how to get the beer out of the keg? I wasn't aware there was a problem. I thought you just held your glass under a faucet and turned it on. Well, Louis Leblanc (like in Mel Leblanc), one of our newest members, tells me that, if not done properly, the keg could blow up and level a three block area and deposit a fine, white foam thereupon. Maybe a little radioactivity, too. What's needed to crack and vent a keg, is a $27 tool that one can make for almost naught. Louis willing, and anxious, to demonstrate the manufacture and use of this tool at the March meeting (March 5rd [sic]). Got an excellent assortment of information, last month, on beer tasting procedures from Fred Eckhardt, including a beer evaluation sheet, a booklet on beer tasting (available thru John), and other information on the same. Some notes he sent contained so much valuable information that I retyped them and have copied them for any one who is interested.

Elhardt's newsletter was for the Maltose Falcons, the homebrewing club he had founded in 1974 in suburban Los Angeles. It was the first homebrewing club in the nation, and it sought to reconnect enthusiasts with a hobby whose high-water mark had been mothered by necessity during Prohibition.

People like Fred Eckhardt's father, with his ten-gallon recipes of sugar, syrup, and water, had created strictly utilitarian brews of strong strength but dubious taste. Elhardt, however, was using all-grain recipes fermented with yeast that he actually cultured at home (he was said to have smuggled some yeast strands out of the Tuborg brewery in Denmark). Such a transition from utilitarian homebrewing was no accident—and no easy, inevitable feat. But it would prove incalculably beneficial to the larger craft beer movement as both a training ground for future commercial brewers and a testing ground for the American palate.

The excerpt from the Maltose Falcons newsletter tells us just about everything we need to know about homebrewing in the mid-1970s, as well as a lot about the would-be American craft beer consumer ("would-be" in the sense that at the founding of the Maltose Falcons, Fritz Maytag's Anchor was the only commercial option).

First, it was a newsletter. That is, it was a typed-out, black-and-white memo to a group of like-minded people, and the group was small enough that Elhardt could reasonably expect to be able to circulate it to enough individuals and still make it worth his while. The world of homebrewing—and craft beer—was then a small one that commanded and demanded the attention of its inhabitants.

Second, the reputation of Fred Eckhardt, 950 miles north in Portland, preceded him. Elhardt gives him no introduction in the newsletter because none was apparently needed. Therefore, while craft beer was a small world—or *because* it was a small world—expertise traveled and experts were emerging.

Third, the expertise of Eckhardt and of Maltose Falcons member Louis Leblanc was recounted by Elhardt. It had to be; information on how to make good beer, we can surmise, had to be shared through word of mouth, printed or verbal. Aside from the older, more technical homebrewing books and Eckhardt's *A Treatise on Lager Beers,* there was *Quality Brewing: A Guidebook for the Home Production of Fine Beers* by Byron Burch, published in 1975 with a borrowed five hundred dollars because Burch tired of repeatedly answering the same questions at the Berkeley, California, homebrewing and wine-making shop where he worked (much the same motive that compelled Eckhardt six years before).

Fourth, Elhardt tossed dashes of humor and whimsy into the newsletter with his talk of radioactivity from a blown keg and the need only for a ready glass to relieve the pressure. This suggests that the original initiates of the American craft beer movement enjoyed their pursuit and found pleasure in it rather than pretention. It was a good time as much as it was a passion.

Fifth, that Elhardt was the newsletter's author suggests he had some expertise recognized by the wider group, and we know that Elhardt's expertise came in large measure through his experience with European beer. The craft beer movement in America, such as it was, followed an undisputed leader: Europe.

Finally, a feeling of expectation infuses Elhardt's paragraphs. It was what a financial analyst might call a forward-looking statement, meant to not only inform its readers but also prep them for something in the near future. The news of Eckhardt's beer-tasting booklet tells us that the Maltose Falcons members knew they had to keep their taste buds in ready shape for the beers that would surely come (the "John" that Eckhardt's booklet was available through was John Daume, the club's financial sponsor, who hosted its meetings from the beginning at the wine-making shop he opened in 1972 in L.A.'s Woodland Hills). Homebrewers like those in the Maltose Falcons—early members included a utility lineman, a PhD student at UCLA, a church deacon, and an artist—emboldened the movement with their growing interest and their growing numbers. (The Maltose Falcons would soon count more than a hundred dues-paying members.) They were by far the largest leg of an emerging three-legged stool: Fritz Maytag's Anchor was the commercial leg and the other was writers like Fred Eckhardt and Byron Burch, who also visited Anchor as he set about assembling his homebrewing guide. Maytag gave him a tour of the Eighth Street brewery that ran to three hours. It was not just generosity on Maytag's part; he knew that the more informed homebrewers there were, the more craft beer consumers there might be.

Information was becoming a premium commodity in the American consumer marketplace. The very notion of the "informed consumer"—the savvy shopper who peers around the corners of advertising to the nuts and bolts of a particular product, including its geographic origin—had only just come into vogue. This was in large part due to Ralph Nader, whose 1965 book *Unsafe at Any Speed* chronicled the campaigns of major automakers against safety improvements, including seatbelts, and made him and his legion of Nader Raider lawyers media darlings. The creation of Earth Day (1970) and new federal bodies such as the Environmental Protection Agency (also 1970) and the Consumer Product Safety Commission (1972) further drove the notion of the informed consumer (as did, in no small measure, the criminality exposed by Watergate in 1974—if you couldn't trust the president to properly police things, who could you trust?). And if consumers' pursuits of information left them particularly skittish about a product, they could decide to opt out of the marketplace in some measure. As Nader pointed out in an October 1975 interview, consumers' skepticism of a food supply increasingly dominated by factory farming was "tied to the fact that twelve million home gardens have been started in this country in the past two years."

We should not overstate this informational shift as it pertains to beer. Americans were not running out to buy all-grain homebrew kits (there weren't any legally for sale then in the United States) or setting up yeast cultures in test tubes next to the toaster. There was, however, a perceptible attitude shift in the early 1970s among those who, like the Maltose Falcons members, were paying attention. Ken Grossman, who would at the decade's end cofound the Sierra Nevada Brewing Company, opened a homebrew shop on the second floor of a former fleabag hotel in Chico, California, in 1976. For him, the hobby gelled with what he called the "other homesteading activities" he and his wife pursued at their small, creek-side stead in the nearby town of Oroville: raising goats for fun as well as for milk and cheesemaking. Charlie Papazian, who would, also by decade's end, cofound the American Homebrewers Association and pen the early draft of what became the bestselling homebrewing guide ever, saw the hobby he took up while a student at the University of Virginia as something that made people happy when they drank it, rather than stupid, which seemed to be the case when they downed sixty-nine-cent six-packs of Big Beer. And Jack McAuliffe simply got a kick out of sharing his now years-old pastime with his father once he shipped out from Scotland for the States.

Along with this shift among homebrewers was a more general Everyman realization that something was missing from the once grandly heterogeneous tradition of American brewing, that barely a hundred breweries was not enough for a nation of two hundred million splashing across a continent and over the Pacific. In early 1973, the *Chicago Daily News*'s Mike Royko, famed for his columns about Windy City politicians and criminals (and criminal politicians) and the recipient of the previous year's Pulitzer Prize for commentary, lamented that "America's beer tastes as if it were brewed through a horse." The column touched a national nerve. How dare he criticize the national drink! One reader gave him a Plan B: "Go to hell, if you don't like this country's beer. Maybe you'll like what you are served there."

Royko responded by organizing what may well have been the first beer taste test by a newspaper. The results, printed on July 9, 1973, were telling. Of the twenty-two beers, including imports, blindly sampled by eleven tasters, Budweiser, the signature brand of the nation's biggest brewery, finished dead last, with Schlitz, then the number-two brewery, just ahead of it (judgments regarding Bud: "a picnic beer smell," "lousy," "Alka Seltzer," "yeccch"). No brands from the nation's top-five breweries finished in the top five (and, we should note, Anchor Steam was not among the twenty-two sampled). The overall winner was a West German pilsner, followed by England's Bass Ale; and the domestic champ was Point Special, a pilsner from the regional Stevens Point Beverage Company in Stevens Point, Wisconsin. "Great flavor and a great beer smell," as one judge put it; "light and lovely," said another. The 116-year-old brewery, which would change ownership several times in the next thirty years and add cola making to its activities, enjoyed a 20 percent sales bump from the win. But it turned down a request by airline TWA for two hundred cases a week because it would deplete its supply and hurt local distribution. When a liquor store in the Rockies requested Point Special, it got the same answer. There were consumers out there; there just wasn't that much variety available unless you made it yourself.

THE MOST INFLUENTIAL BEER
San Francisco | 1974–1978

Though the first Anchor bottles meant for points beyond California had headed out of the Eighth Street brewery on Don Saccani's trucks in 1975, America's only craft brewery still was not turning a profit. What to do? Maytag looked at the calendar and saw a chance for further innovation wrapped in a marketing opportunity: the nation's two-hundreth birthday, which was fast approaching.

Maytag had the year before finally started to brew his signature steam beer consistently enough that it arrived to vendors, whether in kegs or bottles, tasting the same time and again. He had also developed the idea for an Anchor Porter, a darker, richer ale once all the rage in nineteenth-century England (its name supposedly came from its popularity among porters along the new railroads). The brewery that Maytag bought in 1965 had been producing a dark steam beer by adding caramel coloring; he discontinued that and brewed a real porter. To his and his crew's surprise, they learned that no commercial brewery in England was producing one; the Anchor Porter brewed and kegged in the winter of 1972 would be the first new one anywhere in modern times. It was a seminal moment in the nascent American craft beer movement: a brewery from the New World supplanting any in the Old in one of its signature beer styles. Anchor Porter was first bottled on July 17, 1974, and hit the backs of Saccani's trucks.

Around that time, Maytag and Gordon MacDermott traveled to England to survey the beer scene—in particular, to case any good ale styles perhaps worth Anchor's imitation. What they discovered instead was the genesis for an American original that would embitter a generation of beer drinkers. Maytag and MacDermott visited the family-run Timothy Taylor brewery in bucolic Keighley, West Yorkshire, and sampled its Landlord, which one leading critic described as "a bitter with a color of pale honey and a wonderful aroma of hay, earthy with deliciously bready grain flavors lingering in the aftertaste." Landlord was distinguished by its fruitiness and its "very full-flavored hop presence," not by any sweeter malt concentration. It was a bitter beer, but one, oddly enough, refreshing in its bitterness.

At this point, it's important for our story to step back and learn about the importance of hops in beer, as they will come to play an outsized role in the American movement. Unlike grains, which serve a more utilitarian role in brewing, hops, along with yeast, can make or break a beer as far as its style; and many craft brewers would come to define themselves by their use of hops. Hops are the flowers of humulus lupulus plants. Since the Middle Ages, they have been used as the primary bittering agent in beer. Hops also help stabilize a beer's foam (or "head") and act as a preservative. They grow mostly in Northern Europe, particularly Germany and the United Kingdom; Australia and New Zealand; and, especially, the Pacific Northwest. Once harvested, hops can be added throughout the brewing process as pellets or cones, including after fermentation (when their addition is called "dry hopping"). They can be added during the earlier "bittering" stage of brewing or the later "aromatic" stage. Until about the early 1970s, no US-grown hops were considered by even domestic brewers worthy of being used in the aromatic stage to give a beer a certain scent; instead, American hops were used for bittering and European hops for aroma.

Finally, hops are delicate flowers—stored or shipped too compactly or loosely, or under the wrong temperatures, and they can lose their intended flavors and therefore ruin an entire batch of beer. Partly because of this mercurialness, Big Beer after Prohibition stopped using large quantities of hops in their brewing batches; Big Beer's lagers usually had as little as two ounces of hops per barrel.*

---

* Modern craft beers, particularly India pale ales, might average at least two pounds of hops per barrel.

More than anything, though, the American postwar palate—weaned on soft drinks, fruit juices, sugar-packet bins beside automatic coffeemakers, and Tang—had simply grown unaccustomed to bitterness in drinks. A brewer by the early 1970s would be foolish to produce a drink many times bitterer than a cup of coffee. Consequently, most American beers of the time registered on the low end of the zero-to-one-hundred International Bitterness Units scale used to measure beer's bitterness. A bottle of Miller Lite, for instance, was around ten IBUs.

The idea that Maytag took from Timothy Taylor in West Yorkshire back to Anchor in San Francisco would end up creating a beer with as much as four times that bitterness. First, the idea. The nation was turning two hundred, and Maytag figured that a lot of breweries, big and small, would be doing special brews—or, at least special packaging—to commemorate the bicentennial. Maytag decided to opt out of the scrum and brew something to commemorate the two-hundredth anniversary of Paul Revere's April 18, 1775, ride through the Boston area to warn of a British attack. It also undoubtedly imbued what he brewed with a delicious dose of irony, since the beer would be an ale in the tradition of what he had tasted in England, particularly the Landlord at Timothy Taylor.

Maytag found the hop he would use via a friend from his early ownership of Anchor in the 1960s. John Segal was a second-generation hop farmer with land in the Yakima Valley of Washington. Segal's father, George, discovered hops while selling cheese door-to-door in the 1920s, during Prohibition. Hops then were available through retailers, including candy stores—ostensibly for brewing tea. George learned the hops trade from a German business partner, and for a time he had a sales office across from Manhattan's Grand Central Terminal, complete with a walk-in refrigeration room for storing and showcasing varieties. George's son developed a reputation in the industry as someone willing to take risks in the pursuit of new varieties of hops for the marketplace. And it was a risk: for every new variety of hop that made it into a commercial beer, there were several, perhaps dozens, that flopped in the experimental phases.

One of John Segal's contacts, Chuck Zimmerman, ran an agricultural research center for Washington State where he cultivated, among other crops, hops. Zimmerman, in fact, would go on to develop some of the most popular hops varieties in the United States, including Chinook, Centennial and Columbus. On a 1968 visit to the center in Prosser, along the Yakima River, Zimmermann showed Segal an experimental hop variety. It was then known only as "56013." Zimmermann had gotten it from the USDA's hop-breeding farm in Corvallis, Oregon, then run by Alfred Haunold, himself a major force in cultivation. Born in 1956 of a lineage that included Russian and English hops, 56013 had been languishing for years, unused commercially, when Segal rubbed it between his fingers in Prosser and liked what he felt. He took some roots back to his Yakima Valley farm for cultivation. Coors had already approached Segal about using an American-made hop for aroma because of concerns about pesticides in European hops and a blight that hit Central European yields in the late 1960s. Segal suggested 56013. In 1972, Coors brewed a test batch and liked it; the brewer bought Cascades at one dollar a pound, a half to one-third more than what other hops commanded. The exact origins of the name remain unknown (maybe it had to do with the Oregon mountain range), but the Cascade hop as a going concern was born. It was the first widely used, American-made aroma hop and the first hop variety from the USDA's hop research program to be OK'd for sale since Prohibition. Its scent and taste would help define American craft beer.

The first craft beer to use it was what Maytag decided to call Liberty Ale in honor of Paul Revere's ride. It was bitterer than any domestic beer on the market and more robust in flavor than even many imports, especially the German and Czech pilsners that had come to be the rubric for Big Beer. The recipe would evolve over time, and Anchor did not have the capacity to brew it regularly; but that original Liberty Ale was several times the bitterness of the new Miller Lite (the current iteration is forty IBUs). It also had that citrusy, floral aroma that the unfamiliar Cascade hops provided, and it could be consumed by the session, as the industry parlance went. At just under 6 percent alcohol by volume, a drinker could tipple well more than one Liberty Ale in a sitting and not get staggeringly drunk. Most consequently, by being bitterer than most but not *too* bitter, Liberty Ale straddled a coming divide in craft beer. On one side would be the pale ales that the brewery's signature steam beer was more akin to; on the other would be India pale ales (IPAs).

The IPA style, like Anchor Steam itself, has various creation myths, ranging from a single East London brewer named George Hodgson to a recollection that British beers sent to colonial India were dosed with high amounts of hops to preserve them for the long sea voyage to simply a savvy marketing ploy from the mid-nineteenth century. Whatever the origin, IPAs came to be defined as the hoppier, and therefore bitterer, kin of pale ale. And there stood Anchor's Liberty Ale, starting with the first bottles on June 26, 1975, at the root of the coming division, a common ancestor to how American brewers would interpret both styles and how those interpretations would change brewing. Liberty Ale's debut was an Event in culinary America, one that would spawn not only thousands of pretenders and usurpers but also a vocabulary (hoppiest, hoppier, hoppy, hophead), wider interest in hops and their role in brewing (and American agriculture and American agricultural history), and a palatal pivot that would see thousands, millions, of Americans embracing bitterness over sweetness in their favored drinks. Liberty Ale would become quite possibly the most important beer of the late twentieth century.

No one cared. Or at least no one outside of Anchor's still small orbit of two-hundred-case bottle runs and restaurant keg deliveries. There were no mentions of Liberty Ale in the media—no reviews, no stories on the rollout, the backstory, the commercial risk, the pioneer move (Maytag didn't think much of the beer himself; he had to be persuaded to release it). Sales were always modest—the initial bottling produced 530 cases. What had been born Liberty Ale remained on the market as "Our Special Ale," until it reemerged as Liberty Ale again in the summer of 1983.*

On the other hand, more than seventy million cases of Miller Lite would hit the market in 1976, its first full year of sales. Still, something had happened. Mark Carpenter traveled to Europe decades after Liberty Ale's debut. He noticed something curious in the Belgian, Dutch, and French ales he encountered: they were using Cascade hops just like so many beers back home, where they were born.

CHEZ MCAULIFFE
Sonoma, CA | 1976

There was a knock on the brewery door. Jack McAuliffe answered it.

"I've heard of this place," the knocker told him, "can I just look around?"

"Fuck no," McAuliffe replied, his blue eyes running cold, the square jaw clenching that much tighter. "I'm busy, get out of here!"

McAuliffe was not to be trifled with at his brewery, and that included the pilgrims who often showed up with little notice. Normally, if they called ahead, he was happy to oblige. He would personally give tours of the old fruit

---

* The current iteration of Liberty Ale was reintroduced in July 1983 through 2,920 cases (per Dave Burkhart at Anchor).

warehouse off Eighth Street East in rural Sonoma, California,* the first start-up craft brewery in the United States since Prohibition, charging the visitors at the end for the samples of stout, pale ale, and porter; but the trickle had lately broken into a steady stream.

People were showing up so often and without warning that McAuliffe had taken to turning visitors away, sometimes brusquely. He and his skeleton crew needed to focus on brewing and distribution. The New Albion Brewing Company was growing.

It had started modestly enough, without any thunderclap of recognition of its importance to American culinary history, even by its founder. McAuliffe had left the navy in 1968, settling in San Francisco, where he had done his training on Treasure Island. He studied physics on the GI Bill at California State in Hayward, and worked as an electrical technician and an optical engineer. Through it all, McAuliffe kept homebrewing. He had hauled bottles, bottle tops, some ingredients, and homebrewing books back from Scotland; he found additional supplies at wine-making shops in the Bay Area. The situation was just as he had predicted in that Boots in Glasgow in 1966: if he was going to have the sorts of beers he had discovered in Europe, he was going to have to make them himself. There were imports on the shelves—sales nationally had jumped sevenfold in the early 1970s—but six-packs were one dollar to two dollars more expensive than those of the giant domestics; and, for all their growth, imports still represented an infinitesimal slice of the American market.

Plus, some were not imports at all: European-sounding brands such as Andeker, Lowenbrau, and Michelob were brewed by Pabst, Miller, and Anheuser-Busch, respectively, part of Big Beer's "super premium" push meant to capture a more discerning consumer. The super premium push even led to a lawsuit over alleged deceptive advertising because a Chicagoan thought he was plunking down an extra couple of bucks for beer brewed in Munich, not Milwaukee. If we were to behold a typical American grocery store's beer section, circa 1975, we would find that roughly 80 percent of the packaging staring back would be from the nation's top ten breweries; another 2 percent, at most, would come from Canadian or European brands; and the rest from the remaining one hundred or so breweries left in the United States. One of those, of course, was Anchor. It was after a tour of Anchor that McAuliffe got his idea: he would cobble together some money and some material, and start a brewery of his own (and he, too, would use the new Cascade hops).

---

* The full building address was 20330 Eighth Street East.

Why in Sonoma, in the heart of what was rapidly becoming California wine country? McAuliffe had moved there to help a friend construct a custom-built house; he worked as a tradesman, doing electrical wiring, welding, sewage—skills he had started learning at Clay's welding shop in Fairfax County, Virginia. There was another reason, too, and it would grow in significance as the movement that McAuliffe helped launch grew.

Alice Waters had relocated to the Bay Area in the 1960s from East Orange, New Jersey, to attend the University of California at Berkeley. She studied abroad in France and, more than anything, absorbed its food—genuine crepes, Belon oysters, the hard ciders of Normandy—and the culture surrounding it. That culture was moored in the fact that the French took their time cooking; they used local ingredients whenever they could and prepared simple yet pleasantly robust meals. More important, they lingered over their repasts, elevating eating and drinking beyond the utilitarianism it was fast becoming in America. Food in France was slow. Waters took these lessons back to a Berkeley that, in her estimation, did not have any fine restaurants. In 1971, she opened Chez Panisse in an old house on Shattuck Avenue. The restaurant quickly gained a game-changing reputation for slowly prepared, simple French meals culled as much as possible from local ingredients. Francis Ford Coppola, Danny Kaye, and Mikhail Baryshnikov were regulars. The *New York Times* declared Waters "a chef of international repute" whose "cunningly designed, somewhat raffish establishment" was unique in the West. Even the French sang hosannas. Christian Millau, a food critic famous for his guides to Parisian restaurants, took particular note of Waters's use of "good and beautiful products of her native land." McAuliffe knew of Waters's restaurant. He also knew of the Marin French Cheese Company in nearby Petaluma, the oldest cheese manufacturer in the United States, which specialized in French cheeses made with Northern California ingredients. And, of course, McAuliffe knew of the burgeoning wine industry in the area, itself a challenge to the French and to other Europeans.

McAuliffe realized he might just happen to be in the right place at the right time, and he shared with anybody who would listen the revelation he'd had during the Anchor tour. One of those people was Suzy Stern, a Harrisburg, Pennsylvania, native who had driven west from Chicago with her three kids and their dog in a Dodge van for a fresh start; her son had gotten into Stanford, and Sonoma—California in general—seemed as good an option as any in America. Stern had already led a geographically varied life: college at Vassar in upstate New York; work as a United Nations interpreter on Manhattan's East Side; then Chicago; and now Sonoma, where she went back to school at Sonoma State to study music. A friend she met through a local food co-op introduced her to McAuliffe, and Stern became only the latest person in the town of barely five thousand to hear about the shaggy-haired thirty-one-year-old's dream for a start-up craft brewery.

Stern knew little about beer and nothing about brewing. But she was in because it seemed like an interesting idea, and McAuliffe, with his combination of bravado and technical know-how, seemed like just the guy to pull it off. Stern and a friend of hers—Jane Zimmerman, who was then the wife of Stern's friend from the co-op—became New Albion's original outside investors. (The two put up $1,200 each, and Jack raised the rest of the $5,000 in seed money; Stern also suspected that McAuliffe appreciated the utilitarianism of her Dodge van.) Zimmerman was on a path toward becoming a successful therapist, and Stern was still studying music; both would take a crash course in brewing from McAuliffe, the ex–nuclear submarine mechanic turned optical engineer turned contractor. This unlikely trio would, in their happenstance way, create a model for future craft beer entrepreneurs, which advised, "Your background in brewing or your knowledge of beer does not matter—what matters is your drive and determination."

They had both in spades, McAuliffe especially. After completing an onerous approval process with the county—which often referred to New Albion as a "winery" on official forms (what bureaucrat had ever heard of a start-up brewery?)—in the fall of 1976 McAuliffe found part of a corrugated-steel warehouse to rent on a ranch owned by the Batto Fruit Company, a large local landowner known mostly for harvesting grapes. The warehouse was at least a mile from downtown Sonoma in a remote industrial spot shaded on the west by towering eucalyptus trees, with direct sunlight from the south and east; the North Coast Mountains could be seen in the distance. The permits and the real estate out of the way, McAuliffe concentrated on a name and some know-how.

The name came rather easily and quickly. Just as Maytag had the "Since 1896" on the Anchor label, McAuliffe decided on a little historical alchemy of his own. English explorer Francis Drake combed what would become the Northern California coast in the 1570s, claiming the area for Queen Elizabeth I as Nova Albion (or "New England," Albion being an ancient name for the British Isles). As McAuliffe would tell the beer writer John Holl, "History is important in the brewing industry—but, if you don't have a history you can just make it up." And so he did: Drake's ship, the Golden Hind, would stare out from the New Albion label, with the California coastline in the background and NEW ALBION BREWING COMPANY/SONOMA, CALIFORNIA above it. History—and, by association, tradition—would be paired with a sense of place.

As for the know-how, McAuliffe headed about an hour northeastward to see Michael Lewis at UC-Davis. McAuliffe had a homebrewer's understanding of brewing; that is, he knew how beer was made and what could ruin it as well as improve it. But he knew all this only on a smaller scale. It was one thing to make five gallons on a kitchen stove, it was another entirely to make several times that amount, over and over, and have it taste the same each time. Lewis found in McAuliffe "a vacuum cleaner of information," and McAuliffe in particular made a beeline to the older books on brewing in Lewis's library, some from the nineteenth century. Lewis's program would also be instrumental in advising McAuliffe on the all-important yeast strains that would give New Albion's porters, stouts, and pale ales their flavors.

The old brewing books also provided McAuliffe a template for building the brewery in the old fruit warehouse. It is difficult for us today to imagine the odds McAuliffe and his crew faced, but nothing illustrates them better than the effort involved in fabricating New Albion's equipment and the physicality of the brewhouse. With limited funds and the knowledge going in that New Albion's production would not be that voluminous, at least not at first, the charming copper kettles of European breweries or smaller

Jack McAuliffe next to an old-fashioned barrel cleaner outside New Albion. He got it cheap—for about fifty dollars—and made it work himself. Copyright © Michael E. Miller and Jack McAuliffe

American operations were out of the question; and the large, industrial-size equipment of Big Beer was pointless. So McAuliffe went foraging. He took special advantage of Northern California's contracting dairy industry and salvaged a lot of discarded milking equipment. His biggest score came when PepsiCo—ironically enough, the spurned suitor of Miller five years before— decided to stop shipping syrup in fifty-five- gallon drums; McAuliffe got hold of several, bending and welding the drums into a mash tun, a brew kettle, four primary fermenters, and ten secondary fermenters.

Once he assembled the equipment (or at least located it) over those nine months, McAuliffe set about building the brewhouse within the warehouse, with Stern and Zimmerman helping. It was lonely, long work in the country-side quietude. McAuliffe designed the brewery with gravity as the main power source (there were no pumps at first), setting the starting point of the brewing process on the roof. Hot water would flow from there into the mash tun (the vessel for mixing the cracked malted barley with the hot water to produce wort), then to the brew kettle so the hops and whatever other ingredients could be added, and then from there to primary and secondary fermenters on a lower level, where the wort could be cooled and the yeast added. Finally, it would move to the cellar for aging the wort-turned-beer. When you walked in, you found yourself in a small office with a coal-burning furnace, and a bottling line took up the middle of the brewhouse. The fermentation room was the size of a walk-in closet. There was a laboratory as well, with framed photos of physics and chemistry giants like Einstein, Oppenheimer, and the revered Pasteur. Finally, well above it all was Jack McAuliffe. He had fabricated an apartment for himself over the brewhouse, which he climbed a ladder to reach and where he bunked "like a spider," with a self-made stove and shower. The founder of America's first start-up craft brewery lived literally above the shop.

New Albion Brewing Company filed for incorporation with the State of California on October 8, 1976. Almost exactly seven months later, on Saturday, May 7, at 3 PM, the company hosted "the Consecration of the New Albion Brewery," with an after-party nearby. It would prove to be rare time off. McAuliffe, Stern, and Zimmerman were working ten to twelve hours daily, six to seven days a week, to produce a barrel and a half, or roughly 495 bottles, at a time. And, despite a marketing pamphlet in which McAuliffe welcomed visitors so long as "you telephone me a day or two before," the unannounced visits started soon after.

THE BARD OF BEER

London | 1976–1977

As McAuliffe built beer history in Sonoma, California, Michael Jackson was giving it a lexicon seven thousand miles away. Born and raised in a working-class household near Leeds in West Yorkshire in northern England, Jackson had his first beer, a lower-alcohol mild, at fifteen at the Castle Hill Hotel in Huddersfield. He dropped out of high school a year later, in 1958, to support his family, working newspaper and magazine jobs into the late 1960s, when he also worked as a documentary producer and a program editor for British TV host David Frost. In 1969, he was covering a carnival near the Dutch-Belgian border as part of a long gig in the Netherlands that took him away from his London home. There he tasted an ale brewed within the walls of a Trappist monastery in Belgium and found it was nothing like the English beers he had been drinking since his teens. Struck by its complexity and intrigued by its history, the next day Jackson rode the bus less than a mile and a half and, as beer writer Jay Brooks put it, "crossed the border—his Rubicon—and began exploring Belgium's beers and culture."

What Germany and the Czech Republic are to lagers, Belgium is to ales. For a variety of reasons, including a sixteenth-century German dictate that beer be made only with water, hops, and barley (they didn't know about yeast's role then), the Maryland-sized kingdom has long boasted a rich, complex tableau of ales, from those dark as the chocolate they taste like to ones as effervescent and fruity as any sparkling wine. Brewers there, unlike in Germany, felt free to experiment boldly, often using the hops indigenous to Belgium, especially its northern region of Flanders. Belgium indisputably made the world's most interesting ales. So it was no surprise that Belgian beer enthralled Jackson, who had grown up in an England where lagers increasingly dominated the market. That the experience propelled him to become the most famous and influential beer writer ever—perhaps the most influential food writer on any one subject of the twentieth century—was almost as improbable as Jack McAuliffe birthing a brewery by hand in the hinterlands of a small town on the western fringe of the American empire. But that's what happened.

Michael Jackson in a publicity photo for his book *The World Guide to Beer*. Courtesy of Running Press, an imprint of the Perseus Book Group

In the same year McAuliffe began building New Albion, Jackson took over the writing and editing of a guide to English pubs when the original author balked. The slim volume allowed him his first stabs at lengthy beer writing. His pièce de résistance emerged the following year, when niche publishers released *The World Guide to Beer* on both sides of the Atlantic.*

It boomed across 255 pages of photos and fine print, detailing in plain yet densely packed prose the genesis and provenance of hundreds of brands covering myriad styles, from not just the Northern Europe that had captured his fancy the decade before and that dominated world beer, but also to far-flung locales in the Caribbean and the South Pacific. The very fact that

---

* *The World Guide to Beer* was originally published in the United States by New Jersey–based educational publisher Prentice-Hall. The author quotes from and references a May 1978 edition published by Ballantine.

Jackson wrote about beer styles was revolutionary by itself in the most literal sense. His was the first work, at least in English, to explain beers as "styles." "If a brewer specifically has the intention of reproducing a classical beer, then he is working within a style," Jackson wrote, somewhat matter-of-factly given his originality, early on in *The World Guide to Beer*. Before Jackson, writers who gave beer a wine-like vetting used nearly every other etymological construct under the sun but "styles"—"divisions," "species," "types," "varities," "classes," and so on.

Beer in the twentieth century had its piper. Never again would budding brewers, critics, and connoisseurs be without a roadmap. Charles Finkel, a Seattle wine merchant who would in 1978 begin pioneering the importation of fine European beers to the United States, including many from Belgium, told the beer writer Stan Hieronymus that *The World Guide to Beer* "was to me like a heathen discovering the Bible. It answered all those questions that I had about top and bottom fermentation, about hops, about yeast, about the nature of beer and the history of beer, and traditions of beer and beer culture." British beer writer Martyn Cornell put it this way:

> [Jackson] invented the expression "beer style," which was found nowhere before *The World Guide to Beer* appeared, forcing brewers and drinkers to think about the drink in a way they never had before, when they talked merely of "varieties" or "types" of beer. He introduced drinkers to beers they would probably never have heard of without his work, and he encouraged brewers, directly or indirectly, both to revive old styles and to push the envelope until, sometimes, it tore in their efforts to come up with new styles.

Jackson's coverage of American beer ran to fourteen pages, three of them full-page illustrations or photographs (Denmark, by comparison, got ten). A certain melancholy infused much of that coverage. After noting in the first paragraph that "there are single breweries in the United States which produce as much beer as entire European countries," he took the reader rather quickly through the sad decline of centuries of brewing tradition.

> Biggest can also mean fewest. For all its great output, the United States has little more than 50 brewing companies, owning less than 100 breweries. Some of these breweries use a great many labels, but few of them produce more than three or four beers. Nor is biggest necessarily best.

Jackson laid the blame for homogeneity squarely at the feet of Prohibition. He did, however, choose to end his American section on a positive, prescient note, alerting his flowering band of followers to the little brewhouse on Eighth Street.

> No beers in the United States are more idiosyncratic than those produced by the Anchor Steam Brewing Company [*sic*] of San Francisco. . . . The smallest brewery in the United States has added a whole new dimension to American brewing.

It would be several years before this most important book on beer in the English language, updated and expanded, with several more pages on American beer, would be a commercial success among enthusiasts in the United States (for one thing, no major American newspaper or magazine appears to have reviewed the 1977 first edition). But people such as Cornell and Finkel realized the potential that the book's exhaustiveness offered. Beers could be assessed, using the histories of their styles, as exactingly and as vibrantly as wines—and by third parties independent of the breweries that created them. (Robert Parker Jr., a lawyer in suburban Baltimore, was doing much the same for wine through a bimonthly newsletter he launched in 1978 called *Wine Advocate*.) Jackson had reached back, past the middle decades of the twentieth century, to pull beer from the depths of homogeneity and, in many cases, obscurity. He launched a revolution in thinking about beer, and it would eventually join the revolution in *making* beer that was under way in Northern California.

LONG DAYS, LONGER ODDS
Sonoma, CA | 1976–1977

In 1976, Anheuser-Busch opened a brewery in Fairfield, California, that would have the capacity to turn out four million barrels of beer a year. About thirty miles to the west, New Albion was toddling along toward an annual output of four hundred barrels. And this only because McAuliffe, Stern, and Zimmerman brewed nearly every day (Wednesday was bottling day), forty-five gallons at a time, about nine times the typical homebrew batch. The first beer that New Albion produced was a pale ale, and it was put into bottles with a blue label featuring Francis Drake's ship. They used a manual labeler—one blue label at a time—and self-delivered the beer into a marketplace that didn't quite know what to make of it.

Nothing illustrates this disconnect better than a visit that an Associated Press reporter paid to New Albion in the late autumn of 1977, shortly after McAuliffe finished the nine months of creation. The comments by him and Stern, and the reporter's attempts to make sense of the brewery in 455 words for the readers at home, show bravado versus bafflement.

> Something is brewing amid the golden fields and aromatic vineyards of California's lush wine country—but it sure ain't vino. It's ale, brewed by a man and two women in what may be the nation's smallest commercial brewery, located outside this small rustic town 20 miles north of San Francisco.

"Most of the domestic beers have adjuncts, like corn and rice," Stern told the reporter, "instead of the pure ingredients we use: hops, yeast, malt, and water." She went on to label Big Beer in America "a national disgrace," a blizzard of "chemicals, stabilizers, and all sorts of things" that hide beer's true and ancient nature.

It was not hyperbole on Stern's part. The Food and Drug Administration earlier in the year had moved to require that ingredients be displayed on the labels of alcoholic beverages. The move came in response to the years-long crusade of one-time Nader Raider Michael Jacobson, a microbiologist by training who argued that beer was full of potentially toxic additives. A lot of his research turned out to be more sensationalistic than scientific, buoyed by that culture of the informed consumer popularized by his old boss Ralph Nader. For instance, Big Beer did famously use gum arabic, the hardened sap of some species of acacia tree in sub-Saharan Africa, as well as the appetizing-sounding propylene glycol alginate—seaweed extract—to goose the size and duration of the heads on beers. They did this only because their watery pilsners would never form the sort of natural head that all-malt beers could, especially after they'd been shipped hundreds of miles. But the seaweed extract and the hardened sap and other shortcuts, like corn syrup, never killed anyone (beer's ethyl alcohol, in abusive amounts, could do that without any help). However, the Reagan administration scotched the FDA's requirement in 1981, after years of court battles and before it ever took effect. Still, such background noise could only bolster New Albion's claims to purity versus Big Beer. "You can really taste the balance between the hops and the malt," Stern explained that autumn day. Alas, the craft was beside the article's point; about halfway in, the reporter turned to the odds that New Albion faced as a business.

> The three [McAuliffe, Stern and Zimmerman] work 12-hour days, brewing, bottling, cleaning, and bookkeeping. New Albion turns out about 45-50 cases a week and sells them to Pay Area [sic] retailers at $14.16 a case. Liquor stores sell New Albion at about [a] 90-cent deposit, a price that "compares with those of imported beers." McAuliff [sic] thinks that's a bargain. "Ours is much better than the imports you get here," he said. . . . "Like most things, you can make it cheaply or you can make an excellent product," he said. "Corporate brewers chose the first path."

We can easily read between the lines to see the length of New Albion's odds: twelve-hour days to craft an unfamiliar product retailing for more than its competitors. And McAuliffe could—and did—look eastward to the new Anheuser-Busch plant turning out in under an hour what New Albion would be able to produce in a year. However, we can read quite clearly the swagger inherent in the enterprise, a determination to soldier on in the service of fine ingredients for a fine product, one that was defiantly local. Present, too, was a clear dose of humor like we saw in Merlin Elhardt's Maltose Falcons newsletter. While McAuliffe told the AP reporter that the brewery wasn't looking to compete with the bigger brands, Stern deadpanned, "Maybe we'll become rich beyond the dreams of avarice."

That same winter, a Bay Area native named Don Barkley decided to return to school. He had spent the last few years as an electrical-mechanical draftsman and had long had an interest in homebrewing, which he settled on after a dalliance with wine making that proved too tedious—you had to wait months, sometimes more than a *year*, before sampling your creation. Barkley's brother-in-law was taking a wine-making course through UC-Davis's extension program, and suggested he check out the school's brewing courses. Barkley, his long hair flowing, met with Michael Lewis in the professor's office.

"I want to learn about making beer," he said, "and I want to start my own little brewery sometime."

Lewis looked at him quizzically. Most students wanted to study at UC-Davis so they could land a management-level job at one of the big or regional breweries. What other options were there, really? "Well," Lewis began, "there is this guy over in Sonoma by the name of Jack McAuliffe who is starting a little brewery." He explained that McAuliffe spent hours at a time hoovering up the university's brewing library. "You may want to go talk to him."

So Barkley went to the warehouse to see McAuliffe and explain himself. And McAuliffe, as was his wont, promptly showed him the door. Yes, he understood that the eager young Barkley would work for free, that he just wanted the hands-on experience of a commercial brewery, but McAuliffe had too much on his plate right now, so would Barkley please leave?

Barkley left. He would not return until the following year, which was lucky for him, as it turned out to be the most important one so far in the American craft beer movement.

PART II

TIPPING POINTS

Boulder, CO; Washington, DC | 1978

The year 1978 was the first undeniably pivotal one in the American craft beer movement. Hindsight shows that as that year dawned, the movement was headed inexorably toward a reckoning. Commercial pioneers like Fritz Maytag and Jack McAuliffe, evangelists like Michael Jackson and Fred Eckhardt, and eager disciples like Mark Carpenter and Don Barkley were all in place as if actors on a darkened stage as the audience gathered. Our script even had an appropriately omnipotent villain in Miller Lite and the rest of Big Beer's imperious consolidation. And the audience! An audience the likes of Merlin Elhardt and his Maltose Falcons in John Daume's wine-making shop; of patient tutors like Michael Lewis and John Segal; of frustrated Everymen like Mike Royko and his band of blind-tasting judges; of outlier inspirations like Alice Waters and every Belgian who had ever brewed; and of those primed to care about the content of their foodstuffs, those already standing athwart TV dinners and toward more appetitious alternatives that their older selves would one day call locavore—they were out there, waiting. The play really needed only two things to start.

It needed a legal imprimatur, as if in days of old when German princes and Spanish archdukes decided which ingredients could go in which beers and at what amounts. And it needed some sort of organization, a tent for the tribe to gather under and rally around, both professionally and amateurishly. Just as humankind may very well have ceased millennia of hunting and gathering to grow grains to brew beer, so too did the craft beer movement need its own reason to stop going in isolated directions and rally around something larger. Both would occur in 1978.

It was a year of fateful visits, tribal gatherings, and organizational flexing that we can now look back on as essential to the decades that came after in American beer. And it all started with a teetotaler's pen stroke.

Charlie Papazian grew up in a rural area of northern New Jersey about forty miles west of New York City and walked the mile and more to school past working dairy farms. The long walks presaged a lifetime of outdoors activities that would leave him a model of physical fitness, slim well into middle age. One of three brothers, he enjoyed science classes and gym the most, and world and modern European history, too. He was a solid B student, with some As sprinkled in, enough to land him a spot in the late 1960s at one of the nation's top public colleges, the University of Virginia in Charlottesville. He intended to study chemical engineering during a five-year program, but chemistry got in the way—Papazian didn't get the language of it, so to speak. He switched to nuclear engineering because he had a felicity with math and physics. He was in naval ROTC for two and a half years and took graduate-level courses in bio-medicine, preschool and early education, art, and philosophy while keeping up with the math, physics, and engineering training. Into this academic rigor in 1970 a wrench was tossed.

A friend of Papazian's, whom he had met through his education classes and who ran a preschool nearby, mentioned during a visit to his apartment near campus that one of his neighbors homebrewed. Would Papazian ever be interested in trying some?

He would.

They walked to a place off Montebello Circle in Charlottesville and met the neighbor, an older man who had been homebrewing since Prohibition. He used a very simple recipe, which he shared with the visitors: one can of hop-flavored Blue Ribbon malt extract, five or six or seven pounds of sugar, some yeast, mix with water, and ferment for five gallons or thereabouts. The neighbor pulled some bottles from his basement that he had been aging for probably a year. It tasted decent to Papazian, better than what he was buying for sixty-nine cents a six-pack.

Papazian and his circle were soon brewing beer themselves. They brewed in the dirt-floor basement of his friend's preschool, in a fourteen-gallon trash pail and right next to a coal-fired furnace that shot sooty rockets now and again. The results were awful. Scholarship was in order. Papazian read up on homebrewing, discovering he could substitute corn sugar for cane sugar and could use something called dried brewer's yeast instead of dried bread yeast. Pretty soon what he and his pals were brewing in the preschool basement was turning out tasty. Word got around Charlottesville, and they threw some fantastic parties powered by their homebrew. It was during these parties that Papazian, the would-be nuclear engineer from the wilds of northern Jersey, realized what turned out to be his most impactful theorem: when people drank homebrew, they got happy, not stupid.

Papazian's homebrewing experiences in the 1970s were pretty typical no matter the location. As we have already seen, while Papazian was jiggering recipes in the basement trash pail in Charlottesville, the early Maltose Falcons members were appraising homemade concoctions in a Los Angeles wine-making shop. They all felt their ways along using the literature available to them, like the limited-run American books by Fred Eckhardt and Byron Burch, or the older British ones; they became, by necessity, amateur organic chemists and microbiologists. They also shared information via word-of-mouth or by hastily scribbled lists, a dipsomaniacal game of telephone, started during Prohibition forty years before and seemingly ceaseless so long as the vast supply of commercial beer remained, in the words of one of Mike Royko's judges, "lousy." Finally, they all cadged and cobbled what they could ingredients-wise, mostly through wine-making shops; there may have been as many as one hundred or slightly more by the late 1970s nationwide, with most carrying brewing supplies as well, with a nod and a wink.

Homebrewing was illegal in the United States; wine making was not. It appears to have been a simple oversight of federal lawmakers in 1933, when they may have been distracted by the Great Depression and the rise of fascism in Europe. In any case, the oversight would spur the explosion in creativity that homebrewing clubs such as Los Angeles' Maltose Falcons, lower New England's Underground Brewers, launched in 1975, and San Francisco's San Andreas Malts, founded in 1978, exemplified, as did individuals such as Papazian and McAuliffe. Homebrewing was a calling, a passion, something more than a hobby, and the illegality might only heighten the thrill. "The difference is gargantuan between my beer and commercial beer," a thirty-seven-year-old photographer from the Philadelphia suburbs told a newspaper reporter. "I know what's in mine. My brother-in-law likes a dark beer, and I make it to his taste. . . . Describe it? Describing homemade brew is like describing a rainbow to someone who is blind. No, you have to taste it." And it was cheaper than commercial beer; it might cost thirty-one cents in the Philly area to brew a quart of homemade beer, and seventy cents to buy the same amount in a store.

So why did it matter if homebrewing was illegal? It didn't, really. Papazian wound up teaching homebrewing classes out West a few short years after he learned it himself in Charlottesville. If the feds did come busting down the door, he figured, the publicity around his arrest would popularize homebrewing a lot more than he could alone. Fred Eckhardt in Portland didn't think about it, issuing only practical warnings about not selling any homebrew commercially or to minors. Fritz Maytag in San Francisco told Byron Burch after that three-hour tour of Anchor in 1974 not to mention that he had shared his expertise, lest the feds make trouble (it was only in an updated 1992 reissuing of *Quality Brewing* that Burch thanked Maytag). The federal Bureau of Alcohol, Tobacco, and Firearms essentially adopted a hear-no-evil, see-no-evil approach to enforcement, and there is no record of any American, including those who ran homebrewing shops, being arrested for homebrewing when it was illegal. "It's been a very low priority item," as an ATF technical adviser noted at the time. An aide to California US senator Alan Cranston put it more bluntly: "It's a dopey law." But it was an obnoxious one. And it could stifle the entrepreneurial juices of homebrewers perhaps considering turning pro. Finally, as Eckhardt pointed out in *A Treatise on Lager Beers* in 1970, if homebrewing were legal, "a number of new brewing materials and chemicals would be a good bit easier to obtain; indeed, we might find access to some of the famous German malts and any number of brewing aids available now only to the commercial brewers."

Whatever the reason, it had to go. Lee Coe, a homebrewing instructor and a member of the Maltose Falcons in California, and Nancy Crosby, the Connecticut-based head of a national trade group representing wine-making shops that also surreptitiously sold homebrewing supplies, lobbied Cranston to introduce a bill legalizing homebrewing. Cranston grew up in Los Altos, worked as a newspaper reporter, and served in the army during World War II, returning home to make a living in land investment and home construction—lucrative pursuits in postwar California—before being elected state comptroller and then senator in 1968. The Democrat was as good a legislator as any to push for the change and it only seemed appropriate that the effort at legalization should come from the Golden State, where so much commercial innovation was then happening.

Legalization, though, was not an inevitability no matter how busy homebrewers were underground. Similar legislation had failed in Congress before, and a bill brought up by the House of Representatives in 1976 would have limited a household to no more than thirty gallons of beer at a time and two hundred gallons over an entire year. Homebrewers found that unacceptable—it would mean less aging time, worse beer. "The worse your beer, the more you could make—the better your beer, the less you could make," Lee Coe told the Associated Press. Coe, whom Eckhardt described as "a California homebrew curmudgeon" from Berkeley, had written his own homebrewing guide in 1972. "The faster you could drink it, the more you could make—the slower you would drink it, the less you could make." We can note in the comments of Coe and others the evolution in the purpose of homebrew itself—during Prohibition, it was made almost entirely to pack a kick that could not be had commercially. Forty years later, it was made to savor and as an alternative to commercially available products. Cranston's key role came when that House bill wended its way to the upper chamber. He proposed an amendment, No. 3534, that deleted the thirty-gallon limit, and, on Friday, August 25, 1978, the Senate passed a reconciled bill by voice vote with no dissent. The part about homebrewing, nestled between one about home wine making and one about illegally produced beer, read:

(c) BEER FOR PERSONAL OR FAMILY USE—Subject to regulations prescribed by the Secretary, any adult may, without payment or tax, produce beer for personal or family use and not for sale. The aggregate amount of beer exempt from tax under this subsection with respect to any household shall not exceed—

1. 200 gallons per calendar year if there are 2 or more adults in such household,

or

2. 100 gallons per calendar year if there is only one adult in such household.

For purposes of this subsection, the term " adult" means an individual who has attained 18 years of age, or the minimum age (if any) established by law applicable in the locality in which the household is situated at which beer may be sold to individuals, whichever is greater.

The bill went to president Jimmy Carter, the devout Southern Baptist said to be a teetotaler,* who signed HR 1337 into law on October 14, 1978. It took effect February 1 of the following year.

It was perfect timing for Papazian. After graduation and a summer at a boys' camp in Maine, he had relocated to Boulder, Colorado, in the fall of 1972; a college roommate's brother was attending the University of Colorado

---

* Interestingly, Carter took up wine making after he left office (per Scott Benjamin, "Life After the White House," CBS News, February 11, 2009). Still, during the 1976 presidential campaign, the media many times reported that Carter never drank alcohol.

and had a floor for him to sleep on. He wanted a change, and he figured it was to be found out West, not on the East Coast. He found a job as a preschool teacher, as well as an apartment, and in 1973 he began teaching evening homebrewing classes in the kitchen. Papazian earned a reputation in those early Boulder days as "a magnet," according to one contemporary, a sort of amiable, bearded eccentric who might organize a marbles tournament or a pig roast for hundreds of his closest friends. The homebrewing classes, which he taught through the Community Free School ("where anyone could teach whatever they wanted"), fit snugly with this crunchy, up-from-the-people ethos. His first class had four students, and one of those was Charlie Matzen.

Matzen was, like Papazian, a schoolteacher in his late twenties who was also given to the outdoors, as well as a bit of what we would today call a foodie—or, at least, he could be known to throw parties with a lot of food, much the same way his new teacher and fast friend could throw parties with a lot of homebrew. The two started hanging out and traveling together, camping and chatting and plotting ways, as men of that age will do, of making more money, preferably at something they enjoyed. They found a way during a trip together to Hawaii, where Papazian joined Matzen, who was fixing up some condos that his parents owned. They went camping and talked of experiences in homebrewing—a full, five-gallon carboy of Matzen's had recently exploded, sending shards of glass into the walls and bubbly wort into a closet of the condo below—and an idea flashed: something for the homebrewers of America! The hobby was still illegal, but both men knew that it was growing in popularity. Still, aside from the one-off instruction books of Eckhardt, Burch, and a handful of others, there was little for homebrewers to tap into editorially for expertise and inspiration.

Thus *Zymurgy* magazine was born (the word refers to the study of yeast fermentation, especially for beer and wine). Papazian and Matzen pieced together the first issue back in Boulder with a few volunteers and a shoe-string budget of $4,000 (they each put half toward the venture). It ended up at twelve pages with two advertisements, one for a local wine-making and homebrew shop (which was also a coupon for 10 percent off), another for Green Mountain Herbs ("We've got hops—and more!"). The masthead on the second page consisted of Papazian as editor, Matzen as assistant editor, and Bob Telischak, a commercial artist in Nederland, Colorado, as "Art." An annual subscription and a yearlong membership in the newly formed American Homebrewers Association together cost $4; an extra $2 got you a copy of Papazian's self-published guide *The Joy of Brewing*, offered in the same issue for $2.50 by itself.

The contents revealed the template that had arisen by 1978 for writing and thinking about craft beer: *Zymurgy* was history, frequently of the personal kind, mixed with often highly technical how-to, all done to a whimsically friendly beat throughout. Papazian's backstory and recipe for "Stuffed Whole Lobster A-la-mazing"—"a shrimp and stuffed lobster feast for ten people"— ended with an exhortation to "smile when you drink homebrew." A detailed recipe for a seven-gallon batch of Vagabond Black Gingered Ale cautioned followers twice not to worry about the effort involved and to "have a beer, get relaxed" while the wort boiled. It was homebrewing presented as a calling since time immemorial, a club you wanted to join. The main story, "The Lost Art of Homebrewing," which Papazian had picked up and reprinted from a local library and which started on the cover and jumped to two interior pages, was by Karl F. Zeisler, a newspaperman turned journalism professor at the University of Michigan–Ann Arbor. He wrote it in 1935, two years after Prohibition ended, when the discovery of old brewing equipment in his basement from "pre–New Deal times" triggered a Proustian recollection of an often frustrating yet rewarding hobby:

> Homebrewing was practiced in upstairs halls, bedrooms, broom closets, telephone booths, and dumbwaiters, but my own technique required an entire basement. Mere dilettantes brewed only five gallons at a time—the quantity made from one can of malt—producing about 45 twelve-ounce bottles. But more sophisticated fermenters like myself made a double batch, netting approximately 85 bottles at a single ordeal. Purloining the bottles was one of the sobering elements in the whole business, for only plutocrats laid out good money for them, and many a nocturnal scavenging expedition up alleys was undertaken to meet the needs of a confirmed Brewer.

The rest of the inaugural *Zymurgy* unfolded in a similarly fun, instructional way, with hints at coming attractions such as recipes for "stouts that taste like stouts" and "the First Annual National Homebrew Competition sometime during the month of May, 1979." More passionate than professional, *Zymurgy* was literally not trying to be slick—it was rubber-cemented paper, rather than bound glossy pages—and a homebrewer in Brooklyn or Berkeley might be hard-pressed to recall, exactly, why he should care about this new publication out of Boulder. There wasn't much news about beer or homebrewing in it. It wasn't even the first of its kind—Fred Eckhardt had been publishing from time to time the *Amateur Brewer* journal since the late

1960s. It was part magazine, complete with news about breweries and reviews of brewing kits, and part detailed recipe book (*Amateur Brewer* number six in the summer of 1979 was the "special yeast issue").* Moreover, there were industry trade magazines such as *Brewers Digest,* which nearly every month pumped out sixty-plus pages of glossy beer coverage, including of smaller brewers; and the venerable *Modern Brewery Age,* a statistics-heavy newsletter and magazine going back to 1938.†

Charlie Papazian homebrewing.
Photo by Jay Quadracci, courtesy of Charlie Papazian

What Papazian and Matzen did have with *Zymurgy* was impeccable timing: volume one, number one, was dated December 1978, less than two months after President Carter signed HR 1337, with Alan Cranston's crucial amendment, into law. Zeisler's story shared a corner of the cover with part of an article, "Congress Passes Homebrew," that led with, "It's official. If you're eighteen years or older, you may legally brew one hundred gallons of beer for

---

* This *Amateur Brewer* should not be confused with a later, larger magazine of the same name.
† *Modern Brewery Age* was an exhaustive source for this book. The author would like to take this opportunity to commend it for its statistical thoroughness.

personal use each year—tax free! This probably isn't an astonishing piece of news, as beer-making has been legal in the minds of homebrewers for years."

Doubly fortuitous in *Zymurgy*'s timing was that its publication marked the launch of the American Homebrewers Association (AHA), the somewhat pretentiously grand title that Papazian and Matzen gave to their new conclave of . . . well, fellow Boulder-area enthusiasts and whatever wine-making shops nationwide they could locate through the Yellow Pages at the library. The magazine, though, offered a hint of the association's aspirations to have its grasp match its reach. The article on the homebrewing legislation ended with comments from "a high-ranking representative of the AHA" on the lawmakers "championing our cause on the floor of the Senate" and urged readers to remember those who voted against homebrewing the next time they went to the polls.

There were other beer organizations, much older than the AHA, that did their own arm-twisting on Capitol Hill. The United States Brewers' Association (USBA) dated from the late nineteenth century, when German immigrants who had turned to brewing organized, and the Brewers Association of America dated from World War II, when smaller regional breweries got together to ensure they were able to get supplies during wartime austerity. Between the two, they claimed as members just about every brewery in America. The USBA, in particular, held powerful sway in the halls of government. It had been led since 1962 by Henry King, a gregarious Philadelphia native and food industry executive who had won a Silver Star and a Purple Heart fighting in the Pacific Theater, and whose favorite drink was known to be a whiskey-based Rob Roy. King had proven particularly instrumental in lobbying for a tax break in 1976 that would turn out to be a godsend to craft brewers, beginning with Fritz Maytag's Anchor. The break reduced the federal excise tax on beer from nine dollars to seven dollars per barrel on the first sixty thousand barrels—so long as a brewery produced no more than two million barrels annually. Similar legislation had failed several times over the previous thirty years, but when it came up this time, King led behind-the-scenes lobbying that included fundraising from Big Beer and calling in favors from organized labor as well as other industries. It passed Congress in September 1976, and Stroh Brewing chairman Peter Stroh nudged fellow Michigander Gerald Ford to sign it without fanfare.

Papazian and Matzen's American Homebrewers Association had a long way to go if it hoped to be that influential. We find them instead on a December day in Boulder, one foot of snow already covering the ground and more falling. Papazian had driven his 1969 Toyota Corona to pick up the first two thousand copies of *Zymurgy* from the printer. Back at his place, volunteers helped organize and label the first mailing. About eight hundred homebrewers and their partisans in the Boulder area would receive copies; another one hundred would hit those wine-making shops nationwide that Papazian and Matzen had found in the Yellow Pages. Those shops soon would be able to legally sell the homebrewing supplies they had been selling anyway. Their inventories of such supplies, and those of vendors that sprouted entirely new after 1978, would grow in volume and quality, touching off a symbiotic role that resonates to this day. President Carter's pen stroke had been good news to the merry band of libationary eccentrics huddled in Papazian's home, news that would help their dim salvo echo well beyond the muffle of that snowy Colorado day.

"SMALL, HIGH-QUALITY FOOD PLACES"
Sonoma, CA | 1978

Don Barkley returned in the spring of 1978 to the warehouse on the outskirts of Sonoma. This time Jack McAuliffe was away, probably down in Davis doing more research or in San Francisco picking up grains from the city's last malt house, the Bauer & Schweitzer Malting Company. Suzy Stern greeted Barkley in the small office at the warehouse entrance.

He pleaded his case again: he was a student of Michael Lewis at UC-Davis and wanted practical experience this summer in small-scale commercial brewing because he hoped to found his own small brewery someday.

"Sure," a delighted Stern said, "come back! And you want to work for free, right?"

"Yeah, well, maybe for some free beer."

Barkley that summer fell into a grueling work rhythm with McAuliffe, Stern, and Zimmerman. Workdays often started around 6 AM with the milling of about one hundred pounds of malted barley in a wooden mill that McAuliffe had built, working off nineteenth-century designs. They would then mash the barley in hot water piped in from the nearby mountains to release the sugars that the yeast would convert to alcohol. While it mashed, they might sit around the small office, drinking coffee in the heat provided by the soot-belching stove (the local feed store sold stacks of coal, so fire was never a problem during the bitter winter months—warmth might be, but fire wasn't). Then they would boil the mashed barley and add hops, depending on the beer type. New Albion got its hops, mostly the Northern Brewer and Cluster varieties, from the family-owned Signorotti Farm in Sloughhouse, east of Sacramento; one or two bales would last an entire year.*

After the boil, the wort would be cooled and then left to ferment. Within a few weeks it would be time to bottle. Unlike Big Beer—unlike most commercial beer in the world—New Albion's ales were not pasteurized. Instead the yeast went into the bottles along with everything else, providing a further fermentation punch and a generally more complex beer. The beer was sold in returnable twelve-ounce bottles labeled by a machine built in 1910—"We don't believe in throwing things away," McAuliffe told a reporter—and packaged in twenty-four-count wooden cases made and silk-screened by McAuliffe himself. New Albion's ales were then sent out to a Bay Area that was apparently quite thirsty for them, no matter the price.

Bottles of New Albion might retail for ninety-five cents to $1.05 each, making them perhaps the most expensive beers produced in the United States. As with Anchor, most of the brewery's accounts were local (New Albion and Anchor occasionally shared shelf space, the first time since Prohibition two craft beers did), though McAuliffe started getting requests from other parts of the country. He could not deliver. The twelve-hour days were barely keeping up with the beer's popularity locally. McAuliffe had already upped production to pay for Barkley—the curious student became an increasingly masterful employee for $150 a week and all the beer he could drink. And it was not like the company was full of frills: Stern's van still served as the main distribution vessel, as well as the conduit for supply runs, and McAuliffe still lived arachnid-like above the shop. It was just that, perhaps primed by Anchor, the marketplace wanted its craft beer. The company lost $6,000 its first fiscal year and was on its way to falling just short of breaking even in its second. As the *Washington Post* noted in a Sunday story in July 1978:

> From the first week New Albion beers were available, the brewery has been unable to meet demand, selling every single bottle every single week despite the fact that the rate of production has already doubled. And some time this summer, McAuliffe will begin distributing kegs to local bars for the first time. As with the bottled product, the keg

---

* A hop bale weighed around two hundred pounds.

beer will be fermented in the container, making it America's only noncarbonated draft beer.

Was McAuliffe worried? Nah. "It's real beer," he assured the *Post*. "All you have to do is make a good beer, and it will sell." And, like Fritz Maytag down in SoMa, he would not advertise. "We don't really have to. If you make good beer—if you put money into the ingredients of your beer—you don't have to pay for advertising. It's when you get into the mass market that you can't tell your beer from the others except by the difference in advertising." He then harked back to Alice Waters's operation, also in the Bay Area. "It's just like cosmetics, or bread, in the big mass market. That's why we don't advertise; small, high-quality food places don't have to."

How such a quote must have gone over in the boardrooms of John Murphy's Miller. "Great Taste, Less Filling," "It's Miller Time"—these worked on the public. How dare this upstart! Big Beer's trade voice did, in fact, push back a bit. In a letter to his father dated August 1, 1978, McAuliffe recounted with a certain insouciance his run-in with Henry King's USBA for further comments he'd made about ingredient shortcuts. The letter, too, showed a son not yet thirty-five tell his father that he was part of something—something that was growing, that was directly related to the after-school hours at Clay's welding shop back in Fairfax and to the hobby he had dragged from Scotland and that they had engaged in together. Even the media coverage was growing—and its quality, too. Gone was the editorial wonderment of the year before at this strange thing called small-scale commercial brewing. It was replaced by earnest descriptions, clips from the time brim with explanations of such terms as "bottle fermentation," "cellaring temperatures," and "wort."

Dear Pop—

Here's a clipping from the *Washington Post*. I got my hand slapped by the United States Brewers Association, Augie Busch president, for saying all that stuff about rice & enzymes. I told them I was going to be good from now on.

We're getting new malt storage capacity—15 tons, so I won't have to go to the city [San Francisco] every two weeks to pick it up.

I think we'll show a profit this coming year.

Love,
Jack

THE BEARDED YOUNG MAN FROM CHICO
Chico, CA | 1978

Byron Burch listened to the twenty-three-year-old from Chico, California, go on about his plans to open a small brewery. Burch, the author of *Quality Brewing* and the co-owner by then of a homebrewing shop in San Rafael, was familiar with such a storyline; he knew Jack McAuliffe and Fritz Maytag and had heard of plans for other small breweries, though the idea still seemed novel, even foolhardy. The young man from Chico had written to him because of his book, and the two ran into each other at a wine-making trade show at the Claremont Hotel in the hills of Berkeley. They headed to Burch's place in the nearby Oakland flatlands to get away from the conference for a bit and to shoot the breeze over some of their own homebrews. The homebrews turned into dinner, and the young man ended up crashing there.

For the young man, the trade show in the spring of 1978 was a tipping point in a short life that seemed somehow to have been inexorably aimed toward craft beer. He had grown up in downtown Los Angeles and in the more suburban Woodland Hills, the middle child of three in a middle-class family of 1950s and 1960s America. He had a fascination with taking things apart that started in the cradle—the toaster, electrical outlet covers, even the washing machine, usually with kitchen knives or tweezers, anything in arm's reach and while his mother wasn't looking. Eventually, he came to learn how to put them back together as well, although not always in the same places: a neighbor's lawnmower engine once became the power for a go-cart. By adolescence he could build things from bare-bones ingredients; he would never forget the time he built a screwdriver from scratch in junior high shop class, something much harder than it sounds. He also would never forget the neighbor who homebrewed and made his own wine, the rows of carboys on a side porch with air locks bubbling away, the weekend pop-ins to discover pots of boiling malt and hops on the kitchen stove.

In the summer of 1969, he gave it a go himself. He spent less than twenty-five dollars at John Daume's wine-making shop in Woodland Hills to buy an open-top plastic fermenter (like what McAuliffe bought in Glasgow a few years before, it was a glorified trash can), a five-gallon glass carboy to ferment the beer, a hydrometer to meaure its alcohol content, a short length of plastic tubing, and a crude bottle capper. He bought the ingredients at the grocery store down the road: canned Blue Ribbon malt extract and a lot of cane sugar. He was aiming for high alcohol content, not high quality. That changed in 1970, when, while at a homebrewing shop, he discovered Fred Eckhardt's *A Treatise on Lager Beers*. Now a high school student who had little use for his classes, he devoured the information and switched to all-grain brewing, the technical know-how that had been building since before he could walk gelling nicely with his newfound passion to produce not-terrible concoctions that he and his friends could enjoy.

Shortly after graduation—he skipped the actual ceremony—our young man, now conspicuously bearded even though not yet eighteen, commenced a couple of seemingly random journeys that in fact turned out to be as life altering as the neighbor who homebrewed. The first trip was a ten-hour drive to Chico, about 175 miles northeast of San Francisco, so a couple of friends could check out the local college there. They ended up in the impossibly seedy La Grande Hotel downtown, with no air-conditioning in the sultry June night-time, an oddball assortment of permanent residents, and a shared bathroom down the hall spattered with blood. It was not an auspicious welcome to the town of thirty thousand. The young man decided to stay nonetheless; it was as good a redoubt as any to plan his post–Southern California life. He looked in the Yellow Pages for bike shops—he had been working at them on and off since junior high—and landed a job at a local Schwinn store. He and his friends the next day found a five-bedroom house to rent on the south end of town, and he called his mother to tell her he was moving in two weeks.

The second journey then commenced. He and a friend biked their way roughly ninety miles from Novato to Ukiah, stopping along the way to sample the wares of a burgeoning Northern California wine scene—and to discover, almost by accident, commercially produced craft beer. Our young man had heard of the particular brand, maybe even knew a bit about its recent history as a resurrected example of pre-Prohibition brewing. Regardless of what he knew, the timing was perfect, as the brewery had only a short time before begun distributing bottles, and it was in a small restaurant off Highway 1 that Ken Grossman had his first Anchor Steam.

We can with hindsight trace a straight line from Grossman's encounter with Anchor Steam to his development of what became the definitional pale ale of the West Coast—what made "West Coast" an adjective in craft beer. He spent the next few years studying chemistry as well as other sciences at Chico State and a nearby community college, working on and off in bike shops, and honing his skills as a homebrewer to the point where he was able to malt his own barley. Part of this was necessity, as ingredients were scarce; another part was that Grossman and new wife Katie were leading an up-from-the earth existence in their one-room house next to a little creek in the foothills above Oroville, California. They raised goats for milk and made their own cheese. Homebrewing meshed nicely with such a slow approach to food. By 1976, Grossman and a next-door neighbor were co-owners of a homebrew shop in Chico, paying fifty-seven dollars a month to rent a second-floor space in the La Grande Hotel, the same dive he had crashed in right out of high school his first night in town. (When money was tight, they paid their rent in janitorial services for the building.) Grossman taught homebrewing classes at the shop, building up a customer base that, along with a side gig brokering the sales of wine grapes, allowed him to quit his second job at the bike shops. The line was almost complete: Ken Grossman could now focus on beer full-time.

The 1978 trade show in Oakland provided him an entrée into what he would later call "my community." He met Fred Eckhardt, Byron Burch, and many of the homebrew-shop owners who had supplied his own venture early on. He also met Fritz Maytag, who acted as the tour guide during a group visit to Anchor's Eighth Street brewery, which struck Grossman as "fairly crude" with a "small, cramped bottling line. It had only a few open fermenters and a handful of aging tanks in a dank cellar." No matter. He understood its significance—the only other brewery he had ever toured was the gigantic Anheuser-Busch plant and Busch Gardens in Van Nuys, California, as a child. Anchor was something much different. So was its beer. At the end of Maytag's tour, Grossman bought cases of Old Foghorn; initially brewed in November 1975, it was the first new barleywine a domestic brewer had produced since Prohibition, reviving perhaps the world's strongest, most complex ale style for American palates. He had never tasted anything like it before.

Grossman's tour of Anchor came at a transitional time for the brewery. It was outgrowing the Eighth Street location; Anchor's production had increased twenty times over, from six hundred barrels annually in 1965 of iffy steam beer in kegs to 12,500 barrels of consistently high-quality beer in different styles, available from kegs or bottles. Maytag, after a long search, would move the twelve-employee operation in the late summer of 1979 about a mile southward, to an old Chase & Sanborn coffee roastery at Mariposa and De Haro Streets. In the new facility, Anchor's bottle runs could jump from 70 a minute to 275. While other operations were in their infancies, just toddling forth into the unforgiving beer market of consolidation and homogeneity, such growth was a sign of Anchor's entry into a confident adulthood. General Brewing, the only other brewery left in San Francisco, capped its last bottles of Lucky Lager at the end of March 1978 and closed for good, leaving Maytag's operation supreme locally. Nationally, Anchor was distributing as far as Wisconsin and New Jersey, and it was leading the way in fresh styles with Liberty Ale, Old Foghorn, Anchor Porter, and, since November 1975, the first seasonal ale by an American brewer since Prohibition.* More than that—and more important for the larger movement—Maytag had developed a reputation as an approachable godfather of craft brewing, the man you could see or at least telephone for free advice.

If his 1978 visit to this transitioning Anchor opened Grossman's eyes, a visit that same year to Jack McAuliffe's New Albion changed his life. Grossman's older brother had before the Berkeley trade show introduced him to a fellow homebrewer and cycling enthusiast named Paul Camusi. Grossman and Camusi eventually fell into talking about opening their own commercial brewery, though neither was quite sure what that meant. The visit to New Albion, which they planned after the Berkeley trade show, clarified things immensely. They saw in McAuliffe's gravity-flow system of secondhand equipment, cobbled together by pluck and luck, a homebrewing kit writ slightly larger. It brewed forty-five gallons at a time; Grossman was brewing fifteen gallons at a time at his home in Oroville, having fabricated a refrigerated cabinet on the covered porch. A little elbow grease, some start-up capital, a willingness to, like McAuliffe, work tortuous hours—it didn't seem so far-fetched. Grossman and Camusi, epiphany in hand, finished the New Albion tour with McAuliffe, who charged them for the samples at the end and was eager to get back to work.

McAuliffe would not remember the bearded young man from Chico stopping by—so many people did in those days and, besides, Grossman had toured with a group. But Grossman never forgot. His visit to New Albion was one of the tipping points of that tipping-point year for American craft

---

* The 1975 seasonal ale was called Our Special Ale and became known over time—with regular tweaks to the recipe—as Christmas Ale. It began life modeled after Liberty Ale, which became a standalone brand for the second time in 1983 (per Dave Burkhart at Anchor).

beer, an event that was by no means inevitable but that changed the course of our culinary history.

THE FIREMAN AND THE GOAT SHED

Novato, CA; Hygiene, CO | 1979–1980

The June 1979 newsletter of the Maltose Falcons carried this report:

> The California Steam Brewery has just begun under the watchful eye of Rich Dye. The DeBakker Brewing Company owned by Tom DeBakker [*sic*] has just gotten underway. That makes four small breweries, all located in the Greater San Francisco Bay Area! We all welcome you as worthwhile additions to the fine art of brewing and look forward to trying your product. If some of you good people "up north" could furnish the Maltose Falcons with their addresses, we would be grateful.

The other two small breweries, of course, were Anchor and New Albion. De Bakker and California Steam were the third and fourth American craft breweries since Prohibition. The latter disappeared quickly—not least because the name and the label may have been all-too-similar to Anchor's—and was notable largely because Dye was a vintner who ran a winery out of the same warehouse that held his brewery; he was the first to make the leap from fine wine to craft beer.* The other brewery mentioned in the newsletter had sturdier staying power.

Tom de Bakker did not know of Jack McAuliffe's operation until he read about it in the papers. He just knew, ever since he had tasted imports like Pilsner Urquell and Bass, that he liked good beer. The son of a San Francisco socialite and a Dutch-born father, de Bakker grew up with one sibling, a sister, in the city's Presidio Heights neighborhood. He went northward to study

---

* California Steam was as short-lived as its second word. It ran into legal trouble very early on because of the similarity of its name to Anchor's signature brand (though there is no record in California of a court case involving the companies). The Maltose Falcons newsletter may signify the most thorough reference to California Steam in its time.

fine arts, particularly sculpting, at Sonoma State University, where he met his wife, Jan. The couple spent about a year in Hawaii after graduation, and then returned in 1973 to hunt for work. De Bakker joined the fire department of Marin County, about thirty minutes north of San Francisco; he would rise to captain and then chief before his mid-thirties. All along, on and off, he homebrewed, producing drinkable batches from the get-go with the usual amalgam of canned syrups and secondhand know-how. This homebrewing, in an increasingly familiar pattern, led to commercial brewing. De Bakker built a gravity-flow brewery in about two thousand square feet of warehouse space in Novato, around twenty miles north of Sonoma, using secondhand equipment, including a chiller for the wort from an old dairy farm, a grain grinder he pieced together from junkyard parts, and a mash tun and kettle from a liquidator. The barrels for aging he fabricated from old soda ones. De Bakker got his grains from the Bauer & Schweitzer Malting Company in San Francisco, positioning his pickup truck in the same spot where the railroad cars would await deposits, taking on a ton or so, and then fishtailing it back up to Novato.

In July 1979, the DeBakker Brewing Company capped its first bottles of pale ale with a six-hundred-dollar contraption its founder got for fifty dollars from the Falstaff brewery on Tenth Street when it closed the year before. The bottles themselves were overstock from a company that supplied the Olympia Brewery in Seattle. Their labels included a sharp red seal at the center, with an eagle clutching barley and hop twines (the ATF made him remove a shield with the Stars and Stripes across the eagle, arguing it was too close to symbolizing the USA, which was de Bakker's whole point). Around the seal ran not only a description of the beer but also a little education for the consumer, who might be scared off by that pulpy film undergirding the beer: "The fine sediment at the bottom of the bottle is the result of a natural bottle conditioning using the krausen process." Five hundred cases hit the shelves of Bay Area retailers, selling for ninety cents to $1.20 a bottle. The de Bakkers knew what they were up against but, like the pioneers down Highway 101 in Sonoma, proceeded with a dash of swagger. "What Suzy Stern, Jack McAuliffe, Jan, and I are doing is just the beginning," he told the *Los Angeles Times* for a front-page story on the "resurgence of small breweries." "I think tiny breweries like DeBakker and New Albion will be springing up all over the United States just as boutique wineries have in recent years. It is just a matter of time."

The twenty-nine-year-old firefighter, who kept his day job through it all, was on to something. As the Maltose Falcons newsletter suggests, with its request for basic information like addresses, the American craft beer movement, for all the flurry of 1978, remained a diffuse one, often still dependent on word of mouth and lacking much commercial infrastructure (in the de Bakkers' case, they replaced McAuliffe's discarded PepsiCo barrels with discarded Coca-Cola ones for aging). The twenty-first century may have been fast approaching, but the communication, with its mailings and phone calls, remained more akin to the nineteenth.

Fortuitously, though, in the same Northern California where the craft beer movement was taking its first baby steps, the American fine wine movement was at a toddler's trot. Prohibition had never decimated the winemaking industry as it did the brewing industry. Loopholes allowed for the ongoing production of sacramental wine and for households to order up to two hundred gallons of grape juice annually—ostensibly for the juice itself, but invariably for home wine making. Such end runs around Prohibition allowed many wineries and vineyards, especially in Northern California, to keep operating, however limited their options. When Repeal came in 1933, then, the industry was able to more easily pick up right where it had left off thirteen years before. That is not to say that Prohibition did not stymie commercial wine making in the United States—it did—but not as much as it did commercial brewing, which all but disappeared, save for low-alcohol near beers, for more than a decade. Still, much of the wine these post-Prohibition wineries produced was utilitarian and undistinguished. They came from lower-quality grapes rather than from higher-quality varietals such as merlot and cabernet sauvignon, the sorts born in Europe and undergirding the famed French wine industry. What's more, these wines were fortified—essentially grape juice high in alcohol and sold from screwtop jugs. They were popular with an American public largely unfamiliar with the likes of merlot and cabernet sauvignon, which were not widely available anyway. Then, beginning around the time Fritz Maytag saved Anchor, wineries started popping up in the same San Francisco Bay Area dedicated not to the reigning fortified plonk popular with the masses, but to those European styles so prized overseas and among a small coterie of domestic consumers. Robert Mondavi, scion of Napa Valley wine-making family that specialized in more utilitarian fare, launched in 1966 the first groundup winery in the United States since Prohibition dedicated to European styles. His eponymous operation, which won plaudits early on for its cabernet sauvignon and a white release it called Fume Blanc, sparked first a trickle in smaller, boutique wineries and then a flood beginning in the 1970s. Coverage of wine blossomed during the decade, too—publications such as the *New York Times* added wine critics and outlets such as *Wine Spectator* and *Wine Advocate* launched—and soon fine wine, the corked European styles and some American counterparts such as zinfandel, were outselling the fortified screwtops. By 1975, more acres of the Sonoma County where the de Bakkers brewed were covered by wineries and vineyards than were ever covered before Prohibition, most of the grapes grown to produce delicately dry wines meant as much to inebriate as to impress. Tom de Bakker in particular, who had happily discovered the burgeoning wine industry and culture while in college in Sonoma, could be forgiven for thinking the same pleasant fate awaited craft beer.

Grossman and Camusi believed there was an audience out there, too, so much so that they took their time in building what became the Sierra Nevada Brewing Company. They knew of other breweries starting up in 1979 and into 1980, including DeBakker, California Steam, and Cartwright Portland, further up the road in Portland, Oregon. Founded by Charles and Shirley Coury, who had owned a vineyard for thirteen years in nearby Forest Grove, Cartwright Portland ("Cartwright" was Shirley's maiden name) debuted from a building on SE Main Street in the late spring of 1980 with about 150 cases of a mild ale in the English style. It sold for one dollar a bottle and did not get the warmest reception from consumers. "The beer wasn't great and the bottling was downright poor," went one account. Still, local enthusiasts really wanted it to work—the Courys' enterprise represented the first craft brewery not only in Oregon but also in the entire Pacific Northwest outside of Northern California.

Randolph "Stick" Ware, David Hummer, and Al Nelson were the first to open a craft brewery beyond the West Coast—and the first to open one in a goat shed. For Ware, it all started back in his junior year of high school in South Pasadena, California, when a friend's uncle—one of fourteen siblings of the friend's mother, all born on the Louisiana bayou—blew into town to avoid some legal entanglements back home and took the boys to Los Angeles to buy homebrewing supplies. Uncle Slim showed them the ways of bread yeast and Blue Ribbon extract, and the boys made some pretty terrible beers. The bug had bitten, however, and Ware continued to tinker with homebrewing through college and graduate school in experimental physics, right into his postdoctorate at the Joint Institute for Laboratory Astrophysics out of the University of Colorado in Boulder. The institute's chairman was David Hummer, a theoretical astrophysicist of Amish stock who was married to a British woman. Hummer himself had made the leap beyond extracts and syrups to all-grain brewing; he crushed the malted barley with a rolling pin and used a bridal veil to dip them into a five-gallon thermos cooler. *Voilà*—mash tun! The pair of PhDs brewed some fine batches this way, so much so that colleagues came up to them in the cafeteria after one particular party and asked for any more of the beer that had fueled it. Ware looked at Hummer.

"Hey, we ought to start a brewery," he said, more than half-joking.

As these sober boasts go, though, Ware soon found himself on the phone with the Bureau of Alcohol, Tobacco, and Firearms (ATF) office in Denver. A helpful voice on the other end sent a two-foot-thick stack of papers that Ware promptly left for weeks undisturbed on the kitchen table of the small farmhouse he shared with a fellow musician named Otto Zavatone (Ware played sax and Zavatone the piano in a local band called the Fornicators). He had his work at the institute, his music gigs, and the small farm where he and Zavatone grew and raised what they could eat (they once hit a monthly low of ten dollars in groceries)—he didn't have time for red tape. Eventually, he confronted the stack and called the ATF back. The same helpful voice directed him to the parts that he absolutely had to fill out, and on September 25, 1979, he and Hummer and a third partner, an engineer named Al Nelson, had the forty-third brewery license in the United States.

They then sought materiel and advice. Ware visited Jack McAuliffe at New Albion and got further help, including with supplies like grains and hops, from what would seem like an odd choice: Jeff Coors, scion of the increasingly cultish Big Beer brand (Coors was available only in eleven states by the mid-1970s, and no less than Henry Kissinger and Gerald Ford were said to have had cases of it flown to Washington, DC). Coors's grandfather and Ware's grandmother had dated—plus Jeff Coors thought it would be good for legislative lobbying purposes to have a second brewery in Colorado. Ware, Hummer, and Nelson also retrieved in Denver an old stainless-steel food-processing kettle that could hold a barrel and a half at a time. And they named Zavatone, who had worked as a chef and a fisherman, brewmaster. Finally, Nelson had a farm near Hygiene, at the edge of the Rocky Mountain National Park, and on that farm he had some goats, and next to the goats was a steel shed that they then turned into the Boulder Brewing Company's first brewhouse. In it, they brewed a stout that won a blue ribbon at the American Homebrewers Association's first-ever national competition, held in the brewery's nearby namesake city. It was a nice little confidence builder.

The partners were soon spending $25,000 on the construction of a three-story, one-thousand-square-foot brewhouse, also on Nelson's farm, to supplant the goat shed. They didn't have the local government green-lights for it, but they figured—correctly, it turned out—that once it was built, it would be hard for the authorities to order it shuttered. When the authorities did get wind of the brewhouse, they were actually helpful and a tad bemused by the whole enterprise. Their response was like the one from Sonoma County that Jack McAuliffe encountered in setting up New Albion four years before: Who had ever *heard* of such a thing as a new small brewery? By July 4, 1980, Boulder Brewing had twenty cases of hand-labeled, hand-filled bottles to sell at the Gold Hill Inn, a rustic resort near the Rocky Mountain National Park. The American craft beer movement was no longer a West Coast thing.

THE WEST COAST STYLE
Chico, CA | 1979–1981

Ken Grossman and Paul Camusi reassessed their plans. They knew they needed to talk to Jack McAuliffe again. They drove the three hours from Chico to Sonoma and analyzed the mechanics—and, more subtly, the finances—of the nation's first start-up craft brewery. McAuliffe and Suzy Stern—Jane Zimmerman had bowed out by then to pursue what became a successful career as a therapist—were still working long days alongside Barkley and a handful of others, including those brought in to bottle on Wednesdays. And the output was still relatively small, with the forty-five-gallon batches translating into about twenty cases of beer at a time.

The only big thing that had changed at New Albion by then was that it had switched grain suppliers—from the soon-to-close Bauer & Schweitzer Malting Company to the soon-to-move Anchor nearby. As he often did in his role as munificent godfather, Fritz Maytag cut a deal with McAuliffe to supply New Albion with grains. Every six to eight weeks, someone would drive Stern's Dodge van to San Francisco, with a bin hooked up to the back that could hold as much as sixteen hundred pounds of malted barley. The driver would spray about that amount from Anchor's silo and drive it right back to Sonoma.

Otherwise, things in the corrugated-steel warehouse continued apace, with fame lapping at the edges of Jack McAuliffe's dream. Michael Lewis, by then renowned in the industry for regularly placing his UC-Davis graduates at some of the nation's most well-known breweries, routinely led classes of ten to twenty through the brewery, with McAuliffe, in these instances, an obliging tour guide willing to answer numerous questions. Stern once found an envelope in the office mail addressed simply as "The Brewery, Northern California." *Newsweek* mentioned "America's smallest brewery" in a story about the big ones ("The people who sit at a bar and drink eight or nine bottles of Budweiser are not going to be the people who drink New Albion," Stern told the weekly). And one day, someone knocked on the door—someone who had written some of the era's more memorable pop songs. James Taylor was a beer fan and had heard of the little brewery; might he look around? Beer writer Michael Jackson, too, dropped by. Tom de Bakker picked the critic up at the San Francisco airport and showed him first around his own brewery in Novato, then he drove him twenty miles in his 1968 Triumph 250 to New Albion. There Jackson signed a copy of his book *The World Guide to Beer*. Finally, none other than *New York Times* wine critic Frank Prial paid a visit in late spring and liked what he saw, telling the Old Gray Lady's influential readership of "what may be one of the country's best beers." Prial took refuge amid the brewing terminology in a wine simile: "Because New Albion is not filtered, it is not crystal clear like most mass produced beers. It also contains small amounts of yeast. Like true Champagne, New Albion's final fermentation literally takes place in the bottle."

These were heady times for New Albion, and Grossman and Camusi at first sought to emulate McAuliffe's approach of rendering their homebrewing operation into a slightly larger commercial one. But then they thought harder about it. New Albion's output in 1979 was sufficient to cover the brewery's operating expenses, but not enough to fund much growth. If they wanted their own commercial venture to be profitable, then they would have to brew more beer at a time. They settled on a ten-barrel system, which could produce roughly 315 gallons per batch, and set about physically and financially building what became Sierra Nevada Brewing Company in Chico. Their efforts are illustrative of the challenges that start-up craft breweries still faced fourteen years after Maytag saved Anchor and more than three years after McAuliffe built New Albion. There simply wasn't the equipment available; and traditional funding, from commercial or investment banks and private equity firms, was a nonstarter. What institution in its right fiscal mind would loan someone thousands—maybe hundreds of thousands—to build a small, inherently fragile company to compete with Anheuser-Busch and Miller?

Even Maytag, with his profitability since 1975, confronted a bankruptcy scare involving Anchor's move to Mariposa Street in August 1979. In fact, that first year at the new location was déjà vu all over again: Anchor lost money. Worse yet, Maytag had pledged his own assets, including real estate and stocks, to build out the Mariposa site, designing and buying equipment before any financing came through, leaving him with sleepless nights. Then one morning, he woke up, got dressed, went downstairs, and couldn't leave. He went back to bed. The larger plant, though, did allow Anchor to expand its production and therefore its distribution; soon it regained its financial footing. Still, in a way as pioneering as much of what Maytag had done to that point, the bankruptcy scare served as an unspoken cautionary tale to the second wave of American craft brewers that came after him: watch your growth, kids. Some in the second wave (and third and fourth) would heed this tale. Others would not.

As for McAuliffe, as heady as the times were for his little warehouse operation, he did not recommend the business. He told the *Washington Post* that first full year of operations:

> You know, you have to either have a great deal of money—an unbounded amount of capital—or you have to be able to weld and do water chemistry and build the place and go get money and write business plans and do design, mechanical analysis, structural analysis, and all that stuff . . . and then run the brewery. There aren't too many of them out there like that.
>
> You have to be totally committed. The only thing you think about is beer and brewing. You work 10 hours a day, eight days a week. That's the way it is.

Grossman especially possessed such mechanical know-how from his work with bicycles as well as from his homebrewing. What he and the other second-wave craft brewers lacked was access to capital—the other route to a semblance of stability, according to McAuliffe. It was not just the incredulity of traditional money sources, it was the trend of things, the very notion of where beer as an industry was going, the strivings of the early craft movement notwithstanding. Bob Weinberg was the era's most respectable industry analyst and was often quoted by a media that understood beer through the prism designed by Miller's John Murphy or August Anheuser Busch III.

A former air force officer, Department of Defense analyst, and MIT lecturer with a formidable knack for number crunching, Weinberg went to work for Anheuser-Busch in 1966 as a vice president of corporate planning; five years later he struck out on his own to produce for clients exhaustive surveys of the brewing industry. By 1980, Weinberg was predicting that only a handful of breweries would remain by the new millennium. It was a pervasive and persuasive shorthand. Bill Coors, grandson of the Big Beer founder and driving force behind the aluminum can that did so much to change the way Americans consumed beer, told Henry King of the USBA that there would be only five breweries by the year 2000. "I was simply extrapolating the death curve out," Coors said later.

Steve Dresler, Sierra Nevada's brewmaster, adds hops to the early brew kettle that Ken Grossman fabricated. *Courtesy of Sierra Nevada Brewing Company*

To get capital in this climate meant to get it from yourself, friends, or family (or, most likely, a combination). Grossman and Camusi decided after visiting McAuliffe again that they would need $50,000 to start up Sierra Nevada in Chico (another early decision after other locations around San Francisco were ruled out). They foolishly tried banks first—Grossman did not own any credit cards and had run his homebrewing shop on the good graces of his own prompt bill payments to nonmainstream venders; Camusi may have had a gas card but not much else. Still, they buttoned up and went into banks—and were duly turned away. It was not merely the lack of credit but the state of the brewing industry that banks could read about via Weinberg, Coors, and others. A brewery—a small one in a relatively remote area of Northern California at that—was simply not a sound investment. At this point, we can almost step back and see the American craft beer movement as a doomed venture by 1979 and 1980, one that was by no means assured of stumbling out of the decade of stagflation and oil crises in any kind of fighting shape. The country, like a listing ship in rough seas, was about to turn into a major recession that would make borrowing all the more difficult, for craft brewers and everyone else.

Grossman and Camusi dug into their own pockets—Grossman sold the homebrewing shop in the old La Grande Hotel for a few thousand—scrounging just over $15,000. Then, as their original $50,000 projection doubled, they hit up family, arranging for them to invest through a limited partnership. The business would lose money, the two figured; with a limited partnership, at least their relatives could claim the losses on their taxes. It was a relentlessly stressful time. The two drove to Mount Vernon, Washington, one day to pick up a secondhand bottle filler, washer, and labeler for a total of $5,250. On the hours-long drive back, Grossman, then a married father of one, had plenty of time to mull over the fact that he had just spent nearly all the money he had to his name—and for only a part of the operation. Maybe this whole brewery thing was a mistake. Look at Jack McAuliffe and his crew—ten- to twelve-hour days for twenty cases per batch, even three-plus years in. Look at Fritz Maytag, like a duck, gliding along on the surface, paddling furiously just below. Or look at . . who? Ware, Hummer, and Nelson in the Rocky Mountain goat shed? The de Bakkers, where Tom worked on his days off from firefighting and Jan on the others?

Still, the pair pressed on, downsizing the physical size of their brewery, a converted metal warehouse on Gilman Way in Chico, to avoid additional city fees; soaking up information from Michael Lewis and the UC-Davis brewing library; and scooping up future fermenters and refrigerators from old dairy farms in Northern California that themselves had fallen victim to industrial consolidation. Then Grossman and Camusi settled on a recipe for what would become their signature beer, a fateful decision they made simply because they liked the taste and because Grossman had been visiting Washington's Yakima Valley regularly to pick out favored hops for his homebrewing shop. They did several test batches of various beers, including stouts and pale ales, using different hops, and finally they settled on a pale ale with generous helpings of Cascade.

Grossman and Camusi brewed the first batch of what became known as Sierra Nevada Pale Ale in the third week of November 1980.* They spent

---

* The first beer the pair tried to brew commercially was, in fact, a stout, with the pale ale attempts starting a few days later (per Ken Grossman to the author in an e-mail, July 2012).

time tweaking it, however, and it was not until the eleventh batch of the recipe the following March that they were satisfied they should sell it commercially. Released in the spring of 1981, Sierra Nevada Pale Ale was a bold, bitter statement in more than recipe: The start-up had chosen a distinctly American, and slightly more expensive, hop variety to power its pale ale's taste, one developed, cultivated, and popularized commercially in the western United States. The Eurocentric conception of what a bitter beer could be would change forever. The West Coast was prepared to define the style for the world.

MAYFLOWER REFUGEE
Boulder, CO; Manhattan | 1981–1984

Daniel Bradford was restless. He had spent the last dozen years on a headlong run from his roots on the East Coast and now found himself directionless in the Rockies. The second child of six and the eldest son, he had grown up in New England acutely aware of being a direct descendant of William Bradford, who came over on the *Mayflower* and was an early governor of the colony that became Massachusetts. When he was eleven, his father, who had bought a firm that manufactured papermaking machines, moved the family from that state to Maine, where they lived in a house dating from 1694 on one hundred acres of land fertile with pheasant, fox, and moose. It was isolated—enough to drive a young man to romantic daydreams of escape. Bradford chose the West; it was more of a concept to him than a geographic destination (aside from a visit to an uncle in Minnesota, he had never left the region his ancestors pioneered). So, after graduating with his high school class of seventy-two in 1968, the tall, wiry young man went west, to the University of Colorado at Boulder. It was the first time he'd been on an airplane.

Hippies were rare in Maine. In Colorado, they were de rigueur. Within a few weeks, Bradford was part of the counterculture. He protested against Vietnam and for civil rights and women's lib; there were sit-ins and demonstrations, confrontations with the police and speeches to the masses (Bradford delivered one on campus, though later he would not be able to recall the topic). He also worked jobs in the publishing industry, including for a bookstore, an academic publisher, and a magazine wholesaler. The whole time he studied the social sciences, intrigued by people's decision-making processes: Why do we do what we do? The coursework qualified him for more coursework, and he pursued first a master's and then a PhD at Colorado before becoming disillusioned with the snippy infighting of academia and walking away "totally disoriented" at the end of the 1970s. Friends connected him with a job selling books door to door, which was fine for the intellectual refugee—he hustled enough in the summer to take the fall and winter off. During that time he hoofed it around Europe, including France, Italy, and Britain, handed off from friend to friend and couch to couch, now past thirty and still searching for something that he knew wasn't anywhere near rural Maine. After he returned to Boulder in 1981, a friend made what seemed like an odd suggestion, even with Bradford's publishing background: become a literary agent. Not only that, but the friend had a particular client in mind: Charlie Papazian.

Papazian's six-page syllabus for his early homebrewing classes in Boulder had grown to a seventy-eight-page, self-typed, self-published title in 1976 called *The Complete Joy of Homebrewing*, which sold a couple of thousand copies. In that fateful year, 1978, he revised it to about one hundred pages and again self-published it. This was the edition that Bradford picked up on the recommendation of their mutual friend. He was blown away. He knew little about beer and less about brewing, but he got that Papazian's breezy, conversational style nonetheless exposed a wealth of technical know-how. Plus, as with the launch of both *Zymurgy* and the American Homebrewers Association, it was all just such perfect timing. Legalization at the federal level had opened up the pipeline for higher-quality ingredients and now allowed for a freer flow of ideas between commercial brewers and the homebrewers who might want to join them. Papazian himself was a charming evangelist, the same "magnet" who had arrived in Boulder almost a decade before, sleeping on other people's floors as he traveled to deliver lectures and tutorials and setting up the AHA's office on his approximately fifty-square-foot back porch. When Bradford met Papazian, the AHA's staff consisted simply of volunteers plus Papazian and Charlie Matzen, neither of whom paid themselves in the first couple of years. Papazian was able to quit his day job teaching kindergarten and preschool in Boulder in 1981, though Matzen continued to teach sixth grade in nearby Longmont. Matzen left the AHA soon after to pursue a successful real estate career, though he did serve as a judge at early homebrew competitions and on the association's eventual board of directors.

It was clear to Matzen that his friend was more passionate, seeing the AHA as a real nationwide venture, a way of professional life.

Papazian's association was determined, certainly, but was still in start-up mode more than two years on. And it was far from nationwide—outside of the Boulder-Denver area, you would have been hard-pressed to find many card-carrying AHA members. The evangelist needed an evangelist. Bradford became the AHA's first full-time hire as marketing director. He stood out, especially in contrast to the bearded, breezy Papazian: the wiry Bradford was usually clean-shaven and could even be found in a snugly knotted tie if duties demanded it. His first order of business would be finding a mainstream publisher for *The Complete Joy of Homebrewing*.

It was an arduous, at times insulting task. Bradford traveled early on to the pitiless concrete canyons of Manhattan, where he kept a ridiculous schedule, taking meetings with nineteen publishers over three and a half days, animated by the belief that Papazian's booklet from the 1970s could be a bona fide book in the 1980s—and not just a book, a brisk seller powered by a now-bicoastal movement that had added several comers to its commercial ranks in recent years. The AHA by 1984 was claiming more than three thousand dues-paying members—a startling swell in less than five years that nevertheless seemed rather paltry to publishers in Gotham. Bradford confronted a skepticism similar to what craft brewers confronted from retailers and distributors: Craft what? You mean a whole book on brewing your own beer? For national release? On a major imprint? You can't do that; there aren't enough possible buyers to justify it. Bradford had never worked Manhattan before. He was sleeping on friends' floors. He was rushing everywhere. I am going to sell this goddamn book, he thought. Faced with his persistence, every publisher smiled and told him they were interested. He flew back to Boulder satisfied and took up his marketing duties again at the AHA. Not a single publisher responded over the next two weeks. He had been sold slow no's.

Bradford pressed on. He had little to lose—he was living in a basement apartment and driving a car that didn't go in reverse. He secured one more sit-down with Avon, a publisher best known for romance paperbacks and comic books. Back in Manhattan, he resolved not to leave the publisher's offices without a firm commitment. "You'd be stupid not to do this deal," he told them. Papazian's book was so . . . *there*. It was a countercultural memo to the yuppie decade, Maynard G. Krebs teaching Gordon Gekko how to homebrew—more than that, how to get back to the earth a bit and away from the plastic fantastic, an urtext for the locavore movement. It might have been overselling, but it worked. Avon offered a small advance, and Papazian got on with it back in Boulder. Through the late spring and summer of 1983, he spent the mornings and afternoons writing in longhand, and then, after everyone else had gone home from the AHA offices at his place on Nineteenth Street, he would input the writing into the word processor via the association's lone computer.

The 331-page book he produced, which was published nationally in 1984, became rather quickly the bestselling book on homebrewing ever, an expanded update to the earlier works of Fred Eckhardt and Byron Burch and their British counterparts from yesteryear.* There were an estimated 1.4 million homebrewers in America by then, and many responded to Papazian's tone in *The Complete Joy of Homebrewing*, just as Bradford expected. That tone was set in the book's introduction, especially the last three words of its third paragraph, part of a mantra that would become inextricably linked to Papazian:†

Making quality beer is EASY! Don't let anyone tell you any differently. At the same time, making bad beer is easy, too. The difference between making good beer and bad beer is simply knowing those little things that make a big difference and insure success every time. Above all, the homebrewer should remember not to worry because worrying can spoil the taste of beer faster than anything else. Relax. Don't worry.

The tone belied the technical knowledge, including detailed recipes, that Papazian sought to impart from his years of homebrewing and teaching homebrewing. The book's sections for the beginning, intermediate, and advanced homebrewer were divided into careful demarcations. Witness the table of contents for "The Secrets of Fermentation" starting on page 102, under the intermediate section:

- Temperature
- pH
- Nutrients and food
- Oxygen
- Good health
- Life Cycle: Respiration
- Fermentation

---

* Its status as the bestselling homebrewing book takes into account sales from subsequent editions.
† The full mantra became, "Relax. Don't Worry. Have a Homebrew."

- Sedimentation
- Listening to your beer

And, for those paying particularly close attention to the American craft beer movement in 1984, *The Complete Joy of Homebrewing* got some added gravitas via a preface by Michael Jackson, who was by then an advising editor and regular contributor to *Zymurgy*. The critic noted the renaissance taking place in beer in the United States and urged fledgling homebrewers to not let any perceived lack of supplies or technical capabilities daunt them. He then bolstered this encouragement with a concluding anecdote that we should note at length, as it shows just how sinuously deep the movement that Jackson and Papazian helped foment could run by mid-decade:

> Wherever my travels take me in the United States, and whichever commercial beers I am asked to taste, whether by a magazine, a scientific institute, or a brewer, I always seem to finish up in someone's garden at the weekend, enjoying their own home-produced vintage. My hosts always turn out to be members of the American Homebrewers Association. It happened again the other day, in Washington, DC. My hosts were a physicist and his schoolteacher wife. They had friends present, an executive in a government agency and a couple of journalists from a famous newspaper. We enjoyed that same pleasure usually experienced cooking together, except that we were brewing. While we went about it, we sampled the recently matured product of their last brew.

The craft beer movement had drawn an English critic to a backyard in the American capital, named for one of the nation's original homebrewers, to share ideas and a passion that might very well then spin off into a commercial enterprise. (Who knew? That was the way of things!) It was as sure a sign of progress, of awareness, as any roster of craft breweries or sales statistics (which were by and large guesstimates anyway due to the iffy distribution). There was a catch, though. Just as the year 1978 in hindsight appeared to be especially pivotal, so would the mid-1980s. The congenial vibe summed up in Jackson's anecdote for his friend Papazian's book, born as that vibe was in the San Francisco of the 1960s, was about to run headlong into an entirely different one on the East Coast of the 1980s.

HOW THE BREWPUB WAS BORN
Yakima, WA | 1981

It was sometime shortly after Bert Grant filed incorporation papers with the State of Washington in 1981 to open the nation's first brewpub since Prohibition that he and Michael Jackson were blasting through the Cascades in a Rolls Royce with a license plate that read "Real Ale." It was entirely appropriate given Grant's personality—as was the fact that he opened that first brewpub in an old opera house in Yakima in the heart of central Washington State's hop-growing bull's-eye. Grant was a bit operatic himself, given to wearing kilts and waving a claymore at anyone who dared break his brewpub's smoking ban. A brash, brassy Scotsman from Dundee, his family moved when he was a boy to Toronto, Ontario, where he got his first job in beer at age sixteen during World War II: as a taster in a brewery. Others would follow, in Canada and the United States, including a fifteen-year stint as a brewing chemist at Canadian Breweries and then several years as research director with Stroh Brewing, then one of the largest breweries in the United States. He left that job in 1963, did some consulting work, and then joined the Yakima-based hop-grower S. S. Steiner in 1973. He was older than most of the twenty- and thirty-something first- and second-wavers in the American craft beer movement and the only one with true European roots who would end up an owner. He also fell outside the orbit of mentorship and word-of-mouth that had cultivated our characters to this point—he had come from decades within the brewing industry and not from a hobby or happenstance. Whatever his route, Grant had long dreamed of opening his own brewery, and legislative changes wrought by the legalization of homebrewing at the federal level opened an opportunity for him.

President Carter's signature on HR 1337 in October 1978 did little beyond freeing homebrewing suppliers from fears of a federal raid and allowing enthusiasts to congregate more openly. At the state level, things remained murky regarding the legality of homebrewing—or of brewing simply on a small scale, either for commercial sale off-site or, in the case of a brewpub, on-site. In Carter's home state of Georgia, for instance, homebrewing remained illegal for years even as legislators in Atlanta OK'd home wine making. In Washington State, the legislature passed Senate Bill 3722 in 1981, making it legal to transport homemade wine for exhibitions and tastings, but did not move on the legality of beer at the state level for many more years. Still, the tweak to the law involving wine seemed to be all Grant needed—or he had always planned to go ahead regardless, serving under the radar. Until the law caught up with—or on to—them, he and others would be making up the definition of an American brewpub as they went along. Loosely, though, it can be understood at first to have simply meant making and serving beer under the same roof. Grant filed state incorporation papers for the Yakima Brewing and Malting Company on December 23, 1981. Early the following year, he set up Grant's Pub in the lobby of the town's old opera house and brewed four barrels at a time; he justified the "malting" part of the name by frying some early barley on a skillet in the kitchen.

Jackson was one of the operation's biggest and most important fans from the start. He praised Grant's eccentricities along with his beers, painting for his readers the picture of an iconoclast loose in the hop fields of America. Grant was undoubtedly partial to bitter ales, having come to despise the blandness of Big Beer lagers (he often carried a vial of hop juice to spice up any pale pilsner that crossed his transom); and Jackson would eventually declare his India pale ale "the hoppiest beer in America." Grant's first beer at the brewpub was, appropriately enough, a Scotch ale—but not in the traditional sense.

"Isn't this on the hoppy side for a Scotch ale?" Jackson asked him in those early days of Rolls Royce rides.

"Yes," Grant replied, "all beers should be hoppier."

The world's leading beer critic pressed him. "Is it really fair to sell it as a Scotch ale?" Scotch ales were traditionally lighter on the hops and heavier on the malts.

"It is Scotch ale because I created it," Grant said. "I am Scottish."

"When did you leave?"

"When I was two years old."

Clearly the iconoclasm redefining American beer was not limited to the craft brewers of Colorado and California. That Scotch ale would win second place in the Great American Beer Festival's consumer preference poll in 1984. Grant also took first place with his Russian imperial stout, which outpolled seventy-four other beers. He accepted the wins wearing a kilt. (Yakima Brewing and Malting also broke ground with its 1983 release, Bert Grant's India

Pale Ale. It was the first time an American craft brewery—or a brewery any-where in the world in decades—had debuted a beer explicitly called "India pale ale" or "IPA." According to Michael Jackson, that move "brought back the historic name and made it part of our beer vocabulary again.")

As for those brewers in California and Colorado, they were finding them-selves increasingly limited businesswise. Distribution, for one thing, remained both a hurdle and a hassle. Grossman and Camusi were able to get their Sierra Nevada Pale Ale onto the shelves and into the bars of Chico, but when they tried to expand into the Bay Area proper they found slim pickings amid the available distributors. Most were in the pockets of Big Beer and had little use for what were considered risky brands that would never sell as reliably as more established ones. The only distributors even interested in Sierra Nevada were those trading in esoteric imports. Sales of foreign beers had tripled from 1975 to 1981 nationally as more brands arrived, including higher-end ones from Belgium, many for the first time in the States. The sorts of distributors willing to take these brands, themselves risky bets, were more apt to take on domestic craft brands as well. Grossman realized the distributors were utiliz-ing a throw-it-against-the-wall-and-see-what-sticks approach; little marketing was involved. Tom de Bakker found the going equally rough, though he was able to sign on with two similarly niche distributors—only to have disbeliev-ing retailers oftentimes plunk his beer on the import shelves. A backhanded compliment in a way, it was at least proof that more craft brands were feeling their ways into a wider marketplace. It was a positive.

THE FIRST SHAKEOUT

Sonoma, CA; Novato, CA | 1982–1983

On June 6, 1979, Jack McAuliffe wrote this letter to his father and included a copy of Frank J. Prial's *New York Times* story on New Albion. Its stouts, porters, and ales were selling well in the Bay Area, and McAuliffe and Stern were even planning to haul samples to the august Great British Beer Fes-tival that autumn—as symbolic a move by any American craft brewery as there could be. Moreover, the brewery had added a new level of forward-looking professionalism with an official board of directors, including Stern and McAuliffe as well as people culled from other areas of expertise. Unlike the letter of last August, this one was written under a New Albion letterhead that included the re-creation of Francis Drake's Golden Hind:

> Here's a clipping from *The New York Times*. As you can see from the photo, the labor involved here is brutal.
>
> We've recovered from a brush with bankruptcy and are now mak-ing money—it's good to have a banker on the board.
>
> We have a crew from Davis here for [work study] for the summer. I am working on the plans for the next brewery and we are going to look at property Saturday. I have written to brewery architects & they say it is going to cost between $900K & $1 million. I'm going to get the money . . .
>
> Love,
> Jack

It was a race. Since 1980, the brewery had been profitable, but not profit-able enough. Employees like Barkley made peanuts, plus beer; McAuliffe and Stern made barely anything, maybe forty dollars a week each, enough to buy food. For the fiscal year ending June 30, 1980, for instance, New Albion's profits were $8,262.52 from sales totaling $79,639.80. It could not go on like this, and McAuliffe had looked to expand starting as early as 1979, the second full year of operations. He sought out potential investors; he approached com-mercial banks with business plans; he got a right of first refusal on property for what was supposed to be a nice, English-style brewpub in downtown Sonoma. He outlined the plan to Prial, sketching like a zymurgical da Vinci a picture describing not only every brewpub that would come after, including Bert Grant's more than two years later, but the ideal habits of people like Waters, people who we decades later would call locavores:

> At New Albion, water must be trucked in once a week or so from a well in the nearby mountains. "We'd like to go to 50 barrels a day eventually," Mr. McAuliffe said, "so we have to get nearer a good water source." Actually, his plans are more ambitious than that. He hopes one day to open a country inn with a small brewery attached. "We'd lease the restaurant, of course," he said, "but they'd be closely connected. Guests in the restaurant could see the beer being made." But that's still not all. "I'd like to have a farm as part of the property.

Then we'd grow our own barley and malt it. It would be a totally contained operation. There is nothing like it anywhere."

The usual twelve-hour days continued. There were bright spots, too, amid the stress and worry over expansion. On the same trip that Stern and McAuliffe hit the Great British Beer Festival, they traveled to breweries in England and Scotland, the birthplace of McAuliffe's interest in fine beer. There were parties with Anchor employees such as Gordon MacDermott and Mark Carpenter, usually on or around the winter solstice and usually involving heaping amounts of pork and generous volumes of beer; one year the Anchor guys showed up with a pallet of low-fills, bottles that didn't quite get filled to the top—Barkley figured they must have been saving them up. There was more media coverage and more visits by Michael Lewis and his students. And there was even a Bay Area beer-tasting contest in February of 1982 that a pair of PR and advertising executives hosted; New Albion's pale ale won, followed by its porter, and then a tie for third between New Albion's stout and Anchor's signature steam beer (we should take the results with a grain of salt, however—McAuliffe and Carpenter were among the judges). Through it all there was that race for more money. At least one acquaintance of New Albion promised to find investors; that never panned out. McAuliffe mostly encountered responses such as these from traditional lenders:

"You're taking on Augie Busch and all of his friends?"

"Are you guys nuts?"

"We're not going to give you $750,000 for something as loony as that!"

It looked as if New Albion was going to lose.

So were others. Tom de Bakker's eponymous brewery was turning a profit by 1982, producing eighty to one hundred barrels annually out of the warehouse in Novato, with two distributors running it to shelves throughout the Bay Area. As many as four other people worked at the brewery at a time, and visitors popped by, like they did at New Albion, including homebrewing clubs and reporters. The brewery then appeared to be a victim of its own success. It was a Catch-22: de Bakker knew he had to expand to keep the profitability going, but in order to expand he needed loans; and traditional lenders, as we've seen, had no interest in propping up a small commercial brewery. In addition, the deep national recession meant a spending crunch among consumers—with the unemployment rate at more than 10 percent, higher than at any time since World War II, tipplers were increasingly unwilling to dig into their pockets for DeBakker bottles at ninety cents to a dollar or more a pop. Plus, if Americans were going to spend more on alcohol then, it was most likely going to be on vodka or white wine, not beer. Per capita wine consumption reached a post–World War II peak of nearly two gallons per American in 1979, the same year McAuliffe wrote his father. Softer, juicer white wines, especially Chardonnay, led this boom. The era also saw the advent of wine bars in major cities and the first spikes in sales of accoutrement such as corkscrews and aerators. As for vodka, Absolut, a Swedish brand introduced in the United States in that same 1979, revitalized the market for clear spirits and especially the cocktails with which they mixed so easily. Meanwhile, beer was headed toward an all-time domestic production high in 1983, with light beer driving much of the growth. A gradual rollback would soon take hold, as beer confronted vodka and white wine's popularity. The de Bakkers, tiny players in a contracting industry and a struggling economy, ran the numbers and decided to close in early 1983.

The Courys in Portland had shuttered their Cartwright Portland Brewery the year before. The California Steam Brewery, which had opened in San Rafael, just down the road from DeBakker, disappeared way before that. The years 1982 and 1983 were proving to be the first shakeout of the American craft beer movement, as second-wave entrants with plenty of spirit and skill buckled under the expenses of production and the challenge of distribution in a marketplace that simply was not ready for their bitter creations. It was an appropriately bitter coincidence, indeed, that in March 1982, Anheuser-Busch rolled out in forty states Bud Light, the Goliath's long-anticipated answer to Miller Lite. The debut would lift the nation's largest brewery to a market share of 32.5 percent and sales of 60.5 million barrels the following year—more than all the beer sold by all the craft breweries since Fritz Maytag took over Anchor in 1965. And all against an industry backdrop of six brewers controlling more than 80 percent of American beer sales. As a "grim, determined and serious" August Anheuser Busch III—"the word relax doesn't seem to be in his vocabulary"—told an apparently awed reporter that year: "There are no easy answers to gaining market share. Only constant pressure, constant attention to the marketplace."

When New Albion finally did shut down in late 1982, it closed with none of the attention you might expect would accompany the demise of the first start-up brewery in America since Prohibition. No reporters traipsed to the rural reaches of Sonoma to cover this aspect of the curious business. There would be no more students from UC-Davis, no more pop stars popping in, no more letters addressed to "The Brewery, Northern California," no more disciples seeking wisdom, Englishmen and Scots paying attention, anyone to note the culinary bridge Jack McAuliffe had thrown up between local food and local beer. It all just went away, the bottles of pale ale, porter, and stout disappearing from Bay Area shelves shortly after the brewery that crafted them disappeared. There were meetings in the old fruit warehouse throughout the year about the money race. No one would remember much of what was said beyond the sad mechanics of going out of business. Everything had to be out; the former New Albion Brewing Company had to vacate the premises. McAuliffe and his crew did that by hand, too.

"THAT'S A GREAT IDEA, CHARLIE"
Boulder, CO; Denver | 1982–1984

Byron Burch knew just about everyone in the American craft beer movement by the time he climbed aboard the red double-decker bus in Boulder. It was June of a tumultuous 1982, as some in the movement struggled and others started to soar. He was in Boulder for a concoction of Charlie Papazian's: the first Great American Beer Festival. However, like "the American Homebrewers Association," the national adjective in the name, as well as "great," seemed optimistically grandiose—just about everyone who attended the festival could fit on the bus with Burch. That included Michael Jackson.

An expanded version of the English critic's canonical *The World Guide to Beer* would be republished in the United States later in the year, and he was writing regularly now about beer for European publications, as well as acting as an advising editor for *Zymurgy*. Jackson by 1982 was well known to the domestic craft beer movement, an avuncular eccentric given to outlandish sartorial combinations, particularly when it came to his colorful ties, and sonorous descriptions of his favored beer. He was also generous with his time and advice. It could be argued that no one would be sitting on the bus on its way out of Boulder had Papazian not run into Jackson at the Great British Beer Festival in London the year before. He talked to Jackson about the possibility of a similar festival in the United States. Would it work? "That's a great idea, Charlie," Jackson replied. "Only what will you serve for beer?"

Papazian returned to the States confident despite the odds. He would make two crucial tweaks. First, the Great British Beer Festival was all about cask ale, the unfiltered and unpasteurized beer beloved in British pubs. The

Great American Beer Festival would simply be about all and any beers brewed in the United States. Second, while the festival would be full of competitors, Papazian decided they would be asked not to behave as competitors—it was a bit of a departure, to say the least, from the lusty million-dollar marketing wars of Miller and Anheuser-Busch. Papazian hosted organizational meetings in his living room, where ten to fifteen people—mostly volunteers, as well as Daniel Bradford, who would be considered the cofounder of the festival—discussed how they were going to foment a tide that would lift all boats. It would be about talking beer, not talking brands. They settled on June 4 as the festival date, toward the middle of the annual homebrewers conference.

The bus ride out of Boulder, at the end of the festival, was to visit Boulder Brewing, launched in the goat shed three years before by "Stick" Ware, David Hummer, and Al Nelson. Burch spotted Jackson on the bus's lower level and positioned himself behind him. He listened to Jackson talk about how he was then writing a book on British restaurants. Burch couldn't resist.

"Now that you can talk your way into any brewery in the world," he said, "now comes the book on restaurants; and then about five years it'll be Michael Jackson's attempt to supplant *The World Atlas of Wine*. And about five years on it'll be *The World Guide to Brothels*."

Jackson grew quiet.

"Actually," he said in his slow northern England accent, "I wrote a piece called 'The Consumer's Guide to the Brothels of Amsterdam' some years ago for *Oui* magazine."

Everyone laughed. Underneath the mirth and camaraderie, however, was something meaningful and financially very serious. The festival—and the homebrewers conference, for that matter—allowed the likes of Burch, who by then co-owned two homebrewing shops and had written *Quality Brewing*, one of the most influential works on the subject, to mingle freely with the world's leading beer writer. Personalities were gelling, alliances were forming, and ideas were being exchanged. The homebrewers could buy the commercial brewers a few rounds at night and pick their brains in service of their own dreams of turning pro. Nascent commercial brewers could learn from brewers and principals at older, more-established companies. Charlie Papazian's confab was a trade show, yes, but also a meeting of what could and would one day be described as a tribe.

Logistically, it wasn't much. Page eleven of the program for "The American Homebrewers' Association's Fourth Annual National Homebrew and Microbrewery Conference National Homebrew Competition and the Great American Beer Festival 1982" listed the schedule for the festival portion on

Friday, June 4, as follows: "4:30–9:30 PM. The Great American Beer Festival 1982—see details on page 16." Page sixteen offered a five-sentence hello introducing the festival and its beers "selected for their quality, unique and special character," followed by a glossary of beer terms and descriptions of the forty-seven beers available from twenty-four different breweries at twenty-two different spots in the five-thousand-square-foot ballroom of the Hilton Harvest House on Twenty-Eighth Street in Boulder.

We see in these descriptions not only the first inklings of the adjectival redolence that would come to define beer criticism (the program might mark the first time that a beer's aroma was described in print as "flowery") but also a care and concern for the elements of beer that was rare in America. The descriptions tell of specific ingredients (in Sierra Nevada Pale Ale: "traditional top-fermenting ale yeast, and Cluster, Cascade, and Tettnanger hops"), of history (regarding Boulder Porter: "traditionally a darker, heavier beer popularized in London during the eighteenth century by the porter tradesman who drank porter beer"), and of attention to storage and serving (for Anchor Steam, the ideal "serving temperature is around forty-five degrees F"). Beer was being accorded respect in a collective way for the first time in a long time.

Each of the approximately 850 attendees could move through the twenty-two tasting points in about an hour, if they cared to, and take the rest of the time to absorb information from exhibits on brewing and from fellow attendees. Sapling craft brands like Sierra Nevada and Boulder rubbed commercial shoulders with surviving regionals like Genesee and F. X. Matt, both out of Upstate New York, and G. Heileman and Jacob Leinenkugel, both from Wisconsin. The oldest brand in attendance was D. G. Yuengling & Son, the Pottsville, Pennsylvania, regional with roots in the 1820s; the largest—and the only sign of Big Beer—might have been Colorado's own Coors. Representatives from these, as well as luminaries of the craft beer movement—Fred Eckhardt, Ken Grossman, Michael Lewis, Papazian, Bradford, Burch, and Jackson—mingled with aficionados, budding and hard-core, from both coasts and from interior places like Minnesota, Michigan, Ohio, and Indiana (the only region from the contiguous United States that appeared to be unrepresented at the first great national beer festival was the South). These attendees could then return to their home ports, confident in the knowledge of a wider, growing movement at their backs—one buoyed by an increasingly professional AHA. For one thing, the association was preparing to move its physical address from Papazian's porches on Nineteenth Street to honest-to-God offices on Pearl Street in downtown Boulder; and there was a full-time marketing director in Bradford (albeit with his roles as office assistant and

Zymurgy circulation director still voluntary), as well as ambitions to effect legislative change regarding homebrewing and commercial brewing in all fifty states.

There would be stumbles along the early way, some of them nearly fatal. In June 1984, a little more than three thousand people attended the third GABF. A respectable number, sure—but the AHA, in a fit of hubris or simply wishful thinking, had switched venues, from the Hilton Harvest House in Boulder to the much larger Currigan Exhibition Hall in Denver. One attendee remembered that "the cavernous building had all the ambiance of an airplane hangar," and its vast size seemed to render the attendance paltry. Papazian would pronounce the move "a disaster," as the forty breweries present, including Big Beer arrivistes like Anheuser-Busch and Stroh's, couldn't really fill out the hall, and the ticket sales weren't enough to cover the rent or the insurance. An embarrassed AHA had to borrow money to cover not only the festival but also its basic operating expenses for a time.

Still, the signs of healthy, sustained progress were unmistakable: The AHA by 1984 had started buying its toilet paper in bulk rather than from a nearby convenience store. A moment could not be spared as they built a clearinghouse for a movement that rather suddenly found itself in a bicoastal growth spurt.

THE THIRD WAVE BUILDS

Manhattan; Virginia Beach, VA; Portland, OR; Hopland, CA | 1982–1984

Matthew Reich flew to Boston and pitched his idea for a New York City brewery to Joseph Owades in his apartment. Owades had worked at the last New York brewery to close, Rheingold, which shut its Brooklyn operations in 1976. By the time Reich sought his counsel at the start of the 1980s, Owades was one of the most successful consultants in the brewing industry through his Center for Brewing Studies and his reputation as the biochemist who invented the basis for light beer. He was also a quiet, immensely respected force in the nascent craft beer movement, having advised Fritz Maytag at Anchor.

Reich was a Bronx native who went to the University of Massachusetts and in 1971 cofounded the Boston Food Cooperative, which became the East Coast's largest members-owned food market, with an emphasis on locally grown and organic foodstuffs. He moved back to New York and was a lending officer at Citibank before becoming a top executive on the business side of Hearst Magazines in Midtown. Along the way, after an epiphany about the grape in France, he taught wine-tasting classes at Manhattan's Harvard Club, the Yale Club, and the New School, where he also taught a brewing course. Reich knew of Maytag's Anchor, and he had read enough stories and heard enough anecdotes to imbibe the notion that a craft brewery could work on the East Coast as well.

It was a notion that seemed oddly radical. The American craft beer movement at that point was just a few operations in the San Francisco Bay Area, some of them about to fold, plus the hive of activity in and around Boulder and a couple of colonies in Oregon and Washington State. For whatever reason, aside from some Anchor beers, it had not really penetrated east of the Mississippi. Coors was novel to New Yorkers and New Jerseyans; Anchor was downright exotic; New Albion and DeBakker would have been stupefying. Still, there was a rich tradition of East Coast brewing, especially in the North, pre-Prohibition. That Rheingold brewery, to take an example, had been one of nearly fifty operating in Brooklyn by the turn of the twentieth century. Yuengling in eastern Pennsylvania had been in the same family since 1829. Upstate New York once produced more hops than anyplace else in the country. It wasn't so far-fetched, a craft brewery on the East Coast. Why should the Californians and Coloradans have all the fun?

There was the cost. Owades heard out his young visitor—Reich was barely into his thirties—and then heard how much he could raise from friends and family: roughly $350,000. It would not be enough to open a physical brewery, especially not within New York City, which was gradually recovering from its nadir of urban decay and municipal bankruptcy in the early 1970s. Its industrial spaces, including the grand, old breweries of Brooklyn, were set on a twenty-year march toward upscale condos and alternative office space.

Owades had a solution, though, one that would reverberate through craft beer, not without controversy, opening up avenues to would-be brewers high on enthusiasm but just short of capital. It was called contract brewing. Reich, Owades explained, should pay an existing brewery for the labor and equipment to brew his beer. He could in the meantime raise money to open that physical brewery in New York City. It was like borrowing someone's kitchen to make one of your recipes, he explained. Owades had a particular kitchen in mind. The F. X. Matt Brewing Company was started as the West End Brewery in Utica, New York, about 240 miles north of Manhattan, by F. X. Matt, who immigrated to the United States in the late nineteenth century after learning the brewery trade in Baden, in southwestern Germany. His grandson, F. X. II, who had served in the US Army in Germany during World War II, was running it by 1980, when it was one of the last great regional breweries (he renamed it for his grandfather). He had a reputation for bluntness but, luckily for Reich and others, also a soft spot for entrepreneurs in the mold of his grandfather. Besides, Matt had already contract-brewed at least one brand: Billy Beer, the short-lived libation of President Carter's kid brother. Reich contacted Matt about a contract to brew his recipe.

"This is the dumbest idea I've ever heard," Matt told him.

But he was in, the wheels of commerce greased in no small part by Owades, who knew Matt and signed on with Reich as a consulting brewmaster. In the summer of 1982, Matt brewed seven thousand cases of Reich and Owades's amber lager recipe; Reich had to pay for the labels up front and agree to buy all seven thousand, regardless of whether they subsequently sold, at roughly eleven dollars a case. His business plan revealed the modest yet ambitious sales goals of craft brewers then: "To sell four thousand cases per month by the end of the first operating year; six thousand cases per month by the end of the second year; and eight thousand cases by the end of the third year."

It was this modesty that especially defined Reich's plan as a craft brewery, rather than, say, just a clever way to create another brand for a regional brewery (Big Beer did not even enter the equation). Where a regional like F. X. Matt might produce five thousand barrels per day, Reich was aiming for much less than that per month and giving himself years to get there; and, unlike many regionals at the time, Reich's beer was to be brewed with traditional ingredients only, no adjuncts, and sold solely in draft or bottles. This traditional brewing approach and the modest production goals set the tone for every contract craft brewer that came afterward—for a time, anyway.

Reich rented a warehouse in Manhattan's Meatpacking District, hired two guys to drive the delivery truck as well as a salesman with a background in wine, and, along with him, started marketing the bottles in October 1982 to Manhattan restaurants under the New Amsterdam brand. It was much the same approach as Fritz Maytag had taken going door-to-door in San Francisco more than fifteen years before, and like then, it was a tough sell. The amber lager defied categorization in New York. It wasn't premium, super-premium, or import; it was something different. This was a Manhattan, too, that was still years from the specialty food stores and farmers markets full of locally grown produce, artisanal cheeses, and wines made from grapes pressed on Long Island that would change the conception of grocery shopping in the city. Plus New Amsterdam was more expensive, about twice as much as a bottle of Bud. Reich's pitch was simple yet meant to be game changing: try it. Try it, he would tell skeptical bar owners and restaurateurs. Sure it costs more, but you drink less; it's the antidote to light beer. As for the name, it was taken from the Dutch moniker for what the English would redub New York. Reich had followed a path hewed by Jack McAuliffe at New Albion, though he was not familiar with that brand's backstory.

There was little that McAuliffe might have been able to really teach Reich. That was because, with the birth of contract brewing, the nature of the American craft beer movement was changing. It was moving away forever from the archetype set by McAuliffe, de Bakker, the founders of Boulder, Grossman and Camusi at Sierra Nevada, even Maytag in his original primitive Eighth Street spot in SoMa. Then a craft brewer needed to know not only what ingredients to get for a certain recipe but also how to scrounge for material, how to weld it into something usable, how to position it in a system that would produce beer born from that recipe—all of this in the end requiring at least a passing knowledge of biochemistry and microbiology. It would be years before a craft brewery seemed even remotely like a sure investment of such time and money. But newcomers such as Reich now had shoulders to stand on, and contract brewing solved the Sisyphean challenge of capital. (Reich even *looked* different from these other pioneers. Whereas many of them were given to beards and shaggy miens, never mind blue jeans and sneakers, Reich was clean-cut and clean-shaven, comfortable with suits and in boardrooms; his closest sartorial kinsman in the movement might have been Fritz Maytag, who, though surrounded for decades now by easy-breezy San Francisco, still wore a tie to the Anchor Brewery and kept his hair trim.)

Whatever the fate of contract brewing, others were still trying the old-fashioned way, albeit with readier access to material than Jack McAuliffe had ever had. A couple hours' drive up the Hudson River from Reich's dream, a budget analyst for the state of New York, William S. Newman, was opening the first stand-alone craft brewery in the eastern United States with his wife, Marie. Tall and lanky, with owlish glasses and shaggy hair parted slightly off-center, Newman had actually filed incorporation papers with the state as early as October 1979—almost a year to the day, in fact, since President Carter signed the legislation legalizing homebrewing federally. Newman was beyond that stage by the time his Wm. S. Newman Brewing Company opened in an old warehouse in Albany's industrial district with an annual capacity of five thousand barrels (though it would at first produce half that). He had apprenticed at the Ringwood Brewery in southern England, bringing back a taste for that country's pub culture and its milder ales. Newman's pale ale debuted in February 1982, described in the *New York Times* with quotation marks around the adjective "hopped." He insisted at first that local establishments serve this and subsequent beers warm, at about fifty degrees Fahrenheit, in the English style, which the vendors were not always happy to do. Newman realized this insistence was a problem for the all-draft operation when an amber ale he brewed, which was meant to be served cold, began to outsell the pale ale. "Americans like their beer cold," he concluded. Newman sprung into action in 1983, acquiring a bottling line and tweaking the pale ale recipe a bit to make it acceptable for serving at cooler temperatures (thirty-seven to forty degrees). He rolled out the East's first specialty craft beer since Prohibition, Winter Warmer, in 1983, a brown ale of nearly 6 percent alcohol per volume that he compared to a Guinness-like stout, though not as bitter.

Farther down the East Coast, in the Virginia Tidewater, an orthodontist and a veterinarian, both in their mid-thirties, were putting the finishing touches on what would become the first craft brewery in the South. Jim

William Newman in his brewery in downtown Albany. Courtesy of Charlie Papazian

Kollar, a Penn State linebacker turned veterinarian, had been homebrewing since before the federal law change, creating increasingly larger batches until he and his friend Lou Perrin, the orthodontist, decided to make the commercial leap with a few other investors, all relatives, and a brewmaster hired from West Germany. They were prepared to put up as much as $250,000 to make the Chesapeake Bay Brewing Company work from the ground up at an old industrial park in Virginia Beach. That would allow them to produce twenty-five hundred cases a week eventually of a signature amber lager they planned to brew using Cascade hops. As Perrin told a reporter in the winter of 1982 as he poured cement at the brewery site, those expecting a "locally brewed Budweiser" would be disappointed. "It will be made from only malt, hops, yeast, and water," he said. "That means no corn syrup, no corn flakes."

Back West, more California craft breweries were in start-up mode. Jim Schlueter ran across Michael Lewis's brewing curriculum while browsing the course catalog as an aimless freshman at UC-Davis. He earned a degree in that curriculum and went to work in Wisconsin for Schlitz, then one of the biggest breweries in the country. Wanting, however, to "brew beer by tongue rather than by computer," he cobbled together $350,000 in loans and started the River City Brewing Company in an old upholstery shop in downtown Sacramento, California. It was the first American craft brewery to focus on lagers rather than ales. In Mountain View, California, amid the microchips and venture capitalists of Silicon Valley, a father and son were using what they saw working in the burgeoning computer industry in the making and marketing of craft beer. Kenneth Kolence had in 1967 cofounded Boole & Babbage Inc., one of the world's first computer software concerns. His son Jeffrey had written his senior paper at California Polytechnic on the operations and layouts of small breweries and the mistakes they made in both. The younger Kolence then spent six weeks studying at a small brewery in England while his father raised $400,000. By the end of 1983, their Palo Alto Brewing Company was selling ten to fifteen barrels a week of their flagship London Real Ale, a bitter, to a half-dozen or so bars in San Mateo and Santa Clara Counties south of San Francisco for $2 to $2.40 a pop. Nearby, in Berkeley, another family brewery, albeit on a smaller scale, was inching forward. Charles Ricksform started brewing small batches of ale in his basement in 1981, with his two sons and a daughter, under the name Thousand Oaks Brewing Company.

Also in California, the nation's second and third brewpubs, after Bert Grant's in Yakima, Washington, were opening. (Governor Jerry Brown had signed legislation in 1977 that allowed for on-premises sales of beer up to certain amounts, removing the sort of legal ambiguity that would continue to haunt brewpubs and would-be brewpubs in other states.) That third brew-pub belonged to Bill Owens, a slender photojournalist with a shock of thick salt-and-pepper hair, who homebrewed so much that, on his fortieth birthday in 1978, a friend suggested they start a brewery. Owens went to his accountant and asked how one raised money these days. The accountant reached into his desk drawer and pulled out a form meant for another client. "White out 'almond farm' and put in 'brewery,'" he said, explaining a limited partnership.

Owens rented an old camera store in downtown Hayward, southeast of San Francisco, and renovated it using about $90,000 he raised through selling thirty-three shares through the limited partnership. The equipment came in the usual way: from a candy company, a food manufacturer, and, of course, a dairy, with sixty-two feet of pipe laid from the brewhouse to the bar with the help of an investor who normally worked on nuclear bombs. The brewhouse was visible through a picture window that allowed the customers up front to see where the beer they were drinking was coming from. Buffalo Bill's Brewpub opened on September 9, 1983, with annual production reaching about three hundred barrels. As Owens told the writer William Least Heat-Moon a few years after opening, the money came in the ingredients-to-sales

Bill Owens in the summer of 1985 in his Buffalo Bill's Brewpub
in Hayward, California. Courtesy of Bill Owens

ratio, something that would hold true for other brewpubs nationwide. "For $130 worth of ingredients, I can make a $2,500 profit," Owens explained. "A glass of lager—that's all I brew now—costs seven cents. I sell it for a dollar and a half. Compare my profit on a bottle of commercial beer—forty cents."

One hundred and twenty miles to the north, California's oldest brewpub had already been under way for a month by September 1983 in the impossibly appropriate town of Hopland. It also claimed remarkable parentage: the start-up equipment for the Mendocino Brewing Company came from Jack McAuliffe's New Albion. So did its first brewmaster, Don Barkley. It was the founders and first employees of Mendocino that did McAuliffe the grim favor of absorbing the equipment he had fabricated when the old fruit warehouse in Sonoma had to be vacated. McAuliffe went with it, for a while—he left the new brewpub pretty soon after arriving, and then he left the craft beer movement altogether. Barkley, along with Mike Lovett, another old New Albion hand, and the company's three founders, Michael Laybourn, Norman Franks, and John Scahill, quickly built Mendocino's Hopland Brewery, Tavern, Beer Garden, and Restaurant into a success. They were soon brewing 120 cases of beer a week on the old New Albion equipment, and it was selling out in as little as three days, all out of this novel thing called a brewpub. The location didn't hurt, either—ninety miles north of San Francisco, off one of the nation's busiest highways, 101.

A couple of hours down the 101 from Hopland, in Emeryville, two recent University of California-Berkeley graduates, Tad Stratford and Maureen Lojo, launched Golden Pacific Brewing Company out of an old General Motors engine factory using a recipe they'd perfected at their Berkeley apartment. The pair started out in 1985 selling their Bittersweet Ale from cardboard boxes with bladder-like plastic bags inside. They would use a hot-glue gun to solder the boxes at the edges to contain the carbonation, and Stratford himself would often personally deliver them to events like so much pizza, their contents gushing forth after the initial opening. Golden Pacific's packaging approach encapsulated the American craft beer movement's very short-lived flirtation with beer in a box. The technology then worked much better with flatter wine. Golden Pacific eventually switched to bottling, the boxes available only if customers specifically requested them.

Farther north, in Oregon, two vintners were picking up where two other vintners had left off. Dick and Nancy Ponzi owned Ponzi Vineyards near Portland, and they hired a native of the area, Karl Ockert, an avid homebrewer fresh out of Michael Lewis's program at UC-Davis, to fashion the first craft brewery in Oregon since the Courys' Cartwright Portland closed in 1982. The

Columbia River Brewery brewed its first beers, ones more on the malty than the prevailing hoppy side, in late 1984 in an old, three-story cordage factory in Portland's industrial northwest. With an annual capacity at first of six hundred barrels, it was eventually renamed the BridgePort Brewing Company.

On the same unremarkably grungy side of the Willamette River, two brothers in their twenties who learned homebrewing from an uncle were pushing toward their own brewery, unhappy with the commercially available beers in Portland. Kurt and Rob Widmer had drawn up a business plan that set as a goal twenty draft-beer accounts. They quickly surpassed that after their April 1984 opening and came to help define American beers that used wheat instead of barley as the primary grain. Together, BridgePort and Widmer—with no small help from Portlander Fred Eckhardt, who continued to write regularly about beer in local media and his own publications—would spark not only one of the more significant local craft beer booms but also a renaissance of that area of the city.

To the north, in Washington State, three craft breweries joined Bert Grant's groundbreaking brewpub. Inspired by Fritz Maytag's Anchor, the aptly, almost defiantly named Independent Ale Brewing Company opened in a former transmission shop in Seattle in the summer of 1982, serving a signature beer called Redhook Ale. It was supposed to be modeled after richer English ales but was born of a Belgian yeast strain, discovered by one of the brewery's founders, that produced a spicy, fruity beer; locals took to calling it "banana beer" because of the spice. Cofounders Paul Shipman, a former door-to-door wine salesman out of nearby Woodinville and the discoverer of the Belgian yeast strain, and Gordon Bowker, a one-time writer who a decade before had cofounded the Seattle coffeehouse that became Starbucks, sold less than one thousand barrels of it that first year. But a porter in 1983 and an IPA in 1984 changed everything, and their five thousand-square-foot brewery soon reached capacity.

Around the same time, about 350 miles to the northeast, a twenty-something Washingtonian, back from bicycling through southern England and tasting what local breweries had to offer, was readying his first beer for sale. Mike Hale, who was also inspired by Jack McAuliffe's New Albion, called that first beer Hale's Pale American Ale and chose July 4, 1983, for its debut. In January 1985, Andy Thomas and Will Kemper poured the first beers from their new Bainbridge Island brewery, Thomas Kemper, at the Roanoke Park Place Tavern in Seattle. In another corner of Washington, right on both the Oregon border and the banks of the Columbia River, husband-and-wife team Tom Baune and Beth Hartwell built by hand Hart Brewing Company in an old general store in a logging town called Kalama (population twelve hundred); they called their first beer, a pale ale that debuted in 1984, Pyramid.

Finally, in the old clocktower building of the small lower-Michigan town of Chelsea, about twenty miles west of Ann Arbor, a thirty-one-year-old cook and choir director named Ted Badgerow started the Real Ale Company, the first craft brewery in the Midwest. It was a milestone for the state that had been the first to ratify the Twenty-First Amendment and that had had as many as 128 breweries before Prohibition. By the time Badgerow came along, the region was best known brewing-wise for the Stroh's plant in Detroit. His ethos, as he told *Time* magazine in July 1983, was simple: "I just crank up the stereo, stoke up the boiler, and brew some ale." He had been doing that on one scale or another for a few years, ever since a friend in Grand Rapids, Michigan, served him a tasty ale that Badgerow, fresh off a long bike ride and thirsty, took for an import. No, the friend said, it was his own creation—homebrew. Badgerow himself undertook the hobby just as it became legal at the federal level, and before long friends suggested he started a brewery; one friend was a dairy farmer near Sparta, Michigan, named Gordon Averill, whose family concern was struggling. Badgerow worked there in the summer of 1981.

"I'm going to get rid of all of this," Averill said one day as the pair surveyed the equipment, "and I probably won't make ten, twenty bucks on it. What am I going to do?"

Badgerow had an idea. "If we filled it with beer, think how much we could sell that for."

The clocktower space as well as the hardness of the town's water made Chelsea the best location for the brewery in Badgerow's mind. Friends kicked in $12,000 as seed money, and he and Averill poured in sweat equity. They got busy right away brewing—one of the first calls Badgerow made was to Otto Zavatone at Boulder Brewing for advice—while awaiting the proper state licensing (dealing with the federal ATF had been fairly easy). The state-licensing warren might have been familiar to Jack McAuliffe and Suzy Stern at New Albion in California seven years before. No one had applied for a commercial brewing license in Michigan in about twenty-five years. What form did you even fill out? A friend of Badgerow's from the choir had a brother who was a state lawmaker, and he helped them push things through. Badgerow skipped down the glazed marble of the state government building, license in hand, a bemused Averill walking more slowly beside him. They sold several cases right away of English-style bitters, bottled by hand four at a time in old Bass, Guinness, and Harp bottles that Badgerow got for cents on the dollar. The new brewery, novel as it was for the middle third of the country, had a stream of visitors (drawn as much, Badgerow figured, by the choice dartboard they had as by the possibility of free samples). The partners from the Chesapeake Bay Brewing Company traveled from Virginia Beach, Virginia, to check out the new arrival, and, oddly enough, pop-rock group Hall & Oates dipped in from a Canadian tour to buy seventy cases. Unbeknownst to Badgerow and Averill, other would-be commercial brewers were part of the stream as 1983 turned into 1984.

By the end of 1983, there were fourteen craft breweries and brewpubs, including contract concerns, selling beer in the United States. Seven were in California, three in Washington State, two in New York, and the remainder in Colorado and Michigan. (Others such as Hart and BridgePort would start selling soon.) There were rumors of more breweries in Iowa, Maine, Michigan (again), northern New Jersey, Texas—even Utah and the Outer Banks of North Carolina. What tethered them despite the differences in size, geography, and temperament? A few things. Foremost, they shared, intentionally or not, the definitional qualities of craft beer set forth by Fritz Maytag in the 1960s at Anchor. They were small, by necessity; independent, also by necessity and sometimes to the extreme of starting without proper legal green lights; and traditional, often fiercely so—witness William Newman's insistence that his beer be served warm or Lou Perrin of Chesapeake Bay assuring future consumers his beers would not be made with "corn flakes" or Mike Hale's determination to mimic the local ales he encountered in England. They were each beachheads in their own ways, helping to turn palates toward a bitterness Americans simply could not seem to abide in large numbers and reanimating the notion of the local brewery. They had also either survived or started just after that first shakeout in 1982 and 1983 that saw the closure of DeBakker, Cartwright, and, most significantly, New Albion (the Real Ale Company in Michigan would barely make it into 1984). Collectively, then, they now represented a movement.

It is not insignificant that a term arose around this period to describe them in relation to the rest of the brewing industry. As the *New York Times* explained to readers the week before Thanksgiving 1983, "micro-breweries" were those small operations "that have sprung up over the past few years to produce a few thousand barrels of specialized beers each year for limited distribution." The same story dismissed much of the movement: "Despite admirable intentions and some pretty good products, many of the new beers are pretty awful. . . . Most microbrewery founders are just beer-lovers who want mainly to make their own idea of the perfect beer. They pick up most of their brewing experience in kitchens." Quality control, though, was not the biggest hurdle. Back-of-the-envelope calculations show the entire craft beer movement was producing no more than fifty thousand barrels of beer annually in 1984—and about half that total would have belonged to the long-established and recently expanded Anchor. That is, whatever the quality of the beer (and the evidence shows that most of it was, in fact, quite well received), the movement was small. Each start-up was tenuous, and the competition from Big Beer fierce. Not that the large breweries noticed. They would have little noted what Steve Harrison, an early Sierra Nevada hire on his way to becoming its sales director, said at the second Great American Beer Festival in June 1983, held once again in Boulder. (Sierra Nevada won the top two spots and Anchor the third in the festival's sole award, a consumer preference poll introduced that year.) At the tail end of the homebrewers competition,* Harrison remarked, "Basically, the whole idea of homebrewing and microbrewing is a reaction against the Budweiserization of America. There's nothing wrong with Budweiser beer. There's nothing wrong with McDonald's hamburgers or Holiday Inns, either. It's just that every beer today tastes exactly like Bud, and every hotel looks exactly like a Holiday Inn."

The American craft beer movement was trying to change that. Its philosophy—small, independent, and traditional—was sound enough to attract converts. The definition of who could become a craft brewer continued to expand with each new operation. And they stood together amid the vanguard of a larger movement awaiting its vocabulary: slow food, artisanal, locavore. But could craft beer really work as a business, or would it, like the drink itself, always have a shelf life of five or six years at the maximum? The answer was about to come—but from the East, not the West.

---

* The homebrewers competitions were crowning their own winners. The very first, in 1979, was a man from Boulder named Tim Mead. It was an ironic surname, given that mead is the name for the beer-like drink made from fermented honey. Nancy Vineyard of Santa Rosa, California, would win in 1983.

THE LESSON OF THE NYLON STRING

Newton, MA; Boston | 1983–1984

Jim Koch watched in quiet amazement as Michael Jackson asked for a second pot of coffee. The revered critic, seated before Koch's kitchen table in the tony Boston suburb of Newton, was clad in a rumpled bathrobe and what must have been a terrific hangover—were he showing it. Instead, Jackson talked energetically as he downed cup after cup of coffee, perhaps four to every one Koch drank. The two men picked up their conversation of the evening before for a few more hours.

Koch, a Harvard-trained management consultant, had invited Jackson to stay with him on his visit to the Boston area because he had had an epiphany about beer. Jackson, whose first book was about that certainty of English life, the pub, had told his host it was a shame America lacked such a staple. Koch set out to prove him wrong—he took him to pubs like Doyle's, a local bar that three Irish American brothers ran in Boston's then-gritty Jamaica Plain neighborhood. The two tied one on, Jackson's significantly tighter than Koch's, and discussed the host's epiphany regarding the freshness of beer, which he illustrated using one of the English ales Jackson had labeled a world classic.

"Michael, this is crap," Koch told him.

The beer was several months old, he figured from its taste, so stale through oxidation that Koch was picking up a dryness not unlike sherry. It couldn't possibly be the same beer that Jackson raved about.

The critic didn't argue. He explained to Koch that he had dubbed it a world classic after drinking it near its Yorkshire brewery, where it was freshest. In a pub in Boston thirty-two hundred miles away, it could taste different.

The information confirmed Koch's hunch about American beer, which he knew something about: his family had a long history in brewing. His father had been a brewmaster with concerns in the Midwest, his grandfather had worked at Anheuser-Busch, and his great-great-grandfather had run the eponymous Louis Koch Brewery in St. Louis in the nineteenth century. Koch grew up in Cincinnati knowing about brewing and knowing brewers, including Adolf Merten of Ems Brewing Company, a friend of his grandfather's and one of the authors of *The Practical Brewer: A Manual for the Brewing Industry*, the oft-reissued 1946 work that was exactly what its title suggested. But it all faded to background noise, something in familial lore rather than something in family life, as Koch headed to the foliaged environs of Cambridge, Massachusetts.

After he graduated from Harvard in 1971, Koch made the masochistic decision to enter the university's dual law and business degree program. It was partway through that four-year track, while living on campus and working as a tutor and prelaw adviser, that he realized he was barreling toward a career whether he liked it or not. Koch had done nothing but school his entire short life, so he took a break. A friend, a rugby player from the Australian Outback who was studying Matthew Arnold under Lionel Trilling, had gotten him into rock climbing and suggested he become an instructor for Outward Bound, the nonprofit that coordinates wilderness expeditions. Koch found himself over four straight summers leading groups of eight to ten people, sometimes younger than his twenty-four years, into the wilds of the West on climbing and hiking expeditions. He climbed Mount McKinley in Alaska, North America's highest peak, and its South American counterpoint, Argentina's Mount Aconcagua. The Outward Bound treks (as well as the vegetarianism he would adopt in the 1980s) not only contributed to a compact, sinewy frame that would last well into middle age, but they also taught Koch a valuable lesson via nylon string. The expeditions had only so much string; on his first one, he gave his charges more string than they needed. At the end of the twenty-eight-day trip, they didn't have enough string, having cut it, lost it, or otherwise taken it for granted. The next expedition, Koch handed out less string than his charges needed, and there was a surplus at the end. They had learned to take heed and care of their resources, or to substitute others.

Koch returned to Harvard after three years and wrapped up his dual degree. He landed a plum job at the Boston Consulting Group, joining the ranks of what was then one of the more coveted post-MBA tracks in the United States: management consulting. It didn't sound sexy, but it placed its people at the nexus of what passed for business innovation at the time. And business was innovating—in Japan. That country's long, Western-backed return from the ruins of World War II was starting to crest in a wave of faster factories and more efficient workers, and Koch studied the trends and causes with a fascination that treated its progenitors like rock stars. This was the business era when Japanese automobile manufacturers cut the hours it takes to make a car from eighty to thirty-five—something, to Koch's consternation, that most American executives dismissed as the results of anything but greater efficiency: robotics, docile unions, calisthenics. Japan's economy, with far fewer domestic resources (that nylon-string lesson again), was on its way to growing at a much faster pace than that of the United States by the end of the decade.

Koch's focus was American companies, and his base was one of the world's most prestigious management consultancies. BCG was a rapidly growing concern that fellow Harvard Business alum and former Bible salesman Bruce Henderson founded in the early 1960s; by the early 1980s it had offices as far afield as Dusseldorf, Tokyo, and Los Angeles, with others planned for New York and San Francisco. The names of the firm's hundreds of consultants, past and present, read like a crystal ball Who's Who of American business: alumni would include Jeffrey Immelt, CEO of General Electric; Indra Nooyi, CEO of PepsiCo; Austin Ligon, cofounder of CarMax; George David, chairman of United Technologies; and Mitt Romney, of Bain Capital, the Massachusetts governorship, and presidential politics. (Koch, after returning to school, had interviewed with Romney, an old Harvard classmate, for a summer position at Bain; he didn't get it.*) Their missions were simple while at BCG: to make their clients' businesses run more profitably. Strategies included the "advantage matrix," introduced a few years into Koch's tenure. The advantage matrix was:

> a framework that categorizes competitive business environments in four distinct categories or quadrants. It correlates the size of the competitive advantage each offers with the number of possible approaches to achieve that advantage available in that quadrant. The resulting matrix helps companies recognize when their strategies are or are not appropriate for their competitive environments.

This was the environment in which Jim Koch, soon to become the most successful craft brewer in America, worked. The environment paid handsome returns on both macro and micro levels. BCG's revenue from consulting topped $50 million in 1982, right as its growth really took off; Koch himself was pulling in at least $250,000 annually after six years of advising clients as prominent as General Electric and International Paper on manufacturing

---

* Koch actually ran against—and lost to—Mitt Romney for the presidency of their Harvard Business School class.

efficiency and quality control. He developed a fervent belief in what made a company successful: the product it made or service it provided had to be better or cheaper. Marketing didn't matter; quality mattered, and quality could be measured by whether a company made or provided what it intended to. Koch liked that his work afforded him these insights; he liked learning about how things were made and how they could be made better; he even liked, on occasion, the traveling. It was during these travels that he encountered the craft beer movement. The background noise of his youth grew loud again—he read about Fritz Maytag and Anchor; he sampled what he found, particularly in the Northwest. He began to think it through. He would give the American consumer the freshest glass of beer he or she could get. That was his epiphany: a better product no matter where it was encountered, and the product was beer.

His father thought he was crazy. "We've spent twenty years trying to get the smell of a brewery out of our clothes," Charles Koch said.

Born a few years into Prohibition, the elder Koch's own beer career had run the industry's very timeline, from work as a brewmaster at independent regional breweries (he had a BS in chemical engineering as well as a degree from the prestigious Siebel Institute in Chicago) to disenchantment with Big Beer's rapacious consolidation and the bland-tasting beers that resulted. Koch, who was the fourth-eldest son in a row in his German American family to become a brewmaster, left the industry in the late 1950s to cofound a company in Cincinnati that distributed brewing and industrial chemicals.

As trepidatious as he was about his eldest son's decision, he became his first investor and an informal adviser—an unpaid management consultant, if you will. Charles Koch had two pieces of advice upfront. They were meant to defray the costs of a start-up brewery, especially in the postrecessionary climate of 1983, one that would see the closings of more craft breweries, including the Real Ale Company in Michigan, and the near-closings of others like River City in California and Boulder Brewing in Colorado. "Don't worry about the marketing," Charles Koch said. "People don't drink the marketing, they drink the beer. Make sure the beer is good." That was the first piece of advice, given as the younger Koch was considering plans to open a physical brewery with whatever parts he could find. His father had a way through that challenge, too. "Look," he said, "there are plenty of breweries that can make really good beer. You don't need to a build a brewery. There are plenty of breweries with quality control and excess capacity."

Charles Koch was right. The American brewing industry—Big Beer, the regionals, and the fledgling craft movement—was nearing an all-time production peak in 1983 of around 195 million barrels, but a handful of brewers produced nearly all of it. Jim Koch would discover what Matthew Reich had a couple of years before in New York: the smaller breweries, especially the regional ones built out in past decades to handle many more accounts and customers, simply did not have as much need of their equipment or as much work for their employees as they once did. Another brewer, then, could rent the equipment and the labor. Koch intended to do just that. First, he needed to find some investors beyond his father. And he needed to join his patrilineage—it was time to brew.

"THIS CONNOISSEUR THING"
Manhattan — Estes Park, Colorado | 1983–1985

M atthew Reich always intended to open a physical brewery in New York City. The contract brewing at F. X. Matt in Utica was just supposed to get his Old New York Brewing Company and its flagship New Amsterdam amber lager off the ground. It did. Within two and a half years of the first cases rolling out of that Meatpacking District warehouse, New Amsterdam was available in 350 Manhattan restaurants, with 107 of those carrying it on draft. High-end grocers carried it as well for as much as nine dollars a six-pack (Big Beer brands might go for less than half that). The company in 1983 moved seven thousand barrels for $1.2 million in sales (and a tidy $50,000 in profits). Moreover, New Amsterdam had taken third place in the consumer preference poll at its first-ever GABF appearance in 1984, making it the most popular lager, as the top two finishers were ales from Bert Grant's Yakima Brewing.

It was the sort of chi-chi product Manhattanites, then and now, adore as much for its novelty as for its quality. Reich knew that. "This is yuppie beer, I guess," he told the *New York Times* in February 1985, rattling off some of the more fashionable neighborhoods where bottles could be had. "Yuppies drink it." One yuppie in particular, who happened to run a venture-capital firm, had a New Amsterdam one day in 1984 at Harry's Bar on Hanover Square in downtown Manhattan, and called Reich. He told Reich he really liked it, that his firm drank it all the time. What were Reich's plans? What was that about a brewery that he had read about in the papers? The venture-capital firm partnered with Reich and raised $2.2 million toward opening a brewpub at Twenty-Sixth Street and Eleventh Avenue; about $50,000 of that went into buying equipment from a brewery in southern West Germany. The firm took majority control of Old New York Brewing, with Reich retaining a 25 percent stake and remaining the handsomely young face of an effort to return brewing to New York City for the first time since 1976. The 110,000-square-foot brewpub opened with the capacity to produce thirty thousand barrels annually (it did about one-third of that the first year) and food fare like a sixteen-ounce sirloin for $15.95, blackened filet of redfish for $10.95, homemade quiche for $6.75, and the New Amsterdam Burger, "plain and simple," for $5.95.

Matthew Reich at his New Amsterdam brewpub on Manhattan's West Side in the mid-1980s. Courtesy of Charlie Papazian

The New Amsterdam brewpub also opened with a competitor two miles away. Richard Wrigley, a thirty-seven-year-old British transplant from Manchester who could not find a decent beer in New York (he once likened Anheuser-Busch's Michelob to "a soft drink"), cobbled together investors and opened in the fall of 1984 a five-thousand-square-foot brewpub. His Manhattan Brewing Company was located in an old electric-company station at Watts and Thompson Streets in Soho. Wrigley planned to brew up to sixty barrels a day in a system also acquired from a West German brewery. Setting prices at $2.50 a mug, he'd offer two ales and one lager—and maybe even take a stab at a recipe written out by George Washington and archived at the New York Public Library. The opening stole Reich's thunder by almost two years, and the two brewpubs would circle each other in a rocky relationship for years. Most of the rancor, played out in a local media apparently very friendly to the idea of craft beer, stemmed from both companies' use of contract brewing. F. X. Matt continued to brew a lot of New Amsterdam in Utica, and Wrigley contracted with the regional Lion Brewery in Wilkes-Barre, Pennsylvania. This allowed New Amsterdam to claim New York parentage on its bottles (as in New York State). "We were brewing [in the city] first, and Reich copied everything we did," Robert D'Addona, a Brooklyn businessman and one of Wrigley's partners, told *New York* magazine. The claim of copying seemed especially thin, as Reich had contracted with F. X. Matt before Manhattan Brewing opened. "We didn't deceive anybody," he told the same magazine. "The label said, 'Made in New York,' and we always intended to open in the city." It was a decidedly different atmosphere than the conviviality that prevailed in the San Francisco Bay Area, and the sniping presaged one of the great rifts the following decade in the American craft beer movement.

New Amsterdam's move also heralded a sea change in the perception of craft beer as a business model. Gone could be the days of do-it-yourself start-ups studying texts by Byron Burch and Fred Eckhardt and the nineteenth-century Brits and Germans and then cobbling together old dairy barrels and secondhand labelers from dying regional breweries. Partner with private equity or venture capital and pull the tap on serious cash flow!

The Boulder Brewing Company had undergone something similar some two thousand miles away. After initial success following its July 4, 1980, debut, the brewery born in a goat shed hit some bad batches due to bacterial infections of the beer, and it struggled financially, so much so that Stick Ware had trouble sleeping. How would he and his partners get themselves and their investors out of what looked like a money loser, one as doomed as New Albion, DeBakker, and others of that early era? It was the same damning macroeconomic environment of high interest rates and recession-level unemployment besides. The path seemed grimly predictable.

Then a chance encounter at a diving-equipment shop changed everything: Ware met a stockbroker with the improbable name of Jerry Smart. The physicist-cum-saxophonist-cum-brewer told Smart what he did; Smart told Ware what he did and suggested that he give him a ring sometime if he needed help. To him, the brewery sounded like a curious idea. Ware did just that in the spring of 1983. By the fall, Smart and his partners had bought control of the company and were preparing to take it public, when it would rake in $1.7 million, enough to unburden Ware and other early investors and to steer it toward a tenfold increase in production. Within a couple of years, the brewery relocated away from Al Nelson's farmland near the Rocky Mountain National Park to a fourteen-thousand-square-foot castle-like structure in northeastern Boulder that cost $1.5 million to build. The brewery was operating with $600,000 of debt and a hungry outlook for growth that included more money for advertising and sponsorships. The Boulder Brewing Company was by mid-decade most definitely still the second word in its name, but it was increasingly the third as well.

Why did moneymen like Smart and Reich's venture-capital backers want in—especially when they might have little to no knowledge of beer and their focus was on high returns in a sector that remained largely a money loser? There were a couple of likely reasons. Charlie Papazian thought it might have to do with a change in the public's perception of beer that the craft beer movement had largely caused (a recent AHA seminar had attracted more than thirty people who wanted to start craft breweries). Beer was no longer "a workingman's drink—take a six-pack to the ballgame, or sit and drink in front of the TV." There was now "this connoisseur thing. It's more acceptable at social gatherings to pull out beer instead of wine or drinking a cocktail." Howard Hillman, a wine and travel writer, tapped the same French-derived adjective for his *Gourmet Guide to Beer*, a 255-page book that Simon & Schuster published in late 1984: "Beer connoisseurship today is where that for wine was twenty years ago. Remember then? Most of us thought of wine as either red or white, or, perhaps, dry or sweet." David Bruso, a brewer at William S. Newman's operation in Albany, thought this wider newfound appreciation for beer flowed from the bottom up. "We have a better-educated, better-traveled public that has been exposed to quality beer in Europe, and they want it here." There was something to that "better-traveled" bit. The deregulation of the airline industry in the late 1970s (enacted the same month as the change that legalized homebrewing) led to double-digit percentage drops in international ticket prices. Routes increased, too. Residents of midsize American cities who had never had a direct flight found they could drive thirty minutes to the airport and then wake up less than half a day later in London, Paris, Brussels, or Rome. The unprecedented opportunities surely helped expose more Americans to what were then considered the best beers in the world.

Perhaps the biggest expression of this connoisseurship aspect was the creation in early 1985 of the Beer Judge Certification Program. Pat Baker co-owned a wine-making supply company that sold products through the mail and through a retail shop in Westport, Connecticut. Baker's business partner was Nancy Crosby, whom he'd met through playing bridge. The pair went on to cofound the Home Wine & Beer Trade Association, a group for home wine-making supply companies that also quietly sold homebrewing supplies and expertise—and that became instrumental in pushing the legalization of homebrewing in 1979. Five years after that milestone, Baker approached Charlie Papazian at an AHA conference with an idea: an examination-based program to certify beer judges for competitions, including homebrewing contests. "Do you really think people will pay money to take an exam?," Papazian asked Baker. Baker pushed forward, Papazian's AHA a passive partner to Baker and Crosby's trade association. Baker administered the first BJCP exams on May 31, 1985, during the AHA's annual conference, held then in Estes Park, a town in Rocky Mountain National Park. Fifty-one people paid thirty dollars a pop to take the exam, which consisted of twelve questions—half on brewing and half on style. Questions included "Name two Trappist beers and describe the style" and "What is the difference between a Marzen, Oktoberfest, and a Vienna style beer?" (The latter was a bit of a trick question: There was very little difference.) Within two years, 153 people had taken the BJCP exam, including commercial brewers. One in five failed, a hefty share that Baker thought might have something to do with the lack of a study guide.

Finally, the shift in perception aside, craft beer also showed a certain savvy from the start when it came to branding. As Jack McAuliffe had discovered with New Albion, a label could say so much in the blending of history with place. Fritz Maytag made a similar discovery with the retention of "since 1896" on bottles of Anchor despite the brewery's rebirth following his 1965 takeover. Craft beer as a relatable business idea like any other, coupled with the dawn of contract brewing, meant that you did not necessarily have to have studied under Michael Lewis at UC-Davis or at the Siebel Institute in Chicago. You didn't even have to have been a homebrewer. The growth of the movement in terms of attention to styles and tastes meant the growth of the movement as a business model. The tab was open for the go-go 1980s.

BECAUSE WINE MAKING TAKES TOO LONG

Belmont, CA | 1985

Pete Slosberg had a twelve-week paid vacation coming up in 1985. He had been working since he was sixteen and had been logging particularly long hours at his current employer, ROLM, which made computerized telephone systems for businesses and which had recently been acquired by IBM, and before that at Xerox. The latter company had saved him from the bleak weather of Rochester, New York, by transferring him to the San Francisco Bay Area in the late 1970s (and it had a policy of twelve weeks' paid vacation every seven years of employment). Up to that point, Slosberg had been a northeasterner. He grew up in Norwich, Connecticut, and studied engineering and business at Columbia University, earning a BS in 1972 and an MBA in 1974, taking odd jobs along the way, including brief work during graveyard shifts as a New York City cab driver. (The first part of the medical exam? Roll up your sleeve so they could check for needle marks.) His first job out of school was in Xerox's Rochester office.

By that time, Slosberg had developed a bit of a palate for wine through Amy, his girlfriend-turned-wife. The beer he had had in college turned him off to the taste, and the most popular brand in Rochester was Genesee. Slosberg marveled at the fervency with which Upstate New Yorkers bought up cases of the regional brewery's spring beer, Genny Bock, believed (erroneously) to be made from the built-up crud inside the regular tanks. He found Genesee's flagship cream ale to be faintly sweet; that was pleasant enough. Otherwise, beer just did not do it for him. Wine did. He and his wife would make it a point to sample local wineries, and after the move to California, Slosberg had a go at wine making in the basement of their house in Belmont, about twenty-five miles south of San Francisco. Through Wine and the People, a wine-making and homebrewing shop in Berkeley, he bought two hundred pounds of cabernet grapes from a Napa Valley winery, and then ritualistically hand-squeezed them using cheesecloth. He added the yeast; he studied the fermentation; he siphoned the finished product into glass carboys for maturation; he looked at the calendar. Because this was a cabernet, it might take as long five to ten years to age before drinking. Wine making would not work as a hobby. He called Wine and the People and recounted his impatience. The guy on the line suggested white wine—it would only take one or two years to age.

No.

Then how about homebrewing? "Have you ever had a homebrewed beer?" "I have not," Slosberg said.

"If you haven't had a homebrew, then you haven't had real beer!"

That did it. Slosberg bought a basic twenty-dollar kit and brewed an amber ale using malt extract and hops. The result was edifying and illuminating:

Six weeks later, I opened up a bottle, a couple of weeks before I was supposed to, but I couldn't wait any longer. The amber liquid developed a glorious head as I carefully poured it into a pint glass, and the aroma was actually quite inviting. The first taste surprised me because it didn't taste like anything I had ever had before. Sure it was odd, but the oddness evolved into a realization that this stuff did taste good. Maybe I hadn't had all that many different kinds of beer in my life, but this beer was far superior to anything I had ever tasted. I knew, then and there, that I was going to become a beer lover. Twenty-nine years old, and I finally became a beer drinker.

The malt taste in the amber ale took Slosberg back to childhood milkshakes on the Connecticut shore. It also spawned an obsessive beer can collection and the seemingly inevitable march toward a commercial brewery. Slosberg moved in the circles of what was fast becoming the late twentieth century's most storied and lucrative industry: computers. He knew people through ROLM and IBM, and through what for a few years now had been called Silicon Valley, with its vast financial resources as well as oftentimes vaster skill sets. It was not an assemblage of bearded back-to-the-earth types (though Slosberg had stopped shaving after he cut himself badly on his wedding day and would sprout a black beard forevermore); it was instead a breeding ground for entrepreneurship. Like Jim Koch a continent away, whom he would compete with in the coming decade to be America's biggest craft brewer, Slosberg was an Ivy League MBA with an interest in homebrewing, not a tinkerer by trade like Jack McAuliffe, Ken Grossman, and others in the early waves of the movement. As his twelve-week vacation approached in 1985, Slosberg had a feeling something in his life was about to change.

MORE THAN IN EUROPE
Boston; Kalamazoo, MI | 1983–1986

I t was the morning after St. Patrick's Day in 1985, and Rhonda Kallman was a little hungover. Jim Koch, a boss at the Boston Consulting Group and now her business partner, had an assignment for her nonetheless: buy a computer. Every reputable business surely needed these desktop devices, and their company should be no exception. Kallman, who had no idea where to start, set about her task. Later that day, Koch got a phone call. It was his mother's cousin, whom Koch considered an uncle and who was a partner at New York investment bank Goldman Sachs and one of Boston Beer's investors. "So, what did you do today?" he asked.

Koch replied that he had started the search for a computer. "Why?"

To keep track of things like sales and payables—all the miscellany of a business.

"Oh yeah," Koch's uncle said. "Sales. By the way, have you got any?" No.

"So what the hell are you doing buying a computer? You know, Jim, I've seen a lot more businesses go broke because they didn't have enough sales than I've seen go under from lack of computers. Why don't you work on first things first?"

That jarred Koch. Why *was* he looking for a computer? The company didn't even have an office! He and Kallman had spent much of 1984 and now early 1985 working around their schedules at BCG, and now were working out of their respective homes. No, his uncle was right: they needed some accounts. The first five batches of their signature lager were aging in tanks in Pittsburgh, set for delivery in five weeks. What then?

Koch was most certainly no natural salesman. There were two big reasons for this. One was Harvard. His business education there had focused heavily on marketing to the exclusion of sales—who got an MBA to be a salesman? It was an abstraction at best to Koch and his fellow grad students, something that just sort of happened at a company after the marketing team got done targeting the product. At worst, salesmanship was seen as a grimy, grubby thing you did as a last resort in the business world. He had lived professionally within this mindset during his six years as a management consultant. The work he pursued for his manufacturing clients at BCG kept him, as one later profiler put it, "by choice and by assignment . . . as far away from actual customers as a Douglas fir tree is from a *New York Times* reader. Selling was something he did his 'best to avoid.'" That wouldn't do. Not when he was out on an entrepreneurial limb.

Koch called Kallman back. Scratch the computer—we need a list of potential accounts instead.

Such had been the learning curve for the Boston Beer Company, which filed with Massachusetts in December 1984 but had been going as a two-person operation for at least a year before then. Kallman was a secretary at the Boston Consulting Group, working for seven different consultants, including Koch. A bartender by night and on weekends, Kallman was a native of Lynn, Massachusetts, and was raised in Peabody. With a ready smile framed by blond hair, she was an extrovert—as natural a salesperson as Koch was not. When he was starting the company and hunting for investors, including among the verdant financial fields of BCG on the upper floors of One Boston Place, a gleaming skyscraper that counted law firms and private-equity groups as other tenants, someone suggested Kallman as a partner. Barely into her twenties, she turned down the opportunity to help start BCG's New York office to work with Koch on this door-to-door beer-selling concern.

The beer itself sprung from Koch's earlier epiphany: he would make the freshest glass of beer the American consumer could get, and he would do it over and over. He turned, like Matthew Reich at New Amsterdam before him, to Joseph Owades. Koch's father, Charles, had known Owades when he worked as a brewer, and Owades happened to live in the Boston area at the time. The two hammered out a deal, with Owades getting 2 percent of the company as compensation, and then set about crafting a late-twentieth-century equivalent of a Koch family lager recipe from the mid-nineteenth. Much as Charles Koch served as business mentor to his son, Owades served as brewing mentor—and he had a willing and eager protégé.

Jim Koch not only homebrewed but also connected by phone with commercial brewers like the Boulder Brewing Company and Wm. S. Newman, where he apprenticed for two weeks. The apprenticeship reaffirmed his hunch: for all its pioneering, Newman, like most of the early craft breweries, struggled with quality control. Dust from the different grains drifted across the downtown Albany warehouse space, settling in beers where it wasn't called for in the recipe. Bacteria was a constant foe. The beer could be inconsistent, the best on the East Coast one batch, cloudily unappetizing the next. Koch knew if he could make the same high-quality beer time and again, he would have an advantage over other small-scale brewers (he was not even thinking of competing with Big Beer directly; they could have their business model). To gain that advantage, he brought on Owades. (Newman would file for Chapter 11 in August 1987, under crushing debt tied to a bottling deal that went wrong. F. X. Matt continued brewing the brand for a while, and Newman's Albany space, which had housed the first brewery in the New York State capital in sixty-five years, became a Bruegger's Bagels factory.)

Koch and Owades picked for his contract brewing the Pittsburgh Brewing Company, a regional founded in the 1860s by German immigrants. It would prove a fateful decision affecting the entire industry. For the time, it seemed a superb choice—the Boston Beer Company's signature brand produced there eventually started to sell itself.

First, though, Koch and Kallman were selling it bit by bit, beginning with the local bar and restaurant list they made the day after Koch's phone call with his uncle. They figured they would need thirty accounts to make the business work initially. Thirty accounts—it didn't seem like much. One day shortly after they made the list and while Kallman was visiting her brother in California, Koch rolled reluctantly out of bed in Newton, the call with his uncle in the back of his mind, and put on his weekday uniform: a dark pinstripe suit. He would face his fear head-on: he would do his first solo cold call. He had bought Tom Hopkins's salesmanship how-to book, *How to Master the Art of Selling*, at the Harvard Co-op across the street from his alma mater and committed a sales pitch to memory. Later that day, though, Koch's mind clanged with doubt during the long elevator ride down from his cushy office with its magisterial views of Boston Harbor, through the skyscraper's polished, sunny lobby, and out onto Washington Street, where people had a million places to be and none of them a brewery. Why was he doing this? What was the point? The failure rate—the failure rate was so high! He wasn't a natural salesman!

Koch couldn't find any bars on Washington. He took his first right—you always turned right—and there, down State Street, he found a bar. It would have to do. The Dockside Restaurant and Bar sat amid the Faneuil Hall Marketplace, a Boston nightlife and shopping district that had been revamped to much success the decade before. Koch walked into the Dockside before 11:30—he knew restaurants and bars did not want to have to deal with a sales pitch during lunchtime. He was carrying his briefcase full of ice packs and lager test-batch bottles with black-and-white labels that said "Sample Beer." He also had with him a couple of early articles from the media to paint his venture with some legitimacy. The bar was empty except for one man behind the railing. Koch began reciting his memorized pitch to the man, who said nothing in return. Remembering a lesson of the salesmanship book, Koch started asking questions—you were supposed to keep the conversation going. Still no answer; urban quietude was the only noise coming from the street. He thought of his office back at BCG. Then another man stepped from the shadows. He was the manager, and he wanted to know what this besuited fellow was doing fast-talking up his staff. Koch started his pitch over: "Hi, I'm Jim Koch. I'm starting this new brewery, and I have a new beer, and it's called Samuel Adams Boston Lager. Have you heard of it?" He poured some for the manager, who took it, held it to the light, tasted it, and promptly ordered twenty-five cases.

Koch was elated. Back at the office, he called Kallman in California. "I sold an order for twenty-five cases!" he said. "But I told the guy I couldn't deliver him twenty-five cases, so he's going to take five and we'll take it from there!"

The Boston Beer Company had its first account. Bit by bit, Koch and Kallman, eventually full-time yet without an office, sold their way toward the magic number of thirty. Both dressed smartly—they were occasionally mistaken for IRS or board of health agents. Lugging the ice-packed samples—in Kallman's case, within an oversized Lancôme bag she'd earned—they hit prospect after prospect, sweetening any pitch with the offer to return for free and educate the bar or restaurant's staff about the beer they would be pouring. The pouring was the big thing. Koch and Kallman knew that if they could get the beer in the glass in front of a manager or an owner, they could get the account. That sometimes took two, three, four visits, but the pour worked like a charm.

The flagship brand, Samuel Adams Boston Lager, was, as one contemporary in the craft beer industry put it, "a clean, clean beer. It was gorgeous. [Koch] put it out there: nice color, good head. All of a sudden, it was like, 'Oh that's good draft beer.'" For Koch, the lightbulb was the control behind that quality. That Samuel Adams Boston Lager was so clean and therefore appealing to a general consumer audience was no accident; it was something Koch, ever the consultant as much as the brewer, sought so as to distinguish his product from the rest of the slowly growing market. Incidents of infections—the brewing process was a five-star hotel for bacteria—had hit other craft breweries, had even helped drive some out of business, like Charles and

Shirley Coury's Cartwright Portland, or very near it, like Boulder Brewing (which Koch had visited while planning Boston Beer).

Plus, most craft beers in the United States at the time were ales, which could be naturally cloudier than lagers, with the sort of yeast sediment at the bottom that Tom de Bakker had sought to warn drinkers about on his labels. The cloudiness did not mean the ales were bad or off, just that they were a different creature than their more slowly, more coolly fermented brethren. To an American beer consumer in the mid-1980s, however, when more than eight in ten beers sold were an exactingly clear shade of yellow that would not tolerate even the faintest gossamer of wavy sediment, Samuel Adams Boston Lager was a masterstroke of presentation. It didn't hurt that it tasted good: malty and slightly sweet on the finish, with a crisp bitterness throughout. Koch, with the help of Joseph Owades, had crafted an archetypal beer from his ancestor's recipe, what Michael Jackson would declare "an American classic."*

And Koch had crafted a seemingly airtight brand to back it. The goofy eighteenth-century man on the label, which Boston ad firm Gearon Hoffman designed, was the culmination of careful research; Koch showed mocked-up labels to bar patrons, to fellow business travelers on airplanes, to potential investors such as his uncle at Goldman Sachs, to just about anyone who would give constructive feedback. He went with "Samuel Adams" over other contenders, like "New World," because it connected on some level with consumers. Koch knew of Jack McAuliffe's defunct effort, New Albion, though he was not aware of that pioneer's formula for a beer label and name: history plus location can equal authenticity in a drinker's mind, and if you don't legitimately have the former, "you can just make it up." Koch had both history and location in the Samuel Adams Boston Lager label. "The Boston Beer Company" splashed across the top; the city, redolent as it was of all things Revolutionary in the mind of any American who had passed through grade school, again in the beer's very name; the chisel-chinned patriot smiling knowingly just below, hoisting a frothy tankard of history and cheer. Brewer. Patriot. Clear and clean. Tasty. What wasn't to like? Even if it did cost twenty-five cents more than a bottle of Heineken.

Koch and Kallman delivered the bottles—they couldn't afford to do draft—themselves, having not been able to find a distributor willing to take Boston Beer on. Kallman drove an orange Chevy Vega with a white interior,

---

* Jackson's highest accolade was "world classic," however. According to the critic Stan Hieronymus, Jackson declared only one American craft beer a world classic in all seven editions of his *Pocket Guide to Beer*: Anchor Steam (http://appellationbeer.com/blog/a-short-history-of-jacksons-world-classics/).

Koch a yellow Plymouth Reliant station wagon that his kids took to calling the "Beer Mobile" (a rented truck came later, after the magic thirty accounts, and more, provided some revenue). Early promotional materials turned on Kallman's homemade signs—eleven-by-fourteen- or sixteen-by-twenty-inch poster board with six beer labels each, red tape around the edges as a frame, and the name of the establishment followed by the tag, "Proudly serves Samuel Adams Boston Lager." Here, too, they soon graduated to real tabletop umbrellas, menu boards, even sixty-second radio spots featuring Koch's gravelly baritone talking about the qualities of the beer, a complete refutation of the typical beer spot with its ex-jocks and bikini models. As for the sales and payables that post–St. Patrick's Day computer was supposed to handle, labeled shoeboxes on Koch's kitchen table sufficed for the time being.

Samuel Adams Boston Lager was one of the few of that type in the craft beer movement by the mid-1980s (Jim Schlueter's River City in Sacramento had been the first craft brewery to focus on lagers). The overwhelming majority remained ales—porters, stouts, pales, IPAs, seasonals such as Anchor's Christmas ale, even some wheat ales, a specialty of Widmer Brothers in Portland, Oregon. Ales could be easier to make. The yeasts were heartier and could ferment at higher temperatures; that saved craft brewers the trouble and expense of keeping a fermentation kettle cool for days and sometimes weeks.

When it came to Big Beer in most of the United States, however, it was, as Larry Bell put it, "straight lager country." Bell was a native of the Chicago suburb of Park Forest, a Cubs fan with neatly combed blond hair and a beard that would eventually shrink to a goatee. He had first encountered beer during a bicycle road trip at age sixteen, when he and a friend came upon some unopened cans of Old Milwaukee, a lower-end Pabst brand, at a campsite. Bell encountered decidedly better-quality beer when his older brother invited him years later to Washington, DC, where they hit the Brickskeller, a bar near DuPont Circle that once held the Guinness world record for largest selection of commercially available beers (1,072). After attending college in Kalamazoo, Michigan, Bell picked up homebrewing via a coworker at the Sarkozy Bakery in that city in 1980. He visited the Real Ale Company shortly after its launch a couple of years later in Chelsea eighty-five miles away and asked the usual questions of Ted Badgerow, who, if you had pressed him later, would not have been able to remember Bell in particular among the many who popped in to talk shop. Bell had an interest in food and might have become a chef or even a farmer, had the Real Ale Company tour not intervened. He, like Ken Grossman at New Albion twenty-three hundred miles away and four years before, took away from this visit to the Midwest's first craft brewery the notion that the distance between homebrewing and a commercial itera-tion was navigable. Besides, there wasn't that much competition in between the coasts and people already wanted to buy Bell's homebrew. A commercial leap did not seem so far-fetched.

Bell incorporated an eponymous brewery with the state of Michigan the week after July 4, 1983; the brewery was actually a homebrew supply shop in Kalamazoo. Soon, however, Bell was collecting investors, including two hundred dollars from his mother, and a fifteen-gallon soup pot for a brew-ing kettle. By August 1985, in three rooms of an old plumbing warehouse on East Kalamazoo Avenue that he rented through trading the landlord stock in his new brewery, he was brewing test batches of English ales. Sales via secondhand bottles began the following month. By that time, Ted Badgerow's Real Ale Company in Chelsea had closed down, broken by some iffy batches and the same financial pressure that had weighted earlier craft breweries, with a dearth of lending sources making expansion all but impossible even as demand stayed relatively high. Bell's operation, called Kalamazoo Brewing Company, had become in its first full year the oldest craft brewery between Colorado and the East Coast.

Reaching this milestone underscored a strange new reality in the craft beer movement. Yes, the Stroh Brewery in Detroit could produce in thirty minutes what Kalamazoo could produce in a year (520 barrels). But just as Bell supplanted Badgerow, there was a flow of new craft entrants that meant competition was now coming from within the movement, as well as from without, with a breadth no one had seen before. The AHA's Daniel Bradford explained it like this in the summer of 1986: "You can now get more beers in places like Boulder, New York, Madison, and Berkeley than anywhere in Europe. There are about three hundred brands available in some of these cit-ies. Because of that," he went on, "a market segment is opening up that can't be dealt with by major breweries because it is basically too small. The larger breweries require a certain volume to keep plants going, and they can't handle this." The American craft beer movement by its third wave in the mid-1980s had its niche marketplace all to itself, which proved a blessing and a curse.

BEER, IT'S WHAT'S WITH DINNER
Washington, DC; Portland, OR | 1983–1987

O ne September evening in 1985, on the ground floor of an old hotel off Washington's tony DuPont Circle charging sixty dollars a night, a Bethesda,
Maryland, schoolteacher stepped to the microphone and told the fewer than
three dozen people assembled about the first beer of the tasting: Tsingtao out
of China. Bob Tupper was the MC for the evening at the Brickskeller, the
family-owned restaurant dating from 1957. It was owned, as was the Marifex
Hotel upstairs, by the Coja family, one of whom, Diane, had married Dave
Alexander a few years before; Alexander and his father-in-law, Maurice, set
about making the Brickskeller a beer Mecca. It amassed a reputation as the
place in the District to find hundreds of brands from across the globe and
the place *not* to order a Miller Lite.

When the local wing of the Cornell University alumni association
approached Coja about holding a beer tasting, he approached Tupper, who
he knew had an encyclopedic collection of tasting notes and, owing to his
career as a history teacher at a private school in Maryland, had no fear of
public speaking. Tickets were fifteen dollars a pop and included a modest
buffet to go with the ten beers, including German and English ones meant
more to illustrate the styles than to showcase the brands. It turned out to
be the first commercially run sit-down beer tasting with food in the United
States, unwittingly sparking a trend that would redefine the parameters of
American craft beer.

Other tastings at the Brickskeller followed in the new year, with Tupper
adding a dollop of multimedia to the proceedings with slides, some from
photos he had taken during brewery visits; and eventually the restaurant
drew none other than Michael Jackson as a regular lecturer at the tastings.
Anchor beers, too, became a regular in Tupper's tasting lineups, as did other
craft brands as they became available in the District (or before they did:
Tupper's mother-in-law put three cases of Samuel Adams Boston Lager in

a nondescript brown box and paid its Greyhound bus fare from up north). The tastings were as much a way to introduce the curious to good beer as it was to stay one step ahead of the neo-Prohibitionists. The Washington city council was considering requiring that new liquor-license applicants gain the approval of a majority of residents living within sixteen hundred feet. "If we did have to justify our existence," Dave Alexander figured, "we could say we were here for the education."

The education of the would-be craft beer consumer was a real thing by the mid-1980s. This was distinct from the education of the homebrewer or of the homebrewer looking to make the leap to small-scale commercial brewing. This was education in the more general and pressing sense: how to draw more consumers. This push, subtle and sporadic as it was with events such as the Brickskeller's, chose to position craft beer as part of a well-rounded palate (if not diet). Why not? Fine American wine in the previous decade had grown as a respected accompaniment of fine food or as a culinary end in itself. For instance, wine bars sprang up in major cities starting in the late 1970s and early 1980s, catering to aficionados and novices alike.

There were few such equivalents in beer. The Brickskeller was one. The Horse Brass in Portland, Oregon, was another. Don Younger, the regional office manager for consumer products giant Lever Brothers, launched the Horse Brass in 1976, and the following year began carrying New Albion, a formidable achievement considering the Sonoma, California, brewery's limited production and reach. Soon, the Horse Brass had four taps for craft beers and imports, a draft lineup that made Younger nervous—how would he ever find enough beers to keep all of them flowing? Judy Ashworth did not face quite so difficult a challenge a decade later in her Lyon's Brewery Depot in Sunol, California, just southeast of San Francisco. There was a relative bounty of craft beers and choicer European imports to choose from when Ashworth decided to throw a "Farwell to Bud" party in 1986 and forgo carrying Big Beer brands. The ex-head of her own commercial janitorial business, Ashworth had acquired the Lyon's three years earlier with copious loans and would likely have been fine with those selections of Budweiser, Miller, et al. But a patron introduced her to homebrew and that launched Ashworth on a self-tutorial about the craft brewing happening throughout Northern California. The pivot away from Big Beer in 1986 would prove fortuitous for that region's craft brewing scene, and therefore for the nation's at large (given the eventual reach of early Lyon's selections such as Sierra Nevada, Anchor, and Pete's Wicked). For one thing, the Lyon's then-huge tap run—at least nineteen and eventually forty-five at a new location north of Sunol in Dublin—provided a lot of breweries a platform for reaching curious consumers (and Ashworth was an obliging host, often driving personally to pick up kegs). More important, the Lyon's served as an educational hub in perhaps the nation's busiest hive of craft beer activity. Here was a place to not only drink the latest offerings, but to learn about them, too. The Lyon's and the Horse Brass proved by the mid-1980s that one could build an evening around craft beer. The leap that the Brickskeller made, in marrying craft beer to food, was not so gapingly wide, particularly since Americans' attitudes toward food and drink in general were starting to change.

"There is a new gourmet influence," the brewing consultant Joseph Owades told a reporter in the summer of 1984. "People now are exposed to so many new tastes. They want fresh pasta, more flavorful wine—and richer beer." The education also offered a crucial marketing peg for the fledgling industry, one that would only grow in leaps and bounds. Call it an aspiration quotient, one summed up beautifully by Matthew Reich, who was fond of saying that his New Amsterdam was "not for the six-pack drinker. It's the beer to have if you're having one. With dinner." This was very important for the craft beer movement: Wine for a long time had held an exalted place in popular culture, the provenance of elites, worthy of critics empaneled by major publications such as the *New York Times*; beer had not. The coverage of it mattered.

As was his custom by now, Michael Jackson stood at the vanguard. He wrote for the *Washington Post* in November 1983 what was very likely the first article in a mainstream American newspaper about pairing beer with food, and vice versa. The *Post* was still in its Watergate afterglow of nine years before, the third-largest daily US newspaper by circulation, which not only the denizens of the White House and Congress read but also a wide regional audience from central Virginia through Maryland. On November 16, 1983, the week before Thanksgiving, they awoke to a discursive, at times humorous, essay meandering through four pages on which beers to have with which foods on the big feast day. Jackson eased his readers into the unfamiliar territory with wine as well as with an emphasis on the geographic origins of different beers, which in itself might have seemed unfamiliar. For the main course:

With the centerpiece of the meal, the turkey, the wine-drinker has a difficult choice. Should it be a medium-dry white? Or a drier medium-bodied red? Among beers, I would opt for a pale but medium-dry brew of the type produced in the city of Munich and elsewhere in Bavaria. . . . With just a hint of sweetness to match some of the turkey's accompaniments, these Munich Light beers have plenty of body without being too filling. Their alcohol content is pretty ordinary, at well under 4.0 percent by weight or 5.0 by volume. As for serving temperatures, the simplest rule to observe is that any beer from Munich or elsewhere in Bavaria should be served chilled but not to American popsicle level; not less than 48 degrees, in fact.

It was something any person with healthy taste buds could get right away: certain beers went well with certain foods. But it was a matter of getting consumers to pair the beers with the foods in the first place. The era of light beer—not to be confused with the "Light" that Jackson referred to, which had to do with the German beers' color—was in full force, with tens of millions being spent on television and print ad campaigns to move tens of millions of barrels. Anheuser-Busch had debuted Bud Light (formerly Budweiser Light) in 1982, with a commercial of a mighty Clydesdale running through a seemingly endless pasture, a deep, unseen voice intoning, "A light beer worthy of the King of Beers." Miller Lite, the brand it was meant to usurp, inaugurated the celebrity-studded Lite Beer Bowling Tournament in September of the same year. Beer was still seen as a beverage to be consumed when you're having six, with or without dinner, and as close to "popsicle" as possible. As for its geographic origins, it was not important if it wasn't local. Attempts to integrate American beer with gourmet food seemed as hopeless as Rodney Dangerfield's attempts to roll a strike in the Lite Beer Bowling Tournament (he couldn't down a pin).

The sit-down beer-food tastings and Jackson's articles were a start, though. He would write more for the *Post* and other American publications throughout the decade and would host pairings at venues that included the swanky Pierre hotel in Midtown Manhattan, where four Belgian chefs devised the lunch menu; Monk's Cafe in Philadelphia's Center City as well as at the metropolis's Museum of Archaeology and Anthropology; and the Century House in the hamlet of Latham, New York. That one, on November 4, 1986, even got a little advance press.

English beer authority Michael Jackson will visit Albany Nov. 4 to conduct "The Quintessential Beer Tasting," at 8 PM at the Century House in Latham. The international beer tasting, sponsored by Albany's Newman Brewing Company, will be open to the public. . . . For the Albany show, he will lead a guided tour through a selection of

13 international beers. Tickets at $6 per person are available through
Newman's Brewery . . . and at the door.

Largely, though, press for the tastings or for craft beer generally was slim
to none. From consumer media, it was mostly of the parachute variety: The
reporter would be assigned to cover an event such as the Great American
Beer Festival; he would arrive, gather what background he could, garner some
quotes from attendees and organizers for color, and be gone as quickly as he
arrived. Rare, too, was the byline with any gravitas in the industry or with
readers. Frank J. Prial's spring 1979 visit to Jack McAuliffe's New Albion
was so far the most storied example—the *Times*'s wine critic stomping about
the wilds of Sonoma, scribbling notes on craft beer! When T. R. Reid of
the *Washington Post* phoned Daniel Bradford to tell him he was coming to
Boulder for the second GABF in June 1983, it was all Bradford could do to
not shout across the office to his boss, "Charlie, the *Washington Post* called,
and they're sending a guy to cover this!" The silver lining in consumer coverage was that it had long ceased writing of craft beer as if it were a blip in
the marketplace or a mere curiosity; knowledge about the brands and the
brewing process was diffuse enough, and sources plentiful enough, that these
parachuted reporters could get up to speed quickly.

From trade media, the coverage was more in-depth, and followed the
conversational, we're-all-in-this-together tone set by homebrewing club newsletters like those of the Maltose Falcons in Los Angeles or self-published
memoranda like Fred Eckhardt's *Amateur Brewer* out of Portland or Charlie Papazian's increasingly professionalized *Zymurgy*, the quarterly out of
Boulder. As we've seen, they all mixed recipes and reviews with whatever
news, including information on upcoming events, that could be amassed
in the pre-Internet age, when even a long-distance phone call could be an
event. Wider industry trade publications covered craft beer as well. The three
most prominent were the monthly magazine *Brewers Digest*, the multifaceted
Modern Brewery Age, and the bimonthly magazine *All About Beer*, which
Los Angeles printing executive Mike Bosak and investors launched in early
1979 with a sixteen-page issue that included news of homebrewing's federal
legalization and Anchor's production at its new Mariposa Street location.
Despite a stable of heavy hitters such as Jackson and James D. Robertson, an
engineer who while working in Germany in the early 1960s discovered beer
"so well made" it found its way regularly onto dinner (and lunch) tables, the
industry often dismissed Bosak's publication because it sometimes sold editorial space, including the cover. With a claimed readership of one hundred

sixty thousand by 1983, however, *All About Beer* did likely have the widest reach of these larger trade magazines.

It was Fred Eckhardt, though, even more than Jackson, who dragged craft beer coverage over the hump from esoteric toward commonplace. On April 25, 1984, a Friday, tucked onto a page of Portland's daily newspaper, the *Oregonian*, with ads for Diet 7-Up and Atta Boy dog food as well as a call for contestants for a rice-cooking competition, were two brief stories and one photograph, what those in the newspaper trade call a thumbnail. The shorter of the two articles was headlined BEER EXPERT WRITES COLUMN, and it gave Eckhardt's CV in digestable nuggets: "Eckhardt is a 'self-taught' amateur brewer who started making his own beer in 1969 [*sic*], in the fashion his father did during Prohibition." It was the warm-up for the longer article: MOST AMERICAN BEERS LACK ONE THING: TASTE. The ensuing column marked the opening of what would be the first regular American newspaper coverage of craft beer. The type of writing that Michael Jackson championed out of England had found a domestic expression in Eckhardt in the *Oregonian*, which was one of the most respected midsize dailies in the country, with a weekday circulation of 249,000. And the ex-Marine did not hold back.

From that first column on April 25: "When drinking San Francisco Steam Beer [Anchor Steam], or a well-made dark beer, you notice the taste. Most domestic brews taste alike and many of us are forced to look to imports for the kinds of taste we used to find in American beer." The list of "Twenty Beers with Class" at the end of the column included Anchor Liberty Ale and Sierra Nevada Pale Ale.*

From a June 20 column after Eckhardt returned from the third GABF: "Since the voting was limited, and somewhat chauvinistic as a popularity contest, I am taking the liberty to list my choices for the twenty top beers at the festival. And, yes, I did taste all of the thirty-six beers which are not available in these parts. . . . Rumor mills say the New Amsterdam Amber (already in California) will come north this fall."

And this one on the Fourth of July of the same year:

Anyone who thinks that great beer has to be brought into Portland from a great distance just hasn't been paying attention. Some of the best beer in the world is made within 200 miles of Portland, where

---

* The rest of the list was mostly imports as well as a few regional brewers such as Weinhard's and Rainier.

there are six breweries. . . . Good beer is becoming stylish, and if we hang in there, there'll be real taste in American beer again. In fact, it is here now. We have Redhook and Grants [*sic*] brewing world-class beer, but only on draft. The new Ponzi operation, Columbia River Brewing [later BridgePort], is set to produce beer by mid-August, but also only on draft.

Fred Eckhardt speaking at the old Brickskeller beer bar in Washington, DC, in 2002. Courtesy of Dave Alexander

Eckhardt's *Oregonian* columns continued through the 1980s and set a precedent in mainstream outlets not only for opinionated, conversational coverage of craft beer but also for sometimes putting the cart before the horse when it came to writing about brewers and their beers. Eckhardt, for one, would sometimes suggest a particular style to one of the Portland breweries—a winter ale, say—and then write about it once it was produced. Or he would write about a style that was unavailable from local brewers as a none-too-subtle nudge. Like Jackson's coverage, Eckhardt's combined a genuine desire to educate the consumer with a soft spot for mentoring these start-up breweries.

William Least Heat-Moon also had ulterior motives. He wanted something to write about that might require a road trip. Ex-Navy, with a PhD in English from the University of Missouri, he had crafted a bestselling memoir in the early 1980s called *Blue Highways*, about traveling America's back roads after he lost his job and his estranged wife on the same winter's day. Critics compared it favorably to John Steinbeck's *Travels with Charley* and Jack Kerouac's *On the Road*. The pursuit of rediscovering something in America—namely areas empty of strip malls and fast-food joints, and the characters who inhabited them—perhaps uniquely qualified Heat-Moon to write the first long-form consumer magazine story about beer since the craft movement began. Besides, the third paragraph of *Blue Highways* could all but serve as a credo for the movement's entrepreneurs: "A man who couldn't make things go right could at least go. He could quit trying to get out of the way of life. Chuck routine. Live the real jeopardy of circumstance. It was a question of dignity."

Heat-Moon's 6,978-word chronicle of his visits to nearly every brewpub and craft brewery in the country in the mid-1980s—Ken Grossman's Sierra Nevada was the big exception, owing to time and traveling expenses—was published by the 130-year-old *Atlantic Monthly* in November 1987 under the entirely appropriate headline A GLASS OF HANDMADE. Heat-Moon and a friend, whom he called The Venerable Tashmoo,* not only sampled myriad glassfuls but also learned the brewers' back stories and techniques, starting in Albany.

> One September afternoon The Venerable and I watched Bill Newman work; we gnawed grains of his various malted barleys; we helped him stir the mash; we tasted the sweet wort, the hopped wort, the green beer, and the finished ale fresh from the maturing tank. Young Newman (to be a micro-brewer is to be under forty) wanted to give his city a choice of flavors, to fill a cranny that the industrial breweries left as they bought up regional companies.

The underlying theme of the story was one of the underlying themes of the craft beer movement: local variety versus mass production that had engineered out the former and eschewed the latter. With this came the challenges, and Heat-Moon recorded those, too. It was a daily grind with distributors, retailers, and especially consumers, even in 1987—twenty-two years after Fritz Maytag walked into the old Anchor on Eighth Street, eleven years after Jack McAuliffe started building his gravity system in the grape warehouse, and

---

* Heat-Moon and his friend, Scott Chisholm, were both partly of Native American descent. Chisholm died in 2007.

five years after Charlie Papazian and Daniel Bradford launched the Great American Beer Festival.

> I told the bartender what I'd seen at lunch in a cafe downtown: a man—fifties, blue blazer, penny loafers, *USA Today* under his arm— ordered a Hale's Pale American Ale, took a single sip, and handed it back to the bartender, who dumped it and then passed across a bottle of Heineken. The bartender said, "I don't see many conversions of middle-aged people. The beer a man's drinking when he's thirty is the one he tends to believe in the rest of his life."

It was also around the time of Heat-Moon's *Atlantic* piece and Eckhardt's first *Oregonian* columns that a writer in Seattle named Vince Cottone began using a term that he thought best described the breweries he had begun writing about recently, including for the *Seattle Post-Intelligencer* newspaper, the Association of Brewers' *New Brewer* magazine, and a guide to breweries and bars in the Northwest, published in 1986 and featuring a foreword Michael Jackson wrote. In that guide's introduction, Cottone sought to define his topic: "I use the term Craft Brewery to describe a small brewery using traditional methods and ingredients to produce a handcrafted, uncompromised beer that is marketed locally."

Cottone had also used "craft brewing" and "craft-brewery scene" as early as 1984, very likely making him the first person in the United States to do so publicly. It was his 1986 attempt to actually define "craft brewery," though, that would prove a watershed in terminology, eventually sweeping all other monikers before it, including "micro-brewery" and "boutique brewery," which Jackson himself used in a pocket guide to US beer that Simon & Schuster published, also in 1986. "Craft brewery" quickly spawned "craft beer," too, though Cottone in that same guide tried to sell "true beer" as the phrase describing the fruits of these smaller operations' labors. When Cottone was asked why he had settled on "craft brewery"—especially that first word—he pretty much shrugged. Maybe he had heard it during recent visits to the UK, he wasn't sure. "Craft brewery" just "seemed to fit best."

VATS AND DOGS

San Francisco | 1986–1987

The call could not have come at a worse time for Pete Slosberg. It was Bob Stoddard on the line; Stoddard had taken over Palo Alto Brewing in Mountain View, California, from father-and-son founders Kenneth and Jeffrey Kolence. Now, at the beginning of 1987, it was going out of business in a rather messy way. Stoddard told Slosberg, who was brewing his first batches of beer under contract there, that he was going into Chapter Seven bankruptcy. It was a Wednesday evening; the sheriff would arrive on Monday to lock the brewery's doors; everything inside would be off-limits. Slosberg and his business partner, Mark Bronder, had to get their beer bottled and out the door before then.

It was Bronder who had suggested they start a business. An Omaha native who grew up in Minneapolis and Nashville as the son of Johnny Carson's one-time radio partner (his dad later became an advertising executive), Bronder had an MBA from Northwestern and had logged time in IT for a steel firm in Chicago. He left that job when he realized the managers had all been there for a decade or more—and were still managers. He went to consulting power-house Booz Allen and then was lured by the glam of Silicon Valley. Porsches and Ferraris studded the parking lot outside of ROLM. You didn't have to wear a tie in the office—you could even grow a beard, like his nearby cubicle neighbor, Pete Slosberg. The unfailingly gregarious Bronder and the slightly reserved Slosberg became friends. One Friday, Bronder asked Slosberg what he was doing over the weekend. Slosberg told him he was competing in a homebrewing contest. Bronder wished him luck in that half-listening workplace way—and promptly asked him on Monday what he had done over the weekend. Slosberg reminded him about the homebrewing competition.

"How'd you do?"

"I came in third," Slosberg replied.

"Well, that's pretty good," Bronder said like the Little League coach of a losing team. "How many people entered?"

"Five hundred. It was statewide."

Five hundred, Bronder thought, and you placed third! Bronder was not a beer drinker—he had not had a drink in his life—but he realized Slosberg's homebrew must be pretty good. Bronder, who would leave ROLM to go into venture capital, pitched the idea of going into business together before— and during—Slosberg's twelve-week sabbatical from ROLM. The sabbatical allowed him to travel widely, including in South America. He and his wife and their two children crossed the Andes from Argentina to Chile; they spent spells in Peru and Bolivia; Slosberg sat atop a mountain overlooking Machu Picchu, Andean pipes playing about him, and knew he could not go back to ROLM when he returned to the Bay Area. He reached out to Bronder—he was in. The pair began brainstorming for business ideas.

They knew of the craft beer movement. It was Northern California in 1985—you couldn't miss it. Fritz Maytag's twenty-one-person operation on Mariposa Street in San Francisco was still the largest craft brewery in the United States, with forty thousand barrels of six different types of beer annually. Ken Grossman's Sierra Nevada out of Chico was brewing more than ten thousand barrels annually, mostly of its flagship pale ale, which was becoming the archetype for not only hoppy West Coast beers but also for the American interpretation of the English-born style. And there were the Bay Area's vaunted brewpubs, like the Mendocino Brewing Company in Hopland and Buffalo Bill's in Hayward, the second and third oldest in the nation (Bert Grant's original brewpub, in Yakima, Washington, was up to three thousand barrels annually). There were by 1986 as many as twenty-six craft breweries, including brewpubs, touching every region of the nation, save for the Deep South and Hawaii (and those were not far behind). And for every one that closed, as we've noted, there seemed to be another ready to start up in its place. Still, distribution for most remained severely limited, often to the immediate vicinities; and the production, even aggregated, paled next to Big Beer's output. Anheuser-Busch on its own was producing more than sixty million barrels a year.

It helped, then, that Slosberg and Bronder were dreaming in the Bay Area, where American craft beer was born and where it was in relative abundance. Had they been in, say, Rochester, New York, Slosberg's old home, or even in New York City, where he went to college and graduate school, it's entirely possible an entirely different industry could have scratched their entrepreneurial itch. As it was, the pair settled upon craft beer—it was a growing industry, especially where they were; it looked fun; and, besides, Slosberg was a good homebrewer with a beer-can-collecting habit that often meant sudden stops on family vacations. Plus, Bronder's ad-man father had taught him that creativity could make a difference, that a little company could break through with just the right angle and amount of fun. Bronder more than anything wanted to have fun with the advertising.

They examined the economics and, like Matthew Reich in New York and Jim Koch in Boston, decided on contract brewing. Enter Bob Stoddard, a local sales rep for Miller who bought the Palo Alto Brewing Company in 1985 from the Kolences, when its annual production was about fifteen hundred barrels with a seven-barrel system. The Mountain View brewery was near Slosberg's house, and Stoddard's expansion to a twenty-barrel brewhouse with an old soda-bottling line spawned enough excess capacity for Slosberg and Bronder's first batches. Away went much of the start-up costs—the pair raised an initial $21,000 and incorporated what they called Pete's Brewing Company on April 23, 1986. They got the necessary licenses only after resistance from the state, which initially balked at allowing the company to make its commercial beer using someone else's equipment.

Pete Slosberg in front of the very first case display
of Pete's Wicked Ale, at the Liquor Barn in Mountain View,
California, in 1986. His English terrier can be seen
on the packaging. Courtesy of Pete Slosberg

The first beer brewed late that year in Stoddard's kettles came from a recipe Slosberg stumbled upon trying to imitate Samuel Smith's Nut Brown Ale. Deep brown, with a nutty finish and brewed by the oldest brewery in Yorkshire, it was first introduced to the United States by Charles Finkel's Merchant du Vin importing company in 1978. Slosberg's fourth attempt at a suitable knockoff eight years later instead produced a brown ale with a reddish color and a bitterer taste. He and Bronder eschewed calling it Pete's Brown Ale or, simply, Pete's Ale—what was memorable about either? They wanted something zippier for the increasingly crowded beer shelves of the Bay Area (the region was a hub not only of the growing craft beer movement but for imports, too, which were enjoying their briskest growth since Prohibition). Then Bronder heard a bit on San Francisco radio by comedian Bobcat Goldthwait, who threw around the adjective "wicked"—"wicked" this and "wicked" that. Slosberg liked it, too, and they slapped it in between "Pete's" and "Ale." Bronder got the graphic designer who did the brochures at his venture-capital firm to mock up some packaging and paraphernalia with pictures of Slosberg and his white-and-black bull terrier named Millie. The designer didn't care for Slosberg's mug—"The dog's a kick," she told Bronder. Millie became the face of Pete's Wicked Ale.

Slosberg and Bronder got that endangered batch out of the doomed Palo Alto Brewing Company with more than a little help from their friends. Beer and pizza powered a two-and-a-half-day, round-the-clock bottling, labeling, and packaging spree that produced another couple of hundred cases of beer to join the first ones at Bay Area retailers, produced months earlier by Stoddard without a hitch.

The narrow escape revealed a problem with contract brewing. Six craft breweries had come and gone in the past ten years: New Albion, DeBakker, Cartwright, Real Ale, River City, and now in early 1987, on its second owner, Palo Alto. Meanwhile, more of the larger regional breweries continued to succumb to the industry's consolidation. Miller, in a perfect example of both the targets and the goals of this consolidation by the 1980s, bought the 120-year-old, family-owned Jacob Leinenkugel Brewing Company in Chippewa Falls, Wisconsin (population 13,108), around the same time Palo Alto went bankrupt. Why? Leinie's, as locals called it, produced sixty-one thousand barrels annually to Miller's 38.7 million. No matter: Miller wasn't after size; its executives said it wanted the regional simply to reach those Leinie drinkers who would never pick up a Big Beer brand. The sweeping consolidation of the past thirty years had given way to one of attrition. Bit by isolated bit, Big Beer was going after the last vestiges of independent breweries, to the point where analysts could now speculate there would be only a few breweries in the entire country by the new century. Craft brewing was barely on anyone's radar, perhaps less than 2 percent of the beer bought in the United States (who was even tracking it?). For contract craft brewers, this meant fewer and fewer hands controlled the physical breweries that remained; and not all were amenable to contract brewing, excess capacity or not. It would take Slosberg and Bronder six months to locate another set of kettles and pipes. They found them more than two thousand miles away—and just in time.

TO THE LAST FRONTIER AND BACK

Juneau, AK; Amana, IA; Baltimore; Boston | 1985–1986

Geoff and Marcy Larson could not have contract brewed had they wanted. The nature of their particular chosen environment, Alaska, did not allow it. The Last Frontier was pretty much that in the early 1980s as far as craft beer went—or any beer, with European imports often arriving past their freshest dates and craft brands like DeBakker, Sierra Nevada, and Anchor distributive rarities. Shipping distances even within the state could be immense; it was a day's drive between Juneau, the capital, and Anchorage, the largest city, for instance (and that included a ferry ride). A start-up craft brewery was a capital and an organizational hurdle anywhere else in America; add to it this unique crucible of remoteness, and the prospect was positively frigid.

Still, Geoff Larson had taken that turkey run with Fritz Maytag. That meant something, he remembered.

Larson, who sported a Beatles haircut and whose smile seemed to cock to the right, had grown up all over as the son of a foreign-service officer, periodically landing for spells in Washington, DC, before college at the University of Maryland, where he studied chemical engineering. In his last summer before graduation, he decided to hitchhike to Alaska but ran out of money in Montana. He ended up as a short-order cook at Glacier National Park, where he met a blond-haired Florida native named Marcy Bradley who had just graduated from college with plans to be a photojournalist. To pay the bills, she worked as an auditor for the park. Marcy's and Geoff's schedules lined up—she worked nights, he worked mornings, and by noon their days were their own. The two became hiking buddies and soon much more. After the summer, Geoff returned to finish his five-year program and Marcy headed to Alaska, to another national park and another auditing job.

Geoff had been into cooking and homebrewing, and as a chemical engineering student knew the vagaries of fermentation well. He had even joked with college friends about starting a brewery. He tried the mainstream job route for a year after graduation. But something bit, and in 1981, on a trek back to Marcy in Alaska, he found himself on Greyhounds and couches, visiting breweries to soak up information. He visited F. X. Matt II at his eponymous brewery in Utica, New York, and as he would be with Matthew Reich and others, Matt was patient with the young visitor who had written him, showing Larson around and taking him on a further psychological tour of what he thought it meant to be a commercial brewer at that point in America. Matt talked in particular and at length about the shared heritage brewers had. "If you brew beer, you represent the entire industry," he told Larson. "Brew the best beer you can."

Larson heard a similar message shortly afterward on a trip west to Anchor on the Wednesday before Thanksgiving. Unbeknownst to Larson, Matt had

Marcy and Geoff Larson of Alaskan Brewing at a Great American Beer Festival in the early 1990s. The GABF was often the first time a geographically isolated craft brewery such as Alaskan got its shot at a wider consumer audience. Courtesy of the Alaskan Brewing Company

written Fritz Maytag about him; now it was that brewer's turn to seek out the would-be entrepreneur for an afternoon of mentorship. Maytag then drove Larson to the Greyhound depot, where he would catch a bus to Seattle and a ferry to Juneau. On the way, Maytag stopped to buy his Thanksgiving turkey. It was that kind of industry.

Back in Juneau, the couple got down to gathering investors. The banks all said no way, but after thirteen months Marcy and Geoff ended up accumulating eighty-eight backers from across Alaska. Few were interested so much in craft beer as they were in something new and invigorating in a decidedly bleak economic climate. In 1985, the couple rented from a neighbor two thousand square feet in an unfinished warehouse in an industrial area of Juneau. They were able to get new brewing equipment through JV Northwest, a manufacturer based in Canby, Oregon, that would end up supplying many craft breweries. Geoff spent two weeks apprenticing at the Millstream Brewing Company in Amana, Iowa. Carroll Zuber, a financial planner, and brothers James and Dennis Roeming, both restaurateurs, had launched what became the Cornhusker State's first craft brewery in 1985. Zuber had gotten the idea for a brewery a decade before while tasting beers during a visit to West Germany, and Millstream initially specialized in the cleaner, crisper lagers endemic to German beer culture. That was what Geoff Larson learned how to make when he apprenticed there shortly after Millstream's launch. In total, the Larsons spent $310,000 getting what they called the Alaskan Brewing Company off the ground in 1986, including on secondhand bottling equipment (they eschewed kegs at first). The twenty-eight-year-olds, who married in that eventful 1985, held the nation's sixty-seventh brewing license. Even after all the start-up stress, the couple still looked young and effusive enough to pass for college students.

The first 253 cases of their Alaskan Amber ale that rolled out of the Juneau warehouse with the help of ten volunteers in December were especially important for the wider craft movement for two reasons. First, the amber was a more malty flagship beer than had been seen in a while; only slightly hoppy in taste, it was certainly an anomaly for the West Coast start-ups; that was deliberate on the part of the Larsons. The beer was based on a popular local recipe from the early twentieth century that used Saaz hops from what is now the Czech Republic; the hops were difficult to come by in then-territorial Alaska, and so were used sparingly. Second, the brewery represented a logistical triumph: the first cases distributed outside of Juneau went first by ferry to Haines and then outward via truck. The Larsons' Alaskan Amber was a boundary pusher; it proved that while the craft beer movement was reasserting the importance of geography in American beer, geography did not preclude its conquests. It was a sign of the movement's potential that Alaska clearly would not be its last frontier.

Commercial brewing in any of the great cities of the East—Washington, Baltimore, Philadelphia, New York, and Boston—*would* have been an anomaly as late as the mid-1980s. Washington's last brewery, the Olde Heurich Brewing Company, closed in 1956 and was razed to make room for a national cultural hub on the Potomac that became the Kennedy Center. In Baltimore, the last brewery behind the apropos American Beer brand closed in 1973, leaving vacant a gorgeous eleven-story building dating from 1887. As we've seen with New York, Brooklyn alone had dozens of breweries by the turn of the last century. None remained in that borough, and barely any in the city at large. And, in Philadelphia, there may have been more than one hundred breweries, big and small, in operation at any one time in the 1800s and early 1900s. By the mid-1980s, there was just one left, Christian Schmidt and Sons; it would close in 1987. There were, though, two contract breweries operating in Philadelphia. On June 23, 1986, bartenders poured the first glasses of Pennsylvania Pilsner, which a business consultant named Tom Pastorius had developed with the biochemist Joseph Owades, already industrially famous for developing the recipe for what became Miller Lite and codeveloping the ones for Samuel Adams Boston Lager and New Amsterdam Amber. Pastorius had worked in West Germany for a decade, and missed the beers he discovered there. He incorporated the Pennsylvania Brewing Company in March 1986, and brewed that inaugural pilsner through the Pittsburg Brewing Company in western Pennsylvania. In January 1986, Jeffrey Ware, a restaurant manager and former pastry chef, and Rosemarie Certo, an English teacher and photographer, incorporated the Dock Street Brewing Company, and contracted upstate New York's F. X. Matt to brew Dock Street Amber Ale. The couple released it in the second half of 1986, with the ale finishing third in the Great American Beer Festival's consumer preference poll that fall. Dock Street would at the end of the decade open as a brewpub off Philadelphia's Logan Square.

As for Boston by 1987, New England's biggest city, like Baltimore and Washington (and soon Philly), would have no physical brewing presence. Boston's last brewery, Haffenreffer in the Jamaica Plain neighborhood, closed in 1964, ending centuries of brewing in Boston. When Carling in Natick closed in 1975, commercial brewing disappeared altogether from Massachusetts, where it had been woven into the socioeconomic fabric since just after the *Mayflower* finished its voyage from England in 1620.

Then, in the summer of 1986, the Commonwealth Brewing Company opened in Boston's West End, a block from the Boston Garden. Its proprietor? Richard Wrigley, the English transplant who had likened Michelob to "a soft drink" and who had opened New York City's first brewpub (the East Coast's, really) in the fall of 1984. As with his Manhattan Brewing Company, Wrigley saw the Commonwealth Brewing Company's mission as one servicing "serious beer drinkers," some of whom were not alive when Boston lost its last commercial brewery. Along with a seasonal with ginger in it, the pub planned to brew five beers regularly—a golden ale, an amber ale, a porter, a stout, and what Wrigley dubbed Boston's Best Burton Bitter—in the basement, with bar food, including smoked meats and fish, served upstairs. The beer selections were likely to find a thirsty audience. As a *Boston Globe* article on the brewpub's opening noted, "Wrigley isn't the only successful Boston brewer." Taking cues from the Maltose Falcons and other, older West Coast homebrewing clubs as well as from the personal computer age, Boston's two-year-old Wort Processors had won an award at the American Homebrewers Association's latest national competition. Moreover, Jim Koch and Rhonda Kallman were growing the Boston Beer Company well beyond those original thirty accounts they needed to launch. Boston, among the great cities of the East, seemed poised for the biggest craft beer renaissance.

Rich Doyle, Dan Kenary, and George Ligeti certainly hoped so. On August 12, 1982, the Dow Jones Industrial Average dropped to what would turn out to be a recession low of 776.92. It had nowhere to go except up: the bull market run of the 1980s was snorting and pawing at the gate. The three young men, all Harvard graduates, could stand to make a financial killing. All had already started down particularly lucrative roads: Ligeti worked in oil and gas, Kenary as a corporate lending officer, and Doyle in New York at the precursor to the financial services firm Lehman Brothers. But they pivoted. Doyle went back to Harvard to earn his MBA, and to avoid more class time he signed on for an independent study project that involved drawing up a business plan. He chose beer. Like fellow Harvard MBA Jim Koch around the same time, he had read an article on Fritz Maytag, and he had heard about Bill Owens's Buffalo Bill's brewpub in Hayward, California. Doyle had also traveled in Europe and to other parts of the world—even working for a spell as a bartender in New Zealand—and had discovered the pleasures and poignancies of locally produced beers. Why couldn't the beers he and his buddies drank in the Boston area also be locally produced? Killian's Irish Red, the Coors stab at a red ale introduced at the Great American Beer Festival in 1982, was perhaps the most exotic thing going in the area. With his roommate and through the independent study, Doyle began drawing up a business plan for a start-up brewery in greater Boston.

He enlisted Kenary, a Worcester, Massachusetts, native who had earned an MBA from the University of Chicago and whom Doyle had known since before college; and Ligeti, a Canadian who was also passing through the Harvard program. Part of the plan's research involved visits to craft breweries out west. Kurt and Rob Widmer, clad in coveralls, talked brewing at their Portland, Oregon, operation; so did Richard and Nancy Ponzi in nearby Bridgeport, Connecticut. Paul Shipman of the Independent Ale Brewing Company, brewer of the increasingly popular Redhook Ale, met the visitors in the former transmission shop in Seattle; and Doyle by himself popped in on Mike Hale's brewery farther south in Washington State. At different times, he and Kenary made it northward in the state to visit Thomas Kemper by the Canadian border; and then they went over the border.

Canada had had its own brush with Prohibition. Before and during World War I, provinces and territories in the Great White North began banning alcohol production to some degree, as well as forbidding imports from south of the border and elsewhere. After the war ended in late 1918, provincial and territorial governments began repealing their prohibitive measures, starting with

Rich Doyle, left, and Dan Kenary. Courtesy of the Mass. Bay Brewing Company

Quebec the following year. Prohibition had left its mark, though, and it would be a generation before Canada had really replaced the hundreds of breweries, wineries, and distilleries it lost. The first Canadian craft breweries began opening in the early 1980s, inspired in part by American ones. Canada did, however, beat America to the first brewpub on the continent. Opened in 1980, two years before Bert Grant's brewpub in Yakima, Washington, John Mitchell and Frank Appleton's Horseshoe Bay Brewery and Roller Inn Pub, on British Columbia's Howe Sound, about thirty miles north of Vancouver, was also the country's first craft brewery. Doyle and Kenary stopped nearby in Victoria at another creation of Mitchell's, Spinnakers Gastro Brewpub and Guesthouses, which opened in May 1984 and which served classic English-style ales from hand-pumped taps.

Doyle, Kenary, and Ligeti were not homebrewers—just what we would now call beer geeks—so the visits were a technical eye-opener. The plan moved forward, often during brainstorms in Doyle and Ligeti's Watertown, Massachusetts, apartment or at local bars. They set a production goal in their business plan of sixty-five hundred kegs and eight thousand cases annually by year five, with nearly $2 million in revenue. As for the first year, they would be ecstatic with one hundred draft accounts. In the spring of 1986, the trio began raising funds from family, friends, and friends of friends, eventually amassing $430,000 from thirty-five people. The trio, like the young couple behind Alaskan Brewing, the Larsons, found that beer got an emotional reaction from people—a gut feeling, whether they knew much about it or not. That came in part, Doyle, Kenary, and Ligeti realized, from the growing popularity of other foodstuff start-ups that stood athwart the homogeneity of their particular niches. These included Ben & Jerry's, the ice cream brand started by two Vermont hippies in 1978 with $12,000 (one-third of it borrowed), and, of course, Starbucks, then a quirky, almost quaint chain out of Seattle, many years from its hegemony. This was a fresh context in which newcomers could think about craft beer—as another foodstuff that was tastier and created in a more hands-on way, often locally, and therefore costing a little bit more than the bigger brands.

Funding incoming, Doyle called Michael Lewis at UC-Davis. He asked for recommendations for brewmasters. Lewis listed several of his students, and Doyle headed westward to interview them. He hired twenty-three-year-old Russ Heissner, who had worked at a California winery. They found and fixed up a couple of thousand square feet of warehouse space in an old navy yard on the South Boston waterfront. It was still the Southie of mobster Whitey Bulger and gang turf wars, a gritty, largely industrial swathe the general public avoided; the city was happy to have the Mass. Bay Brewing Company as a tenant. They bought the kettles from JV Northwest in Oregon and a secondhand soda-bottling line. They also bought a truck to do distribution themselves, as every wholesaler in the area turned them down ("Five thousand cases? Not big enough"). Heissner's first recipe was for what the company called Harpoon Ale, a sweet, citrusy amber. The first two commercial kegs of it, delivered by Doyle and Kenary, were tapped at bars in Beacon Hill and Jamaica Plain on June 2, 1987, a Tuesday. Breweries were back in Boston.

WEEPING RADISHES, SCOTTISH LORDS, AND ROLLER COASTERS

Portland, ME; Park City, UT; Missoula, MT; Plano, TX; Abita Springs, LA; St. Paul, MN; Manteo, NC; Vernon, NJ | 1982–1986

D avid and Karen Geary were, like the Larsons in Juneau, another husband-and-wife team keen on bringing a craft brewery to a particularly geographically inhospitable place: in this case, Portland, Maine, with its long winters and a population of just over sixty-one thousand in a state still mostly rural. The Pine Tree State's last commercial breweries had closed with Prohibition—and never came back. In March 1986, longtime homebrewers Hugh Nazor of Georgetown and Jon Bove of South Portland introduced Portland Lager, a recipe they arranged to have contract brewed by the Hibernia Brewing Company in Eau Claire, Wisconsin. It proved popular with locals, even at five dollars or more a six-pack, though not popular enough for investors—Nazor and Bove spent fruitless years trying to raise funds for a brewery for their Maine Coast Brewing. David Geary's path proved more successful. It all started when the twentieth laird of Traquair stayed with him in Portland, Maine. Peter Maxwell Stuart had in 1965 revived the brewery at his family's estate, a dictatorially ornate Scottish castle dating from 1107, complete with a hedge maze and priest holes. Geary knew Stuart's American importer. After a pleasant enough stay in Portland, the laird told Geary that if he ever wanted to learn the brewing trade, he should drop him a line—Stuart would set him up with an unpaid job at the Traquair brewery and give him letters of introduction to other breweries in Britain. Geary did just that after the company he sold medical supplies for went bankrupt, and at thirty-eight he could not stomach the process of sending out résumés. He incorporated the D. L. Geary Brewing Company in October 1983 and then split for Scotland and England for three months. The hours were long—mash would happen around 6 AM—but the lifestyle was beyond quaint for the former salesman from Maine. There was tea at 10, a beer at 11 (in line with the British custom of elevenses), and the camaraderie of craftsmanship. The bearded, blond-haired Geary almost forgot it was a business, as cutthroat in Britain, where the brewing industry was also consolidating, as it was in the New World.

> After the mash, we went into the storage room where Peter Lennox made tea for the four of us. We discussed beer, sports, and politics and I felt very comfortable. At one point the Laird called my name from outside and I could see George and Ian become tense about the prospect of being caught away from their duties. It surprised me somewhat. I guess I thought this whole estate was a storybook affair, but it's clear that it's a business, and a large one at that.

Back in Portland, Geary and his wife embarked on a fundraising tear. In a year and a half, they raised $300,000, including from the doctors who had been Geary's clients. Everyone thought it was a cool idea. Other than the odd bottle of Samuel Adams, there just wasn't local beer on the shelves or from the taps in Maine (and Samuel Adams Boston Lager was being brewed in Pittsburgh besides). They built a space in an industrial park in Portland's more rugged western reaches and hired Alan Pugsley, a lanky, spectacled Englishman from Manchester. A biochemist by education and a brewer by training, Pugsley was gaining a reputation as a top brewing consultant in the United States in much the way another biochemist, Joseph Owades, had almost a generation earlier. Pugsley was most noted for helping popularize the so-called Ringwood yeast, which was used to make clear, crisp English ales. He set about under David Geary's direction to develop just that sort of ale for the new brewery's flagship.

Pugsley poured a glass for Geary after the first batch was completed in the early autumn of 1986. Geary brought it to his lips. Somewhere in the back of his mind, he knew this whole start-up brewery in the wilds of an old port city had to work—he didn't really have, or particularly want, a Plan B. And for the brewery to work, the beer had to be good. Quality counted. That was, Geary knew, the price of admission to the industry. He closed his eyes and took a sip.

"Ah." Geary smiled. "D. L. Geary's Pale Ale." Pugsley smiled back, relieved.

The first six-packs and kegs of D. L. Geary hit Portland shelves and bars shortly afterward. The brewery would score its biggest distributive coup when the supermarket chains Hannaford and Shaw's agreed to stock the beer, beginning in 1987.

D. L. Geary was soon joined in New England by Catamount Brewing Company, which became Vermont's first brewery since Prohibition when it started producing an English-style pale ale in early 1987 in an old meat warehouse in White River Junction. The brewery was started by ex–PE teacher and longtime homebrewer Stephen Mason, bluegrass musician Alan Davis, and businessman Stephen Israel with $750,000 from thirty-two investors and a Small Business Administration loan.

In the Midwest, an operation out of St. Paul, Minnesota, joined Larry Bell's Kalamazoo Brewing Company. That most American variety of angst birthed the new brewery: the frustrations of a middle manager. Mark Stutrud was an intermittent homebrewer by night and on the weekends; by day he was a clinical social worker in a large hospital, a role he would describe as "classic middle management with a lot of responsibility and no authority." He saw two ways out: graduate school or medical school. And then a third way emerged through his hobby: he began in the early 1980s to read about craft beer pioneers. The bug had bitten. In July 1984, he incorporated with Minnesota the Summit Brewing Company. It would become the first new brewery in the Twin Cities since Repeal in 1933, joining only a handful of regionals and Big Beer outlets in the entire Gopher State that either survived Prohibition or opened afterward. Stutrud raised $500,000 by selling thirty thousand shares to twenty investors, including a local ad agency, which helped with promotion (the marketing budget was about five dollars per barrel). Summit set up shop in an old truck-parts warehouse on University Avenue in St. Paul, and Stutrud bought a Bavarian brewhouse with a capacity for six thousand barrels annually. The first kegs of pale ale and porter hit Minneapolis and St. Paul bars in September 1986, retailing at about $1.50 a glass. Drafts from the James Page Brewing Company, a homebrew supplier and craft brewery that a Minneapolis lawyer started, quickly joined them. Minnesota, which had begun the year with no craft breweries, closed it with a pair of them.

Utah also opened 1986 with no craft breweries—no breweries, period (Minnesota's August Schell regional dated from 1860). The last Utah one, Salt Lake City's A. Fisher Brewing Co., had shuttered in 1967. Enter a hippie from Milwaukee, the Wisconsin city positively steeped in beer, thanks to Big Beer operations such as Pabst, Schlitz, and Miller. Greg Schirf was unsure of what to do after graduating from Marquette University in 1974. So, hair down to his waist, he hitchhiked to Park City, Utah, to visit his older brother, who had gone to college in California and Colorado (their mother had dropped Schirf by the side of the Milwaukee freeway herself). He encountered a Park City where many of the storefronts along Main Street were boarded up. The ski town was still relatively undeveloped compared with the likes of Colorado's Telluride and Aspen, and there was a lot of tension between newer hippies such as himself and longer-established miners. Mining was the big industry, skiing a boom-and-bust seasonal affair at best.

Schirf worked construction and in real estate development and brokerage with his brother. He started an alternative weekly newspaper with a friend, one aimed at the growing counterculture they represented. He realized he did not want to do real estate for the rest of his life, and he eventually sold his friend his stake in the newspaper. Along the way, he took up homebrewing and began talking ceaselessly about launching a brewery. He had traveled to San Francisco in the early 1980s to see the Grateful Dead in concert, and visited Anchor Brewing while there. He'd also spent a year studying abroad in Rome while at Marquette, and that experience had whetted his appetite for better beer. The taste stayed with him.

Schirf incorporated the Schirf Brewing Company with Utah in July 1982, and then not much happened until John Morse, an old college friend, invited Schirf to visit him in Seattle for Thanksgiving in 1984. "You're always talking about beer," Morse said, "and how you're going to start a brewery." In that case, Morse said there was someone he wanted Schirf to meet. The someone was Tom Baune, who, along with his wife, had in 1984 launched the Hart Brewing Company in Kalama, Washington, with a flagship pale ale called Pyramid. Baune and Schirf hit it off, and Schirf hired Baune as a consultant on his brewery plan. He could not afford to pay him a regular fee, so he agreed to pay him a royalty on each barrel of beer Schirf sold. (As for Morse, he and his brother, who ran an ice cream company, would buy out Baune in the late 1980s with other investors and grow the reminted Pyramid brewery significantly.) Schirf also consulted Ken Grossman at Sierra Nevada, who helped him solve the riddle of several stuck fermentations—wherein the conversion of a beer's ingredients into alcohol suddenly stops. It turned out that the ingredients were not getting sufficient oxygen because of Park City's high altitude. Grossman suggested an oxygen tank for extra air. That did the trick, and, soon, the Schirf Brewing Co, Utah's first brewery in twenty years, craft or otherwise, was off the ground. It started production on October 24, 1986, in a warehouse at 1250 Iron Horse Drive, its first offering what Schirf called Wasatch Premium Ale, after the local mountain range. Sales were difficult in a state that the alcohol-averse Mormon church dominated. To boost his numbers, Schirf decided to open a brewpub in Park City, one that might cater to the increasing number of skiiers coming through and that would cut down on distribution costs. He had explored the phenomenon firsthand in Northern California, but he soon ran into a problem familiar to other craft brewing pioneers: Brewpubs were illegal in the Beehive State. Schirf, with the aid of a symphathetic state legislator, would have to change the law before he could open the brewpub. This he and the legislator did, and in 1989 Schirf opened Utah's first brewpub on Park City's Main Street. A copper brewing kettle loomed from a window overlooking the once-blighted drag.

Also out West and around the same time that Greg Schirf was starting up Utah's first craft brewery, Reinhard and Trudy Schulte, a wealthy couple originally from the German region of Bavaria, were laying the groundwork for Montana's first modern, ground up craft brewery, one that put forth an eclectic lineup compared with much of the nation's beer. The brewery was born of the necessity of finding decent beer not only in an America awash in lackluster lager, but in one of the nation's most sparsely populated states. Montana had roughly eight hundred thousand people in its nearly one hundred fifty thousand square miles. Whether there would be a sufficient customer base for the brewery the Schultes had planned for Missoula, a city near the Idaho border where the last local brewery had shuttered in 1964, remained to be seen. The pair lived on several hundred acres outside of Missoula, the home of the University of Montana, and they initially hired a consultancy to get the brewery off the ground in a building they owned in that city. They already leased space in the property to a bar and a restaurant—a potentially built-in customer base in an otherwise inhospitable climate for more traditional beers. The consultancy only took the Schultes so far: a basic setup with small-scale brewing equipment. To make the brewery a truly self-sustaining concern, they looked eastward. Trudy Schulte came from a brewing dynasty in what's now Germany, and her family's brewery had routinely tapped Doemens, a brewing school near Munich, for talent. So that is where the couple looked.

And they found Jürgen Knöller. Knöller was in his early twenties and finishing a brewing degree at Doemens (he had started in the industry as an apprentice in 1979). The mustachioed, hazel-eyed Knöller planned to work for German brewing giant Spaten, particularly in its international operations. He wanted to see the world and Spaten needed people on the ground in central China. That position was not going to open up for several months, and so Knöller took up the Schultes' offer of a six-month job in Missoula. Before he accepted the position and left West Germany with two suitcases—one full of books, the other of clothes—he got out a map. Montana was "on the upper left corner" of America, near Calgary, Canada, which would be the site of the 1988 Winter Olympics. Knöller figured he could bum around ski slopes while helping launch a brewery, which the Schultes called Bayern, after the German word for Bavaria. Bayern launched in August 1987. It was a brewpub in all but the legal sense, as Montana did not allow such operations. Bayern had to go through a distributor to sell its beers at the restaurant and bar right on the other side of a glass wall separating the businesses—a perfect illustration of some of the juridical inanity regarding alcohol left over from Prohibition. The brewery specialized in lagers, and its offerings from the get-go were exotic for much of the United States. Its Amber Lager was a marzen, for instance, a German style that would become best-known in the States as the basis for Oktoberfest beers. In December 1987, Bayern released a strong, dark doppelbock, a lager style rarely found in the United States even through imports. There was also that first year a wheat ale, a departure from the company's lager lineup and one of American craft beer's first wheat-based offerings, period.

Bayern's startup phase complete, Knöller prepared to return to preparing for China. On a trip home for Christmas, however, Knöller found that Spaten had pushed the China start date back again. Then, the German brewery nixed the plan entirely, following the Chinese government's massacre of protesters in Beijing's Tiannemen Square in April 1989. Knöller would stay in Montana. By that point, too, the culmination of the Cold War had shredded the Iron Curtain, and the Schultes were looking to invest in the soon-to-be former East Germany. They divested themselves of their American holdings, including Bayern. Knöller stepped in with a loan from a friend and acquired the brewery in January 1991. Knöller's expertise ensured success for Bayern. Its presence, however, was not really felt outside of Montana, a common refrain in these still-early days of American craft beer. Isolation, both geographic and psychological, was a theme—some areas of the country simply were not that hospitable to newer breweries and funkier (for America) styles. This was especially true in what Michael Jackson tactfully described as "the conservative South" in a 1988 guidebook for Simon & Schuster. "Where the summers are long and hot," the critic wrote, "real men suck on Schlitz popsicles and watch out for signs warning, 'Last beer before dry county.'"

The particular environment for Don and Mary Thompson was not quite that dire when the couple launched the Reinheitsgebot Brewing Company in the Dallas suburb of Plano in late 1985. But, early on, the going was lonely. Reinheitsgebot—boldly named after a sixteenth-century German beer purity dictate—was one of only two craft breweries in the entire South. The other was the Chesapeake Bay Brewing Company that Jim Kollar and Lou Perrin started in Virginia in 1982. It was in February of that year that the Thompsons registered their startup with a Texas that had yet to legalize homebrewing or brewpubs, and that was perhaps best-known beer-wise then for Miller's Fort Worth outpost, where Miller Lite was first brewed on a large scale in 1975. The couple had met in October 1973 at Munich's Oktoberfest and had then traveled Europe for a year before returning Stateside, marrying, and pursuing their idea of a brewery based on the beers they'd so liberally sampled overseas. Don studied at the University of California-Davis—and also visited Sierra Nevada in Chico—and Mary studied at the Siebel Institute, and the pair started brewing in late 1984 in a Plano warehouse. The following year, Reinheitsgebot's first offering, a golden ale based on one of Don's homebrewing recipes and named after the surrounding Collin County, debuted before a typically indifferent marketplace. A local news segment from October 29, 1985, accentuated the challenges the couple—and other craft brewing pioneers—then faced, especially outside of relative hotbeds such as Northern California and the Boulder area of Colorado. A reporter's voiceover introduced the brewery as decidedly exotic: "The latest premium beer to hit the Dallas-Fort Worth area is not from Holland or Canada or Germany—it's imported from Plano." And it was made in infintesimal amounts, as the segment went on to explain: "The Thompsons produce about six hundred barrels a year, and hope to expand to sixteen hundred barrels soon. In contrast, a major Fort Worth brewery"—a reference to the Miller plant—"packages thirty thousand barrels a day." Mary Thompson was optimistic. "At only eight hundred cases a month, surely there are enough people that could buy our beer to keep us going."

One southern state over and in that same year, Rush Cumming and Jim Patton, two homebrewers, were launching the South's third craft brewery in a Louisiana town of barely one thousand souls on the other side of Lake Pontchartrain from New Orleans. The Abita Brewing Company was also the only other brewery in Louisiana after the Dixie Brewing Company out of New Orleans, which dated from 1907 and which, with a production level barely one-third of its 1985 capacity, was in the same straits as other struggling regionals—as one reporter put it, they were "like ghosts in a Pac-Man game." The arriviste, which boasted a Munich-trained brewmaster in Mark Wilson, was named after its original location in Abita Springs, a town where the water was supposedly some of the purest around and could therefore go right into making the brewery's first two lines, all draft, no bottles: an amber lager and, to placate potential customers who might prefer "Schlitz popsicles" in the soupy Louisiana heat, a golden-colored lager.

Joining Chesapeake Bay, Abita, and Reinheitsgebot in the South was a most unlikely entrant in our story of the American craft beer movement. Uli Bennewitz was a trim, young Bavarian who came to the United States in the late 1970s to manage vast farmlands for European and American clients. He had studied agriculture, was interested in it, and was good at what he did; it kept him busy. Then his brother called from England. A brewery near Munich was looking to expand and wanted to rid itself of a five-barrel, electric-powered system that it used for test batches. Bennewitz had complained to his brother about the poor quality of American beer— nothing like the German bock, helles, and pilsner they grew up on. Why not buy the set and have it shipped to his home base in North Carolina? Bennewitz did just that, and thus he planted the seed for the South's first brewpub and eventually one of the largest brewery-restaurant hybrids in the United States.

Bennewitz partnered with a retail store for the space and set about creating what was known as a brewpub—not that he knew that. To him, the small-scale operation was just a chance to meld fine German-style beers with German-style cuisine. He also did not know that the Tar Heel State did not allow you to serve the beer you brewed on-site. He thought the

Uli Bennewitz at Weeping Radish. Courtesy of Weeping Radish Brewery

"ABC" that people suggested he check with was some sort of school-related thing (it was not—it was the Alcoholic Beverage Control commission). The law would have to change, which Bennewitz set about pushing with the help of a state senator and a cooperative ABC. The change in hand, he and his partners, with brewers imported from West Germany, opened the Weeping Radish in Manteo on July 4, 1986. That brought two more revelations: they should have brewed ales, which Bennewitz discovered were all the rage in the nascent craft beer movement (ales would have taken significantly less time to make); and the lagers they did brew, including a brightly colored, lighter-tasting helles, a schwarzbier (or dark lager), and a pilsner, were not to the liking of American palates, particularly those of the neighbors. North Carolina's first commercial brewery since Repeal in 1933 had been an outpost of the Atlanta-based Atlantic Ice and Coal Company in Charlotte. That shuttered in the 1950s. Stroh's opened a brewery in Winston-Salem in 1970, and then Miller opened a plant in Eden eight years later. The vast state—the longest east of the Mississippi—was a fecund environment for Big Beer, not to mention fast food. "If we had had Budweiser and sold chicken wings," Bennewitz realized, "we would have had a chance with the locals."

As it was, the Weeping Radish was packed in the summers and dead in the winters; customers on average came from at least two hundred miles away, from Ohio, Pennsylvania, and the like, often for their first sight of a working brewery. That it churned away on the North Carolina coast, in a remote area best known as the testing grounds for the Wright brothers' flights, only added to the allure. The brewpub, named for the Bavarian practice of salting white radishes to dehydrate them, produced four to five hundred barrels annually those first couple of years. They moved as much as they could during the summers and picked back up again with the brewing around Christmas.

It was around Christmas in 1986 that the *New York Times*, in an article on the launch of Catamount in Vermont, also noted the existence of a craft brewery even more unlikely than Bennewitz's Weeping Radish. Gene Mulvihill had amassed a fortune from fields as disparate as cellular broadcasting, mutual funds, robotics, skiing, and carnival rides. It was the latter two that he combined in 1978 to create Action Park in Vernon, New Jersey, near the New York border. Mulvihill began adding amusement rides to a ski resort he already owned. The attractions were often slipshod—Action Park's Alpine Slide sent riders down a zipping concrete incline atop puny cars with shoddy handbrakes, and the suction on the wave pool was often frighteningly intense. At least six visitors would die due to injuries sustained at Mulvihill's park, and, at one point, emergency workers were carting away as many as ten wounded patrons a day. Many might have seen a cartoonishly unacceptable level of danger for an amusement park. Mulvihill saw opportunity: He started a Cayman Island–based insurance company to cover his creation, turning his liability into an asset. The businessman also saw opportunity in the festivals that Action Park occasionally hosted—particularly, the opportunity to sell beer to huge captive audiences.

The idea came to Mulvihill during a visit to the world's biggest beer festival: Bavaria's annual Oktoberfest. Wanting to recreate the smorgasbord back home, he acquired a tent big enough to shield five thousand and then set about trying to find the sorts of unfiltered lagers he had amply sampled overseas. Unable to find them domestically—and unwilling to import them—Mulvihill did what to him seemed natural, but what was actually quite radical for the time and the place: he set a brewery within Action Park, complete with a brewhouse and a brewmaster, Stephan Muhs, from West Germany. The barley, hops and yeast for what Mulvihill incorporated as the Vernon Valley Brewery in February 1985 also came from the land of the Reinheits-gebot, the German edict dating from April 1516 that required beer be made solely from water, hops, and barley (the creators of the Reinheitsgebot did not know yet about the role of yeast). The only American ingredient, really, was the water.

The results of New Jersey's first craft brewery were apparently spectacular. "The most uncompromisingly traditional lagers in today's America emerged from an unlikely place—a ski resort in Vernon, New Jersey—in the mid- to late 1980s," wrote Michael Jackson in an updated edition of his *World Guide to Beer* three years after Vernon Valley's launch. "The Dark Lager is surely the finest produced in the United States in living memory."

Jackson also cheered the early efforts of another Northeastern startup that specialized in lagers. Carol Stoudt's husband, Ed, had long run a popular steakhouse and beer hall in Lancaster County—that's where Carol met him, when Ed bought her an apricot sour at the eatery—and she had developed a taste for decent beer during the couple's travels through West Germany, including on their honeymoon. She had left teaching to raise the pair's five children, and when the fifth child started school Carol decided to start a new career—in brewing. The brewery would be attached to the existing restaurant and would specialize in Central European lager styles such as clear, crisp pilsner and darker, stronger bock. Carol threw herself into learning about brewing, including through an apprenticeship at Louisiana's Abita, a course at the University of California-Davis, and visits to dozens of breweries in central

Europe and the Pacific Northwest. She ran into a now-predictable wall when it came to financing what she would call the Stoudt Brewing Company Commercial banks turned her down, and she ended having to raise around $150,000 from friends and relatives—and from selling to Ed her share of their Victorian mansion in Adamstown, Pennsylvania. They also further separated their assets and finances to get around the Keystone State's notoriously labrynth alcohol laws, which included a prohition against an individual owning a brewery and a restaurant where the brewery's beer would be sold. Stoudt, then, launched in May 1987 under Carol's ownership—and stewardship as brewmaster, making her one of the few women in the United States up to that point to weild such power over a brewery. That brewery had the capacity to produce up to five thousand barrels annually, with nearly all of it sold at Ed's restaurant.

HERE, THERE, AND EVERYWHERE
Denver | 1987

Daniel Bradford thought they were about to set a world record. It was the first year, 1987, that the Great American Beer Festival used a single draft system for all the entries—perhaps the largest single draft system ever devised. There were 120 beers from seventy breweries for the two-day festival, which had recovered from the 1984 debacle that nearly croaked the whole thing.* Bradford went to the Merchandise Mart in Denver the Saturday morning before the festival for that day started. He was alone with the single draft system, alone in the hall as the sun streaked through the bank of windows, shining bright light on the best beer in America. *He was alone with the best beer in America.*

He liberally sampled several, and it hit him then: the growth in the movement, the growth in the industry. It was something now decidedly different than the planning sessions in Charlie Papazian's living room. It was an increasingly professionalized segment of a distinct part of American cuisine.

---

* The GABF had not entirely escaped organizational flubs. The following year, 1988, several breweries were left out of the program, and the medals did not arrive in time for the awards ceremony. Per Vince Cottone, "Movement in the Right Direction," *American Brewer*, fall 1987; Maureen Ogle, "First Draft Follies: Early History of the American Homebrewers Association and Brewers Association, Part 8."

As if to put an exclamation point at the end of that realization, Bradford recalled that this would be the first GABF with a blind tasting panel of professionals: two brewmasters from Big Beer, one craft brewer, three beer writers, and Charlie Papazian as president of the Association of Brewers. Attendees could still vote in consumer preference polls, but the panel and its parameters signaled a shift. The GABF had come up with criteria for twelve different categories, defining for the first time at the festival what constituted a porter, what constituted a wheat beer, and so on.* Like with the popularity contests of previous years, there would be three winners in each—but this time, à la the Olympics, each would be awarded a specific medal rather than a numerical ranking. And the panels were meant to be exacting and unforgiving; if, for instance, an entry did not pass the initial smell test for a particular style, a judge would nix it from the competition without so much as tasting it. The panels meant that relative unknowns could win big right out of the box; they didn't need the brand recognition that might have helped others over the hump in the consumer preference polls. In its very first GABF,

The team from the Association of Brewers (now the Brewers Association) before the Great American Beer Festival in the mid-1980s. Daniel Bradford is center, with beer; Charlie Papazian is on the far left, standing. Courtesy of Daniel Bradford

---

* Interestingly enough, the twelve original categories did not include one for India pale ale, which has become the beer style for which American craft brewers have become most famous for interpreting.

for example, Mark Stutrud's Summit out of St. Paul won the gold in the porter category.

It had come to this in a few short years: gold, silver, and bronze; professional panels; convention halls. The American craft beer movement by the end of 1987 was finally touching nearly every region of the country—even distant Alaska, the Great Plains, and the Deep South. Hawaii couldn't be far behind. Each successive start-up seemed more routine. It was still a challenge from a business standpoint; the industry had seen several closures. Entrepreneurs as disparate as Geoff and Marcy Larson in Juneau and Dan Kenary, Rich Doyle, and George Ligeti in Boston couldn't get banks to back them, and the founders of Boulder Brewing and New Amsterdam, two thousand miles apart, sought refuge in the plush arms of venture-capital firms. Still, the business model of a craft brewery seemed, in less than half a generation, a plausible one.

It might sound crazy, except it wasn't in practice. There were paths to emulate; people to go to for advice, for supplies, for equipment, for brewmasters; timed gatherings of the tribe like the GABF and the now-separate homebrewers competition; media from trade publications to regular columns in major newspapers, with some of the coverage waxing as poetic as any baseball writing. And now there were style guidelines, molds for subsequent generations to bend to or, as often as not, break. The play that opened in that pivotal year of 1978 was wrapping its early acts. The scenes to come would prove just as interesting for the audience.

For now, though, exeunt Americans. Let the curtain rise on the Spanish Steps in Rome.

PART III

UNHAPPY MEALS
Rome | 1986

On Monday, April 21, 1986, on the 2,739th anniversary of the founding of
Rome by the sons of the God of War, thousands of Italians gathered before
the Spanish Steps to receive their heaping plates of penne pasta cooked
flawlessly *al dente* in giant skillets. The skillets sizzled near a stage where
politicians and celebrities railed against the "degradation of Rome" and the
"Americanization" of their country's culture. Many in the crowd in front of
the stage wore T-shirts or carried posters with pictures of Clint Eastwood
with the message, CLINT EASTWOOD, YOU SHOULD BE OUR MAYOR, written
underneath. The actor and director, recently elected mayor of the California
town of Carmel, had made it a point to crack down on the proliferation
of fast-food restaurants. The protesters were trying to do the same. Four
weeks earlier, the largest McDonald's in the world had opened a block from
the eighteenth-century Spanish Steps; it had 450 seats and was the eighth
fast-food restaurant to open in the area in recent months. Worse, it was
owned by a Frenchman! Moreover, it replaced a popular local coffee bar
and cafe, as perfect a symbol as there could be for the protesters' fears that a
certain homogeneity was set to devour Italian cuisine. The city council had
entertained the notion of shutting the McDonald's down because of what it
called a "degradation of the historic center" of the Eternal City. The fashion
designer Valentino sued for the same end, claiming the joint, which abutted
his headquarters, caused "significant and constant noise and an unbearable
smell of fried food fouling the air."

The McDonald's survived. It did brisk business, its hundreds of chairs
often all filled, its location, the chain's 9,007th worldwide, a hangout for Italian
youth in particular, not to mention the ceaseless stream of tourists. The eat-in
and the earlier efforts to shutter the restaurant had captured imaginations,

however, including that of Carlo Petrini. He was, in that inimitable Italian way, both a left-wing journalist and a noted wine expert from the country's north. Petrini had been part of the crowd outside the McDonald's on its opening day chanting, "We don't want fast food, we want slow food!" The protests gave him an idea.

SECOND CAREERS
Brooklyn | 1986

Shortly after mayor Ed Koch pulled a tap and hoisted a mug on May 13, 1986, to officially mark the opening of the New Amsterdam brewpub, Matthew Reich received three visitors in rapid succession. The first was Jim Koch, who had recently launched Boston Beer Company and its well-received flagship lager; he wanted to talk brewpubs and distribution with Reich. The second and third visitors were Tom Potter and Steve Hindy, who wanted to open a brewery in Brooklyn. Though the idea made historical, almost spiritual sense—before Prohibition the borough had as many or more breweries than Milwaukee or St. Louis—Reich did not welcome the intercity competition and the meeting did not end with wishes of good luck. Still, Potter and Hindy by 1986 were committed to returning brewing to its one-time American capital.

Hindy in particular had taken such a winding route to the idea that turning back no longer seemed an option. A goateed native of an Ohio River town between Pittsburgh and Cincinnati who went to college at Cornell, Hindy worked as a reporter at small newspapers in Upstate New York and northern New Jersey. He figured he'd hit the jackpot financially with a $20,000 salary at the Associated Press bureau in Newark in the late 1970s. But one day on the New York City subway, thinking about a change of scenery, he decided to study Arabic (his surname came from a Lebanese great-grandfather) and eventually put in for a transfer with the AP to covering the Middle East. It was, in its way, invigorating. He lived for two years in Beirut and three in Cairo; he was kidnapped and shot at and along the way covered international crises such as the Israeli invasion of Lebanon, the Iranian Revolution, and the Iran-Iraq War.

One October day in 1981, he was standing on a grandstand in Cairo next to a colleague from the *Washington Post*, taking in a military parade, another flexing of Cold War–funded muscle by Egyptian president Anwar Sadat. French-made Mirage jets streaked overhead; spectators craned their necks to look. Just then, a truck towing an artillery piece halted before the grandstand and several men from it dressed in military uniforms strode forward, led by a lieutenant. Sadat rose as if to receive his salute—and instead was met with a grenade. The men fired semiautomatic weapons and lobbed more grenades, killing twelve, including Sadat, and wounding several times more. Hindy and his colleague were not among the victims, but the invigoration of the Middle East beat was wearing on him, as he explained years later:

> Most correspondents, including me, were rogues and adventurers addicted to the big story. Most were divorced, getting divorced, or getting remarried. Most drank too much, or took drugs, or stopped drinking and became real psychos. We all started out thinking we knew who the good guys were and believing we were on their side. . . .
>
> But the more wars I covered and the more I learned of the roots of conflict, the less sure I became of who the good guys were—and the less sure I was of the nobility of my role.

When the AP offered an assignment in the Philippines covering what would be the last torturous years of Ferdinand Marcos's regime, Hindy said no and returned to the United States with his family. He also took with him a curiosity regarding a hobby that had roots going back millennia in the Middle East. A friend of his in Cairo had homebrewed while working in Saudi Arabia, where Western companies might provide employees with instructions for homebrewing to circumvent the kingdom's ban on alcohol, with the ingredients coming through the diplomatic post. Hindy was taken with the dark, rich, and hoppy beer produced.

When he settled back in the United States in 1984—in the Park Slope neighborhood of Brooklyn, which was far from the fashionably hip enclave it became but still safer than Beirut—Hindy gave homebrewing a shot. He got a copy of Charlie Papazian's recently published *The Complete Joy of Homebrewing*, studied it, gathered some ingredients, and thought fondly of the beers he had tasted in Europe, the Bavarian lagers in particular. He settled in for the day in his family's two-bedroom apartment on Eighth Street . . . and promptly brewed himself right into a disaster. To top off the bottles, Hindy used a crude metal gadget called a hammer capper, which was exactly that:

a bottle-capper powered by a hammering motion. He ended up smashing thirty of the forty-eight bottles on that first batch, making a terrific mess, even frightening his family into gathering at the other end of the apartment. To his credit, Hindy took a deep breath, recalled Papazian's mantra—"Relax, don't worry, have a homebrew"—and tried again. He got better and better at homebrewing, sharing his concoctions with his new colleagues at *Newsday*, the Long Island newspaper where he was assistant foreign editor, and with his Park Slope neighbors. One of those neighbors—the thirstiest, in fact—was a mustachioed assistant vice president at Chemical Bank named Tom Potter. Potter had bought the apartment downstairs in 1985; he and Hindy, and their families, became fast friends. The two men would drink Hindy's homebrew in Potter's backyard on summer weekends, watching the Mets on a black-and-white television swing their way improbably to a World Series win in 1986.

All the while, something stuck in the back of Hindy's mind. He had subscribed to *Zymurgy*, and he had learned about Jack McAuliffe's former operation at New Albion and about Fritz Maytag's expanding one at Anchor. He knew, too, of Matthew Reich's successful New Amsterdam launch via F. X. Matt (local media loved it) and of William S. Newman's eponymous brand in Albany. The craft beer movement was real to Hindy, albeit from a distance. He was an ex–foreign correspondent now working the domestic side of the beat. What did he know about starting a brewery? He mentioned the idea to Potter, a recently minted Columbia MBA. That was as far as the planning went.

Then, as was his wont, one rainy day Hindy went for a jog through nearby Prospect Park. He passed another runner wearing an old T-shirt that read, in classic Victorian font, BREWERIES OF BROOKLYN. He ran into the guy again on the other side of the park and this time asked him about the shirt.

"Oh, this," he said. "It's a book I wrote. It's been out of print for ten years." The guy was Will Anderson, a chronicler and a collector of arcane brewing odds and ends who had taken it upon himself to detail Brooklyn's beer history just as the last breweries in the borough closed in the mid-1970s.

"I'd like to talk to you," Hindy said. "I'm starting a brewery in Brooklyn."

"Yeah," Anderson said. "You and everybody else."

The chance encounter with Anderson refocused Hindy on opening what would become Brooklyn Brewery within two years, with Potter as his partner and the New York City borough of more than two million as both customer base and marketing tool.

DAVIDS AND GOLIATHS
Boston | 1986

Jim Koch wasn't sleeping. He and Rhonda Kallman were working around the clock growing the Boston Beer Company. They had moved well beyond the thirty original accounts they thought they needed for the business to succeed; their flagship lager was being distributed to around two thousand spots on the East Coast and in West Germany, home to some of the most sacrosanct soil in the beer universe; the three-year-old lager, too, had already captured a handful of plaudits from Charlie Papazian's organization in Boulder. Samuel Adams Boston Lager had topped the consumer preference poll at the Great American Beer Festival in 1985 and 1986 and then won the gold medal in the continental pilsner category in 1987, the

Jim Koch outside 1600 Pennsylvania Avenue. The writing on the photo reads, "1986 IN THE WHITE HOUSE FRIDGE!!!" Courtesy of the Boston Beer Co.

first year of the blind-tasting panel of professional critics and brewers. As for the consumer preference poll, Boston Beer nabbed that in 1987 too, this time with what the company cryptically called "Festival Lager" at the GABF and which Koch later unveiled at a press conference as Boston Lightship. Though heavier in texture and taste, it was clearly introduced to compete with light beers as well as thinner-tasting imports like Heineken and Beck's; it marked the craft beer movement's first foray into the hitherto verboten light beer market. Boston Lager was even being distributed to the White House, Camp David, and Air Force One! Koch had arranged the deals himself through an old colleague at the Boston Consulting Group, who knew the head of the White House Mess. Secret Service agents would show up at a distributor, pick several cases at random for security, and be on their way.

Closer to home, Boston Lager was available on draught for the first time in 1987, and Kallman's homemade signs had been replaced by slicker ones that carried news of the GABF wins along with the beers' availabilities. They even had a warehouse—appropriately enough, the old Haffenreffer facility in Jamaica Plain, the last regional brewery to close in the Boston area in 1964. And a truck! More than one! Koch's Plymouth Reliant station wagon and Kallman's orange Vega with the white interior had become now part of the backstory of a successful start-up. Koch found himself in a position that perhaps only Fritz Maytag at Anchor had ever otherwise occupied, and then only intermittently: he was a comfortable commercial success in American craft beer. He had worked off Matthew Reich's idea—via Joseph Owades, who also worked with Koch—and cranked up the production to eleven. Koch should have been sleeping like a log.

It was the multimillion-dollar bids that kept him awake. A goal had been from the company's founding to build a physical brewery and to stop relying on contract brewing through the Pittsburgh Brewing Company. Koch, who by now was running all the business operations except sales, had raised $3 million from industrial bonds and venture capital to purchase and to begin renovating the old Haffenreffer site in the inner-city Boston neighborhood of Jamaica Plain. He ordered $2.7 million in equipment, including thirty tanks, and began telling people he planned to open a 225,000-barrel operation in the first half of 1988—the largest craft brewery in America. Then the renovation bids started coming in. They were millions over what he had funding for—costs to get the brewery up and running could run to as much as $14 million. It was enough to sink the whole company if things didn't work out. Koch, ever the consultant, stepped back. Jeez, he thought, I'm almost forty, and I just wrote off more than I've made in my whole life. Riskier yet, the new brewery would not necessarily have made his beers any better. He opted to continue contract brewing, with the Jamaica Plain site used for storage, a small test brewery, and tours. Koch would continue to focus his considerable energies on marketing the beers.

Armed with a Harvard Law–trained mind and a masterful publicist in Sally Jackson of Boston, Koch was by now one of the more vocal proponents not only of his own brand but also of the little guys, so to speak, on the American brewing scene. He could be relentless when painting this David-versus-Goliath tableau. Take this testy segment on PBS's normally staid *Mac-Neil/Lehrer Newshour* in August 1986. Reporter Paul Solman in a voiceover introduced a blind taste test that Koch organized at a Boston restaurant. The tasters? Local bartenders. The contestants? Koch's signature lager and major imports like Heineken and Beck's.

Solman [*voiceover*]: Koch charged that the imports have been adulterated for the American market with corn, sugar, and preservatives. As a result, he claimed, these beers couldn't meet the standards Germans apply to their own domestic beers. While his competitors were understandably reluctant to play into his hands, they simply couldn't let Koch's charges go unchallenged. Philip Van Munching, importer of Heineken:

Van Munching: His contention in his ads that Heineken is outlawed in Germany for using illegal adjuncts certainly sounds dramatic. Well, the truth is rather boring . . . . [T]he German law that Jim Koch cites is a trade restriction. They want . . . to protect their smaller breweries. Well, that's fine. But to call it a purity law and state somehow that our beer is impure, other beers are impure, is ludicrous.*

Koch: What I'm doing is obviously very risky. I'm directly attacking very powerful, entrenched interests—imported beers and imported brewers, beers that sell hundreds of millions of dollars worth of beer here. And I'm pointing the finger directly at them and saying they're a fraud.

Boston Lager won that day's taste test; Heineken placed fourth.

---

* Philip Van Munching never really got over confronting Jim Koch. After he left the beer business when his family firm was bought out, Van Munching wrote a book about his experiences, with a chapter called, "Sam Adams: Brewer, Patriot, Pain in the Ass."

FIVE HUNDRED MILES IN A RENTED HONDA
New Ulm, MN | 1986–1987

Pete Slosberg and Mark Bronder and other early investors met often at the Jew and Gentile Deli in Mountain View, California, in those six months after the Palo Alto Brewing Company went so eventfully bankrupt. They had bottled and shipped hundreds of cases of Pete's Wicked Ale—and, as with the last batch in late 1986, the cases had moved briskly off area retailers' shelves. The brown ale Slosberg had stumbled onto trying to mimic Samuel Smith's Nut Brown Ale was popular with consumers and respected by critics (it would take the silver in the ales category at the 1987 Great American Beer Festival). But it was a scarce commodity growing scarcer. They needed another place to brew it.

And it would not be their own. Like Jim Koch and Rhonda Kallman with the Boston Beer Company, Slosberg and Bronder had started out planning to eventually open a brewery, though that was never the main goal. The main goal was liquidity—making a handsome profit. Contract brewing saved them time spent locating a site and the subsequent construction costs, which could have run into the hundreds of thousands in the Bay Area. The realization comforted Slosberg as a homebrewer who wanted to go to the next level. "You don't have to own your own brewery to make great beer," he thought. "I guess some people have to hug their very own vessels and pipes every day in order to feel good, but that wasn't a requirement for us." It also afforded them the flexibility to keep their day jobs and run Pete's Brewing in their spare time.

In those six months after the Palo Alto rescue mission, Slosberg and Bronder sought out older regional breweries with excess capacity. They wanted to avoid what had happened with the start-up craft brewery and figured a more established name would give them less of a chance of a sudden emergency phone call. They returned to Bronder's roots to search, flying to Minneapolis and staying the night at his mom's. The next day, they drove five hundred miles in a rented Honda to visit different breweries, aware that a decision had to be made soon enough to keep the brand going two thousand miles away in the Bay Area. They were resolute about finding a brewer who took their product seriously and not simply as another brand. One candidate had a big office and a new brewery he named after his Irish heritage. Bronder and Slosberg didn't like that—too much about the brewer, not enough about the beer. They settled on the August Schell Brewing Company, a family-run concern in New Ulm, southwest of Minneapolis, dating from just before the Civil War. Pete's Brewing was back on.

NEW YORK MINUTES
Brooklyn; Manhattan | 1987–1988

"**D**o you know who Milton is?" the snooty voice on the other end of the line asked Steve Hindy.

He did know who Milton Glaser was. He was one of the best graphic designers alive, the hands behind the "I Love NY" logo and innumerable magazine covers. That was why Hindy wanted to talk to him. Could he?

"Absolutely not," Glaser's receptionist said. "He doesn't talk to anyone who just walks in the door."

It was that kind of year for Hindy and his partner, Tom Potter. They had been trying to start Brooklyn Brewery since late 1986 and were running into obstacles at nearly every turn. Their plight was a common-enough thing in the craft beer movement but ironic given their locale: the global capital of capitalism. Instead, Gotham threw up problems, not least the real estate costs for the physical brewery itself. The pair decided to start out contract brewing, and, as fellow New Yorker Matthew Reich had done a few years before, they sought out F. X. Matt Brewing in Utica, which meant seeking out F. X. Matt II. Hindy cold-called him one day.

"What makes you think you can sell beer just because you make five gallons on your kitchen stove?" Matt asked him. "My family has been doing this for one hundred years and we are having a very hard time."

Hindy asked Potter to try. His call was greeted with the same forceful no. Hindy gave it one more try. Matt started into another harangue about the difficulties that even established brands faced. His company was itself at a crossroads as one of the last regional breweries in the nation. It would lose more than $1 million in 1988 and was operating at less than half its potential capacity (which explained the room for contract brewing). Contrast that with the Miller plant eighty miles to the west in Fulton, New York: the Philip Morris division was spending $23 million to rejigger the plant so it could produce 1.5 million barrels annually of Miller's new hit, Genuine Draft. Big Beer's marketing budgets had convinced many consumers that brands like Genuine Draft were superior to Matt brands like Matt's Premium and Utica Club. Moreover, Matt could not compete with lower-priced brands like Old Milwaukee and Milwaukee's Best for one reason that was very simple (and, to newer brewers like Hindy and Potter, endearing): Matt couldn't and wouldn't make beer that cheaply.

It was an ominous situation. The regionals' market share was shrinking. You could see how this was supposed to end, so why would you jump in now? Hindy pressed on in the phone call. Matt asked him what he did for a living. Hindy explained his time as a foreign correspondent.

There was a pause.

"Really?" Matt said. "I always wanted to be a journalist."

They talked for the next fifteen minutes about the news business and literature—Matt had studied it at Princeton and wrote poetry as a hobby. He was even known to write apologetic verse to consumers in response to those rare complaints about his beer and to carry a copy of Henry James's novella *Daisy Miller*, about a romance in Europe, in his breast pocket during walks around the brewery. He invited Hindy and Potter to Utica to discuss contract brewing.

Hindy and Potter devised the recipe with a brewing consultant named William Moeller, who had recently taken early retirement from Christian Schmidt and Sons, the last brewery to close in Philadelphia. Moeller, whose grandfather had been a brewer in Brooklyn at the turn of the century, saw the venture as a refreshing change. "For thirty-five years," he told Hindy and Potter, "I have listened to brewery owners tell me to make a beer cheaper and faster. This is the first time in my career that an owner has ever asked me to make the best damn beer I can make." They leafed through Moeller's grandfather's notebooks, fiddling with different combinations over a two-month period in Moeller's Boyertown, Pennsylvania, basement, before settling on a recipe. Moeller would take it to Utica and, in a departure for Matt, would be on hand when the initial batches were made.

Hindy and Potter raised $300,000 from a variety of sources in 1986 and 1987: lawyers, bankers, friends, relatives, even low-paid journalists that Hindy had known in his soon-to-be former life (the two would both turn full-time by the end of the year, though Hindy returned briefly to *Newsday* during the first Gulf War in 1991). They hit their goal at an unimaginably lucky moment: right before the stock market crash on October 19, 1987. The market lost more than 20 percent of its value in that single day, taking investor confidence down with it.

Hindy and Potter also paid for services through stakes in the company—Bill Moeller got one, for instance. So did Milton Glaser. Hindy finally got through to the graphic-design legend, approaching the end run around the receptionist as a dogged reporter chasing a scoop. Glaser got the concept immediately, more than Hindy or Potter, really. Beer in Brooklyn. Brooklyn beer. Brooklyn. Brooklyn, New York. America's fourth-largest city. The Borough of Kings. Known worldwide. A brand in itself. Hindy and Potter had pitched the iconic imagery of the borough, including the Brooklyn Bridge and even the *Brooklyn Eagle*, a newspaper that Walt Whitman once edited. Instead, Glaser went with a simple yet elegant *B*—no cheesy graphic, just the perception of Brooklyn, what it meant to people. His clients were underwhelmed when he unveiled it. "Don't say a word," Glaser said. "Take this home and show it to your wives. Put it on the counter in your kitchen and live with it for a while."

The first cases of Brooklyn Lager, with Glaser's design, were delivered to the company's first five accounts on March 30, 1988. By June there were 150 accounts, and a fanfare-filled delivery of the first bottles to Manhattan via water taxi was planned for August. Hindy and Potter had rented space in an old warehouse formerly used by the Hittleman Brewery, one of the dozens of breweries that had once dotted Brooklyn. It was on Meserole Street, which used to be known as Brooklyn's Brewers Row—and would be again.

Brooklyn Brewery debuted just as the brewery portion of Matthew Reich's beautiful New Amsterdam brewpub on Manhattan's West Side closed. Reich, not yet forty, was the acknowledged pioneer of contract brewing—Hindy and Potter sang his praises, along with Jim Koch (even F. X. Matt, a hard man to impress, would tip his hat to the newcomer). The expense of a physical brewery in a large metropolitan area, however, proved too high. Construction costs ran hundreds of thousands of dollars over budget; and then operating a restaurant alongside the 110-barrel brewery took a toll, even as New Amsterdam reached fifteen thousand barrels in annual sales and distribution in twenty-two states (far better than what Reich reached for in his original business plan). It was a New York minute rendered ironic. "How long do you think it takes to unload a truckload of malted barley in

New York City?" Reich asked Hindy after the two had become friends. "It takes a lot longer than it does anywhere else." Plus, the venture-capital firm backing him scored big on another investment (a railroad) and had no desire to extend more credit for his concern. Reich sold the restaurant portion of the old brewpub in 1989, and though New Amsterdam continued as a brand contract brewed once again out of F. X. Matt, its outer-borough rival would soon eclipse it as New York City's most famous beer.* That rival's ascension was not only notable for its location, although plunking a craft beer flag atop the summit of American media and finance didn't hurt the movement. More important, Brooklyn Brewery would place itself at the vanguard of the wider public's understanding of craft beer. And not a moment too soon, it would turn out. The number of craft breweries and brewpubs was about to balloon, upending the entire industry in the process. Things were about to get very interesting and very messy.

THE REVOLUTION, TELEVISED

San Francisco; Cleveland; Chicago | 1987–1990

Regal trumpets blare; goblets, flutes, steins, chalices, mugs, and bottles rush past with beer brands from England, Belgium, West Germany, Czechoslovakia, the Netherlands, and America emblazoned on their glass. A man's hand reaches down to cradle the last vessel in the pantheon; he brings the beer inside it, a Trappist ale, to his nose and then to his lips. The music shifts to ragtime jazz. Episode two of Michael Jackson's series *The Beer Hunter* can now begin.

And it does, with sweeping shots of the San Francisco Bay and of Jackson walking resolutely amid hilly streets with cable cars, on his way to a festival with almost two hundred beers on tap. We see tables with banners and wares from Sierra Nevada, Boston Beer, and the Mendocino Brewing Company. We see the taps running, the glasses passed, brimming with beer. "They come from a generation of tiny breweries," Jackson's voice explains over the images

---

* The restaurant portion of the New Amsterdam brewpub went out of business, too, shortly after the 1989 sale.

to American viewers watching the Discovery Channel, "that have sprung up all over America in the last decade."

With his rumpled suit, owlish glasses, salt-and-pepper goatee, and circlet of unkempt curls, Jackson looked like anyone's favorite professor. His classroom for this particular lesson was a Discovery Channel show that reached into about thirty-eight million households. Even if Jackson reached a fraction of those eyeballs, he would reach a wider audience than American craft beer had ever enjoyed to that point. (Foreigners augmented this audience, too: *The Beer Hunter* had run in the United Kingdom the year before, and aired in Belgium the same time as it ran in the United States.) Jackson wandered the festival floor in San Francisco and confronted for his viewers a resurgence in brewing and interest in beer unlike anywhere else in the world, in his opinion. "To a Beer Hunter, America's Northwest beckons like a new frontier, and Americans are beginning to discover that there's more in the kingdom of beer than a standard six-pack from the supermarket." Festival-goers smilingly explained the libations in their sampling glasses for the charming, curious beer bard from Yorkshire: a lager by way of Santa Cruz, California; an extra special bitter from Hood River, Oregon; an amber ale from Mendocino County in California.

The episode aired on the Discovery Channel on August 30, 1990. It showed an American craft beer movement in seemingly full and unstoppable bloom. The movement certainly appeared so on a macro level. It was in the midst of a four-year run that would see the number of craft breweries and brewpubs increase tenfold. The stories of the entities' origins—and their geographies—were becoming ever more diverse, the plausibility of their individual success more and more assured. Americans were catching on and catapulting craft beer sales.

Or so it seemed. Scratch a little bit, and we see that none of the above was really true. Of the more than 120 craft breweries and brewpubs in the United States, about half were along the West Coast and one-third were in California. For all the growth in numbers through the 1980s, one in four beers sold in the country came from Anheuser-Busch, and other Big Beer rivals such as Coors absorbed most of the rest of the market share. Brewpubs were illegal in nearly half the fifty states. Craft sales as a percentage of overall American beer sales could be measured in the very low single digits, whether they came from retailers or from taps steps away from the kettles and tuns (brewpubs made up the majority of newer operations). Craft breweries and brewpubs produced an estimated 120,000 barrels in 1988 and 180,000 in 1989, according to the Association of Brewers, the trade organization for the smaller operators that emerged out of Charlie Papazian's American Homebrewers Association and became the go-to media source on craft brew statistics. It was all so many specks on Big Beer's windshield.

Jackson was unequivocally correct that "the kingdom of beer" now had many more mansions and that many of these new houses were distinctly American. Jackson was also spot on that America remained a "new frontier"—enough so that fresh ventures nearly a quarter-century into the movement could still claim pioneering "firsts" on their entrepreneurial CVs. These included the Samuel Adams Brewhouse, a brewpub that Jim Koch co-owned that opened in December 1989 with three beers made under the supervision of brewmaster Jim Pericles: a lager called Ben Franklin Gold, Poor Richard's Amber, and George Washington Porter. Samuel Adams joined the Dock Street Brewing brewpub that year as the first breweries in Philadelphia since Christian Schmidt's closed in 1987.

An earlier first on the other side of the continent was the Hood River Brewing Company, started in Hood River, Oregon, right across the Columbia River from Washington State, by Jerome Chicvara, Meg Roland, Irene Firmat, and partners. It became the first craft brewery in Oregon to bottle its beer for sale. Chicvara, who worked for a distributor selling beer, had wanted to contract brew what he called Sasquatch Ale. Finding no breweries willing to do it, he set about raising $50,000 from thirty-three people, mostly relatives, as well as another $150,000 from one of the state's economic development engines, and he opened a physical brewery in an old fruit-canning warehouse. Homebrewer David Logsdon, who owned a laboratory in nearby Parkdale that made, among other products, yeast cultures for wineries, devised Hood River's flagship beer, Full Sail Golden Ale, with the first kegs released in the late spring of 1987 and the first bottles shortly before Thanksgiving.

There was also the Great Lakes Brewing Company that brothers Patrick and Daniel Conway founded in late 1986. Patrick Conway had studied abroad in the early 1970s in Rome; from that base he had soaked up the pub and brewery culture of West Germany, Belgium, and Britain. The brothers raised money and supplies throughout 1987 and early 1988 and opened in September of that year Cleveland's first brewery since Christian Schmidt and Sons closed in 1984. The city had once hosted as many as eleven breweries after Prohibition and nearly thirty in the decade after the Civil War. The Conways' one-thousand-barrel, 140-seat brewpub at the 120-year-old Market Tavern building near downtown also signaled the first craft brewery in the Buckeye State entirely. Thaine Johnson, a brewer at the shuttered Christian Schmidt, was coaxed out of retirement to oversee the production of three initial beers retailing at $2.20 a glass, including an amber ale named after Clevelander Eliot Ness, best known for enforcing (or trying to, at least) Prohibition.

There was also the Connecticut Brewing Company, a contract operation started by John Foley, a twenty-six-year-old Wall Street bond trader and friend of Mass. Bay Brewing Company cofounders Rich Doyle and Dan Kenary. His Nathan Hale Golden Lager, a recipe culled from the state's pre-Prohibition era and brewed through the Lion Brewery in Wilkes-Barre, Pennsylvania, became the first craft beer based in Connecticut; it hit shelves and bars in the winter of 1989.

There was also the Deschutes Brewing Company, which Gary Fish started in Bend, Oregon, in June 1988. Fish had grown up in the California wine business and started in the restaurant industry as a dishwasher in high school and a waiter in college. He relocated from a restaurant in Salt Lake City to start the brewpub in Bend, with John Harris as brewmaster (Harris would later move to the Hood River brewery that became known as Full Sail).

In Vermont, Long Trail Brewing Company joined Stephen Mason, Stephen Israel, and Alan Davis's Catamount Brewing. Specializing in German-style beers, Long Trail was started by Andy Pherson in the fall of 1989 in the impossibly small town of Bridgewater Corners—the brewery joined a general store and a post office as the main commercial ventures. Across the country, in Palo Alto, California, Dean Biersch and Dan Gordon, who had spent five years studying brewing in Munich, were into their second year of running Gordon Biersch Brewery Restaurant, a 185-seat brewpub carved from an old theater; the pair talked openly of turning the concept into a chain. And on the central Oregon coast, the Rogue River Brewing Company, founded by Jack Joyce, Bob Woodell, Rob Strasser, and Jeff Schultz (Schultz was Woodell's accountant and a homebrewer), was in its first year at a new location. The company's initial brewpub in Ashland, a sixty-seater with a ten-barrel system in the basement, proved too small, so they moved the business 270 miles northwestward to Newport. The new brewpub opened in May 1989 with John Maier, a Siebel Institute graduate and former assistant brewer at Geoff and Marcy Larson's Alaskan Brewing Company, as brewmaster.

A year and a half before that, Sierra Nevada had completed what may have been a first in the movement as well: a physical brewery's major expansion involving at least one conventional loan source. In part with funding from Bank of America, Ken Grossman and Paul Camusi's concern opened a twenty-five-thousand-square-foot brewery on East Twentieth Street in Chico, California, and, in 1989, added an adjoining twenty-seven-hundred-square-foot brewpub. The complex featured a beautiful, light-drenched, cavernous, one-hundred-barrel brewhouse capable of producing sixty thousand barrels annually under the direction of brewmaster Steve Dresler, though the founders doubted the company would ever reach that capacity. For now, it was simply satisfying to have undergone such a growth spurt after shakeouts in the wider industry. Grossman was especially pleased his brewery did not need to sell its soul to grow—the decision to open later rather than leap in during the late 1970s had made a difference. So had a cover story in the *San Francisco Examiner* Sunday magazine. On May 25, 1986, readers throughout the Bay Area awoke to a big, blocky headline, THE BEER THAT'S MAKING CHICO FAMOUS, and a photograph of Camusi and Grossman that absorbed the magazine's entire cover. They were out in a sown field, the California sky stretching away toward the horizon, the two young men in jeans, T-shirts, and sneakers, sitting atop boxes of beer, stacked kegs beside them, their hair unkempt, a bearded Grossman holding a half-full glass, Camusi holding a bottle, the craftsmen taking a breather—clip the photo and the two could literally be the poster boys of the craft beer movement to that point. The subsequent story by Michael Castleman, which covered Sierra Nevada's history and hinted at the expansion to come, helped immensely in getting their brands into more hands than any West Coast brewery in the second or now third wave.

Closures and readjustments had thinned that second wave considerably (the first wave, Anchor by itself, pushed merrily on). This late-1980s third wave was diffuse geographically and divergent in background, just as it may never had read an issue of *Zymurgy* or heard of Jack McAuliffe's New Albion. Bond traders, restaurateur refugees from the wine industry, beer salesmen, accountants—all were all in on what looked from the outside like that growing industry that Michael Jackson marveled at in *The Beer Hunter* and Grossman and Camusi so coolly personified on that magazine cover. On the inside, too, it seemed a rather burgeoning industry. The seventh annual National Microbrewers and Pubbrewers Conference and Trade Show, as it was called, was held over three days beginning on August 30, 1989, in the San Francisco Hilton.* The theme was "Brewing into the Future," and the registration fee for members of the Institute for Brewing Studies, a wing of the Association of Brewers, was $392 ($462 for nonmembers). Session topics included,"Which to Choose: Brewpub or Microbrewery?" hosted by David Geary; "Brewpub Packaging for Premise Sales—Why, How, and Special Regulations," hosted by Don

---

* The Association of Brewers would change the name to the Craft Brewers Conference in 1996. This conference replaced earlier microbrewer meetings, which were often part of the annual homebrewers competition.

Barkley; and "Practical Brewery Sanitation," hosted by Michael Lewis, still the nation's only full professor of brewing science. More than two hundred brewers, vendors, and others related to the industry attended. It was a far cry from the first conferences as well as the first homebrewers competitions and Great American Beer Festivals—much larger numbers-wise, more regimented, and decidedly, necessarily, more forward-looking and less amateur. As big a harbinger of the shift as anything was the discontinuation after the 1989 GABF of the consumer preference poll—from now on, every competition would be decided by a panel of judges.*

It was no small thing, either, that by now the Microbrewers Conference was held in a different city each year; 1988's had been in Chicago, which in under a year caught up to New York in its number of breweries. The first—and the first brewery in America's third-largest city since the Peter Hand Brewing Company folded in 1978—was Sieben's River North, which could seat four hundred people in its pub and brew up to five thousand barrels. It was started by Jim Krejcie, who got the idea after attending an AHA conference in 1982. He borrowed $10,000 from his mother, enough for the brewing equipment, the space in an old warehouse near the North Branch of the Chicago River (he made the landlord a partner to get lower rent), and the name of what had been Chicago's oldest beer garden, Sieben's. He also collected as partners Bill and Ron Siebel, the brothers who ran Chicago's august Siebel Institute, which had been training brewers since the late nineteenth century. Sieben's River North's first brewmaster was Peter Burrell, a geologist by training taking courses at Siebel. The brewpub opened in September 1987 to fifteen-minute waits for tables. It was followed within a year by the Tap and Growler in Chicago's Greektown neighborhood and Goose Island about two miles north of Sieben's. Attendees at the 1988 Microbrewers Conference visited each one, as they would visit Mendocino, Gordon Biersch, and other brewpubs in the Bay Area a year later.

They also dropped in on Anchor Brewing on Mariposa Street. Fritz Maytag's operation was as pivotal as ever in the movement, and Michael Jackson made it a point, along with his producer and director Bob Bee, to make it the focus of that second episode of *The Beer Hunter*. If Jackson were the rumpled English professor, Maytag was every bit the English department's chairman—physically trim in middle age and crisply dressed, tactfully restrained in his enthusiasm, slow in picking his words, frowningly serious about the bottom lines, financial and otherwise. He and Jackson walked about the copper kettles

---

* Boston Beer Company's beers had won the consumer preference poll in 1985, 1986, 1987, and 1989.

of the beautifully apportioned Anchor brewhouse. Maytag explained for a second generation that first encounter with the old, struggling brewery in August 1965. "I found it to be intriguing that it was an entity," he said, "and that it was a local thing. It was a real, local entity; and the idea of saving it appealed to me from the beginning."

Later in the episode, Jackson accompanied Maytag and his crew on a more than three-hundred-mile bus ride to Tulelake, near California's Oregon border, to the single field on the one farm that produced the barley used in Anchor Christmas Ale. Maytag used the annual trip to remind his crew—and himself—that the beer they crafted came from the earth, the local earth at that, and should the earth not cooperate in birthing the proper ingredients, everything could go awry. The riders played cards and guitars, sang and laughed, talked and sipped—it was a trip everyone watching would have liked to have been on. Maytag sat slightly apart, glancing at the Northern California landscape as it rolled from brushy to verdant, flatter to hillier. He shared his American perspective with his foreign guest: "I think there's a dangerous closeness to having beer almost become a commodity in our country. For a while there, we had almost lost the idea that beer could be wonderful and that there were different styles of beer, and that brewing companies could have personalities. I think we were very close to losing that. It's coming back now."

A MANIFESTO AND ARNOLD SCHWARZENEGGER

Venice, Italy | 1990

"**I am fed up with restaurants!**" declared the poet Folco Portinari. The eyes of the delegates from fourteen nations swung to him. "All restaurants should be closed for one year. Journalists are the only ones who eat in restaurants. The rest of the people eat what they make at home."

Portinari went on to propose a promotion of a "realistic cuisine" that would help "recover" people who no longer ate locally, who no longer cooked for themselves, who were no longer in tune with what wasn't mass-produced and marketed to them. He ended his remarks, which had stopped the first International Slow Food Congress in its officious tracks, on an almost fatalistic, yet pragmatic note. "It is useless to fight against fast food, but we must support tradition."

That the delegates had gathered in early December 1990 in Venice was no accident. Carlo Petrini had picked it because, as he told a reporter, it was "the slowest city in the world." Petrini had not been able to forget the protests outside of the new 450-seat McDonald's off the Spanish Steps in Rome in 1986. In the interim, he and Portinari started a group dedicated to the enjoyment of locally produced food and drink, envisioning it as a deliberate reaction to the rise in fast food, in mass-produced foodstuffs, in the growing distances between producers and consumers wherever they happened to be in the world. Slow Food, as it was called in any language, was a mix of tongue in cheek and deadly seriousness. It even had a manifesto, written by Portinari and signed the previous December in the Opéra Comique in Paris by delegates from fifteen nations, including the United States. The first two paragraphs stated the group's grievances:

> Our century, which began and has developed under the insignia of industrial civilization, first invented the machine and then took it as its life model. We are enslaved by speed and have all succumbed to the same insidious virus: Fast Life, which disrupts our habits, pervades the privacy of our homes and forces us to eat Fast Foods.

Toward the end of the 248-word manifesto, Petrini and Portinari, and their partisans, got to what they were trying to effect.

> Our defense should begin at the table with Slow Food. Let us rediscover the flavors and savors of regional cooking and banish the degrading effects of Fast Food. . . .
>
> That is what real culture is all about: developing taste rather than demeaning it. And what better way to set about this than an exchange of experiences, knowledge, projects?

That first congress brought earnest discussion of the goals laid out in the manifesto. It also brought suggestions that showed a certain bravado as well as naivete: a journalist from Austria proposed bringing the recently liberated nations of Eastern Europe onboard; a delegate from Venezuela said his country would host a cooking school based on Slow Food's principles. Americans were skeptical about the movement. As Sheldon Wasserman, an authority on Italian wines, asked at a New York press conference announcing the manifesto, "Why does there have to be an organized movement for this?"

"To share the enthusiasm," replied Nino Beltrami, a math professor at the State University of New York at Stony Brook and one of Slow Food's American organizers. "Concertgoers," Wasserman went on, "share a love for music by going to a concert, and those who enjoy good food share their interests by going to dinner together at some place other than McDonald's. There are already plenty of food and wine organizations for those who want to join them."

Beltrami was left to explain that Slow Food wasn't meant to be elitist. It was meant, as the manifesto said, to promote the enjoyment of food and drink made as close to a consumer as possible from the finest ingredients available (it was meant to be affordable as well, though this wasn't said in the manifesto or in much of the movement's first months). Slow Food was reactionary, much like the American craft beer movement; both drew inspiration and guidance from earlier times and set themselves in opposition to what seemed like their ages' prevailing and inevitable norms. Slow Food—what was the point? A small-scale brewery, Mr. McAuliffe? You must be kidding; the state of California doesn't have a form for that!

Slow Food also arrived in an America coming off a decadelong fitness craze. Hundreds of exercise videos designed for the advent of the VCR hit shelves and were hawked in magazine ads and late-night television commercials; some sold into the millions and actually spawned sequels. Gym chains such as Bally Total Fitness, Crunch, Planet Fitness, and Equinox started in the 1980s opening hundreds of locations, including several in each of the nation's largest cities. Home-gym suppliers did tens of thousands of dollars in business per month. C. Everett Koop dusted off the bully pulpit of the national surgeon general, intoning through the Reagan administration like the voice of a vengeful God against smoking and sloth. George H. W. Bush reinvigorated the President's Council on Physical Fitness and Sports by making Arnold Schwarzenegger, the world's highest-paid movie star and recently minted Kennedy in-law, its chairman. The council condemned millions of school kids to compete through pull-ups and sprints for certificates from the president, who made it a regular point to be seen jogging, buff Secret Service agents in tow, a habit his successors were compelled to adopt. The fitness craze almost appeared an inevitable successor to the consumer concerns that arose the decade before over the nation's food supply, the same concerns that sparked those twelve million home gardens in the mid-1970s. It would be years, though, before Slow Food and the locavore movement it championed—and grew in tandem with—joined this emphasis on fitness in the United States. But there were Americans paying attention to Petrini, Portinari, and their disciples, enough to note the delicious symbolism (probably intentional) during that first night of the first International Slow Food Congress. A banquet was held at the Palazzo Pisani Moretta, a fifteenth-century palace along the Grand Canal in Venice, reachable by motorboat. The 250 delegates, press, and guests dined beneath chandeliers and sconces lit only by candles. It evoked, as one observer noted, an "earlier, slower" time.

THE VALUE OF GOLD
Utica, NY | 1991

T hings were slow at the F. X. Matt Brewing Company—and not in a good way. Nick Matt had joined his brother F. X. at the family regional in 1989, a year after its one hundreth birthday and after a career that included a stint as a top executive at Procter & Gamble. Nick Matt also came aboard just after he, his three brothers, and their sister bought out a family trust to gain control of the brewery their grandfather had started.

It was a precarious time. Like the handful of other older, family-run regionals, F. X. Matt was losing money, operating under capacity, and being squeezed by Big Beer. It couldn't compete as strongly on the marketing end, and it couldn't, in many instances, produce its brands cheaply enough to compete with Big Beer's cheapest labels. F. X. Matt faced the additional challenge of having the largest Old Milwaukee franchise outside of Milwaukee in its hometown of Utica, New York. The Stroh's brand almost dared F. X. Matt to price its Utica Club and Matt's Premium more cheaply. What to do?

The brothers streamlined where they could and upped their marketing game. They changed their packaging, including the labels, to make them pop more from retailers' shelves. They turned their down times into money with contract brewing for craft operations like Matthew Reich's New Amsterdam, Jeffrey Ware's Dock Street, and Tom Potter and Steve Hindy's Brooklyn Brewery. They got local and state tax breaks. They even started exporting to Japan and brewing a nonalcoholic beer. A mild optimism set in amid the 130-plus employees. Through it all, F. X. Matt (the man and the brewery) refused to compromise on product quality. Cuts and savings might come elsewhere, but not on the ingredients and the time taken to brew their own beer. It turned out to be a crucial decision, though it seemed like a suicide pact. The marketing changes were unlikely to make a big enough difference, and the contract brewing wasn't by itself going to keep the brewery going. Then the Great American Beer Festival intervened.

F. X. Matt had been making an all-malt lager it called Saranac 1888 since 1985, named after a lake in Upstate New York and the year of the brewery's founding. It was not one of their main brands and was more akin to the craft beers starting to circulate than to Utica Club or Matt's Premium. The brewery entered it in the GABF in 1987 and, to its surprise, walked away with a silver medal in the Continental Pilsners category (losing to Samuel Adams Boston Lager but edging out a pilsner from fellow family-run regional August Schell). That was a nice spot of good news amid the bad, though it did little to nothing to stem what seemed like a slide into oblivion. A headline in the February 6, 1989, metro section of Syracuse's *Post-Standard* seemed to say it all about Upstate New York's biggest breweries: MILLER, BUD TO BOOST PRODUCTION; MATT HOPES TO SURVIVE. Then, again, the GABF intervened.

F. X. Matt had another beer in its Saranac line called Saranac Amber Lager. Like the 1888, it wasn't a big part of the brewery's repertoire, accounting for perhaps 1 percent of its sales. At the 1991 GABF, the amber won the gold medal in the American premium lager category. The silver medalist? The Jacob Leinenkugel Brewing Company, which Miller had bought in 1988. Nick Matt remembered the news reaching Utica from Denver; it gave everyone pause. "If this is such a great beer," they thought, "maybe we should spend more time focusing on it." So that's what F. X. Matt did. The brewery swung its marketing squarely behind the Saranac line, which also included a black and tan, a pale ale, and a pilsner, pushing it in place of less expensive brands like Matt's Premium and Utica Club. Sales of Saranac grew several years in a row. The main marketing tool? The GABF gold medal. It was not so much that F. X. Matt's brewing expertise shifted—Saranac had been part of its lineup, their brewers knew what to do—but that the focus shifted. The medal showed the regional, which made its bones in the last golden age of American brewing, a path away from consignment to the history books.

So there it was to many inside and outside the industry: craft beer could be a great business move. It was the way, the truth, and not the light. What could possibly go wrong if you marketed everything right?

"THE TYRANNY OF FAST GROWTH"

Baghdad, Iraq; Marin County, CA | 1991–1994

A merican, Saudi Arabian, British, French, Italian, and Canadian warplanes tore through the desert sky. They attacked Iraqi targets at a rate of more than one sortie per minute, searching for the Scud missiles that Iraqi dictator Saddam Hussein had been lobbing into Israel. The patricianly grim president George H. W. Bush, architect of the international force now in its third day of attack, vowed "the darndest search and destroy mission that's ever been undertaken." He urged patience, however, and his military men echoed him, telling reporters the war would be a slog, not a sprint. Twelve warplanes had been shot down, including four American ones; seven crew members from those planes were missing. The bombing continued day and night.

Back home, despite the dire warnings from the president and the generals, the grainy images of the bombing that the relatively new cable news channel CNN beamed into living rooms, diners, bars, and basements enraptured viewers. What was coming to be called the Gulf War was almost a moment of national catharsis, the country whipped into a fervor of patriotism that many expected would wipe away lingering doubts of US military might left by Vietnam only sixteen years before. The United States seemed to be winning and winning big, never mind the cautions emanating from the White House and Central Command. It was January 1991, and the country had caught war fever.

For Tony Magee, it was more of a pounding headache. He was just into his thirties, newly married, recently a homeowner (though with a sizable mortgage), and the financial walls had begun to close in. The war had interrupted the accidental business the Chicago native fell into around San Francisco, after a years-long stab at music netted him lots of touring in a reggae band and musical-arrangement credits for Pizza Hut, Bud Light, and Hallmark commercials. The business was a commission-only printing-sales job, an incongruous fit for Magee, a spectacled multi-instrumentalist more at home with a set list of Slim Harpo and Blind Willie McTell, or discussing Beethoven in terms of Brahms; but it worked handsomely financially. Now, because of the war, his biggest client, a San Francisco bank, decided not to print and mail a Visa card solicitation; not only that, the bank would soon move Magee's projects to Seattle and thus away from him. Everything went from bad to worse. Magee and his wife confronted bankruptcy. It brought to his mind that line from Martin Sheen's character, Willard, in *Apocalypse Now*, the one about how "bullshit piled up so fast [that] you needed wings to stay above it." He would sort through his anxiety only years later:

> I went from earning in the strong six figures to the feeble fives over-
> night and the rebuilding, which would eventually occur, would take
> years. The repo guy would call nightly about the car, the Amex card
> went away, the mortgage went into default, planned vacations evapo-
> rated, the IRS and the state tax board letters all appeared like new
> roommates. . . . The stink of foreclosure, divorce . . . and dissolution
> filled the air, and I just didn't want to become one of the bitter, old
> foreclosed, divorced, and dissipated 65-year-old printing trolls that
> I'd seen in the afternoon bars of San Francisco's financial district.

Enter craft beer. Magee's younger brother worked at a brewpub in Oregon and bought him a homebrewing kit for Christmas in 1992, when Magee was just then pulling his household back from financial ruin and looking for something else to delve into besides printing. The aesthetics of brewing equipment appealed to him, reminding him in a way of the sensual shapes of musical instruments like guitars and saxophones. The functionality of the tuns and kettles appealed to Magee as well: here was something a man could work with. That quality was in the equipment at the Marin Brewing Company, the oldest brewpub in Marin County, just north of San Francisco, where Magee had become a regular. Marin Brewing was part of the second wave of brewpubs; it was started in April 1989 by Craig Tasley, who worked in restaurants, and Brendan Moylan, who was a buyer for a liquor store and who had his own beery epiphany while visiting Bill Owens's Buffalo Bill's Brewpub in Hayward, California, a few years before. The sessions at Marin Brewing and the homebrewing kit from his brother in the Oregon brewpub business planted a kernel that very nearly drowned in the first batch Magee made: a California common beer mimicking the style that Anchor popular-ized. The next batch, though—a straight-ahead pale ale—turned out much better, and soon Magee was asking what he thought were entirely appropriate technical questions of his local homebrew vendor.

"Which yeast strain might convert the most sugars to alcohol?" he wanted to know. He wanted to make stronger beers.

The vendor turned away from him, unimpressed. "That is not a question a brewer would ask."

We'll see about that, Magee thought—styles were for academics. He read Charlie Papazian's *The Complete Joy of Homebrewing*, Byron Burch's *Quality Brewing*, and newer works such as *Brewing Lager Beer* by Greg Noonan, the co-owner of a brewpub in Burlington, Vermont, and brewpub pioneer Bill Owens's 1982 handbook, *How to Build a Small Brewery*. He bought a three-tier homebrewing system and rented 750 square feet in a building nearby. He spent evenings and weekends on his living room floor, guesstimating the start-up costs of a commercial brewery, compelled to pursue something he knew could be as risky or more so than the boom-and-bust printing business he was already in. Magee was aware of the wider craft beer movement—how could one not be in Northern California?—and he knew the start-up costs could run quickly into six figures. The numbers didn't necessarily jibe, but he barreled ahead through much of 1993 nonetheless. The need to start a brewery was almost a compulsion, an entrepreneurial infection contracted unwittingly through airborne happenstance.

Magee's big break came when he spied an ad in the back of *New Brewer*, the bimonthly magazine of Papazian's Association of Brewers, posted by a man named John Cross. Cross was one of the main American importers of what had been called the Model T of brewing tanks: the Grundy. They were not much to look at, squat and gray, a far cry from the beautiful copper kettles that occupied postcard places in brewers' hearts. Grundy serving tanks were mass-produced for pubs and restaurants across Europe and could hold up to 210 gallons. They eventually fell out of favor on the Continent and in the United Kingdom as pub owners figured out how to jimmy off the tops and water down their beers. Brewers switched to kegs. Cross and a few others bought up the used Grundy tanks, brought them to the United States, fixed them up as needed, and began unloading them to craft brewers like Magee for relatively cheap. In April 1993, he responded to Cross's ad in *New Brewer*; drove five hours south to Porterville, California; and promptly lost hope after talking with Cross. Magee knew he would need more than Grundy tanks to get his brewery going, and he just could not afford the equipment Cross described. He told him as much.

Cross grew quiet. He looked Magee up and down, rubbed his chin. He then told him about a brewhouse that he had built for a Russian brewery that no longer needed it. It was a fifteen-foot-long rectangular, stainless-steel box with a hot water tank, a mash tun, and a two-hundred-gallon kettle—it was all Magee's for $5,000. Deal. Magee took the Russian-made brewhouse and two Grundy tanks back with him to Lagunitas, California, and named his new brewery after the area. He was the only employee, though he kept his day job as a printing salesman. It was going to be all draft, not wedded to conventional styles, and sold only locally.

By the summer of 1994, Magee had a schedule down. He would mill grains around 9:00 the night before he knew he would brew, then wake up at 3:00 AM to start mashing the grains around 3:30. He would do the boil within a few hours and be cleaned up by ten, ready for his day job in printing sales. The job still paid relatively well, a lot better than a start-up craft brewery in the 750-square-foot space in an unincorporated area of western Marin County, though it often took him on overnight flights to Los Angeles to OK printing runs. Those trips couldn't be allowed to interrupt the brewing, and the schedule, predictably enough, turned brutally exhausting. By June, he was ready to hire some help.

A line of refitted Grundy tanks, the cheaper surplus vessels from England that so many American craft brewers used. Courtesy of Tony Magee

The beer he was producing with the weird, seven-barrel electric brewhouse that was meant for Russia and the two converted Grundy tanks from England was of uneven quality by Magee's own admission: it ranged from vile to barely drinkable to wonderful to elegant to questionable-at-best. The wonderful and elegant batches afforded him enough growth; he was on pace to brew roughly one thousand barrels that first year, all of it draft via a keg machine he got for $5,000, and all of it personally distributed to around twenty accounts in San Francisco and the tourist-heavy Marin County coastal areas. The pale ales and ambers were stronger than much of what other brewers produced. Some of Lagunitas's beers would top 7 percent alcohol by volume—a number so high that more than a few retailers (even in the Bay Area, with its more sophisticated beer palate) refused to carry them. They were worried about selling too few glasses, as people would get drunk faster.

Lagunitas would eventually stake its claim to market share by being the first California craft brewery to make an India pale ale its signature beer. It was a hoppier homage to what had emerged in the last ten years as the prototype for what the new crop of beer writers was starting to call West Coast style: Ken Grossman's Sierra Nevada Pale Ale. What was West Coast style? It was bitterer beers made so by more hops, especially the Cascade variety that Anchor first used in craft brewing in 1975 for its Liberty Ale (Sierra Nevada also used Cascade in its pale ale). That was West Coast style defined in a nutshell (or hop cone, as it were): bitterer because of more hops. There were West Coast beers that weren't that hoppy, of course—porters and Anchor's Christmas Ale jump to mind—but when people began talking about a "West Coast style," they meant hoppier, bitterer beers.

And why the West Coast? No one really knew. One theory was that the East Coast breweries were closer to Europe and its milder English ales and Czech and German pilsners (air travel and the Midwest never seemed to throw doubt on this theory). Another held that the most verdant hop fields in America, including the Oregon one that birthed Cascade, were on the West Coast, so craft brewers could perhaps get their hands on fresh ones more cheaply and easily (which wasn't actually the case as, like with other commodities, a worldwide market set the prices and shipping costs were passed on to all brewers by vendors, not just those farther away from the source). In the end, it may have been nothing more than the West leading the way again in another national palatal shift. Just as the region had birthed the entire craft beer movement, it was now working up the thirst of Americans weaned on sugary sodas and sweet juices for a much bitterer libation. Whatever the reason, Magee decided Lagunitas would lead with an IPA. It would be the same hot, wet work to brew as it had been to produce the earlier styles, and for those first months it was Magee with nothing but constant worry as a companion.

It was eerie in a way, déjà vu all over again. Here was Magee in Marin County in the midst of a one-man operation that absorbed all the time he could give it to brew, bottle, and distribute, and it seemed so precarious as to invite concerns over his professional sanity. It seemed so like what Jack McAuliffe went through just over the county line nearly twenty years ago with New Albion. Why would anyone do this given the failure rate, the debt, the capital-intensive equipment that needed rejiggering, the increasingly crowded shelf space? These were still questions being asked despite the craft beer movement's leaps and bounds over the last few years in sales and production; despite its first cadre of genuine business stars, like Jim Koch, Pete Slosberg, Ken Grossman, and Fritz Maytag, who now received a seemingly obligatory reference in any article about the movement's growth; despite that financial backers had grown exponentially to the point where venture-capital firms and Wall Street traders would want in on pales ales and porters. Somehow it could still be a solitary man and a dream in the relative middle of nowhere. Magee explained it to himself as some kind of compulsion, one you could almost be embarrassed about having: "I didn't really ask anyone if this was a good idea or not. I knew what the answer would be. I read once where the entrepreneurial urge is, in its purest incarnation, a sort of seizure—nearly involuntary, like speaking in tongues or getting married in Vegas. It was like that for me, and this was the moment where reality and finance parted ways."

Lagunitas would grow, like other craft breweries in the 1990s, in an almost manic fashion, with the growth arrow pointed upward, never mind the financial strains; Magee couldn't find a bank, for instance, to lend him money for more equipment (a new fermenter became as necessary as those first hires). It was a strange, heady experience—to grow so fast while financial ruin seemed to stalk you like the rattle of Jacob Marley's chains. But that's what was happening for Magee and other start-ups. They might sell $20,000 worth of beer one month and then $30,000 the next; but with production costs running to 65 percent of the sales price for the beer, that meant frequent shortfalls when the money coming in from the sales didn't cover the costs. Bills to vendors—equipment, grains, hops—get pushed back; payroll becomes paramount; the work could be around the clock; debt and angel investors such as venture capitalists become ever more tempting. Magee came to call it "the tyranny of fast growth."

Others in the industry saw it more benignly. They saw more beer going out the door and a growing movement as evidenced by more brewing companies, bigger attendance figures at the Great American Beer Festival, more stories, more critics, more pilgrims pounding on the warehouse doors wanting a peek. Like they had wanted a peek at New Albion fifteen years before.

FINDING ROLE MODELS, DEFYING LABELS
Philadelphia; New Glarus, WI; Burlington, VT; Fort Collins, CO | 1991–1993

The billboards began popping up in the Philly area in the fall of 1993. "Philadelphia Is Putting Blondes Behind Bars," they read, a deliberate double entendre to grab the more lascivious minds in the City of Brotherly Love. The "blondes" actually referred to bottles of a new beer that would be hitting shelves and bars that same season. Called Red Bell Blonde Ale, it was the brainchild of a twenty-eight-year-old ex–college football player named James Bell. "I know bonds and stocks," Bell, an executive at a securities brokerage, told a reporter that October. "I'm starting to know beer."

He was an exuberant frontman for a brand that had investors, including Philadelphia Eagles safety Ray Ellis, before they even had a prototype to taste. Bell amassed more than $200,000 in start-up money and used $60,000 of that for the promotional push, which included not only the cryptic billboards but also radio ads, tasting parties, and PR (another slogan rolled out: "Put a blonde at your table"). The idea, the red-haired frontman explained, was to make Red Bell "the next Sam Adams."

And why not? Jim Koch and Rhonda Kallman's Boston Beer Company seemed as ubiquitous as any consumer product introduced in America in the last quarter-century. The company brewed 275,000 barrels in 1992 and was now distributed in nearly every state and the District of Columbia. The days of Koch and Kallman going door-to-door to cold-pitch skeptical merchants on Samuel Adams Boston Lager seemed so utterly distant as to have passed into folklore; Bell was not even of legal drinking age when the pair was doing that. Besides, nowadays, there were more than two hundred craft breweries and brewpubs in the United States, with more in the pipeline.

And what growth! Sales volumes for these breweries and brewpubs were jumping by double-digit percentages annually, leaving them, as the *New York*

Times noted, "heady as prom queens with their local popularity." The public's pivot to health foods and exercise, and to a growing willingness to pay a little bit more for what it considered fresher, more local products, only buoyed the confidence of fresh arrivals like Bell. You could make a killing in craft beer, whether you were an old hand like F. X. Matt, set in your century-old ways, or a newcomer to the industry like, well, like everybody! Hadn't Ken Grossman worked in bicycle shops before he started his homebrewing supply store in Chico and then cofounded Sierra Nevada? And hadn't Sierra Nevada's sales grown every year since the company's commercial launch in 1981?

Never mind the cautionary tales that recent flops such as Jersey Premium Lager told. Another contract brew—like Red Bell, through the Lion Brewery in Wilkes-Barre, Pennsylvania—it was started five years earlier by two Brooklyn wine salesmen and headquartered in Bordentown, New Jersey, thirty miles north of Philly. It captured quite the buzz upon its debut, selling its first thirty-five hundred cases in six weeks. But Jersey Premium Lager was out of business by the time Bell had his idea, as was William Penn, another contract-brewed brand distributed in the Philly area. As for other defunct craft breweries—if Koch and Kallman's early Boston Beer Company was folklore, then Jack McAuliffe's gravity brewing system in Sonoma, California, was science fiction. Who even believed it these days?

Anyway, there had been sturdier additions to the movement in just the last couple of years. Dan and Deb Carey had moved to New Glarus, in southern Wisconsin, to open a craft brewery named after the town in the spring of 1993, with the initial capacity to make three thousand barrels annually. Its line of beers, particularly a cherry-infused Christmas ale, had proven extraordinarily popular since. Dan Carey was one of Michael Lewis's pupils at UC-Davis and later studied at the Siebel Institute in Chicago; he went on to apprentice at a small brewery near Munich and then work as a production supervisor for Anheuser-Busch near Fort Collins, Colorado. Deb Carey grew up in Milwaukee, studied graphic design and marketing while at college in Montana, and raised the $400,000 for the brewery as a gift to her husband. The couple founded the brewery largely as a reaction to the homogenization they saw all around them; foodstuffs from mass producers (including Dan Carey's one-time employer Anheuser-Busch) struck them as boring. "It's like eating fast food every night of the week," he would tell people. It was time to join the change.* On nearly the same latitude as New Glarus, though more than twelve hundred miles away, Alan Pugsley had

---

* The Careys would adopt "Drink Indigenous" as their brewery's motto.

teamed with Fred Forsley in early 1994 to start a new brewery near the busy waterfront of Portland, Maine, called the Shipyard Brewing Company. Its origins actually dated from 1992, when Forsley, a Gray, Maine, native and real estate entrepreneur, opened the Kennebunkport Brewing Company and the Federal Jack's brewpub above it in that coastal town, with Pugsley consulting on the equipment setup and the beers.

Out in Colorado, ranchers George Stranahan and Richard McIntyre were partnering in a new brewery in Denver, in an old laundry building at Broadway and Market Street, that would capitalize on the success of Stranahan's Flying Dog Brewpub, which opened in Aspen in 1991. Stranahan was a polyglot—a rancher, a physicist, a photographer, an artist, an Ohio-raised heir to the Champion Spark Plug fortune—and nothing illustrated this more than where he got the name for his brewpub: from a painting of a flying dog in a hotel room in Rawalpindi, Pakistan, after climbing K2. Flying Dog's brands would become particularly noteworthy for label illustrations by the English artist Ralph Steadman and musings from legendary writer and local resident Hunter S. Thompson.

Back east, around the same time James Bell was erecting his billboards about blondes barely thirty-five miles away, two childhood friends, Ron Barchet and Bill Covaleski, were preparing to launch what they called the Victory Brewing Company in an old Pepperidge Farm cracker factory in Downingtown, Pennsylvania. Covaleski learned homebrewing from his father, and he gave Barchet a kit for Christmas in 1985. The two eventually fled their corporate jobs to study and work in brewing, including spells in Munich and at the Baltimore Brewing Company, a brewpub started by Dutchman Theo DeGroen in 1989. Their brewpub would open the day after Valentine's Day in 1996, with forty-two seats, a seventy-foot-long bar, and a brewhouse that produced twenty-five hundred barrels that first year.

While Barchet and Covaleski were training for what would become Victory, serial entrepreneur Alan Newman and Bob Johnson, who worked in the mail order business before turning to brewing, were putting the finishing touches on their Magic Hat Brewing Company in Burlington, Vermont. It would start production in late 1994 and expand into a new brewery in South Burlington within three years, by which time it would be one of eighteen craft breweries in the state. It was a stunning, decadelong march from the first one, Catamount Brewing Company in 1987, especially considering that Vermont had fewer than six hundred thousand residents.

Finally, in Fort Collins, Colorado, about an hour's drive north of Denver, Kim Jordan was passing her Fridays thusly: she would call customers in the morning and see what beers they needed; she would spend the afternoons distributing it by way of her Toyota Tercel station wagon, picking up her son from first grade along the way; he would do his homework in the passenger's seat while she finished deliveries in the early evening; then it was home for dinner; later she ran out again for a Kinko's run to make marketing materials like table tents. The rest of the workweek, she kept her day job as a social worker; her husband, Jeff Lebesch, kept his as an electrical engineer. In whatever free time he could create, however, he was the brewmaster for the New Belgium Brewing Company, which the couple started in 1991 out of their basement using old dairy equipment that Lebesch had rejiggered and around $60,000 in start-up costs. They did only bottles at first, in part so as not to compete with two other craft operations in Fort Collins, both then all-draft: Odell Brewing, started in 1989 by brother and sister Doug and Corkie Odell and Doug's wife, Wynne, in an old grain elevator downtown; and CooperSmith's brewpub, also downtown and opened shortly after Odell. Lebesch and Jordan's idea sprang from trips to Belgium in 1989 and 1991, where they bicycled about, imbibing what was then the world's most esteemed beer selection. New Belgium sold its first beers on June 28, 1991, at the recently launched Colorado Brewers Festival. Their production would near twenty thousand barrels annually by 1994—or less than what the 130-acre Anheuser-Busch plant just north of Fort Collins could churn out in a week.

New Belgium was the first craft brewery to stake its reputation on Belgian-style beers, including a rich, malty ale in the style of the Trappist monks of Belgium called Abbey Ale and a mildly bitter amber ale they called Fat Tire in honor of the bicycle trips. While it may not have been surprising that they went the Belgian route, it was not auspicious, either. Never mind that the beers were nothing like the watery lagers of Big Beer, they were also out of step with the more popular craft brands, like Pete's Wicked Ale, a brown ale; Sierra Nevada's hoppier pale ale; and Samuel Adams Boston Lager. So out of step were they that initially New Belgium literally defied categorization at the Great American Beer Festival down in Denver, failing to fit into any designated styles. In 1993, the festival added a catchall "Mixed, Specialty" category, and New Belgium's Abbey promptly won the gold. It was around that time, too, that Jordan ceased doing the distribution. Pregnant with their second child, she realized it probably wasn't best to be performing the door-to-door unloading.

Lebesch and Jordan were not models for James Bell in Philadelphia—nor were any of these other newer arrivals in the early 1990s. He instead took as his model Jim Koch, who made building a craft beer company seem if not easy at least fun in a pugnacious way, with his public takedowns of imports and his lessons on hops and barley. Bell was so confident he could mimic this model that he was planning to make his brand an export as well as a domestic: Red Bell Blonde Ale would be marketed as Buccaneer Gold in the Cayman Islands. The beer (or beers, as the dual brands would have it) was a light-bodied golden ale modeled on the German style Kölsch. Bell contracted with Lion to produce as much as seven thousand barrels annually, and he planned to offer the beer on Philly-area shelves at less than what a case of imports would cost (or a case of Samuel Adams); Red Bell would retail for under nineteen dollars a case. Its namesake was prepared for three years of losses but eventually expected to turn a $200,000 profit at a 38 percent return on investment. "If we can get people in Philadelphia emotional about the beer," Bell explained, "it will fly."

GHOSTS AROUND THE MACHINES
Washington, DC | 1993

The nation's "center of attention," as the front page of the *New York Times* put it, shifted to CNN's Washington studios on Tuesday, November 9, 1993.

That evening, in front of what would turn out to be the largest cable television audience of the twentieth century, vice president Al Gore and Texas billionaire Ross Perot were to debate the North American Free Trade Agreement on *Larry King Live*. NAFTA, heavily supported by the Clinton administration and Wall Street, would open up trade with Mexico and Canada, ostensibly lowering prices on consumer goods and boosting companies' bottom lines to spur more job creation. Opponents like Perot, as well as a sizable chunk of the nation's organized labor, worried NAFTA would mean the loss of American jobs to Mexico, where labor costs were significantly cheaper than in the United States. Perot had colorfully described the prospect as "a giant sucking sound" during the recent presidential race. The agreement was expected to come to a congressional vote before the end of the year. The debate took on the portentous aura of a major sporting event; only one side, it was assumed, could emerge the winner in the ring of public opinion. Not surprisingly, it turned contentious at times. The two men basically called each other liars, like in this exchange early on:

> *Perot:* Do you guys ever do anything but propaganda?
> *Gore:* Isn't it your business also?
> *Perot:* Would you even know the truth if you saw it?
> *Gore:* Oh, yes, I—
> *Perot:* I don't believe you would. You've been up here too long.

NAFTA did pass, and President Clinton signed it into law before the new year—not before the controversy loosed a national reckoning over America's manufacturing sector. Once the envy of the world, providing job security for tens of millions of Americans and goods that were sold domestically and exported to dozens of countries, the sector as of late had been frighteningly contracting. Industries previously thought impervious to major job losses were confronting them and the concomitant losses in disposable income and tax revenue from displaced workers. Steel, automobiles, textiles, furniture, industrial machinery, even the hardware of the computer industry—all were seeing jobs go elsewhere, partly because of greater automation but mostly because of companies chasing cheaper labor and proximity to recently stronger markets like Eastern Europe and South America. Between 1979 and 1992, the year before the NAFTA debate, America lost more than three million manufacturing jobs. And they weren't coming back; there simply weren't enough being created to overtake the losses, and all the growth was in the professional and service sectors, a trend that would continue into what was being called, hopefully, the Second American Century.

Soon enough, the Gore-Perot debate would recede into memory, and the manufacturing sector's ills would be overshadowed by the go-go economic optimism spurred by what was about to become one of the most bullish stock markets in American history. Dozens of stocks from a new technology were about to become the surest things. As odd as it seemed, this boat would lift craft beer, too.

CHERRY BREW AND NAKED HOCKEY
Manhattan | 1992–1993

Sam Calagione kept going. He had sterilized two dozen twenty-two-ounce bomber bottles by heating them in his apartment oven for twenty minutes—and they had promptly stuck to the rug he placed them on. No time to stop, though, lest bacteria wrest the better of his first five-gallon batch of homebrew and sour everything. He poured the beer, a pale ale infused with cherries, into the bottles; capped them; and then dragged them and the rug they were stuck to toward a dark corner to age. A week later, he cut the bottles loose from the rug, melted remains sticking to the bottoms of each, and put them in the refrigerator. A tasting party shortly thereafter proved the so-dubbed Cherry Brew a success and straightened Calagione's circuitous route toward craft beer.

It was one that commenced as these things sometimes do: with copious amounts of Big Beer poured down teenage throats. Calagione was a wild child growing up in the north-central Massachusetts town of Greenfield. For one thing, he had a side gig at his tony prep school selling to classmates beer that he had finagled from what he would remember as "sympathetic western Massachusetts libertarian hippies." Such endeavors—and others that included naked ice hockey and sitting cross-legged atop a Winnebago going sixty on its way to crash the prom—got him kicked out of school weeks shy of graduation. His father, an oral surgeon who made wine at home, was not amused. Still, Calagione managed an English degree from Muhlenberg College in Allentown, Pennsylvania, and went to New York City in 1992 to study writing at Columbia, with some acting on the side (muscular and tall, with a square jaw and thick, dark-brown hair, Calagione had done some postcollegiate modeling, too).

It was in Gotham that he graduated from Big Beer to craft. He got a job waiting tables at a Mexican restaurant a couple of blocks from the gates of Columbia in the Morningside Heights neighborhood of upper Manhattan.

While the restaurant could morph into one of the neighborhood's rowdier college bars by nightfall, not everyone was clamoring for Corona: the restaurant was one of the few in the city then with a menu, albeit small, of fine beers, including craft brands like Sierra Nevada Bigfoot Barleywine and Anchor Liberty Ale as well as choicer imports like Chimay Red, brewed in a Trappist monastery in southern Belgium. Calagione befriended the restaurant owner behind the menu, Joshua Mandel, and that led not only to the Cherry Brew but also to an encyclopedic knowledge of craft beer. He became blissfully insufferable on the subject; the Cherry Brew tasting provided him one such soapbox:

> The beer was the hit of the party. More than that I had created something unique that people enjoyed. I had given people something that, at that moment, they really needed. That evening I spent as much time as my friends could stand talking about all the different beers in the world, the ingredients used in making them, and all of the small breweries that were popping up around the country.

Later in the evening, as the Cherry Brew flowed and Calagione settled from his soapbox, thoughts crept across his young mind. He likely would never write the Great American Novel. He could, however, produce an interesting beer that others might enjoy. That was artistry in itself, one that could reward risk taking and coloring outside the lines as much as any other medium of expression. Yes, of course it could! Calagione stood up and declared to those still in his apartment: he would become a brewer.

The next day, head foggy but memory clear, he walked several blocks from his apartment in Chelsea to the main New York Public Library in Midtown, its stone lions standing stern guard against ignorance on either side of the entrance, and began reading up on brewing. Crucially for the craft beer movement and for himself, Calagione had little idea what he was doing, both business- and brewing-wise. He knew enough about the ingredients of beer to lay down a basic formula for a little zing to walk on (in the case of his first batch, which he made with cherries from a local bodega).

Calagione was not nearly far enough removed from his restless youth, however, to sit intellectually still for strict recipes. It was the Winnebago and the naked hockey and the underage-beer-selling racket all over again—rule-breaking time.

IN PRIME TIME
San Francisco | 1994

Pete Slosberg had not counted on the cop. One of the executives who ran the ad agency that Pete's Brewing had hired, Goodby, Silverstein and Partners, had told him to show up at a red-draped table that was set up on a sidewalk in downtown San Francisco and stick a radio piece in his ear. Slosberg did what he was told and sat down at the table beneath a sign that read, in blocky letters, PICTURE WITH THE REAL PETE $1.00. Two rows of bottles of Pete's Wicked Ale stood to his right. Slosberg, never a natural salesman, was wearing a dark short-sleeved shirt in breezy, cool weather, adding to the discomfort of the odd setup. The executive from the ad agency began talking in his ear, telling him what to call out to unsuspecting passers-by as the cameras rolled.

"Morning! How'd you like a picture taken with the actual Pete, maker of Pete's Wicked Ale?"

Nothing. Just an awkward shake of the head.

"How would you like your picture with the real Pete?" "No." "No!" "Nah."

The conceit of the commercial was clear: you might be able to recognize a Clydesdale at quick glance or identify a Miller commercial blindfolded just by its opening banter, but the namesake and cofounder of one of the fastest-growing companies in the United States—beer or otherwise—was practically invisible.* If there was any doubt, enter the cop. Or that's what Slosberg thought. Unbeknownst to him, it was an actor dressed as a cop. He stood over Slosberg and asked him if he was serving anyone the beer. Did he have a permit for the table? How long was he going to be in the middle of the sidewalk anyway? Slosberg stammered some explanations as the earpiece fell stone silent. The commercial ended with the actor/cop sauntering away,

---

* People did, in fact, stop during Slosberg's session at the table; crowds even gathered at some points. That was not the effect the ad agency was going for, and it instructed Slosberg through the earpiece to disperse them (per Slosberg, *Beer for Pete's Sake*, 136).

wishing Slosberg a good day and swinging two bottles of Wicked Ale next to his holster.

The ads—which also included one where Slosberg, again at a red-draped table on a sidewalk, autographed photos that were then hastily crumpled and tossed by their takers—aired in 1994 in major markets like Seattle, Boston, San Francisco, and Minneapolis during prime-time hits like *Seinfeld, Northern Exposure,* and *Melrose Place.* They were watersheds for craft beer: the movement's first national television advertising campaign. And though relatively low-budget—Pete's account with Goodby, Silverstein was $1 million and Anheuser-Busch eventually hired them away with a $31 million offer—they were impactful, both financially and creatively. Stuart Elliott, the longtime advertising reporter for the *New York Times,* named the Pete's campaign as one of the year's top ten, right up there with pushes for Nike, Ikea, Bud Light, and McDonald's; the same article also listed campaigns for Budweiser and Bud Dry as among the ten worst. Financially, the spots were helping lift Pete's to $44 million in profits in 1994. The company, which was now led day-to-day out of Palo Alto by former Seagram marketer Mark Bozzini, would by the end of the year sell 2.5 million cases of beer in forty-one states, no small feat for an operation that distributed just ten thousand cases in 1988, mostly in the West.

For all the money and the plaudits, the ads' conceit still spoke to fundamental tenets of the American craft movement that went all the way back to Fritz Maytag at Anchor in the 1960s: independent and traditional. Slosberg and Mark Bronder's Pete's Brewing, along with Jim Koch and Rhonda Kallman's Boston Beer, were growing exponentially compared to their competitors; Boston Beer was by now actually America's fourteenth-largest brewer, period. Together, not even ten years after each of their starts, the two companies accounted for well over one-third of all craft beer produced in the United States, and they were the only ones with widespread advertising. But Boston Beer and Pete's always felt the need to pay more than lip service—and gladly so—to the ideas that they were small, independently run operations compared with Big Beer and that they brewed with only classic ingredients as dictated by old-world norms.

The two sometimes competed to seem the most David against the Goliaths. In the run-up to the thirteenth annual Great American Beer Festival in Denver in 1994, Koch and Slosberg argued through the media the merits of medals and debated the reasons for their brands' success. The GABF, which would draw twelve hundred beers from 265 breweries (up from 207 the year before), was prepared to bestow 102 medals in thirty-four categories, a far cry from the consumer preference poll that had stood alone at the earliest festivals. To Koch, whose Boston Lager and Boston Lightship swept four of the final five consumer preference polls, the medals were well and fine (Boston Beer had captured seventeen so far).* But the quality alone moved his beers—which meant that his marketing, including radio spots with his voice that had been airing for years, mattered little as well. "Industry writers can't get it out of their heads that it's not marketing that makes you buy a beer," he told the *Denver Post.* "It's because you like the taste. The people who will survive are the brewers who have the highest-quality standards." The medals mattered a little more to Slosberg, who noted to the same paper that Koch's indifference to marketing didn't stop him from advertising. "It's the judgment of your peers, it's an accomplishment," Slosberg said of the GABF medals. "We like to think people are impressed by medals."

Jim Koch in a tasting room of the Boston Beer Company's brewery in Jamaica Plain, Boston. Courtesy of the Boston Beer Company

No matter how they moved so much beer in an industry still dominated by the likes of Anheuser-Busch, Miller, and Coors, the sizes of Boston Beer and Pete's were together the single, biggest boost to craft beer since perhaps

* The seventeen included the consumer preference polls.

the legalization of homebrewing at the federal level in 1978. Simply put, the two were able to put craft beer in more consumer hands than any other thing or combination of things, with the possible exception of Michael Jackson's Dicovery Channel series. It was not just the radio ads or the national television spots: there were bar and restaurant promotions manifested in thousands of cozies, stickers, coasters, sandwich signs, banners and boards; T-shirts and glassware; stunts like Koch sitting over a dunking booth filled with Boston Lager or Slosberg in a tub of bottles of Wicked Ale; Slosberg presenting Pete Wilson with a Pete's jacket in front of reporters at his inauguration as California's governor; Boston Beer in the White House Mess and on Air Force One (the youthful new president, Bill Clinton, was said to prefer Samuel Adams); holiday tie-ins, like Pete's advice for surviving Valentine's Day through beer ("Skip the fattening desserts and instead indulge in a good beer with your valentine"); and both Slosberg and Koch holding forth to audiences big and small—or to a single reporter—on the nuances of craft beer and the brewing process. They both subscribed to the idea that a rising tide would lift all boats, that greater consumer knowledge about craft beer meant greater sales for everybody in the industry, themselves included. Their efforts were not universally appreciated. "I resent it," Bill Owens of the now-legendary Buffalo Bill's brewpub in Hayward was known to say. "Those people are just top-notch salesmen."

Neither Slosberg nor Koch could get out from under the accusation that contract brewing was not really craft brewing. It was true that they had avoided the capital costs of starting a physical brewery, costs that were prone to rise with each expansion and ones that had already helped fell many a predecessor.

Koch, for his part, had opened a brewery in early 1989 at the old Haffenreffer location in Boston for research and development as well as tours; he placed inside it the cornerstone from the old Louis Koch Brewery that he, his father, and Charlie Papazian had found in St. Louis. The Boston brewery, located as it was just off the region's subway system and with powerful champions like Governor Michael Dukakis, who was at the ribbon-cutting, proved remarkably popular with visitors and helped revitalize a run-down area of the city (one of Boston Beer's earliest neighbors was given to killing cats and mounting their bodies on stakes; it was that bad).

But most of Koch's beer was still brewed elsewhere, and all of Slosberg's had been brewed thousands of miles away from the company's nondescript offices since 1988, near Stanford University, although the company would talk about plans for a brewery, perhaps in Northern California. Still, in the early 1990s, there was absolutely no ignoring the sales success of Boston Beer and Pete's and the impact of that success on the movement. It had upped the game just as more players joined—and more spectators than ever watched.

CRITICAL MASS
Durham, NC | 1995

I n the summer of 1995, the Discovery Channel released a CD-ROM based on Michael Jackson's series *The Beer Hunter*. The disc, which retailed for forty dollars, contained Jackson's top twenty-four American beers (one-eighth were from Anchor), as well as history lessons on brewing that went all the way back to ancient Mesopotamia; there was even a section on "how hobbyists can set up their own home-brewing operations." You could simply pop the disc into your computer—PCs only to start, available soon for Macintoshes—sit back, and watch the world's leading beer authority explain the American craft beer movement with a mix of still photos and short videos. One more thing: you would need at least eight megabytes of RAM for it to run properly.

The CD -ROM, though primitive by today's standards, was light-years beyond the fifteenth-century technology behind Jackson's seminal 1977 book, *The World Guide to Beer*. The disc illustrated not only the craft beer movement's toe dipping into the computer age but also the confidence of producers and platforms like the Discovery Channel in the consumer market for such products. The CD-ROM, then, was not so much a natural progression for Jackson's work—articles to book to software—but one in tandem with a growing awareness of craft beer. Jackson was not the only shepherd of this new awareness, even if he was by the 1990s the acknowledged master of the beer-writing medium. Frank Prial, a beat reporter who became the *New York Times*' first regular wine critic in 1972, wrote on and off about beer. Robert Hillman, a Harvard MBA turned wine and travel writer, also wrote occasionally on the subject, most thoroughly in his 1984 *Gourmet Guide to Beer*. In that book, amid guidance on how to serve, taste, and store beer, Hillman rated five hundred different ones. Only four American beers rated his highest accolade, five mugs: Anchor Steam, New Amsterdam Amber, and Sierra Nevada's porter and stout. James D. Robertson, who had been writing beer guides since the late 1970s, continued to write about the subject, particularly for *All About Beer* magazine, where his discursive, hyper-descriptive reviews could contain paragraphs that stretched an entire page column; and books such as his 1982's *Connoisseur's Guide to Beer* enjoyed updated editions.

Other figures from the earlier days continued to produce criticism and exegesis on the small, but growing universe they'd helped nurture. These figures included Fred Eckhardt, who continued to write his regular columns for the *Oregonian* in Portland; Byron Burch, who updated his *Quality Brewing* for a 1994 reissue; Bill Owens, the brewpub owner who, throughout the 1980s and into the next decade, became a prolific chronicler of the brewing trade from a business perspective; and Charlie Papazian, perhaps the most well-known (and oft-quoted) American expert on the movement, whose Association of Brewers now published the *New Brewer* bimonthly as well as *Zymurgy* and whose *The Complete Joy of Homebrewing* would get its own CD-ROM in 1998. The regular newspaper reader, too, about now would have noticed the articles on the state of craft beer in America that seemed to coincide every autumn with the association's Great American Beer Festival.

Daniel Bradford, the marketing maestro behind so many of those articles from the early 1980s onward, had left the Association of Brewers at the start of the new decade. It and the American Homebrewers Association were growing rapidly, and Bradford figured he was not the person to be Papazian's right hand anymore. Besides, he had gotten married. His wife, Julie Johnson, held a PhD in evolutionary biology—she had studied with Jane Goodall in Tanzania—and had accepted a faculty position at Duke University in Durham, North Carolina; the couple went east. Durham sat sandwiched between the North Carolina capital of Raleigh and the quintessential college town of Chapel Hill, equal parts a technology and academic boomtown and a gritty city struggling with the decline of the tobacco and textile industries. And the beer sucked. For Bradford, who only a few short years before had stood lovingly alone amid the hundred or so best beers in America before that first day of the GABF in 1987, central North Carolina offered little in the way of libations— Uli Bennewitz had opened the Weeping Radish along the coast a few years earlier, but otherwise there were no other craft brewers in the longest state east of the Mississippi. Bradford enjoyed introducing himself to the couple's new friends, many culled from the academic community surrounding Duke. What did he do? Well, he was the cofounder of the Great American Beer Festival. He was also the owner of a magazine called *All About Beer*. Bradford had stepped into a deal to buy the magazine and threw himself into running out of his Durham house what had become the premier glossy publication for the craft beer movement largely by default. There were no real competitors on the consumer side and the magazine seemed to have succeeded despite itself. For one thing, McMullen Publishing, an Anaheim, California, outfit that had bought the magazine from original owners Mike Bosak and his partners in 1982, had continued the practice of selling editorial space. Each issue's editorial angles, reviews especially, became suspect. Bosak reacquired *All About Beer* in 1990, and three years later Daniel Bradford bought it from him. Bradford stopped the practice of selling editorial inches, due partly to advice they got from beer writers such as Randy Mosher.

Mosher was part of a third wave of beer writers and critics that also included Stan Hieronymus, Jay Brooks, Lew Bryson, Don Russell, Alan Eames, Jack Erickson, Stephen Beaumont, Gregg Smith, Lucy Saunders, and Bill Brand. They came of age in the 1960s and 1970s; were introduced to better beer in the 1980s, usually through a friend or through happenstance and often via imports, not craft brands; had other jobs, usually related to writing; were all homebrewers or at least familiar with homebrewing; and were all enthusiastic about the growth in craft beer that they found themselves covering by the 1990s. They each became, like Jackson nearly two decades before and Eckhardt before that, part evangelist and part journalist.

Mosher's first big beer work was *The Brewer's Companion: A Source-Book for the Small-Scale Brewer*, published in 1993; he did his research in the pre-Internet way, traipsing to libraries and exchanging photocopies with other brewing enthusiasts through the regular mail or at festivals.

Hieronymus, a veteran newspaperman (when he started in the trade, the minimum wage was $1.25), turned to beer writing along with his wife, Daria Labinsky, in the early 1990s, after the two chucked their full-time gigs in favor of traveling the country while freelancing and running a newsletter about concert tours and festivals. By 1993, he was pretty much writing about beer full-time; he became editor of RealBeer.com, one of the first websites on the beat, the following year.

Bill Brand was for years a reporter and then editor at the *Oakland Tribune*, and he covered considerably soberer subjects like the Unabomber and the Columbine school shooting. He started a newsletter called *What's On Tap* in 1994, and it eventually became a column for the *Tribune* and other Bay Area papers.

Jack Erickson was a former congressional aide and speechwriter who wrote on a variety of subjects before discovering England's Campaign for Real Ale during a vacation. His *Star-Spangled Beer: A Guide to America's New Microbreweries and Brewpubs*, published in 1987, was the first stab at a written history of the movement; in 1995, he launched *The Erickson Report*, a regular newsletter about the industry.

Gregg Smith would also carve out a prominent role as a beer historian, and not just for craft ones; his *Beer in America*, published in 1998, delved into the libation's nation-building role in what the book's subtitle called "The Early Years—1587–1840."

Lucy Saunders was a pioneer for women beer writers and one of the first overall to focus on the relationship of craft beer with fine food: Time-Life published her recipe and pairing guide, *Cooking with Beer*, in 1996.

Don Russell was a corruption-scooping general-assignment reporter at the *Philadelphia Daily News*. He began writing a regular beer column under the moniker Joe Sixpack in 1996, after earlier attempts at beer writing convinced his editor there was an audience for it.

A native of southeastern Pennsylvania who went into the navy and was stationed for a time in New York City in the 1970s, Jay Brooks published *The Bars of Santa Clara County: A Beer Drinker's Guide to Silicon Valley*, about the beer scene in his adopted Northern California, in 1991.

Lew Bryson, who was also from southeastern Pennsylvania, worked as a librarian before turning to beer writing in 1995; like other scribes in the third wave (and like Jackson, who became a renowned expert on whiskey, and Eckhardt, who became the same on sake), Bryson would also write about spirits, particularly whiskey.

A native of central Canada, Stephen Beaumont thought he knew everything about beer by his mid-teens, only to discover his ignorance while slinging drinks at a pub in midtown Toronto, Ontario; like his fellow beer writers after their own epiphanies, he would thereafter become a sponge for American beer arcana, at one point writing nine regular columns for eight different publications at the same time, with a particular focus, like Saunders, on beer's place among food.

Alan Eames's path was the most peripatetic of the bunch. A one-time magician, he ran a successful art gallery in Manhattan, a liquor store in Massachusetts legendary for its beer selection in the 1970s, and later the Portland, Maine, pub Three Dollar Dewey's, where he insisted on quiet, refined enjoyment of good beer, often buying the Sunday *New York Times* to spread among the tables and railings. The pub exercised immense influence on the etiquette of future beer bars: these were not to be loud nightclubs or lusty singles joints. He also did consulting for companies such as Pete's Brewing, Boston Beer, and D. L. Geary (David Geary was a regular at Three Dollar Dewey's). All along, Eames wrote about beer, appearing on radio and television to explain his research—he would visit forty-four countries in swashbuckling pursuit of it, earning the sobriquet "The Indiana Jones of Beer." His best-known work came in early 1995 with the publication of *The Secret Life of Beer*, a thunderstorm of trivia covering centuries of the drink.

It was Jay Brooks's approach, however, that best illustrates how the third wave of critics came at beer: in specific, drilled-down contexts. In the cases of Brooks, Bryson, Russell, and Brand, these were largely geographical; in the case of Hieronymus, who would write popular guides to Belgian beer, the context was stylistic. Gone were the sweeping logs of Jackson; unnecessary were the impartations of a wide yet long-forgotten body of knowledge provided by the likes of Eckhardt, Burch, and Papazian. People had a sense of what was going on now. It was time to sort out the additions and subtractions, all the changes that seemed to affect the craft beer movement every month. The new wave wanted to make sense of a movement that might now offer consumers and hobbyists several brands and vendors to choose from just in their hometowns; these critics could assist those who wanted to start homebrewing but couldn't distill the wealth of instruction that had accumulated in the last several years. The options could be baffling and the information hard to get in these years just before the World Wide Web.

Finally, the new critics were having fun. It was hard not to, and it was part of their branding (who wouldn't want to get paid to write about beer?). Plus, they knew they were fairly early to the party, able to enjoy a vantage that would simply not be available to later arrivals. Beer in America had never had so many writers. Hieronymus's New Beer Rules numbers five and six formed a kind of working rubric for everybody: "It *is* only beer," and "The best beer was in the empty glass." And here was Russell with some buddies on an "Ultimate Beer Run" on Super Bowl Sunday to a legendary suburban Philly beer store called Shangy's, run by an Iranian American family named Hadian:

> For the next 90 minutes, we wander the aisles, and Hadian answers every question. He tells us of the entrepreneur who imports only those rated as the best by beer guru Michael Jackson. . . . He even points us away from ordinary brews like Oldenburg of Fort Mitchell, Ken., advising us to try better brews from Weeping Radish of Roanoke Island, N.C., and Smuttynose of Portsmouth, N.H.
>
> He claims about 75 percent of his sales are specialty beers, but just then a customer walks in and asks for a case of god-awful Coors.

"What can I say?" he shrugs. "The Philadelphia region is the biggest Coors Light market in the world."

Now it is time to make some tough decisions. We settle on 10 cases for about $380. We'd have bought more if Eric, in an uncommonly selfish act, [hadn't] declined to give up his seat for three more cases of ale. But before we stomp on the gas, a quick question.

"Hey, Nima. What's Shangy mean?" He smiles. "It's Iranian, for 'happy.'" Ooooooo, beer!

Bradford's newly acquired and editorially improved *All About Beer* joined two other glossy magazines, both published by brewpub legend Bill Owens: the higher-brow, graphically ambitious *BeeR* and the venerable trade quarterly *American Brewer*, which Owens acquired in 1986.* All three titles brought together the best-known beer writers, sometimes in the same issue, whatever their vintage. Eckhardt became a columnist at *All About Beer*, often penning first-person essays full of the sort of name-dropping earned from nearly thirty years covering beer; and Jackson was a regular contributor to *All About Beer* and *BeeR*, writing in his usual erudite fashion about beers both local and exotic. Burch showed up in both those titles, too, as did Bradford's old boss, Papazian, either as a contributor on homebrewing or as a source on the industry, his Association of Brewers having become not only the coordinator of its grandest festivals and (not without controversy) the definer of its styles but also a lobbying force in state capitals and Washington.

While barrels of ink were being spilt upon dead trees on behalf of brewing, breweries, and brewpubs by the mid-1990s, another medium was emerging that would prove markedly more influential. When it came to craft beer, it would be democratic, dictatorial, illuminating, confusing, accurate to a tee and rife with errors all at the same instantaneous time. At first, it was cumbersome to read and nothing much to look at—Bill Owens's art would most certainly not work with it. For consumers, there was a considerable barrier to entry, too, compared with the cost of a magazine or even a book. You had to have a computer or at least access to one—and that computer had to have access to the Internet. Still, for those who mastered it, the new technology provided a fount of fast information and exchange, rendering not only quaint but obsolete those paper newsletters of early homebrewing clubs

---

* Owens changed the name from *Amateur Brewer* as both the magazine and the movement became more professionalized.

like the Maltose Falcons—and, for those paying attention, it drew a bead on the print publications.

Daniel Bradford in 1994, a year after he took control of *All About Beer* magazine. © Durham Morning-Hearld Co., Used with permission

Rob Gardner started the first Internet site for the craft beer consumer in late 1986 out of his home in Fort Collins, Colorado. He set up and ran manually from his computer an e-mail newsletter, called *The Brewsletter*, that would grow by the decade's close into the *Home Brew Digest*, a forum for homebrewers and beer enthusiasts worldwide. Gardner, to keep up with the subscriber volume, wrote code that could handle routine tasks such as dealing with those subscriptions and sending out the digest; it had quickly moved beyond what could be run manually. Most of the subscribers were college students or staff (thus the access to Internet connections). And, difficult as it is to imagine, there were none of the graphical bells and whistles of today's web; the digest was largely an all-text, black-and-white compendium of messages that Gardner had received or that had been e-mailed to the subscriber list. The site's exchanges were also regularly reposted on other early Internet beer forums, like AOL's Food and Drink Network and brewing forums hosted by Prodigy and CompuServe. The exchanges usually followed a question-and-answer format, with someone from Massachusetts, say, sending in a list and someone from New York sending in a correction—as happened on Halloween of 1988, shortly after 5:00 PM Eastern time, when someone from the Rensselaer Polytechnic Institute in Troy, New York, wrote:

> Subject: nice list, changes needed
>   hey thanks to jmiller for putting together that micro and brew-pub list. Please note that Bill Newman's brewery is now defunct. He contracts through F. X. Matt in Utica. You stand a better chance of getting a response by writing them. I know I long ago gave up waiting for him to return my calls.

Or this message on Veterans Day of the same year, which showed just how far and wide the movement had reached. It came from someone at Clemson University in South Carolina, which had yet to legalize homebrewing at the state level and which contained no craft breweries as of 1990:

> Subject: Ginger Beer/Honey Beer
>   Does anyone have a recipe for ginger beer or for a honey beer? A friend has recommended that I try both of these, but neither one of us has a recipe. I am fairly new to this hobby, so any general advice would also be appreciated.

THE POTATO-CHIP EPIPHANY

Kailua-Kona, HI | 1993–1995

At the Association of Brewers' annual craft brewers conference in Austin, Texas, in April 1995, Charlie Papazian asked the ballroom of attendees how many were planning or wanted to open a brewery but had not yet done so. Most of the people in the ballroom raised their hands. As we have seen, the craft beer movement was growing across the country, making its way into areas that would have seemed commercially inhospitable—or just plain bizarre, as in the case of Geoff and Marcy Larson's Alaskan Brewing Company in Juneau. Another such area: the other noncontiguous state.

Cameron Healy grew up in Bend, a small city in central Oregon. His father, Bill, had moved everyone there in the 1950s to run the family furniture store, but Bill soon turned to a new line of work in the windy taluses of the nearby Willamette National Forest by opening a ski resort. Mount Bachelor became one of the nation's leading ski resorts when it came to technology, with high-speed chairlifts and a computerized ticket system. Cameron Healy worked at the resort until he left Bend to attend the University of Oregon in Eugene. It was there his story became a kind of microcosm of the 1960s. While pursuing a social sciences major, he took up yoga, converted to Sikhism, and changed his name to Nirbhao Singh Khalsa. In the process, the sleepy-eyed Oregonian, with curly hair running from the top of a prominent forehead to just above his collar, swore off alcohol and simplified his life, tilting it to revolve around the yoga commune. How to help pay for that commune, however, and yet not compromise its back-to-the-earth ethos? Healy invested $1,000 in a bakery called the Golden Temple, which opened in Eugene in 1972, and produced exactly what you might expect: whole grain breads, granola, and other healthy, natural foods of a sort that seemed novel in an America with an increasingly homogenized cuisine.

After a year and a half, Healy donated the bakery to the commune and moved on to his next venture, one as crunchy as the last but savvy. He knew he and his compatriots would age, a wave of baby boomers growing old with ideals and practices picked up in college towns like Eugene throughout the nation. Those practices would need to be serviced and those ideals respected; and both would have to be done in a convenient, uncomplicated way as the baby boomers traded "Get Clean for Gene" pins and George Harrison LPs for bourgeois respectability in car-dependent communities. Healy started a natural food distribution company out of Salem, Oregon, that grew by 1978 into a natural-food manufacturing concern called the N. S. Khalsa Company. The company, which started with a $10,000 bank loan and with Healy selling roasted nuts, trail mixes, and cheeses to outlets along Interstate 5 out of an old van, grew by the late 1980s into one of the most successful natural-food brands in the country. Its signature became the potato chip, and it's through that, unbeknownst to the teetotaling Healy, that his story began to intertwine with the craft beer movement.

Americans loved their potato chips, Healy knew, and, through a wave of consolidations that saw smaller firms gobbled up by larger ones, most were produced through a handful of companies by the 1980s. The largest potato chip producer in the United States, Frito-Lay, was formed by the merger of two different firms and grew to forty-six production plants by the time of its own 1965 merger with Pepsi-Cola to form PepsiCo. While their nineteenth-century predecessors might have been produced by hand one slice at a time—the potato chip was said to have been invented by a chef at a Saratoga Springs, New York, resort—those of the late twentieth century were anything but. The chips produced in Frito-Lay's dozens of plants were deep-fried by the hundreds per minute, laden with trans fats, heavily salted, and sealed in cellophane bags for shipment to all corners of the country. Americans inhaled them; potato chips reigned as the nation's top snack food by the end of the 1980s, with sales growth twice that of any other. But consumers had little idea of the chips' origins and couldn't care less about what obtuse ingredients preserved them on their journeys to supermarket shelves and vending machines. If I could create a distinctive-enough product, Healy thought, there would be a mystique about them.

He set about in 1982 crafting some more natural potato chip prototypes in his home nut roaster using only Oregon-grown potatoes. The chips found a market: N. S. Khalsa's sales hit $3 million within two years of those first home batches, mostly because of what it called its all-natural potato chips, made with local spuds, no trans fats, and, eventually, all organic ingredients. It was certainly different from what consumers were used to in a snack food, though it was not without its pratfalls. The small batches didn't always work out taste-wise, and Healy's company found itself pulling some bags from shelves because the quality was bad. Gradually they reached the upper end of the manufacturing learning curve, turning out consistently good batches that found their ways first into natural-food stores and then into other retailers— and without having to buy shelf space. The sales of Kettle Foods (the company changed its name in 1988) were largely due to word of mouth, consumers nudging one another about this curious addition to an American staple. The company opened plants in Ohio, Ireland, and England, and, in 1993, it scaled a personal summit for a Healy: revenues beat those of his father Bill's ski resort. Cameron Healy started looking around for something else to do.

Luckily, he had started drinking again. A 1987 trip through northern Europe introduced him to Belgian beers in particular, and he had long been familiar with the American craft beer brands on the West Coast. Here was a whole segment of an industry that seemed to approach its production the same way he had approached the production of potato chips and other foodstuffs since the 1970s; it even had the same mystique about it. Craft beer brands had colorful owners and local foci in their production. Not only that, but also just about every brand, even the contract brewers, chose to anchor their imagery to their localities and to stress the craftsmanship, the natural ingredients, the wholesomeness of their ingredients. Healy started assembling a business plan for a craft brewery. His son, Spoon Khalsa, had the perfect spot: Hawaii's Big Island. Father visited son there over Thanksgiving 1993 to kick the entrepreneurial tires all over again.

The state did have a brewing history that stretched back to the early nineteenth century with the arrival of the first Europeans; but any breweries it had going were wrecked by Prohibition in 1920 as surely as it wrecked breweries on the mainland. A handful of breweries reemerged after Repeal; the Hawaii Brewing Corporation's new location at Kapiolani Boulevard and Cooke Street in Honolulu, which opened in May 1934, was the first brewery to be completely constructed west of the Rockies post-Prohibition. The brand it produced, Primo, however, became the last one standing in Hawaii by the 1960s—and it was made under the aegis of Chicago-based Schlitz. On May 15, 1979, Schlitz shipped the last cases of Hawaii-brewed Primo and transferred production to a plant in Los Angeles; the moves marked the end of commercial brewing in the state.

Aloysius Klink and Klaus Haberich brought brewing back to Hawaii in the summer of 1986 with their Pacific Brewing Company's Maui Lager, proudly brewed according to the strictures of the German beer purity law, the Reinheitsgebot. Their beer was a hit. The brewery sold more than four thousand barrels annually after its first year, including in California, and garnered regular media attention that could not resist noting the barley, hops, and yeast came from Belgium, Germany, and Canada, while the water was Hawaiian. Still, Pacific Brewing collapsed in late 1990. It seems to have vanished without much of a trace, its closure likely due at least in part to shipping costs, including distribution to and on the mainland.

This was the situation facing Cameron Healy and Spoon Khalsa when they launched the Kona Brewing Company. It was a potential consumer gold mine—Resorts! Luaus! Tourists, locals, more tourists!—though isolated geographically, even more so than the Larsons' Alaskan Brewing Company. Healy saw opportunity in this isolation. Hawaii had no commercial breweries after Pacific Brewing; here was an opportunity to repeat the successful formula of the potato chips: craft on a small scale a foodstuff that can appeal to those looking to pivot away from its mass-produced versions and to enjoy something with local roots. It was a chance to try out the locavore approach with no real competition. Healy believed they had the winds at their back.

THE BREWPUBS BOOM
Denver; Palo Alto, CA | 1993–1995

C ameron Healy and Spoon Khalsa's Kona Brewing Company launched operations in an old newspaper pressroom in Kailua-Kona, on the western edge
of Hawaii's Big Island, in the spring of 1994; its first beers, Pacific Golden
Ale and Fire Rock Pale Ale, rolled out in (mostly) kegs and bottles on February 14, 1995. Healy brought in Mattson Davis from Portland, Oregon, as
the CEO and president within two years, and the brewery enjoyed steady
though modest growth with three thousand barrels produced in 1997. It
didn't make a profit for the first few years and had to battle a state government that taxed brewers like they were going out of style (which, of course,
they had been): Hawaii charged brewers ninety-two cents for every gallon
of beer produced. Kona would not move into the financial clear until it
entered the brewpub business late in the decade. That also meant tango-
ing with the state, which capped production for brewpubs at five thousand
barrels annually.

Brewpubs were very much in vogue by then nationally. In 1993, 70 brewpubs opened; in 1994, 101 (only six closed); and more than 360 were in
operation by the spring of 1995, besting the number of craft breweries by
more than three to two. These numbers were helped in no small part by
legal changes in big states such as Florida and Texas,* and the ranks now
included legendary pioneers such as Bill Owens's Buffalo Bill's in Hayward,
California; Bert Grant's in Yakima, Washington; and the Mendocino Brewing Company's Hopland off Highway 101 north of San Francisco alongside
appendages of the most notable early standalone breweries. Not least among
these was Ken Grossman's Sierra Nevada, which opened a brewpub next to
its new Chico, California, brewery in 1989 that quickly became popular not
only with the locals but also with hikers, bikers, and sundry fellow travelers
venturing north from San Francisco.

---

* Texas joined forty-four other states and DC in legalizing brewpubs.

However prolific brewpubs might have become, they were still new enough in some places to produce firsts, just like breweries. John Hickenlooper was a Colorado geologist who had just gotten laid off from an oil company—with two years' severance—when he visited his brother in Berkeley, California; they went to the Triple Rock Brewery and Alehouse on Shattuck Avenue, a brewpub that two brothers in their mid-twenties, John and Reid Martin, started in March 1986. They had had to first convince even America's arguably most liberal city that what it considered a factory was not a bad thing for the downtown area. The beer blew Hickenlooper away and he returned to Denver with the idea of opening the Mile High City's first brewpub. The Wynkoop Brewing Company opened in October 1989, after Hickenlooper and his partners raised $575,000 through a bank loan and investors (including an aunt in Scotland who put up $10,000). The brewpub at Eighteenth and Wynkoop Streets helped transform a blighted area of Denver into a fashionable enclave, and inevitably became a major tippling point every time the Great American Beer Festival came to town.

Finally, there was the phenomenon of the brewpub chain. The idea of a restaurant serving beer that it brewed on-site was novel enough in the decade before, but now owners of different temperaments and levels of business savvy had proven it time and again in different locations. Frank Day saw an opportunity to take it up a notch. Day was a Harvard MBA and former Chicago ad man who started in the food-and-drink business with a run of popcorn concessions in the Midwest. He eventually grew a chain of pizza parlors specializing in Chicago deep dish and then tried brewpubs with the Walnut Brewery and Restaurant, which opened in Day's adopted Boulder (he was born in Denver), in 1990. The following year, he and his partners took over the struggling Boulder Brewing Company.

The ballyhooed brewery that began in 1979 in the converted goat shed on Al Nelson's farm was by 1990 on its sixth ownership group in five years. Nelson, Stick Ware, and David Hummer's decision to turn to venture-capital money had saved the brewery and paid back original investors; it also unleashed a romping ride through craft beer's growth spurt, where the brewery increased capacity to keep up with demand. Its profit margins ultimately suffered—it was the "tyranny of fast growth" that Tony Magee described in his own experience with Lagunitas in California. In 1990, $2 million in debt, Boulder Brewing declared bankruptcy, and Day and his partners, including Boulder city councilman (later mayor) Bob Greenlee, stepped in. Under the direction of Gina Day and Diane Greenlee, Frank and Bob's wives, they changed the name to the Boulder Beer Company, went private, and added a restaurant to make it the city's first brewpub.

The Walnut and Boulder Beer served as catalysts for what many of the same investors opened next: the Rock Bottom Restaurant and Brewery. Located thirty miles southeastward in Denver, it opened in November 1991 in nine thousand square feet of the first floor of Prudential Plaza, off the Sixteenth Street Mall, and quickly became a major hangout. Lines queued out the door; there were even crowds on Sunday nights. Inside, patrons could see jazz bands and brew kettles simultaneously, and bartenders put on their own show, with twirling glassware and trivia centered around the five beers overseen by Mark Youngquist, the brewmaster brought in from the BridgePort Brewing Company in Portland, Oregon (the red ale was a particular hit). It was a party as much as a restaurant-brewery. Revenues soon exceeded $1 million annually; the formula seemed invincible. Plans were soon made to expand nationwide. The Rock Bottom in Houston, Texas, would have twice as many seats as the original in Denver; Portland, Oregon, and Minneapolis were early additions, too; four more Rock Bottoms were slated for 1994 and at least three more for 1995.

Rock Bottom was at the vanguard of the brewpub-chain trend. Jon Bloostein, a one-time Wall Street investment banker, spent $2 million renovating an old kayak store in Manhattan's Union Square and another $250,000 on brewing equipment to open Heartland Brewery in 1995. That a brewpub would be part of the city's mid-1990s gentrification under the Giuliani administration struck nobody as unusual. The *New York Times* mentioned Heartland, which would grow to seven brewpubs in the city, in the same breath as the neighborhood's Barnes & Noble, the incoming House of Blues nightclub, and the regular farmers market in Union Square that featured local produce from New Jersey and Upstate New York.

Hops Bistro and Brewery had four locations in California and Arizona by the spring of 1995, including in San Diego and the original eighty-five-hundred-square-foot spot in Scottsdale, Arizona. A similarly named though different operation, Hops Grill and Bar, had nine in Florida. The latter, which would grow into the largest brewpub chain in the country, was started by David Mason and Tom Schelldorf, two restaurant executives who logged time at the Steak and Ale chain, founded by the man behind Bennigan's. Wynkoop's John Hickenlooper was said to be involved in a total of eleven brewpubs, including ones in Nebraska, Kansas, and Oklahoma.

Gordon Biersch Brewing started in an old theater in downtown Palo Alto, California, in 1988. Dan Gordon had worked in restaurants since he was fifteen, and Dean Biersch had studied brewing in Munich before internships at the Spaten Brewery there and Anheuser-Busch back home. The pair's idea was a knockout almost from the get-go; the venture grew to five locations in under eight years, including Hawaii's first brewpub, which opened in late 1994 with expectations of as much as $7 million in revenue annually.

It was that kind of business—its growth seemed to have no end in sight, and financial expectations were high from opening day. And why not? The beer produced could be sold at a considerable markup: pints selling out front for three to four dollars each could be made in the back for twenty cents. The model was not without its critics. The kitsch came in for tongue-clucking, with comparisons to the faux Irish bars that had begun springing up nationwide starting in the 1970s; like those, with their O's and Mc's in the names and the beer-brand mirrors on the walls, the brewpub chains seemed at times a tad too formulaic: slightly higher-end bar food, a little music, and the beer. Trade media's comparisons to other restaurant chains such as Chili's and Red Lobster that were meant to be favorable were instead taken as warnings of what Larry Baush, publisher of the *Pint Post* newsletter out of Seattle, called the "McDonaldization of brewpubs. I think that's the real danger to the whole brewpub sector, especially if we see the restaurant chains get into it, and there's definite interest in that."

But the focus on the beer was undeniable and redeeming, regardless of the decor and the sound system. These chains, like other lone brewpubs, produced some of the nation's most celebrated and coveted beer. Most important, they provided perhaps millions of Americans with their first encounters with craft beer. Rock Bottom's four-hundred-seat Houston location alone could whet the palates of more consumers in a month than most craft breweries could in a year through their tours and tastings. Still, the restaurant chains were circling; so were the investment bankers. Like with standalone craft breweries, the business of brewpubs seemed too sure a thing to leave alone.

SUDS AND THE CITY
Brooklyn | 1995

It was like a scene straight out of *Goodfellas*. Two big limousines pulled up in front of a development project in a gritty, isolated area of Brooklyn. Somber, serious men in bulky overcoats got out as construction workers scrambled for cover. In heavy New York accents, the men from the limos asked to speak to "the man in charge." That man was Steve Hindy, the construction super told them, but he was out to lunch. That was OK, the men said; they could wait.

The construction project was for the new Brooklyn Brewery. Hindy and Tom Potter's operation by 1995 had made a leap that other contract brewers routinely talked of making though rarely did: creating a physical brewery to take over a large chunk of production. They had found an old warehouse space in the Williamsburg neighborhood of Brooklyn, which, a century before, had served as the nexus for the city's brewing industry. The neighborhood, although it would in a few years become synonymous with hip (in no small part owing to Brooklyn Brewery), was then far from fancy, which was why Hindy and Potter were able to plant their flag there. They had looked first in Manhattan. Through real estate agents, they sized up an old jazz club in Greenwich Village. The original estimate to build out the space into a brew-pub was $3 to $4 million; Hindy and Potter showed the estimate to Milton Glaser, the legendary graphic designer who had been given a stake in the brewery in exchange for designing its logo. Glaser told them it would cost almost twice that much. The pair abandoned Manhattan for their brewery's namesake borough.

And why not? Brooklyn resonated as a brand in itself the world over. Hindy especially knew the borough's reach from his former life as a foreign correspondent. A friend of his from the *New York Times* had been seized without any press credentials by the Palestinian Liberation Organization during the 1982 Israeli siege of Beirut. A hooded interrogator asked him where he was from. Brooklyn. What street? Flatbush Avenue. What was the name of the baseball team that left? The Dodgers.

"You seem to know something about Brooklyn," the *Times* reporter said. "Yes, I live there," the hooded interrogator replied.

The brewery space that Hindy and Potter found in the fall of 1994 was actually across the street from the windowless, gas-heated office they were using to coordinate the distribution and marketing of the now more than eleven thousand barrels annually being brewed at F. X. Matt in Utica. What looked like one red-brick building was actually an old matzo factory over three smaller, adjoining ones totaling around twenty thousand square feet and including a five-thousand-square-foot space with twenty-five-foot ceilings and no columns: a perfect brewhouse. Hindy and Potter arranged a five-year lease with an option to buy the space for $1.1 million. The landlord included the option to buy only reluctantly: there was a sense in the mid-1990s that New York City was changing for the better and that the right kind of business in a space like this could really do well—for itself and for the neighborhood.

Deal in hand, throughout 1995 Hindy and Potter, along with brewery staff as well as the contractors and subcontractors, planned and renovated the space. The partners were careful of cost overruns, like those sustained by Matthew Reich's old New Amsterdam brewpub in Manhattan. The costs, however, did run away from Hindy and Potter at times: new floor drains, $13,000; a new sidewalk, $20,000; new wood beams in the crawl space to support the brew kettles and tuns, another twenty grand. It was a common refrain in brewery build-outs. Still, the construction work heralded something big for the area, and that's what the papers wrote about—and the somber men from the limos read about.

The overcoat-clad men wanted to wet their beaks through unionized construction jobs. They leaned on the brewery for a sit-down, and Hindy obliged them for what turned out to be a solo meeting with the boss of the Brooklyn building trades union and several of his associates. Hindy kicked things off by telling them his life story, emphasizing his experience covering wars in the Middle East. He then suggested going somewhere for lunch. The boss suggested they go to the brewery's warehouse. The warehouse didn't have enough chairs for the boss and his associates, so Hindy said he would fetch more.

"No," the boss said, "at our meetings, the old men sit and the young men stand."

Fair enough. The boss, Hindy, and a union secretary sat down. Hindy began to weave his life story into the brewery's story, highlighting the challenges he and Potter had confronted: the self-distribution, the skeptical investors. He found himself talking about his foreign-correspondent days again. The union treasurer, a plump guy with a shaved head who was standing while Hindy talked, interrupted.

"Yeah, yeah, yeah. We've heard enough of this bullshit. We're here for one thing: J-O-B-S, jobs. You built this brewery without us. The first brewery in Brooklyn in a long time. That's an insult."

The boss cut him off and let Hindy continue. Finally, the boss looked him in the eye. "Look, we don't want to hurt you."

The blood drained from Hindy's face.

"I don't mean physical stuff," the boss said. The blood crept back. "We don't do that. We have lawyers. If we put a picket around your project, no one will come near it. If we put the word out in Brooklyn, no one will unload your products."

"My project is almost complete," Hindy replied. "I'm on a very tight budget and I think you would be destroying a company that will bring jobs and goodwill to Brooklyn."

That set the treasurer with the shaved head off again. He demanded a meeting behind some nearby pallets stacked with beer—without Hindy. Which was fine with him. His shirt was soaked in sweat; fresh doubts about the brewery galloped through his mind, now alongside what the boss might make him do. No-show jobs? What would he say to that? What *could* he say to that?

The union members reemerged. The boss walked up to Hindy, still in his chair, and grabbed the inside of his right thigh, his face inches from Hindy's. "We're going to have to hurt you."

Hindy stared back, trying not to show fear. Then the boss grabbed his shoulders and shook with laughter. "Just kidding!" Everyone else laughed.

"Look, we're going to leave you alone. But if you expand this brewery, or build anything new, we have to be in on it."

Hindy nodded.

"And," the boss went on, "we want you to come to our Christmas party; bring your wife, and take an ad in our journal."

Hindy could live with that.* Brooklyn Brewery was back on, about to ride—as both a driver and a passenger—not only the American craft

---

* It turned out the brewery had, in fact, been employing union construction workers; it was just that the unions did not have enough work for them, so they took the brewery job on the side. (Per Hindy and Potter, *Beer School*, 171–72.)

beer boom but also the renaissance of the nation's largest city and consumer market.

ATTACK OF THE PHANTOM CRAFTS
Denver; St. Louis | 1994–1995

More people than ever, from the mob to the media, were paying attention to
the American craft beer movement, and that included Big Beer. The wider
industry had spent a generation ignoring it or, at best, treating it as a fad.
The number of barrels that the largest breweries produced only grew, after
all, besting that light-beer-driven peak reached in 1983, while the dominance
of the biggest breweries remained seemingly impregnable (in 1990, more than
three-fifths of the domestic beer market belonged to Anheuser-Busch, Miller,
and Coors alone). With market share firm and competition decreasing, why
fret some dreamers in sneakers in their rented warehouse space and glorified
speakeasies? It wasn't arrogance on the part of Big Beer; it was charts and
graphs that showed clear trends through decades now—no matter how clever,
creative, or just genuinely better tasting the craft start-ups were. For all the
Sturm und Drang of the already storied sector, it still accounted for less than
3 percent of US beer sales by the 1990s. Then 1992 rolled around. The productivity levels of Big Beer rolled back; the charts and graphs were no longer
going inexorably upward. There were different causes, not least of which were
the recession of the early 1990s and renewed competition from imports. There
was also the continued popularity of fine wine, now available at all sorts of
price points, from ultra-expensive French imports to everyday Chardonnay
retailing for under ten dollars a bottle. What's more, other premium spirits
brands such as Grey Goose vodka and Bombay Sapphire gin followed Absolut's marketing-heavy formula for quick and enduring success. It was around
this time, too, that Big Beer turned to more aggressive marketing overseas,
including in the recently liberated nations of Eastern Europe no longer behind
the Iron Curtain. More than anything, it appears Big Beer simply overdid it
with the domestic marketing and advertising, and in the end ceded ground
or lost it. Top industry analyst Bob Weinberg called the period from 1991 to
1995 "the brewing industry's Vietnam," when Big Beer could have enticed

more consumers but instead stuck to what seemed tried-and-true measures. "I don't know why the industry doesn't aggressively campaign for intelligent drinking," Weinberg told a reporter. "Less than half of the people who can drink legally, do. None of the brewers do this, however. They go after the twenty-one-to-twenty-four-year-olds instead, and that's just preaching to the choir." The advertising, so potently effective in the 1970s and 1980s, seemed to have run its course, and the overseas market was not going to pick up all of the slack. Where to next?

The name conjured up something ruggedly American: a wild, untamable animal; mountains meant to hold possibilities; a way away from cities and toward something new. In the spring of 1994, Anheuser-Busch debuted its Elk Mountain Ale, a red ale intended to compete, at least according to reports, with Coors's Killian's Irish Red, unveiled at the first Great American Beer Festival in 1982, and Miller's Leinenkugel Red, spun from the Wisconsin regional that it had taken over in 1988.* But there was something about the earnestness with which Anheuser-Busch hawked Elk Mountain: its debut was pushed up several months, moving from the back burner at the St. Louis headquarters to "priority" status. Some in the industry said it was because August Busch IV, great-great-grandson of the brewery's cofounder, had recently ascended to the top marketing spot. "This one is his," one insider whispered. "As August has moved up, so has this idea." Others pointed to something more prosaic: Sales of craft beer had taken off, as had sales of specialty lines by other Big Beer brands. Killian's sales were up 60 percent in 1993 and trending upward again for the new year. Miller took note, too: its Leinenkugel and the Coors brand were going head-to-head in national advertising campaigns, competing to convince consumers which was "the better red."

This new competition was no fad. Coors debuted in March 1994 its first-ever line of seasonal beers, including a wheat and an Oktoberfest; ripping a page from craft beer, the giant was doing little to no advertising for it, instead emphasizing in media coverage the styles themselves and what set them apart from the usual watery lagers. Anheuser-Busch, as it introduced Elk Mountain, was also raising Red Wolf, its first-ever red lager, set for release that fall; according to marketing, it got its color from specially roasted barley malt that added a "subtle, sweet taste." Miller had already rolled out what it primly called its Reserve Amber Ale and Reserve Velvet Stout. There was even a Rolling Rock Bock. It was all a far cry from "Head for the Mountains," Rodney Dangerfield bowling, and "Great Taste, Less Filling."

---

* Anheuser-Busch owned a hop farm called Elk Mountain, hence the name.

Craft brewers noticed this furtive imitation. After being ignored or dismissed for so many years, it appeared that Big Beer was trying to elbow in on their consumers by mimicking their styles and techniques—and by charging a premium: the new beers were priced slightly higher than Big Beer's traditional fare. And they weren't bad, either, richer in taste than the usual bastardized pilsners. "The big breweries are quite capable of making excellent beers," said Bert Grant, founder of the nation's oldest brewpub and a former brewer at Stroh's, at one of the Great American Beer Festivals at the time. "They *did* make excellent beers," he quickly clarified. Others were not so sanguine, seeing what came to be called "phantom micros" or "phantom crafts" as a particularly insidious—and ingenious—threat in the marketplace. "It definitely makes it more competitive out there," noted an ever-diplomatic Charlie Papazian at the same GABF. Ken Allen, a chiropractor who cofounded the Anderson Valley Brewing Company in Mendocino County, California, in 1986, pushed it a little further when a reporter from San Diego broached the subject: "We're much smaller than David—and they're much larger than Goliath. 'The King of Beers'? They want to be the despot of beers." The whole situation was a tad ironic: by ignoring it for so long, Big Beer had allowed craft beer to develop without undue influence or downward pressure; now, during its biggest growth spurt, the largest breweries sought to co-opt craft beer by pretending to be what craft beer had been when they were ignoring it.

Phantom crafts were not initially big sellers for Big Beer. They did succeed, however, in muddying things enough to take a bite out of craft brewers' market share. Simply put, consumers didn't know what they were drinking unless they read the fine print on the packaging (and that's if the packaging even had that fine print telling of the beer's true parentage—some phantom crafts did not). The phantom crafts followed tried-and-true formulas, including homespun labels, names that evoked some sort of back-to-the-earth ethos, an emphasis on ingredients, a painstaking care in the brewing process—in other words, everything but the reality of craft brewers. Given their dominance in distribution already, Big Beer was able to also plant these labels in front of more consumers, especially on retail shelves. While light beer remained the sales leader for Big Beer in the 1990s, it was only a matter of time before one of these phantom-craft brands did break out. That brand was Coors's Blue Moon.

Blue Moon was born in a brewpub behind the right-field stands at Coors Field in Denver, home of the Colorado Rockies. It was there that brewmaster Keith Villa, who studied brewing at UC-Davis and then earned a PhD in brewing and fermentation biochemistry in Brussels, devised the recipes for a string of beers that Coors broke off into what it called the Blue Moon Brewery—as in "once in a blue moon," a nod to how unique the Big Beer operation knew Villa's efforts were. Coors saw to it that Villa's beers got a wider audience. The first Blue Moon beers, rolled out in the fall of 1995, included a Belgian-style wheat ale spiced with coriander and orange peel, as well as what the company called Honey Blonde, Nut Brown Ale, and Harvest Pumpkin Ale, meant to be a seasonal. While the earliest incarnations were served at the Coors Field brewpub, the 1995 rollout involved twenty-two states; six-packs of Blue Moon showed up virtually overnight in grocery stores from New York to Colorado. It was a flexing of distribution muscle that no craft brewery—not even Pete's Brewing and Boston Beer—could hope to compete with in terms of scope and speed.

The beers were an immediate consumer hit, and distribution spread within two years to all fifty states. "Coors" did not appear anywhere on the packaging; for all a prospective consumer knew, here was another entry in that burgeoning craft beer field he or she had heard or read so much about lately. The label for the wheat ale, the most ubiquitous of the new line, showed a big, bright moon looming above a bucolic forest and, beneath it, blue moon brewing company. The beer from inside the bottle was not bad, either. One guide noted, "It's heartening that American drinkers have taken to Blue Moon, since it decidedly does not taste like typical American beer offerings. A moderately soapy coriander nose with slight sour notes wafts from the glass, and the palate is floral, gently malty, with light bitterness." (The same guide's verdict on Coors's flagship pale lager: "A light, sweet nose smells vaguely of white wine, but who swirls and sniffs Coors?") Blue Moon seemed to have it all from the get-go: widespread distribution, consumer enthusiasm, and critical praise. Taken at face value, the Blue Moon Brewing Company could be considered to have overtaken Pete's Brewing as the number two craft operation in the United States by the end of the decade, second only to Boston Beer.

Its success with consumers sent purists like Bert Grant into paroxysms of frustration, though what really drove them nuts was that, for all its success, Blue Moon, like any of the other phantom crafts from any other Big Beer operation, was not really important to Coors's bottom line. The critical and consumer attention was all well and fine, but no one was going to close up shop if a Belgian-style wheat or an ale infused with pumpkin flavor didn't succeed in the marketplace. Pete Coors, the brewery's CEO and great-grandson of its founder, sat down with *Modern Brewery Age* for a long interview in the fall of 1997, two years after Blue Moon's debut. Here was how he saw things vis-à-vis "the specialty arena" of American beer: "We will continue to play in the areas where there is industry growth, and where we see opportunity. Frankly, in the specialty market, when you take out Sam Adams and Pete's, it's pretty small potatoes. It's difficult for a company our size, that puts out twenty million barrels, to get too excited about fifty thousand or one hundred thousand or even three hundred thousand barrels of product."

But get excited they would.

"BUDHOOK" AND THE BULL BEER MARKET
Seattle; Portsmouth, NH; Frederick, MD | 1995–1996

The numbers were enough to stand out even in the 1990s bull market. On Wednesday, August 16, 1995, the Seattle-based company had its initial public offering at seventeen dollars a share. Trading on the NASDAQ under the symbol "HOOK," the company's share price climbed steadily by ten dollars within the first six months as millions from the IPO poured into its operating coffers, and it was able to pay down millions more in debt. It seemed to be following the well-trodden (and well-covered) path of other IPOs in the decade's bull market, including a seemingly ceaseless stream of Internet companies. But the Seattle firm was no Internet start-up. It had begun life thirteen years ago in an old transmission shop as the Independent Ale Brewing Company, with a signature product called Redhook Ale, what the locals quickly nicknamed "banana beer" because of the spiciness provided in large part by a Belgian yeast strain. This, the first Initial Public Offering by an existing American craft brewery, was what had the market agog—and investors such as Anheuser-Busch interested.

The biggest Big Beer operation of them all, which a year before had taken a 25 percent stake in Redhook for $18 million, had pumped in another $9 million to maintain that stake, which was the largest single chunk of shares—nearly three times that of the second-largest investor, GE Capital, a financial services wing of General Electric. The IPO was underwritten by investment houses Smith Barney, Montgomery Securities, and Piper Jaffray. Redhook emerged from the process valued at more than $111 million; more immediately important, it generated $33 million and change for operating costs, including expansion; and, finally, the IPO allowed the brewery to reduce its long-term debt by $3 million. It also made the brewery's founders some tidy bundles. Paul Shipman, the one-time wine salesman and discoverer of that key Belgian yeast strain, made $986,000 from a dividend payout tied to the 6.7 percent stake he owned, which was worth well north of $6 million; and Gordon Bowker, the writer who had been behind the original Starbucks as well, made $369,000 in dividends on his 4.2 percent stake. Other Seattle-area investors also made hundreds of thousands upfront on similar single-digit slices.

It was hard to argue with. Redhook had a track record that investors could tap into for confidence. Unlike, say, an Internet start-up whose only promise for investors was the expectation of consumer demand for a product either recently or about to be launched, the brewery that had sold fewer than one thousand barrels in that first year from its five-thousand-square-foot plant had grown steadily. It had also racked up critical praise: its Redhook Extra Special Bitter won a bronze medal at the 1991 GABF and had become a standard to measure American-produced bitters against. The brewery had just opened a second location in Woodinville, Washington, that could produce 175,000 barrels annually, doubling its capacity; it would soon be distributed in forty-eight states, and sales in 1994 had topped $16.2 million. They would have been higher, Redhook executives like Shipman said at the time, if it weren't for capacity constraints; it simply cost a lot to expand while keeping up with rapacious demand. Enter the IPO and its biggest stakeholder. Suddenly, tens of millions were available to boost capacity and distribution. It seemed like a vindication for Shipman, Bowker, and others who had logged the same worrisomely long hours the last decade and a half as any other second- or third-wave craft brewing company; they had survived, and now came the payoff. Their compatriots were paying attention. Other IPOs by big craft names would soon follow. Craft beer seemed as sure a bet suddenly as the much-touted Pets.com. Rock Bottom, the brewpub chain started in Colorado by Frank Day and other investors, had already gone public in 1993, trading two million shares at $8 a piece; the share price was soon up to $27.50. One analyst in New York called Rock Bottom's IPO "a screaming winner."

But it was Redhook's nine-figure valuation that really served notice to the craft beer movement—that, and who their investors were, namely Anheuser-Busch. Just as with phantom crafts, investment in publicly traded companies seemed like another way for Big Beer to co-opt, even take over, the movement; they could cash in on the sharp growth fomented by techniques and traditions they had scoffed at or ignored for so long. Some in the movement decried the Redhook–Anheuser-Busch deal as a Trojan horse. Jim Koch of Boston

Beer told a reporter he was going to go home and watch the second movie in the original Star Wars trilogy, *The Empire Strikes Back*, because he forgot who won in the end (no one did, but the empire screwed things up royally for the previously successful rebels). He also called the deal's announcement "a declaration of war" that marked the end of "the cozy, fraternal days of the microbrewery business." The fear now was that "Budhook," as a never-shy Koch called it, with its bottomless capital could open breweries all over the country and thereby swamp the craft beer marketplace through almost limitless capacity and steroidal distribution muscle. Redhook's plans seemed to justify these fears.

Shortly after the August 1995 IPO, Redhook laid out plans for a $30 million, one-hundred-thousand-square-foot brewery in central Portsmouth on the New Hampshire coast. Ironically enough, the first new brewery in the Granite State since Prohibition had been the Anheuser-Busch plant in Merrimack, which opened in 1970 and had the capacity to produce six hundred million twelve-ounce bottles annually. The first craft operation in New Hampshire had been the Portsmouth Brewery, a brewpub that siblings Janet and Peter Egelston and Mark Metzger started in 1991 on its namesake's Market Street. Metzger was a partner of the Egelstons in the Northampton Brewery in western Massachusetts, one of the oldest brewpubs in New England, founded in 1987.

Peter Egelston wasn't done. A one-time Manhattan doorman and Brooklyn high school teacher who picked up homebrewing via a magazine ad for kits, he ended up in 1994 buying at auction equipment from the Frank Jones Brewery, New Hampshire's last regional, which went out of business in 1950.* From that equipment grew Egelston's Smuttynose Brewing Company in Portsmouth's southern wilds, New Hampshire's first standalone craft operation, whose Shoals Pale Ale became an instant local favorite upon its July 1994 debut. Some openly worried—complained might be the better word—that Redhook's planned late-1996 arrival in Portsmouth might doom smaller houses such as Smuttynose and the Portsmouth brewpub.

It wasn't so much that Redhook was going to draw a bead on them but that they would get caught in the crossfire of a war with larger craft concerns such as Boston Beer. David Geary, founder of New England's oldest craft brewery, D. L. Geary in Portland, Maine, was a panelist during the three-day Craft Brewers Conference in Boston in May 1996, organized by the Association of Brewers. There he said Redhook's Portsmouth opening would

---

* Frank Jones was resurrected as a brand briefly in the 1980s and early 1990s.

spark "a slash-and-burn marketing blitz" between it and Boston Beer. Nick Godfrey, a marketing executive with the Mass. Bay Brewing Company, the makers of Harpoon and Boston's oldest craft brewery, took it a step further. He verbalized what many in the industry were now thinking, watching both the growth in craft breweries and brewpubs as well as the rise in IPOs and the millions that flowed from them: "Maybe the competition will split the market into different tiers, with Sam Adams and Redhook on one end, but there is going to be a shakeout."

A shakeout, as in something had to give—and would give. Look at what happened to Miller. Bob Weinberg, the noted industry analyst and consultant who had predicted but a handful of American breweries would exist by the century's end, explained to the conference that the Big Beer titan had grown by double-digit percentages throughout its 1970s battle for market share with Anheuser-Busch; then it hit a wall in the early 1980s as its production faltered in keeping up with overall industry growth; it hadn't had a double-digit year since 1981. "The future is in your hands," Weinberg told an assemblage of the conference's more than three thousand attendees. "I have no doubts the market will double in 1996, and I would like to say it will double again, but that is up to you."

Wall Street analysts sizing up some of the craft beer IPOs were starting to question the basic premise behind them: how long could this supply-side growth in craft beer be sustained in terms of consumer demand? In other words, just how many craft beer drinkers were there out there, willing to plunk down a premium for what was still an unfamiliar product to many beer drinkers, never mind to most Americans? Stocks rely on profit growth—and confidence in profit growth—to themselves grow in value and to then hold that value. Too much product and too little demand seemed a recipe for disaster. Still, the valuations achieved by Redhook, and the capital infusions that came even with smaller public launches, made the IPO an irresistible siren for craft brewing companies.

Within seven months of Redhook's IPO, five more would launch, including Hart Brewing Company (symbol: HOPS), which Tom Baune and Beth Hartwell founded eleven years before in an old general store in the Washington State logging town of Kalama. The husband-and-wife team behind the Pyramid line of ales sold the brewery for one million dollars in 1989 to a group of investors that included John and Peter Morse, owners of the Fratelli Brothers ice cream company. The new owners embarked on an expansion that included not only a new sixty-five-barrel Kalama location but also one in Seattle, Washington, with its own brewpub space and a capacity to brew eighty thousand barrels annually. Hart, which would change its name to Pyramid mid-decade, also snapped up the Thomas Kemper Brewery in northern Washington in 1992, one of the first mergers in the craft beer movement (Thomas Kemper by then, though, was best known for its soda-making spinoff, which was also part of the Hart deal). It was Pyramid's IPO in early December 1995, with 2.6 million shares offered at nineteen dollars a piece, that allowed it to leap into the hyper-competitive San Francisco Bay Area; its Berkeley brewhouse and brewpub had the capacity to produce another eighty thousand barrels yearly and was part of what executives described at the time as the "primary phase" of a national expansion.

James Bernau knew something about public offerings and expansion. A one-time lobbyist for independent businesses, he had used an IPO in 1989 to raise funds to open his Willamette Valley Vineyards, selling shares sometimes from booths at county fairs. Indeed, the craft beer IPOs were not happening in a libationary vacuum. Wineries had been going public to similarly ecstatic fist pumps from Wall Street. Napa's pioneering Robert Mondavi Winery offered 3.7 million shares at $13.50 each in June 1993; it was, the winery said, to pay off $65 million in debt and to fund an expansion. The Mondavi IPO followed two smaller ones by the Chalone Wine Group, another higher-end winery out of the Bay Area, and the Canandaigua Wine Company, which produced lower-priced bulk wines from an upstate New York headquarters under the Canandaigua Brands umbrella (the company would change its name to Constellation Brands in 2000). Bernau turned to beer in 1993, raising $3.6 million through a stock offering to open the Willamette Valley Brewing Company in Portland, Oregon, later called the Nor'wester Brewing Company. Bernau's endgame was to raise enough money to open a chain of brewpubs, a goal he undertook with yet more stock offerings by 1995 to fund locations in Irvine, California, and Seattle. An IPO for Nor'wester (symbol: ALES) came in January 1996, with shares opening at seven dollars each. It wasn't all just dollars and shares and expansions for Bernau: he used about $500,000 from that latest offering to endow a fermentation science professorship at Oregon State University.

The final craft beer IPO in this first wave illustrated that a relatively modest valuation meant staggering growth for even far more fledgling operations. Kevin Brannon, a former corporate attorney and homebrewer from Portland, Oregon, and Marjorie McGinnis, the woman he fell in love with on a trip east, had started the Frederick Brewing Company, located in the central Maryland town of the same name, in the spring of 1992 with $800,000 in loans and private investments. Husband and wife worked out of a brick warehouse that ended up needing tens of thousands of dollars in renovations, though their Blue Ridge brand of beers, overseen by brewmaster Steve Nordahl, was well received. Seeking to expand, Brannon and McGinnis arranged an IPO in March 1995 (symbol: BLUE) that raised $4.8 million through six-dollar shares. Money in hand, the sky was the limit: They bought top-shelf brewing equipment from JV Northwest and packaging equipment from Krones, they broke ground on a new $7 million brewery that could produce ten times the twelve thousand barrels they were then selling, and the payroll swelled to thirty as the founders were able to also pay themselves salaries for the first time. Frederick Brewing's distribution grew from five states and the District of Columbia to twenty-one plus DC; they would, for a time, become the biggest craft brewery by sales in the Mid-Atlantic.

As impressive as these numbers and benchmarks were, they and even those of Redhook paled in comparison with the granddaddies of the craft beer IPO wave: Pete's Brewing and Boston Beer. Both companies, as we've seen, experienced explosive, industry-altering growth through the late 1980s and into the early 1990s; together they now produced nearly one hundred thousand barrels annually (though even in this rarefied air there was a further demarcation: Boston Beer produced four times as much as Pete's). The two brands had become the ubiquitous symbols of domestic craft beer to Americans, the likeliest non–Big Beer, nonimport labels to be staring out from grocery store and gas station shelves as well as staring back from tap handles and menus. If one in four American beers consumed was from Anheuser-Busch, a back-of-the-envelope estimate for the mid-1990s meant that one of every two American craft beers consumed was a Pete's or a Samuel Adams. Koch's vociferous aversion to Anheuser-Busch's investment in Redhook notwithstanding, their respective public offerings in November 1995 were probably the least surprising—and the most anticipated.

Mark Bronder and Pete Slosberg didn't want to leave Pete's Brewing to any heirs; they didn't want to own plants in different parts of the country; they didn't want a fancy office full of mementoes of their climb. They wanted to make great beer, sell it widely—and with not a small dose of panache, as another one of their goals was to have fun—and get out when the getting was good. The IPO was a part of that strategy. So was an undeclared price war with Boston Beer.

Time was that a six-pack of Samuel Adams Boston Lager, Pete's Wicked Ale, or one of the two companies' other brands might run toward seven bucks. Shortly after the turn of the decade, consumers noticed the prices dropping: first below the six-dollar mark, then toward the five-dollar mark, and then, in many locations, below even that, until six-packs of the leading craft beer brands in the United States were flirting with the price points of Big Beer's cheaper offerings. Competitors figured out what was going on: Boston Beer and Pete's Brewing were chasing sales volume through lower prices. One company would lower its prices, and the other would soon follow. But neither ever dropped so far as to become confused with a six-pack of Busch Light, and the beer inside was the same quality as that inside higher-priced packs of yesteryear. Still, it was clear the two biggest players were each jockeying for a big valuation post-IPO. And they got it.

"We think that there is substantial volume growth ahead for this company," rating agency Standard & Poor's wrote of Pete's in the second week of November 1995. The agency fretted about the frothy growth in the craft beer industry as a whole and about Pete's switch the past summer to Stroh's in St. Paul, Minnesota, for its contract brewing, fearing the Big Beer operation might not keep as watchful an eye on the smaller batches as the Minnesota Brewing Company had. But S&P nonetheless saw the Redhook offering as proof that other established names could be a healthy investment. Besides, in the first nine months of 1995, Pete's had already surpassed its $30,837,000 revenue figure for all of 1994. It also had its own distribution networks into nearly every state, it was particularly strong sales-wise in California, and it had that national television advertising campaign with Pete Slosberg, a unique thing in the industry.

As strictly a business proposition, Pete's Brewing appeared exceedingly smart. Its three million shares were priced at eighteen dollars each, and Stroh's was given an option to buy 1.1 million; one-third were snapped up by the public (symbol: WIKD). The company emerged from the IPO valued at $254,022,700, and the more than $40 million raised was enough to pay down its debt and get busy building a physical brewery in Northern California that could produce at least 250,000 barrels annually by its launch in 1997. Pete's CEO, Mark Bozzini, talked of growing the company's brand line—there were four year-round Pete's beers and two seasonals—and expanding capacity "at the expense of some of our competitors." It was time to conquer more markets, "like Chicago, Miami, Houston, and Dallas," the way they had conquered California, New England, and the Northwest.

For Jim Koch and Rhonda Kallman at Boston Beer, the summits seemed to have already been scaled by the time of the company's IPO. Kallman's sales team was legendary in the industry by that point, with more than 110 reps in nearly every state, one rep to no more than every five hundred retailers, pushing sales growth by double digits for several years in a row. The success seemed to breed success. For 1993, Kallman instituted a "63 in '93" campaign: 63 percent sales growth for that year; they ended up with nearly 65. Meanwhile, Koch was not only the company's but also the entire craft beer sector's ubiquitous media presence, oft-quoted in print, frequently on the radio or television news, sometimes controversial, invariably self-confident, sunny, and articulate on the merits of his product over Big Beer's. One of the merits Koch liked to push in particular was Boston Beer's supposed connection to everyday beer drinkers, who knew what they were getting into with a bottle of Boston Lager or pint of Oktoberfest (the company now had fourteen beer lines, half of them seasonals). Drinkers could also know what they were getting into with the company's IPO. In a twist, Koch arranged for consumers who were at least twenty-one years old to buy thirty-three shares each at $15 a share ($495 total) through a toll-free number on the beer's packaging. The move was meant to inspire further brand loyalty, and 990,000 of the four million shares were set aside for callers, who responded in droves.

The remaining shares in the IPO that raised $60 million for the company right off the bat went to institutional investors, including venture-capital firms, and to the cofounders as well as those involved since the beginning; that included Koch's father, Charles Koch, who had initially warned his son away from the beer business, then provided key advice; and brewing consultant Joseph Owades, who took the old family lager recipe and turned it into the bestselling craft beer in America. Owades had 162,000 shares; Charles Koch, 500,000; Kallman, 400,000; and Jim Koch more than three million (together with his father, he owned about 40 percent of the company). Those three-million-plus shares included so-called Class B ones, which would enable Koch to control the company long-term; predictably, he left competitors like Redhook's Paul Shipman and Gordon Bowker in the dust when it came to value post-IPO. Jim Koch—who twelve years ago had been fretting whether to leave his day job, keeping the company books in a shoebox, and schlepping ice-packed bottles of beer door to door in a briefcase—was worth more than August Busch III, as Koch's Boston Beer shares were worth $189 million, and Busch's in the Anheuser-Busch that he chaired were worth $108 million. The apples-to-apples comparison could be misleading, though, given the wider Busch family's holdings, including entire distributorships and a 45 percent share of the American beer market (versus somewhere around 1 percent for Boston Beer). "Comparing the worth of Koch to that of Busch is like a gnat on an elephant's butt," said one industry analyst. "Koch has done well, but when comparing the two, the Busch family is on an entirely different plane."

Regardless, the first wave of craft beer IPOs that ended in the spring of 1996 with Frederick Brewing raising $4.8 million off $6 shares for a company not even four years old appeared to give an entirely different impression. It was an era, after all, of quick growth and quick profits, of a bull stock market that everyone could sense was historic, that was seeing more attention than ever thanks to a new medium not only covering it but involved in it as well—the Internet. As incongruous—incomprehensible!—as it might have seemed only a few short years before, craft beer now fit the financial times: fresh, bold, growing by leaps and bounds. And the performance of these stocks and others in the months that followed their initial offerings only confirmed a sense of their staying power: craft beer stocks were trading thirty-seven times higher than projected 1996 earnings, while the average American stock was trading just fourteen times higher. Besides, had Anheuser-Busch not started small, too? Who was to say that Boston Beer's market share would stay around 1 percent? Or that Pete's wouldn't open not only the Northern California brewery but one, two, five more and amp its production exponentially? Or that more Big Beer brands, with a much longer and beefier track record than smaller competitors, would jump in with capital and further investor confidence? To question the wisdom of the market in the mid-1990s, moreover, was to miss out. Wall Street, whose underwriters, lawyers, and analysts were making not-insignificant fees shepherding these IPOs, was bullish on craft beer; that's all a lot of people needed to know. Redhook's IPO, as one analyst put it, "lit the fuse for an exploding new industry. Craft beer has become the 'in' thing."

LAST CALL FOR THE OLD DAYS
Hopland, CA; Portland, OR; Portland, ME | 1995–1997

Sometime in 1984, after Ron Lindenbusch relocated from St. Louis, where he grew up, to Santa Rosa in Northern California, where he had a job, an old friend put a glass of Anchor Steam in his hand. Lindenbusch's beer curriculum had commenced years before with Busch (it was St. Louis, after all, and there was his surname's third syllable) and then had advanced to Heineken Dark, the most exotic beer he could get for a little bar he owned after college. Now he tried the Anchor Steam. "That's the most bitter beer I've ever tasted,"

Lindenbusch thought. He gave it the old postcollege try, though, and halfway through the beer from Fritz Maytag's Mariposa Street operation it began to grow on him. By the end of that first Anchor Steam, Lindenbusch knew it would not be his last. On the way back northward to his friend's place in Humboldt County, they stopped off at the Mendocino Brewing Company's Hopland Brewery, where he tried his first Red Tail Ale; although he liked it well enough, the Black Hawk Stout was the one that really caught his fancy. That, and the surroundings. The brewpub, the second oldest in the nation, struck him as "the coolest place on the planet to drink a beer." The selection of beer brewed onsite was ahead of its time; there was live music, even a sandbox for the kids; and patrons could pluck a cone from the hop trellises growing over the beer garden and toss it in their beers.

Lindenbusch returned to Hopland time and again over the next few years, blasting through the temperate evenings on his Yamaha 750 shaft drive to take in the beer and more than that the atmosphere, especially the music. He was managing Sizzler restaurants one at a time in Santa Rosa and Petaluma, getting gradually fed up with their corporate approaches and running headlong into a quarter-life crisis. One morning when he had about reached his breaking point, his wife handed him the paper; the Hopland brewpub was hiring a general manager. Lindenbusch got the job. The twenty-eight-year-old took his tie off, put on jeans and an "Eye of the Hawk" T-shirt, and never looked back. After the Hopland, he would eventually land a top position at Tony Magee's equally sartorially laid-back Lagunitas Brewing.

Lindenbusch's story would be familiar to so many others who joined the movement professionally in the late 1980s and early 1990s, a movement that was irreversibly changing—though no one quite knew by how much. The Hopland's status was proof of the change. When it opened off Highway 101 in the summer of 1983, it was a revelation, part of only a handful of craft-brewing operations. Not only that, but Hopland could trace its ancestry through brewmaster Don Barkley back to Jack McAuliffe's New Albion Brewing, the first start-up craft brewery in the United States. Fast-forward to just 1989, when Lindenbusch started work there, and several more breweries and brewpubs had joined the party in every region of the country; and, as we've seen, hundreds more would follow in the next five years alone. The Hopland and its ilk no longer seemed so unique.

A newcomer such as Lindenbusch, then, caught the craft beer movement at the very end of its innocence. Larger-scale players like Anheuser-Busch had been circling it for years, awaiting their chances, and throughout the mid-1990s they struck.

In the summer of 1997, a reporter from *Forbes* magazine climbed aboard a 165-foot yacht called *Indian Achiever*, moored off the West Side of Manhattan. The yacht's owner, Vijay Mallya, only just on the other side of forty, sat "lord-like" in an ornate chair, beyond him the sun shining upon the imperious Manhattan skyline dominated by the World Trade Center towers. He talked excitedly about his global conglomerate's latest venture: American craft beer. "The prices at which Bernau was buying glass bottles were ridiculous," he said. "If I control fifteen or twenty microbreweries, I can negotiate better prices."

The "Bernau" was James Bernau, who had undertaken multiple public stock offerings to get his various vineyards and breweries off the ground, including Nor'wester in Portland, Oregon. The plan had been to open a chain of brewpubs and breweries, and, for a while, Bernau succeeded. Locations opened as diffusely as Woodinville, Washington, and Saratoga Springs, New York, as well as in Denver and Irvine, California. Then things went from bad to worse: shares in Nor'wester (still trading under ALES) peaked at $9.50 after opening at $7 in January 1996, and then they dropped precipitously to $2. Mallya called him out of the blue that summer; the two men didn't know each other; Mallya was driving around Napa Valley, checking out vineyards, but he told Bernau he wanted to invest in his craft beer chain. Fine by Bernau. He and Mallya arranged a deal that gave the billionaire a 40 percent stake for $5.5 million, while Bernau retained 10 percent and the remaining Nor'wester shareholders 50 percent. The brewery in Saratoga Springs was put up as collateral for Mallya's infusion.

Mallya's interest wasn't entirely incongruous. He headed a multibillion-dollar firm, UB Group, that had been in his family since the birth of modern India in 1947. It dabbled in fertilizer, computer software, and spirits, but perhaps its best-known brand was Kingfisher lager, which had become synonymous in the West with Indian beer. Through it and thirteen other brands, UB dominated more than 40 percent of the Indian beer market and had made significant inroads abroad, including in the United States, where Kingfisher showed up at many Indian restaurants. It was particularly ubiquitous in South Africa and the United Kingdom, where UB owned half of Shepherd Neame, the nation's oldest brewery, and controlled the venerable Wiltshire Brewing Company, including its dozens of pubs. Mallya, who took over the family business at age twenty-eight, had renamed Wiltshire United Breweries.

Around the time he invested in Bernau's five operations, Mallya also invested $3.5 million in the Mendocino Brewing Company, roughly the amount in sales that the Hopland operation would do in 1996. He also pumped $1.75 million into Humboldt Brewing, started in 1987 in Arcata on the Northern California coast and now producing about eighteen thousand barrels and $4 million in annual sales. These were all small amounts for Mallya—his UB Group was estimated to do $1.4 billion in annual revenue through fifty companies in twenty countries—but he had big, big plans for these IPAs and amber ales. On his yacht that sunny summer afternoon, his future in the American craft beer movement stretching before him, Mallya hinted that those plans might include a direct assault on Big Beer. "I'll have a lot more clout going in with five or six brands, each distinct and not similar," he said in response to a question about challenging Big Beer vis-à-vis distribution, "I'll make sure of that."

On the other side of the country and shortly before Mallya held court on the Hudson River, the owners of one of the most beloved monikers in the craft beer movement were ceding control. BridgePort Brewing Company had been, after its late 1984 opening, the first craft brewery to really take hold in Oregon (Cartwright Portland had already folded after barely two years of dubious quality); BridgePort and the brewpub that opened alongside it in 1986 were instrumental in transforming Portland's industrial northwest into a hip area; and more than anything, BridgePort helped to place both the city and the state on the beer map. That Oregon, along with the rest of the Northwest, would have become a craft beer Mecca without Dick and Nancy Ponzi's operation seemed almost unimaginable. But, ten years in, the Ponzis faced a choice. "We could draw the line at expansion to distant markets," as Dick Ponzi saw it. "We could invest in expansion on our own, or we could sell to a proven sales and marketing organization."

They were victims of their own success in a business that required lots of capital to keep up with consumer demand and, more important, with competitors. BridgePort was producing twenty-five thousand barrels a year— but competitors like the Widmer Brothers, once on that same unremarkable side of the Willamette River and now greatly expanded on the other side, and Full Sail Brewing Company, some sixty miles up the Columbia River in Hood River, Oregon, were producing more. And these were just the nearby competitors; the Ponzis also had to contend with the dozens of craft-brewing companies that now had wide distribution reaches, not least Boston Beer and Pete's Brewing. Then there was the IPO wave of 1995, with these same competitors receiving infusions of capital unimaginable in 1984.

So the Ponzis sold the brewery to Gambrinus in the fall of 1995 for an undisclosed price. Gambrinus was started in San Antonio, Texas, in 1986 and grew quickly into one of the ten largest beer importers in the United States. Its biggest acquisition thus far had been the eighty-six-year-old Spoetzl Brewery, which was in 1989 on the brink of closing like so many other regionals when Gambrinus stepped in. By 1993 it was selling one million cases of beer annually, including its popular Shiner Bock brand—the first time the brewery had ever reached that sales mark.

BridgePort's quality continued unabated under Gambrinus, overseen as it still was by Karl Ockert, who had studied under Michael Lewis at UC-Davis. For many of these craft breweries saved by mergers and acquisitions, or by cash infusions such as those of Vijay Mallya and Anheuser-Busch, life continued as before in the mid-1990s, and it's not entirely clear whether consumers even noticed the changes in ownership. The craft beer trade media had limited reach in this darkness right before the web's dawn, and the deals and the IPOs tended to get more coverage besides in business publications such as *Forbes* and the *Wall Street Journal*. There was nothing to suggest that it was a bad thing existentially for a Big Beer operation—or a bigger operation, period—to step in, especially not when the movement had already had numerous closures and there were rumblings of a gigantic shakeout. It was a boost to marketing and to productivity especially, not to mention a way to quickly pay down debt.

That was basically the pitch the Shipyard Brewing Company, based in the other Portland, made around the same time as the BridgePort-Gambrinus deal. The craft brewery a stone's throw from the ruddy Atlantic that prodigious brewmaster Alan Pugsley and brewpub entrepreneur Fred Forsley started in early 1994 sold a 50 percent stake to a Miller subsidiary in the fall of 1995 for undisclosed terms. What was clear was that Miller wanted in on craft beer. It had watched Anheuser-Busch, its mortal rival throughout the 1970s and 1980s, gain a toehold through Redhook in what was the fastest-growing segment of American brewing—this at a time when Miller's phantom-craft stab, the Reserve series, was dying an embarrassing death, never able to sell more than two hundred thousand barrels annually, a pittance for the Big Beer operation that had let the world have Lite. And, anyway, Shipyard had debt it needed to pay down, and it wanted to expand both its brewery and its production, from 54,000 barrels annually to 108,000, and get into the New York market. Miller's new subsidiary, the American Specialty and Craft Beer Company, could allow it to do all that without sacrificing its quality.

Pugsley said at a Thursday morning press conference announcing the deal that it fulfilled his "lifelong wish list" for what a smaller-scale brewery could be. Miller wasn't Forsley and Pugsley's first choice—they explored an IPO (they were all the rage) but realized Shipyard didn't yet have the financial track record after barely a year in operation. Miller had a spot of a track record besides. In the eight years since it bought the Jacob Leinen-kugel Brewing Company, the northern Wisconsin regional's sales had only grown, and the same Miller subsidiary that bought 50 percent of Shipyard had, earlier in 1995, bought a controlling stake in the well-regarded Celis Brewery. (Celis was started by Pierre Celis, a former milkman who almost single-handedly resurrected the Belgian white style, first in his native Flanders and later through a brewery out of Austin, Texas.) So Miller it was. But just as with the IPO wave, the Anheuser-Busch interest in Redhook, or Vijay Mallya's stakes in Mendocino, Humboldt, and Nor'wester, it wasn't entirely clear yet what Miller's share meant beyond more money for another craft brewery to expand and another toehold for Big Beer.

David Geary, for his part, was magnanimous toward his competitor's move (in stark contrast to Jim Koch's reaction to the Anheuser-Busch deal with Redhook). It made his D. L. Geary, also in Portland and already the oldest, the biggest independent craft brewery in Maine. "I don't think," Geary said at the time, "anything has changed for us."

BIG BEER'S BIGGEST WEAPON

Kansas City; Merriam, KS; Chico, CA | 1996

David Geary's matter-of-fact reaction might have belied the bigger fish that the craft beer movement had to fry—courtesy, again, of Anheuser-Busch.

The world's biggest brewer had launched a squeeze on distribution through what it called by the decidedly Orwellian name "100 percent share of mind." It all started in March 1996, when August Busch III told a national wholesalers conference, "Each of you [must] exert your undivided attention and total efforts on Anheuser-Busch products. If you sell our competitors' products, can you still give us your best efforts? I don't think so." It was threat draped in gossamer: the world's biggest and most reliable brewer was asking distributors nationwide carrying their brands to focus only on those to the exclusion of others. If they didn't, well . . . Anheuser-Busch could not say out loud that they would take their tens of millions of marbles and go home—that might have put them afoul of antitrust laws—but the possibility was clearly put out there. Distributors, starting only months after Busch's comments, began to play ball one by one.

Distribution was already a crucible for craft brewers. More than anything save the capital costs for starting up and (if lucky) expanding, distribution could make or break an operation. "Go home and hug your wholesaler," Fritz Maytag told a gathering of craft brewers earlier in the decade. He meant it—the day that Don Saccani started distributing his Anchor brands was a game changer for the brewery. The problem, however, was that the standard three-tier system in place in most areas of producers, distributors, and retailers did not favor craft brewers; it favored larger, better-known producers who could guarantee turnover. Craft brewers were often treated as a side business that could be ignored or indulged at whim, depending on the distributor. Kim Jordan and Jeff Lebesch, in the early days of their New Belgium in Fort Collins, Colorado, left a couple of pallets with a distributor down in Denver. They called the distributor regularly to see if it needed the supply refreshed, only to be told everything was fine; after a while, incredulous, they dropped in on the distributor unannounced and found both pallets still under their original plastic wrapping. The distributor had done nothing illegal by letting their beer linger and lying to them about it (luckily, New Belgium had not yet signed a contract with the distributor and took the beer back).

A no-less-august defender of the free market than the *Wall Street Journal*, in an editorial, excoriated how the three-tier system stymied competition. The editorial was in response to the so-called Twenty-First Amendment Enforcement Act passed by Congress in 2000, which allowed state attorneys general to use the federal courts to stop alcohol shipments coming from producers outside their states directly to consumers. Ostensibly meant to prevent underage consumers from ordering alcohol online, it seemed to the *Journal* and many others just another way to keep distributors in the middle:

> Think of it this way. You live in Indianapolis and order a flannel shirt from L. L. Bean in Maine. No one would think of saying that you can't do that, or you have to buy it through a licensed Indiana flannel-shirt distributor. But when it comes to California chardonnay or New York cabernet sauvignon, that's the argument. . . . [T]he laws regulating alcohol sales are themselves of dubious vintage, a legacy of post—Prohibition attempts to create a distribution system the mob could not control. Hence the legislation providing for a state-licensed middleman between you and the producer; hence too the dozens of

related laws, such as the one in New York prohibiting alcohol chains, that today raise prices and keep out competition. . . .

In the late summer of 1996, Robert Eilert, cofounder of the Flying Monkey Brewery in the small eastern Kansas city of Merriam, got a letter from an Anheuser-Busch executive. The letter was in response to one from Eilert contending that the Big Beer operation had forced Flying Monkey's distributors in Wichita and Lawrence to stop carrying its only-three-month-old brand. Eilert had returned to the area he had grown up in after spending three years in Breckenridge, Colorado, where he worked at the craft brewery of the same name that avowed ski bum and avid homebrewer Richard Squire founded in 1990. Flying Monkey was the seventh Kansas brewery or brewpub since state legislators changed the alcohol laws in 1987 after more than a century of actual and quasi-Prohibition. Kansas held a special place in teetotaler lore: Prohibitionist Carrie Nation lived in the state for ten years around the turn of the century as her saloon-busting campaign got under way. You could trace a straight line from her fanaticism toward the turn of the century to Prohibition in 1920, though Kansas itself beat the rest of the nation to the punch when it instituted a ban on alcohol production in 1881. At that time, the state might have had as many as ninety breweries, a staggering sum for the Great Plains (neighboring Oklahoma, for instance, had none). The legal changes of the late 1980s led to Chuck Magerl, a University of Kansas graduate student, opening a brewpub, the Free State Brewery, in downtown Lawrence in early 1989—the state's first legal brewery since the 1881 ban.

Others, nearly all brewpubs, followed, though the most ubiquitous craft brewery for the eastern part of Kansas where Flying Monkey opened was actually located in Missouri just across the Mississippi River. John McDonald grew up in the small north-central Kansas town of Osborne (population approximately two thousand), where he began homebrewing at the entirely reasonable age of twelve, he and a friend selling what they could conjure to teenagers at the drive-in (one skunky batch they unloaded on the unsuspecting teens had them laying low for a few days). After studying art at the University of Kansas, McDonald moved to Kansas City, Missouri, to work as a carpenter; then he and his wife won a raffle for a free trip to Europe, including to Belgium and West Germany. It was there that he hatched the idea to do his adolescent hobby on a much grander scale back in Kansas City.

McDonald would in November 1989 deliver the first kegs of the Boulevard Brewing Company's signature pale ale in his own pickup truck, driving from the brewery on Southwest Boulevard near Interstate 35, which included a brewhouse McDonald imported from Bavaria, to a restaurant a few blocks away. Boulevard was the first brewery to open in the Kansas City area since a Schlitz plant closed in 1973, though the 119-acre Anheuser-Busch headquarters in St. Louis dominated Missouri as a whole. It had quite a head start, having been in operation on and off since 1852.*

And Anheuser-Busch's attempt to cement such domination, at the regional and national levels, through 100 percent share of mind was what had prompted Robert Eilert at the new Flying Monkey in Merriam to write to that same St. Louis headquarters, questioning the pressure Anheuser-Busch exerted on Kansas distributors. The letter Eilert got back was nonchalant: Anheuser-Busch did not use any "bullying" tactics to enforce the share of mind, but it did think "it is best for our wholesalers to be exclusive Anheuser-Busch distributors." Nor did the company propagate publicly what incentives it might offer distributors to focus on its brands exclusive of craft ones; instead, as Ed Maletis, president of Columbia Distributing in Portland, Oregon, a big distributor of craft brands as well as Coors and Miller, put it: distributors' "financial incentive is called Budweiser and Bud Light." Lose those and you lose a lot of saleable product you couldn't make up with Christmas ales and Russian imperial stouts.

Though neither Miller or Coors, the other two of the big three, was enforcing any policy similar to 100 percent share of mind (Miller, in fact, distributed Flying Monkey in Missouri), Anheuser-Busch hewed to the party line that its campaign was merely a reminder to distributors, albeit one weighted by bottom lines. In Johnson County, Missouri, for instance, on the Missouri-Kansas border and a major suburban area of Kansas City, Flying Monkey lost its distributor after Anheuser-Busch's reminder, which little surprised Eilert. "Anheuser-Busch has 58 percent of the market share of Johnson County," he explained at the time. "In Johnson County, the bread is buttered on one side with Bud and Bud Light on the other."

It wasn't just smaller, younger craft-brewing concerns impacted by 100 percent share of mind. Anheuser-Busch also targeted the movement's larger companies in its larger markets. Whereas craft beer might claim under 5 percent of the market share nationally or in regional markets like Kansas City, craft brewers might be hoovering around 15 to 20 percent of beer sales in older markets like San Francisco; Seattle; Portland, Oregon; and the state of Vermont. "They want more attention that the craft beers are taking away," according to one distribution consultant. "A-B distributors carry some

---

* Boulevard would cleverly call itself "Missouri's second-largest brewery."

regionals, some waters and imports, but that's never seemed to concern Saint Louis as much as the whole craft phenomenon."

None other than Ken Grossman's consistently growing Sierra Nevada in the Northwest found itself facing pressure on two fronts. First, as they did with smaller and younger competitors, some distributors dropped Sierra Nevada under pressure from 100 percent share of mind. The second front grew from the anemic sales of Anheuser-Busch's phantom crafts. The company was on its way to its twentieth consecutive year of record sales in 1996, giving it a market share of more than 45 percent. But the preponderance of the 91.1 million barrels that would be sold, a 4.1 percent increase over 1995, was of the standard bearers such as Bud Light; that brand was still enjoying double-digit growth, even as it closed in on its fifteenth birthday. Beyond these core brands, things were so-so, as the drinking public failed to respond to Elk Mountain and Red Wolf as well as to the American Originals series that Anheuser-Busch began introducing at the end of 1995 (supposedly based on old recipes and with names such as Faust, Muenchener, and Black and Tan), or even to the Michelob hefewiezen and amber bock. Things had gotten so worrisome on that front that Anheuser-Busch was considering launching a new ad campaign touting Budweiser as the "classic American lager," an implicit admission that its recent commercials, including a 1995 one with talking frogs, had trivialized things a bit too much.

In response to these flaccid phantom craft sales, Anheuser-Busch introduced . . . another phantom craft. This time, it was aimed squarely at the consumers of the hoppier West Coast–style brands, and none at this point embodied the style more than Sierra Nevada Pale Ale. The brewery, eight years into its new downtown Chico facility, was selling 150,000 barrels annually, much of it the signature brand that Grossman and Paul Camusi had cooked up fifteen years earlier by trial and error. The fresh phantom craft that Anheuser-Busch rolled out of its Fairfield, California, plant in late 1996 was very nearly a mirror image of it. A pastoral green, the same verdant hue as Sierra Nevada's, dominated the packaging, which included a body of water amid a forest backed by soaring mountains—again, just like Sierra Nevada's. The brand's name was crowned by the tag "Brewed in Northern California," just like Sierra Nevada was brewed in Northern California. Finally, the name itself, Pacific Ridge Pale Ale, and the ingredients, including the game-changing Cascade hops native to the Northwest, were unmistakable imitations.

As with previous phantom crafts—and with its 100-percent-share-of-mind campaign—Anheuser-Busch's official line was that it was not targeting any specific competitor with Pacific Ridge, though it was slated for distribution only in Northern California. The tactic was clear, though: it was another attempt to muddy the craft beer waters enough to grab a slice of what was still the overall industry's fastest-growing sector. The biggest brewer in history, which had turned brewing into a feat of borderless engineering, even adopted the locavore movement in its marketing for Pacific Ridge. Billboards popped up in Northern California exhorting consumers to "Think Globally, Drink Locally." It was enough to make Steve Harrison, Sierra Nevada's marketing director and very first employee, laugh. But the Pacific Ridge line, coupled with the 100-percent-share-of-mind campaign, was cause for additional worry in a craft beer movement that seemed ever more frothy—and not in the good way.

THE FRENCH LIEUTENANT'S COAT
Brooklyn | 1996

On May 28, 1996, New York City mayor Rudolph Giuliani cut the ribbon on the North Eleventh Street space in Williamsburg, Brooklyn, that Steve Hindy and Tom Potter had battled finances, the unions, and self-doubt to open (it ultimately cost $2 million to build out the space and fill it with top-notch equipment). It was a beautiful, open interior—His Honor quickly hopped behind the tastings bar and began pulling taps, explaining that his family had once owned a saloon—designed as much to foment interest from the community as it was to produce Brooklyn Brewery beers. The brewery would become the site of concerts, art shows, innumerable tours and tastings, and just generally a stop on the literal and psychological route of the renaissance that the borough of two million was about to undergo.

A big part of the physical reality of the new Brooklyn Brewery was due to its brewmaster since 1994, Garrett Oliver. He found the equipment via a Canadian fabricator and, along with the cofounders, conceived of the brewery as less of a simple production plant than as a neighborhood nexus. It was Oliver's second go-around with a New York City brewery since 1989, though his experience with beer in Gotham stretched back much further. He and Hindy had met, actually, on a cold winter's evening in December 1987 at a bar on Manhattan's Lower East Side. The New York City Homebrewers Guild had invited

Hindy to talk about this idea he had for a brewery across the Hudson River; he mingled with the members before he spoke, encountering myriad professionals—lawyers, engineers, professors, journalists like him—who asked if he had met Garrett Oliver, one of the guild's founders. No, he had not.

Then, shortly after eight o'clock, the bar door swung open and heads swung with it: Oliver wore knee-high buckled black boots, with a nineteenth-century French lieutenant's great coat draped over his shoulders. He introduced the crowd to Hindy, who soon realized after talking to him that Oliver's sartorial eccentricities equaled his passion for homebrewing and his knowledge of beer. At the end of the night, he presented the guild's guest speaker with a bottle of homemade raspberry stout, Oliver's Christmas ale that year. Hindy had never seen a more elegant bottle of beer; the parchment label depicted the guild's baroque label, complete with the Statue of Liberty's laurel as a crown, and across the cap a wax seal held in place a scarlet ribbon.

Garrett Oliver inside Brooklyn Brewery.
Courtesy of Brooklyn Brewery

Oliver grew up in eastern Queens in a family that prized good food and drink. His father, a Manhattan ad man, bred, trained, and hunted with German short-haired pointers, taking the family on horseback hunts for

Long Island pheasant and quail. Oliver's father would then prepare the food with the right herbs and the right white wine to go with it. His son studied filmmaking at Boston University in the late 1970s and early 1980s; there he organized concerts for bands such as R.E.M. and the Ramones (he took his fellow Queens natives bowling afterward in the basement of the student union). After graduation, he split for a year in the United Kingdom to stage-manage bands at the University of London. Like many Americans of the era who traveled to Europe, he had his beer epiphany quickly—his first day overseas—and completely. After the year in London, Oliver made it a point to travel to West Germany, Belgium, and Czechoslovakia to sample the other beers Europe had to offer. When he returned to the States in 1983, he found it very difficult, if not impossible, to drink domestic brands.

Oliver worked for HBO and later, at the time he met Hindy, for a prominent New York law firm as its operations manager. By then, he had acquired a reputation as a masterful homebrewer. He and Hindy met a second time in 1988 when a partner at Oliver's law firm, an old college friend of Hindy's, suggested Brooklyn Brewery do a tasting there; everyone again insisted Hindy meet this beer guy Garrett Oliver. By 1989, Oliver was an apprentice at the Manhattan Brewing Company in the Soho neighborhood, working under Mark Witty, who had been a brewer at Samuel Smith's, the Yorkshire brewery beloved by critic Michael Jackson.

Ever since Manchester, England, transplant Richard Wrigley opened it in the fall of 1984 as the city's first brewpub, Manhattan Brewing had struggled. It had shuttered and reopened by 1990, the ownership shifting away from Wrigley; it suffered a second closure in 1991, only to reopen in 1993 under different owners, a real estate investor and his CPA cousin. By the time of that third opening, Oliver was the brewmaster, capping a ten-year trek from his return to New York following his first encounter with fine beer in Europe. All the while, he and Hindy had been running into each other, hanging out, getting into late-night, boozy arguments over brewing and the craft beer movement. It was clear to Hindy that Oliver would be a perfect fit as brewmaster at Brooklyn Brewery, especially as it pivoted toward a physical presence in the city. Oliver joined in 1994, just as the build-out on the Williamsburg brewery got under way.

The Manhattan Brewing Company went out of business again a year later, and another brewpub then took over its space. The Nacho Mama Brewery was started, interestingly enough, by a pair of investors that included Joshua Mandel, the man who had introduced Sam Calagione to fine beer in the Morningside Heights restaurant of the same name. By the mid-1990s, the nation's largest city served as a microcosm of the larger craft beer movement as a whole. It had its pioneer in Matthew Reich's New Amsterdam and an array of successors, including early stumbles like Manhattan Brewing; finally, it had a boom that mostly consisted of brewpubs. The list was long by mid-1996, barely twelve years after Reich first sat down with Joseph Owades in Boston to plot New Amsterdam: A. J. Gordon's Brewing Company, Bayamo, Brooklyn Brewery, the Carnegie Hill Brewing Company, the Chelsea Brewing Company, the Commonwealth Brewing Company, Hansen's Times Square Brewery, Heartland Brewery, Nacho Mama, the Park Slope Brewing Company, and the Neptune Brewery. More would follow.

The second annual New York City Brewpub Crawl Marathon in July 1996, just as Atlanta hosted the Olympics, covered twelve brewpubs and seventy-two beers for those who might finish. It seemed Oliver, Hindy, Potter, and the others could not have picked a better time to open their physical brewery. Everyone, it appeared, was into craft beer or at least familiar with it, especially in heavily populated places that counted the most when it came to potential consumers, New York City chief among them. Big Beer's hegemony had been irredeemably broken, and the innovation of newer arrivals seemed poised, along with the capital infusions of the IPOs, to pull the movement to new heights. For a brewmaster such as Oliver, the biggest challenge now was an enviable one: How could you stand out?

TO THE EXTREME

Rehoboth Beach, DE | 1995–1997

M ariah Calagione readied the disposable camera. Her husband, Sam, drove their old pickup truck onto the sidewalk next to the building in Rehoboth Beach, Delaware, that housed their soon-to-open brewpub, Dogfish Head Brewings & Eats. Sam got out of the cab and stood proudly in the bed with the brewpub's new sign. First, he would have to remove the sign of the last business that had occupied the building, a failed restaurant. Mariah snapped a picture as Sam removed that old sign . . . only to find another old sign from another failed business beneath it. He asked Mariah not to shoot him removing that one. They are not you, Sam thought, psyching himself up—

Sam Calagione, the cofounder of Dogfish Head. Courtesy of Dogfish Head Brewery

again—as entrepreneurs had done since time immemorial. Their ideas were not your ideas.

And Sam Calagione had ideas. He had, after all, learned a lot from his homework at the New York Public Library. He had declared to those assembled at his Manhattan apartment at the tail end of the tasting party for his homemade Cherry Brew that he would be a brewer. Now, barely three years later, in the summer of 1995, he was making good on that drunken boast as he and Mariah prepared to open the draft-only brewpub. He named it after a peninsula in Maine where he spent boyhood summers and picked Rehoboth Beach in southern Delaware because it was Mariah's hometown (the pair had been together since Calagione's rocky high school years). It did not hurt in terms of free publicity, Sam figured, that Delaware had no other craft breweries or brewpubs; in fact, he was to find out only after he leased space that, as in only seven others, brewpubs were still banned in the First State, something he personally lobbied to change.

The brewpub was off the beach's beaten path, a shell of a restaurant vacated so quickly that there were still liquor bottles on the shelves and a couple of onion rings in the fryer when Calagione walked through it—not to mention a few bras, some boxers, and a stiletto heel elsewhere inside. Its location earned him a break on the rent with an option to buy, a clause he sensed the owner included only because she didn't think his business would last. Had she known more about what kinds of beers Calagione planned to produce, the owner's hunch would have been all the more justified.

Calagione's research (Bill Owens's *How to Build a Small Brewery* became a bible) and his own familiarity with craft beers had convinced him that the vast majority were based on interpretations of European styles. He was correct. There were only two distinctly American styles of beer at that point: steam beer, which Anchor had an excusable monopoly on (not to mention a trademark), and cream ale, perhaps most famously interpreted by the regional Genesee Brewing Company based in Rochester, New York. The rest were spins on styles developed in Ireland, Scotland, England, Belgium, the Czech Republic, and especially Germany, with its long tradition of beers brewed under the Reinheitsgebot. It no longer carried the weight of law, but its influence remained profound in Europe and the United States. Calagione saw an opening in this emphasis on European styles by Anchor, Sierra Nevada, Boston Beer—all the brands he was familiar with, admired, and liked to drink. They're doing those sorts of things really well, he thought. We're not going to stand out just trying to copy what they do.

Calagione's research into craft beer had taken him down other culinary avenues similar in approach and scope to what he had chosen to do, the

Dogfish Head's Chicory Stout.

sorts of avenues, like artisan breads and coffees, that would within a decade be associated with locavores and that were already linked with the nascent Slow Food movement. Artisan bread was then being called "the next food craze," with upscale bakery-cafés peppering cities like Boston, San Francisco, Seattle, and New York; there were even chains, like Au Bon Pain and the St. Louis Bread Company (Au Bon Pain would absorb the St. Louis Bread Company in the mid-1990s, repositioning it as Panera Bread). Calagione saw in these other artisan foodstuffs an opportunity to embrace every ingredient under the sun in brewing. There would, of course, be water, yeast, and grain undergirding everything, with hops of different varieties, too. Otherwise, it was open season. It was a sort of Reinheitsgebot for Generation X on the cusp of the twenty-first century.

When the brewpub opened, Dogfish Head was the smallest brewery, craft or otherwise, in the United States, brewing ten gallons at a time in a system rigged from three kegs and heated by propane burners, three times a day, five days a week. (Curiously enough, it was also the first brewery to plunk the phrase "craft brewery" in its actual name.) Dogfish Head's first offering was a straight-ahead pale ale using the four ingredients of barley, hops, water, and yeast in those European traditions. Then, during that first year, the brewpub pivoted toward the likes of Chicory Stout, which it debuted as a winter seasonal. It, too, had barley, hops, water, and yeast; it also had Saint-John's-wort, a plant sometimes used to treat depression; organic Mexican coffee; roasted chicory, a plant that can be ground down into a coffee substitute; and licorice root. In other words, it had ingredients that would have been unfamiliar—anathema, really—to a Bavarian brewer of the nineteenth or even twentieth century. These ingredients produced a dark, peppery beer with hints, not surprisingly, of roasted coffee and chocolate; it was, as one reviewer put it, perfect "if you only want to have one or two stouts."

Part of it was boredom with the status quo; part of it the possibility for experimentation; part of it another way to stand out in an increasingly crowded pack whose production was growing by double-digit percentages yearly. Whatever the ultimate reason, Calagione's Chicory Stout was one of the opening salvos in extreme beer and extreme brewing, though neither term would come into vogue for years yet. What characteristics defined extreme beer? Strength: they were typically higher in alcohol per volume than your pales ales, IPAs, and ambers. Richness, too, could be a defining feature; as with the Chicory Stout, extreme beers tended to be very busy on their back ends, brimming with hitherto unimagined ingredients or with unimagined amounts of those ingredients. Hops would become a favorite tool of extreme brewing, with Dogfish Head pioneering a method for frequently adding hops—sometimes once a minute for two hours—to the boiling wort. Finally, because of the first two characteristics, extreme beers were simply exotic to the American palate, even a palate that may now have spent an intimate twenty years with craft beers. They tasted stranger, their packaging even *looked* stranger, than anything out there, the explanations of their origins and the adjectives that might flow from tasting them unlike anything the beer consumer, in the United States or elsewhere, had ever encountered. The definition of extreme beer seemed destined to mimic the popular one for obscenity: people knew it when they saw it.

Boston Beer was perhaps the first brewery in the nation to present extreme beers as exactly that, beginning in the late 1980s with its interpretations of the strong German lager style called bock and then its Utopias line, some bottles of which, it was suggested by Jim Koch, should be aged like—gasp!—wine. Koch would explain it this way when extreme beer had become a staple of the American craft beer movement: "The world doesn't need one more pale ale or more good porter or hefewiezen. There's enough of that. Craft brewers have to continue to brew unique, distinctive, even surprising beers."

For the time being, extreme beers did not really have a name or a niche. The vast majority of craft beer produced and consumed in the United States was, as we have seen, on the milder, more traditional side, with Koch's own Boston Lager claiming a sizable share. But Calagione was just twenty-five when his brewpub opened, young enough to have grown up around craft beer's wider availability and after the movement's first shakeout in the 1980s. As a newcomer, he took to the possibilities offered by extreme beer for experimentation and innovation on a scale not seen since the heyday of Belgian beer in the sixteenth and seventeenth centuries, when styles now common worldwide were developed by the isolated equivalents of late-twentieth-century start-ups. Still, for all the enthusiasm engendered by these potential avenues, it remained to be seen whether roasted chicory and Saint-John's-wort in unusual packaging could be a successful financial route; extreme beer might just be a particularly innovative way to go broke. Things were uncertain enough already.

The Dogfish Head brewpub grew in popularity despite its location, its growth powered in no small part by the live music that Calagione booked and the general ambiance of a spot that had embraced "Off-Centered Ales for Off-Centered People" as its slogan. Calagione expanded the brewhouse thirtyfold to keep up with demand for the beers, consigning the original, ten-gallons-at-a-time system to lore. And then in 1997, a year after the brewpub began bottling that first pale ale, he moved the packaging from the restaurant to a space seven miles away, in Lewes.

Small as it still was, Dogfish Head ran smack into Anheuser-Busch's 100-percent-share-of-mind campaign. At least two distributors told the brewery they did not want to distribute its brands anymore, and when Dogfish Head, now on its way to producing five year-round beers and garnering $1.6 million in annual sales by the decade's end, tried to distribute beyond the Mid-Atlantic, it ran into similar reticence. When a distributor pressured by Anheuser-Busch wouldn't take his brands, Calagione would approach another big distributor in whatever particular market, only to be told he had too many craft brands as it was. In those cases, he would hunt for smaller distributors and count on word of mouth among consumers to stoke demand, as it had done in Rehoboth Beach.

Or he would have some fun with his company's size. Goliath might have the major distributors and the ad men, but David held an increasing fascination with consumers, from Wall Street to Main Street. On the morning of August 24, 1997, a Sunday, Calagione climbed into an eighteen-foot scull he had spent $1,500 making and drifted into the currents of Delaware Bay with a six-pack of his pale ale beside him. He spent about four hours rowing the seventeen nautical miles from Rehoboth Beach to Cape May, New Jersey, to deliver the first Dogfish Head to be distributed outside Delaware. There were only a handful of people to see him disembark, however, and the publicity stunt seemed like a clever flop. Then jeansmaker Levi Strauss learned about the journey and contacted him to appear in an ad campaign photographed by Richard Avedon. The theme? Plucky entrepreneurs.

THE TOTAL PACKAGE
Petaluma, CA | 1995

Tony Magee knew that everyone in craft beer knew the origin of Oktoberfest. The king of Bavaria threw a two-day festival for his newly married son, the crown prince, in October 1810. Ever since, the Germans, and eventually people worldwide, have marked the occasion each year with their own festivals resplendent in copious amounts of beer and German food. Oktoberfest beers grew from the original festival as well, and Magee's brewery, Lagunitas, was about to debut its own interpretation in October 1995. But first it needed a label, one that would stand out among the other Oktoberfest beers offered by American craft brewers (Jim Koch's Boston Beer had perhaps America's bestselling Oktoberfest interpretation, a lager it introduced in 1989). Magee's backgrounds in music composition and print sales dovetailed nicely as he pored over ideas for what might make a marketplace splash but was also out of the ordinary for a typical Oktoberfest. His was a hoppy amber ale, while most others were lagers on the sweeter side. He wanted a label that stood out both visually and editorially; packaging could be, he realized, as experimental as the stronger beers his brewery was turning out.

It was a realization that other craft brewers, especially the newer ones, were coming to across the country as they eschewed the educational and direct packaging of their pioneer predecessors as much as they eschewed their recipes. The label of a bottle of Anchor Brewing, Sierra Nevada, or Boston Beer—even the more irreverent Pete's Brewing—might tell the origins of the beer and the ingredients as well as the pride the brewery took in presenting the product. The accompanying imagery would be equally simple and often the same through a brewery's various styles, little altered except for the ingredients and the packaging's colors, with maybe an addition or omission here and there. These labels were straightforward—they had had to be in an era when most consumers would have been unfamiliar with what was staring back at them from the grocery store shelf. Too cute or too arcane and it wouldn't matter how good the beer was inside the brown bottle (which could itself be unfamiliar enough). The imagery on Anchor's label for Liberty Ale, revolutionary for its use of Cascade hops, shared the anchor, barley, hops, and "San Francisco" from the label for the brewery's steam beer (but, unlike the steam beer label, it also had an eagle behind the anchor). It read:

San Francisco's famous Liberty Ale was first brewed on the 18th of April, 1975, to celebrate the 200th anniversary of Paul Revere's historic ride. It is virtually handmade by the brewers of Anchor Steam Beer in one of the smallest and most traditional breweries in the world. Liberty Ale is made with the finest barley malt; fresh, whole hops; top-fermenting yeast; pure water; and the natural methods that reflect our exceptional respect for the ancient art of brewing. It is "dry hopped," a classic ale tradition, and slowly completes its fermentation in sealed vats in our cellars. This unique process creates

Liberty Ale's distinctive bouquet and uncommonly delicate, entirely natural carbonation.

Here was Magee's label for the Oktoberfest, Lagunitas's first seasonal:

The original derivation of the word "Oktoberfest" was actually the phrase, "Ach! Tuber Fest!" This antiquious expression refers back to the Dark Age reign of Sir Loin of Boef, during which there existed a brisk European trade in captured Irish slaves. The prevailing Germanic Lords imported Irishmen to work in their central European potato plantations. These Irish slaves were notorious for their endurance in drinking festivals under the new moon and during the potato harvest. They would brew up huge batches of a unique fermented alcoholic Potato Beer. The Irishmen eventually introduced their German masters to this unusual beer-like beverage. The harvest parties centered around this brew, hence the term "Tuber-fest." The slaves were finally freed during the European potato blights of 1252 and 1257. Years later malted barley was substituted for the spuds of old and, well, the rest is history. Honest. . . .

Literally every phrase and sentence on Magee's label was factually incorrect (and "antiquious" wasn't even a word); nevertheless the brewery got calls from credulous consumers asking if this was the true story of Oktoberfest. Magee couldn't help himself. He liked the idea of a backstory. He was familiar with the J. Peterman clothing catalogues (before they were immortalized on the television show *Seinfeld*), and he liked the idea of standing athwart the movement toward talking about beer as if one were discussing wine. He did more creative writing for other Lagunitas brands, and soon the brewery was pioneering not only an IPA as its flagship but also some of the zanier names in the already rapidly expanding craft beer lexicon: Dogtown, Bug Town, Hairy Eyeball Ale, Equinox Ale, the Lagunator. The last, released over the holidays, spoofed the recently released Arnold Schwarzenegger vehicle *The Terminator*, complete with a dog in sunglasses and the tag, "I'll Be Bock." It didn't matter to the brewery that the beer was a brown ale and a bock is a type of lager—it worked. It helped the seasonal sell well in an ever-more-crowded marketplace.*

---

* The marketing material for the Lagunator, a dark brown ale, included the explanation, "We brewed this Special Ale to celebrate the darkness and depression that mar the holiday landscape." That was not included on the packaging.

These beers were rolling out of a new brewery; a moody septic tank at the original location had forced Magee's hand. "In putrid tones," he remembered, "it told me we had to leave, and quickly. The septic tank also called the neighbors. It called the busy street in front of the brewery, the playground behind us, and then it called the county." So he rented space in an old industrial garage about twenty-five miles north in Petaluma, a stone's throw from Highway 101. The move represented an expansion and a step up. He was able to replace the increasingly rickety seven-barrel electric brewhouse once meant for Russia with a newer one fabricated by the same John Cross who had imported Grundy tanks from the United Kingdom, though the fight against the tyranny of fast growth remained.

The label for Lagunitas Sucks Holiday Ale Brown Shugga' Substitute,
what might loosely be called an American strong ale.

Here was how it was working financially for Magee and other start-up craft breweries in this age of multimillion-dollar IPOs and Big Beer takeovers. Lagunitas was still self-distributing all-draft when it moved to Petaluma. Such a brewery might sell a keg to a distributor for sixty-five dollars. Because there were two kegs to one barrel, a fourteen-barrel system, probably the bare minimum to seriously compete and grow, could generate around $1,820 in sales wholesale. The same fourteen-barrel system, however, might generate around

$2,960 wholesale via bottles. But bottling beer introduced an entire new set of costs, including the glassware, the caps, and especially the bottling line, which, as we've seen, could run into thousands of dollars even secondhand. Plus, this was the era of price wars between craft brewers, in particular Boston Beer and Pete's Brewing, as they amped up for and went through their IPOs. So it was not a given that a six-pack of freshly minted bottles would sell at, say, $5.99 when a competitor's in the same display was selling for $4.99. For his part, Magee decided Lagunitas had to price itself at the higher end to send a message that it intended to play with the bigger brands.

Add to this worry over pricing and expansion the actual start-up costs, which never seemed to go away, even after years of growth. Debts had to be paid down, and investors had to be paid up. Even a new location, a new approach to labeling, a new set of styles that might revolutionize the industry, a hospitable local environment such as San Francisco or New York that seemed to manufacture new consumers by the day—none of it was enough for a financial respite. Meanwhile, every time a start-up turned around, it was liable to find a fresh competitor, often one with more capital. The only saving grace for start-up craft brewers at this point seemed the promise of the industrywide double-digit growth continuing into the late 1990s. Thank God for that.

BOOS

Boston; Pittsburgh | 1996

The crowd of craft brewers and brewpub owners booed David Geary. He didn't care—he felt what he had to say needed saying. It was the Association of Brewers's annual conference in May 1996 in Boston, a two-hour drive from Geary's craft brewery in Portland, Maine, the oldest in New England; there were at least three thousand attendees, many of whom had already been fretting openly about the impacts of the wave of IPOs on the industry and the incursion of Anheuser-Busch into Redhook, including the plans for the one-hundred-thousand-square-foot brewery in Portsmouth, New Hampshire, halfway between Boston and Portland. Nerves were frayed, minds were troubled; the industrywide growth was all well and good, but there was a feeling that something had to give. How much craft beer could the American consumer stomach? No one really wanted to hear what Geary ended up saying.

First, he praised Goliath. Budweiser isn't bad beer, he told the crowd; it's great beer.

Boos.

"Listen to me," Geary went on, "you would kill to have the consistent quality that they have. You may not like the style, but it's not bad beer."

More boos.

Then Geary grabbed some salt. He dumped it on a wound that had been festering for ten years.

We have to stop saying that Jim Koch was an impostor, Geary said, an interloper. He's not.

The dig had followed Koch since the launch of Boston Beer in 1985, when it was brewed by the Pittsburgh Brewing Company. After more than a decade of explosive growth, steady revenues, and an epic IPO, more than 99 percent of Boston Beer's Samuel Adams line was still brewed outside of Boston, the brewery in the city's Jamaica Plain neighborhood little more than window dressing for tours and tastings and further branding (though it was also used for small batches as well as research and development). Boston Beer now contracted not only with Pittsburgh Brewing but with Stroh's in Lehigh Valley, Pennsylvania; Blitz-Weinhard in Portland, Oregon; and a Gambrinus-owned brewery in Germany for the European marketplace; and the bocks brewed in Jamaica Plain might age in vats at a winery in Northern California. The company traded 961,000 barrels in 1995, including in Europe, for net sales of $151.3 million, many times its nearest competitors.

All the while, there was Koch in the papers, on the radio, and sometimes even on the TV, talking in folksy tones about history's Samuel Adams and his roots in Boston, and the city's own roots in brewing. (The stuff about Samuel Adams grated on some nerves, too, as Adams was not himself a brewer but the son of the owner of a malting house, a business he quickly ran into the ground after his father's death.) Koch, by ceaselessly recounting these details, as well as his own family background in brewing, crafted what Geary called, not without admiration, "a mythology." It worked. The media repeated it; consumers took to it; it ballasted a brand that went in a few years from experimental bottles on ice in Koch's briefcase and Rhonda Kallman's oversized Lancôme bag to the biggest small-time beer ever. How could you argue with so much Americana, from the patriot on the label to the imagined brewers in their overalls boiling amber waves of grain and one man's devotion to honoring his familial calling at the expense of a cushy job in a big skyscraper?

"So Jim Koch," Geary asked the Boston conference rhetorically, "is not a craft brewer? The man who taught us all how to sell beer? Ridiculous!"

More boos—in Koch's backyard, no less.

The contract brewing particularly annoyed those brewers who had sunk thousands, maybe even millions, into the start-up costs of a physical brewery: the rent on space, the kettles and tuns, the bottling line, the cooling systems, the labs, the insurance for it all. These were costs that contract brewers like Koch largely escaped, freeing them to pour any revenues into more marketing to spur more sales to spur the need for more lower-cost contract brewing . . . and on and on, capacity unencumbered by physical limits. It bred resentment. "Contract brewing is the cocaine of the beer business," Paul Shipman, a cofounder of Redhook, which Koch mocked in the media after the Anheuser-Busch deal, said around the time of the Boston conference. "People who do it deny that they do it; then, when confronted with it, they say they've got it under control." Other brewers lobbed a simpler insult. "He's just an extremely aggressive salesman," sniffed Bert Grant, the founder of the nation's first brewpub. It was meant as a particularly stinging rebuke in an industry that traditionally prided itself on not advertising.

But it wasn't just those who had risked a physical brewery. Pete Slosberg and Mark Bronder, cofounders of the other big-time contract brewery, Pete's Brewing, did not get on with Koch personally or his company professionally. And Koch did not help himself with some of his early tactics. Not only did he understandably target Big Beer and imports in his bid to popularize Samuel Adams, but he also went after the little guys, too. Boston Beer backed the late 1994 launch of the Oregon Ale and Beer Company, ostensibly a start-up contract brewer in the Northwest but in actuality a wholly controlled subsidiary of Boston Beer (Koch had, for one, helped devise the new company's recipes). Some saw it as a direct challenge to Pete's Brewing on the West Coast and as another inroad against the smaller physical breweries—and these smaller breweries said so. "Local Microbrewers Incensed at Imposter," read one ad taken out by the Oregon Brewers Guild and the Washington Small Brewers Association. Explained Michael Sherwood, then the guild's director: "An out-of-state brewer came into Oregon, didn't build a brewery here, appropriated the name, and marketed it around the country to trade on the name that in-state brewers worked hard to make, and then put on the label 'Microbrewed in Oregon'—but it was made at one of the large industrial breweries in the state."

A similar complaint dogged Samuel Adams Cranberry Lambic, which Boston Beer introduced in 1990. Lambics are generally sour beers developed in an area of Belgium southwest of Brussels; to connoisseurs, including brewers, a beer should call itself a "lambic" on the label only if it originated from that area, much like real Champagne must come from a particular region of France. Koch did it anyway, calling it an "interpretation" of the Belgian style.

Then there were confrontations such as this one near Boston's Fenway Park. In April 1992, brothers Steve and Joe Slesar invited their parents to the new beer bar they had just opened across the street from the legendary baseball stadium. Another guest showed up uninvited—Jim Koch, who was peeved about the bar's name: Boston Beer Works. The brothers' father overheard the entire heated argument between Koch and the Slesars, which seemed to hinge on whether the two words "Boston" and "Beer" infringed on the trademark held by Koch's company. The two sides would spend the next year and a half—and tens of thousands of dollars—fighting over the words, with Koch losing his last challenge in November 1993.

And speaking of trademarks, Koch had tried to trademark the phrase "The Best Beer in America" for his Samuel Adams Boston Lager after its run of wins in the Great American Beer Festival's consumer preference poll in the late 1980s. In a November 1993 filing with the US Patent and Trademark Office, Koch cited the more than $2 million his company had already spent promoting the beer thusly, as well as a Rolling Rock promotion that invited consumers to sample "the beer that bested 'The Best Beer in America'" after its bock trumped Samuel Adams in a taste contest. It was, Koch contended, proof that at least one competitor saw Samuel Adams as literally the best beer in America. The trademarks office disagreed—as did a federal court that Koch appealed to—and so did many of his fellow brewers. They were stung enough to have lost the consumer preference poll so many years running (three straight and four in five), but Koch racing to slap the wins on his packaging seemed to them the height of gauche. Such things were simply not done in the American craft beer movement.

Which may have been precisely the problem, as David Geary saw it. The movement had started small and had stayed that way for its first couple of decades, due largely to the challenges faced by the likes of Sam Calagione and Tony Magee in the early 1990s just as they had been faced by the likes of Jack McAuliffe and Tom de Bakker in the early 1980s. Consumers' unfamiliarity with the product, despite the most fervent efforts of Michael Jackson, Fred Eckhardt, Byron Burch, Charlie Papazian, and other evangelists, was one challenge. The capital-intensive start-up costs were a challenge, too, as were the distribution costs and compromises that somewhat cruelly accompanied growth. Finally there was the challenge of finding skilled brewery workers, particularly brewmasters, and controlling quality to produce the same beers consistently.

Then along came Matthew Reich at New Amsterdam and Jim Koch at Boston Beer—and shortly after, Pete Slosberg at Pete's Brewing—with contract brewing, and much of these challenges went by the wayside, freeing revenues for marketing, for educating the public about these newfangled pale ales, India pale ales, porters, stouts, ambers, bitters, extra special bitters, bocks, and wits. That was the triumph of the contract brewers: they brought craft beer to places that had never encountered it and placed it before consumers who may have only read or heard about it secondhand. Suddenly, in a few short years in the late 1980s, craft beer was ubiquitous. To this day, on the web that would in the coming decade help to spread the movement to ever more Americans, stories abound of Pete's Wicked Ale as what we'll call a gateway craft beer. From these first, furtive encounters grew a groundswell of demand as well as an upswing in supply that stood directly crosswise to the trends in American manufacturing in the 1990s.

The grim predictions of Ross Perot in that November 1993 CNN debate with Al Gore appeared to be coming true already—and not just because of NAFTA. That trade agreement was just one part of the relentless march of globalization, which, with its promise of cheaper labor overseas and cheaper goods at home, was upending entire, age-old American industries. Take the furniture industry in central North Carolina. Since the late nineteenth century, it had been a major employer in the region, and by the 1980s, the small city of High Point, near Greensboro, had earned the nickname the Furniture Capital of the World, in no small part because it hosted the world's biggest home-furnishings trade show every year. The furniture its factories produced was a point of local pride and a major economic engine.

But by the mid-1990s, the engine was sputtering; it became clear that employment in High Point's furniture industry was peaking. Overseas competition, particularly from China, where furniture could be made at a fraction of the cost with cheaper materials, was hampering sales. Local politicians and industry executives began talking of greater automation as the key to growth, though that alone could not stem the factory closings and the layoffs. Pretty soon these same pols and executives were talking of the industry's heyday in the past tense and encouraging those laid off to retrain for work in more high-tech fields. A Duke University study of the furniture industry's decline put it this way: "The chance of finding a new job in the furniture industry is probably very low for most displaced workers." Furniture-making in central North Carolina would never be the same, especially when it came to employment.

The same went for manufacturing in general. US Department of Labor statistics were starting to show a looming cliff; the number of factory and other manufacturing jobs had grown since World War II, with muscular peaks in the 1960s and 1970s as Americans created products the world wanted. For those studying such things closely, though, it was clear that the jobs growth was ebbing; entire neighborhoods in major cities like New York, Chicago, Cleveland, and Pittsburgh, where factories once belched smoke, were now either abandoned or becoming pricey loft apartments, their manufacturing pasts mere marketing material for real estate brokers. It would be a few years before manufacturing as a sector of the US economy went over the cliff hand in hand with a sizable chunk of the national psyche. But the writing was starting to scrawl across the wall.

Then there was craft beer. The industry was slapping on jobs with its torrid growth in the 1990s. As many as 115 craft operations, including brewpubs, would start up in 1996, nearly ten a month or one about every seventy-two hours, with most employing at least two people full-time. This was an industry that could not be outsourced, that provided a foodstuff with a long and storied history in the United States, that prized technical know-how and a devotion to accuracy, and that often now served as an economic-development engine on a local level, as most breweries rented space in the less desirable (and therefore cheaper) areas of their communities. Witness the changes wrought by Brooklyn Brewery in its part of the borough or the Mass. Bay Brewing Company's role in turning the public perception of the South Boston waterfront from an area where Whitey Bulger might've clipped enemies to one that produced that tasty Harpoon IPA. Craft beer was a true port in the manufacturing sector's storm, an industry so burning hot that everybody, including Big Beer and Wall Street, wanted in. It just seemed so . . . doable.

This was never inevitable. Those brewers who had come and gone could attest to that. David Geary—and others, though they may have not said so out loud in front of thousands of their closest friends and competitors—knew that the movement's ubiquity was due to the efforts of Jim Koch. He and Matthew Reich and Pete Slosberg, and their partners, including brewmaster Joseph Owades, used the advantages they had gained from contract brewing to spread the gospel of craft beer to the far corners of an America increasingly inhospitable to American manufacturing. In doing so, they lifted the smaller boats that might have been sunk by those weighty start-up costs. They provided a context for consumers to think within. Now we have a category, Geary himself thought once Samuel Adams beers reached Maine by 1988, two years after he started selling his own.

But he was booed at the 1996 Craft Brewers Conference in Boston. No matter how many fresh consumers that New Amsterdam, Boston Beer, Pete's Brewing, and others had brought to the proverbial table, many in the audience, particularly those from the West Coast, were not prepared to acknowledge any of them as one of their own. The entire industry, in fact, had begun to fragment psychologically. Charlie Papazian recognized this and all but pleaded with the same Boston crowd. "There is a controversy now about where beer is being made, and people are getting very emotional," he said. "The issue that really matters is being unique. It's not just about a product, not just about where it's made—but about its spirit." Such an invocation of the collectivist ethos from the movement's earliest days fell on deaf ears; 1978 was a long time ago.

No hair was too thin to split now. The purveyors of what would come to be called extreme beer were dismissed as faddists by brewers in the mold of more traditional European styles. Geary caught more flack by telling his audience there were too many medals for too many categories of beer. The number of categories at the Great American Beer Festival alone had more than tripled in the ten years since medals were introduced in 1987. Moreover, while the GABF was still the highly regarded standard for judging American beer, other entities had sprung up with dubious credentials and criteria; at least one seemed to be simply pay-to-play, a way for brewers to slap news of a gold medal on their next label.

Sour beers in particular annoyed more traditional brewers. Wasn't a sour taste simply the result of bacterial infection, a sign of failure? Yet some newer brewers—and some who would award them medals—were beginning to see sour as its own animal. Long gone were the days when a tiny college of critics, with Michael Jackson their infallible dean, decided the archetypes of beer style.

On and on the recriminations went as the growth ballooned. The older hands from way back in the 1980s eyed the hundreds of new startups suspiciously, sometimes with contempt. The physical breweries disdained the contract breweries. The solo brewpubs dismissed the chains. The West Coast, keeper of the original flame, distrusted the East Coast, a late arrival at the party. The brewers partially owned by Big Beer were anathema to the independents. No one trusted the next nearest guy to make the case to the consumer as strongly.

The American craft beer movement was an undeniable manufacturing and culinary triumph, but one far adrift from its collegial roots. It was all so shrill now. Litmus tests abounded, particularly for newer entrants and anyone, like Jim Koch, who was *too* successful. One was reminded of the answer British prime minister David Lloyd George gave when asked how he had done at the Paris Peace Conference in 1919, when he found himself dealing with the idealistic US president, Woodrow Wilson, on one side and the vengeful French premier, Georges Clemenceau, on the other: "Not badly, considering I was seated between Jesus Christ and Napoleon."

THE MOVEMENT'S BIGGEST SETBACK

New York; Philadelphia | 1996

On Sunday, October 13, 1996, at 7:00 PM Eastern time, the sonorously calm voice of television newsman Stone Phillips eased into around eight million American homes: "When it comes to beer, you've never had more choices on tap."

Colorful images of pull taps and glasses of beer flowed across the screen. An unidentified man at an unidentified bar pronounced his verdict upon a Rhino Chasers Peach Honey Wheat from the William and Scott Company, a contract concern started by Culver City, California, ad execs in 1989 that brewed through the Minnesota Brewing Company in St. Paul and F. X. Matt in Utica, New York: "It's got a hint of berry flavoring."

Phillips again: "But do you know where some of those exotic and expensive specialty beers are really being made?"

Thus the setup for a segment of that evening's episode of *Dateline*, an hour-long NBC newsmagazine broadcast out of Rockefeller Center in Midtown Manhattan. It debuted as a Tuesday program in 1992 and had gradually expanded to four nights, including a Sunday edition added only seven months before. That edition was meant as head-to-head competition for CBS's venerable *60 Minutes*, but lately the time slot was barely pulling ahead of the likes of Fox's *When Animals Attack*.

Even four years on, *Dateline* dragged around the aftershocks of a disgraceful 1992 segment on General Motors pickup trucks. The program backed up its allegation that the trucks' fuel tanks could easily explode in accidents . . . by rigging the trucks' fuel tanks to explode in accidents. Still, the show soldiered onward, adding timeslots as it became a franchise for NBC and a beachhead for a new kind of a documentary-like, confrontational news show, a sort of precursor to reality TV—here was how people *really* lived professionally and personally. The roster of talent behind the show, including Tom Brokaw, Jane Pauley, Katie Couric, Bryant Gumbel, and Maria Shriver, gave *Dateline* gravitas, as did its reach. In the era just before one-thousand-channel cable and satellite packages, not to mention widespread use of the web, *Dateline* could make or break businesses and people.

After the episode's introduction plugged other segments for that evening, including ones on O. J. Simpson's civil trial and the crash of TWA Flight 800 a few months before, it was back to beer. Here was Stone Phillips on-screen now, his chisel-chinned looks and leading-man gaze priming the audience.

> Good evening. From the ballpark to the corner bar to your refrigerator, beer is a $50-billion-a-year business in this country, and making the biggest splash these days are those trendy specialty brews, offering new flavors with a mom-and-pop appeal at premium prices. But how much hype is mixed in with the hops and the barley? How much do you really know about your favorite beer? Just how and where it's actually made? Here's Chris Hansen.

To any craft beer aficionado who might've already tuned in, the inclusion of the contract-brewed Rhino Chasers in the introduction would have been a clue to how this segment, titled "Brew-Haha," was about to go. And on it went.

Chris Hansen, who would the following decade attain a sprinkle of television immortality as the host of the *Dateline* spinoff *To Catch a Predator*, about confronting would-be sex offenders on-camera, gave his own voiceover as more images of exotic taps and glasses washed across the screen. His roll-out was interspersed with further critical pronouncements from patrons and bartenders.

> *Hansen:* The selection is mind-boggling—Seismic Ale and Earthquake Pale, Red Fox or Goat's Breath Bock?
> *Bar patron:* It's got that dark, malty kind of full-bodied taste.
> *Hansen:* They're called craft brews, or microbrews, because, we're told, the beer is carefully crafted one small batch at a time.

Viewers then met Jim Koch. They heard about the Boston brewery and about Koch's patrilineage: "Every oldest son in my family has been a brewmaster for a century and a half." Hansen told the audience of the success of Samuel Adams—the sales, the medals—and of Koch's dedication to the craft of brewing: "Koch says he still samples every batch his company brews, and he wasn't shy about doing so during our visit."

It all sounded so commendable and complimentary, not only to Koch's Boston Beer Company but also to the entire craft beer movement. This *Dateline* segment looked as if it could end up being the biggest single platform the movement ever had to reach the nation, to tell the populace of this manufacturing and culinary triumph, of this return to local craftsmanship using wholesome ingredients and traditional recipes. This looked to be a moment not just for craft brewers and their fans—it looked to be one for craft food producers, period.

However, any craft beer aficionado who might have tuned in—indeed, any viewer who heard Stone Phillips's incredulous questions about craft beer during the introduction—had to have known what was coming. It was as if NBC had painted a big, red bull's-eye on Jim Koch's back. Hansen, after the laudations:

> [T]he bottle invites you to come visit their small traditional brewery in Boston. So we did, and found a small brick building, a photo tribute to previous generations of Koch brewers, and, just as you see in the Sam Adams commercials, the small copper kettles and equipment used to brew the beer. But there's one small problem with this picture: At least 95 percent of all Sam Adams beer isn't brewed here—or anywhere even near Boston, for that matter.
> Shots now of other, much less bucolic breweries.
> It's brewed here, at the Stroh's Brewery in Lehigh Valley, Pennsylvania. Here, at Genesee in Rochester, New York. And at several other large industrial breweries throughout the country. And while it may be handcrafted one single batch at a time like the bottle says, each single batch is brewed in a kettle that can hold up to one hundred to two hundred thousand bottles of beer. That's right—the Sam Adams you buy in the store was likely brewed in the same place as more humble and less expensive brands, like Old Milwaukee, Stroh's, or Little Kings. And Sam Adams is far from alone. Many of the expensive boutique beers that promote themselves as "handcrafted"

or "microbrewed" are actually made in larger commercial breweries like this one; it's called contract brewing.

The boom was lowered. Craft brewers of whatever size or stripe would never forget the *Dateline* segment. On it plunged with its blazing indictment of contract brewing, an indictment that grew throughout the segment to tarnish the entire craft beer movement. If Samuel Adams Boston Lager was brewed in Pittsburgh and it was the bestselling American craft beer brand on earth, then where was any bottle of craft beer brewed? It was all enough to make a consumer stare at the beer in his hand and then back at Chris Hansen, wondering what the extra buck or two per six-pack was really worth. The worst thing about it all was who NBC presented as the aggrieved party, the victim of these dastardly small-scale brewers and their deceptive marketing: Big Beer. Anheuser-Busch in particular put itself forward as a source for NBC.

Hansen: Francine Katz is the vice president of consumer awareness at Anheuser-Busch, the biggest beer maker in the world, one of the nation's biggest television advertisers, and a brewer that's hopping mad about a lot of the so-called boutique beers.

Katz, brandishing a bottle: This one says that it was brewed and bottled by Pete's Brewing Company, St. Paul, Minnesota, but Pete's doesn't own a brewery in St. Paul, or anywhere; Stroh's made that beer.

Hansen: Pete's Wicked Ale is the second hottest-selling microbrew in the US. Anheuser-Busch manufactures some ninety million barrels a year?

Katz: Mm-hmm.

Hansen: Forty-five percent of the market? Why are you so concerned about what little Sam Adams is doing or little Pete's Wicked Ale?

Katz: This comes down to honesty and truth in labeling. You know, I'm not going to stand here and tell you that we don't want to sell beer. All we're saying is, 'Hey, guys, let's agree on some basic rules of honesty, let's be truthful on our labels.'

Hansen then returned to Koch for a classic clinic on gotcha journalism, though he had yet to unsheathe his sharpest weapon.

Koch: Sam Adams beer is brewed by Boston Beer Company. We select the ingredients; we select the recipe; we are the brewer.

Hansen: But the guys actually brewing the beer don't work for you.

Koch: The people brewing beer are brewing it under our supervision and our direction. They do exactly what we ask them to do.

Hansen: But don't you think you create the image in people's minds that Sam Adams is brewed right here in this quaint Boston brewery, when, in fact, it's farmed out all over the country?

Koch: We don't lie to them.

Hansen: Well, it doesn't sound like it's being completely honest, either.

Koch: We tell them who brews the beer. If Julia Child comes to your house, brings her own ingredients and her own recipe, goes into your kitchen, and makes dinner for you, who made dinner, you or Julia Child?

Koch, the nation's biggest craft brewer, came off looking defensive, a little sad even. Anheuser-Busch, the world's biggest brewer, came off looking concerned for the consumer, a dipsomaniacal Ralph Nader. As Katz put it seconds later regarding craft beer packaging: "There's enough on this label to be a small novel; certainly, there's enough room to tell beer drinkers the truth." She did not stray off-message when Koch argued to Hansen that Anheuser-Busch's concern for consumers was nothing more than a pose in the face of a craft beer segment growing then by double digits. "This doesn't come down to the issue of competition," Katz retorted. "It doesn't come down to whose beers are better. I can't think of why asking a beer producer to be honest about who's making the beer could be in some way being a bully."

Hansen then went on to cite a federal tax credit that encouraged smaller brewers to expand, which, he said, was available to contract brewers as well. Craft brewers at this point were able to take advantage of not only this credit for purchasing equipment but also a lower tax rate of seven dollars per barrel up to the first sixty thousand barrels if they brewed no more than two million barrels a year (which everyone then did). Individual states, too, might have fairly generous tax breaks for expanding smaller brewers compared to those for Big Beer. It was something, Hansen explained, that peeved Anheuser-Busch, as well as competing craft brewers. That was because the tax breaks were meant, according to Hansen, for craft brewers who had started capital-intensive physical operations. He introduced Gary Fish, founder of the Deschutes Brewing Company in Bend, Oregon, amid scenes of a busy pub.

Hansen: Fish founded the Deschutes brewpub and restaurant in 1988, putting his and his family's financial future on the line to make it happen. He expanded successfully, building a brewery from the ground up. And, today, the Deschutes name is popular throughout the Pacific Northwest. Deschutes and thirty other small brewers from Oregon have sided with Bud in the battle over truth in labeling.

Fish: Microbrewery is a—is a noun. To me, it means something.

Hansen then showed viewers the label on a bottle of the Boston Beer-backed Oregon Ale and Beer Company, explaining that it was brewed under contract by Stroh's.

Hansen to Fish: How do people out here in Oregon involved in craft brewing react when they look at a bottle of Oregon Ale and it says "microbrewed" on the label?

Fish: I think they feel patently offended.

There it was: the tetchiness of the American craft beer movement that had swelled over the last few years. The rancor, the worries, the mistrust—it had all spilled onto a national, prime-time stage. But who had set the stage?

Jim Koch watched the episode with his kids back in Newton, Massachusetts, just outside of Boston, after watching the Yankees beat the Orioles 6 to 4 to secure their first World Series spot since 1981. He had kind of known what was coming. His last client at the Boston Consulting Group twelve years ago before he left to do beer full-time was General Electric, and GE owned a majority stake in NBC. Koch, following his interviews with Hansen and before the episode aired, contacted an old friend within NBC to try to get a read on what to expect from the final cut.

"Is it going to be objective?" Koch wanted to know. "Is it going to be negative?"

"It's going to be negative, Jim," his friend replied.

He broke it down for Koch like this: Anheuser-Busch was one of NBC's biggest advertisers. It had bought, for instance, 175 commercials for the Olympics in Atlanta the summer before. It wasn't that *Dateline* lacked journalistic standards, but any segment, with just about any set of facts, could be slanted as the show wanted it. Besides, GE management was not wont to interfere with the editorial side of the network, so what was any segment subject like

Koch to do? Phone calls and worrying was not going to get him anywhere. Sit tight. "It's not going to be malicious," the friend tried to reassure him.

Unspoken between Koch and his friend was another possible cause of the segment's slant, one that Chris Hansen brought up in a quick aside: "Anheuser-Busch makes Red Wolf, a specialty lager, and identifies itself as the brewer on the label. Anheuser-Busch is also a minority investor in another specialty beer, Redhook, along with a subsidiary of NBC's parent company, General Electric." Anheuser-Busch and GE were in bed together on Redhook. This would be the same Redhook that Koch had vociferously denounced for its 1995 deal with Anheuser-Busch, which he had called "a declaration of war" by Big Beer and had analogized to the original *Star Wars* trilogy, with Budhook—Koch's nickname—in the role of the evil empire. There was never any clear indication that Redhook, GE, or Anheuser-Busch put a journalistic hit on Koch and the larger craft beer movement, and Anheuser-Busch denied the implication. The interconnectivity was undeniable, though. It appeared the chickens were coming home to roost, and on a national scale.

It wasn't just the *Dateline* segment, either. Around the same time, Anheuser-Busch, along with more than two dozen Oregon brewers, petitioned the federal Bureau of Alcohol, Tobacco, and Firearms (ATF) to force smaller breweries to put on their labels who made the beer and where, a requirement similar to one already enforced for other foodstuffs and household products like cosmetics and medicines (beer had no nutritional value, the thinking had gone since Repeal, so best to avoid things like ingredients and origins on the labels lest the public think otherwise). The petition was seen as an assault on Boston Beer in particular, which countered with a petition of its own asking the ATF to require sell-by or best-before dates on beers as well as where they were brewed (something Boston Beer had been doing on its own since 1989). Beer has a relatively short shelf life as opposed to, say, wine, and the implication was that Big Beer brands routinely arrived in front of consumers old and spoiled, owing to the volumes made and the distances shipped.*

Boston Beer also asked the feds to please define what a craft brewery or microbrewery was. Since the second wave of openings in the early 1980s, the unofficial handle promoted by the Association of Brewers, critics, and brew-

---

* Both Anheuser-Busch and Boston Beer were able to walk away from the labeling controversy claiming some semblance of victory. Anheuser-Busch began voluntarily placing "Born on" dates on their beers (though not necessarily telling consumers the beer might go bad within several weeks of that date); and Boston Beer voluntarily started saying on labels where particular beers were actually brewed rather than just the Jamaica Plain, Boston, headquarters address.

ers themselves was any brewery or brewpub making up to fifteen thousand barrels annually; the rest were regional breweries or craft regional breweries or regional craft breweries. The public at large might also take "craft -brewery" and "microbrewery" to mean any operation that wasn't one of the Big Four—Anheuser-Busch, Miller, Coors, and Stroh's—that controlled nearly 90 percent of the market. This semantic confusion was part of the reason for the recriminations. For its part, Charlie Papazian's Association of Brewers, which had with seeming ease been able to define more and more styles for the Great American Beer Festival, was working on an official definition of a craft brewer, and it looked like it could not come soon enough.

Around the same time as the *Dateline* segment, Anheuser-Busch launched a television, radio, and print ad campaign that further clouded things for consumers. The ads were merciless: "Why does Sam Adams," asked one, "pretend to come from New England when the truth is, it's brewed by contract breweries around the country?" Another all but called Koch a liar: "Time to stop tricking beer drinkers, Jim." And another went for the jugular on the all-important issue of price: "If Samuel Adams is made at the same contract breweries that churn out cheap, blue-collar beers, why does Sam Adams cost so much more than these other products?" Anheuser-Busch also targeted Pete's Brewing as well as, interestingly enough, its longtime archrival Miller in the ATF petition and the ads. Without a hint of irony, considering its own myriad forays into phantom crafts in the last few years, Anheuser-Busch called on Miller to come clean about its Plank Road Brewery, the supposed rustic brewhouse behind its popular Icehouse and Red Dog brands since 1993. With an almost audible sigh to any reporter who read it, Miller felt compelled to release this statement in early 1996 regarding its competitor's calls for full disclosure: "The Plank Road Brewery, the original name of the brewery established by Frederick Miller in 1855, is a separate division of Miller Brewing Company. Plank Road beers differ from Miller in both style and taste. Plank Road's relationship with Miller is well established and well documented. We view it as most unfortunate that the industry leader is looking to use a government agency to stifle competition."

Pete Slosberg's company had already sparred at least twice with Anheuser-Busch—the first time over a dog. The bigger brewer felt that Slosberg's black-and-white English bull terrier, Millie, which Pete's used on its early packaging beginning in 1986, was a tad too similar to its own black-and-white English bull terrier, Spuds MacKenzie, which it introduced in 1984. Although Pete's reach then barely extended through the San Francisco Bay Area, Anheuser-Busch threatened legal action, and the smaller brewer stopped using Millie on its packaging in 1989.* Anheuser-Busch also swooped in and lured away the ad agency that Pete's used for its national television ad campaign in 1994, the first by a craft beer company.

Otherwise, though, the single, biggest fallout from the Anheuser-Busch ambush—the phantom crafts, the 100 percent share of mind, the ATF petition, the ad campaign, and, especially the *Dateline* segment—was a wavering in consumer confidence in craft beer. An industry already swollen with newcomers, given to in-fighting, and growing at a torrid pace suddenly lost its hard-won authenticity in the eyes of millions of consumers or would-be consumers. Some craft brewers understood that immediately. Dan Kenary, a cofounder of the Mass. Bay Brewing Company—which had never shied from reminding consumers that its Harpoon brand was the first beer to be brewed in Boston since the 1960s, not Samuel Adams—knew he would never forget a closing image of the *Dateline* segment: an ugly-looking smokestack at the Stroh's plant. He knew that the brush used to paint Boston Beer and Pete's Brewing, no matter what others may have thought of them, colored everybody in the industry. It was all a whiff of grapeshot aimed to kill competition, no matter how scattered. The lines now had been clearly drawn: it was not physical brewer versus contract brewer anymore, newbie from the 1990s versus veteran from the 1980s, certainly no longer West Coast versus East Coast. It was Us versus Them—and Them had a lot of resources.

There was an almost visceral reaction among craft brewers as a survival instinct kicked in. John Hickenlooper, cofounder of the first brewpub in Denver and now co-owner of others, pulled all Anheuser-Busch brands in the face of the ad campaign. There were smaller acts of defiance throughout the nation. Don Russell, the Joe Sixpack columnist for the *Philadelphia Daily News*, described the angry reaction in the City of Brotherly Love:

> It's been maybe 10 years since Bud last touched Joe Sixpack's tongue. But, now, in the spirit of journalistic accuracy, I find myself on the brink of actually tasting this dreck once more. The occasion is the Budweiser Backlash—a stiff, negative reaction to last year's network television broadside in which Anheuser-Busch claimed the nation's burgeoning microbrewery revolution was a fraud. . . . About that backlash: It actually goes back a few years before A-B's craft-brew assault. Tom Peters, the manager of Copa Too (263 S. 15th St. in

---

* Stroh's had them both beat anyway: its commercials featuring Alex, the beer-fetching dog, debuted in 1983.

Center City), said he stopped stocking the slop about five years ago when he heard how the company was bullying a tiny Czechoslovakia brewery called Budvar over trademark rights to the Budweiser name.

Across town, Dawson Street Pub (Dawson and Cresson Streets in Manayunk) also proudly refuses to carry Bud. The pub's only bottle of the gunk is displayed above the bar, with its familiar red label marked up with the international cross-out symbol.

It was, as the beer writer Jack Erickson put it, an unceremonious meeting between the Big Beer–dominated industry and the culture that had grown up around the movement over the last two decades. Every budding aficionado who knew the name Michael Jackson as synonymous with beer and not pop music; every critic, compensated or not; every homebrewer with his or her dog-eared books by Fred Eckhardt, Byron Burch, and Charlie Papazian; every person behind each e-mail address on the earliest online beer and homebrewing newsletters; every regular at every brewpub in nearly every state—they all had skin in this game. "What we have now is a beer culture," Erickson explained to Russell. "It tends to be young, affluent and opinionated. Beer is an important part of their lifestyle, and they don't like the big boys pushing around little guys. . . . A-B is just trying to take market share—that's the way they do things. The backlash is the beer industry clashing with the beer culture."

Finally, in the spring of 1997, Anheuser-Busch ceased the ad campaign. The influential National Advertising Division of the Council of Better Business Bureaus had, at Boston Beer's request, examined the ads. It said that they contained "contextually inaccurate factual statements" that could be "false, misleading, and deceptive." Both sides claimed victory. Anheuser-Busch could continue to tell consumers that most Boston Beer was brewed outside of its namesake city, if not New England entirely, but it had to stop implying that that fact meant the beers were the same as lower-priced, mass-produced ones that Anheuser-Busch and its Big Beer brethren made. Regardless, the damage had been done. If 1978 was the first undeniably pivotal year in the American craft beer movement, 1996 was the second—though for negative reasons rather than positive. Things would never be the same.

LUCKY BASTARDS
Los Angeles; San Marcos, CA | 1996–1998

G reg Koch certainly remembered the *Dateline* segment as a tipping point—and he didn't even see it. He was too busy at the time.

Koch, no relation to the segment's main target, Jim Koch, was born in Southern California, and his family moved to Ohio when he was four. He moved back west in 1984 to attend the Guitar Institute of Technology above the Hollywood Wax Museum on Hollywood Boulevard in Los Angeles. Koch wanted to be in rock and roll, and he was, for a long while: he worked at one point as a tour photographer for the guitarist Steve Vai and later, after earning a business degree at the University of Southern California, managed bands and owned rehearsal studios in downtown Los Angeles, which musicians could rent by the month.

During his time at USC, Koch frequented a downtown bar at the base of the American Hotel called Al's. It was loud and cramped and still defiantly punk in a new wave world, the sort of place that reveled in being a dive; Thursdays were "No Talent Night," Koch's favorite time to go. Al's had up to four beers on tap at any one time, serving them in the sorts of waxy paper cups you might get from a fast-food joint. One Thursday night, there was only Lowenbrau Dark and Anchor Steam on tap—and Koch chose Anchor Steam. A lightbulb went off in his young mind, a total epiphany; it was the first craft beer he had ever tried, and from then on that's all he drank, becoming a self-described "beer geek" increasingly familiar with a movement that was about to grow by leaps and bounds, particularly in California.

Though not necessarily in *Southern* California. While Northern California was undeniably the movement's Eden, beginning with Fritz Maytag's 1965 acquisition of Anchor in San Francisco and growing from there into dozens of breweries and brewpubs by the mid-1980s, craft beer in the Golden State's bottom half had developed only in fits and starts. The region might have been, by the time the lightbulb went off in Koch's mind, only really notable in the movement as the birthplace of both the nation's first homebrew club, the Maltose Falcons in Los Angeles, and, in the same city, Ken Grossman, cofounder of Sierra Nevada—which he and Paul Camusi chose to open in Chico, way northward near the Oregon border.

San Diego was an illustrative case. Its history with beer ran just about the entire gamut of the nation at large. Before Prohibition, the city had one brewery for every sixteen thousand residents, and a far narrower pub-to-resident ratio. After Repeal in 1933, three breweries were able to reopen: the Aztec Brewing Company on Main Street, the San Diego Brewing Company at Thirty-Second Street and Bay Front Street, and the Balboa Brewing Company on Imperial Avenue—about one brewery per ninety-seven thousand residents. All would close by 1953. It would be pretty much Big Beer only for about twenty years after that, and then came the imports in a big way, particularly from just due south. Mexican brands like Corona, Dos Equis, and Tecate dominated the shelves and menus of San Diego by the 1980s because those were the cheapest imports for distributors to carry. By 1985, with more European brands making the transcontinental trek, 10 percent of the beer sold in San Diego was imported, more than twice the national average.

This would turn out to be the peak of a trajectory that started in the early 1970s as some imports started clocking in at an unacceptable six dollars a bottle. Big Beer reasserted itself; the craft beer movement germinating in Northern California seemed a world away, the odd Anchor tap or six-pack just about the only glimpse a San Diegan might catch of it. Then, in the mid-1980s, two friends, Chris Cramer and Matt Rattner, began toying with the idea of opening a craft brewery after moving to the Mission Beach neighborhood after college. Cramer, who had grown up in San Diego, had an older cousin named Karl Strauss, a German immigrant who had worked his way up over forty-four years at Pabst to head its national brewing operations and later became a noted brewing consultant. Intrigued by his cousin's idea and old enough to remember a pre-Prohibition America, Strauss helped the pair of twenty-somethings design the brewery and recipes as well as train the brewers (he also lent his name to the brewpub).

On February 1, 1989, the Karl Strauss Brewing Company opened with a Vienna lager, a pilsner, and a brown ale on tap and to lines around the block on Columbia Street in downtown San Diego—the city's first brewery since Prohibition. Paul Holborn, a homebrewer who studied under Michael Lewis at UC-Davis, had opened the first brewpub in the wider San Diego County more than a year before, the short-lived Bolt Brewery in Fallbrook, which named its beers after those three San Diego breweries that staggered out of Prohibition. (Holborn would go on to be a brewing consultant at the respected Pizza Port brewpub chain in San Diego in the early 1990s.) Within a year of Cramer and Rattner opening the Karl Strauss brewery, several more entrepreneurs let it be known they were planning their own in the city and surrounding county. San Diego was late to the game, but it had arrived.

So had the rest of Southern California by the start of the 1990s. Its quality and scope still could not hold a candle to Northern California—few regions nationwide could—but Greg Koch, the newly minted beer geek, did have regional options. Most were brewpubs or connected to a brewpub, including the largest craft brewery in Southern California at the time, the Alpine Village Hofbrau in Torrance, which opened in 1988; it specialized in German lagers with its ten-thousand-barrel brewhouse, which sold much of its beer at the adjoining restaurant. Several operations, typical of the time, were firsts for the region since Prohibition: the first brewpub on a beach (Belmont Brewing in Long Beach, summer 1989); the first brewpub in Santa Barbara (the Brewhouse Grill and State Street Brewing, summer 1990); the first craft brewery in Orange County (Heritage Brewing in Dana Point, December 1989); the first in Ventura County (Shields Brewing in Ventura, winter 1990). Southern California's oldest craft brewery was the Angeles Brewing Company in L.A.'s Chatsworth neighborhood. Richard Belliveau, a mechanical engineer who relocated from Maine to Los Angeles in the late 1950s and later opened his own machine shop, filed papers with the state in July 1985 after assessing the sorry state of the area's beer. "Nobody's doing it here," he thought, "I'm going to get rich." It, of course, did not quite work out that way; it would take Belliveau nearly two years to start brewing commercially in early 1987 in an old industrial park, held up by a zoning variance; and then it would not be until the early 1990s that he broke even, when annual sales tipped into the six figures.

Also in Los Angeles, there was Gorky's on Eighth Street downtown, a funky, twenty-four-hour bistro noted for its in-house Russian imperial stout. Steps from the Manhattan Beach Pier was the Manhattan Beach Brewery, which two brothers, Michael and David Zislis, and a friend, John Waters, opened in the summer of 1991 with an eight-barrel system.

These last three operations were largely it for the nation's second-largest city beer-wise in the early 1990s. Luckily for Koch, who then was living in an artist's loft in downtown Los Angeles, he spent a lot of time in the San Francisco Bay Area. It was there that he learned about a Saturday class being offered through UC-Davis's extension program and taught by Michael Lewis,

"A Sensory Evaluation of Beer." Lewis, who in 1970 was the nation's sole full professor of brewing science, now had academic company, as did the UC-Davis program he helped build. Oregon State University in Corvallis, home of the USDA's hop-breeding farm and birthplace of the Cascade hop, had started a fermentation-science degree program in 1996.

In Lewis's class, Koch ran into a guy who played keyboards and bass in a band that used to rent rehearsal space from Koch. Steve Wagner was born in Chicago, and his family decamped to Los Angeles when he was ten. He drank a lot of bad beer in college at UC–Santa Cruz and turned his English literature degree into fifteen years on the road as a professional musician. Like Koch, his beer epiphany came through an Anchor Steam, although he was also able to sample different craft beers on tour throughout the 1980s and early 1990s. One of his bandmates got him into homebrewing, and he gradually became obsessed with it, not only as a hobby but also as a possible avenue out of life on the road and toward more stability. The pair—who hardly knew each other through the rehearsal space because Wagner's band always paid the rent on time—became better acquainted in Lewis's class; eventually, their talk of beer inched toward the commercial edge. After Wagner worked a stint as a brewer at a Pyramid operation in Washington State, the two decided to partner on a new venture.

But where? Wagner didn't want to move back to Los Angeles from his current home in Washington; Koch was not averse to leaving the megalopolis. Still, Southern California had not been that hospitable to craft beer. Even Wolfgang Puck, a pioneer in casual fine dining with local hotspots like Spago and Chinois, had seen his own toe-tip into the movement falter. Largely owing to Puck's imprimatur, Eureka, the 214-seat West Los Angeles brewpub the chef and his partners launched in the spring of 1990, had been one of the loudest salvos so far in elevating the role of craft beer in dining. Dishes like tubular ravioli stuffed with tangy cheese and potato puree and topped with a toasted hazelnut butter, as well as the meats of a skilled sausage-maker Puck lured from Munich to oversee Eureka's charcuterie kitchen, were paired with the fruits of a $6 million brewhouse imported from West Germany, including the brewpub's signature Eureka California Lager. It was all so hip and bold. "Most brewery restaurants have been created for beer drinkers," Puck declared, not entirely inaccurately, "and very little attention is paid to the food."

By May 1992, it was all gone; the brewpub shuttered under approximately one million dollars in debt. The restaurant portion, according to the partners, had done well, but the brewery part had never really caught on, weighing down the entire operation. A plan to reopen with Boston Beer running the brewery portion never quite took, and, by May 1993, Eureka's former manager, an old Puck friend named Mickey Kanolzer, who was now running the chef's pizza company, could tell the *Los Angeles Times*, "It just hurts so bad, but it was one of those things beyond my control. I've been going downhill ever since: I was making beer, now I'm making pizzas. Next thing will be hamburgers and hot dogs, and then what?" We could glean from this lament, then, that craft beer was at least in the middle tiers of fine dining, no matter the risks it might still entail.

Against this inhospitable Southern California backdrop, Koch and Wagner continued to talk about where they might one day put a brewery of their own. Then one idyllic weekend in March 1995, Koch went to Solana Beach in northern San Diego County with some old college buddies. He called Wagner. "Hey, how about the north part of San Diego County?" Wagner was OK with that; his brothers had gone to college in the area. Five weeks later, Koch drove his Mitsubishi Diamante the two hours from Los Angeles to Solana Beach to move in with a friend in a condo, where he began brewing test batches of what became Arrogant Bastard Ale (a name, Koch claimed, that was always in the cosmos' ether, awaiting humanity's incantation) for his and Wagner's Stone Brewing Company. Wagner moved from Portland, Oregon, in October, and the pair rented a warehouse in San Marcos, about

Steve Wagner, left, and Greg Koch, cofounders of Stone Brewing Company. Courtesy of Stone Brewing Co.

fifteen miles inland and about thirty-five miles north of San Diego. They set up shop on February 2, 1996, with Koch, by now sporting a goatee and hair falling over his forehead, focusing on the sales side and the cleaner-cut Wagner on the brewing end via a thirty-barrel system. They sold their first keg, a pale ale, to Pizza Port on July 26. Vince Marsaglia, who owned the chain with his sister Gina and who had introduced in-house brewing in 1992, dropped by personally to pick it up.

It was the frothiest time in the larger movement. The industry was growing annually by double-digit percentages, and the number of new entrants like Stone was swelling by the month. Koch and Wagner found themselves in the midst of fourteen- to sixteen-hour days, fighting the good entrepreneurial fight against what Tony Magee, several hundred miles up the California coast at Lagunitas in Petaluma, called "the tyranny of fast growth." After ten months, Stone started bottling their beers in twenty-two-ounce bombers—Stone Pale Ale in June 1997, Stone IPA later that summer, and, finally, Arrogant Bastard Ale in November. That last one, a strong ale we might place among the earliest extreme beers, displayed the new brewery's swagger right on its logo: a muscular gargoyle which appeared to brook no nonsense. As if to dispel any confusion that might be left by the name and the logo, the brewers put the story, written by Koch, on the label. It was rather smug:

This is an aggressive ale. You probably won't like it. It is quite doubtful that you have the taste or sophistication to be able to appreciate an ale of this quality and depth. We would suggest that you stick to safer and more familiar territory—maybe something with a multimillion dollar ad campaign aimed at convincing you it's made in a little brewery, or one that implies their tasteless fizzy yellow beverage will give you more sex appeal. Perhaps you think multi-million dollar ad campaigns make things taste better. Perhaps you're mouthing your words as you read this.

Not exactly the sort of pitch meant to draw consumers. Still, Arrogant Bastard Ale was a hit; it would prove one of the bestselling craft beers out of Southern California. But it wasn't enough—the company was losing money, around $30,000 a month. It was a precarious time in the industry, but, more prosaically, Stone faced the same challenge that had daunted start-up craft breweries going back to Jack McAuliffe's New Albion: distribution. Stone was losing five dollars a case or thereabouts doing distribution itself (driver, truck, and so forth). Koch started talking to big distributors in the area, most of them tied to one Big Beer operation or another. It was no and no from the Anheuser-Busch and Coors affiliates; the Miller affiliate, to Koch's surprise, said yes. "Maybe our company won't die!" he thought. Then the distributor called in November and said it did not want to start carrying Stone around the holidays—how about January 1998? Agreed. The distributor called back in December and noted that the Super Bowl was in San Diego that coming January; how about February instead? Agreed. Then in January, after the Denver Broncos had dispatched the Green Bay Packers in Super Bowl XXXII, the distributor called to say its employees would need a break; how about March? Fine. Then the distributor called Koch again: On second thought, it was too busy, period, and would not be able to carry any Stone beers. At least that's what the Miller distributor said. What Koch heard was, "You know what, we're going to let your company die." He hung up, walked the fifteen feet to Wagner's office, and recounted the news. What now? Every other distributor had said no, and they had been losing money the whole time.

Then March came and with it spring. The clouds parted, sales picked up, the decision to start bottling the year before paid off, and Stone made its first profit. Koch and Wagner, and their company of around a dozen people, had held on just long enough—and had not had to compromise to do so. Stone was one of the lucky ones.

A TALE OF TWO BREWERIES
White River Junction, VT; Philadelphia | 1996–2000

The old railroad crossroads, White River Junction, rests bucolically right on the Vermont–New Hampshire border. It was there, as we've seen, in January 1987, that Stephen Mason, Alan Davis, and Stephen Israel, with $750,000 from thirty-two investors and a Small Business Administration loan, rolled out the inaugural kegs from the Catamount Brewing Company, the first brewery in Vermont since Prohibition. It had been a long slog to opening day—the state incorporated the brewery on Halloween 1984—but the brewery was quickly both a critical and commercial success. Working out of an old meat warehouse on land that Catamount leased from the Central Vermont Railway, it produced thirty-five hundred barrels that first year with Mason, a former homebrewer and PE teacher, as brewmaster. Its Catamount Amber, a mild English-style pale ale, and Catamount Gold, a hoppier golden ale, inspired fellow New Englanders hip to the craft beer movement. So did Mason's dedication to the craftsmanship side; his willingness to have put in the years of training, including at a brewery in Hertfordshire, England, before the idea even got off the ground; and the hours he logged at the brewhouse that seemed to be in the middle of nowhere. Catamount Gold took a gold medal at the 1989 Great American Beer Festival. Catamount's line of beers grew to include a pale ale, an oatmeal stout, and seasonals; production climbed to twelve thousand barrels by 1993, and annual revenues tickled $3 million.

All the while, as the production increased and its quality impressed, Catamount's sales-and-marketing operation remained basically a one-man show. Davis would drive around to accounts to negotiate orders and payments in person, as distribution had never really grown beyond central New England. After a few years, he started to notice something: the retail shelves once populated only by Big Beer brands and a handful of stale imports were now peppered with other craft brands like Catamount. The marketplace was getting crowded. Davis went to Mason and the brewery's board of directors, which included original investors, to persuade them to hire more salespeople and develop a better marketing strategy, like point-of-sale materials for these stores with more craft brands than ever before. The board said no. The brewery would, instead, focus on production of its award-winning beer.

Davis left the brewery in frustration, and Mason went looking for a way to expand Catamount's capacity. He found it fifteen miles down Interstate 91 in twenty-six thousand square feet on several acres of an industrial park, which also housed a glass-blowing factory that served as a major tourist attraction for Windsor, Vermont. Catamount's second brewery would be about eleven thousand square feet bigger than the original and would serve as the production point for the company's bottled beers, the White River Junction location moving to kegs only. Mason, who had already been buying top-notch equipment from JV Northwest throughout the early 1990s, decided to spend between $3 and $5 million acquiring and outfitting the Windsor brewery. It would be, in the words of a consultant Catamount hired, "a real Cadillac," completely state-of-the-art. Mason announced the Windsor location in the summer of 1996, and started brewing there in 1997. Production jumped to nearly twenty-two thousand barrels the following year.

Within twenty-four months it was all over. Catamount closed its doors in April 2000, undone by debt it couldn't get out from underneath. There had not been a concomitant sales-and-marketing pitch to move all the new beer being brewed in both White River Junction and Windsor. Creditors closed in on both locations as the brewery fell tens of thousands of dollars behind on taxes and hundreds of thousands—perhaps millions—behind on loans, especially loans tied to the Windsor expansion. The Mass. Bay Brewing Company, the maker of Harpoon, which had recently reached its capacity limit at its South Boston brewery, bought Catamount's Windsor brewery from a creditor for $1 million in the summer of 2000. The original site in White River Junction was also auctioned; it was by then, as one observer noted, "in a state of minor disrepair."

During the same years, 350 miles away, in the nation's fifth-largest city, a similar story of decline was writing itself, although the ending would be even grimmer. It had all started promisingly enough for the Red Bell Brewing Company in the fall of 1993. It looked then like James Bell, the ex–college football player and securities broker, and his partner, Jim Cancro, a civil engineer turned brewer, had a smash hit on their young hands with Philadelphia's newest craft beer company.

Bell had amassed more than $200,000 from investors, including local television personalities and pro athletes, and used about $60,000 of that to start a cheeky marketing blanket of the city that included, as we've seen, the billboards that read, PHILADELPHIA IS PUTTING BLONDES BEHIND BARS, and the slogan, "Put a blonde at your table." Although the company started by brewing the approximately seven thousand barrels annually of Red Bell Blonde, a light-bodied golden ale modeled after the German beer Kölsch, and Red Bell Amber, a lager, under contract at the Lion Brewery in Wilkes-Barre 115 miles to the northwest, Philly locals embraced it. Mayor Ed Rendell and other big shots turned out for the company's official launch in January 1995 at the Egypt Nightclub on Delaware Avenue. Consumers snatched bottles from the shelves—happily so, oftentimes paying less for the hometown beer than what they would've had to pay for an import or another craft brand; the same went for bars, where pints of Red Bell retailed for three dollars or less. They were willing to pay a premium at Veterans Stadium, raucous home of the NFL's Eagles and baseball's Phillies, where a cup of Red Bell might go for $5.25. More than eighty thousand people turned out for a monthlong Oktoberfest that the company sponsored. Sales grew by double-digit percentages in 1995 and 1996; the company sold about forty-six hundred barrels in 1995, and Bell estimated that for every twelve hundred barrels sold, his concern made $1 million.

And just a year after the company's launch, Bell and Cancro could boast a physical brewery with a forty-barrel system—in Philly's old Brewerytown section, no less, the nexus of the city's dozens of breweries before Prohibition. Cancro oversaw a talented, young staff that expanded Red Bell's repertoire to include a highly regarded Scotch ale, a pale ale, and a black cherry stout. That same year, 1996, they scored a first for the entire American craft beer movement: a brewpub within a sports arena. In this case, a ten-thousand-square-foot spread capable of producing up to two thousand barrels annually within the state-of-the-art confines of the new CoreStates Center, home to hockey's Flyers and the NBA's 76ers; not only that, but Red Bell also had the exclusive on draft beer at the twenty-thousand-seat arena.* There were plans for more brewpubs around Philly, including one downtown in partnership with a venture-capital firm and five so-called minibrewpubs in Veterans Stadium set to debut during Major League Baseball's All-Star Game that year. There was a flurry of forward-looking press releases and pronouncements and talk of going public, of buying the Lion Brewery in Wilkes-Barre, of merging with the venerable Pittsburgh Brewing Company farther west. Finally, in barely three years, it all seemed to come full circle: Bell told the local press in May 1996 that he planned to contract brew other beer companies' brands at the new Brewerytown location. Yes, Bell seemed well on his way to being, as he had said at the company's launch, "the next Sam Adams." He had even adopted a mantra for all this expansion unknowingly similar to Jim Koch's about quality control: "If you deliver a good product, people will come."

What buoyed Red Bell's swagger, what made it all so deliciously plausible, was the explosive growth in the craft beer industry. It served as a perfect backdrop for a couple of young men with limited brewing experience to talk of chains and exclusive rights, of confidence in continued double-digit growth and, at the same time, of a commitment to quality. Besides, Red Bell dovetailed nicely with its host city's renewal. Philadelphia, like other major US cities, was experiencing a historic drop in violent crime during the 1990s as well as sweeping changes in its real estate, which often involved converting unused manufacturing and other commercial space into housing, particularly downtown. These conversions, coupled with a grateful government's incentives like long-term property-tax breaks, brought, in *Philadelphia* magazine's words, "a sea of first-time buyers lured by cool historic living [and] bringing a jazzy aesthetic and a steady stream of cash that fueled a retail and dining renaissance."

---

* The arena is now called the Wells Fargo Center.

As Matthew Reich recognized more than ten years ago in a changing New York City, craft beer could have a place at this urban-infill table. "Yuppies drink it," Reich explained to the *New York Times* then, and he targeted his sales efforts to the fashionable neighborhoods and retailers frequented by those yuppies, many of them now happily marked with the new moniker "foodie." They may not have been called yuppies by the late 1990s—"hipsters," perhaps—but they were the same type of consumer. Bell knew them. He was one of them, barely into his thirties and head of a thriving company.

Or was he? By 1998, the precariousness of Red Bell was an open secret. Maybe the beer wasn't all that good; the Scotch ale got solid reviews now and then, but the quality of some was hit-or-miss. Maybe the brewery didn't even care. Had not Bell once told Cancro to "come up with something like Budweiser because that sells so well?" And did he not tell a reporter from the city's largest newspaper that he preferred grape Juicy Juice to his company's beer? And all that marketing—didn't Red Bell have to pull the initial double entendre spots about blondes at your table and behind Philly's bars and come back with new campaigns? The answers were all yes. Whatever the company's enthusiasm, one could be forgiven for thinking that Red Bell had merely thrown things against the wall to see what would stick. The emperor had barely any clothes—and the creditors were coming for those.

Red Bell had lost millions of dollars since its founding in 1993, with losses of more than $2 million some quarters. It never did acquire the Lion Brewery or merge with Pittsburgh Brewing or do much contract brewing in the Brewerytown location. That building was headed toward foreclosure anyway, with more than $1 million in mortgages as well as several hundred thousand dollars in liens. The brewpubs? Those made money, though not really enough: after fees to the arena owner and its concessionaire, Red Bell might net nineteen cents on one of those $5.25 cups.

The company did go public. The hope was to raise capital the way that first wave of craft beer IPOs did in 1995 and 1996. It didn't happen. After peaking at well over five dollars, Red Bell's share price dropped below a quarter—and then below a penny. Bell issued statements expressing confidence in a turnaround, but that never came; eventually he resigned and a creditor stepped in as chairman. Finally, Pennsylvania revoked the company's brewing license because of $80,000 in unpaid payroll taxes. The mess left hundreds of dollars in fresh legal fees and barrels of ink of negative coverage from a Philly media that had once cheered on Red Bell's bid to be the city's own Sam Adams. Things got so bad that, when the new chairman considered Chapter

11, he looked at the legal fees involved and realized it was impossible: Red Bell was too broke to go bankrupt.

THE GREAT SHAKEOUT
Nationwide | 1996–2000

The year 1999 would be the first when more US craft breweries and brewpubs closed than opened. Dozens would cease operations from 1996 through 2000, and openings would slow to a trickle. The American craft beer movement had ceased growing by double-digit percentages—had ceased growing much at all—and the dreaded word "shakeout" that Wall Street analysts had first uttered following the start of the IPO wave in 1995 became a definitive part of the movement's lexicon. As much as brewers, consumers, and critics might have talked about before and after Fritz Maytag, or before and after Jack McAuliffe, or before and after the first homebrewers conferences and the Great American Beer Festivals in the early 1980s, or before and after Jim Koch, they now talked about before and after *Dateline*, or before and after 100 percent share of mind, or simply before and after the shakeout of the 1990s. The stories within the shakeout varied, but most were a combination of what happened to Red Bell in Philadelphia and Catamount in Vermont. Debt overtook revenue, supply far exceeded demand, and all in the movement, with the perfect vision of hindsight, would say they saw the fates of doomed breweries coming years away.

Two things were inarguable. There was too much beer, a lot of it of dubious quality, and too many breweries, brewpubs, and contract brewers, the latter dominated by entities that might not have been in the movement for the craftsmanship. One brewer, who started up just as the shakeout began, described these contract brewers as "Milli Vanilli" entrants, citing the pop singers who ended their brief careers in disgrace after it was discovered they lip-synched even in the studio. Some of these entrants had internalized the worst elements of globalized manufacturing: get things done as quickly and as cheaply as possible and hope the consumer doesn't notice until after the sale.

The tenets sanctified by Fritz Maytag when his Anchor was the only game in town—small, traditional, and independent—had been tossed aside in too many cases. It was bigger, faster, stronger for several years. And consumers did notice after the sale. "There was a shitload of awful beer on the market," one member of the movement recalled of the 1980s. Another member, one of the top brewers by the time of the shakeout, followed a similar excremental line, this time including the 1990s: "There was a lot of crappy beer sitting on the shelves." For all the colorful packaging, the shots of bucolic mountain streams and sleigh blades slicing fluffy snow, of men with overalls and beards, of soothing assurances of "highest quality" and "best ingredients," it still came down to taste and consistency. If consumers, especially the newly initiated, plunked down a premium too many times for what turned out to be "crappy beer," they might be turned off to craft brands forever—all craft brands. Just as the *Dateline* segment from 1996 targeting Pete's Brewing and Boston Beer painted the entire industry with a charlatan brush, so too did one too many bottles that looked colorful and inviting on the outside but that evinced wincing, maybe even gagging, once the first sips were taken.

By no means was every shuttered brewery during the shakeout producing poor-quality beer. Stephen Mason's Catamount produced some of the most respected beers in the entire movement. Sometimes the numbers simply did not work out—and did not work out with particularly bad timing. Catamount's grave misfortune was to expand not only before they had wider distribution in place but also just as the entire industry started to falter. On the other side of the country, Greg Koch and Steve Wagner's Stone Brewing, also makers of some of the movement's most respected beers, may very well have met the same fate had they expanded rapidly at the same time; they did not, and they survived to grow in the next decade into the biggest craft brewery in the Southwest. Sierra Nevada, too, was one a handful of craft breweries that saw steady growth through the late 1990s shakeout. Ken Grossman had been careful not to expand too rapidly and therefore was able to spend the shakeout not only acquiring and installing a top-shelf bottling line that could fill 650 bottles a minute but also building a gorgeous new, two-hundred-barrel brewhouse at the Chico, California, headquarters. Copper kettles prefabricated in Bavaria dominated the public areas. Murals depicting the brewing process by the artist Eric Grohe surrounded the kettles, creating a kind of temple effect for visitors. Careful expansion and tightly monitored distribution helped New Belgium, the Mass. Bay Brewing Company (a.k.a. Harpoon), and Brooklyn Brewery, among others, post strong gains as the century ended. The right decisions in the good times meant surviving the bad.

Finally, there were other reasons for the shakeout besides bad beer, tough times, poor timing, and flighty newcomers. There was Big Beer's assault through the phantom crafts; Anheuser-Busch's 100 percent share of mind; the ad campaign against contract brewers; the *Dateline* segment; and the labeling petitions to the federal government. There were also the price wars between the movement's biggest players, Boston Beer and Pete's Brewing, which drove craft beer prices in some areas to the levels of Big Beer brands, further confusing consumers. And there was the movement's own infighting, as we've discussed. The movement, for all its symbiosis, had failed to produce that many benevolent godfathers in the mold of Fritz Maytag and F. X. Matt II. Charlie Papazian's Association of Brewers had served as a rallying point through it all, but its conferences and conventions were voluntary affairs and its efforts, particularly at lobbying various levels of government on behalf of smaller brewers, were overlapping with the larger Brewers Association of America, which the well-connected Henry King had run since 1992. Something had to give there, too.

In the end, the shakeout would seem a necessary thing—and not necessarily as dramatic as it looked. Estimates vary of how many craft breweries and brewpubs the nation hosted by the end of the decade. There were likely just over one thousand in 1996, with brewpubs outnumbering breweries around two-to-one. In 2000, there were just over fifteen hundred, an increase of about 50 percent, with the vast majority again brewpubs rather than standalone breweries. That 2000 number would decline by about one hundred during the next five years, but otherwise remain fairly static into the latter half of the first decade of the new century. Gone, it appeared, were the spikes of yesteryear. Still, fifteen hundred craft breweries and brewpubs, give or take, was more than a respectable amount—especially given that there had been one a mere quarter-century before.

VICTORY ABROAD, DEFEAT AT HOME
Palo Alto, CA; Boston | 1997–2000

The twin announcements from Pete's Brewing came in the late winter of 1997. Mark Bozzini, the CEO who had helped steer the company to its number-two craft-brewing position behind Boston Beer, was leaving. Also, the plans for a physical brewery in Northern California were indefinitely postponed.

The moves were not surprising; Pete's, like everyone else in craft beer, was having its troubles. The popularity of the company's brands over the last several years and the general growth in the industry meant that distributors typically had eighty-five days worth of Pete's beer on hand by early 1997, much too much to move before it started to go bad; the company offered to take back some beer and to slash prices so it might sell more quickly. That year, then, Pete's was able to reduce its distributors' inventories by 23,600 barrels. That helped to "better align inventories to current market trends," as Bozzini's successor, Jeff Atkins, a top executive at Quaker Oats before he joined Pete's in December 1996 as CFO, put it. The realignment, of course, had an effect financially: the company would report a net loss of $6.1 million for the year. Production and sales dropped, too: In the last three months of 1997, Pete's shipped 94,000 barrels versus 114,000 in the same period in 1996; sales dropped annually 21 percent. Pete's stockholders lost thirteen cents per share after at least breaking even in 1996.

The euphoria of the IPO wave was a distant echo as investor confidence waned and Wall Street hustled to find the next Next Big Thing. Redhook, which had kicked off the whole wave, saw its share price drop from a summit of more than $34 in August 1995 to just above $5 by the end of 1997. Boston Beer, still by far the biggest craft brewery, hit $32.50 a share the week of Thanksgiving 1995, and was down to $8 by St. Patrick's Day 1997. And Pete's share price flirted with $30 in late 1995 and now, like Redhook, traded for around $5. All saw their sales ebb right along with their share prices. Rhonda Kallman's legendary sales force at Boston Beer had its first real off-year in 1996: there was growth, but it was in the low single-digits, a long way from "63 in '93."

None of the publicly traded craft beer companies appeared to have a tougher go of it than the Frederick Brewing Company, the central Maryland operation founded in the spring of 1992 by husband and wife Kevin Brannon and Marjorie McGinnis and the biggest craft brewery in the Mid-Atlantic. Their March 1995 IPO afforded them millions for a spending spree on top-shelf brewing and packaging equipment as well as a new $7 million brewery that upped their capacity tenfold. It produced more than fourteen thousand barrels in 1998, an 81 percent increase over the year before. Then, within two years, it was all gone. As with Catamount Brewing in Vermont, Frederick Brewing could not foment enough demand to absorb its new supply. Its sleek, new brewery was running at less than 40 percent capacity; its share price slid below twenty-five cents; its brewmaster quit; and its board went looking for someone to take over. A small conglomerate out of Cleveland, started by technology consultant David Snyder, did just that in the summer of 1999. By then, Frederick Brewing owed hundreds of thousands in back taxes and fees, and it had been delisted from NASDAQ for trading so low. It never did turn a profit after the IPO.

Pete's, even with its troubles, was never in such dire straits. The industry had changed, though, and if cofounders Pete Slosberg and Mark Bronder were going to cash out, now would be the time. With hindsight, we are able to see an arc of recovery in the craft beer movement, with the shakeout of the late 1990s as a trough and the growth of the twenty-first century's first decade as another peak. But for those living it in 1997 and 1998, things looked dire. Competitors and compatriots who were with you one month, whom you perhaps shared a beer with at an Association of Brewers conference the springtime before, were gone, oftentimes with creditors hounding them as they departed, the quality of their beer immaterial to the bottom line. And for all the hullabaloo of the last twenty years, for all the hope and heartbreak, the long hours and the financial risks, domestically produced craft beer still accounted for not even 5 percent of the American beer market. Some craft brewers might have been rock stars, but they were not superheroes.

A few had exited already while the getting was good. BridgePort Brewing in Portland, Oregon, had sold itself to Gambrinus in the fall of 1995. Cofounder Dick Ponzi explained that it was either not expand and maybe even prune distribution, or expand with fresh investments that might mean giving up control of the company, or sell—pretty much the summation of choices all smaller craft breweries faced. The first choice would have likely spelled disaster for anyone as the industry heated up; the last two, on the other hand, proved much safer bets. Gordon Biersch, the brewpub chain started in Palo Alto, California, sold a controlling stake for $17 million to Fertitta Enterprises, a gambling and hotels company out of Las Vegas; the November 1995 sale allowed Gordon Biersch to expand at a time when founders Dan Gordon and Dean Biersch, who kept 30 percent of the company in the deal, had grown the chain to five locations.

The same year, in a deal fraught with inescapable symbolism, the largest winemaker in Washington State bought America's oldest brewpub. The irrepressible Bert Grant—he of the vial of hop oil, the kilt, the Rolls-Royce with "Real Ale" on the vanity plate, the contention to critic Michael Jackson that the hoppy Scotch ale he brewed was a Scotch ale because Grant had been born in Scotland—realized that with craft beer really taking off, he needed to more effectively market his thirteen-year-old, twelve-thousand-barrel Yakima Brewing and Malting Company. According to him, marketing "was never my big suit anyway." At age sixty-seven, Grant would stay in what he described as "anti-retirement," remaining as brewmaster as new owner International Wine and Spirits anticipated quadrupling production while still limiting its distribution to the Northwest.

To drum up cash, Pete's actually spent much of early 1998 looking to make similar acquisitions of smaller competitors when its investment bank, Morgan Stanley, came back with another option: sell. And the bank had a buyer: San Antonio, Texas–based Gambrinus, one of the nation's ten biggest importers, had already saved the regional Spoetzl Brewery and had acquired BridgePort for its first foray into craft beer. It might have seemed to some a bit incongruous for the importer of Corona—the big Mexican brand that was a particular bugbear of Michael Jackson—to snap up the second-largest craft brewing company, whose beers had been the gateway drink for millions of craft beer geeks and had spawned not a few imitators. But Gambrinus made it worth a struggling Pete's while: an affiliate of the importer offered $69 million in cash, or $6.375 a share, when Pete's shares were trading at around $5.80. Gambrinus would keep Pete's recipes—it would even keep Pete; part of the deal, closed in June 1998, was that Slosberg remain for two years as pitchman.

Slosberg was one of the shakeout's graceful exits. So was Rhonda Kallman. The bar-savvy, twenty-something secretary turned beer mogul, leader of the industry's most productive sales force who shared an office with Jim Koch until her final day in late 1999, was done. The last few contentious years had taken a lot of the fun out of the day-to-day work, and besides, Kallman had other opportunities she wanted to pursue.* As for Slosberg, he would remain a presence in craft beer, not only in those two remaining years at Pete's and not only in America, but also by lecturing throughout the world, including in South America, which began taking its zymurgical cues from the States rather than from Old World stalwarts such as Belgium, Germany, the Czech Republic, and Ireland. Over the last thirty years, the student had become the teacher. American beer was now more diverse in style, bolder in flavor, and influential in experimentation than just about anything the European countries had produced or were producing. It was as if American craft brewers had compressed centuries of evolution into mere decades.

Michael Jackson noticed this shift earlier than anyone. Writing for an updated 1988 edition of his groundbreaking book, *The World Guide to Beer*,

---

* Kallman did reemerge in the beer world in 2001 with a short-lived Hingham, Massachusetts–based brewing company called New Century. Its signature brand, however, was a doomed caffeinated beer called Moonshot, which met with consumer indifference and government opposition.

Jackson pegged it all—rightly—to that unique feature of American history, mass immigration: "Far from lacking in a beer culture, the world's most cosmopolitan country is enriched by the traditions of all its founding nations. It made almost every type of beer before Prohibition—and is now beginning to do so again. The rediscovery of beer in the developed world is proceeding faster in America than anywhere else."

American craft brewers, as we've seen, still largely defined themselves stylistically against their European counterparts. And though it would be easy to drift into a kind of obnoxious triumphalism—USA, USA!—it is important to remember that European countries faced their own brewing challenges in the 1990s. Aside from being part of nations sorting out their economic and governmental structures post–Cold War, German and Czech brewers were wedded to the Reinheitsgebot; the beer purity edict had long lost much of its legal teeth, but retained a very strong allure. It was the same in Belgium, that tiny, big arbiter of style: save for the giant Interbrew, maker of Bass and Stella Artois, among others, tradition trumped the pursuit of explosive growth: why fix what had never broken?

As for Great Britain, it was undergoing its own consolidation wave: "The once gentlemanly trade of beer making has fallen prey to big business," as the *Birmingham Evening Mail* delicately put it in December 1998. Nowhere was this more evident than when it came to that staple of British lore and life: the pub. A flurry of deals had by the end of the 1990s left the Japanese bank Nomura as the biggest owner of British pubs: more than fifty-five hundred, including 988 from the Bass estate acquired in a nine-figure deal in February 2001. By the start of the new century, fewer than 10 percent of the kingdom's pubs were owned by breweries like Newcastle, the majority of the rest snapped up like so many securities by investment houses like Nomura. Such consolidation meant a homogeneity in draft beer perhaps unprecedented in the long history of Albion, thousands of supposed locals all with the same taps.

Something similar was happening in Ireland, though with a nasty twist of irony. The faux-Irish pubs that popped up throughout the United States in the 1980s and 1990s now dominated the real Irish drinking landscape; the nation's National Heritage Trust estimated that by the new century there were only twelve to fourteen examples of authentic Irish pubs left in the capital and largest city, Dublin. Add to the fates of the pubs the fact that the number of breweries was rapidly decreasing—thirty closed in the United Kingdom in the 1990s—and you had the story of American craft beer in reverse.

More than anything, though, the old countries lacked the moxie of the new. Americans came at beer from all sorts of walks of life and with all sorts of ideas in hand. They brought panache and swagger, a jones for experimentation and a Manifest Destiny–like hunger to expand (sometimes too much so, as we've seen from the shakeout). Nowhere but in America could or would individuals from so many different backgrounds, with so many certainties as to the way to do things, have gathered as they did at the first homebrewers conventions or Great American Beer Festivals in the early 1980s or at the first beer dinner in that hotel basement in Washington a few years later or at myriad smaller events like the one Charlie Papazian and Jim Koch hosted in Denver in October 1999.

The Denver gathering was a blind taste test for seventy-five people at John Hickenlooper's Wynkoop Brewing Company: five American craft beers versus five European imports. Four of the American beers trumped their European challengers. Koch, who had quickly recovered his own swagger after Big Beer's assault, declared the results proof that "when you take away the fancy bottles and the hype of the import, then the best American craft beers are making better beer." While most Europeans still saw American beer as Budweiser, Miller Lite, and others of that ilk, things had changed stylistically as much as they had changed financially. It was this zest for experimentation and evangelization that would power the American craft beer movement through the postshakeout years and into a fresh period of explosive growth. This time, though, as Koch noted at the Denver taste test, "We're all in this together."

PART IV

PLOTTING A COMEBACK
Atlanta | 1998–2000

I f ever there was an appropriate keynote speaker for the Association of Brewers's annual Craft Brewers Conference, it was Fritz Maytag, godfather to the entire movement. And if there was ever an appropriate time for Maytag to be that keynote speaker, it was during the shakeout.

When the conference opened on April 5, 1998, in Atlanta, the industry's growth had skidded from double-digit percentages to barely single digits—it was just under 5 percent in 1997, according to the association. Dozens of breweries and brewpubs were closing up shop forever. Once the darling of Wall Street and many Main Streets, craft beer was now incongruous to the still economically booming America. Indeed, it was a particularly cruel twist of the knife that the larger national economy continued to do so well as so many craft brewers washed out. It was an era of cheap loans, swelling stock portfolios, and, as president Bill Clinton had been fond of reminding voters during the 1996 elections, the longest peacetime economic expansion in the nation's history. Unemployment was below 6 percent, and the Dow was headed toward a previously unfathomable ten thousand (when it finally broke that ceiling in March 1999, traders at the New York Stock Exchange literally popped Champagne and tossed specially made rally caps). The bull market that had lured so many of Generation X's best and brightest to Wall Street seemed to have no end, no red flag, no matador with a knife to quiet things. For a while, craft beer was a part of that. Now everyone clamored for Pets.com; much fewer wanted an IPA.

Up to the podium in Atlanta stepped the man who started it all. Maytag was not a boisterous public speaker; he was plainspoken, even matter-of-fact, with wry humor not uncommon. He came armed this time with a ladder chart to punctuate a warning for his compatriots who were left:

At Anchor, we're trying not to grow. Each vertical line is capital investment, and each of these leaps signifies a change in the nature of your company. Don't assume that you should make every leap. Your company may not easily make the next jump, and you don't necessarily have to try. Being small is a matter of choice. There is a chasm between levels, and when you make a vertical leap, you may fail before you get to profitable volume. Once you get to be a medium-sized brewery, your business will change. The wives won't be able to come in and visit as much anymore.

It was sage advice, and Maytag himself followed it. After thirty-three years under his control, Anchor was producing one hundred thousand barrels annually, an impressive amount nearly double that of a decade ago, but still a relative pittance even within the movement. Anchor was distributing farther and wider than ever before, though, to several European countries as well as Australia, Japan, Canada, and Hong Kong. Its sales would total $10 million in 1998—again impressive, but again a relative pittance, especially stacked against those who chased IPOs a few years back.

Maytag's advice was, of course, too late for many; and it's unlikely it would have been widely heeded. "Small is beautiful," as he put it at the conference, was simply not an axiom many in an industry that had been growing so explosively wanted to hear. Nor were they likely to heed Maytag's call for beefier pricing, not when some brewers were discounting their brands to spur sales or to simply clear back inventory amid the shakeout. "Most of the wine in the world sells for two dollars a bottle. Quite a bit sells for four dollars to five dollars a bottle, and there are many that sell for ten dollars a bottle. Then you have wines that sell for three hundred dollars a bottle. What the world needs is a beer that's worth five dollars a bottle. I think that would be great. If all beer prices are forced down to the level of Busch Bavarian, none of us will be here."

There were bright spots amid the ruins. Some were simply symbolic, others much more portentous. As much as Maytag emerged amid the tumult to speak at the Craft Brewers Conference, Jack McAuliffe of the long-defunct New Albion emerged, too, in a way. Six months before Maytag's speech, the Mendocino Brewing Company released a small batch of what it called New Albion Pale Ale to honor the twentieth anniversary of the first startup craft brewery in America. McAuliffe, who had long since left the movement, had no hand in the release, but Don Barkley, the Michael Lewis student who became New Albion's first employee in 1978, and Michael Lovett, also an old New

Albion hand, were involved through their ongoing roles at Mendocino. Two kegs were shipped cross-country to the Brickskeller in Washington, DC, where the first beer-tasting dinner had been held in September 1985 and which still boasted one of the biggest beer selections on the planet. The batch birthed a mild burst of remembrance of New Albion—the Brickskeller hosted a beer tasting for journalists—although McAuliffe remained a J. D. Salinger–like figure in the movement, reclusive and legendary.

As for Mendocino itself, freshly minted majority owner Vijay Mallya hit his first roadblock in establishing a national chain of craft breweries and brewpubs. Tiny Humboldt Brewing Company, a brewpub in Arcata, California, started by Vince Celotto and his brother Mario, a former NFL linebacker, rejected the Indian billionaire's $1.7 million offer in December 1997. They decided instead to go it alone by expanding distribution into Southern California and lowering the price of their six-packs from $6.49 to $5.99. Humboldt would just outlast the shakeout and serve as a rebuke to the way things were going.

The same was true for Shipyard Brewing Company. Founders Fred Forsley and Alan Pugsley bought back full ownership of the Portland, Maine, brewery from Miller in April 2000, after four iffy years partnered with Big Beer. Miller's 50 percent stake was supposed to infuse Shipyard with enough capital to grow well beyond the Northeast. Instead, production actually dropped, from 39,500 barrels in 1996, the year of the Miller partnership, to 25,300 barrels in 1998, as Shipyard pulled away from markets where it wasn't selling as well, including nearby New York. Forsley and Pugsley recalibrated the brewery to focus closer to home with three-fourths of its distribution in New England—sales promptly grew by 10 percent.

Such recalibration was all the rage as the shakeout took its toll. Craft breweries once planning for national domination—or, in the cases of the much smaller ones, regional reach—now deliberately pulled back on their distribution and therefore their production. Maybe small was beautiful, as Maytag had said. David Geary of New England's oldest craft brewery, D. L. Geary, put it this way: "The lesson is: Devote your time, your money and your effort to your core market, and you'll be fine." Geary's own distribution extended barely beyond the Northeast, a market with nearly fifty-five million people, more than most countries in Europe—plenty of potential customers there.

The same was true in other regions, especially ones where craft beer's share of the marketplace might be much larger than its sub–5 percent share nationally. Gary Fish's Deschutes Brewery cut distribution in Colorado and the San Diego area and discovered plenty of fans in the brewery's northwestern backyard to pick up the slack. Seattle-based Pyramid Brewing and Breckenridge Brewing in Denver also cut back out-of-state distribution, as did a number of much smaller companies. Steve Hindy and Tom Potter's Brooklyn Brewery happily distributed 80 percent of its thirty-two thousand barrels in 1999 in the New York City metro region, the nation's largest consumer market.

About four hours' drive to the north, a new brewery in Cooperstown, New York, served as the perfect example of the new local focus. Husband and wife Donald Feinberg and Wendy Littlefield ran the import company Vanberg & DeWulf, which brought Belgian brands such as Affligem, Duvel, Frank Boon, and Saison Dupont to the United States. In 1996, they partnered with several Belgians, including the trio of brothers who were the fourth generation in their family to run the Duvel Moortgat brewery, to start Brewery Ommegang on 136 campestral acres of an old hop farm in Cooperstown. The brewery specialized in bottle-conditioned Belgian beers, and Ommegang's brands quickly became whispered-about treasures as they inched their way farther and farther from the so-called Birthplace of Baseball. The New York City tabloid the *Daily News* dutifully instructed readers in the summer of 1998 that Ommegang's new golden ale, Hennepin, named for the Belgian discoverer of Niagara Falls, "was only available in a few places." At the same time, Feinberg and Littlefield, who continued to run their import company, deliberately made the brewery a local nexus, offering tours and tastings and using hops from a local farming museum in a later ale called Centenniale. The couple were also perfect protagonists for media stories about the rise of Belgian-style beers in America in the late 1990s. This newfound enthusiasm for what would soon be known more widely as locavorism was the triumphant reemergence of one of the original conceits of the whole craft beer movement: traditionally made local beers you couldn't easily get anywhere else. It slapped back on a level of romance that was lost amid the red-hot growth of the early and mid-1990s, as beer became more about product than provenance.

Another portentous event during the shakeout was the 1998 retirement of Henry King as the head of the Brewers Association of America (BAA). The move marked King's departure from brewing in general, including a twenty-two-year run as president of the United States Brewers Association that ended in 1983, shortly before its dissolution. In retirement he was recognized rightfully—and belatedly, some said—for the positive impact he had had on craft brewers. Lost in King's regular boosterism for Big Beer, including his chumminess with the likes of August Busch Jr. and his son, was the pivotal role he played in the 1976 tax change that helped keep costs considerably low for smaller American brewers, which spawned eternal envy among their Canadian counterparts.

As we've seen, that change, which had failed in one form or another in Congress several times over the thirty years before King lobbied it through, reduced the federal excise tax on beer from nine dollars to seven dollars on the first sixty thousand barrels, provided the brewery produced no more than two million barrels annually—not a problem for the earliest craft beer pioneers, who recognized King's contribution a lot more keenly than later entrants. "There is no one that I have known in my business life for whom I have more respect," Maytag would say a few years after King's retirement, when in his early eighties the World War II hero was battling cancer. King again provided craft beer a stimulus for growth when he helped keep beer's excise tax at seven dollars in 1990, when Congress doubled the regular one. To King, though, beer was beer was beer, and he often expressed a polite indifference to the craft beer movement. He reserved little sympathy for smaller concerns that couldn't find distribution if they didn't advertise, and he lamented the lack of institutional memory among the upstarts.

King's eventual successor at the BAA,* chosen in a search that association chairman Rich Doyle of the Mass. Bay Brewing Company led, was, on the other hand, steeped in craft beer: Daniel Bradford, Charlie Papazian's right-hand man in starting the Association of Brewers and its Great American Beer Festival nearly twenty years prior. The AB and the BAA had complemented each other now for that long, with the latter throwing its muscle into lobbying and other political activities and the former now industry famous for its festivals and conferences. With Bradford helming one and Papazian the other, the two appeared headed toward a merger as the new century dawned. They would need the firepower. Some were calling the shakeout just the beginning of the end. "At the end of the day, five or six big microbrewers will survive, in my view," Vijay Mallya told a reporter. "The rest of them will be the brewpubs. Everybody in between, according to my view, is going to go. They'll either get bought, or they'll have to close down, or they'll have to merge; they'll have to do something. They cannot stay where they are."

---

* Gary Galanis served in the position for a year before moving on to a job with Guinness.

"MCDONALD'S VERSUS FINE FOOD"

Manhattan | 2000

There had been 1,127 entries from 370 breweries in thirty-seven countries. The Japanese had fared particularly well, tying the vaunted Germans with 8 percent of the medals at the 2000 World Beer Cup, despite until recently having a beer culture as homogeneous as America's before 1980. American breweries and brewpubs accounted for 63 percent of the entries and swept two-thirds of the medals. The biennial World Beer Cup was a de facto brewing Olympics started by Charlie Papazian's Association of Brewers in 1996 in Vail, Colorado. It had grown to become arguably the most prestigious beer awards in the world, not least because the United States was now recognized as the undisputed comer in brewing, shakeout or not.

The AB arranged a panel after the awards ceremony at the Marriot Marquis in Manhattan's Times Square. Michael Jackson, the redoubtable critic from Yorkshire, and Carlo Petrini, the founder of Slow Food from northern Italy, spoke of American craft beer as an unstoppable thing, a part of the brewing marketplace ipso facto. "Mass marketing is a declining dinosaur," Jackson told the audience. It must have been an odd yet reassuring pronouncement to hear, given the rollback in craft beer growth and market share the last few years. "The natural dynamic is to drink less, but drink better," Jackson continued. "There are no longer masses of workers exiting steel factories in Pennsylvania and coal mines in northern England, ready to wash away the day's work with cases of Pabst Blue Ribbon and the like. Most workers sit at computer screens. They still get thirsty, but not for Pabst Blue Ribbon. They want something better-tasting."

Jackson was right about the shift in the American workforce. The cliff that America's manufacturing sector had been barreling toward for decades finally showed itself in 2000. The total number of manufacturing jobs in the United States began a decadelong slide from more than seventeen million to fewer than twelve million; by the start of the new century, there would be, for the first time since records were kept, more white-collar workers than blue-collar, though there were fewer of these as well, fewer of the workers sitting behind the computer screens. The tech bubble on Wall Street had burst in spectacular fashion, and unemployment was creeping upward as the nation's economy sank into recession. The go-go 1990s were over; other industries were joining craft beer in the doldrums. How long might the doldrums last? Petrini pointed to something. It was idealistic, a throwback—but then, he had started a movement that reveled in the ideas of preindustrial consumption. "Craft beer is not a niche," Petrini explained. "It is fulfilled by people. Small production requires culture, and the culture of beer is to know the difference." Did people know the difference? Yes and no. "For most people, there is not a difference in beer. In some countries, there is only one type of beer and many people know only this type. Others are looking for a better-tasting product, and the two can't get along."

And the people wanting the better-tasting product won't know what they've lost until it's gone, according to Steve Hindy, the Brooklyn Brewery cofounder who was one of two Americans on the panel (Papazian was the other). The craft brewery closings the last few years had left a void in the "beer culture," something a nation didn't necessarily get back once it was lost. "The culture of beer will be lost," Papazian warned, "unless the masses understand that it is a cultural item." Jackson pointed to the consolidation that we've seen in the brewing industry of his home country; the genuine culture of the British pub, the subject of Jackson's first book a quarter-century ago, was in danger of disappearing. "It's equal to McDonald's versus fine food, or generic Chablis versus fine wine," he said. "Beer culture is a part of the world of food and drink. It's not just a commodity in cans and bottles, but has value as an agricultural product with good ingredients." Alas, it might prove impossible to get people to think of it that way, especially American consumers who absorbed the Big Beer assault of the 1990s and didn't quite trust what the newer brands said on their labels. Jackson, whose oeuvre was the Rosetta Stone for whatever beer culture there was or could be, sighed at the challenge. "I still see people buying and swilling terrible beer. I sometimes think that my job is like farting against a gale, but I just keep moving forward."

CRAFT BEER LOGS ON

Boston; San Francisco; Atlanta | 1999–2001

On February 9, 1999, the three-year-old website BrewGuide.com published this:

Sierra Nevada Brewing Co.
Chico, California
Known for using insane amounts of hops with all of their brews. Definitely West-Coast style, and catering to the hop-heads of the world.
Porter
- **Category:** Porter
- **Presentation:** 12oz brown twist. Standard SN label with a sky blue label. No freshness date.
- **Appearance:** Rich dark brown (true Porter colour) with tan, creamy head.
- **Smell:** Earthy malt aromas with some aromatic hop presence.
- **Taste:** Upfront there's a semi-acidic twang (black malt) with a citrusy hop flavour, followed by some malt sweetness and a dry/ burnt aftertaste.
- **Notes:** An excellent West-Coast interpretation of a Porter.

We can glean a lot from this ninety-seven-word review about the state of what Michael Jackson, Steve Hindy, Charlie Papazian, and other pioneers were calling "beer culture." First, its medium: BrewGuide.com was the product of two brothers, Todd and Jason Alstrom, who grew up in and around Springfield, Massachusetts, and got into craft beer in the late 1980s through Boston Beer and Pete's Brewing brands. They tried their hand at homebrewing—an early attempt involved pounds of sugar for a brown ale that clocked in at more than 14 percent alcohol by volume—and both partook freely of

European lagers and ales during the years Todd was stationed by the Air Force in England (Jason visited as often as he could—he wasn't underage there). When Todd returned to the States in 1995, the American craft beer movement was hopping, as we've seen, with more brands and styles than he could have dreamed of in his salad days. To help make sense of the new scene, Todd penned his first beer review on a napkin at the end of a dinner with his parents on August 22, 1996, in Northampton, Massachusetts. He gave 3.88 stars out of 5 to the Steel Rail Extra Pale Ale from the Berkshire Brewing Company, the western Massachusetts brewery started two years before by homebrewers Christopher Lalli and Gary Bogoff. Todd's brother took up the habit, too, and together they launched BrewGuide.com in late 1996, using Todd's background in code writing and web design.

It was a propitious time to be involved in both websites and craft beers. In 1989, an English programmer named Tim Berners-Lee created what he christened the World Wide Web. Launched in January 1992, it busted the Internet, for decades largely the provenance of academics and governments, wide open, its templates for the masses and global interconnectivity ready to transform how people shared information. The number of websites quickly exploded, especially after Marc Andreessen, inspired by Berners-Lee, figured out in 1993 how to make uploading graphics and photos to the web easy with his browser Mosaic. BrewGuide in 1999 could have an entirely different look—graphics, including a blocky, black-and-yellow logo—and a much wider audience—anyone with access to a web browser—than the Home Brew Digest in 1989, with its pictureless, black-and-white e-mails between college students.

We can also tell from BrewGuide's Sierra Nevada Porter review that there was now a standard way of talking about beer, whether you were a returning judge at the Great American Beer Festival or a guy on his computer just getting into something other than yellowy, mass-produced pilsner. Beer was to be evaluated, à la Michael Jackson, on its appearance, taste, and smell, even on its packaging. More than that, it was to be understood within how well it hewed to the style it claimed to be, the styles brought back to modern life by Jackson in the 1970s and further delineated for an American audience by the GABF when it adopted categorized, judge-awarded medals in 1987. A porter was an "excellent" porter only if looked, smelled, and tasted like an excellent porter. But the review also tells us that it was now understood that styles could be broken down further. It was like terroir with wine: it mattered where the beer came from, not because, as with wine, the geographic origin of the ingredients could define the taste, but because the geographic origin of the *brewer* could. Thus the Alstroms could type about a definite "West

Coast-style . . . catering to the hop-heads of the world." It was a given that the informed craft beer consumer knew what defined the West Coast style (and that there were enough American craft breweries now to make knowing the geography worthwhile).

A couple more things. The labeling battle of the previous few years between Anheuser-Busch and Boston Beer surely influenced the reference to "no freshness date." Consumers cared because it seemed something they should care about now. And finally, the adjectives: "earthy," "rich," "creamy," "citrusy," "dry/burnt." It was unusual when the program for the first GABF in 1982 described a beer's aroma as "flowery." Now such perspicacious tongue rolling was expected, even important. There were hundreds of different beers out there now, even after the shakeout—more than the United States had seen in nearly a century. They came in all sorts of different styles, some of them dormant for generations, from breweries big and small. You needed all the verbiage you could muster to explain the differences. It was surely one of the ironies of the American craft beer movement that, just as it hit its biggest challenge—the shakeout of the 1990s—more people than ever were offering their opinions on what brewers were doing wrongly or rightly.

The watershed for craft beer online, however, was less editorial page and more news section. RealBeer.com was launched in 1994 by Mark Silva, who first encountered the web while working at an advertising and marketing firm. By the winter of 1995, he and his wife, Darci, a television producer, had quit their day jobs and hit the road in service of research for RealBeer.com; physical visits and phone calls were the norm, after all, not only in the pre-web age but through its infancy. Credit cards maxed, a bit worse for wear some days, the couple trolled around the country in a ten-thousand-pound, thirty-four-foot trailer, with $20,000 worth of computer equipment and America's better trailer parks for temporary addresses, visiting breweries and brewpubs and snapping thousands of photos. After two years on the road, Mark Silva set up shop in San Francisco, California, with Pat Hagerman as a business partner and the site's president (Hagerman's brother had introduced him to RealBeer years earlier after seeing it on a brewery tour).

The pair set about growing it as a one-stop shop: "Everything you could ever want to know about craft beer can be found here, and more!" For the web at the time, RealBeer was remarkable aesthetically, crisply organized, and easy to navigate, with inviting graphics and idiot-proof engines for searching for breweries or for factoids through what it called the "Library." You could click through to the musings of beer writers and critics, including newer names such as Gregg Glaser and Will Anderson. Crucially for the site's business model, there were also ways to connect quickly and easily with various beer-related products: sign up for a ten-week brewing apprenticeship from the American Brewers Guild, a training school that UC-Davis's Michael Lewis cofounded in 1994; buy a CD-ROM of Michael Jackson's series *The Beer Hunter*; or send a gift subscription to newer publications such as *Brew Your Own* magazine and *Southern Draft Brew News*. You could even take a year-by-year virtual tour of the Great American Beer Festival; distant were the days of hearing about it secondhand from a snail-mailed homebrewing club newsletter or print publication. If only for its exhaustive list of craft breweries and how to find them, Silva and Hagerman's RealBeer was the most important informational advance of the craft beer movement since those first newsletters from the likes of the Maltose Falcons.

Print was not dead yet, though. Two brothers-in-law who liked to home-brew, Tony Forder and Jack Babin, mocked up a four-page dummy of a beer newspaper in Forder's northern New Jersey attic; Forder, who had a background in reporting and editing, and Babin, whose experience was in sales and marketing, pitched it to brewers at a beer festival in Boston in 1992. A proper, twenty-four-page inaugural edition of what they called *Ale Street News* dropped that summer; the paper would grow to be the nation's largest-circulation beer publication, with three bimonthly regional editions: New England, the Mid-Atlantic, and the Midwest/West. A couple of years before Forder and Babin's mockup, Tom Dalldorf bought control of the *California Celebrator*, a bimonthly newspaper started by Bret and Julie Nickels out of Hayward in 1988. Dalldorf would serve as editor as well as publisher, growing what he renamed the *Celebrator Beer News* from thirty-two newsprint pages to an average of sixty glossy ones by 2000, after peaking at eighty during the craft beer boom, and expanding its coverage nationally and internationally.

Dalldorf, a blues musician with a wry sense of humor, also set himself up as a sort of sidekick for Michael Jackson. The pair set out in 1995 on the "Iron Liver Tour," a two-week jaunt to every craft brewery and brewpub then in California; the same year saw the debut of the annual *Sports Illustrated* swimsuit parody showing brewers wearing trunks and boots in their brew-houses. (These newer publications could have unintended consequences. One of Dalldorf's writers, Nico Freccia, founded the 21st Amendment brewpub in San Francisco's South Park neighborhood in 2000, with Shaun O'Sullivan, an assistant brewer at the Triple Rock Brewery in Berkeley, California. John Hickenlooper had had his craft beer epiphany there a decade before; Freccia and O'Sullivan met in a UC-Davis brewing course.)

Both *Ale Street News* and the *Celebrator Beer News* would establish online presences, but the web push started with RealBeer and the BrewGuide (which changed its name to BeerAdvocate in 2000), plus a third competitor. Bill Buchanan started RateBeer out of Atlanta in May 2000 to provide "a forum for beer lovers to come together and share their opinions of beer and breweries." Overwhelmed by the user traffic, Buchanan quickly turned the operation over to Joe Tucker, who had helped redesign the site that first year. A UC–San Diego graduate who spent much of the dot-com boom of the 1990s in Silicon Valley, including a stint as a computer-game developer, Tucker set RateBeer on a strict course of user-generated reviews. Anyone could log on and opine; the volume of negative or positive reviews that a particular brewery or beer got decided its rankings. As Tucker saw it, it was a democratization for beer that gelled with the ethos of the industry, where the traditional marketing favored by Big Beer was avoided, even mocked. The sober assessments of RateBeer's reviewers were more akin to Jim Koch's radio spots about barley, hops, and the Reinheitsgebot than Rodney Dangerfield's commercials for Miller. For instance, Anchor Steam, the oldest brand in the movement, would be reviewed forty times by different consumers by late April 2001, drawing a score of 3.71 stars out of 5 and assessments like this: "Banana notes in the aroma. Flavor is mainly dry with a refreshing bitter finish. A good beer for the warm season."

BeerAdvocate and RateBeer both quickly grew to include tens of thousands of reviews of thousands of beers and breweries. Their success inspired the formats and inclusive styles of dozens of imitators, especially web forums for homebrewing clubs that might have before taken the form of an e-mail listserv in the style of the Home Brew Digest. It was like nothing the brewing industry, whatever the sector, had ever seen: the masses weighing in, and frequently. Sometimes that led to legal threats over bad reviews, and both sites struggled at first to draw advertising (print publications such as *Ale Street News* and the *Celebrator Beer News*, both free to readers, had a relatively easier time of it, as advertisers understood the medium much better). But once the floodgates of consumer beer reviews had been opened, it was impossible to dam them. Ironically enough, both websites would father print arms, including compendiums of their reviews and, in the case of Beer-Advocate, a glossy magazine.

Many of the consumer-reviewers were homebrewers—many more, in fact, than there might have been at any point in American history. Homebrewing was by 2000 legal in every state except Alabama, Iowa, Kentucky, Mississippi, Oklahoma, and Utah. There were at least seventeen hundred homebrewing clubs throughout the forty-four states where it was legal (and, though we can't be certain, surely some in the half-dozen holdouts). Some states, California and other Western redoubts in particular, had such active homebrewing scenes that they spawned their own large-scale homebrewing competitions and web-based networks. Nationally, the inaugural National Homebrew Competition, the brainchild of Charlie Papazian and Charlie Matzen, had drawn thirty-four entries in 1979; the number had swelled nearly eightyfold by 2000, with more than three thousand judges evaluating 2,668 homebrews in twenty-eight categories. The competition was so big that preliminary rounds now preceded the final national verdicts.

Of course, with more cooks in the criticism kitchen than ever before and with the web's search engines—Yahoo and Google were years old by 2000—providing ways to learn information faster than ever, an insularity within the beer culture seemed inevitable. While the search engines may have been able to gin up information with instantaneous ease, they often did not provide the context for understanding it. Everyone could fancy him- or herself an expert.

And experts could be insufferable—which meant Tony Magee, again, couldn't help himself. By 2000, his Lagunitas Brewing was one of the most respected craft breweries in the nation, with a new thirty-barrel brewhouse in Petaluma, California, plus an adjoining brewpub where one might happen upon an ale aged in barrels usually used to age pork or a rockabilly band shifting seamlessly into "Okie from Muskogee" before a crowd of unsuspecting California neohippies, the very sort that Merle Haggard had aimed the tune at in 1969. The fresh digs came from a marathon for new investors that Magee had run in 1998, competing against the sour taste among the wider public left by the ongoing shakeout and finishing just before the December 31 deadline for raising a minimum amount of capital lest he have to return earlier investments: "I remember hammering a good guy for the last piece needed to make the minimum capital raise," Magee would recall, "and existentially hearing myself sounding like one of those soulless stock guys you see squeezing blue-haired dowagers for cash in bad Wall Street movies. That last chunk came through on December 27, and I got drunk."

Meanwhile, Lagunitas's beers, particularly its IPA, were among the definitional ones for the West Coast style; and some of the more extreme, complete with Magee's pioneering free-form stories on the packaging, literally defied definition, losing time and again on technicalities at various festivals. Few of the newly empowered consumer-critics could understand Magee's entrepreneurial race for capital; fewer, perhaps, could countenance his brewery's far-out style interpretations. But that's how he and many other craft brewers, particularly the ones started since the 1980s, approached their work: as adding something to an existing style, Americanizing, if you will, what would inevitably be a centuries-old European construct.

Sometimes the brewers' approaches bumped up against the more cocksure attitudes of the consumer-critics. Take when Magee, whose laid-back nature might now be complemented by the occasional thin beard and Hawaiian print shirt, got an e-mail from a member of an Oregon homebrewing club who wanted him to explain the style of Lagunitas's new seasonal. The brewer typed back that it was an "Uzbeki Raga Ale." It was a completely improvised contraption designed to show his shoulder-shrug for canonical definitions; it was also funny. The member, however, was not amused, and quickly shared his chagrin with others on the homebrewing club's listserv. That sparked a weeklong debate over Magee's fake style, an impassioned back-and-forth worthy of record-store clerks perched ever on either side of the Beatles-Stones divide. The largely humorless debate over style became an equally humorless debate over Magee's perceived insouciance. How dare he be so flip about beer! Such was the ridiculous crucible some craft brewers bore as they reinterpreted traditional European styles.

The debates could turn so didactic at points, so shrill even, that brewers might throw up their hands in these same public forums and wade right in. Sam Calagione, whose Dogfish Head, like Magee's Lagunitas, specialized in pushing the style boundaries, would post this missive in the midst of a BeerAdvocate comments thread on supposedly overrated breweries:

> It's pretty depressing to frequently visit this site and see the most negative threads among the most popular. This didn't happen much 10 years ago when craft beer had something like a 3 percent market share. Flash forward to today, and true indie craft beer now has a still-tiny but growing market share of just over 5 percent. Yet so many folks that post here still spend their time knocking down breweries that dare to grow. It's like that old joke: "Nobody eats at that restaurant anymore, it's too crowded." Except the "restaurants" that people shit on here aren't exactly juggernauts. In fact, aside from Boston Beer, none of them have anything even close to half of one percent market share. The more that retailers, distributors, and large industrial brewers consolidate the more fragile the current growth momentum of the craft segment becomes. The more often the Beer-Advocate community becomes a soapbox for outing breweries for daring to grow beyond its insider ranks the more it will be marginal-

ized in the movement to support, promote, and protect independent, American, craft breweries.

For every know-it-all consumer-critic, though, there seemed to be a handful of novices, and web forums like BeerAdvocate and RateBeer provided them ways to explore their newfound interest like no consumers in the craft beer movement could before. They also could not be ignored. The web cut through geography, cut through class, cut through education level, cut right to the heart of what the herd liked. When, in the middle of the decade, RateBeer reviewers ranked a creation of the tiny monastic brewery Westvleteren as the world's best beer, motorists lined up more than a mile and a half deep in front of the monastery in the pin-drop quiet of the Flemish countryside—the only place, along with a bistro across the street, where the beer could be legally sold. When the monks ran out, they then refused, per their traditions, to brew more to slake the newfound demand.

Its influence undeniable, the web remained for that first decade a second read in the craft beer movement when it came to spotting larger trends or to placing the movement within other developments in American cuisine. Print still mattered more. None other than Fred Eckhardt appears to have been the first critic to link craft beer with Slow Food, for instance. Long acknowledged by the new century as a godfather to beer writers much as Fritz Maytag was to brewers, Eckhardt still penned from Portland (though not regularly for the *Oregonian* anymore), where a word or two with him might be as much reason for a craft beer pilgrimage to the city as a visit to one of its pioneering breweries, like BridgePort and Widmer Brothers. He had been writing regularly since the early 1990s for Daniel Bradford and Julie Johnson's *All About Beer*. In a March 2003 column, in a tone as conversational as the one he might have effected in the 1960s, Eckhardt connected a bunch of dots at once: Slow Food and craft beer, the influence of American craft beer now worldwide, the newfound focus by craft brewers on their immediate markets, and beer's place in general at the dinner table.

For some time now, the Slow Food people in my part of the world have acted as though beer did not exist. That's OK, because until very recently I thought of them as an anti-McDonald's group and not much else. I could sympathize with them, but I wasn't ready to squander $60 of my ill-gotten finances on such a narrow philosophy.

It was Garrett Oliver who changed my views. He spoke at length on that subject when I interviewed him a while back at his Brooklyn

Brewery in New York City, where he is a member of Slow Food's New York board. . . .

Carlo Petrini, who started Slow Food, has said that the American microbrew movement is the purest expression he's ever seen of the concept of Slow Food in action—bringing back from the dead a whole beer industry and various beer styles. The United States has become the Ark for beer styles. Many of the Belgian breweries you love couldn't exist without their US sales.

GROWING PAINS AGAIN
Brooklyn; Cleveland | 2000–2003

Jeremy Cowan climbed from the New York City subway into a sticky Monday morning in June. He walked with a bit of a jaunt in his step, ironic given his situation. He had not had a regular job in more than six years, during which time he had married, divorced, and seen his business flop, losing close friends and family a collective $135,000 in investments. Just that month, he had charged $50,000 to two credit cards with no real means of ever paying it off. He was a grown man couch-surfing in Brooklyn, living as of that morning above a wood-burning pizza joint in a sublet with no air conditioning. Cowan, a Southern California native and Stanford grad, really had nothing to lose now, which might have explained his optimism.

He was meeting a sales rep from a local distributor to help move his beer in what was the nation's most populous Jewish neighborhood. That was important: Cowan's beer was a creation of a contract operation called Shmaltz Brewing Company. Its number one brand? He'Brew. It was one of the more remarkable marketing shticks of the American craft movement, a celebration of religious and brewing traditions that everybody, Jewish or otherwise, could enjoy, as well as a gradated affirmation of resiliency. That's because, like the Jews of old, Cowan's Shmaltz Brewing had wandered, dogged by the pharaonic tumult of the late 1990s shakeout.

Cowan had started the company from San Francisco, soliciting advice from Dan Gordon at the celebrated brewpub chain Gordon Biersch and from Pete Slosberg at Pete's Brewing (it turned out Cowan and Slosberg attended the same synagogue) and riffing marketing-wise off a tagline he and his teenage buddies came up with when they had the idea that became He'Brew: "Don't Pass Out, Passover." The first one hundred cases of his premier beer, Genesis, a kosher pomegranate-infused ale tied to Hanukkah in 1996 (pomegranates being one of the seven sacred species listed in the Torah), sold out quickly.

Cowan soon found himself in the familiar entrepreneurial role of doing everything at once, including distribution: Monday in South Bay, Tuesday in Marin County, driving his grandmother's old car and, later, a tan minivan with vinyl seats and no air conditioning wherever fresh supplies were needed. He also perfected the interviewee art of answering the question, Are you profitable? We're on the *cusp* of profits, Cowan would explain, blurring the fact that Shmaltz lost money year after year in the beginning. By 1996, his original brewer, a brew-on-premises store in Mountain View, had tanked, and Cowan contracted with Anderson Valley Brewing, the respected lower–Mendocino County concern started by ex-chiropractor Ken Allen more than a decade before.

Everything appeared to go swimmingly brand-wise for the next few years—Cowan, in fact, found himself turning down two tidy offers from Vijay Mallya to buy Shmaltz—but then the bottom dropped out of the industry, and demand dried up as distribution became more and more difficult. The beer was good and the marketing catchy (the tag for Messiah Stout: "It's the Beer You've Been Waiting For"); the repeat business, however, was touch and go. Cowan arranged to turn over the company to Anderson Valley and then split for some introspection in East Asia. When he returned to the States, he headed east.

An attempt the previous decade to infiltrate the New York City market had stalled; there was too much craft beer clogging the region's already choppy distribution channels. This go-around, Cowan connected with the official subdistributor of Brooklyn Brewery's distribution arm. While the brewery focused on distributing in the region higher-end brands like Ken Grossman's Sierra Nevada, which it rolled out in New York in the early 1990s, the subdistributor focused on mass-market ones like Heineken and Corona.* It was a way to divide up the nation's most competitive market-place. Cowan also switched contract brewers, from Anderson Valley to the

---

* The partnership between Brooklyn Brewery and the subdistributor, SKI, would end acrimoniously within a couple of years as the brewery moved to sever the partnership so it could sell both its New York and Massachusetts distribution companies. Per Hindy and Potter, *Beer School*, 233–254.

Olde Saratoga Brewing Company, a few hours' drive north of New York City. Vijay Mallya, Cowan's would-be employer, had taken the brewery as collateral for unpaid loans he'd made to James Bernau, the vintner turned brewer who had dreamed of a chain of brewpubs and whose IPO for Nor'wester had cratered after 1996. Shmaltz would specialize in six-packs in New York, instead of the twenty-two-ounce bombers of the company's earlier days in the Bay Area. Like the bombers, though, the six-packs needed schlepping, and that's how Cowan found himself striding toward America's largest Jewish neighborhood on that sticky June day in 2003.

Except it wasn't the largest Jewish neighborhood. That would have been the Upper West Side of Manhattan about twenty blocks uptown. Instead, Cowan realized the directions from his distributor's sales rep were taking him to Hell's Kitchen, the old Irish neighborhood that was then decidedly grittier than its northern neighbor, its retail peppered with small shops invariably run by first- and second-generation Muslim immigrants from the Middle East. Cowan met the sales rep, Nidal, at the corner of Forty-Ninth Street and Ninth Avenue. He learned that Nidal was born in East Jerusalem to Palestinian parents who fled to Jordan in 1967 and then to northern Italy, where Nidal went to high school and spent his twenties. He had recently immigrated, settling in Coney Island and marrying a woman born in the Dominican Republic who converted to Islam. The pair popped into their first lead of the day, a standard-issue New York bodega, with the raised deli counter and register behind ostensibly bulletproof plastic, which was papered with voided lottery tickets and other adverts.

"I'd like to introduce you to this man," Nidal said. These were regular stops for his distribution work.

Cowan then started in on his spiel, pitching first himself and then the beer. The man behind the register, a Yemeni Muslim, peered down through a sliding gap in the plastic. "What's the name again?"

It's called He'brew Beer.

"What is this, some kind of Jewish thing?" Well . . .

Cowan pivoted to a fresh angle: the beer was brewed in New York State, great quality, great packaging, a competitive price.

Suddenly, the bodega was packed. Someone rushed from the back room, another from the cooler, still another from the entrance; the man behind the bulletproof plastic and the new arrivals shouted in Arabic to each other. Cowan and Nidal waited. The man behind the register looked at the latter.

"Dude, what's the deal," he said in English.

"I don't know," Nidal said, "It's just beer—just business."

The man looked at Cowan, at Nidal, at everybody else in the bodega. He looked at Cowan's black T-shirt; the He'brew logo was emblazoned in big, gold letters across his chest. He looked at everyone again.

"All right," he said, "send me a case of each and we'll see how it goes." The salesmen exited the bodega. Holy crap! Cowan thought. He had sold a Jewish beer with a Palestinian refugee educated in Italy, the husband of a Dominican woman, to a Muslim from Yemen in a neighborhood famous for Irish gangsters.

Only in America.

Such seemed the resiliency in the fresh, green century of American craft beer. It streaked with surprising speed out of its 1999 nadir, the first year when more craft breweries closed than opened and a year after there was virtually no sales growth to speak of. By 2000, the trend had reversed itself, though just barely, with 100 closings and 102 openings, according to the Association of Brewers. In 2001, the numbers were similarly close: 76 openings, 74 closings. Craft beer seemed to be a bright spot not only in America's dismal manufacturing picture but in the national economy as well. The recession undoubtedly dried up traditional sources of capital, like commercial bank loans, though the breweries and brewpubs that survived the shakeout were clearly growing.

However, they weren't growing more than the larger operations, the veterans that might more properly be called "regional craft breweries" at this point because of their production volumes. These included Kim Jordan's New Belgium (Jeff Lebesch retired from the company in 2001), Gary Fish's Deschutes, and Ken Grossman's Sierra Nevada (he had in early 1999 bought out cofounder Paul Camusi, who then left the movement to pursue other interests such as farming walnuts and harvesting wine grapes). Still without an official definition from either the government or a trade group, most craft brewers defined their sector against the small-brewers tax credit dating from 1976, which set an upper limit of two million barrels annually. No craft breweries or brewpubs came close to two million barrels, of course, so different strata developed.

The larger operations were those producing at least fifteen thousand barrels a year, and their production accounted for well over half the craft beer produced in 2001. (This number from the Association of Brewers was released in tandem with the annual Craft Brewers Conference in April 2002, held this time in Cleveland, Ohio; it did not include the larger brewpubs.) Individually, these regional craft breweries were seeing strong growth; New Belgium's production, for instance, jumped more than 38 percent annually in 2001, Sierra Nevada's more than 8 percent, and Deschutes' more than 7. As for the larger brewpubs, Gordon Biersch, the biggest brewpub chain, saw its production rise annually more than 5 percent.* Much of these jumps could be attributed not only to the steady quality of their brands—the shake-out had, indeed, shaken a lot of iffy product from the marketplace—and also to their expanding physical capacity. John McDonald's Boulevard Brewing announced in August 1999 a $2.5 million expansion adjacent to its existing Kansas City, Missouri, brewery that would boost its capacity by about nine thousand barrels annually. New Glarus Brewing, the brewery that Dan and Deb Carey started in 1993 with a capacity for three thousand barrels, was on its way to more than twenty-five thousand because of a $2.2 million expansion. And Sierra Nevada's late 1990s expansion afforded it a capacity of nearly eight hundred thousand barrels, enough theoretically to do twelve batches a day.

Jim Koch's Boston Beer bought the Hudepohl-Schoenling Brewery, Cincinnati, Ohio's last regional, in 1997. Boston Beer brands had been brewed there for several years, and, in an ironic twist, the new owner continued

Kim Jordan, cofounder of New Belgium, next to the brewery's bottling line in Fort Collins, Colorado. Courtesy of New Belgium Brewing Co.

---

* An investment firm would acquire Gordon Biersch and Rock Bottom in November 2010 and merge them under a firm that Frank Day chaired.

to brew Hudepohl-Schoenling under contract—mostly, though, the brewery became a major producer of Boston Beer, which would pour millions into renovations. The brewery on Central Parkway, a stone's throw from the Kentucky border, would eventually produce more than 40 percent of the beer sold every year by Koch's outfit. It was a nice trifecta for Koch. He had grown up in Cincinnati, where he had first proposed his harebrained scheme of a craft brewery to his father, Charles ("local boy makes good" stories in the Cincinnati media accompanied the acquisition). Charles had once apprenticed at the Hudepohl-Schoenling plant, and the deal helped dispel the nagging criticism of his company as merely a contract brewer. Boston Beer by the new century was still far and away the biggest craft operation, with production at nearly 1.2 million barrels; the next closest in production were Sierra Nevada at 541,000 and New Belgium at 229,000—a ranking that would change little over the coming decade, even as the numbers grew. The ranks of the biggest craft operations by volume throughout the 2000s would be dominated by ones with born-on dates in the 1980s and early 1990s.

In general, the survivors of the shakeout, large and small, were showing positive signs for the years ahead. For one thing, certain pre-shakeout dynamics still held. By 2002, the Association of Brewers estimated there were 1,458 craft breweries and brewpubs, about what there had been in the mid-1990s. The majority were brewpubs (999, or just over two-thirds), just like before the shakeout. Of those remaining, most were small, producing far fewer than fifteen thousand barrels annually, with only about forty-five voluminous enough to be considered regional craft breweries. It was like before, with smaller operations dominating the craft beer landscape, some popping up seemingly overnight.

This go-around was going to be different for everybody, however—it had to be. No more trying to grow as fast as possible to every corner of the country; no more throw-it-against-the-wall-and-see-what-sticks mentality; no more get rich quick off hops and malted barley. As John Hickenlooper, the cofounder of Colorado's oldest brewpub, who would have a more interesting decade than most, explained: "For a while, every Tom, Dick, and Harry got into it not for the love of beer but because they thought they would get rich." At the same time, there was to be no passivity when it came to making consumers understand that it was about the beer. As David Geary had realized when he started the first craft brewery in New England, quality beer was the price of admission—can't pay it, and you get tossed eventually. It was a psychological shift of sorts that existed on two levels.

First, beer quality became holy writ. As a result, brewers poured capital into better equipment and better labor, with training at places such as UC-Davis, Oregon State, and Siebel more in demand than ever. As a result, by the turn of the century, the United States boasted more modern small breweries than any other nation. With the IPO wave played out, the price wars were over except in a few isolated markets. Craft brewers knew they would never really compete price-wise with Big Beer brands and most imports. They could grab consumers with quality, though. Geoff Larson, cofounder of the Alaskan Brewing Company, put it this way: "People ask about growth. Whenever we come to a point of adding equipment or facilities, the primary driver is increasing the quality of our product. . . . Cost is a secondary issue for us, because we know we can't compete on price. We can only compete based on the quality of the product in the glass." By 2000, Alaskan was growing by double digits again.

The second level of this psychological shift was simpler, and certainly cheaper, yet more profound: the craft beer movement tucked in its shirt and dragged a comb across what was left of its hair. For the Craft Brewers Conference in Cleveland, Ohio, in April 2002, Charlie Papazian put together a slide show made up mostly of photos from the 1980s. There were not a few hirsute young men in old T-shirts and frayed blue jeans in the photos; Fritz Maytag looked downright anachronistic in his tie. While the rebel element, a certain swaggering insouciance that comes from knowing you took the road less traveled, would remain in the movement and would still be a draw for newcomers, things did get a bit more professionalized. Just as the brewhouses became as a rule more modern, so too did the business sides. Craft beer pioneers found themselves calling and attending more meetings about matters like production efficiencies and sales strategies than they ever might have before. This was partly because there were more people to do other tasks: hiring jumped after the shakeout and rose steadily as the movement once again began to expand.

States and cities for the first time started calculating the economic impact of breweries and brewpubs on their physical landscapes and bottom lines; attention was finally being paid to craft beer as a jobs generator and tourist attraction. This was true in metropolises such as New York, where city hall and the chattering classes credited Brooklyn Brewery with helping shepherd in the real estate renaissance of the surrounding borough, and San Francisco, where Anchor and newer arrivals like 21st Amendment were quickly becoming the last true manufacturers within the city limits. It was also the case in smaller locales like Bend, Oregon, or the Outer Banks of North Carolina, where brewpubs like Gary Fish's Deschutes and Uli Bennewitz's Weeping Radish, respectively, might be among the top two or three reasons for even visiting the areas at all.

The resiliency was there; it was bolstered not only by the awareness of

David Geary of D. L. Geary in Portland, Maine, with US senator Susan Collins. Elected leaders began regularly touting craft brewers as job creators in the new century. Courtesy of Hollie Chadwick

having run a gauntlet to emerge on the other end stronger and more confident but also by the return of healthy sales growth. Would it last, though? Or was it just another start of a climb to a peak and the cliff right afterward? The keynote speaker at the 2002 Craft Brewers Conference was Michael Jackson. His goatee and curls were more salt than pepper now, the spread around his middle showing the effects of the occupational hazards of his decades of work. He had been traveling again and again to America since the 1970s to study its beer, to give pep talks to its brewers, to all but plead with its consuming public. For all that, he was an endearingly revered figure in the movement, perhaps only matched in regard by Fritz Maytag and Fred Eckhardt. As a critic, as a seer of trends in the global beer world, Jackson had no peer.

His Cleveland speech, then, is worth quoting at length, as it was a truncated history of what had just happened and what could happen. He began by noting the acquisition of Beck's, Germany's biggest export brewer, by the already-large Belgian concern Interbrew as well as the growth of Denmark-based Carlsberg and Netherlands-based Heineken into other markets. For that matter, Coors had snapped up the iconic Bass brand in Britain that February. And Jackson could not avoid mentioning the pending merger of South African Breweries and Miller, a deal that would close in July for $3.6 billion and create in SABMiller the world's second-biggest brewery behind—you guessed it—Anheuser-Busch. (In the United States, the merged entity would operate as MillerCoors.) AB and SABMiller would immediately set about divvying up the global beer map as if playing Risk, competing for companies as varied geographically as Romania, Italy, and China (Jackson noted, too, that SAB already controlled Pilsner Urquell out of the Czech Republic, famed for its archetypal pilsner). The two breweries would also reignite their decades-old tradition of attacks, with Anheuser-Busch, for instance, buying a full page in *USA Today* to remind consumers that Miller was now "South African owned" and Miller taking a full page in the *New York Times* to declare its archrival "the Queen of Carbs." To Jackson, such cattiness represented a boon to American craft beer, a way of creating fresh consumers if only the sector seized the opportunity:

> This notion of the global brewers' fallout benefiting the craft brewer may seem Pollyannaish, but it has already been evident in the Nordic and Baltic countries. Having never quite hacked North America, Carlsberg has been building a dominant position in these countries. In precisely the same period, Denmark has gained a beer movement, with an annual festival and a crop of new products. With the exception of Anheuser-Busch, which has grown organically, the biggest brewers have sought growth by acquisition. Breweries available for sale are usually big but less successful. Thus groups consolidate overcapacity. They then close breweries, centralizing production in fewer plants and lengthening the road to market at a time when preservatives and other additives are under scrutiny by the consumer. The growth to global from national ambition also lowers the common denominator of flavor. This is already so low that many young consumers see aroma and flavor as being faults, distractions on the path to feeling drunk. The same follows for super-premium vodkas and gins. . . .
>
> The big brewers made some very good specialty beers for a time, in an effort to benefit from the success of the micros. Their head brewers knew what they were doing, but the cost accountants and marketing people could not think micro.

For them it seems to have been the road not taken. They chose "beer as soda pop." Craft brewers are "beer as wine." That is the road we must take. We must stick to it, and climb higher along the way.

We have come a long way already. When I started writing about beer, there were fewer than fifty brewing companies in the US. . . .

There are now more breweries in the US than in any other country, including Germany: about 1,500 make beers in more than fifty styles, many more authentic than the European originals upon which they are modeled. This is a remarkable achievement, an astonishing success story. Why don't we tell the story? Were we distracted by the opportunists who came into the business when it was being hyped by Wall Street? Remember them? "Mr. Jackson, I don't know much about brewing, but I know that Americans enjoy a beer like Budweiser." I would point out to them that someone had already noticed that market, a man named Busch. They were all going to overtake A-B in two, three, or four years. They've all gone now, telling the world that they got out just in time. It is their absence that makes this such a pleasant conference. . . .

"Everybody knows about microbreweries," someone said at this conference. No, they don't. I have even met people in Seattle or Portland, Oregon, who are unfamiliar with the phrase "microbrewery." Far more are familiar with the phrase, but unsure what it means. Or whether it is a good thing. Some people still get a bit giggly about having been to a brewpub, as though it were somehow not "normal" beer. Would they feel the same way about visiting a cook-from-scratch restaurant as opposed to a McDonald's?

We understand the differences because we love, live—and no doubt breathe—beer. It is easy to forget that not everyone shares our passion. . . . As a young television producer, I persuaded James Baldwin and Norman Mailer to appear on a program. Thrilled with achievement, I asked an aunt what she thought of the program. "I liked the black man," she said, "but that feller with the curly hair was a bit of a loudmouth." The names James Baldwin and Norman Mailer had meant nothing to her. We have to allow for the fact that millions of people drink without thinking, as though they were sleepwalking, but could be awakened to the pleasures of good beer.

Jackson did not need to spell it out for his audience: however it looked now, future growth was not a given.

STILL THE LATEST THING

Guerneville, CA; Oklahoma City, OK; Houston | 2002–2005

By all rights, given what we know now, Vinnie Cilurzo's decision in May 1994 should have caused the heavens to open and a ray of deific light to bathe his plastic fermentation tank. As it was, nothing much happened; Cilurzo's decision produced a pretty decent beer. What was the decision? To double the hops and to up the malt a bit in a pale ale recipe he had. Why? To cover any off-flavors in a batch that simply had to work. Cilurzo, a twenty-four-year-old with close-cropped brown hair and big, almond-shaped eyes, was one of three partners and the brewmaster for a new, four-thousand-square-foot brewpub called the Blind Pig, the name a play on Prohibition-era bootlegging, in Temecula, California, about sixty miles north of San Diego. He didn't have much experience brewing at the professional level, though he had known for a while that he wanted to be a brewer. He grew up around wine—his parents owned a winery nearby with nearly two dozen peacocks—and he had homebrewed in college as well as in the winery's basement. He hopped around Europe, including an illuminating spell in Belgium, and worked at his parents' winery before embarking on what would become the Blind Pig with $160,000 from investors.

The brewpub launched with three beers: the obligatory pale ale, a golden ale, and a seasonal, the Blind Pig Inaugural Ale. This last one was where Cilurzo's decisional alchemy came in. The equipment was secondhand, thanks to Electric Dave down around the Mexican border. Electric Dave was Dave Harvan, a one-time electrician who blew into the former mining community of South Bisbee, Arizona, in an old Volkswagen van in the late 1970s. Ten years later, off State Route 92, off an unmarked road and through a tunnel made of corrugated metal, in a part of the Old West where mounds from the old mines gave the landscape an apocalyptic feel, Harvan started the first craft brewery in Arizona since Prohibition.

The Grand Canyon State's brewing history reflected the larger national changes, especially when it came to consumer tastes. The only Arizona-brewery to make it out of Prohibition for any length of time—eight tried—was the Phoenix-based Arizona Brewing Company. It shed consumers, however, as its home city's population boomed after World War II; then as now the Phoenix region was one of the nation's fastest growing. The newcomers brought with them tastes for the homogenized Big Beer brands they'd grown accustomed to elsewhere, and the Arizona Brewing Company was acquired in 1964 by Canadian conglomerate Carling. The Phoenix brewery closed in 1985; one of the fastest-growing states in the union was without any semblance of local beer.

Enter Harvan in 1987 with a tie and some wingtips he got at the Salvation Army to personally lobby state officials to follow the growing trend of legalizing small breweries and brewpubs. The state did just that, authorizing operations that produced a minimum of ten thousand barrels annually. Chicago transplants Joe and Addie Mocca opened the state's first brewpub in the spring of 1988, Bandersnatch, in downtown Tempe, with another partner, making it a popular hangout for students at nearby Arizona State University. Soon after, with $ 25,000 from investors, some of them teetotalers by necessity, Harvan began producing beer in his South Bisbee garage with a seven-barrel brewhouse he rigged himself that included plastic fermentation tanks. A reporter who made the trip out described the brew as having "a rich, slightly intoxicant quality to it, full-bodied, lacking the watery blandness characteristic of macrobreweries." Harvan happily drank at least six bottles' worth a day and self-distributed the rest in kegs with his white Dodge pickup for seventy-five dollars each. An arrest for marijuana smuggling soon put Electric Dave temporarily out of business—he would reopen on the same small scale in 2000—and his equipment in the hands of other brewers, including Vinnie Cilurzo at the Blind Pig.

Cilurzo called the seasonal he crafted from Electric Dave's equipment a "double IPA." It was about 6 percent alcohol by volume and ninety-two IBUs in bitterness—that is, it was about the same alcohol content as Anchor's landmark 1975 Liberty Ale but more than twice as bitter. What had seemed a curiosity not even a generation ago was coming into its own as a distinct style. As we've discussed, the so-called West Coast style was already largely defined by its bitterness; Ken Grossman's Sierra Nevada Pale Ale might be the archetype, with Fritz Maytag's Liberty Ale the urtext. But what Cilurzo had crafted was so much more bitter that in time his creation, along with those from a handful of other brewers on the West Coast and elsewhere, would redefine the style. Bitterness became almost a badge worn by consumers who had a jones for it: they were hopheads and proud of it.

Whether Cilurzo's moniker, double IPA, constituted a brand-new, distinct beer style remains an open question. The first mainstream-media reference to "double India Pale Ale" or "double IPA" did not appear to have come until nearly a decade after Cilurzo's first batch. The reference was to a Double IPA Festival in February 2002, hosted by Victor and Cynthia Kralj, owners of a pub and beer garden in downtown Hayward, California, called the Bistro. IPAs had to be at least ninety IBUs to enter. The following year, the Great American Beer Festival added a category called "Imperial or Double India Pale Ale," as official an acknowledgment as brewers of double IPAs could get. (The Pizza Port brewpub chain out of San Diego, California, would win the first gold and silver medals in the category.)

Cilurzo would gain his widest audience for hoppier beers after the Blind Pig, which, like so many other brewpubs and breweries of the era, went out of business in the late 1990s. He then connected with the Russian River Brewing Company in Guerneville, California, about seventy-five miles up Highway 101 from San Francisco. The fifteen-barrel brewhouse opened in May 1997 within the Sonoma County vineyard of its owner, Korbel Champagne Cellars. The company used Centennial and Cascade hops grown on the vineyard in its beer, which was served out of a new on-site restaurant and to local retailers.

Korbel was not the first vintner to segue into craft beer. Charles and Shirley Coury at the short-lived Cartwright Portland and Richard and Nancy Ponzi at BridgePort Brewing, both in Portland, Oregon, had pioneered that pivot at least fifteen years before. Others followed, including up and down California's esteemed wine country. Along with Korbel in Sonoma, there was the Sonoma Mountain Brewery, opened a couple of months after Russian River Brewing and owned by the Benzinger family, which had made its name in California wines. Downstate, in Santa Barbara County, there was the Firestone Walker Brewing Company. Brothers-in-law Adam Firestone and David Walker spent months studying brewing at UC-Davis and started the brewery in 1996 on the Firestone family's vineyard in Los Olivos (the family had actually crafted a nonalcoholic beer as far back as the late 1980s). Almost as a nod to an adjective now beloved by beer geeks and wine snobs alike, Firestone Walker was known to ferment its ales in sixty-gallon oak barrels, which could leave—wait for it—an "oaky" taste.

While Firestone Walker would expand twice within six years, eventually relocating farther north to Paso Robles, California, the Benzingers and Korbel would turn back to wine full-time in the same period. The former simply converted its brewing equipment to wine making. In Korbel's case, however, there was a handoff: The winemaker in 2002 sold its Russian River brand to Cilurzo and his wife, Natalie. The couple, along with partners Jerry Warner and Jim Muto, reopened Russian River as a seven-thousand-square-foot brewpub in downtown Santa Rosa, California, in April 2004 after investing $750,000 in startup costs, including $75,000 for old brewing equipment from a defunct North Carolina operation. The reborn Russian River, like the old Korbel-controlled brand, produced fifteen hundred barrels annually at first but grew its production to slake demand, especially for its Pliny the Elder, a double IPA named after the Roman naturalist that won the gold medal for Imperial or Double India Pale Ale at both the 2005 and 2006 GABF. (Pizza Port had captured it again in 2004, the category's second year; through 2011, with one exception, California breweries won every gold and silver medal in the category—West Coast style, indeed.)*

The Cilurzos were part of what we might call the craft beer movement's fourth wave. It was one of relative youngsters—the Cilurzos and Jeremy Cowan were barely into their thirties by the new century—not really old enough to have known an American beer scene without Samuel Adams or Sierra Nevada, without sincerely earnest debates over style at BeerAdvocate or RateBeer. Despite their ages, it was also a wave populated by those tested, sometimes even broken, by the shakeout of the late 1990s. They were, then, cognizant of being part of a wave, of something that might either continue to crest or to crash messily. They often proceeded accordingly, this new batch of craft brewers, keeping their distribution close to home and their eyes on innovation. This innovation might come through different styles, or it might simply come through geography: the movement, now at least a generation old on the West Coast and getting there on the East, could still seem like the latest thing in the middle of the country.

When the Bricktown Brewery opened in downtown Oklahoma City, Oklahoma, in the fall of 1992 as the Sooner State's first-ever brewpub, patrons would invariably ask Luke DiMichele, the UC-Davis-trained brewmaster, "You brew the beer right there?" The novelty lingered through the next decade, to when Rick and Shaneen Huebert opened the first start-up brewery in Oklahoma since voters endorsed statewide repeal in 1959, in a sixty-five-thousand-square-foot space in Oklahoma City's Capitol Hill neighborhood. The *Daily Oklahoman* carefully explained the Hueberts's eponymous opera-

---

* The GABF in 2009 renamed the category "Imperial India Pale Ale." The only exception was also a West Coast brewery: Hopworks Urban Brewery of Portland, Oregon, which won the 2009 gold.

tion to its readers in May 2004: "Huebert Brewery produces about 45 barrels of beer every two weeks. . . . The facility is capable of producing fifteen barrels at a time. Brewers use the barrel as their standard of measurement, and 330 bottles can be made from one barrel."

When Saint Arnold Brewing Company released a golden ale called Fancy Lawnmower in the summer of 2002, the oldest craft brewery in Texas had to explain the joke: "'Lawnmower beer,'" according to the August 7 food section of the *Fort Worth Star-Telegram*, "is a term used by some microbrew fanciers seeking to denigrate the watery, industrially produced, mainstream lagers that most American drinkers happen to prefer." That such a lead would run in a Texas newspaper was a testament to the craft beer movement's growth in what had become by 2000 the second most-populous state in the union. A lot of that craft beer growth was due to the efforts of two thoroughly disgruntled investment bankers in Houston, Brock Wagner and Kevin Bartol, who chucked their day jobs to open Saint Arnold in the summer of 1994, near the Hempstead Highway in Houston. They put in half a million of their own money and raised $400,000 more, visiting most of the craft breweries then in existence (this was right before the boom), soliciting advice, and knowing full well the Lone Star State was the land of actual watery lawnmower beers, not craft ones.

Texas may have had nearly sixty breweries in the decade after the Civil War, but then it underwent its own miniwave of consolidation as Big Beer precursors like the early Anheuser-Busch barged in and the number of breweries sank to the single-digits before 1900; after a post–World War II spike, the number stayed that way, with six breweries in operation in Texas by the early 1980s. Outside forces owned most of these, including Anheuser-Busch's 126-acre Houston plant, which could produce 3.2 million barrels annually, and Miller's in Fort Worth, which could produce more than twice as much. Even the locally beloved Lone Star brand was owned by G. Heileman out of La Crosse, Wisconsin. Don and Mary Thompson's Plano-based Reinheitsgebot brewery, the very first stab at craft brewing in Texas, had fizzled out in 1990, after five years. The original reception, then, for Saint Arnold in the vast state in 1994 ranged from incredulity to ignorance, with Wagner and Bartol, homebrewers since their days at Rice University, pressing on through guerilla marketing and a radio ad a few years in that Wagner estimated boosted sales roughly 0.0001 percent.

Lost in all the consolidation was the steady fact that Texans liked to drink beer: about thirty gallons per Texan per year in the 1980s and 1990s. Eventually, Saint Arnold tapped into this thirst, thanks in part to favorable media coverage and word of mouth, as well as Houston's own population growth via newcomers from elsewhere (the city in the 1980s surpassed Philadelphia as the nation's fourth-largest). The brewery, which resolutely stuck to Texas in its distribution, was pushing the production limits of its original location, closing in on ten thousand barrels annually. Wagner, who bought out Bartol and other investors in 1998, found himself happily planning for an expansion in a new Houston location.

On March 19, 2005, Don Alan Hankins, the founder and brewmaster of Olde Towne Brewing Company, was on hand at the Costco in the Birmingham suburb of Hoover to explain his amber ale to fellow Alabamans. He and assistant brewer Darren Evans-Young even had some literature on it. Alabama was part of a handful of states that still had anachronistic, even punitive, restrictions on beer, whether prohibiting homebrewing, capping alcohol content, or limiting the sizes of bottles to no more than a pint—in Alabama's case all three. Hankins's Olde Towne sold its beers in twelve-ounce bottles by the case. The day at the Hoover Costco was particularly productive: the store moved thirty-one cases of Olde Towne Amber. Hankins was especially pleased that more than twenty cases went to people who had never heard of his year-old operation, the Yellowhammer State's oldest craft brewery.

Around the time of Hankins's good day at Costco, forty-four hundred miles away Garrett Marrero was filing with Hawaii to open a small brewpub in Lahaina on the island of Maui. Opened later that year with wife Melanie Oxley, the Maui Brewing Company was locavore all the way in its production and ingredients, a rare enough combination still in the craft beer movement and unheard of at that point beyond the contiguous forty-eight states. Hawaii's biggest brewery, the Kona Brewing Company founded by Cameron Healy and Spoon Khalsa in 1994, and now run and co-owned by Mattson Davis, had been brewing on the mainland since 1998 as well as on the Big Island, becoming one of the ten largest craft breweries in the country; like Sierra Nevada and New Belgium, Kona's growth never really slowed during the shakeout. Marrero, a longtime homebrewer and former investment consultant who split from San Francisco to the islands after a trip to Maui in 2001, and Oxley strove to brew all their beer in Hawaii with only Hawaiian-raised ingredients (even the packaging was local) and seemed to rarely miss an opportunity to remind consumers of that. Given its location and its owners' fervency, Maui Brewing pushed the locavore envelope in American craft beer farther than it had ever been pushed.

CRUSHING IT

Lyons, CO | 2002

Along with geography and style, innovation in American craft beer now came through packaging. By this we mean not necessarily the garrulous labels of the likes of Tony Magee's Lagunitas or Sam Calagione's Dogfish Head, though those were increasingly the norm in the movement: bright, bibulous vignettes trying to make sense for consumers of increasingly boundary-pushing beers. Instead, we mean the actual physical contraptions for storing craft beer: namely, cans.

Cans had a negative connotation in craft beer culture. Cans were the purview of everyone's paunchy uncle or dad, pounding Big Beer brands by the case during yard work or while watching the big game in the Barcalounger, anachronistic throwbacks to every cheesy commercial that ended with a burly, hairy hand plucking a sweaty beer can out of a buddy's cooler or, better yet, from a crisp mountain stream. Bottles, on the other hand, evoked a certain romance, inviting comparisons to fine wine, which was always bottled (only the cheap hooch was boxed) and conjuring images of dusty old-world brands on worn wooden shelves in dusky Belgian monasteries and English pubs (though the latter was farther away now than ever from small-batch brewing). Beyond the perception, craft beer consumers and brewers had concerns about the potential seepage of metals into canned beer, ruining the flavor, even causing health hazards. Never mind that technological advances since the Newark, New Jersey–based brewer Gottfried Krueger introduced the first tin beer cans in January 1935 had largely eliminated this threat. Still, cans just seemed . . . off. Besides, with prices starting at around $250,000, canning machines were another big capital investment most craft brewers simply couldn't make.

Enter again, in our tale, the Great White North. In 1999, Calgary, Alberta–based equipment manufacturer Cask Brewing Systems introduced a manual canning machine that could can two twelve-ounce beers at a time and that was small enough to fit on a tabletop. The machine was originally targeted to brew-on-premises retailers, though the American shakeout might be called the true mother of this invention. As the brew-on-premises trend fizzled in both Canada and the United States, Cask Brewing Systems shifted its focus to American craft breweries. The company knew that many needed to up sales to survive but might be wary of any more big capital investments anytime soon; at no more than $10,000 a pop, the manual canner could cut through the price anxiety. After all, a small operation in Canada's Yukon Territory had become, in 2001, the first craft brewery in North America to can its beer using the manual canner.

American craft brewers proved more skeptical. Cask Brewing Systems reps pitched the machine at the 2002 Craft Brewers Conference in Cleveland and were told it was the "dumbest idea" and that "nobody will put their craft beer into aluminum cans."

History up until 2002 seemed to bend toward the skeptics. In June 1991, the Mid-Coast Brewing Co., a contract brewery based in Oshkosh, Wisconsin, debuted its Chief Oshkosh Red Lager in cans at a press event at the Oshkosh Hilton. The beer, brewed at the Stevens Point regional seventy miles northwest of Oshkosh, was the revival of a brand that the Oshkosh Brewing Co., one of those regionals that industry consolidation had swept away, had put out until the early 1970s. The recipe, though, was the creation of Mid-Coast founder Jeff Fulbright, who studied at the Siebel Institute and launched his company in early 1991 after talking to Jim Koch at a Great American Beer Festival. Fulbright's decision to can his beers was purely financial: it was cheaper to have Stevens Point can the beers than bottle them (Fulbright had started Mid-Coast with "way under" $100,000). Chief Oshkosh Red Lager in cans caused a minor stir, but the company itself foundered after thirty-six months. Distribution peaked at thirteen states. Miller-owned Leinenkugel in Chippewa Falls, Wisconsin, three hours to the west, helped thwart a national distribution push, and understandably so—Leinenkugel had introduced its own red lager in 1993.

Subsequent attempts at canning craft beer were similarly short-lived and reliant on contract brewing. In the late 1990s, Koch's Boston Beer briefly allowed its cream ale sold in the United Kingdom to be canned;* Pete's Brewing canned its Summer Brew through the Minnesota Brewing Company and then Stroh's, both in St. Paul, in the mid-1990s; and, around the same time,

---

* Whitbread did the brewing and canning under license from 1996 to 1999, with "modest production" (per Boston Beer Company).

the Minneapolis-based James Page Brewing Company, which the founder sold in 1995, canned some of its beer under contract at August Schell in nearby New Ulm. Otherwise, any hopes of canning American craft beer seemed perpetually crushed.

Then a brewpub twenty miles north of Boulder bought one of Cask Brewing Systems's manual canners and in true Colorado fashion (given the goatshed birthplace of the Boulder Brewing Company in 1979) got to work with it in an old nearby barn. Dale Katechis had gotten into craft beer in the late 1980s while a student at Auburn University after getting a homebrewing kit for Christmas. In the craft beer desert that was Alabama and much of the South, he stood out, known for making hoppy homebrews and driving two hours northeastward to Atlanta to stock up on Pete's Wicked Ale. After earning a finance degree, Katechis left for Colorado, worked at a backpack manufacturer, and bartended on the side before opening his Oskar Blues Cajun Grill in Lyons (population fourteen hundred) in 1997. At the urging of a new business partner, he added the brewery component two years later. A recipe born in Katechis's college bathtub, Dale's Pale Ale, became the brewpub's flagship; that and other recipes proved popular enough that pretty soon Katechis was looking at packaging options. A bottling line, even used, might cost in the low six figures; same for a canning line. Both would take up precious space. The manual canner from Cask Brewing Systems was the breakthrough. Katechis's canning of Dale's Pale Ale in six-packs, beginning in the old barn in the fall of 2002, rocked the craft beer movement—after the laughter died down. Katechis and brewmaster Brian Lutz found themselves in an explanatory slog.

The critics: Why can?
Katechis: We like pushing the envelope and stretching the boundaries. We like hearing about something that can't or shouldn't be done and then doing it. That's what craft brewing is supposed to be about.
Was it better than bottles?
Katechis: Unlike bottles, cans eliminate the risk of light damage and oxidation to our beer.
Lutz: Cans are far more environmentally friendly than bottles, they're much easier to recycle. They also make it easier for outdoor enthusiasts to take great beer into the back country, in the canoe, the ski pack, anywhere they want to.

Dale's Pale Ale. Courtesy of Oskar Blues Brewery

OK, but what about that metallic taste? Won't the aluminum ruin the beer? You're getting your cans, after all, from the Ball Corporation, the biggest can manufacturer in the country, the guys who supply Coors over in Golden?

Katechis: The cans' glass polymer lining ensures the beer never contacts metal.

Once craft brewers absorbed this fact, the demand for canners grew. Cask Brewing Systems eventually found itself with a backlog of orders from American craft breweries; the company developed other canner models, larger and faster ones that were still priced competitively against bottling lines (a five-at-a-time canner introduced in 2004 and also adopted by Oskar Blues cost about $45,000). Within eight years, more than one hundred craft operations would be canning beer. As for Katechis's brewery, its production jumped from three-figure annual barrelages to twenty thousand, and its distribution wove its way out of Colorado, to both coasts and higher-end grocery chains like Whole Foods, as well as to high above the Earth: Shortly before Christmas 2002, about a dozen years after Katechis got that homebrewing kit, Oskar Blues inked a deal with Denver-based Frontier Airlines to carry Dale's Pale Ale on all flights. It was the first time a commercial airline carried beer canned in a craft brewery;* Frontier cited the lighter-than-glass packaging as key in its decision. More than anything, the numerous plaudits that the canned Oskar Blues brands won in subsequent years, including medals from the Great American Beer Festival and glowing results from a *New York Times* blind taste test, put to rest any lingering doubts over canning craft beer.†

As the number of craft breweries and brewpubs began to expand rapidly after 2002, innovations like canning, the double IPA, and the opening of operations in farther-flung corners of the nation became more and more pronounced in their influence. More innovations were coming, too. So were more big changes.

WITH GUSTO
Manhattan; Boulder, CO | 2003–2005

Shortly after the turn of the century, Garrett Oliver was at a party in Manhattan's West Village hosted by Rob Kaufelt, the owner of New York institution Murray's Cheese. As often happened in small talk, someone asked him what he did. He said he was the brewmaster at Brooklyn Brewery, an intriguing job description that usually prompted follow-up questions. His interlocutor in this case was a literary agent, and the two fell into talking about books about beer. Oliver mentioned that he had wanted for a while now to write a book about beer and food. He had recently begun hosting beer dinners at the brewery in Williamsburg and elsewhere, and he had seen what he called the "aha moment" spread across hundreds of faces as they realized the potential in pairing the right beer with the right food. Imagine codifying that somehow and sharing it with a mass audience. "The beer is here," Oliver explained, "the food is here. Why aren't people putting two and two together? I feel literally bad for people who don't know the combination of beer and food."

The conversation would lead to the publication by HarperCollins in 2003 of *The Brewmaster's Table: Discovering the Pleasures of Real Beer with Real*

---

* At times in the late 1990s, Continental Airlines carried Pete's Summer Brew, and Northwest Airlines carried James Page beers, both of which were contract canned in Minnesota.
† Dale's Pale Ale topped twenty-three other pale ales that the tasting panel sampled (per Eric Asimov, "Crisp, Complex and Refreshing," *New York Times*, June 29, 2005).

Food, an effort to educate the general public about exactly what the subtitle implied: what beer went best with what foods. It was not new territory. Jack Erickson had written and published the 146-page book *Great Cooking with Beer* in 1989; Lucy Saunders's 154-page *Cooking with Beer: Taste-Tempting Recipes and Creative Ideas for Matching Beer & Food* had come out seven years later; Candy Schermerhorn's 86-page *Great American Beer Cookbook*, published in 1998, included a foreword by Michael Jackson; and there had been myriad shorter pieces within other beer books before and since, as well as extensive writing by Jackson, perhaps most prominently his 1983 piece for the *Washington Post* on which beers to pair with which parts of a Thanksgiving feast.

What set Oliver's book apart was not simply its heft (384 pages) but its holistic approach. It was not just a way to enhance the dining experience by complementing that Thai dish's spiciness with the bitterness of an IPA; it was instead a manual on how to weave beer into one's lifestyle, how to, as Oliver put it in the introduction, use beer to amplify the "symphony" that eating should be: "Great beer from around the world is now available everywhere, and, unlike wine, it's an affordable luxury. You can enjoy it literally every day. Once you discover traditional beer, your 'food life' will be transformed into something fascinating, fun and infinitely more enjoyable."

If Oliver's words sounded like Folco Portinari's 1990 Slow Food manifesto, it was no accident. By 2003, Oliver was very familiar with that tract, which saw the understanding and resultant appreciation for good food and drink as essential for the "slow, long-lasting enjoyment" of life. He had learned about the Slow Food movement in the late 1990s from a flier about its biannual trade show in Turin, Italy, called Salone del Gusto, and wrote movement cofounder Carlo Petrini directly, asking how he could get involved. Petrini wrote back that the next Slow Food event was a cheese festival in Bra, a town in northern Italy's wine country.* Why didn't Oliver come up with something for that? The brewmaster then connected with Rob Kaufelt, and the two flew to Italy on different flights, each with a suitcase full of cheese should one or the other get stopped by security (Kaufelt did, though he and his cheese still made it). The Americans were a hit in Turin.

From there, Slow Food asked Oliver to get involved in setting up the movement in the United States, which became Slow Food USA in 2000, the same year Petrini declared from Midtown Manhattan that American craft beer was the purest expression of Slow Food's principles; Oliver found him-

---

* Bra is also Petrini's hometown and Slow Food's international headquarters.

self on its board and later on the board of the entire international body. Oliver's partner at Brooklyn Brewery, Steve Hindy, had also been involved in Slow Food early on, serving as a judge for its 2002 international awards, which included traveling to Bologna, Italy, to help present the top award to a beekeeper from rural Turkey. After that, Hindy went to his first Salone del Gusto in Turin and was pleased to find "an astounding gathering of artisan food producers—tiny producers of traditional cheeses, game, vegetables, fruits, breads, wines, beers, liquors, oils, vinegars, and all manner of prepared foods. It was nourishing just being in the presence of so many like-minded people."

Salone del Gusto in Turin, Italy, the biennial trade show for Slow Food. This one in 2000 marked the second that American craft brewers attended. Courtesy of Slow Food International

Two years before, Sam Calagione of Dogfish Head had attended Salone del Gusto as a panelist, the happy convergence of travel funds from the state of Delaware as well as an interest by the movement in his and other American craft beer (the Association of Brewers helped defray the shipping costs of craft beers). Calagione, like Hindy, was pleasantly surprised by what he found in Slow Food. With its rebellion against fast food in all its iterations and effects, Slow Food, Calagione saw, was "exactly in step with what we were revolting against at Dogfish—which was bland, industrialized, monochromatic beer." The Association of Brewers had been sending representatives to Salone del

Gusto since the second one in 1998; Charlie Papazian, in fact, stepped in then to lead a Belgian beer tasting when Michael Jackson's Alitalia flight was delayed, and Papazian later lectured on artisanal brewing. By the 2004 Salone del Gusto, American craft brewers who made it to Turin, usually through the Association of Brewers, were being treated like rock stars by their Italian hosts, peppered with compliments and questions.

Along with the Slow Food movement, Oliver's book reflected Jackson's work—every beer writer's effort did, really—and *The Brewmaster's Table* could be read as an American update on *The World Guide to Beer*.* Oliver wrote lovingly detailed descriptions of the various European beer styles, country by country, often interwoven with his own first encounters with them. Of course, he also gave a thorough tutorial on how to pair food with beer, and he did so in a conversational, almost conspiratorial tone no one had effected before at book length. Here was Oliver writing about pairing beer with after-dinner food, like sweets:

> Quit chuckling and listen up, because I've got a secret for you—beer is brilliant with dessert. In fact it's unbeatable. I once hosted a beer luncheon attended by New York's top sommeliers. . . . As dessert was served, I issued a challenge—that none of the guests could think of a single wine that could match these desserts as well as either of the beers I was serving. . . . My challenge was a bit unfair—wine never stood a chance. I served my own Brooklyn Black Chocolate Stout, an Imperial stout with a huge complex dark chocolate and coffee flavor, and Lindemans framboise, a sweet Belgian lambic fermented with outrageously fragrant raspberries. . . . The sommeliers conceded my challenge, and they hadn't even tasted my vanilla ice cream and chocolate stout float.

There was also a fair amount of sprightly contempt for Big Beer throughout the book. In a section about proper storage and glassware (and years before the craze of young-adult books and movies about vampires!), Oliver wrote:

> Some American mass-market brewers do use clear glass bottles. They avoid the "skunking" problem by avoiding hops altogether; instead,

---

* Michael Jackson's influence on Slow Food was acute. He wrote so much and so well for its magazine, *Slow*, that in the autumn of 2007 his work was translated into Italian and published as a book, *Storie nel bicchiere* (Stories in the Glass).

they use chemically altered hop extracts that won't react with light. How very appetizing. Somehow, this reminds me of Dracula, and the idea that you can't see him in a mirror. The undead have many tricks at their disposal, so beware.

Again, though, it was Oliver's holistic approach to beer that would prove so influential, that would put an exclamation point on years of trying to convey to consumers a wider appreciation of craft beer. If Jackson's writings put a craft beer bottle in someone's hands, Oliver's put that bottle next to a plate. So many would cite *The Brewmaster's Table* as influential in their thinking of craft beer's place in not only what they ate but often their daily lives as well. Charlie Papazian called it "a masterpiece." Critics spoke of it in the same breath as Jackson's *World Guide*. Mario Batali, the celebrity chef and restaurateur, wrote that the book whetted his formidable appetite "for more than ale and beer, but also for the whole lusty experience of true satisfaction at the table." People just seemed to *get* it. As Oliver fervently noted, "Real beer *can* do everything. Mexican, Thai, Japanese, Indian, Cajun, and Middle-Eastern food, and barbecue, are far better with real beer than with wine. Even with traditionally wine-friendly foods, beer often shows superior versatility and flavor compatibility. The range of flavors and aromas in beer is vast—it's deep and wide and tall, and it easily surpasses that of wine."

These were observations Jackson had been trying to get across for what seemed like ages—his "farting against a gale," as he'd put it three years earlier. Now here they were spelled out with gusto and confidence by an American working in what had become, and what had survived to remain, the world's most robust beer culture. No one could argue with Oliver: "The heady mix of a newly vibrant food culture, the wide availability of imported classic beers, and the emergence of excellent American craft brewing have made the United States the most exciting place in the world to enjoy the juice of the barley."

This success, tested it as it was by the shakeout, was a big reason for what became of the Association of Brewers and the Brewers Association of America: After a two-day meeting in October 2004 at the Boulder headquarters of the Association of Brewers, the two bodies announced a merger set for early January. It had been a long time coming. The BAA had been a formidable force in the entire American beer industry since its original efforts during World War II to ensure that brewers got their fair shares of coveted material, including tin and barley. It had then served as the main trade voice in lobbying the government through the ups and many downs of its members, which for decades included the majority of American brewers;

of the twenty-eight breweries from thirteen states represented at what would be considered the BAA's first meeting in May of 1942, only two were left by the late 1990s—and they were under different owners. Still, as the industry consolidated, regional breweries relied on the BAA more than ever, as did many of what became the regional craft breweries; and after he was picked as its president in 1999, Daniel Bradford, the first employee of the AB way back in the early 1980s, restored a sizable portion of the BAA's oomph. But it was just Bradford and one other employee, and annual revenues of $395,000 versus the AB's $2.6 million in revenues and twenty-three employees led by Charlie Papazian, Bradford's old mentor. Plus, the AB had created a juggernaut in its Great American Beer Festival, which was now the world's biggest beer festival outside of Europe; the biannual World Beer Cup; the conferences and competitions of the American Homebrewers Association (which itself huddled under the AB's umbrella); *Zymurgy* and *New Brewer* magazines as well as an emerging web presence; the Craft Brewers Conference, which seemed to happen at every major recent pivot in the industry; and a book-publishing arm drawing some of the top critics of the day. In addition, due largely to its in-house research institute, the AB was the eminently quotable source on so many statistics and trends in not only craft beer but also the wider American industry; a newspaper or magazine reader of the early 2000s might be forgiven for thinking the craft beer movement and the Association of Brewers were one and the same. As with American interpretations of European styles and Jackson to Oliver, this was another torch-passing moment that spoke to the strength of the movement.

Besides, many of the nation's most prominent craft brewers wanted a merger. The board selected to oversee the merger, culled largely from the boards of both associations, read like a Who's Who of the past thirty years in American beer: Jim Koch of Boston Beer, Gary Fish of Deschutes, Steve Hindy of Brooklyn Brewery, Kim Jordan of New Belgium, Ken Grossman of Sierra Nevada, Rich Doyle of Harpoon, Sam Calagione of Dogfish Head, Nick Matt of F. X. Matt, Brock Wagner of Saint Arnold, and the beer writer Randy Mosher, representing the homebrewers association. It just did not make sense anymore to have two organizations working toward the same goals, especially if the strengths of each could augment the other under the same letterhead. The BAA, especially under Bradford, had lobbying acumen; the AB, under Papazian, was the undisputed face of all non–Big Beer in America.

Nerves frayed during the more than eighteen months it took to plan and execute the merger, but everyone was all smiles as it went through in January 2005, with Papazian as the first president of what was dubbed the Brewers

Association (BA) and Bradford returning full-time to *All About Beer* magazine and its annual World Beer Festival, which Bradford and Julie Johnson launched in 1995 and now took place in cities around the South. (The Brewers Association would launch yet another festival three years after the merger called SAVOR, a sort of mini–Salone del Gusto, celebrating craft beer's role with food and held in Washington, DC.) One effect of the merger came in a long-sought definition of just what a craft brewer was in America. The BA's board, which Kim Jordan chaired, voted in the fall of 2005 to define an American craft brewer as:

> **Small:** Annual production of 2 million barrels or less.
>
> **Independent:** Less than 25 percent of the craft brewery is owned or controlled (or equivalent economic interest) by an alcoholic beverage industry member who is not themselves a craft brewer.
>
> **Traditional:** A brewer who has either an all-malt flagship (the beer which represents the greatest volume among that brewer's brands) or has at least 50 percent of its volume in either all-malt beers or in beers which use adjuncts to enhance rather than lighten flavor.

The annual barrelage amount was based on the tax exemption dating from 1976, but the rest of it could have read like a checklist from Fritz Maytag's earliest days with Anchor Brewing. Though no one at the Brewers Association actually attributed the definition to Maytag (and he was not on the board that approved it), the connection was unmistakable: His actions beginning forty years before regarding what went into Anchor Steam and how it was brewed set the tone for the industry that grew up afterward.

A GREAT PASSING
London | 2007

On Tuesday, August 7, 2007, a typically partly cloudy summer day in the British capital, the Belchertown, Massachusetts–based beer importer Daniel Shelton rode the Tube from where he was staying to the west London home of Michael Jackson. He planned to interview Jackson on camera not so much about beer but "about him, his life and work, and what it was like for him now, living with Parkinson's disease."

Jackson had suffered from the ailment for more than a decade, but only intimates were aware. He had kept it largely secret, though he was concerned that he had started to skirt what to him was an uncomfortable line of suspicion: the disease's symptoms, including tremors and slowness of movement, might make his wider audience think he was drunk. The situation came to a head when Jackson blacked out at the Denver airport around the time of the Great American Beer Festival in 2006. He wrote about the experience for Daniel Bradford's *All About Beer* in a column published in August 2007, titled "Did I Cheat Mort Subite?" (It was a play on the meaning of the last two words, "sudden death" in French, as well as the name of a famed Belgian beer.) The first half of the column showed Jackson hard at his typical globe-trotting evangelization over the preceding year, his sixty-five years not seeming to slow him. He went on a trip to Turkey, two to Poland, and one long one to Italy to promote the new anthology of his writing about Slow Food ("to whom I was originally introduced by Charlie Papazian"), and he had plans for a fifth edition of his seminal guide to great Belgian beers. Then Denver, where his collapse had people concerned that his "profession had taken its most obvious toll"—that Jackson was drinking too much.

> I was not. I hadn't had an alcoholic drink that day or the day before.
> . . . When I woke up, I was in a hospital bed. It was just like it is in the movies. I was surrounded by people in white coats, one of whom asked me: "What is your name?" When I replied, "Michael Jackson," there was none of the usual sniggering. People in Denver know who Michael Jackson is. Nonetheless, he asked again. . . . "The Artist Formerly Known as Prince." He looked at another of the white coats whom I later came to know as a neurologist. "I guess he's OK," he said.
>
> Then, addressing himself to me, he asked whether I was hungry, and what I fancied to eat. I suggested a large mimosa and a Denver omelet, though I think something less extravagant was eventually provided.

It was vintage Jackson: witty, conversational, aware, specific, and appreciative in its culinary allusions. It would be the last column he ever wrote. Jackson died of a heart attack on August 30, 2007. The dialogue with Daniel Shelton, too, turned out to be the last on-camera interview he ever gave. It would have been just as affecting an experience without the mortal hindsight. Jackson, though frail and haggard looking, was typically gracious, inviting Shelton and a friend into his cluttered office, fortressed with stacks of papers and books. Its walls were plastered with plaques and awards, its shelves with rows of rare bottles. A big suitcase sat by the front door, as if ready at a moment's notice for another trek. The only nod to real modernity was an opened laptop behind his desk.

Jackson talked of the Belgian bus trip in the late 1960s that "changed my life. . . . I knew nothing about Belgium." He talked of pitching his newspaper editor at age sixteen a series called "This Is Your Pub." "So you're asking me to finance you on a lawbreaking escapade?" the editor said to the underage cub reporter. "Yes." The editor replied, "I like your style. Those are the kinds of reporters we want." And of those first forays into writing about beer, confronting the drag of novelty with each early pitch, then discovering the satisfaction of having set the parameters all others operate within: "I write the way I write, and, at this point, people can take it or leave it." The interview ended at a pub, where Jackson told Shelton he planned to write a book called *I Am Not Drunk*, to dispel any doubt about his Parkinson's. The two made plans to meet again.

Jackson's death loosed a torrent of tributes across the pond. His was the biggest passing yet in the American craft beer movement, and recollections started rolling in almost immediately to craft beer websites and print publications, from those long established in the movement to those who might not have even been alive when *The World Guide to Beer* debuted in 1977. A healthy portion of the tributes were seasoned with recollections of having met the critic—in the restroom at a festival, at the airport, in a pub (seemingly a sort of accidental Everest for any American beer geek), during a dinner where Jackson was the star lecturer—and always of coming away with a sense of his warmth and generosity. A September 14 memorial service in London drew Americans such as Garrett Oliver and Steve Hindy of Brooklyn Brewery; Tom Peters of Monk's Cafe, the Philadelphia pub that had hosted lectures by Jackson; Dave Alexander of Washington's Brickskeller; Charlie Papazian; Daniel Bradford; and importers Charles and Rose Ann Finkel.

A national toast was quickly organized for September 30 to honor Jackson and to raise money for the National Parkinson's Foundation. Tom Dalldorf, publisher of *Celebrator News* and Jackson's companion on their 1995 "Iron Liver Tour" of California breweries, led the toast at the Toronado, a San Francisco bar barely two miles from the original Anchor location where Fritz Maytag kicked off the movement Jackson was so instrumental in boosting.

Dalldorf spoke of how Jackson's boosterism for the American movement annoyed his fellow Englishmen: "'Michael, why don't you ever write about English beers?' And he said, 'Because what they're doing in America is so much more interesting.'" As for Maytag himself, he would say of the critic, "I think Michael Jackson did more for the brewing industry than anybody since Louis Pasteur."

BEER, PREMIUM
Durango, CO; New Orleans | 2006–2008

O ne evening in July 2006, Ray Daniels, Randy Mosher, and Lyn Kruger were awaiting their orders at a basement bar known for its beer selection in Durango, in southwestern Colorado. Daniels worked in the marketing and publishing wings of the Brewers Association and had written books on home-brewing; Mosher, too, had written extensively on homebrewing and was on the inaugural board of the BA; and Kruger was a trained microbiologist who was the president and COO of the Siebel Institute, the august Chicago brewing school where Mosher and Daniels also taught. They were in town to teach a course through Durango's Fort Lewis College and Siebel.

Their beers arrived. One, a Sierra Nevada Pale Ale, ordered precisely because it might, due to its popularity, be one of the fresher beers at the bar, looked cloudy and, worse, tasted sour and buttery—not at all the way Ken Grossman or his brewers in Chico, California, intended. The trio knew this was likely evidence of draft lines that had not been cleaned in a while. They called it to the server's attention.

"No," she told them, "this was how the beer always looks and tastes." Well, they replied, that is not the way the beer is supposed to look and taste.

"I'm sorry," she said. "There's nothing I can do."

They asked to speak to the manager; the manager never came. Daniels, Mosher, and Kruger paid their bill, did not tip, and left their beers on the table. They would never return to the bar.

For Daniels, it was the last straw—and the catalyst for an idea he'd been batting around in his mind for a while: a training program for everyone standing between a brewer and his or her customers. It would be similar to programs that certified wine sommeliers, some of which had been going since the 1950s. It would differ from the Beer Judge Certification Program launched in 1985. Those exams, focused on styles and the science of brewing, targeted people who wanted to judge competitions. Daniels would gear his idea toward service workers such as the one in that basement bar in Durango, training people in industries such as hospitality and restaurants not only on styles and brewing, but especially on how to store, serve, and talk to consumers smartly about beer.

Daniels, like many who had come to the industry in its second, third, and fourth waves, had led a bit of a roving professional life, studying biochemistry at Texas A&M, earning an MBA from Harvard, working in pharmaceutical marketing, and, then, on a business trip to Washington, DC, in the late 1980s, having a Samuel Adams Boston Lager. It changed his life. Sporting a goatee that would turn salt and pepper in the new century, with eyes that collapsed into squints behind rectangular lenses when he explained anything libationary, Daniels became the sort of lovable beer geek who insisted on proper ways to pour different beers and threw himself into homebrewing in 1989. He published a well-received book on the topic in 1996. By 1999, he was working for the Association of Brewers, commuting between Boulder and Chicago.

Daniels suspected, then, that he had the credibility to pull off a certification program. Still, he shopped the idea around the industry, soliciting advice and getting mostly positive feedback. So, in the summer of 2007, working out of his home in Chicago, where a stainless-steel kegerator sat in the living room, he devised a syllabus as well as bought the requisite website names and filed for trademarks. He picked "Cicerone" as the name of his certification program—it could be translated from Italian as meaning "tour guide"—and made the syllabus available online for those who wanted to take the multiple-choice certification exam, which covered the proper care of beer, the history of beer styles, and what differentiated those styles. The first exam, to become a "Certified Beer Server," was administered over the web to a little more than a dozen people on January 3, 2008; each had paid forty-nine dollars. There were questions like:

Which of the following flavors is NOT a sign of stale beer?
    a) Papery
    b) Cardboard
    c) Banana
    d) Sherry

Draft beer lines should be cleaned every fourteen days.
a) True
b) False
The methods for lager brewing began in what city and were established by what year?
a) Munich, 1900
b) Pilsen, 1842
c) Munich, 1600
d) Vienna, 1700*

Daniels quickly developed two higher levels of certification, "Certified Cicerone" and "Master Cicerone," which not only required longer, more detailed exams but tasting tests, too, and were to be administered in person rather than over the web. He left the Brewers Association to administer the program full-time. The first Certified Cicerone exam was given in April 2008, with all seven examinees coming from the brewing industry, including brewpubs, and paying $345 each. The first Master Cicerone exam—a two-day, twelve-hour affair—was administered later in the year at a cost of $595. In its first three years, Daniels's program designated 1,400 certified beer servers, 120 Certified Cicerones, and a grand total of one Master Cicerone (out of seven who had attempted the exam): a salesman named Andrew Van Til at a Kalamazoo, Michigan–based distributor, who finished in early November 2009. "It was probably the most mentally exhausting two days of my life," Van Til said. He recognized the upside of the designation: "The whole status of beer is elevated when you have people recognized as experts who can drive education." Over the next few years, hundreds of Daniels's successful examinees like Van Til would filter through the industry, to distributors, to breweries, to fine restaurants in big cities, to higher-end retail chains, to the corner pub.

Expertise was the name of the game now. The craft beer movement, as we've noted, was becoming more professionalized than ever and, following the rebound after the shakeout, more confident. This was no longer an industry for voyeurs or toe-dippers. This was completely serious. In 2003, Garrett Oliver flew to New Orleans to talk about beer-food pairings before the more than three hundred attendees of the Cheers Beverage Conference, an annual gathering of representatives from the wine, spirits, and beer worlds as well as concerns like Chili's and Red Lobster. The attendees were incredulous. "I

---

* Answers: C; true; C. These were examples of questions that might be on the certified beer server test, although not necessarily questions that did appear on the test.

run a big place, we've got twelve hundred stores," one told Oliver. "You want to know what my beer program is? I take the top fourteen beers in sales in the United States—and that's my beer program. You guys with your craft beer, you must be joking."

"All those top fourteen brands," Oliver replied, "taste the same. There's no point in having the rest of them." He pressed on. "Do you serve Wonder Bread in your restaurants?"

"Of course not."

"Why not?" Oliver said. "Wonder Bread's the top-selling brand of bread."

"Well," the attendee said, "our customers, they come out to our restaurants, they expect something better."

"Oh," the brewmaster said, "you're saying your customer doesn't expect something better when it comes to beer."

The attendee shrugged. "I don't think so."

A few years later, Oliver drove the same point in early morning talks to distributors—this time with different results. "There are some of you here who have been doing this for twenty or thirty years," his standard stump speech would run, "and you're watching the world change around you, and you say you're three or five years from retirement and you don't have to learn about craft beer. I'm here to tell you that I respect what you've done, but you are not going to make it. You are not going to make it. You do not have three years; you're going to be fired." It was not something anyone wanted to hear. But what did the owners of the distributors typically say to Oliver after the talks? "Thank you, that was a great talk."

The confidence was not mere braggadocio—there were numbers. Craft beer sales were up an estimated 5.8 percent by volume in 2008 over 2007, according to the Brewers Association, and more than 10 percent by dollar amount sold ($6.34 billion versus $5.74 billion); the number of craft barrels produced in 2008 was 8,596,971, a quarter-million more than in 2007. Most auspiciously, the movement cracked 4 percent of market share nationally—the first time, it was thought, that that had ever happened (though over the years different regions of the country, particularly the Northwest, had seen market shares double, perhaps triple that).

These healthy numbers were especially important because of two trends ambling along with them in the last half of the first decade of the twenty-first century. First, breweries were expanding, both physically and productively. In November 2006, Greg Koch and Steve Wagner quietly opened a 385-seat brewpub in Escondido, California, just a few miles from the original brewery ten years ago in San Marcos and alongside a new brewhouse capable of producing fifty thousand barrels annually of their Stone Brewing brands like Arrogant Bastard. Around the same time, across the country, Sam Calagione's Dogfish Head was arriving on shelves in Georgia, the first new state added to its distribution in more than two years, bringing its total to more than twenty. In late 2002, Calagione added a one-hundred-thousand-square-foot brewery in Milton, Delaware, to keep up with what became *triple*-digit annual percentage sales growth for brands like 90 Minute IPA and 120 Minute IPA (they were exactly what they sounded like: India pale ale with hops added every minute for however long the brewing took). In Colorado, in the summer of 2008, the first twelve-packs of New Belgium's Fat Tire Amber Ale in cans began appearing—the brewery had become the largest yet to embrace canning, this time with a machine that could fill fifty to sixty cans a minute.

These breweries expanded among a second trend: rising operation costs. The Brewers Association estimated it cost nearly 40 percent more by the end of 2008 to operate a craft brewery, particularly a smaller one with limited distribution, than it had at the end of 2007. The rebound in the number of craft operations meant the usual elbowing for retail space and tap handles, though now there was a new wrench: raw materials and ingredients cost more.

That one particularly definitional American beer ingredient, hops, had become especially prone to scary price spikes. As recently as the late 1990s, a brewer could call a hops supplier directly and place an order; there was a surplus nationally into the next decade. Within a few years, many of the larger craft breweries started getting their hops through long-term contracts with suppliers; this ensured they got their loads of Cascade, Centennial, Columbus, Chinook, and others, with the onus of supply falling on the suppliers. Smaller operations often did not have these long-term lock-ins, and a hops shortage in 2007 and 2008 hit them especially hard. The previous decade's surplus had driven hops prices down and then hops farmers out of business or into other crops. That was bad enough. Then a huge warehouse fire in Yakima, Washington, in October 2006 destroyed about 4 percent of America's hops supply. Finally, calamitous weather overseas, including droughts and hail storms, tightened the supply further, as did a strong euro against the dollar, which meant European brewers could get American hops for a song.

It was the perfect storm of bad luck. America's hops supply in 2007 dropped to its lowest level since the mid-1980s, and prices shot up. Hops that might have traded in the States for ninety-nine cents an ounce tripled in price after 2006, some reaching seven to eight dollars an ounce (or five to six euros). Jim Koch's Boston Beer, the nation's biggest craft beer concern, tried to fill the void, especially for smaller breweries without those long-term dealer contracts, by selling tens of thousands of pounds of its own hops at below-market prices; the first round of bidding in March 2008 drew 212 brewers, and a second one was planned for that November. Ultimately, until American hops yields recovered starting in 2009, brewers and brewpubs were often simply forced to pass along the rising costs to consumers; prices went up on pints, bombers, six-packs. It became one of the ironies of the growing-again movement that the interpretations on European styles that had made American craft beer so popular, such as the double IPA, had made it that much more expensive to compete against European counterparts.

Judging by the sales growth of not just 2008 but also subsequent years, one can see that American consumers were willing to pay that premium. Craft beer became regularly talked about as "an affordable luxury," a status symbol of sorts just as early pioneers like Matthew Reich at New Amsterdam had envisioned: yuppies drank it then; now their hipster children did. Gone was the iffy product of the pre-shakeout years; ascendant were breweries with quirk and history, run by experienced hands, some of whom were routinely described as "rock stars," complete with groupies in several cases (though not necessarily in the carnal sense). The movement took to new social media platforms such as Facebook, launched in 2004, YouTube, launched in 2005, and Twitter, launched in 2006, in droves.

By the summer of 2009, at least 170 breweries and brewpubs would have regularly updated Twitter feeds. Many times that number of consumers and publications would have feeds by then, too, with craft beer groups no longer delineated largely by geography, as in the homebrewing clubs of yore, but by style preferences (hopheads here, fans of cask ale there) and common traits (several groups dedicated to spreading the craft beer gospel among women in particular sprung up). One could now while away an evening following the tweets of Jason and Todd Alstrom of BeerAdvocate as they reviewed beer after beer in a sitting, or get updates on upgrades at Tony Magee's Lagunitas, or follow Greg Koch as he toured behind a new book about Stone, or see what the Brewers Association was lobbying Congress for on behalf of the industry. One could also take those seemingly ceaseless arguments and counterarguments about tastes and styles to social media; it never seemed to get old.

The new-media platforms created an intimacy and an immediacy that could translate into sales ("like" your favorite brewer!), and, especially for the smaller startups, offered low- to no-cost marketing. They also offered a way to integrate quickly and cheaply the movement as a whole into others, such as the locavore and Slow Food movements. Tweets and Facebook updates could be used to direct consumers to food-beer pairing dinners; to festivals dedicated to local food-stuffs, including the products of area breweries; to new partnerships between brewers and area farmers, cheesemongers, and the like. Suddenly, it was all one big virtual universe with faces put to names and personalities to brands.

Of course, the very ease with which the movement slid into social-media use only highlighted its natural stomping ground. Craft beer had become one of the accoutrements of the modern American elites, though, crucially, not necessarily elitist—unlike, say, fine wine or French cuisine. Following the spate of very public tetchiness that preceded the shakeout, the movement personality-wise now seemed positively serene. As Paul Philippon, a one-time philosophy professor who started the Duck-Rabbit Craft Brewery in Farmville, North Carolina, in the summer of 2004, memorably put it in a speech at the 2010 Great American Beer Festival: "The national brewing community is asshole-free."

The highbrow London-based magazine the *Economist* used craft beer as a way to describe the hipper and more mobile inhabitants of twenty-first-century America: "They drink wine and boutique beers (and can discuss them expertly) but only in moderation, and they hardly ever smoke cigarettes." No less a social barometer than the *New Yorker* cottoned to craft beer with a 9,775-word piece in its annual food issue right before Thanksgiving 2008. Written by Burkhard Bilger, whose work included a book on the more eccentric eating and drinking habits of southerners and a magazine piece on the Madagascar gem trade, it starred Sam Calagione as he pursued ever more extreme beer. It also swept in all the major trends in the movement over the past four decades, from the first saplings of growth to the late 1990s shakeout to a counterrevolution against extreme beers, represented by Garrett Oliver. The piece was perhaps the most important mainstream magazine article on craft beer since William Least Heat-Moon's "A Glass of Handmade" in the *Atlantic Monthly* twenty-one years before. The last section of Bilger's article was set at the Great American Beer Festival in 2007, the first year it sold out of tickets. About twenty-eight thousand attendees paid fifty dollars a pop to sample more than eighteen hundred beers over three days.

> Wandering through the hall in the hour before it opened I saw signs for beers called Goat Toppler, Chicken Killer, and Old Headwrecker, Incinerator, Detonator, Skull Annihilator and Obamanator. Many were double IPA's that seemed to be competing for the highest IBU rating. But others were faithful recreations of ancient recipes, or else beers invented whole cloth. "When you're making an extreme beer,

it's like pushing beyond the sound barrier," Jim Koch told me. "All of a sudden, everything is silent. I remember when I first tasted my Triple Bock. It dawned on me that beer has been around for thousands of years, and I am tasting something that no brewer has ever tasted. It was inspiring, beautiful, almost reverential." Even Garrett Oliver seemed to be bowing to the trend. His booth featured two wonderful bottle-fermented ales and a pale ale called BLAST!, with eight kinds of English and American hops. "No, this is NOT a double IPA," a sign beneath the tap read. "Even if you believe in those."

In his last on-camera interview in August 2007, a couple of months before the GABF, Michael Jackson said one of his motives for writing so extensively about beer when no one else was doing so was to preserve "threatened traditions." Had he lived to read Bilger's article, to scroll through the tweets, to amble again amid the GABF or any number of other beer festivals every year, to peruse the forums of RateBeer and BeerAdvocate, to see the passion in the converts and the confidence in the veterans, he would have surely been pleased that America's beer traditions were far from threatened anymore. Instead, they represented a major culinary achievement that was now an undeniable part of the nation's popular culture. Still, the movement that Jackson had so inspired had seen its ups before—and its downs. As Bilger's article noted:

> For all its success, craft beer has yet to reach the mainstream. Ninety-six percent of the market—about sixty-seven billion bottles a year—still belongs to non-craft beers and imports. Oliver remembers talking to a brewer at Anheuser-Busch a few years ago, when sales of Michelob had fallen to about a third of a billion bottles a year. "He told me, 'I wish that brand would just die.' And that one beer was the size of the entire American craft-brewing industry."

EXIT THE GODFATHER
San Francisco | 2009–2010

O ne July evening in 2009, in Harris's Restaurant at Van Ness and Pacific Avenues in San Francisco's Nob Hill, five men sat down to gin martinis and medium-rare steaks. Two of the men were there to discuss an idea with the other three, the oldest of whom was just past seventy and looked as if he'd stepped from a casting call for a Great Plains patriarch.

Fritz Maytag knew Keith Greggor and Tony Foglio from their reputations in the spirits trade. The pair had met at International Distillers and Vintners, the precursor to Diageo, the alcohol beverage behemoth that would come to control brands like Guinness, Smirnoff, Johnnie Walker, and Captain Morgan; Greggor and Foglio were no slouches themselves while at IDV, overseeing the sales and marketing of brands like Baileys, Jose Cuervo, Smirnoff again, and Bombay from a high perch at 30 Rockefeller Plaza in Manhattan (and, later, from across the Hudson River in New Jersey). The pair truly made their reputations after taking over Skyy Spirits in 1998, growing it over eight years into several flavored iterations of the eponymous vodka brand as well as the US distributor of labels like Cutty Sark and Campari (its Milan-based corporate parent beginning in 2002). In 2007, the pair sold their Skyy interests to Campari, and Greggor left to start the Griffin Group, a boutique concern that would look for ways to invest in the various drinks industries; Foglio followed him in 2008. The new group was based in Novato, in the San Francisco Bay Area, where both men had relocated in the late 1990s.

For Greggor in particular, it was a sweet move. Born on the south English coast, he spent much of the 1960s as a teenager in Singapore, where his father was attached to the British army. Greggor found it a rather dreary, paternalistic place, and his youthful eyes gazed thousands of miles away to San Francisco, to where everything seemed to be hip and new and cool in that swinging decade. He missed the sixties in San Francisco by about fifteen years, working instead as a civil engineer, including a stint in pre- and post-revolution Iran, where he was briefly taken prisoner by the Khomeini regime and forced to bribe his way to safety. After that ordeal, he left engineering for marketing, earning an MBA in the early 1980s and finally arriving in San Francisco in 1984 to visit a college buddy. The friend suggested a local beer that Greggor might like: Anchor Steam. It was, as for so many people, Greggor's first encounter with American craft beer. He tried other brands as they crossed his path in the next twenty years, but it was never something he thought much about. He and Foglio were spirits guys, with encyclopedic knowledge of the brands and the businesses that distilled them.

They made their first big move with the Griffin Group in October 2008, when they bought control of Preiss Imports, an importer with a wide array of spirits and liqueur labels, mostly high-end, produced by thirty-five concerns. The acquisition could not have come at a worse time: a month before, Lehman Brothers had collapsed and dragged the global economy into recession with it. Few investment bankers were throwing fifties around for celebratory bottles of single-malt. The group began to lose money, recovering only as the economy did and just in time for its first foray into craft beer—Scottish craft beer. Greggor and Foglio bought a minority stake in BrewDog, a small brewery started in 2004 outside of Aberdeen that was best known for making some of the world's strongest beers with cheeky names such as Speedball, a nod to the heroin-and-cocaine cocktail. BrewDog, with the capital infusion and Greggor on its board, quadrupled production and expanded its distribution. The onetime spirits kingpins had a taste for a beer.

Which is how they ended up sitting in Harris's in July 2009, with Maytag; John Dannerbeck, Maytag's nephew and a top executive with the brewery; and John Fisher, an investment banker who Maytag, Foglio, and Greggor all knew. The quintet quaffed Anchor Steams at the bar before heading to their table and getting down to business. Greggor and Foglio had an idea for a so-called Center for Excellence, based in San Francisco—a sort of consultancy that would cull from the worlds of craft beer and artisanal spirits and include their own varied portfolios. What did Maytag think? They talked about it, and one thing led to another, and it turned out that Maytag was thinking of selling his iconic operation.

The possibility of Anchor's sale was an open secret by 2009. Maytag had put out feelers as early as 2005, though he was not necessarily pleased with the responses he was getting. Some suitors hinted that they would move Anchor out of San Francisco, to a cheaper location—a deal breaker for Maytag, who saw the brewery as a creature of the city, the two inextricably linked. He was also worried about the employees, some of whom, like Mark Carpenter, had been with the brewery for decades; a takeover by another craft brewer might mean a wholesale housecleaning. Either scenario would mean the end of what Maytag had built into not only San Francisco's most famous brewery but also its largest manufacturing business.

Like the rest of America, San Francisco had seen its own manufacturing cliff-drop. In 1990, the sector employed 29,000 people in the city; by 2009, the number was 9,356, with the biggest drops coming just after the turn of the century. Anchor's approximately fifty employees meant something more than just great beer. So a months-long dance, which Maytag initiated, began after the steak dinner. Greggor and Foglio were outside the American craft beer movement, though very much inside the Bay Area. Moreover, they had experience with spirits, and Maytag had started a distillery in 1993, producing brands such as Old Potrero rye whiskey, named after the San Francisco neighborhood where Anchor was located. By April 2010, Maytag, Greggor, and Foglio were ready to make a big announcement.

"These are the right guys," Maytag said during an interview on National Public Radio on April 30, 2010, a Friday. The news had been out since that Monday: the Griffin Group would buy the nation's oldest craft brewery for an undisclosed amount. At eight in the morning on the thirtieth, Maytag and Greggor had met at the Mariposa Street brewery to commence a mild PR blitz. A caller to the NPR show, the pair's second radio appearance of the morning, echoed the sentiments of many when she worried aloud that the sale meant the end of Anchor as nearly two generations of consumers had known it. Maytag tried to assuage those worries, reminding listeners that Griffin was not a big company, that it was highly specialized, and that he had talked to several other suitors over the past five years and found them wanting—but not Greggor and Foglio. He also modestly placed himself on a continuum that now included the new owners: "The brewery has had many, many owners over the years. It has been in six locations in San Francisco. . . . The brewery has had a long, colorful history in San Francisco."

Greggor, for his part, acknowledged the likelihood of a modest expansion in production from the current 86,000 barrels annually and certainly in distribution. While Anchor had reached into forty-nine states as well as Canada, Japan, and parts of Europe, according to Greggor, "a lot of people tell us they just can't find it the way they used to be able to find it. Our task is to get the beer into more people's hands." As for what would happen to the recipes and the craftsmanship behind Anchor Steam, Liberty Ale, Anchor Porter, and other groundbreakers: "I feel an utter sense of awesome responsibility in looking after the Anchor beers. And to follow in Fritz's footsteps is very alarming, I must admit."

It was as amiable a public handoff of an institution as one could hope for. Still, the movement Maytag was so essential in spawning fretted for days afterward. The very scope of the debate over Anchor's future showcased how far the movement had come in Maytag's nearly forty-five years at the brewery's helm. When he took it over in 1965, no media noted the shift. For years afterward, the only attention came from local newspapers, from the odd allusion in a Charles McCabe column in the *Chronicle*, or from beer writers like Fred Eckhardt, who visited from Portland in the late 1960s, camera in hand, to see this curiosity. Now it was dissected in terms of business and social contexts—from what it meant to make a foodstuff locally to what it meant for San Francisco's employment picture to whether the new owners would relinquish the trademark to "steam beer"—that would have been unimaginable to the twenty-seven-year-old Maytag.

Writing nearly two weeks after the announcement, Don Russell, the longtime beer columnist for the *Philadelphia Daily News*, first listed Maytag's accomplishments with Anchor: first porter since Prohibition, first barleywine, the IPA precursor that was Liberty Ale, the revival of the Christmas ale tradition. Then he tried to convince himself that the new owners ("money guys with big-alcohol DNA") would maintain the same standards, quoting fellow beer writer Jay Brooks, who had lunched with Greggor and returned this assessment to *Oakland Tribune* readers: "I think fans can rest assured that the brand will be in good hands that have no intention of messing about with it." Still, Russell wrote:

> Maytag's departure is a harbinger of broader generational change. Much of the American microbrewing revolution was built on the strong, idiosyncratic personalities of visionary, risk-taking home-brewers who turned their hobby into a thriving industry. Instead of advertising on TV, they connected with their customers, one by one, by sharing their stories and personally pouring samples. Today, the brewers are the brand. So, you can't help but think: What happens when they're gone? Remember, Pete Slosberg sold his trendsetting Pete's Wicked, and it caved; the founder of America's first brewpub, Bert Grant, retired, and his brewery disappeared.

Other ownership structures had changed in the craft beer movement with continuity maintained. Rhonda Kallman had left Boston Beer, and it remained by far the nation's number-one craft operation. An increasingly disinterested Paul Camusi had been bought out of Sierra Nevada, and it was number two. Miller had come and gone as a fifty-fifty partner in Shipyard Brewing in Portland, Maine. Myriad investors, partners, cofounders, and so forth had moved out or moved on from different breweries and brewpubs. Companies had survived, even thrived postchange, introducing new brands and altering distribution.

Perhaps the biggest example was the merger cinched in the summer of 2008 between Widmer Brothers and Redhook, forming what they called the Craft Brewers Alliance. It still included not only principals from both northwestern breweries, like Kurt and Rob Widmer as well as Paul Shipman from Redhook, but also Anheuser-Busch, which owned more than 30 percent of the new company. Around the time of the Anchor announcement in 2010, the Craft Brewers Alliance announced it had absorbed Kona Brewing for $13.9 million, the same Kona run by Mattson Davis, who remained as CEO, and still headquartered on the western edge of Hawaii's Big Island. There were grumblings about Big Beer's fractional involvement, faint echoes of Jim Koch's pre-shakeout cries of "Budhook" after Redhook's initial partnership with Anheuser-Busch. Otherwise, all three breweries remained among the biggest sellers in the industry, suggesting that whatever the feelings about ownership changes, consumers had voted approval with their wallets.[*]

The terms of the Anchor deal, shrouded in secrecy as they were by the two private sides of it, seemed immaterial to the dissection. We might extrapolate from Anchor's 2009 production numbers and distribution that the deal's value was surely in the seven figures at least. Moreover, the Brewers Association in 2010 placed Anchor at number twenty on its annual list of the top fifty craft brewers. Kona, which merged into the Craft Brewers Alliance for $13.9 million around that same time, was number thirteen. Lastly, the Griffin Group took as a partner on the distillery side Berry Bros. & Rudd, the United Kingdom's oldest wine and spirits merchant, finally closing the deal announced in late April on August 3. From that day forward, Maytag was out of the office, making a clean break with the day-to-day operations, though retaining the title of chairman emeritus. Greggor named Mark Carpenter Anchor's brewmaster, succeeding Maytag.

---

[*] Anheuser-Busch's ownership stake did technically remove all three breweries from the Brewers Association's definition of a craft brewery. By 2012, the renamed Craft Brew Alliance was the ninth-biggest brewery in the United States, right behind New Belgium and ahead of Gambrinus, which had absorbed BridgePort.

One reason the worry of obsolescence perhaps hung over the Anchor deal was that Maytag had never tried to grow really big. He had briefly considered an IPO during the mid-1990s to raise capital—it was the thing to do, after all, and an Anchor IPO would have undoubtedly been one of the hottest of the era—but he eventually decided against it, worried that investor demand would force moves he didn't want to make. Instead, he came to revel in eschewing too much growth, preaching a gospel of Small Is Good that seemed downright heretical, especially during the go-go 1990s, before the bust. "At Anchor, we're trying not to grow," he told the Craft Brewers Conference in 1998. "Small is beautiful. At our brewery, one time we all just left—we all went to Europe, and studied wheat beer; deducted the whole thing." With the flamekeeper of such a self-restrictive ethos exiting stage left, and the industry growing once again in terms of sales, production, and number of operations, why not worry that a lot about the oldest craft brewery was about to change—and not for the better?

The people who knew the most about running craft breweries were not worried. Most of Maytag's peers were as surprised as consumers by the announcement, though they welcomed Greggor and Foglio, especially after they insisted they would keep Anchor in San Francisco. It was a testament to the godfatherly role Maytag had so long played so well. "I didn't think at this point he was ready to move on," Ken Grossman told the *San Francisco Chronicle*, perhaps recalling his revelatory tour of the Eighth Street Anchor location thirty-one years before. Tony Magee at Lagunitas reached out to Greggor and Foglio early on. If there was anything he could do, Magee told the new owners, don't hesitate to ask. This collegial spirit of the movement was another legacy of Maytag's, along with something else now, as Don Russell put it at the end of that column fretting the end of Anchor Brewing as the world knew it: "I'd like to think this is Maytag's final accomplishment: a legacy that encourages change."

BIG CROWDS AND THE NEW SMALL
Santa Rosa, CA | 2010–2011

It was the first Friday in February 2010, and that meant the annual first pours of Russian River brewpub's Pliny the Younger, a so-called triple IPA from the accidental progenitor of the double IPA, Vinnie Cilurzo. The beer had debuted in 2005 and had, according to Cilurzo's operation, "gobs of IBU"—well over the 90 IBU threshold generally thought to define a double IPA (or what the Great American Beer Festival called an Imperial IPA). It had proved popular enough each February it was released. Patrons could come in and buy ten-ounce glasses of Pliny the Younger for $4.50 or new half-gallon growlers for $37; supply usually lasted two to three months.

But 2010 seemed different. Cilurzo and his crew had heard rumblings for about a week. Pliny the Younger had scored a perfect 100 rating on both BeerAdvocate and RateBeer. It had only five days before won the People's Choice Award at the tenth annual Double IPA Festival at the Bistro in nearby Hayward. Still, Russian River prepared as if this second Friday in February would be like the last five: the beginning of a gradual sellout of Pliny the Younger. No more, no less.

Then, around 6 am, the line started. It snaked through Fourth Street in downtown Santa Rosa, and those in it could be seen tapping their smart phones, pecking out texts and e-mails to others who might come. Even the weather cooperated; it was the dead of winter, but it was fifty degrees by 11:00 AM, with nary a breeze beneath partly sunny skies. The line grew; the brewpub opened.

The day was a blur. It was all hands on deck as one patron after another stepped through the door. Even husbands, wives, girlfriends, boyfriends, and buddies were drafted by Cilurzo into filling glasses and growlers. Friends of his from Kern River Brewing near Bakersfield had come up for the pour; he put them to work pouring. Cilurzo drilled holes in the back of the cold box in the brewhouse to open up another filling station; he yanked other beers from the taps and ran those lines to Pliny the Younger. Natalie Cilurzo filled growlers without a break all day. Russian River would sell its entire supply of Pliny the Younger—twenty barrels, or forty kegs, a supply that had every previous year taken at least two months to run dry—in eight hours. They forbade growlers the next year and had more staff for the pour.

Such scenes were reenacted in the new decade at craft breweries and brewpubs throughout the nation on an almost monthly basis. More operations than ever before were releasing special annual brands or lines of beers that loosed happy clamors upon their release dates, followed quickly by the now de rigueur debates on the web and through social media. If brewers like Cilurzo were rock stars, their specialty beers were hit songs. Many of these—nearly all, in fact—could be classified as extreme beers: big, brassy, unapologetic recipes with lots of different ingredients, some used in no other beers on the planet, and packing alcohol punches.

Sam Calagione at Dogfish Head remained the Mick Jagger of extreme beer. Like Michael Jackson almost a generation earlier with *The Beer Hunter*, Calagione even had his own Discovery Channel television show, *Brew Masters*, in late 2010. He introduced as many as one million viewers an episode to concoctions such as Chateau Jiahu, based on a nine-thousand-year-old recipe culled from ancient pottery jars found in China; the first season ended with episode six highlighting the Italian craft beer movement, and America's influence on it,* as well as Dogfish Head's collaboration on beers for a new brewpub called Eataly atop the old International Toy Center in Manhattan's Flatiron District. Calagione also published his own memoir-cum-business-advice-book in 2005, during a run that saw others, like Steve Hindy and Tom Potter at Brooklyn Brewery, Jeremy Cowan at Shmaltz, and Greg Koch and Steve Wagner at Stone pen theirs.†

Calagione, Koch, Cilurzo, Cowan, Garrett Oliver, and others also often found themselves at the pouring end of long lines at the Great American Beer Festival and other events, fans patiently waiting for what seemed like eternities for a quick word with their heroes. The GABF bespoke the continued growth in the industry. After almost collapsing in 1984, when it leaped from Boulder to Denver, it set an attendance record in 2010, with forty-nine thousand people tasting twenty-two hundred beers from 455 breweries representing forty-eight states and the District of Columbia, as 3,523 beers

---

* That sixth episode never aired in the United States, though it was broadcast in other parts of the world.

† Pete Slosberg beat everybody. His *Beer for Pete's Sake* was published in 1998.

total competed in seventy-nine style categories. The festival then tied the attendance record in 2011, its thirtieth year, selling out in one week. It shattered the other numbers, adding a brewery from Puerto Rico for the first time in the process. (The most competitive category both years, according to the Brewers Association, was the American-style IPA, suggesting that, yes, Maytag and his crew were on to something with Cascade hops and Liberty Ale in 1975.) John Hickenlooper was the latter year's surprise speaker at an industry luncheon that included several beer writers; he spoke not only as the cofounder of Denver's first brewpub, Wynkoop, but also as its former mayor—and Colorado's governor, elected in 2010. Some of the same faces at the GABF, too, could be found later in the year, every other year, at Salone del Gusto in Turin. Calagione and Charlie Papazian shared the dais there at a lecture on Italian craft beers in October 2010, when Salone del Gusto set its own attendance record.

Things were moving further and further from the point where anyone could remember America as *not* the world's innovator in beer and brewing. At the same time, though craft beer's market share still paled against Big Beer's, the segment's reach was growing as the wider industry's was shrinking. For three years in a row, beginning in 2009, the wider industry sold fewer barrels of beer; at the same time, craft beer sales were growing by double digits. In 2011, the nation's 1,063 brewpubs and 877 craft breweries sold 13 percent more beer than the year before, while the entire industry's sales were down more than 1 percent, similar to a drop in 2010. As for market share, it was 5.7 percent by volume in 2011, an almost 50 percent increase from three years before. The healthy growth meant more jobs than ever before in American craft beer (an estimated 103,585) and more breweries operating in the United States than at any time since the 1880s (and more than in any other country). "The smaller brewers' activity," the *Wall Street Journal* noted right before New Year's Day 2012, "is a bright spot in an economy still struggling to kick manufacturing and construction into higher gear." It was a role the movement was familiar with, one that stretched once again the definition of a "craft brewer."

On December 20, 2010, the Brewers Association changed the definition of a craft brewer by raising the amount that one could produce annually from two million barrels to six million. That was the new "small"; the terms "independent" and "traditional," which Fritz Maytag heralded in the 1960s, remained intact. While some complained it was a sop to the association's larger members, which were closing in on two million barrels a year, others said it was a sign of the times. "A lot has changed since 1976," said Nick Matt of F. X. Matt, who chaired the board that voted in the change. "The largest brewer in the United States has grown from 45 million barrels to 300 million barrels of global beer production." (The 1976 nod was to the Henry King–backed tax change that helped ease costs considerably for smaller brewers.)

The definition change reflected the Brewers Association's efforts, under new COO Bob Pease, to change the law itself to move the annual cap to six million barrels and to halve the tax rate on small brewers from seven dollars per barrel on the first sixty thousand barrels. As it was, the definition swept together every iteration of commercial brewing in America outside of Big Beer and the handful of remaining regionals—from the likes of Boston Beer and Sierra Nevada to the smallest licensed operations, nanobreweries, which were now popping up and which were, with their small batches, homebrewer founders, and self-distribution locally, a throwback to the movement's earliest days.*

Perhaps nothing stamped the ubiquity of the craft beer movement in the new century's second decade than the nation's very officialdom. In April 2010, the 111th Congress passed a resolution in praise of American Craft Beer Week, citing the movement's contributions to the economy and to the national palate by championing "historic brewing traditions dating back to colonial America." The week itself, which the Brewers Association started, dated from 2006, when Congress passed a similar resolution. Satirist Stephen Colbert spoke of the gravity of the milestone on his Comedy Central show, which reached more than 1.2 million viewers four nights a week: "This isn't one of those fake holidays, like Grandparents Day or Women's History Month—no, this is officially sanctioned by Congress as of 2006!" And, in February 2011, for Super Bowl Sunday, President Barack Obama and the first lady served a honey ale that the White House Mess made using the fruits of a beehive on the mansion's grounds—the first time anyone had brewed at the White House in its 210-year history.

---

* There may have been as many as eighty-four American nanobreweries in operation by June 2012. They were defined almost entirely by size—no more than a couple of barrels produced at a time.

"THE ALBION BREWERY"

Sonoma, CA; Denver | 2011–2012

The Vineburg Deli & Grocery comes up suddenly on Napa Road in Sonoma County. By the time you reach it, you're more than fifteen miles east of the 101 and nearly a mile from downtown Sonoma, worlds past the Golden Gate and well into the bucolic blur of one vineyard after another. From your perch on two-lane roads, heading northeastward, you see the rows of grapes punctuated by warehouses and small houses, with hardly any souls appearing to be in or about them. Then a plastic yellow sign says the deli's straight ahead on the right. You find it just behind a surprisingly crowded gravel parking lot, before Napa intersects with Eighth Street East—right along a vineyard and before another. This is wine country, undoubtedly, though every so often at the Vineburg counter someone asks directions to "the Albion Brewery."

More than thirty years had passed since Jack McAuliffe had his idea for opening a brewery. For seven years, the idea burned bright as a dream come true, inspiring others to follow in his footsteps and loosing the American craft beer movement as it would come to be understood. Then it flamed out rather suddenly in 1982, for reasons even decades on not entirely clear, though evidently having a lot to do with the capital-intensive nature of brewing and the crucible of distribution to a marketplace that still didn't know what to make of the pale ales and porters. What equipment that could be salvaged from the New Albion Brewery on Eighth Street East, the equipment that McAuliffe, spiderlike and solitary, had rigged into a gravity brewhouse, was disassembled and shipped off to the new Mendocino Brewing Company in Hopland. That's where McAuliffe ended up for a time, though he left, not content to be a hand on someone else's ship, and faded from the movement he had done so much to build. Early pioneers such as Ken Grossman, Charlie Papazian, and Steve Hindy would remember McAuliffe's name, although those who arrived in the 1990s and the new century would likely have never heard of him. He worked as an engineer after leaving Mendocino, moving to Nevada at one point and to Squaw Valley, near Fresno, California, where the author Maureen Ogle found him.* Her writing on McAuliffe in the mid-2000s shined a much-deserved spotlight on his contributions.

McAuliffe was sanguine about the newfound fame. Just as visitors who did not phone ahead were apt to have New Albion's door slammed in their faces, McAuliffe did not like undue attention, especially from a crowd; he wasn't introspective, wasn't the kind of person to ask himself "what if." He could be blunt, though he had a sense of humor about the whole affair. When asked during a question-and-answer segment at the 2011 Craft Brewers Conference in San Francisco why he chose Sonoma for his brewery, McAuliffe replied, "It's really simple—that's where I lived!" Still, he knew people would ask those things—people would want to know. He was back in the papers, thirty years after the *New York Times* and the *Washington Post* wrote about him, back in the trade publications that had grown up since New Albion closed, his legacy for the first time scrutinized in online forums and in social media unfathomable when McAuliffe's operation was getting snail mail marked simply "The Brewery, Northern California." In 2007, the Brewers Association bestowed its

Ken Grossman pours a Jack & Ken's Ale for Jack McAuliffe at the Sierra Nevada Brewery in Chico. Courtesy of Sierra Nevada Brewing Co.

---

* McAuliffe eventually moved to San Antonio and then Arkansas.

Recognition Award on McAuliffe, an accolade that the likes of Fritz Maytag, Jim Koch, Michael Jackson, and Bert Grant had previously won. He was part of the pantheon; he couldn't avoid it.

McAuliffe did enjoy the visit to Sierra Nevada. In December 2009, to mark its upcoming thirtieth anniversary, Ken Grossman's brewery announced it would be releasing four specialty beers based on collaborations with the titanic figures of the American craft beer movement: Fritz Maytag, Jack McAuliffe, Charlie Papazian, and Fred Eckhardt. The proceeds from sales would go to the namesakes' charities of choice. Brewing day in Chico for the McAuliffe collaboration was in May 2010, and he showed up wearing jeans and a blue, short-sleeved shirt. McAuliffe sipped on a Sierra Nevada Kellerweis, a wheat beer, while a video crew documented his story. More interviews with him and Grossman followed, and, finally, a ceremonial dumping of hops from a white plastic pail into a copper brew kettle took place. About one thousand barrels of Jack & Ken's Ale, more than twice the annual barrelage of New Albion at its busiest, would hit shelves that July, packaged in elegant winelike bottles capped with caged corks. Later, during a lunch, Grossman brought out some original New Albion bottles—dusty, old longnecks with that label featuring Francis Drake's Golden Hind and California in the background. McAuliffe looked at it and let himself smile.

A year and a half later, McAuliffe was at the restaurant Marlowe's on the Sixteenth Street Mall in downtown Denver. Boston Beer was hosting a breakfast to announce the winners of its annual homebrewers competition, and Jim Koch was the MC. About one hundred people, including several prominent beer writers such as Stan Hieronymus and Jay Brooks, stood or sat about, eating French toast and biscuits and other early-in-the-day fare, all cooked with Samuel Adams beer; the lines for seconds snaked down Marlowe's steps from its top level. Most of the conversation had to do with the thirtieth Great American Beer Festival, which would be winding down that day. Koch stepped up to a microphone to announce the competition winners. Before he did, though, the biggest independent brewer in America wanted to say something.

"I know we have Jack McAuliffe here," Koch said. He paused, and the restaurant fell silent; murmurs swept the room. The name rang a bell, a loud one. Koch continued: "For those of you who don't know, Jack started the first microbrewery after Prohibition." He sketched quickly the history of New Albion. "He really served as an inspiration to the rest of us." The restaurant erupted in applause. McAuliffe stood slowly. He smiled sheepishly, clearly surprised at the homage. "Thank you," he said softly.

Thank you.

FORTY-TWO HUNDRED AND COUNTING
Nationwide | 2012–2016

In June 2012, Anheuser-Busch InBev announced it would buy complete control of Grupo Modelo, the Mexico City–based maker of Corona, among other brands, in a $20.1 billion deal. One-third of the money would be paid in cash. The deal came a few years after Anheuser-Busch itself had been taken over by the Leuven, Belgium–based InBev. The maker of Stella Artois, Beck's, and other brands, InBev itself was the result of a 2004 merger between Belgium's Interbrew and Brazil's AmBev. South African Breweries had controlled Miller since a 2002 deal with Philip Morris. Then, around the same time as the Anheuser-Busch–InBev deal, SABMiller partnered in the United States with Molson Coors, which—notice a trend here?—was formed in 2005 when the Colorado brewery merged with Molson, out of Toronto. The new MillerCoors was also tasked with brewing the brands of Pabst, and it might have stayed number one in global market share had InBev and its $52 billion in cash not come along.

Anheuser-Busch did not willingly want to be part of this fresh consolidation wave. Instead, the King of Beers had been forced into an endgame not of its choosing. August Anheuser Busch IV, the brewery's forty-four-year-old chairman, with dark eyes and dark hair straight out of central casting, declared in an April 2008 speech to distributors, amid rumors of a takeover, that the brewery his great-great-grandfather had founded would never trade "on my watch." But it wasn't his family's watch anymore, really. The biggest shareholders were the likes of the British bank Barclays and the investment juggernaut Berkshire Hathaway, controlled by Warren Buffett, and they were quite unhappy with Anheuser-Busch's flat share price over the past several years. Busch found himself conceding the buyout on July 13, 2008, ending 156 years of family control. While the obvious reason was the somnolent share price, investors' pessimism was a factor, too. Few believed that Busch and company could turn things around on their own; they needed fresh blood with fresh capital—damn any national pride amid a global economy. As one analyst put it in terms any American familiar with the country's manufacturing decline could understand: "Anheuser-Busch would have run the risk of becoming the next GM, where market share in the fifties may dwindle down into the teens." Why such pessimistic projections? Because of the machinations of Anheuser-Busch's longtime archrival, Miller, and because of those pesky craft brewers. Their market sector was growing, while Big Beer's was not.

In May 2012, amid the titanic consolidations, the Brewers Association announced that the number of American breweries had surpassed two thousand, all but fifty-one of them craft operations. It was the most American breweries since the 1880s, nearly a half-century before Prohibition. The nation had been flirting with the milestone since at least 2008, and reached it despite the lingering effects of the Great Recession—and the latest wave of consolidation.

As momentous as that two-thousand-brewery milestone was, the nation breezed comfortably by it within barely four years. In December 2015, the Brewers Association announced that the number of breweries the month before had reached 4,144—13 more than the previous record, set in 1873, eight years after the Civil War and just when innovations such as refrigeration and yeast cultures were making themselves felt in the industry. Like then, the vast majority of these breweries now were smaller operations making be in more traditional ways. And, just as soon as the industry notched this craft-driven record, it appeared to be exceeding it. The number of breweries grew to 4,269 by 2016, with more than 4,200 fitting the Brewers Association's definition of a craft brewery. The trade group estimated that more than two American breweries were opening *per day* by the end of 2015. More important, very few were ever closing—the net gain in the number of breweries had been steady year after year since the late 2010s. By 2015, fifteen states hosted more than one hundred breweries; these included the usual suspects such as California, Oregon, Colorado, and New York, but also spots such as Indiana, North Carolina, and Virginia, where there may have been two or three breweries each twenty-five years before. Finally, sometime in the fall of 2016, the number of breweries nationwide slipped past five thousand.*

An unprecedented financial openness helped drive this growth. Commercial banks, private equity firms, and other financing vehicles were more willing than ever to underwrite smaller-scale brewing, including the expansion of existing companies. Breweries that might have struggled to maintain

---

* The Brewers Association numbers include only brick-and-mortar operations, not contract ones, so the tallies might be even higher.

one production facility a decade or two ago now plotted multiple locations. Single brewpubs became chains, small chains added locations.

At the same time, government at every level was only too happy to assist craft brewers with property-tax incentives and small-business loans to fill empty storefronts and industrial spaces, and to hire residents for all facets of a successful operation. Governments were also queuing to slice red tape, some of it stretching back to Prohibition. In 2013, Alabama and Mississippi became the last two states to legalize homebrewing. As if on cue, the number of craft breweries in each marched upward dramatically: In Alabama, the number of craft breweries went from ten at the start of 2013 to nineteen in 2015; in Mississippi, it went from three to seven. In Minnesota, lawmakers in 2011 allowed craft breweries to open in-house taprooms. They quickly obliged, the square footage of taprooms where visitors could amply sample the wares of the breweries growing from 20,000 to more than 480,000—or about one-third of the square footage of the North Star State's tallest building.

Together, this financial openness and government assistance fostered an economic and regulatory climate unfathomable to the American craft beer movement's earliest pioneers. Everyone seemed to be on the same page for the first time as the second decade of the twenty-first century barreled along. People in and out of the industry began talking hopefully of abolishing the three-tier distribution system where it existed, and truly blowing the whole thing wide open.

More than anything, though, simple demand fueled the growth in craft breweries. American craft beer accounted for just over 14 percent of the dollars spent on beer overall in the United States in 2012. In 2015, that market share had reached 21 percent. It wasn't just the steady climb to claiming one-fifth of the dollar value of all beer sold in the United States, it was the pace of that climb: Craft beer market share was growing by double-digit percentages as demand for beer overall stayed flat or declined. Craft beer production was also growing. Craft breweries' share of beer produced in the country increased 13 percent annually in 2015, while the overall market confronted a slight decline in production. The volume share had crested 10 percent for the first time ever in 2011, according to the Brewers Association, and then 12 percent in 2015. Simply put, craft breweries were together producing a lot more beer to slake growing demand.

This was familiar territory, of course. There had been similar double-digit percentage growth in the 1990s, and a concomitant growth in the number of breweries. And, then: shakeout. Dozens of American craft breweries and brewpubs closed around the end of that decade, many abruptly and heavily in debt. What was making the 2010s different (so far)? Or, put another way, why wasn't this demand proving just as faddish as twenty years ago? There were several reasons—all events and trends not really present in the 1990s. Like a fantastically chosen aroma hop, these realities ballasted the American craft beer movement's newfound trajectory, giving it a prominence it never had before and a financial footing surer than ever.

Yet, for all the success and all the growth, there were grave threats, some even existential. They stalked the American craft beer movement, intent on overtaking their prey once and for all.

"DRINK SOCIALLY"

Santa Monica, CA; Roosevelt Island, NY | 2010–2016

For Greg Avola, it was the worst possible time for his plane to be stuck on the tarmac. It wasn't so much that the flight out of New York's John F. Kennedy Airport was delayed, but that the plane would not activate its in-flight WiFi until it was in the air. Therefore, Avola had no Internet connection—and a big problem that could only be solved online.

Untappd, the social-media app dedicated to beer that Avola had cofounded in late 2010, had crashed. It was a Thursday evening during the summer of 2013. Like Friday and Saturday nights then, it was a particularly busy timespan for Untappd's users to check in their beers, rate them, comment on them, and perhaps exchange messages about them with other users. Luckily, Avola's plane soon took flight, the wireless Internet kicked in, and he was able to get his app up and working again.

That app was still in its early days, a side project for both Avola and fellow founder Tim Mather (though each held somewhat grandiose titles: Mather CEO, handling the business end, and Avola, CTO, working the technical side). They had built up a formidable database already of beers to rate, using a kind of Wikipedia-style approach that let users submit brands. The initial database held about five thousand beers, though that would grow mightily in the coming few years. Eventually, the Untappd search box that Avola developed would be able to find just about any beer brand under the sun. Untappd crested first one million users in 2014, then two million, and, finally, by 2016, three million. Three in four of those users hailed from the United States.

That share did not surprise Avola and Mather. They were very aware of the growth in popularity of American craft beer, though neither twenty-something was particularly versed in the beverage at the beginning of their venture. They had connected years before over Twitter—Mather lived in Santa Monica in Southern California, and Avola on New York City's Roosevelt Island—about creating a kind of Twitter-like app unrelated to beer. They ended up instead searching for a way to clone Foursquare, a popular app launched in 2009 that allowed users to check in from venues, particularly eateries and bars. That led the pair, still working in web design and programming on opposite coasts for different companies, to collaborate on what became Untappd. Its tagline said it all: "Drink socially." Its relatively rapid ascent made the forces behind more conventional craft beer media, including print publications and websites, nervous. It also further diluted the power of critics to evaluate and inform on styles and new releases. Just as forums on earlier arrivals such as BeerAdvocate and RateBeer empowered consumers to share information and opinions, so, too, did Untappd. Its design was cleaner and clearer than its predecessors, though, and more easily interactive—a user could register a globally available rating and opinion on a beer in a matter of seconds.

Such democraticization of criticism, as in the past, increased the risk of both misinformation masquerading as fact and of an insularity about what was good and what was not. Most BeerAdvocate forum users, for instance, still touted hyper-hoppy, stronger IPAs as the best beers made in America. Given the website's popularity over nearly twenty years now, BeerAdvocate forum reviews of styles often led the results of Google and Bing searches of particular styles. Consumers doing the searching invariably discovered very high ratings for these IPAs and lower ones for milder or more unfamiliar styles. Thus, there could still be demand for cutting through the increasingly loud echo chamber with more objective evaluations and industry coverage.

Conveniently enough, more media than ever was attempting to slake that demand. Forty years before, a self-publishing Fred Eckhardt had stood virtually alone. Then came a handful of other critics and writers, most prominently Michael Jackson, covering craft beer regularly—and for money—through new publications such as *All About Beer* and column inches in newspapers. A boom in the industry in the 1990s brought a boom in the trade, and, then, further growth in the new century saw dozens of writers, editors, and assorted raconteurs sounding off on craft beer and brewing in numerous online, print, and radio outlets, some of them only a few years old. There is no hard number as to just how many journalists and other writers in America would classify themselves as beer critics or writers, but given the unprecedented breadth of coverage, it's safe to assume that the number is at an all-time high. Several of these writers—including Lucy Saunders, Jay Brooks, and Stan Hieronymus, veterans of an earlier wave of beer journalism—relaunched the North American Guild of Beer Writers in 2011 to showcase writing on the subject, including through annual awards. The guild as of fall 2016 had about 250 members, most from the United States. Its earlier iteration, which had launched in the early 1990s and petered out, was much smaller.

There were not only a lot more people covering American craft beer, the subject itself found its way into coverage of other alcoholic beverages. Whereas once fine wine had been used as a quick descriptor of this newfangled trend called microbrewing or craft beer, now journalists routinely employed craft beer to describe craft spirits and craft cider. Both libations thundered onto the marketplace and the foodie landscape in the 2010s. The popularity and presence of craft spirits—whiskeys, gins, vodkas, etc., made from more traditional ingredients with more traditional methods at often smaller, independently owned distilleries—had gradually grown since the 1960s. The number of craft distilleries numbered perhaps a couple of dozen by 2000 and then several hundred by 2016. As for craft cideries making relatively small amounts of what had been the nation's favorite tipple during its earliest decades, there were perhaps fewer than five by 2000. By 2016, like with craft distilleries, there were several hundred. Craft distilleries and cideries invariably resembled craft breweries—the equipment, the facilities, and the people looked similar. More important, so did the ethos. Here were often small-scale, independent producers trying to craft certain drinks in the most traditional ways possible and then sell those drinks to an often indifferent public familiar only with those from larger concerns. Plus, several craft breweries also produced spirits and ciders. Fritz Maytag's Anchor had established a one-still distillery as far back as 1993 within the brewery's walls in San Francisco. Jim Koch's Boston Beer Company rolled out a brand of cider called Angry Orchard in 2011; it quickly claimed the biggest share of the cider market. Though, in another echo of craft beer, some would argue that Angry Orchard's size precluded its inclusion under the "craft" umbrella. Definition debates rippled through craft spirits, too. One thing was clear, though: craft beer provided an inescapable shorthand for describing what was happening in spirits and cider. Publications often dubbed either "the new/next craft beer," with little explanation of the implication necessary, so ubiquitous was craft beer.

And craft beer consumers needed little prodding to add spirits or cider to their bibulatory repertoire, much as many breweries embraced the production of the drinks. If Untappd was any guide—and it was a good one—craft beer enthusiasts had no problem sidling up to craft cider in particular. Greg Avola and Tim Mather's app allowed users to rate that beverage, but not spirits (or wine, for that matter). Whatever the number of cider reviews, however, the pair kept Untappd's focus on beer, craft beer in particular. It was a focus that their own embrace of the trend heightened, an embrace that strengthened as they built their app. In short, they became fans of craft beer. Avola, in particular, experienced an epiphany about its possibilities in early 2012, more than a year after cofounding Untappd, when he sipped Ommegang's Rare Vos, an amber ale from the Cooperstown, New York, outfit.

They certainly looked the part of the typical craft beer initiate by then: college-educated, on the younger side of forty, male, white, living in two of the nation's larger urban centers, and with disposable income to spare. A 2014 Brewers Association report noted diversity increasing in the craft beer marketplace, including among women, the less-affluent, and Hispanics, but the typical consumer nevertheless looked a lot like the founders of what was likely that consumer's favorite craft-beer app—and had looked like that for a while. The median craft beer consumer fifteen years before was a thirty-nine-year-old white male with "high education" and "relatively high income," and one who was likely to be geographically concentrated in certain areas, particularly larger metropolitan regions and the East and West coasts, according to the Brewers Association report. Despite that increasing diversity, the median craft beer consumer still lived in those areas and still looked like that thirty-nine-year-old white male.* Avola and Mather even had beards, a modern symbol, rightly or wrongly, of urban hipness.

In January 2016, Avola and Mather announced a merger with Next Glass, a three-year-old startup based in Wilmington, North Carolina, that delivered personalized beer and wine recommendations to consumers and retailers. The pair, in an open letter posted on Untappd, said the merger would allow Untappd to expand its features and options—and to allow Avola and Mather to turn to their app full time. The first big expansion came in April 2016, when the app formally unveiled its Untapped for Business feature. It allowed restaurants and bars to post their beer menus for quick sharing through Untappd and other social media outlets, including Twitter, which turned

---

* The author of this book was, as of 2016, a thirty-nine-year-old, college-educated, white male in a major urban area (Greater Boston)—and a craft beer consumer. Statistics do not lie.

ten in 2016 and which, along with Facebook, remained the preferred social media outlet for most craft breweries and consumers. The American craft beer movement was more connected socially than ever.

Such connectivity among consumers and their favorite breweries and tippling holes came as the industry started to splinter—more than at any time since the nearly fatal late 1990s.

CRAFT BEER TURNS 185
Pottsville, PA | 2014–2016

On March 3, 2014, a Monday, the Brewers Association announced its second set of changes to the definition of a craft brewery in less than five years. The last changes had come in December 2010, when the trade group that Charlie Papazian still led expanded the annual production limit for members from two million barrels to six million, thereby keeping bigger craft breweries such as the Boston Beer Company eligible for membership. That move was controversial enough. Some saw it as shameless payola for those larger members, whose hundreds of thousands, if not millions, of barrels a year were worlds away from the production levels of most craft breweries, which produced fifteen thousand barrels at most. Yet others saw it simply as a way to avoid punishing craft breweries and their principals for success. Why shouldn't they be allowed to grow larger and still enjoy the benefits of Brewers Association membership?

The 2014 changes had nothing to do with size, at least on the surface. They instead had to do with the kind of beer a brewery could make and still retain the adjective. Born of a two-day Brewers Association board of directors meeting in February and of months of feedback from members, the new definition still fit within the tripartite rubric of small, independent, and traditional, the parameters that Fritz Maytag had unwittingly set nearly a half-century before at Anchor Brewing. Small still meant fewer than six million barrels, tops, and independent still meant that most of a craft brewery's ownership was just that—independent. The bombshell came in the final section. The Brewers Association now defined traditional brewing thus: "A brewer has a majority of its total beverage alcohol volume in beers whose flavor derives from traditional or innovative brewing ingredients and their fermentation. Flavored malt beverages (FMBs) are not considered beers." It was that "traditional or innovative brewing ingredients" part that would change the craft brewing landscape. The previous definition of traditional had held malted barley almost sacrosanct. Adjuncts such as corn and rice might be used sparingly—"to enhance rather than lighten flavor," as the old definition went—but they were not to be the foundational element in a true craft beer's recipe.

Not anymore: adjuncts were in, and so were the smaller, independently owned breweries that used them. "The revised definition," the Brewers Association said in its March 3 announcement, "recognizes that adjunct brewing is quite literally traditional, as brewers have long brewed with what has been available to them." That was true. Many American breweries in the nineteenth century had started out using corn as a barley substitute likely because the latter was not so readily available in the New World as it would become. Some of these breweries survived into the twenty-first century and, of course, continued to make the same corn-infused beers that had made the breweries popular and financially stable in the first place. To them, adjuncts were part of a long tradition, never mind the half-century of history behind American craft brewing.

Under the revised 2014 definition, a handful of previously regional breweries were able to call themselves craft and largely wasted little time in doing so. These regionals—including the two oldest family-run breweries in the United States, D. G. Yuengling & Son out of Pottsville, Pennsylvania, and the August Schell Brewing Company in New Ulm, Minnesota—slapped "craft" on marketing materials, advertisements, and webpages. Their principals and brewers granted interviews and tours to inquiring critics and other journalists and just generally talked up what had become the very voguish notion of craft beer and craft brewing. It was sort of like what had happened to the F. X. Matt Brewing Company twenty years before—without the switch in beers. Whereas that Utica, New York, regional had pivoted its focus to the all-malt Saranac line and away from lower-quality beers such as Utica Club, Yuengling and August Schell continued to lead with lager recipes that were at least decades old, if not more than a century so.

No regional after 2014 embraced the craft ethos more than Yuengling. The brewery was already more than a century and a half old when the fifth generation of the Yuengling family took over in 1985 in the person of Dick Yuengling Jr., who succeeded his ailing father. The younger Yuengling had grown up around the business, which was one of the largest businesses in the approximately fourteen thousand–strong eastern Pennsylvania town of Pottsville, about halfway between Scranton and Harrisburg, in the Keystone State's coal country. He worked at the brewery as a teenager and while briefly attending Lycoming College in Williamsport, about an hour and a half to the northwest. He had a falling-out with his father about the direction of the brewery—Yuengling the younger wanted to speed up its modernization, Yuengling the older did not think there was money for it—and the son left to take over a local beer distributorship, which he ran for eleven years. That experience taught Yuengling Jr. that his father's brewery, nearly bankrupt and averaging a paltry 137,000 barrels annually, was probably doomed. The American beer marketplace in 1985 was an evermore consolidated and competitive place, and regionals such as Yuengling were getting gobbled up no matter the pedigree—in this case, one that stretched back to its 1829 founding by German immigrant David Yuengling and that Prohibition barely interrupted (David's grandson, Frank Yuengling, made low-alcohol "near beer" and dabbled in dairy products to survive).

Dick Yuengling Jr., barely past thirty and with a dark, deep mane above piercing blue eyes, faced a choice upon his purchase of the family conern: pack up or double down. He chose the latter. Yuengling sped up the modernization his father had undertaken. That meant not only updating the brewery's equipment but also introducing new products, including a so-called Black & Tan born of combining existing lager and porter recipes and a light beer as an inroad into the most popular style America had yet produced. In November 1987, the brewery resurrected a decades-old amber lager, too. Yuengling Traditional Lager would prove to be Yuengling's best-selling brand, but early on in Dick Yuengling Jr.'s tenure it appeared nothing could save the brewery from extinction. Production in 1989 was 127,000 barrels—below the dismal annual average when son took over from father and about 73,000 barrels less than the brewery's capacity.

The following year, in what looked from the outside like a last desperate push, Yuengling hired its first sales and marketing manager. Dick Yuengling Jr. charged David Casinelli with two things: grow the brewery to its two hundred thousand barrel capacity and "don't turn us into IBM." That was a reference to the once-mighty computer concern then struggling to adapt to a fast-changing technology industry. The brewery switched distributors, revamped its labels and other packaging, and generally refocused its efforts on getting the beer to more consumers. Within three years, production reached 245,000. By 1996, there was more demand for Yuengling beers than the brewery could possibly satisfy. It pulled back in markets such as New

York City and New England, and instead focused on its traditional territory of eastern Pennsylvania, New Jersey, and Delaware. A distribution push in the Philadelphia area turned out particularly successful, making Yuengling the best-selling beer on draft in the region before the end of the decade. Indeed, in parts of eastern Pennsylvania, "Yuengling" became literally synonymous with "lager"—order the latter and invariably get the former without having to specify a brand. To slake the demand, the brewery laid plans for two new production facilities: a bigger addition elsewhere in Pottsville and one carved out of an old Stroh's brewery in Tampa, Florida. Its production started to tickle one million barrels annually, its name landing amid the top handful of brewing companies in the United States—well behind the likes of Anheuser-Busch, but still snugly amid the top ten. Annual revenue reached $65 million. Continued success was not assured—the beer marketplace was still a tough, unforgiving place for a regional focused on lower-priced brands—but the specter of collapse now seemed distant. It looked likely that Yuengling would see the twenty-first century, and talk soon started of Dick Yuengling Jr.'s daughters becoming the sixth generation to head the company.

All the while, Yuengling moved outside the orbit of the burgeoning craft beer movement. It was a conscious move in many respects. "We make products that are a little unique, but not too exotic," Casinelli, the brewery's marketing force, told a reporter in early 1997. "People always ask what our demographics are, and not to be smart, we always say, 'Males and females, ages twenty-one to eighty-five.' We still have the old-timers drinking the sixteen-ounce returnables and we have the new drinker looking for trendy products." Part of this arm's-length approach was strategic. Craft beer in the late 1990s and early 2000s brimmed with trendy products, too many of them too much so and not all that tasty—hence a big reason for the sector's great shakeout, which led to dozens of closures during that period. Yuengling had no desire to hitch its wagon to what looked very much like a falling star, especially when the brewery was barely a decade beyond the threat of bankruptcy. Instead, it concentrated on slow and steady growth, building out the two new breweries and slowly expanding distribution to nineteen states.

It continued to price its beers more like the products of Anheuser-Busch than, say, the Boston Beer Company and to use adjuncts in its brewing. This in particular kept it out of the craft club. Again, not that Yuengling minded. The critic Lew Bryson, who had been drinking Yuengling beers since the early 1980s as a southeastern Pennsylvania native, interviewed the brewery's longtime brewmaster Ray Norbert in 1995, and asked him point-blank why he did not brew at least one all-malt recipe, a hallmark of any craft brewer.

Norbert shot Bryson a pitying look. He explained that the rejuvenated brewery was running at capacity, barely able to satisfy current demand, its beers more popular than in many years. "What's broken that I need to fix?" Norbert said.

Nothing, it seemed. And, yet, Yuengling as the twenty-first century marched onward, started to slowly swim in the craft beer stream. That stream had opened from a trickle at the start of the 2000s to become a rushing river, the fastest-growing sector of an overall brewing industry that saw its sales flatline or fall. Yuengling resurrected a recipe for a bock, that strong lager style born in Germany, that the brewery had not used since 1970. It reintroduced its Lord Chesterfield Ale, a pale ale with roots stretching back to the early 1800s. The brewery also vastly expanded the distribution of a porter it had made off and on since the early 1800s as well, revamping its packaging so that it popped visually from shelves and tap handles. Finally, there was a new Oktoberfest, a wheat beer for the summer, and even an India pale lager, an esoteric spin on the near-hegemonic India pale ale style that continued to enthrall craft beer consumers. Yuengling appeared to make each of these beers with some of sort of adjunct, and none came anywhere close to approaching its Traditional Lager in sales—that 1987 rerelease accounted for about 90 percent of the brewery's output by the century's second decade (and that output was closing in on three million barrels annually).

Yet, these new releases signaled Yuengling's clear embrace of the American craft beer movement, one that the Brewers Association's 2014 definition change only tightened. The brewery embraced the language of the movement in particular. Here was the August 2011 press release for its Oktoberfest: "This medium-bodied beer is the perfect blend of roasted malts [and] just the right amount of hops to capture a true representation of the style." And the description of the IPL, rolled out in spring 2015: "Bursting with complex hop notes like an IPA, but with a well-balanced lager base that allows the Bravo, Belma, Cascade, and Citra hops to truly shine." As the critic Don "Joe Sixpack" Russell, another longtime Yuengling drinker from his perch in Philadelphia, put it, "With this newfangled hybrid India pale lager, Yuengling . . . appears to have finally succumbed to the lingo and conventions of craft beer. Where Pottsville's finest was once content with plain ol' Lager or Premium, it now speaks of dry-hopping and wonky IBUs and trendy Citra hops." Yuengling also publicized its unique history as the nation's oldest brewery, adopting a sizable chunk of the craft beer ethos that emphasized tradition, especially when it persevered against long odds—namely competition from Big Beer and the convulsive industry changes that had dispatched so many other regionals. In early 2016, Yuengling launched its biggest marketing push ever with the aid of advertising house Allen & Gerritsen. Rolled out in all eighteen states that Yuengling then distributed to, the television, print, and digital ads were nothing busier than a bottle or a pint of Yuengling Traditional Lager next to two taglines: "America's Oldest Brewery" and "Respect. It's Earned."

Whether existing craft beer consumers, and brewers, respected Yuengling as one of their own depended on whom one asked in 2014 and 2015. That was when the Brewers Association's definition change took effect and Yuengling and other operations such as Minnesota's August Schell and Naragansett out of Rhode Island became some of the biggest craft brewers in the United States. Jim Koch, whose Boston Beer Company Yuengling unseated in 2015 as the nation's biggest craft brewer under the new rubric, was positively magnanimous in a statement: "As a matter of fact, I'm a sixth-generation brewer and Dick Yuengling is a fifth-generation brewer, so brewing is in our blood. I'm personally happy to see craft brewers succeed because it means as an industry, we're all continuing to grow and follow our passions for brewing." Others were less forgiving. The owner of a brewery in Berkeley, California, told National Public Radio in 2014 that the inclusion of larger breweries that used adjuncts such as rice and corn had damaged the entire sector. "I think the Brewers Association has watered down the meaning of craft beer, and of good beer," said Dan Del Grande of Bison Organic Beer, one of several dozen breweries nationwide brewing beers almost entirely from organic ingredients.

Some pointed out that the Brewers Association's change may have had little to do with ingredients and more to do with lobbying and with goosing its statistics. The entrees of Yuengling, August Schell, et al., allowed the Brewers Association to report that much stronger annual growth in craft beer production and sales. Also, the trade group was pushing Congress for a further cut in the federal excise tax, including pushing it as low as $3.50 per barrel from $7.00 for breweries producing fewer than 7,143 barrels annually (there would also be reductions for breweries making up to six million barrels, the production cutoff for Brewers Association eligibility). Iterations of the legislation had been on Capitol Hill since 2011, and sympathetic legsilators had reintroduced a version in early 2015. This was right around the time the Brewers Association definition change took effect. That change brought Yuengling, now the nation's fourth-biggest brewery behind Anheuser-Busch InBev, MillerCoors, and Pabst, into the craft fold—not an insignificant ally to have in a political battle, especially since the opponent was Big Beer, which had its own tax-cut legislation pending. Under this theory, the Brewers Association's definition change appeared like a sudden and all too convenient about-face—though, as far as growth was concerned, it had been rather steady before the 2014 changes. Still, the pivot was stark. The Brewers Association had in late 2012 released and publicized a list of "domestic non-craft brewers" and chastised some on it for claiming the craft mantle. Among those beyond the small, indepdent, and traditional pale in 2011 were phantom crafts such as Blue Moon, Big Beer acquisitions such as Leinenkugel, and the regional likes of D. G. Yuengling & Son, which the Brewers Association said could not be considered craft because of its use of adjuncts.

That was then, this was now. Yet, whatever the theories behind the definition change, and whatever the extreme reactions, most consumers and those in the industry appeared to greet it with a collective yawn. The growth and the creativity in this particular sector of American brewing seemed to have overtaken the power of a phrase to describe it and its products. Look no further than the styles capturing consumer interest—and dollars—in the second decade of the twenty-first century. Gose, an extremely sour, deliberately bitter, lower-alcohol beer born centuries ago in northern Europe, became one of the most talked-about styles of 2015, with several breweries releasing versions of gose, and trade and consumer media rushing to cover them. In particular, beers infused with grapefruit, lemon, and watermelon (or at least the flavoring of those fruits) stormed shelves as did hard root beer, a quasi-beer often compared with craft beer in terms of ingenuity. It was exactly what it sounded like—a spiked version of the popular soda. Several craft breweries, including Boston Beer, Stone, and Dogfish Head, also introduced nitro beers during the 2010s, either entirely new brands or one-offs, including for an annual Nitro Fest that Colorado's Left Hand Brewing Company launched in 2014. Nitrogen powers the carbonation in nitro beers, rather than carbon dioxide, creating a smoother, rounder mouthfeel. And a session beer craze swept out of California around 2010, celebrating lower-alcohol offerings in an American craft beer movement that stronger beers still denominated (hoppy IPAs remained the nation's bestselling craft beer style into the middle of the decade, easily outpacing all comers). Entire brewing companies sprang up to produce session beers, and older breweries developed year-round session releases.

As for stronger beers, they continued to approach a kind of end-of-history moment. Dogfish Head in November 2015 released a beer with 658 international bittering units—about 558 above the level of bitterness a human can actually detect. And the Shmaltz Brewing Company in April of the same year needled the session craze with a so-called session double IPA, a strong version of what was supposed to be a lower-alcohol style. And on and on went the envelop-shredding, craft brewers free of the regulatory constraints of their distilling and vintning brethren and enjoying a marketplace that was at least receptive to new ideas, if not fully supportive. There seemed no end to the styles that the market might bear. The Great American Beer Festival included 145 styles in its judged categories in 2015, up from 138 two years before and barely 130 in 2010.

Such variety rended the canvas upon which so many pioneers had painted over the decades. A half-century on from Fritz Maytag's rescue of Anchor Brewing, the picture looked more Pollack than Copley. The cover of *All About Beer* magazine in March 2015 declared, "Craft Beer Is Dead, Long Live Craft Beer." In the issue, critic Stan Hieronymus unpacked the curious etymology of "craft beer," "craft brewing," and "craft brewer," tracing it all the way back to Vince Cottone's first usage in the mid-1980s through the more recent definitional battles. Like the double IPA or steam beer, America appears to have developed the phrase and exported it to the world. The seeming ubiquity of "craft" had robbed it of its descriptive effectiveness. Here was Hieronymus in that March 2015 essay:

> The words craft beer are part of dozens of book titles and several magazine names; it seems every city has a craft beer week; many breweries have made it part of their names; there is a chain of stores called Craft Beer Cellar; the "I am a craft brewer" video has been watched uncounted times at various Internet sites; and the Colorado Brewers Guild recently began to promote Colorado as "The State of Craft Beer." The term has spread to England, Brazil, Japan, Argentina, Italy, Poland, Germany, China and likely three other countries since you began reading this paragraph. The century-old Palm Breweries in Belgium were recently rebranded as Palm Belgian Craft Brewers. The Global Association of Craft Beer Brewers was founded in 2013, with its own criteria for what qualifies as a craft brewery.

It was now fashionable instead to describe craft beer as simply beer—a better-tasting, more painstakingly made version of the same beverage that Anheuser-Busch InBev and other Big Beer producers made. Or, as Stone Brewing cofounder Greg Koch tweeted in December 2013, "A dream: We stop calling fizzy yellow beer 'beer' & real actual beer 'craft beer,' & begin calling them 'fake beer' & 'beer,' respectively." Jocular as Koch's oft-retweeted dream was, it actually presaged what the Brewers Association would try to do the following year with its tweaked definition. The definition left it up to consumers to decide what made a particular beer "craft." Some might rail at the inclusion of adjuncts in the leading definition of craft beer, others might not—the Brewers Association said it no longer cared, especially when the tweak added larger producers such as Yeungling to its membership arsenal. What the association did double-down on was what made a *brewery* "craft." Independent ownership and relatively small production became that much more sacrosanct in the association's eyes and in the eyes of many consumers who read about, and argued about, the changes. It was a masterstroke of semantics, divorcing the product from the producer.

It was a break a long time coming. Craft brewers had desired for years "to change the way people think about beer," according to Brooklyn Brewery's Steve Hindy, who had been there when the Brewers Association first tried to define its niche. Even then, in 2004 and 2005, with decades of growth and a shakeout behind it, Hindy knew there was a palpable need in the movement for "a whole different way of defining beer or characterizing the consumption of beer." With its emphasis on the brewery rather than the beer, the Brewers Association's 2014 change seemed an attempt to finally settle things. Pity it didn't work.

CONQUERING EUROPE

Fraserburgh, Scotland; London; Rome; Grimstad, Norway; Moscow | 2002–2015

One day in 2002, James Watt, a nineteen-year-old law and economics student, bought a Sierra Nevada Pale Ale from a Tesco's convenience store in the Scottish town of Stonehaven, south of Aberdeen, to go along with that quintessential British snack, fish and chips.

The hoppy concoction from Chico, California, changed his life.

Until that point, Watt had been a whiskey drinker—he was partial to the great American-born variant bourbon—having wearied of both the blander, mass-produced lagers that dominated the British beer market and the rarer, richer cask ales that fans holding a candle for the kingdom's dying brewing traditions long championed, the critic Michael Jackson among them. This Sierra Nevada Pale Ale was something entirely different than both, a striking middle ground with immense floral aroma and sweetly bitter flavor. The "bomb of flavor," as Watt later described the beer, set him on a path that would have been familiar to Ken Grossman, the cofounder of Sierra Nevada who developed the pale ale that so enthralled Watt.

The balding university student with arched eyebrows and slim build became a homebrewer. His first concoction, naturally, was a clone of Sierra Nevada Pale Ale. He initially pursued the hobby out of his Edinburgh apartment, which he shared with a high school friend named Martin Dickie. Dickie was studying brewing and distilling at a university in Edinburgh and would go to work for a brewery called Thornbridge in northern England. Watt himself lasted a few weeks at a legal affairs job after he completed his degree, and thereafter joined the family fishing business, spending two weeks out of every four in the North Atlantic. The pair did not see each other that regularly, then, but when they did get together beer and brewing were major topics. They continued to homebrew, separately and together, focusing, like American homebrewers more than a generation before, on styles they simply could not easily find. That Sierra Nevada Pale Ale at Tesco's had been a bit of a retail coup in itself, as Grossman's brewery had not yet started to distribute widely in the United Kingdom. One of the styles Watt and Dickie attacked was imperial stout—basically a stronger version of the dark, roasty English style, an iteration American brewers had been playing around with for years. In early 2006, the pair took a bottle of it to a tasting event in London that Michael Jackson had organized—Dickie knew him through the Thornbridge brewery—and poured a glass for the critic. "Guys," Jackson replied upon tasting the imperial stout, "you need to give up the day job."

The following year, Watt and Dickie, then both twenty-four, pooled their savings, borrowed twenty thousand pounds, and opened a brewery called BrewDog in a desolate area of the Scottish town of Fraserburgh, north of Aberdeen, in between a needle exchange for drug addicts and a salesman who proclaimed himself the "godfather" of carpeting. Dickie quit his day job at Thornbridge, but Watt kept fishing to bring in some outside income. Their first commercial release, an IPA they called Punk, took three tries to get just right. The first failed because the novices dropped a phone, some keys, and a thermometer into the brew, and the second because a garden hose they used to sipon the beer left the batch tasting of plastic. The final came out just as Watt and Dickie intended: a strong IPA that tasted citrusy and almost sweet, not unlike those IPAs from the far-off West Coast of America—an area they visited prior to the 2007 launch to sample its beers firsthand. Like the then-novel Cascade hop a generation before that powered those releases, a newer hop from New Zealand called Nelson Sauvin powered BrewDog's Punk IPA. Like the Cascade, Nelson Sauvin was especially noted for the fruity, floral aroma and taste it was supposed to impart.

While the hop did just that for the IPA, the taste and the strength—6 percent alcohol by volume—made BrewDog's inaugural release a virtual marketplace pariah. They humped the beer in a used Fiat Punto and a Skoda pickup to farmers' markets and pubs across northeastern Scotland, indifference meeting them at nearly every turn. "It was hard," Dickie would remember. There was "zero interest" in a heavily hopped, unusually strong India pale ale, whatever the style's birthplace in the United Kingdom. Then the pair caught a major break through Tesco, that same chain that years before had sold Watt his epiphanal Sierra Nevada Pale Ale. Tesco held a blind-tasting of British beers, the prize a place on its shelves nationwide. BrewDog Punk IPA cleaned up, winning several spots, including the top one, in the blind tasting. Watt and Dickie now had more demand than their current supply could meet.

From this break in 2007, BrewDog would scale rapidly upward. It would switch its main production to a gleaming new brewery in Ellon, again near Aberdeen, the original spot turned over to experimental batches. Some of those batches made Punk IPA seem rather quaint. There was the End of History, a blonde Belgian ale that clocked in at 55 percent ABV and that BrewDog produced only eleven bottles of, each container snugly fitted into dead stoats and squirrels. The beer, which Watt and Dickie billed as the world's strongest beer, retailed for five hundred to seven hundred pounds each (or well more than one thousand dollars). There was Speedball, a strong ale named after the sometimes fatal narcotics cocktail that included heroin. Speedball drew sharp criticism from an alcohol-beverage industry watchdog in the United Kingodm, which called for retailers to scupper the beer and accused BrewDog of "profiteering from the scourge of illegal drugs." And there was "Royal Virility Performance," brewed for the 2011 wedding of Kate Middleton and Prince William Windsor and said to contain natural aphrodisiacs, including an herbal form of Viagra. BrewDog also loosed plenty of outlandish promotions in service of these and other releases, including driving a tank down a busy retail strip in northwest London and dropping from a helicopter literal fat cats (again with the taxidermy) on the metaphorical ones in the capital's financial district.

Such antics, and such unconventional beers, drew rebukes from pockets inside and outside of the British brewing industry. "BrewDog have surpassed themselves with their over-inflated egos and naked ambition," wrote long-time British beer writer Roger Protz in November 2009, when the brewery unveiled a release that was 32 percent ABV on the day the Scottish Parliament debated a minimum price for alcohol. "Naturally, the wild buckeroos in Fraserburgh claim this is the world's strongest beer, even though technically it's not beer at all . . . Clearly, the new product, called Tactical Nuclear Penguin (what were you smoking last night, chaps?), was finished with a wine or Champagne yeast." Protz's criticism was mild compared with what others had to say, often in the online comments sections of numerous articles about the fast-growing upstart. "I'm a manager at a bar in Northern England," wrote one anonymous commenter in 2008, "and let me tell you, there's absolutely nothing 'punk' about BrewDog. It is not the perception in the bar trade at all. We're just sick and tired of their shit marketing and faux-persecution complex. First, and most importantly, their beer is total shite. Everything is overhopped, overcooked and overpriced." When Watt called for an official craft beer definition for the United Kingdom in October 2013, one commenter summed up the feelings of many critics toward the brewery and its approach: "BrewDog are horrible marketing-type suit people who make terrible beer. Can we all stop doing their bidding and giving them free publicity every bloody time they do something stupid like this?"

Mostly, though, it was the oddness of it all that seemed to irk people— and it was only odd stacked against the staid British brewing industry, which Watt had long ago correctly diagnosed as being a zero-sum game between industrialized lagers from Big Beer producers and traditionalists who adored cask ales, generally heavier, richer beers served in special kegs without added carbonation. This duality caused a decades-long decline in the British brewing industry, especially when it came to variety. Then, in 2002, a tax break for smaller producers unleashed a steady rise in the number of breweries and the diversity of styles available in stores and, crucially, in pubs (this arc was very similar to what happened in the United States following that 1976 per-barrel tax cut for smaller breweries). Were BrewDog operating in America in the second decade of the twenty-first century, they would be considered at times outlandish, if not a little saucy, but would elicit nowhere near the vitriol they engendered on their home turf. In fact, they would likely be celebrated, given the lionization of the likes of Dogfish Head and Lagunitas, breweries that led with stronger, hoppier beers, the sorts that defied easy categorization and that came, in some cases, to be called "extreme beer." Moreover, BrewDog had just about followed the trajectory of those two American craft breweries, from struggling startup facing marketplace indifference, to insouciant disruptor in that same marketplace, to successful pioneer in the public eye.

As it was, though, BrewDog was a Scottish brewery operating largely in Great Britain. That meant a different way of doing things than in the former colonies. The Campaign for Real Ale, the group that had rescued cask ale from near-extinction beginning in the 1970s and that organized the annual Great

British Beer Festival, would twice ban BrewDog from participating—in part because its beers did not fit the cask-ale rubric, but also because they were in many cases so nontraditional. And the same industry watchdog that had criticized Speedball outright banned the sale of Tokyo Imperial Stout, which was 18 percent ABV. BrewDog seized the prohibition as another marketing opportunity: it released a beer very low in alcohol and called it Nanny State.

Within three years of that 2009 release, BrewDog was the fastest-growing food-and-drink producer in the United Kingdom and the fastest-growing bar operator, with more than thirty locations nationwide and several more overseas. It took on new investors, including Keith Greggor and Tony Foglio, who bought Anchor Brewing from Fritz Maytag in 2010, and thousands of consumers, who bought shares in exchange for discounts—a 2015 round of crowdfunding raised five million pounds in twenty days. That original Punk IPA, too, became the country's best-selling craft beer. For many outside of the United Kingdom, Punk became as synonymous with British craft beer as Samuel Adams Boston Lager had with American craft beer to many outside of the United States. Whatever the bafflement and hostility of critics and traditionalists, it was hard to argue with BrewDog's commercial success.

That success had everything to do with American craft beer. "We really wanted to make beers like the American brewers who follow their muses," Watt recalled of BrewDog's earliest days, just after that pilgrimage to American craft breweries on the West Coast. Even after several years as a commercial brewer, he still believed that British breweries were "light years behind the US, and California in particular." BrewDog's rapid rise represented the starkest example yet of a trend that would have been unfathomable a generation back: America setting not only the stylistic trends for Europe, birthplace of all but a handful of styles, but the very way of going about making craft beer and selling it. The number of breweries in Europe increased 73 percent from 2008 to 2013, to more than fifty-six hundred. France and Spain led the increase, with the number of breweries quadrupling in those countries during that time period. In Italy, Poland, and Norway, the number doubled.

Most of these new breweries were small and deliberately more traditional than the Continent's macro-producers. And many were consciously—proudly—aping hoppier, stronger, more experimental American offerings, and doing so with a certain heedless confidence despite confronting marketplaces as indifferent as the United States was to craft beer thirty years before. "Up until maybe a year and a half to two years ago, you still had to really search for the craft beer scene," a brewmaster at a craft brewery in Berlin told a reporter in early 2016. Yet, change was sweeping even the birthplace of the

Reinheitsgebot, that purity dictate that for centuries had rendered most German beers straightforward mixtures of water, barley, hops, and yeast. By 2015, the craft beer section was the fastest-growing segment of Bar Convent Berlin, Europe's largest trade show for bars and alcoholic-beverage makers. Leading the growth were operations specializing in "hop-heavy ales inspired by West Coast breweries." Said the same Berlin brewmaster: "American-style IPAs are hugely popular in the beer scene, and they are slowly making their way into well-curated bars and restaurants in the big cities."

Call it an unintended fruit of an increasingly globalized world, one where products, capital, and people, at least within the more affluent, industrialized regions, traveled with little difficulty. Or maybe it was the result of the influence of a small band of expatriates who started American-inflected craft breweries in Europe. This included the Rome Brewing Co., which Mike Murphy, a homebrewer originally from Philadelphia, launched in 1999 and which introduced the first India pale ale for sale commercially in famously beer-averse Italy. Or perhaps it was simply the result of the ease of information-sharing that the web provided. Whatever the reasons, a Berlin brewmaster could cite "American-style IPAs"—a phrase that itself had only entered the lexicon in the late 1990s—as a major influence on the brewing industry and beer culture of a Germany that Michael Jackson had lauded in *The World Guide to Beer* as the global leader in beer style. Make no mistake: German beer was diverse before the rise of American craft beer, the nation, divided or united, home to perhaps a dozen distinct styles "divided into several categories," according to Jackson. It was just that American craft beer pushed the Germans, and other Europeans, to in turn push the boundaries of what those and other styles could smell, look, and taste like. More than that, American craft beer exemplified how to overcome the indifference of consumers. "We said it was brewed in Russia, and people literally laughed at us," Denis Kovalyova, co-owner of a successful craft brewery just outside of Moscow, told a British newspaper in 2011. "'Good beer can't be made in Russia,' they said."

Kjetil Jikiun faced a similarly arctic reception in Norway. He was an airline pilot whose routes often took him to the United States, where he fell in love with craft beer. He started homebrewing, at first using ingredients carted back from the States, and cofounded a craft brewery called Nogne O in Grimstad, on the southern Norwegian coast, in 2002. Its offerings included, among other novel releases, Norway's first IPA. "For the first two years," Jikiun recalled, "we were just about to go bankrupt every second month or so. Nobody believed in us, nobody believed in our idea." Nogne O and other European craft breweries not only survived in their home countries, but thrived beyond them, some becoming sought-after brands in the United States, Australia, throughout the Continent, and in East Asia, especially Japan. Their slow, steady spread internationally echoed that of American craft brewers years before.

So, too, did the concomitant rise in craft beer cultures in just about every European nation, often most active online and clustered in major urban areas. The number of craft-beer bars in such urban areas became an excellent barometer of the beverage's popularity nationally. In Moscow, for instance, a leading entertainment and culture magazine announced in August 2015 that it would stop reviewing new craft beer bars in the Russian capital. The reason? The sheer number of new ones. It was too hard for the magazine to keep up.

THE STOCKHOLM AFFAIR
Stockholm; Hallertau, Germany; Berlin | 2013–2016

The volume of American craft beer exports cleared one hundred million dollars for the first time annually in 2015, according to the Brewers Association. That involved the shipping of nearly 450,000 barrels, with the biggest growth at mid-decade coming in exports to Western Europe, Brazil, East Asia, and the Pacific, including Australia. These figures did not include collaborations between American craft breweries and their European counterparts that also found their ways into continental and British pubs and stores. A 2010 collaboration on a dry, bubbly ale between the Boston Beer Company and Weihensephan, a nearly nine-hundred-year-old Bavarian concern considered the world's oldest operating brewery, was perhaps the most well known. Other, smaller breweries, including Russian River and Brooklyn, also partnered with European breweries on one-offs.

Some of the biggest American craft breweries, beginning in the 2010s, went beyond exporting or collaborating and simply set production roots overseas. Brooklyn Brewery was the first. In January 2013, the company that Tom Potter and Steve Hindy founded in those now so very distant days of the mid-1980s announced a partnership with D. Carnegie & Co. to open an eight-thousand-barrel brewpub in an old lightbulb factory facing the harbor in the Swedish capital of Stockholm. Brooklyn had long distributed its beers in Sweden and the rest of Scandanavia through Carlsberg Sweden, D. Carnegie & Co.'s corporate parent. The brewery and restaurant, New Carnegie (in English), opened in spring 2014, with the New York company the managing partner. The brewpub produced specialty beers specifically for patrons. Brooklyn brands sold in Sweden—the brewery's biggest export market and the second-biggest, behind Canada, for all US craft beer—were still produced in the States.

Not so the Bavarian outpost of the Urban Chestnut Brewing Company Former Anheuser-Busch employees David Wolfe and Florian Kuplent started Urban Chestnut as a brewpub in St. Louis's midtown area in January 2011. They added a separate brewery in the city about two years later, and, in January 2015, announced plans to acquire and retool an existing European brewery that one of Urban Chestnut's hop suppliers told them about. The brewery, about a thirty-minute drive north of the downtown area of the Bavarian capital of Munich and with a capacity for up to five thousand barrels annually, had essentially gone bankrupt. Its equipment, though, was still fairly new and Kuplent himself was from Bavaria. It was there that he grew up around German beer culture and entered the industry through an old-fashioned brewer's apprenticeship at a small Bavarian brewery. He then collected degrees in brewing, and worked at various European and American operations before ending up at Anheuser-Busch. He worked there for several years as a brewer and met Wolfe, who worked on the business side developing strategies for drawing more consumers. Their own brewing company was decidedly more modest than the world's biggest and reflected the business reality for most newer craft breweries in this era of once-again torrid growth. In 2012, its first full year of operation, Urban Chestnut produced thirty-five hundred barrels of beer, an amount that would nearly double the following year, but that still placed it among the majority of craft breweries producing fewer than fifteen thousand barrels annually. Urban Chestnut would crest that volume even before the retooled German acquisition started brewing under Kuplent's supervision in the late spring of 2015. Urban Chestnut Hallertauer Braurei initially brewed the company's longtime flagship, an unfiltered lager called Zwickel, and two novel offerings as a nod to the surrounding landscape: a pale ale made with newer German hop varieties and a cross between a classic Pilsner and a German Helles, or pale lager.

All would be offered in Germany starting in June 2015, making Urban Chestnut the first American craft brewery to not only launch an entirely separate brewery in Europe, but to make American-born brands there for distribution. In an interesting twist, Urban Chestnut also planned to eventually export to the United States that pale ale and pale lager-pilsner hybrid born at the German brewery (its beers had been traveling the opposite direction, from the United States to Germany, since 2013). As for selling that new brewery's products to a German audience, Kuplent and Wolfe encountered a situation that would have been familiar to many European craft brewers. "It does take that effort to explain it," Kuplent told a reporter back home in St. Louis.

A year after Urban Chestnut's first beers rolled off the line near Munich, the Stone Brewing Co.'s first beers—cans of Stone IPA—rolled off a new line in Berlin. The June 2016 milestone marked a culmination of years of effort on the part of the San Diego County–based company to open a brewery in Europe. Stone cofounder Greg Koch marked the public start of that effort in 2012 by crushing a pallet of non-craft brands with a forklift and a boulder at the former gasworks plant his company planned to turn into a brewery. It was an unsurprising stunt from the pioneering brewery that gave the world Arrogant Bastard Ale, and Koch, who was emerging as a particularly truculent critic of Big Beer and the craft entities that did business with them, was unapologetic. "The real harm was done at those breweries by making cheap, pale facsimiles of beer," he said. "That's the insult." Germany's Reinheitsgebot also came in for particularly withering criticism from Koch. The beer purity dictate turned five hundred in April 2016, and, while it had for two decades ceased to carry the weight of law, its spirit still hovered over one of the world's great beer nations. "The beer scene is better than average in Germany," Koch told a reporter from the United States, "but it has a lot of room for improvement as alternative styles have very limited presence … Drawing parellels with California, I think Berlin's scene is ten to twenty years behind." Koch promised that the new Stone brewery, which included an attached tasting area and a bistro to form a kind of smorgasbord of American craft beer, would help mightily to drag German beer and beer culture into the present. This "camaraderie approach," as Koch labeled it, echoed the approach that had, especially early on, enlivened smaller-scale, more traditional brewing in the United States. Brewers helped each other, materially and intellectually, and the changes came.

A television series that debuted in 2013 showcased the fruits of these changes. The show itself could not have happened without American craft beer: James Watt and Martin Dickie of BrewDog hosted it. The show, a branding coup called *Brew Dogs*, parachuted the amiable Scotsmen into often over-the-top situations involving brewing and beer. It debuted on September 24, 2014, a Tuesday, as part of the primetime lineup of the Esquire Network, a channel that NBC Universal had launched the Monday before in partnership with the venerable men's magazine. While the cable network's nightly offerings barely averaged more than fifty thousand household viewers during its initial several months, *Brew Dogs* represented the first major television showcase for American craft beer since the short-lived *Brew Masters* on the Discovery Channel in 2010. The conceit was similar to that show, which starred Dogfish Head's Sam Calagione as he sought to create unusual recipes— except that *Brew Dogs'* one-hour episodes took things to predictable extremes.

That September 24 premiere found them in San Diego County, brewing with exceptionally hot chili peppers and recently harvested sea kelp, as well as stirring boiling wort, or unfermented beer, with Stone's Greg Koch while barreling between San Diego and Los Angeles on a rickety Amtrak train. Other episodes would follow in other American cities—the second saw the duo decamping to American craft beer's birthplace, San Francisco, and the first season ended in Boston, with Watt and Dickie, and Boston Beer's Jim Koch, jumping into a mash tun of unfermented beer half-naked to provide the necessary bacteria for a sour, lobster-infused brew. Such hijinks, coupled with the careful inclusion of local breweries at each stop and the nervous charm of the hosts, ensured media coverage of *Brew Dogs'* stops well beyond what the show's ratings probably warranted. The whole affair was not without critics, who eye-rolled at the antics much as some British critics had kvetched about the early BrewDog beers. "*Brew Dogs*, a show about regional craft beer brewing is so casual and informational that it possibly gives craft beer drinkers too much knowledge," wrote one critic, "which will probably make their conversations about hoppiness even more insufferable." Still, local newspapers and online publications covered the show's arrival to their towns, sometimes breathlessly; and blogs targeting craft beer aficionados dissected episodes afterward, with special attention paid to the eccentric beers that Watt and Dickie made with their hosts. The eccentric beers, and the means to create them, aside, *Brew Dogs* appeared at heart as a jaunty celebration of American beer and beer culture, one hinging on the fulcrum of craft beer in particular. The movement and the industry offered Watt and Dickie an immense and diverse playground. It would not be until the start of *Brew Dogs'* third season, in the spring of 2015, that the the duo shot outside of the United States, on their home turf of Aberdeen, in fact.

It was during this time, too, that BrewDog, the brewery, finalized plans for its first US production hub on forty-two acres in Canal Winchester, Ohio, a city just to the southeast of Columbus, with an opening set for 2017. The one-hundred-barrel brewhouse was a mere beachhead for BrewDog's Stateside plans: Watt and Dickie envisioned a wave of brewpubs nationally and a second brewhouse eventually, enough with the original Ohio brewery to produce more than one and a half million barrels of beer annually—or more than all the craft breweries in Ohio combined. The production would also easily eclipse what BrewDog brewed in the United Kingdom, a goal with which the company's founders were perfectly comfortable. America was "the land that helped inspire a generation of U.K. craft brewers—not least ourselves," read a press release about the preliminary Canal Winchester plans. "It's been a long time in coming, but we are proud to declare that we are heading to the land of Independence."

LESSONS FROM HERACLITUS
Azusa, CA; Amsterdam | 2014–2016

For those familiar with his earlier work, in both beer and writing, Tony Magee's 2,214-word blog post on September 7, 2015, a Monday, was not surprising at all—at least structurally. Like the labels he had penned for his Lagunitas Brewing Company for decades, the post, published through Lagunitas' address on the blogging platform Tumblr, was digressive and rambling at times, wryly funny at others, and in general quietly informative.

It began with Magee acknowledging that day's big news: that Lagunitas had formed a fifty-fifty joint parntnership with the Amsterdam-based brewing giant Heineken. Magee then spent the remainder of the punctuation-averse post justifying the decision, placing it within a context of an industry and a marketplace that were both changing rapidly—and whose change made both juicy targets for businesspeople who might not share Magee's ethos. "Our time in craft brewing didn't begin on craft's first day, that day came thirty years before we started," read the first sentence of his second paragraph, an apparent reference to Fritz Maytag's rescue of Anchor Brewing. "However, from the first day the world of craft resembled the river in the proverb by the Greek philosopher Heraclitus which says that 'You can never step in the same river twice; It won't be the same river and you won't be the same person.'" And the craft beer movement he and his brewery had done so much to foster wasn't the same, either.

In total in the U.S.A. Craft Beer still represents only 9% of all the beer enjoyed. That's less than one-in-ten. Yet, in places like San Francisco and the Pacific Northwest it approaches and even exceeds 50% of the world of beer. This past February, for one week, our IPA 12-packs were the #1 beer package in the whole of the Bay Area. Number 2 was a big brewer's 30-packs and #3 was another big brewer's 24-pack. That kind of thing was not even dreamt about just 5 years earlier. I believe that the West Coast scene is a forecast for the rest of the country and even the rest of the world. It'll take time, but it is entirely possible.

To Magee, that was the point of the Heineken alliance. Lagunitas itself had grown from its once-struggling Petaluma base just north of San Francisco to include a Chicago brewery and taproom, both of which opened in 2014, and a Southern California brewery slated to launch in 2017 in Azusa, about twenty-five miles east of Los Angeles. The brewery's beers were available in all fifty states and a handful of other countries, including the United Kingdom, Ireland, Canada, Japan, and Sweden. It was the sixth-biggest craft brewery in the United States by sales volume and the eleventh biggest overall. Once all three breweries were up and running, Lagunitas would have a capacity for nearly two million barrels annually, a phenomenal sum for a craft beer sector where most breweries produced under fifteen thousand. More than the raw numbers, critics and consumers coast-to-coast and internationally rightfully recognized Lagunitas as a craft beer pioneer, in particular as a progenitor of the ultra-hoppy Americanized iteration of the India pale ale style that still dominated the sector's sales and the imagination of that sector's most diehard fans. At the start of 2015, Magee surveyed the breadth of his domain and realized that there were still more worlds to conquer. In particular, he had a driving epiphany that year in Ireland, shortly after Lagunitas started exporting to the celtic republic. "I met people there who were big fans of U.S. Craft flavors," Magee wrote in his Tumblr post, "some of whom were themselves newly minted brewers, and I realized that the whole damn world of humans may well want to enjoy these same flavors. When I got back home I thought long and hard about how to aim at that truth, how can we get there, to the whole world?"

For Magee, the answer lay in a partnership with Heineken. The arrangement was fairly straightforward: Lagunitas would remain an independent entity under Magee's control and Heineken would distribute its brands worldwide; they would then share fifty-fifty in the fruits of the labor. Not that Heineken needed the money, even if it clearly wanted the American craft beer entrée. Heineken was the world's second-largest brewery by revenue—nearly $23 billion in 2015—with more than 250 beverage brands, including beer, in more than seventy countries. In the United States, Heineken was known mostly for its green-bottled flagship lager, but it also controlled Dos Equis and Tecate as well as a few hard cider brands. It was not known as a craft brewer—but it was also not known as an antagonist of that sector. Heineken had never targeted craft beer in the same direct and unrelenting manner as had Anheuser-Busch, Miller, and Coors (though craft beer had sometimes targeted Heineken, as when Boston Beer's Jim Koch labeled the company "a fraud" on PBS's *MacNeil/Lehrer Newshour* in 1986). Heineken was for the most part a benign presence to most craft beer consumers. It played in a different marketplace sandbox and its beers bore little resemblance taste-wise to the craft beers it largely ignored. It did have that international reach, though, and that's what Magee wanted. Plus, as he explained in the Tumblr post, he liked the vibe of the company, including the fact that Charlene de Carvalho-Heineken, the great-granddaughter of its founder, still controlled it (de Carvalho-Heineken had almost exactly a year before rebuffed a takeover bid from SABMiller). "More to the point," Magee wrote, "we met a company that saw and understood that we could only work together if we could continue as we are, steering our own ship here and abroad, being ourselves and exporting exactly that to communities all over the world, beginning with Mexico . . .! [Heineken] wanted what it is that we wanted."

That might have been, and the deal might indeed send Lagunitas's revered brands to the ends of the earth, beginning with America's southern neighbor, but the deal rankled plenty of people. "We will no longer be serving @ lagunitasbeer in any of our bars," BrewDog cofounder James Watt tweeted the day after Magee's Tumblr post. The Brewers Association in early 2016 booted Lagunitas from its stable of craft breweries because of Heineken's 50 percent ownership. In 2015, Lagunitas had ranked sixth among the nation's fifty largest craft breweries. A year later, it was still sixth—but with an asterisk that directed consumers to a note informing them Lagunitas would soon exit the list altogether. Finally, ordinary beer drinkers as well as critics registered their displeasure with Lagunitas's agreement with one of the world's largest breweries, especially on social media. Curiously, though, many could not quite put their finger on what upset them. The recipes for Lagunitas's beers had not changed (though some questioned how fresh they might end up if they're shipped too far and too wide); and the company itself, its founder included, still commanded respect for what it, and he, had achieved. Lagunitas stood for West Coast IPAs and extreme beers, oddball packaging and a laissez-faire approach to marketing. The Heineken deal had not corporatized it overnight. And, yet, even Magee acknowledged in his post-announcement exegesis that some people would have trouble digesting the news. "One beer writer commented to me that he was struggling with the 'having our cake and eating it too' quality of this relationship, but that's exactly what we achieved."

One of the reasons people reacted so strongly to the Lagunitas-Heineken deal is because it happened amid a slew of ownership changes elsewhere in the industry. These changes seemed to once and for all shred attempts to define craft beer or craft breweries, including the Brewers Association's 2014 tweak, at least in the popular mind. The already-voguish notion that it was all beer, not craft beer versus other kinds, took even stronger hold. "Magee's announcement is a spectacular Trump-like masterpiece of overstatement, and for me it was the moment craft jumped the shark into over-seriousness," wrote the critic Jeff Alworth in *All About Beer*. Drinkers did not care about the ownership change nearly as much as Magee thought they did, Alworth wrote, and would not unless the beer Lagunitas produced changed. Others begged to differ. To them, ownership mattered mightily in an industry such as craft beer. "There are two ways of operating a business—commodity or artisan," Greg Koch told a reporter the same month as the Lagunitas-Heinekan announcement. "We operate as an artisan . . . Anybody that thinks commodity can operate as an artisan is ignoring the basic facts about how businesses operate."

The debate about what made craft "craft"—and whether that mattered— not only reignited the sort of acrid public bickering that pervaded the industry in the late 1990s, right before the great shakeout, but also obscured what really was an existential threat to the decades-long movement. Brewers, and especially their partisans, seemed to be rearranging the definitional deck chairs on a Titanic that the original craft beer bully was about to swallow.

BIG BEER FEASTS

Chicago; Long Island; Los Angeles; Tempe; Seattle; San Diego | 2011–2016

In early 1988, John Hall, a former executive at a corrugated-box manufacturer, launched Goose Island Beer Company as a brewpub in the Lincoln

Park neighborhood of Chicago (it was named for an island in the Chicago River). It quickly grew in popularity, being one of the first craft breweries in America's third-largest city, and began bottling its wares in 1995. Goose Island survived the shakeout at the end of the decade, but that growing popularity soon overtook its capacity. In 2006, Goose Island sold a 42 percent stake in the company to Widmer Brothers out of Seattle—which also meant selling part of itself to Anheuser-Busch, which had long owned a nearly 40 percent stake in Widmer. As part of the deal, Anheuser-Busch took over distribution of Goose Island, beginning with Illinois. Distribution grew to twenty-four states, including Illinois, plus parts of Europe. Demand increased even more. In an attempt to further satiate this demand, Goose Island in 2011 started contracting out some production. It also simply ceased brewing certain brands, including an oatmeal stout and a Christmas ale, instead focusing on more popular ones such as its Honker's Ale and 312 Urban Wheat Ale. None of the changes quite cut it.

Finally, in February 2011, Goose Island hired an investment banker to find fresh financial backing so that the brewery could expand. "Good beer doesn't do you any good if you can't get it," Hall reasoned. With its 1988 launch date, Goose Island was positively elderly by craft beer standards, especially for the Midwest. Better to bring in moneyed muscle than to cut back further or, worse, risk collapse. Instead of a backer, though, the banker returned with a buyer: Anheuser-Busch. In a deal reflective of how complicated things had become in craft beer, the world's largest brewing company, now operating as Anheuser-Busch InBev, acquired for $16.3 million that 42 percent stake that Widmer Brothers had acquired in 2006—but not from Widmer necessarily. Instead, AB InBev bought the stake from the Craft Brewers Alliance that Widmer, Kona, and Redhook launched in 2008 (in a further twist, AB InBev already owned minority stakes in each of those breweries before their alliance). Anheuser-Busch InBev then paid $22.5 million for the remaining 58 percent of Goose Island. The buyer promised that Goose Island would remain in Chicago and that not much would change, with John Hall still in charge. Also, the deal did not include Goose Island's two Chicago brewpubs—Hall would contine to control those.

Reassurances aside, the March 2011 acquisition unleashed anxious ripples through craft beer—one wag dubbed it "the honk heard round the world" in a play off that Honker's Ale brand. Critics, fellow brewers, and consumers fretted that the deal presaged another front in Big Beer's long war with craft: namely, the wholesale purchase of a craft brewery rather than stealthy stake buys or phantom craft brands. Allegations of "selling out" abounded, and opponents of the Goose Island sale mercilessly mocked its takeover. The head of Goose Island's barrel-aging program received a text from a friend in the industry asking when the brewery was expecting its first shipment of rice, the notorious adjunct Anheuser-Busch InBev used in such macro-brands as Budweiser. A Twitter feed quickly appeared pretending to represent the inner-workings of the Goose Island public-relations operation. A sample: "Thinking of coming out with a line of sour beers. Not that we're making sour beers, just realized we can bottle bad choices. #CaChing." Earnest articles instructed consumers on other Chicago-area beers they could turn to that fit the more traditional definition of craft. For that was what most people chose to focus on: whether Goose Island still qualified as craft and what the answer meant. A relative few went a step further and wondered aloud about what it meant that the world's biggest brewer, which accounted for nearly half the beer sales in the United States, had gradually, and then suddenly, taken over a brewery that sold a relatatively paltry 127,000 barrels annually, the majority of it in its home state of Illinios. "We are market share," Sam Calagione told the critic Don "Joe Sixpack" Russell as far back as 2006, when Widmer, which Anheuser-Busch partially owned, bought a minority stake in Goose Island. "They want to buy us, then indoctrinate us."

That really seemed the case. The overall beer market was flat or in slight decline in the United States, while the craft sector was booming in the new century, with its annual sales doubling between 2007 and 2012, and its share of the national market finally tipping toward a double-digit percentage. It was an old story, then, a kind of rerun from the 1990s, when Anheuser-Busch had first really noticed the growth of what was then called microbrewing and answered with those phantom crafts such as Elk Mountain, a momumental distribution squeeze, marketing campaigns designed to undercut craft beer's credibility with the public, and stake purchases such as the ones for Widmer and Redhook. This time was different, though. For one thing, the share and the growth of craft beer were that much bigger and steeper than in the 1990s. For another, Anheuser-Busch's distributors were clamoring for the company to pick up the slack for declining sales of previously reliable brands such as Bud Light. Initially, the macro-producer answered with dozens of new alcoholic beverages, including the short-lived Spykes, tiny shot-sized bottles of flavored alcohol criticized for its supposed appeal to young people. In the end, it appeared that with the Goose Island acquisition Anheuser-Busch was adopting an if-you-can't-beat-'em-buy-'em approach. The company would simply snap up smaller competitors wholesale, ramp up their production, and widen their distribution—and count on the fact that most consumers wouldn't notice. After all, Anheuser-Busch and its nearest domestic competitor, MillerCoors, still dominated the US market, regardless of craft beer's impressive growth. The Goose Island purchase, and others to come in the new decade, were more of a downpayment on what looked like the future of beer in America.

And the way Anheuser-Busch InBev ran Goose Island post-purchase illustrated how the brewing industry might operate in that future. Despite the reassurances of quasi-independence following the early 2011 takeover, Goose Island's new parent quickly moved to solidify its control. By the end of 2012, John Hall was out as president. Tony Bowker, Goose Island's chief operating officer under the old regime, also exited the company. Both joined a new entity called the Anheuser-Busch Craft Advisory Board. Hall's replacement as head of Goose Island was a thirty-year AB veteran best-known for helping popularize Shock Top, a phantom craft line the macro-producer rolled out during the previous decade. Anheuser-Busch InBev also by the end of 2012 outsourced the brewing of Goose Island's best-selling brands, including Honker's Ale and 312 Urban Wheat, to plants in New York and Colorado. The company, too, announced that Goose Island would soon be available in all fifty states, thanks to the increase in production. Plus, the brewery would launch its first advertising campaign ever in 2013, complete with digital videos, billboads, and print ads in publications as varied as *Rolling Stone* and *All About Beer*. Finally, in February 2016, AB InBev bought the original Goose Island brewpub in Chicago's Lincoln Park, which had remained independent following the 2011 deal (Hall closed the other brewpub, in the Wrigleyville neighborhood, in December 2015). These changes quickly, and predictably, translated into massive sales bumps for Goose Island. Sales of Goose Island brands increased 62 percent from late 2012 through late 2013, the first year they were available nationally. That figure did not account for draft and bottle sales at restaurants and bars, suggesting the increase was even steeper than it appeared.

Anheuser-Busch InBev and other Big Beer conglomerates, including longtime archrival MillerCoors, sought quickly to duplicate the Goose Island arc. Suddenly, the acquisitions were coming at their most dizzying pace since the 1990s, amid an overall mergers and acquisitions climate that was positively scorching by 2015, when more than $3.8 trillion in M-and-A deals closed worldwide. In 2014, Anheuser-Busch InBev acquired the Blue Point Brewing Co., the oldest craft brewery on Long Island, and 10 Barrel Brewing Co., a Bend, Oregon, operation dating from 2006. Then, in 2015, Anheuser-Busch InBev snapped up control of Golden Road Brewing, the largest craft brewery in Los Angeles; Tempe, Arizona-based Four Peaks Brewing Co., the biggest one in Arizona; Breckenridge Brewery, a twenty-five-year-old craft brewery in the Colorado Rockies; and the Elysian Brewing Co., a Seattle brewery that also operated multiple pubs in that city. Also in 2015, MillerCoors bought a majority stake in the Saint Archer Brewery, a San Diego outfit barely two years old. Then there was the Lagunitas-Heineken deal and a similar partnership for the United States between the twenty-year-old Santa Barbara County, California, brewery Firestone Walker and Belgian giant Duvel Moortgat. (The family-run Duvel Moortgat had long owned upstate New York's Ommegang Brewery, and, in October 2013, bought the Boulevard Brewing Co., Missouri's oldest craft brewery.)

Such acquisitions continued into 2016—AB InBev alone would own eight craft breweries before the middle of the year—as did smaller deals for minority stakes in craft breweries. Most of these moves involved relatively small amounts of money, at least for Big Beer. Anheuser-Busch InBev purchased Blue Point for $24 million, for instance, and MillerCoors' takeover of Saint Archer was estimated to have valued the craft brewery at $35 million. Very rarely did a bigger buyer spend in the nine figures for a craft concern—media reports estimated Lagunitas's valuation for the fifty-fifty Heineken partnership at $1 billion, suggesting a $500 million deal. Then a deal sealed just before Thanksgiving of 2015 raised the stakes considerably.

BILLION-DOLLAR WORRIES
San Diego | 2015–2016

Jack White started homebrewing while a student at UCLA. Finding it difficult to locate the proper supplies, he later launched a homebrewing store in San Diego's Morena neighborhood in 1992. Four years after that, he founded a brewery he called Ballast Point, after a local harbor, out of the shop's back room. Peter A'hearn, White's UCLA roommate who had studied brewing at the University of California–Davis, acted as brewmaster. Like so many other freshly minted craft breweries that launched in the 1990s, Ballast Point scaled quickly upward, surviving the great shakeout and expanding its capacity repeatedly. By mid-2014, Ballast Point had four breweries in Southern

California and was producing around three hundred thousand barrels of beer annually (as well as a line of spirits through a craft distillery started in 2008). It sold just under three hundred thousand barrels annually in thirty states and ten countries. Its grapefruit-infused IPA was a particularly popular and influential offering, spawning several imitators. Yet, White and Ballast Point hit the same fiduciary wall as other craft breweries. Expansion was capital intensive and the brewery needed more capital.

Enter Constellation Brands, a family-run, upstate New York–based alcoholic-beverages concern quite familiar with bullish acquisitions. In 2013, it spent $5.3 billion acquiring Mexican brands Corona, Modelo, and Pacifico from Anheuser-Busch InBev. That deal instantly made Constellation the nation's third-biggest beer company, behind AB InBev and MillerCoors. It was already one of the three largest wine companies due to a string of sometimes blockbuster deals. Nearly ten years before the AB InBev trade, Constellation acquired the Robert Mondavi Winery, the most influential post–World War II wine-making company in the United States, for $1.3 billion. That takeover had been Constellation's fifteenth acquisition since 1991. Most of them had been wineries, but the Constellation umbrella also came to cover spirits such as Black Velvet Canadian whisky and Svedka vodka. It was the Anheuser-Busch InBev deal in 2013 that whetted Constellation's appetite for beer—craft beer in particular. Corona and Modelo were as low as Constellation was prepared to go in its beer business. The biggest step up from imports in the United States was into the fast-growing craft realm.

It took that step with Ballast Point. In mid-November 2015, Constellation announced it had acquired Ballast Point Brewing & Spirits Company for $1 billion. It was the biggest sale yet of an American craft brewery. "We have no interest in anything below the high end of beer, so this is a particularly good opportunity," Constellation CEO Robert Sands, who had led the company's acquisition tear since the 1990s, told a reporter after the deal. "Ballast Point is so premium that it actually enhances our premium position in beer even above where it is."

Whether it enhanced Ballast Point's position in the American craft beer movement was another matter. Soon after the November 2015 deal, in what was quickly becoming a familiar pattern following such acquisitions, Constellation expanded its new brewery's distribution to all fifty states from thirty, and began laying the groundwork for an East Coast brewery. It picked a location just north of Roanoke, Virginia, in May 2016. A couple of months after that, White and other top executives at Ballast Point exited the company, with Constellation replacing them with its own people. The reaction to Ballast

Point's sale as well as to the expansion and the management changes appeared more muted than the reaction to Anheuser-Busch InBev's takeovers since 2011, or to Lagunitas's partnership with Heineken. Perhaps it was that Constellation was not nearly the bogeyman that AB InBev was to so many craft beer consumers or that Ballast Point was not quite the cultish favorite that Lagunitas was—it certainly lacked its fellow California brewery's distribution reach at the time of Constellation's takeover. However muted the reaction, the Ballast Point–Constellation deal was inescapably noteworthy: Craft beer in America had ascended into the ranks of ten-figure mergers and acquisitions, the sort of territory in the alcoholic-beverages market once reserved for much more ubiquitous wines and spirits (witness Tokyo-based Suntory Holdings' $16 billion takeover in January 2014 of Beam Inc., maker of such spirits as the bourbons Jim Beam and Maker's Mark).

There seemed no turning back from a business context. The biggest craft breweries—those producing at least a few hundred thousand barrels annually—had become big business, in the context of their own times and the decades-long arc of American craft beer. When Bloomberg News minted Boston Beer's Jim Koch as a billionaire in September 2013, based on the sixty-four-year-old's net worth, it produced little surprise. "What he has done is amazing," David Geary, whose D. L. Geary Brewing Company in Portland was now the oldest craft brewery east of the Appalachian Mountains, told the news service. "He's very focused, a brilliant marketer, and he sort of taught us all how to sell beer." Nor was anyone visibly shocked when Sierra Nevada's Ken Grossman and Yuengling's Dick Yuengling joined the billionaires club two years later—except perhaps the initiates themselves. "Even though we are a big small brewery," Grossman told a reporter, "we are still just half a percent of the U.S. beer industry."

That a brewery as ubiquitous and valuable as Sierra Nevada still had immense room to grow sharply illuminated the potential of craft beer, the very potential that saw bigger players such as Anheuser-Busch InBev, MillerCoors, and Constellation Brands pouring in during the 2010s. (Constellation had apparently made an unsuccessful play for Lagunitas, too.) "Where else do you see 17 percent growth in a consumer product?" a mergers-and-acquisitions analyst asked rhetorically at the time. "And this 17 percent is not an anomaly. This has been going on for almost ten years. It's got a growth profile that is very rare."

This very rare growth profile made craft beer attractive to private equity firms as well—or, more attractive, as the case was. Private equity firms, including venture capitalists, wealth managers, and angel investors, had been buying huge, if not controlling, stakes in craft breweries since at least the early 1980s, when they rescued the Boulder Brewing Company and powered the expansion of the New Amsterdam brand in New York City. Private equity's pace of craft beer stake purchases accelerated in the 2010s, however, with numerous well-known breweries finding financial backing in these flush firms and individuals. Colorado's Oskar Blues, the first craft brewery to can its beer in-house with its Dale's Pale Ale; Dogfish Head, the Delaware-based pioneer of extreme beer; Victory Brewing Company, the Pennsylvania affair launched out of an old Pepperidge Farm cracker factory; SweetWater Brewing Company, a prominent brewery based in Atlanta; the Schirf Brewing Company, maker of the Wasatch beer line and Utah's oldest craft brewery; upstate New York's Southern Tier, which dated from 1996; and the Long Trail Brewing Company, one of dozens of craft breweries in tiny Vermont—these were some of the companies throwing their hand in with private equity in the new decade.

Anxiety often accompanied the partnerships. "Never in my wildest dreams did I think I was going to do business with a private equity firm," Dale Katechis explained in early 2016, a year after Fireman Capital, a private equity firm based in the Boston suburb of Waltham, bought a majority interest in his Oskar Blues. "I thought they were guys that had horns and came in and raped your business and ran away with all your money." Like with other craft brewers that had taken the private-equity plunge, capital needs for expansion and worries about the future forced Katechis's hand. These worries included a lack of succession plans. Those craft brewers who had started in the 1980s and 1990s were a graying bunch now, not all of them with heirs willing to step in or employees able to take over; nor did they wish to go public or to sell their life's work, especially to a Big Beer conglomerate. Private equity provided a kind of third financial way between burning out and selling out (though Lagunitas's Tony Magee would likely argue a fifty-fifty split was just as assuaging). And, as often as the deals spurred anxiety, they turned out to be fairly benign. The single, most noticeable change for consumers may have been recipe tweaks—fewer hops per batch, powdered flavoring instead of actual fruit—but these might prove imperceptible to most palates.

For most, especially newer consumers, the products marched merrily onward, tasting as they always had. Besides, unlike with most Big Beer takeovers, the principals at the craft breweries, often the company's founders, remained intimately involved in its management and planning. In the cases of minority private-equity purchases, the brewers remained in near-complete control. Still, they reaped the benefits of the capital infusions, expanding facilities and increasing production. Wider distribution often followed, pushing brands into territories they would never have otherwise reached—for Oskar Blues it meant distribution to every state (Montana was the last) and into eight more countries, including Japan and New Zealand. And, given that most private equity players did not stop at one craft acquisition, breweries were often able to tap into each other's resources, never mind the geographic distances. Victory and Southern Tier, which the same Manhattan-based private equity fund backed, combined distribution, sales, and marketing efforts. Fireman, which former Reebok CEO Paul Fireman ran with his son Dan Fireman, created a holding company that it centered on Oskar Blues and began acquiring controlling stakes in other craft breweries, most notably Cigar City, a Tampa, Florida, outfit dating from 2009 that Anheuser-Busch InBev toyed with going after until the private equity firm stepped in. The newly constituted Oskar Blues Holding Company produced 262,000 barrels in 2015, well ahead of the 149,000 Oskar Blues produced in 2014, the first full year after the deal with Fireman, with the total sure to rise due to the Cigar City takeover.

There was a danger in these deals, though, one somewhat hidden from the public at large. Private equity was an opaque affair, that adjective in the name rendering most deal terms unknown to the public, and the entities set up to execute them often tediously labyrinthine—investors underwriting funds that controlled holding companies that in turn owned breweries, which could also have other, outside investors. Never mind that it was a far, far cry from craft beer's earliest days, when one or two, maybe three, owners would launch a small, isolated concern as a corporation. The private equity arrangements seemed far removed from a relatively simple Anheuser-Busch InBev takeover. That might make it difficult for consumers to hate a private equity fund or investor, one they had likely never heard nor read of, like they could hate AB InBev, et al., which proved the perfect villain time and again. Not so for people in the industry, some of whom saw the private equity takeovers, especially those that involved controlling stakes, as essentially the same as selling out to Big Beer—or worse. Jim Koch was not necessarily a vocal critic of these deals, but the Harvard Business–trained Boston Beer chairman knew how the murkier world of private equity operated. In March 2016, he reminded a forum of Pennsylvania brewers that a fund typically ended in a "liquidity event" after a finite period, usually no more than a decade, if that. Such a liquidity event might be a sale or an initial public offering—some transaction to close out the fund and disburse its assets, meaning that these new stakeholders in craft beer had no intention of holding for the long haul. They wanted to—had to, in some cases—cash out in the nearer-term. Such events might doom breweries in a liquidated fund, should no buyer or public offering emerge. No one knew for sure, and decisions were years off anyway in 2015 and 2016.

This was the more cerebral take on the threat of these private equity deals. Others in the industry went with their gut. In a February 2016 op-ed for the *San Diego Union-Tribune*, Greg Koch of Stone Brewing mocked "the requisite 'We're Not Changing Anything' press release" that breweries often put out following an acquisition by a larger company. Koch, who now sported a heavy, dark beard and long hair, had become a particularly trenchant critic of Big Beer–craft beer deals, a kind of guru down from the mountaintop to remind everyone of the ethos of the old days. Whereas some pioneers might be silent on the deals, or others supportive, especially if their breweries were the ones Big Beer was buying, Koch was not silent and not supportive. Though that did not stop him from throwing in his own brewery's lot with private equity, at least partially. In early May 2016, Koch announced the formation of a new company with the not-so-subtle name True Craft. Nearly $90 million of its initial $100 million in financing came from a San Francisco–based private equity firm called VMG Partners, with Stone putting up about $10 million dollars of the rest. Curiously enough, the brewery did not disclose VMG Partners as the primary investor in True Craft in the original spring 2016 news—that came later through federal securities filings. Whatever the source of the money, the essence of True Craft was clear and of the time. It would, Koch explained, "give craft brewers another option than selling a majority interest to private equity or selling out to Big Beer," Koch explained. To him, such actions were a kind of spiritual suicide. "Three local SoCal brewers recently sold controlling interests of their companies," he wrote in the *Union-Tribune*, citing Ballast Point, Golden Road, and Saint Archer.

> In purchasing small, "local" brands, Big Beer is able to capitalize on the purchased brand's reputation, while many consumers are too distracted to pay attention or care. . . . It's going to be weird and sad to know that former craft brewers are now being used as a tool to throw elbows at remaining craft bewers. My good friend Sam Calagione of Dogfish Head reflected on this in a recent article: "They're using these once-craft brands as pawns in their game to knock the true indie breweries off the board." On the surface these brands may look the same, but the soul behind the eyes is . . . different. (*last elipses Koch's*)

The opinions of Koch and Calagione were not extreme. While it was complete nonsense that such takeovers and stake acquisitions were a new thing in American craft beer—as media reports often suggested—there was an element of existential threat in their pace. It went beyond the potential liquidation of a fund or the fickleness of a larger company in maintaining quality or staff. No, the gravest and most immediate threat came from that old albatross that had long saddled so many craft brewers: distribution. At the same time as it was collecting craft breweries like so many nickels and dimes, Anheuser-Busch InBev was also buying up distributorships, adding to its already sizable stable of avenues for getting beers from the production line to the grocery store shelf or bar tap. In the span of a few months in mid-2015, AB InBev bought five distributors in three states. The world's biggest brewer also dusted off its 100 percent share of mind policy launched in the 1990s to pressure distributors, even independent ones, to stop carrying craft brands in favor of AB InBev beers.

The twin activities spurred the US Justice Department to launch an antitrust probe in the fall of 2015. Fortunately for craft beer, the department had some particularly strong leverage at just that moment: AB InBev's proposed takeover of SABMiller, the London-based parent company of, among other breweries, MillerCoors, the number-two brewery in the United States. The more than $100 billion takeover would give AB InBev control of around 70 percent of the domestic beer market (in some areas, that share might swell to 90 percent, strengthening its distribution muscle that much more). "It will have even more power to strong-arm independent distributors to carry rival brands and exert pressure on retailers to cut back on, or even refuse to carry, competitive brands," Bob Pease, the Brewers Association's president and chief executive, wrote in a *New York Times* op-ed in early June 2016.

In the end, the Justice Department did not abide. In late July 2016, it approved the takeover—under certain conditions. AB InBev would have to sell SABMiller's 58 percent stake in MillerCoors, cease incentivizing independent distributors to move only its beers, and allow antitrust regulators to review any future acquisitions of distributorships and craft breweries. That last caveat highlighted the very real threat an even pared-down Anheuser-Busch InBev posed to craft beer (the tweaked SABMiller deal left it with about 50 percent of the American market). Normally, many of the distributorship and craft brewery deals would be so small as to not warrant federal examination. Regulators seemed to realize, though, that such deals, bit by bit, could stifle that much more competition in a still heavily consolidated domestic beer market.

For all its spectacular growth during the past half-century, American craft beer could still quiver at the whim of much larger players, whose distribution clout in particular made them all but unassailable, Justice Department or not.

"In most markets, brewers have two choices, a so-called Blue and Silver distributor, who sells MillerCoors brands, or a Red distributor, who sells Anheuser-Busch brands," Brooklyn Brewery's Steve Hindy wrote in an op-ed for CNN.com in December 2012, when AB InBev was about to acquire the Mexican brands it would sell the following year to Constellation. "Craft brewers constantly struggle to get the attention of these distributors." The possibility was clear, then, as the acquisitions continued: without a regulatory firewall, there could come a time very soon when one Big Beer company's myriad craft brands dominated grocery store shelves and bar tap runs in locales throughout the land—with the consumer none the wiser.

"THE FUTURE WILL NOT BE LIKE THE PAST"
Nationwide | 2015–2016

The Anheuser-Busch InBev commercial commenced with scenes of one of its breweries at work, including an anonymous pair of hands crinkling hops. The words "Budweiser Proudly a Macro Beer" popped onto the screen over the scenes, which also went on to include the famed Clydesdale horses and friends enjoying the brewery's finished product. Then came the commercial's unmistakable angle with the words, "It's Not Brewed to Be Fussed Over." The ad superimposed those last two words over an earnest-looking man with a handlebar mustache and glasses dipping his nose over the rim of a goblet of dark beer. In case any viewers missed the point, another shot of tweedy men analyzing their obvious craft beers in what looked like a trendy urban bar followed further shots of casual enjoyment of an ice-cold Bud, as did the words, "It's Brewed for Drinking, Not for Dissecting." On and on it went for a full minute: "Let Them Sip Their Pumpkin Peach Ale: We'll Be Brewing Us Some Golden Suds."

The commercial aired during what turned out to be the single most watched television show in American history to that point: Super Bowl XLIX between the New England Patriots and the Seattle Seahawks on February 1,

2015. More than 114 million people tuned in for the game, and presumably many of that number saw the commercial, too—or at least saw it later, if thousands of YouTube replays are any evidence. It was clearly designed to mock, as one AB InBev executive put it, "the overwrought pretentiousness that exists in some small corners of the beer landscape that is around beer snobbery." It worked. "The whole ad was uncalled for," Larry Bell of Bell's told the *Chicago Tribune*. His brewery went so far as to release forty-eight bottles of what it called Pumpkin Peach Ale, made with peach puree and a pumpkin Bell gew on the roof of his Chicago home. "It's a fuck you to Anheuser-Busch because they sent us a fuck you," the owner of the Midwest's oldest craft brewery told the *Tribune*. Even fellow Big Beer titan MillerCoors let AB InBev have it, lecturing its archrival in a tweet: "We believe each and every style of beer is worth fussing over."

Also, it seemed to some that AB InBev had singled out for lampoonery millennials, that generation of approximately seventy-five million Americans born after 1980 and now coming into their financial own. "This is a some-what odd approach to winning over young drinkers, which, presumably, is AB-InBev's goal," one writer noted. Many industry observers, too, pounced on the fact that one of AB InBev's recent craft acquisitions, Seattle's Elysian Brewing, had recently produced at least two pumpkin-infused beers. "I find it kind of incredible that ABI would be so tone-deaf as to pretty directly (even if unwittingly) call out one of the breweries they have recently acquired, even as the brewery is dealing with the anger of the beer community in reaction to the sale," Dick Cantwell, a founder of Elysian who opposed the craft brewery's sale, wrote amid the fallout. "It's made a difficult situation even more pain-ful." Finally, the whole thing smacked of desperation. Here was the world's largest brewery spending $9 million—the cost of a sixty-second Super Bowl commercial—to tell the world that it did not feel threatened by craft beer. Yet Anheuser-Busch InBev likely got the last laugh. Reaching more than one-third of the American populace all at once, the Super Bowl ad was the single, biggest burst of press American craft beer had yet gotten. It was just that, to the tens of millions who did not follow the industry that closely, it was bad press, a sign of little love lost between craft beer and its longtime Moriarty.

Not that craft beer in the 2010s needed any help with unfavorable pub-licity. There were the wider interrelated controversies regarding the defini-tion of craft beer (and brewing) and whether some companies still fit that definition. And then there were multiple smaller controversies that seemed big to those involved and that, taken together, fostered a kind of tinny static not endured in two decades. Yuengling's freshly minted craft status and continued distribution expansion rankled smaller competitors. The company's rollout—it spilled into six thousand Massachusetts bars, resturants, and stores pretty much all at once in late 2014, for instance—meant other brands got bumped. In perhaps the most ironic instance, a Yuengling tap replaced one for a beer called Slumbrew Porter Square Porter, from the Somerville Brewing Company in the Boston suburb—at a bar in Somerville's Porter Square. Also in Massachusetts in late 2014, Dann Paquette, the owner of a Boston-area craft brewing company, accused two bars over Twitter of essentially accepting bribes in exchange for carrying beers from certain breweries. The accusations of pay-to-play—or, more accurately perhaps, pay-to-pour—rended the normally collegial New England craft beer scene and led to a state investigation. That investigation, in turn, led to an approximately $2.5 million fine against the largest craft beer distributor in Massachusetts.

On the other side of the continent and a couple of months later, Tony Magee's Lagunitas sued Ken Grossman's Sierra Nevada over supposed copyright infringement. At issue was a new Sierra Nevada release called Hop Hunter IPA, the packaging for which Lagunitas contended in federal court looked strikingly similar to the packaging for its own flagship IPA, which had done so much to not only establish Magee's brewery but the very IPA style in the United States. After a storm of criticism, including over social media, Magee announced a day after his company had filed it that he was dropping the lawsuit. "I went home feeling like I had been beaten up, and all I did was stare at the screen," Magee told a San Francisco publication. The Lagunitas–Sierra Nevada dust-up highlighted similar disputes in an American craft beer movement with more beer names, and explanations for them, than ever. Simply put, the industry appeared to be running out of words and images to describe what it was producing. This led to infighting over the use of certain puns related to common terms such as "hops" and to the names of beers themselves. One of the more noteworthy instances again involved Lagunitas. Atlanta's SweetWater, whose flagship was an extra pale ale called "420" (a common code phrase for smoking marijuana), sent a cease-and-desist letter to Magee's outfit, which had for years used "420" in its beer descriptions. Lagunitas dropped the term—SweetWater owned the commercial trademark for 420.

Craft brewers found grounds for conflict even on an issue that seemed tailored for unity: further excise tax breaks from the federal government. The original per-barrel excise tax cut in 1976 had helped spur craft beer's tremendous growth. Its preservation in 1991 was instrumental in sustaining that growth—a lower tax bill meant more money for equipment, ingredients, space, etc. In 2013, the Brewers Association and its congressional allies started pushing another tax cut. It would halve the amount, to $3.50, that breweries paid on its first sixty thousand barrels annually and reduce by $2.00 a barrel the tax on all subsequent barrels up to two million. Each barrel above two million would be taxed at the regular rate of $18.00. And only breweries producing fewer than six million barrels annually would qualify for the tax breaks. This last facet of the proposal is what irked some craft brewers (and observers outside the industry). It was one thing to support a cut for the industry's legion of smaller breweries—most operations easily fell below that annual sixty-thousand-barrel cutoff—but it was another to help breweries such as Boston Beer, Yuengling, and Sierra Nevada that produced millions of barrels a year and whose principal owners were billionaires on paper. That these already-flush companies would reap most of the benefits of the proposed tax break thoroughly annoyed certain of their colleagues. Besides, as many inside and outside of the industry noted at the time, craft beer was growing comfortably in the new decade. Did it really need a tax cut to spur growth? In the end, and due in part to significant pressure from Big Beer's lobbying for its own tax reduction, the Brewers Association in mid-2015 swung behind revised legislation that reserved most of the benefits for breweries making no more than two million barrels annually, rather than six.

This sparring between larger and smaller operations also manifested itself in marketshare. In October 2016, Stone Brewing, one of the biggest craft breweries, announced it was laying off about 5 percent of its approximately eleven hundred employees. The company explained in a statement that competition from Big Beer's newly acquired craft breweries and "the further proliferation of small, hyper-local breweries" forced its hand in the layoffs. That latter reason—the launch of so many smaller breweries—underlined a bitterly ironic trend in the craft beer movement circa 2016. Localness had been one of the defining features of the movement early on—beer as a local product from a local company for largely local consumers; a return to the old days of American brewering in general, before the post–World War II rise of the Big Beer conglomerates. Now, though, these thousands of smaller breweries with their local fanbases were eating into the bottom lines of bigger craft beer pioneers who had leaned in part on localness to grow during their own early days. What's more, it wasn't just sales these upstarts were claiming, it was reputation, too. The verdict from younger consumers could be particularly unforgiving. Few people alive had done more to popularize American craft beer than Jim Koch. Yet a January 2015 *Boston Magazine* cover story, shared widely on social media, explained that "local beer geeks—the industry's connoisseurs—think [Koch's] lost his edge." Their main rationale? Like with other larger craft breweries, the beer was just . . . too familiar. The co-owner of a Boston beer bar pronounced the entire Sam Adams line "mediocre," in fact, mostly because he saw it as so "middle-of-the-road" compared with what else was now out there.

Finally, some familiar arguments found their ways back into the American craft beer movement. Occassionally, owners of physical breweries would publicly criticize contract brewers or those, such as Boston Beer, that initially built themselves up through contract brewing before launching their own facilities. And numerous brewers mounted vigorous assaults against that stylistic hegemon, the India pale ale and its interations, which remained the top-selling craft beer style in the United States, a status that Anheuser-Busch InBev's takeover of IPA producers such as Goose Island only enhanced. Hence the rise of esoteric styles such as gose and the session beer fad that, though faded a bit, continued into the latter half of the 2010s.

The disputes, the Big Beer and private equity takeovers, the definitional challenges, the reactions and counterreactions to major trends—it all fomented a general sense of an American craft beer movement in flux, as did a spate of transitions in the upper ranks of breweries and organizations beginning in 2014. Daniel Bradford sold *All About Beer* and its World Beer Festivals to Chris Rice, a business-side executive at the magazine who became its president and publisher. Charlie Papazian stepped down as president of the Brewers Association he had been so instrumental in building up, with Bob Pease, its chief operating officer, succeeding him. New Belgium's Kim Jordan stepped down as CEO to become executive chair of the brewery's board of directors. Greg Koch made a similar move at Stone, transitioning from his day-to-day role to fill a newly minted executive chairman position. Stone's longtime brewmaster, Mitch Steele, also left the company to found his own concern. Steve Dresler, Sierra Nevada's brewmaster since the early 1980s, also announced his exit due to retirement in 2017. Rich Doyle, a founder of the Mass. Bay Brewing Company (better known as Harpoon) and its chief executive for years, stepped down as part of a stake sale to the company's employees. Doyle in early 2015 launched a private equity fund to invest in craft brewers wishing to avoid takeovers by entities not as steeped in the business as him. The fund's first acquisition was Louisiana's Abita Brewing Co., now the South's oldest craft brewery.

As much as change seemed the only constant, though, there was a fair sense of déjà vu in the controversies and the complaints, and in the change itself. The American craft beer movement since Fritz Maytag's rescue of

Anchor Brewing in 1965 had seen many exits, a lot of them abrupt, as well as shakeouts, one of them huge. It had felt the financial hammer of a disgruntled Big Beer sector and the avaricious indifference of financial markets. The tax debate was a rerun of a rerun. Prodigious growth was nothing new, nor were struggles with distribution, government red tape, or defining just what the whole thing was supposed to be. And, while many analysts and breweries sought to credit or blame craft beer's explosive growth for the trends and challenges in the second decade of the twenty-first century, there might have been much simpler explanations. The global market for mergers and acquisitions was hotter than at any time in modern business history. Craft beer was but one of many industries that the bullish atmosphere and access to cheap financing affected. This suggested that the pace of Big Beer and private equity acquisitions might ebb. What then? The same question could be asked of the transitions underway at breweries, a trend less to do with the industry's growth than with simple actuarial tables—people aged, moved on. Jim Koch, when asked in late 2014 about his strategy for continuing to run the Boston Beer Co., the still-trim sixty-five-year-old replied, "To not die." Whatever the reasons, the repeats and the changes were being enacted—and reenacted—on a much grander scale than ever before. It was a scale that ensured that more people than at any previous time were paying attention and that, finally, the nation's palate might tip decisively away from watery bastardizations of pilsners to the kaleidoscope of styles American craft beer did so much to promote.

In that September 2015 Tumblr post explaining the Lagunitas-Heineken deal, Tony Magee wrote:

> Beer is an old biz in the U.S. and it used to be very orderly. Craft disrupted that and now the old order wants to find a way back to the past. It won't work, but it's going to try.

Magee was right. Craft beer had upended decades-old ways of doing things in the beer industry and marketplace, and, in doing that, helped mightily to chart a mesmerizing new direction in food and drink. What came next was anyone's guess—more of the same, slightly different; something entirely new; a mixture of both. Maybe an America where IPA outsold light lagers? The American craft beer movement had long ago pushed into uncharted territory and was now further from the shore than ever, the end nowhere in sight, the start now slightly fuzzy, and only one thing certain. As Magee headlined his explanation of his own seismic shift, "The future will not be like the past."

EPILOGUE

Most of the characters in this book continue, as of 2016, in the roles where last we encountered them. Some, like Tony Magee at Lagunitas, have seen major changes.

Don Barkley

Don Barkley left the Mendocino Brewing Company after twenty-five years to become the master brewer at the new Napa Smith Brewery, which opened in Napa, California, in 2008.

Larry Bell

The founder of what's now the oldest craft brewery in the Midwest named his daughter, Karen Bell, as chief executive in February 2017. Larry Bell remains as president of Bell's Brewery, which commenced a two-hundred-thousand-square-foot expansion in 2015.

Uli Bennewitz

Uli Bennewitz's Weeping Radish Farm Brewery now unfolds over twenty-four acres near Grandy on the Outer Banks of North Carolina. It is a veritable locavore paradise, with a master butcher, fourteen acres for raising produce and chickens, the brewery, and a "Goodness Grows in North Carolina" section in its retail store. For Christmas 2011, Weeping Radish produced the first-ever commercial beer made entirely from North Carolina–grown ingredients.

Byron Burch

The homebrewing instructor, shop owner, and author died in August 2015 at age seventy-five.

Sam Calagione

After initially scaling back distribution at the end of last decade, Sam Calagione's Delaware-based DogFish Head now reaches thirty states and the District of Columbia.

Jeremy Cowan

Jeremy Cowan remains the CEO of Shmaltz Brewing, which opened a physical brewery in the Albany suburb of Clifton Park in early 2013. To mark the occasion, the brewery produced a black IPA called "Death of a Contract Brewer."

Fred Eckhardt

The homebrewing author and pioneering beer critic died in August 2015 at age eighty-nine.

David Geary

In early 2017, Geary sold what is now the oldest craft brewery east of the Appalachian Mountains to a Maine businessman named Alan Lapoint. The Geary family cited increased competition from other craft breweries as a reason for the sale of the Portland operation.

Bert Grant

Bert Grant died in July 2001 at age seventy-three, six years after selling control of his brewpub. Yakima Brewing and Malting changed ownership one more time before finally closing in late 2005.

Ken Grossman

Grossman's Sierra Nevada launched its East Coast brewery, in the western North Carolina town of Mills River, in early 2014. Grosssman remains chairman of the company.

John Hickenlooper

The brewpub pioneer was re-elected Colorado governor in 2014.

Steve Hindy

Hindy stepped down as president of Brooklyn Brewery in late 2014. He remains its chairman. Fellow founder Tom Potter retired as CEO in 2004. In late 2016, Kirin, Japan's second-largest brewery, bought an approximately 25 percent stake in Brooklyn for an undisclosed sum.

Kim Jordan

New Belgium released the first bottles brewed at its East Coast brewery, in Asheville, North Carolina, in spring 2016. Jordan remains executive chair of the company's board of directors.

Jim Koch

Koch stepped down as CEO of Boston Beer in 2001 but remains chairman and controlling shareholder. Koch's father, Charles, who had served on the brewery's board, died in June 2011 at age eighty-eight.

InBev's 2008 takeover of Anheuser-Busch left Boston Beer for a time as the largest independently owned American brewery.* Asked during a spring 2012 interview, in a tasting room at the Boston Beer brewery in Jamaica Plain, if he harbored any ill will toward August Busch and his company for the attempts to put him out of business, the normally loquacious Koch turned quiet. Noise from a raucous brewery tour seeped through the tasting-room door. No, he didn't. Why should he? "I'm still here," Koch answered slowly, a wry smile emerging. "And he's . . ."—he dragged out the next words—"all gone."

Geoff Larson

In May 2016 Larson stepped down as CEO of the Alaskan Brewing Company he and wife Marcy founded thirty years before. He remains its chairman.

Michael Lewis

Michael Lewis became professor emeritus at the University of California at Davis in 1995 and retired from heading its brewing curriculum. In 2008, the university, using monies donated by the brewing industry, created an endowed fund in his honor.

Wendy Littlefield

Wendy Littlefield and her husband, Don Feinberg, sold the portfolio of their Vanberg & DeWulf import company in March 2014 to Total Beverage Solution for an undisclosed sum. The couple had sold the Ommegang brewery to Duvel Moortgat in 2003.

---

* It ceded the title in 2011 to D. G. Yuengling & Son.

Vijay Mallya

In April 2016, the government of India issued an arrest warrant for Vijay Mallya for debt tied to the collapse of his Kingfisher Airlines. Mallya at the time was living primarily in a grand mansion he had built in Sausalito, California. The majority owner of Mendocino Brewing in the San Francisco Bay Area and Olde Saratoga Brewing Company in upstate New York has yet to make the direct assault on Big Beer that he talked about that summer day in 1997 on his yacht off the shores of Manhattan.

F. X. Matt II

F. X. Matt II died in January 2001 at age sixty-seven. He had stepped down as brewery president in 1989 and was succeeded by his brother Nick, who is now the chairman and CEO. F.X.'s son Fred is the brewery's president and COO.

Jack McAuliffe

A couple of days before the Fourth of July 2012, Jack McAuliffe flew from Arkansas, where he was living, to Boston to participate in a ceremonial brewing of New Albion Ale through Jim Koch's Boston Beer. Koch first broached the idea during that breakfast at the 2011 Great American Beer Festival in Denver, and New Albion Ale debuted at the 2012 GABF. The brand, which used Cascade hops, hit shelves nationwide in January 2013, with all profits going to McAuliffe.

He reportedly made $200,000 initially, and Koch legally licensed the trademark to McAuliffe following Boston Beer's six-thousand-barrel run—which was more than New Albion produced in its entire lifetime. McAuliffe then turned the license over to his daughter, Renee DeLuca, who continues to brew the brand under contract through the Platform Beer Company in Cleveland.

Garrett Oliver

Garrett Oliver remains the brewmaster and a partner at Brooklyn Brewery. Oliver was the editor of the encyclopedic *Oxford Companion to Beer*, published in September 2011.

Joseph Owades

Joseph Owades, the inventor of modern light beer and adviser to several craft breweries, died in December 2005 at age eighty-six. Jim

Koch delivered the eulogy at his funeral, which Fritz Maytag and Pete Slosberg also attended.

Matthew Reich

After working for a couple of years with F. X. Matt as president of the division that handled the New Amsterdam brand, Matthew Reich left craft beer altogether in the early 1990s. He continued to work in the food business, including as an executive at New York charity City Harvest and at Tom Cat Bakery, an artisan bakery also in New York. He is now an adviser and an investor to nonprofit food concerns.

Greg Schirf

The founder of Utah's oldest craft brewery retired in April 2015 from its parent company, Utah Brewers Cooperative, which Shirf formed with fellow Beehive State operation Squatters in 2000. Schirf's retirement came three years after Fireman Capital Partners, the private equity firm based in the Boston area, bought a major stake in the cooperative.

Pete Slosberg

Pete Slosberg still lectures regularly about beer, including overseas, and judges competitions. Gambrinus discontinued the Pete's brands in March 2011 due to "rapidly declining sales volumes."

ACKNOWLEDGMENTS

I**t was a pleasure to update** this book. First and foremost, I would like to thank Chicago Review Press and my longtime editor, Yuval Taylor, for the opportunity to do so. The Chicago crew were instrumental in seeing this to completion, in particular project editor Michelle Williams, as was my agent, Adam Chromy.

I would also like to thank the many people in the American craft beer movement who have given me their time and expertise over the past several years, including recently. As with the first edition of *The Audacity of Hops*, I approached this book as a journalist uncovering a story, and the following from the movement were the most important in helping me do so: Tony Magee and the entire crew at Lagunitas, especially Ron Lindenbusch; Jeremy Cowan; Pete Slosberg; Mark Bronder; Jim Koch and the team at Boston Beer; Jack McAuliffe; Suzy Stern Denison; Keith Greggor and the wonderful people at Anchor, especially Mark Carpenter, Bob Brewer, and Dave Burkhart; Ken Grossman and the entire crew at Sierra Nevada; Rhonda Kallman; Vinnie Cilurzo; Sam Calagione; Steve Hindy; Garrett Oliver; Tom de Bakker; David Geary; Dan Kenary; Rich Doyle; Alan Pugsley; Greg Koch; Nick Matt; Wendy Littlefield; Gary Glass and the entire staff at the American Homebrewers Association; Daniel Bradford; Charlie Papazian, Bob Pease, Paul Gatza, Julia Herz, and the wider Brewers Association, keeper of statistics and organizer of the Great American Beer Festival, a venue that provided ample opportunity for wide-ranging interviews; Kim Jordan; John McDonald; Cameron Healy; Matthew Reich; Geoff and Marcy Larson; Wendy Littlefield; Bill Owens; Dave Alexander; Ray Daniels; Michael Lewis; Ted Badgerow; Paola Nano of Slow Food International; John Segal Jr.; Greg Schirf; Jeff Fulbright; Tad Stratford; Nico Freccia; Florian Kuplent; Jürgen Knöller; Mary Thompson; and Greg Avola.

I would also like to thank once again the many fellow writers who helped me on my discoveries, including Stan Hieronymus; Jay Brooks; Maureen Ogle; Randy Mosher; Greg Kitsock; Julie Johnson; Don Russell; Eric Asimov;

Joshua Bernstein; John Foyston; Todd and Jason Alstrom; Lucy Saunders; Erika Bolden; and Joseph Tucker. Also, I was lucky enough to have interviewed Byron Burch and Fred Eckhardt before their deaths weeks apart in 2015. I feel particular gratitude, too, to my editors at *All About Beer*—John Holl, Jon Page, and Daniel Hartis—who gave me the opportunity to write a regular history column for the magazine. That has spurred my research in directions it may not have gone. My editors at Food Republic, Richard Martin and Chris Shott, did much the same when it came to covering the current state of beer in America.

I would also like to thank Paddy Gunningham and Samantha Hopkins, as well as Donald Marshall at Oxford Brookes University, for essential background on the late, great Michael Jackson, whom I never met nor interviewed, but who remains my favorite character in the now-long history of American craft beer.

And this book, like its predecessor, would not have been possible without the support of my family, particularly my wife, Elizabeth. She was pregnant with our first child during the release party at Brooklyn Brewery for the first edition of this book, and there have been many changes in our lives since. But her constancy endures.

Finally, the second edition of *The Audacity of Hops*, like the first, is dedicated to my parents, this time in particular to my mother.

TJA
Cambridge, Massachusetts
September 15, 2016

NOTES

Author's Note

Statistics on growth Brewers Association, www.brewersassociation.org/.
Number of craft breweries in 2012 New Yorker map, http://projects.newyorker.com/story/beer/ (accessed May 30, 2016).

Prologue

Nation's five biggest brewers Walter Adams and James Brock, eds., *The Structure of American Industry*, ninth edition (Englewood Cliffs, NJ: Prentice Hall, 1995), 145.
Number would crest Bryan Miller, "American Beer: How Changing Tastes Have Changed It," *New York Times*, May 12, 1982, Late City Final Edition, Section C, Page 1, Column 4.
"Alcoholic soda pop" Jim Koch, interview with the author, March 12, 2012.
A-B headquarters "Largest Brewery in the World," *Spokane Spokesman-Review*, April 4, 1903.
Twenty-one gallons United States Brewers Association.

Part I

The Last Shall Be First

Early Maytag Patrick Cain, "Tapping a Fresh Beer Market," *Investor's Business Daily*, February 24, 2010, A03.
Maytag's first Anchor, Kuh details National Public Radio interview with Fritz Maytag, accessed June 12, 2012, www.devilscanyonbrewery.com/industry-news/fritz-maytag-keith-greggor-talk-about-anchor-steam-brewery-on-npr/.
When the deal closed Robert Sullivan, "Head of Steam," *Stanford Magazine*, September–October 1996.
Used those Holsteins Jean Thilmany and Robin Mather Jenkins, "Blue Heaven," *The Chicago Tribune*, January 24, 2007, 1.
"Less than the price of a used car" Cain, "Tapping a Fresh Beer Market."
From the end of the Civil War US Brewers Association, *1979 Brewers Almanac*, Washington, DC, 12–13.
The average American adult Ibid.
Every big city Ibid.

From 1865 to 1915 Ibid.

To present Mayor Angelo Rossi Carl Nolte, "S.F. Toasts the Repeal of Prohibition Again," *San Francisco Chronicle*, December 5, 2008, A1.

The number of unemployed Charmaine Go, "Unemployment Relief Distribution in the Bay Area During the Depression," University of California at Berkeley.

That market share would grow Martin H. Stack, "A Concise History of America's Brewing Industry," Rockhurst University.

"That so many breweries" Roger Fillion, "Bill Coors: 69 Years and Still Brewing," *Rocky Mountain News* (Denver), May 23, 2008.

Over eight in 10 beers US Brewers Association, 1979 *Brewers Almanac*, Washington, DC, 20.

Neither knew much about Maureen Ogle, *Ambitious Brew: The Story of American Beer* (Orlando, FL: Harcourt, 2006), 260.

Sullivan, "Head of Steam." Ibid.

Ogle, *Ambitious Brew*, 261.

Definition of a craft brewer The Brewers Association website, "Craft Brewer Defined," www.brewersassociation.org.

Sullivan, "Head of Steam."

Do It Yourself

Polaris details "Polaris Goes to Work," *Time*, November 28, 1960.

They knew how to fix them Jack McAuliffe, interview with the author, December 18, 2010.

Fairfax by the time For land area and 1970 population from Fairfax County website, fairfaxcounty.gov. For 1950 population, the Fairfax Economic Development Corporation website, fairfaxcountyeda.org.

In part to keep him busy Cathy McAuliffe Dickerson, e-mail message to the author, April 23, 2012.

Welding and Navy details McAuliffe, December 18.

The pull-tab for aluminum Heather McPherson, "Canned Food Turns 200 and Shows No Signs of Being Shelved," *The Dish* (blog), *Orlando Sentinel*, August 25, 2010.

He did it more McAuliffe, December 18.

"Many times I added" William Lowe, e-mail message to author, June and July 2011.

The homebrewing and its popularity Jack McAuliffe, interview with the author, September 30, 2011; Gary Flynn (who served with McAuliffe in Holy Loch), interview with the author, November 23, 2011.

Beer for Its Own Sake

Fred Eckhardt loved the book Fred Eckhardt, interview with the author, November 27, 2010. Archivist of Carlsberg, which now owns the Tuborg brand, confirmed its availability in Japan in the early 1950s (e-mail message to the author, November 9, 2011).

And while Portland by 1965 "1967 Census of Business, Volume V, Part 3," US Census Bureau.

Blitz-Weinhard John Foyston, "Ale and Farewell," *Oregonian* (Portland), October 14, 1999, E01.

Oregon's best-selling beer William McCall, "After 140 Years, Blitz Weinhard Finally Closes," Associated Press, August 28, 1999.

Weinhard had made his way westward "Henry Weinhard (1830–1904)," The Oregon History Project of the Oregon Historical Society, www.ohs.org/education/oregonhistory/historical_records/dspDocument.cfm?doc_ID=B6C30BC3-1C23

-B9D3-686A0541C39727CB. Details of Eckhardt's visit and his correspondence and influence with McCabe confirmed by Fritz Maytag through e-mail coordinated by Maureen Ogle.

Eckhardt-McCallum conversation Eckhardt.

Details from A Treatise on Lager Beers Fred Eckhardt, *A Treatise on Lager Beers*, rev. ed. (Portland, OR: Hobby Winemaker, 1970), introduction, 7, 9.

Who would be able to decades later Prominent craft brewers, e-mail messages to the author, November 2011.

Eden, California

Lewis's life and trip Michael Lewis, interview with the author, December 1, 2011.

Added more than 9 million residents US Census Bureau, "Resident Population and Apportionment of the US House of Representatives."

Boeing was the only "A Brief History of the California Economy," California Department of Finance, www.dof.ca.gov/html/fs_data/historycaeconomy/index.htm.

Lewis and other faculty culled Michael Lewis, interview with the author, fall 2009.

McAuliffe visit Lewis, December 1, and McAuliffe, December 18.

TV Dinner Land

Carpenter Mark Carpenter, interview with the author, November 2011.

Opened what was New Hampshire's "New Hampshire's Brewery Map," State of New Hampshire's website, www.visitnh.gov.

"A crude and primitive, old brewery" Ken Grossman, *Beyond the Pale: The Sierra Nevada Brewery Story* (Hoboken, NJ: Wiley, 2013). This quotation was taken from an advanced, unpaginated copy shared with the author.

Anchor was still just getting by Ibid.; Sullivan, "Head of Steam."

Most of Anchor's local accounts A. Richard Immel, "Snatched from Extinction," *Wall Street Journal*, January 2, 1975.

That new Anheuser-Busch brewery "Watch It Made in the U.S.A.," webpage on touring the Merrimack Anheuser-Busch brewery, www.factorytour.com/tours/anheuser -busch-merrimack.cfm.

Schlitz brewery details "Schlitz Dedicates Carolina Brewery," *Milwaukee Journal*, May 8, 1970, 27.

It worked so efficiently David C. Berliner, "Employees Bitter Over Schlitz Closing in Brooklyn," *New York Times*, February 18, 1973, 150, column 1.

9,600,000 new cars Census Bureau, economic indicators, 1900–2002 www.census.gov / statab/hist/HS-45.pdf; www.census.gov/statab/hist/HS-40.pdf.

A record 13.3 million TV sets Gene Smith, "Appliance Sales: What Slump?," *New York Times*, March 8, 1970, section 3, page 1, column 1.

More than 60 million households Paul B. Johnson, "Computer Age Causes Shift in TV Industry," *High Point (NC) Enterprise*, December 12, 2011.

Sales of the countertop microwave countertop microwave Southwest Museum of Engineering, Communications and Computation website, www.smecc.org/.

The first 200 cases of Anchor rolled Dave Burkhart at Anchor, e-mail message to the author, February 1, 2012.

Maytag-Saccani conversation Sullivan, "Head of Steam."

Maytag still refused to advertise Immel, "Snatched from Extinction."

Maytag likened such brewing advice Ibid.

There were a few such bottles Carpenter.

"Consistently marvelous stuff" Sullivan, "Head of Steam."

Lite Up Ahead

Murphy-Weissman dinner; "Murphy was right" Rob Walker, "Let There Be Lite," *New York Times*, December 29, 2002.

The thorough fermentation Michael Jackson's Beer Hunter website: www.beerhunter.com. The site is maintained by Stan Hieronymus.

Modern light beer: There had been other light beers, or at least beers that tasted much lighter than most available lagers and ales (per Ogle, *Ambitious Brew*, 229-31). Nothing compared sales- and marketing-wise to Miller Lite and its Big Beer imitators, though.

Miller sued successfully Wall Street Journal, November 3, 1975, 19, column 2.

Gablinger's Diet Beer, developed Mary Rourke, "Joseph L. Owades, 86; Created 1st Low-Calorie Beer, Became a Consultant to Microbrewers," *Los Angeles Times*, December 22, 2005.

"Not only did no one want to try" Adam Bernstein, "Joseph Owades Dies at 86; the Father of Light Beer," *Washington Post*, December 21, 2005, B11.

Meister Brau had been Ibid.

"There was a woman" Walker, "Let There Be Lite."

To nearly a quarter of a billion dollars Paul Gibson, "The George Weissman Road Show," *Forbes*, November 10, 1980, 179. $250 million adjusted for inflation from 1978 dollars to 2010.

The exclusive beer spots Robert Flaherty, "We Missed the Boat . . . We Were Unsmarted," *Forbes*, August 7, 1978, 36–38.

$4.6 billion Economist, "And Then There Were Five," July 22, 1978, 36. $4.6 billion adjusted for inflation from 1977 dollars to 2010.

"Brewed Through a Horse"

Who had for years Fred Eckhardt, *Amateur Brewer* 6, Summer 1979.

Newsletter excerpt Maltose Falcons newsletter, February 1978, www.maltosefalcons.com/brews/1978/197802.

Eckhardt history "Maltose Falcons' History," Maltose Falcons website, www.maltosefalcons.com/content/about-falcons.

With a borrowed $500 Byron Burch, interview with the author, January 6, 2012.

Who hosted its meetings Maltose Falcons website; John Daume, interview with the author, December 28, 2011.

Not just generosity on Maytag's part Burch.

"Tied to the fact" "A Progress Report on Consumer Issues," *U.S. News & World Report*, October 27, 1975, 26.

"Other homesteading activities" Grossman, *Beyond the Pale*.

Something that made people happy Charlie Papazian, interview with the author, July 13, 2010. Papazian e-mailed the author recording files on this date in response to e-mailed questions.

"Go to hell" Mike Royko, "Big Taste Test Is Brewing," *Chicago Daily News*, July 6, 1973. The author acknowledges the Newberry Library's assistance in locating these Royko columns.

Judges' reactions Mike Royko, "Worst, Best by Taste Test," *Chicago Daily News*, July 9, 1973.

The 116-year-old brewery Don Russell, "Newspaperman Mike Royko's Beer Ratings Caught on Nationwide," *Philadelphia Daily News*, November 3, 2011, 35; Jerry Apps, *Breweries of Wisconsin* (Madison: University of Wisconsin Press, 2005), 147.

The Most Influential Beer

Porter idea and schedule Carpenter; official brewery timeline from Anchor.

Described by one leading critic Garrett Oliver in *The Brewmaster's Table: Discovering the Pleasures of Real Beer with Real Food* (New York: HarperCollins, 2003), 127.

No US-grown hops were considered John Segal Jr., interview with the author, December 29, 2011.

Details on hops, including where they grow Stan Hieronymus, e-mail message to the author, January 10, 2012. New York State was the nation's largest hops producer in the nineteenth century, before mold and Prohibition ruined the industry (it has recently begun to recover). Hops are usually used in pellet form, rather than flower, by commercial brewers.

Maytag's decision Carpenter.

Cascade hops, Segal discovery through Zimmermann Segal Jr. interview (John Segal Sr. died in 2004); Thomas Shellhammer and Alfred Haunold, "Cascade (hop)," *The Oxford Companion to Beer* (New York: Oxford University Press, 2012), 226–27; "How Adolph Coors Helped Launch the Most Popular US Aroma Hop and the Craft Beer Revolution," *In Hop Pursuit* (blog), January 25, 2010, http://inhoppursuit. blogspot.com/2010/01/cascade -how-adolph-coors-helped-launch.html; author's email exchange with Segal Jr., June 3, 2016.

George Segal eventually split with that German business partner. According to his grandson, John Jr., George spoke enough "intellectual Yiddish" to eventually figure out his partner was ripping him off. John Segal Sr. would sell one million Cascade roots to fellow members of the Washington State Hop Producers Co-op, thereby establishing the variety on a wider scale in the United States. (per Segal Jr. interview).

First bottles on June 26 Author's e-mail exchange with Dave Burkhart; official brewery timeline.

Maytag didn't think NPR interview with Maytag, accessed June 12, 2012.

More than 70 million cases Philip H. Dougherty, *New York Times*, May 27, 1977, section 4, 6, column 3.

Something had happened Carpenter.

Chez McAuliffe

Situation just as he had predicted McAuliffe, December 18; Julie Johnson, "Pull Up a Stool with Jack McAuliffe," *All About Beer*, September 2011.

Canadian or European brands William J. Schmick Jr., "Homemade Imports," *Forbes*, October 15, 1977, 33.

"Good and beautiful products" Craig Claiborne, "Cuisine Bourgeoise Out West," *New York Times*, June 3, 1981, C1.

Marin French Cheese Company details Johnson, "Pull Up a Stool."

Biographies of Stern and Zimmerman Suzy Stern Denison, interview with the author, January 7, 2012.

"History is important" McAuliffe, December 18.

"Vacuum cleaner of information" Lewis, December 1.

New Albion construction and layout McAuliffe, December 18; Don Barkley, interview with the author, January 3, 2012. McAuliffe also generously furnished the author with photos from that time period.

"Consecration of the New Albion Brewery"; "you telephone" Marketing material McAuliffe provided to the author, including an invitation to the consecration.

The Bard of Beer

Had his first beer Stan Hieronymus, "Michael Jackson Drank Here: 25 Historic Beer Sites," *All About Beer*, March 2005.

First Trappist ale tasting Daniel Shelton, "Michael Jackson, The Beer Hunter—Interview Preview," August 7, 2007, accessed on YouTube, www.youtube.com/watch?v=DLohwMW7qjU.

"His Rubicon" Jay R. Brooks, "The King of Beer Writers," *Beer Connoisseur*, Spring 2011, 15.

the first work Martyn Cornell, "Michael Jackson and the Invention of Beer Style," *Zythophile*, October 23, 2010, https://zythophile.wordpress.com/2010/10/23/michael-jackson-and-the-invention-of-beer-style/(accessed August 4, 2016).

used nearly every other Ibid.

"[Jackson] invented the expression" Ibid., 16.

Coverage of American Beers Michael Jackson, *The World Guide to Beer* (New York: Ballantine, 1978), 202–15.

Robert Parker Jr. William Rice, "An Ombudsman for the Wine Consumer," *Washington Post*, September 28, 1978, E18.

Long Days, Longer Odds

Associated Press reporter visit Robert McEwen, "American Style: The Best Brew," Associated Press, December 26, 1977.

FDA and Michael Jacobson Ogle, 267; Josh Rubin, "Gum Arabic," *The Oxford Companion to Beer* (New York: Oxford University Press, 2012), 413.

The Reagan administration scotched Judson O. Berkey, "The History of Alcoholic Beverage Labeling Regulation and Its Implications for a Health Claim on Wine Labels," Harvard Law School, Winter Term 1998, 7–9.

Barkley-Lewis conversation and Barkley-McAuliffe conversation Barkley.

Part II

Tipping Points

Papazian background Papazian.

Cadged and cobbled what they could Ibid.

"The difference is gargantuan"; it might cost 31 cents Murray Dubin, "Folks Who Brew Are Doing It at Home and Illegally," *St. Petersburg (FL) Independent*, January 19, 1979, 7A.

The publicity around his arrest Papazian.

Eckhardt in Portland didn't think about it Eckhardt, *A Treatise on Lager Beers*, 6.

Fritz Maytag in San Francisco Burch.

"It's a dopey law" Dubin.

Cranston background "Cranston, Alan," Biographical Directory of the United States Congress, accessed January 3, 2012, http://bioguide.congress.gov/scripts/biodisplay.pl?index=c000877.

"A California homebrew curmudgeon" Fred Eckhardt, "Craft Beer—State of the Union, 2010," *All About Beer*, vol. 31, no. 6.

"The slower you would drink it" "Homebrewers Want Tax Break," Associated Press, June 10, 1976.

He proposed an amendment Jim Luther, Associated Press, August 25, 1978, AM Cycle.

Bill excerpt Public Laws Enacted During the Second Session of the 95th Congress, 1255–56.

He wanted a change Papazian.

"Where anyone could teach" "Kakes Studios Has It's [*sic*] Roots," accessed January 5, 2012, www.kakesstudios.org/profile.html. Note: The studios were opened by a former teacher with the Community Free School.

The idea for Zymurgy *magazine* Stan Hieronymus, "*Zymurgy*: AHA at the Beginning," Appellation Beer website, August 2003, accessed January 6, 2012, http://appellation-beer.com/blog/zymurgy-aha-at-the-beginning/.

A newspaperman turned journalism professor "Memorial, Karl F. Zeisler," University of Michigan website, accessed January 5, 2012, http://um2017.org/faculty-history/faculty/karl-f-zeisler/memorial.

Henry King Joe Holley, "Henry B. King Dies at 84," *Washington Post*, April 29, 2005, B07.

Excise tax Stan Hieronymus, "Henry King: Another King of Beers," *New Brewer*, Fall 2004; reproduced at Appellation Beer website, accessed June 12, 2012, http://appellationbeer.com/blog/henry-king-another-king-of-beers/.

Zymurgy *mailing* Papazian; Charlie Papazian, "A Beer Milestone—American Homebrewers Association Turns 30," Examiner.com, December 5, 2008, www.examiner.com/article/a-beer-milestone-american-homebrewers-association-turns-30.

"Small, High-Quality Food Places"

Stern-Barkley conversation; workday routine details Barkley; Denison.

Upped production and requests from across the country McAuliffe, December 18; Barkley. Media coverage at the time also suggests that New Albion was in demand beyond the Bay Area.

$150 a week and all he could drink Barkley.

The company lost $6,000 "Profits Soar at New Albion Brewery," *Brewers Digest*, October 1980, 56.

"It's just like cosmetics, or bread" William Ristow and Michael E. Miller, "Brewing 'Real Ale' Is a Yeasty Business," *Washington Post*, July 9, 1978, G9.

The Bearded Young Man from Chico

The homebrews turned into dinner Burch.

Grossman background Grossman, *Beyond the Pale*.

Trade show and Anchor visit Ibid.; Burch.

Anchor's production Chris Hartman, "The Alchemist of Anchor Steam," *Inc.*, January 1, 1983.

Anchor's bottle runs Ibid.

Chase & Sanborn coffee roaster Tom McNichol, "Anchor Aweigh, Full Steam Ahead," *Los Angeles Times Magazine*, March 10, 1996, 22.

Supreme locally Anchor timeline.

Anchor was distributing Hartman, "The Alchemist of Anchor Steam."

Visit to New Albion Grossman, *Beyond the Pale*.

The Fireman and the Goat Shed

de Bakker background; early brewery Tom de Bakker, interview with the author, January 20, 2012.

was at a toddler's trot For details of the Northern California wine industry in the 1960s and 1970s, the reader is directed to the author's book, *American Wine: A Coming-of-Age Story* (Chicago Review Press: 2015), 123-35.

Near beer had to be less than 0.5 percent alcohol by volume.

"beer wasn't great" Andrew Jones, "Craft Brewing Defines Oregon as U.S. 'Beer Capital," *National Geographic News*, August 10, 2001.

Capped its first bottles; de Bakker quotes Charles Hillinger, "Small-Label Beers—More Are Brewing," *Los Angeles Times*, June 24, 1980, A1.

100 more acres of Sonoma County "History of Sonoma County Wine Country," accessed January 13, 2012, www.sonomawine.com/about-sonoma-county/history-of-sonoma-county-wine-country.

Grossman and Camusi knew Grossman, *Beyond the Pale.*

First craft brewery not only in Oregon Andrew Jones, "Craft Brewing Defines Oregon as US Beer Capital," *National Geographic News* website, August 10, 2001, http://news.nationalgeographic.com/news/2001/08/0808_oregonbrewing.html.

Ware background; Hummer-Ware conversation; 43rd brewery license Stick Ware, interview with the author, January 19, 2012.

Increasingly cultish Big Beer "Coors Beer, Tastes Right," *Economist*, May 17, 1975, 62.

Boulder Brewing start up Ware. The name would change to Boulder Beer Company.

Brewery construction and Gold Hill Inn delivery Ware; Roger Fillion, "Small-Batch Craft Brewer Taps Coors for Tips on Getting Started," *Rocky Mountain News* (Denver), May 23, 2008.

West Coast Style

Reassessed their plans Grossman, *Beyond the Pale.*

45-gallon batches Ibid.

Grain pickups Barkley.

Routinely led classes Michael Lewis, interview with the author, winter 2012; McAuliffe, December 18.

"The Brewery, Northern California" and James Taylor was a beer fan Denison.

Jackson trip de Bakker.

Prial excerpt Frank J. Prial, "In California Wine Country, a Rare Beer," *New York Times*, June 12, 1979, C14.

Thoughts on New Albion and a 10-barrel system Grossman, *Beyond the Pale.*

Even Maytag Hartman, "The Alchemist of Anchor Steam." Maytag had also lost his son, Matthew, in a climbing accident in 1978.

He told the Washington Post Ristow and Miller, "Brewing 'Real Ale.'"

Weinberg was predicting Grossman, *Beyond the Pale.*

"I was simply extrapolating" "The New Age," *Modern Brewery Age*, March 27, 2000.

Fundraising, equipment and maybe this whole brewery thing Grossman, *Beyond the Pale.*

Lewis visit and recipe decision Ibid.

Not until the eleventh batch Rob Burton, *Hops and Dreams: The Story of Sierra Nevada Brewing Company* (Chico, CA: Stansbury Publishing, 2010), 186; Ken Grossman, e-mail message to the author, July 2012. The old Ballantine IPA also inspired Sierra

Nevada Pale Ale, in part. Grossman was a fan of that beer (per Tom Acitelli, "Sierra Nevada Pale Ale: A Cascading Effect," *All About Beer*, September 1, 2015).

Mayflower Refugee

Bradford background Daniel Bradford, interview with the author, September 30, 2011.

Evolution of The Complete Joy of Homebrewing Papazian. In that first issue of *Zymurgy*, it was called *The Joy of Brewing*.

Bradford's reaction Bradford.

Matzen left the A.H.A. Hieronymus, "*Zymurgy*: AHA at the Beginning."

Could even be found Charlie Papazian, "Daniel Bradford Comes on as a Hired Gun," Examiner.com, April 9, 2009, www.examiner.com/article/daniel-bradford-comes-on-as-a-hired-gun.

Bradford efforts to sell the book Bradford.

Through the late spring and summer Papazian.

Estimated 1.4 million homebrewers Brad Smith, "Now That Home-Brew Beer Is Legal, Americans Savor Their Own Suds," UPI, June 19, 1984.

The tone was Charlie Papazian, *The Complete Joy of Homebrewing*, 3rd. ed. (New York: Quill, 1983), 1.

"Wherever my travels take me" Papazian, *The Complete Joy of Homebrewing*, preface.

How the Brewpub Was Born

Blasting through the Cascades Michael Jackson, "How Bert Grant Saved the World," Beer Hunter website, accessed January 17, 2012, www.beerhunter.com/documents/19133-001575.html.

Grant background Peter Reid, "Keeping the Faith: Bert Grant of Yakima Brewing & Malting Co.," *Modern Brewery Age*, November 18, 1991.

In Carter's home state "Georgia Homebrewers Fight for Legality," *Modern Brewery Age*, February 3, 1992, 3. It would not be until 1995 that homebrewing was legalized in Georgia.

In Washington State Washington State Legislative research office, interview with the author, January 18, 2012.

Yakima launch, early support Jackson, "How Bert Grant Saved the World"; Scott Sunde, "Micro-brewery Pioneer Bert Grant Led Northwest Beer Revolution," *Seattle Post-Intelligencer*, August 1, 2001. The brewpub would eventually move to an old Yakima train depot.

Jackson-Grant conversation Jackson, "How Bert Grant Saved the World."

Wearing a kilt Shelley Davis, "The Best of Brew," *Washington Post*, June 24, 1984, D2.

first time; "brought back" Joshua Bernstein, "The IPA Through the Ages," Punch, November 8, 2016, http://punchdrink.com/articles/the-ipa-through-the-ages-beer-history-india-pale-ale/ (accessed December 26, 2016).

Only to have disbelieving retailers de Bakker.

The First Shakeout

For the fiscal year ending "Profits Soar at New Albion Brewery," *Brewers Digest*, October 1980, 56.

Promised to find investors Leo DeKinis (a banker who knew McAuliffe), interview with the author, January 12, 2012; Denison.

Responses such as these Barkley.

wine consumption reached "Wine Consumption in the U.S.," the Wine Institute, www.wineinstitute.org/resources/statistics/article86 (accessed August 16, 2016).

The de Bakkers ran the numbers de Bakker.

Rolled out in 40 states "Budweiser Debuts New Light Beer," Associated Press, March 1, 1982.

Market share of 32.5 percent PR Newswire, January 10, 1985.

"There are no easy answers" Michael A. Verespej, "It's Hard to Beat the Busches," *Industry Week*, July 12, 1982, 52.

No one would remember much McAuliffe, December 18; Barkley.

McAuliffe and his crew McAuliffe, both interviews with the author. Brewery counts in this book are based on media reports at different times; interviews with contemporary observers, including those in the industry; and data that the Brewers Association (and its predecessor, the Association of Brewers) compiled. Effort was made to be as accurate as possible, but given the obscurity of some craft breweries and of the craft brewing industry in general until around 2000, exact counts were sometimes not available. Also, the Brewers Association from time to time revises its own count of breweries and brewpubs. The association's counts do not include contract breweries.

"That's a Great Idea, Charlie"

"That's a great idea, Charlie" Burkhard Bilger, "A Better Brew," *New Yorker*, November 24, 2008, page 88.

Papazian decided Bradford.

Papazian hosted Papazian; Bradford.

Jackson-Burch conversation Burch.

Festival logistics "A Beer Drinker's Program to the American Homebrewers Association Fourth Annual National Homebrew and Microbrewery Conference & National Homebrew and Country Homebrew Competition," American Homebrewers Association, 1982.

In about an hour Burch.

Mingled with aficionados and the only region "A Drinker's Program."

"All the ambiance" and "a disaster" Dick Kreck, "The Association," *American Brewer*, March/April 1988, 56.

Had to borrow money Vince Cottone, "Movement in the Right Direction," *American Brewer*, Fall 1987, 28; Maureen Ogle, "First Draft Follies: Early History of the American Homebrewers Association and Brewers Association, Part 8," accessed June 3, 2012, maureenogle.com/tag/first-draft-follies.

Buying its toilet paper in bulk Papazian.

The Third Wave Builds

Flew to Boston Matthew Reich, interview with the author, January 20, 2012.

Reich background Sandra Salmans, "A Local Beer Not for Everyone," *New York Times*, February 19, 1985, D1, column 3; Matthew Reich, "The Old New York Beer Company Business Plan and Market Research," 1982.

F. X. Matt Brewing history "Brewery History," Saranac, accessed June 3, 2012, www.saranac.com/page/brewery-history; "Matt Generations Brew Utica History," Utica (NY) Observer-Dispatch, April 2, 2007, 1.

Reputation for bluntness Reich; Steve Hindy, interview with the author, September 9, 2010.

"Dumbest idea" and wheels of commerce greased Reich.

To sell 4,000 cases Reich shared his business plan from the time with the author. Subsequent details about the start-up phase from Reich and other material provided.

He was not familiar Reich.

Newman details and "hopped" Bryan Miller, "American Beer: How Changing Tastes Have Changed It," *New York Times*, May 12, 1982, C1, column 4.

Vendors were not always happy Hindy.

"Americans like their beer cold" Doug G. Miller, "British-Trained Brewer Learns 'Americans Like Their Beer Cold,'" UPI, January 4, 1983.

Chesbay details and "no cornflakes" Dan McCoubrey, "Virginia 'Chesbay Beer' to Challenge Imported Lager Market," *Washington Post*, January 3, 1983, 9.

"Brew beer by tongue" T. R. Reid, "High Hopes for Home-Brew," *Washington Post*, June 6, 1983, B1.

First American craft brewery Charlie Papazian, "Trailblazers of American Craft Brewing, 1983–1987, Part 1," Examiner.com, August 16, 2011, www.examiner.com/article/trailblazers-of-american-craft-brewing-1983-1987-part-1.

Palo Alto Brewing "A High-Tech Beer from Silicon Valley," *New York Times*, November 15, 1983, D5, column 1; *Erickson Report*, vol. 1, no. 9, accessed January 23, 2012, www.realbeer.com/redbrickpress/tomb.html.

Thousand Oaks The Microbrewed Beer of the Month Club newsletter, vol. 2, no. 10, April 1996, www.beermonthclub.com/newsletters/vol2no10.htm.

"White out 'almond farm'" Bill Owens, interview with the author, May 2012.

"I sell it for a dollar and a half" William Least Heat-Moon, "A Glass of Handmade," *Atlantic Monthly*, November 1987, 260.

Brewing 120 cases of beer Barkley.

Golden Pacific Brewing Co., very short-lived flirtation Author's interview with Tad Stratford, May 20, 2016; Tom Acitelli, "Delivering Beer in a Box," *All About Beer*, May 23, 2016. There are several breweries, big and small, that sell their wares in boxes as of 2016. Golden Pacific was unique for its time.

Bridgeport Brewing Karl Ockert and Dick Ponzi, interview with the author, spring 2010.

Widmer Brothers Widmer Brothers website, accessed January 23, 2012, http://widmerbrothers.com; "Rob Widmer Interview, Part I," *Brewpublic*, accessed January 23, 2012, http://brewpublic.com/beer-events/rob-widmer-interview-part-1/.

Born of a Belgian yeast strain Christine Frey, "A Moment with Paul Shipman, Founder of Redhook," *Seattle Post-Intelligencer*, August 28, 2003.

Soon reached capacity and other Redhook details "About Redhook Brewery," 7G Distributing, accessed January 24, 2012, www.abwholesaler.com/group04/7gdistributingllc1/OurBrands/Redhook; Michael Kaplan, "Tiny Breweries Work to Build Big Impact," *Advertising Age*, April 7, 1986, S-12.

Who was also inspired "The Story Behind Hale's Ales Brewery and Pub," Hale's Ales website, accessed January 24, 2012, http://halesbrewery.com/about_full.htm.

Poured the first beers Alf Collins, "Fresh Today," *Seattle Times*, January 2, 1985, F5.

In an old general store "Brewing a National Image," Associated Press, February 20, 1996.

128 breweries before Prohibition Brian Yaeger, *Red White, and Brew: An American Beer Odyssey* (New York: St. Martin's Griffin, 2008), 49.

"I just crank up" "Small Is Tasty," *Time*, July 25, 1983.

Badgerow-Averill conversation and other Chelsea details Ted Badgerow, interview with the author, February 2, 2012.

"That have sprung up" "A High-Tech Beer from Silicon Valley," *New York Times*.

The whole idea of homebrewing T. R. Reid, "High Hopes for Home-Brew."

The Lesson of the Nylon String

Koch-Jackson conversation and Koch hunch confirmed J. Koch.

A friend of his grandfather's and faded to background noise Ibid.

A rugby player from the Australian Outback Ibid.

Outward bound and lesson of the nylon string Jim Koch, written with Glenn Rifkin, "A Less-Is-More Lesson," New York Times, July 20, 2003, section 3, column 5, 12; J. Koch.

Koch's consternation J. Koch.

The advantage matrix Boston Consulting Group website, accessed February 8, 2012, www.bcg.com/about_bcg/history/history_1981.aspx.

The firm's revenue John A. Byrne, "Are All These Consultants Really Necessary?" *Forbes*, October 10, 1983, 136.

Advising clients as Rolodex prominent Gregory K. Ericksen, *What's Luck Got to Do with It? Twelve Entrepreneurs Reveal the Secrets Behind Their Success* (New York: Wiley, 1997), 45.

That was his epiphany J. Koch.

"We've spent 20 years" Bob Weinstein, "From Beer to Eternity," *Entrepreneur*, February 1, 1997.

Charles Koch biography "Charles Koch, Director of the Boston Beer Company, Dies at 88," PRNewswire, June 15, 2011.

"People don't drink the marketing" and "plenty of breweries" J. Koch.

Nearing an all-time production peak "A Mixed Forecast for Beer," *Modern Brewery Age*, 10. The chart from which the 195 million statistic is taken was printed in April 2006.

"This Connoisseur Thing"

New Amsterdam availability and sales Salmans, "A Local Beer Not for Everyone."

Most popular lager Davis, "The Best of Brew."

"Yuppies drink it" Salmans, "A Local Beer Not for Everyone."

One Yuppie in particular Reich.

VC takeover and brewpub Ibid.; Salmans, "A Local Beer Not for Everyone."

"A soft drink" and Manhattan Brewing details "A Success Brewing," *New York Times*, December 3, 1984, 38; Joe Klein, "Mr. Wrigley Brews His Dream Beer," *New York Times*, July 16, 1984, 16.

New Amsterdam–Manhattan Brewing rivalry Joe Dolce, "Battle of the Brews," *New York Times*, March 23, 1987, 26.

Ware met a stockbroker Ware.

New Boulder Brewing facility Steve Raabe, "Boulder Beer Takes Pride in Its 'Intimacy,'" *Rocky Mountain Business Journal*, July 29, 1985, 4.

"Beer connoisseurship today" Howard Hillman, *The Gourmet Guide to Beer* (New York: Facts on File, 1987), vii. This is a subsequent edition of the 1984 original. The quotation appears in the original as well.

"A workingman's drink" and "We have a better-educated" Mike Leary, "New Brand of Beer Is 'Fresher,'" *Boca Raton News*, September 18, 1983, 13C.

BJCP; "Do you really think"; questions; failure rate Author's e-mail exchange with Pat Baker, July 2016; Lauren Clark, *Crafty Bastards: Beer in New England from the Mayflower to Modern Day* (Union Park Press: May 2014), 20–21. Baker also founded the Underground Brewers, the second-oldest homebrewers club in the nation. Per Clark, 21. The BJCP program became independent of both of its founding groups in the mid-1990s. It started developing a style-heavy study guide around that time, too.

Because Wine Making Takes Too Long

Slosberg biography and "you haven't had real beer" Pete Slosberg, *Beer for Pete's Sake: The Wicked Adventures of a Brewing Maverick* (Boulder, CO: Brewers Publications, 1998), 3–27; Pete Slosberg, interview with the author, March 5, 2012.

"Six weeks later" and took Slosberg back Slosberg, *Beer for Pete's Sake*, 20.

More than in Europe

A little hungover and an assignment for her Rhonda Kallman, interview with the author, February 17, 2012.

Koch-uncle conversation James Koch, "Portrait of the CEO as Salesman," *Inc.*, March 1, 1988, 44; J. Koch.

"By choice and by assignment" Ericksen, "What's Luck Got to Do with It?" 46.

Kallman background Kallman. BCG would move to Exchange Place in Boston after that tower's 1985 completion.

Koch-Owades relationship and Boulder/Newman apprenticeships J. Koch.

Became a Bruegger's Bagels factory Cailin Brown, "Bagel Firm Purchases Old Brewery," *Albany (NY) Times-Union*, June 15, 1989.

Koch's first sales call J. Koch.

Koch began reciting his memorized pitch J. Koch; Koch, "Portrait of the CEO as Salesman."

"Sold an order for 25 cases" Kallman.

Lugging the ice-packed samples Kallman; J. Koch.

"A clean, clean beer" Bradford.

Koch showing mocked-up labels and New World as runner-up Robert A. Mamis, "Entrepreneur of the Year 1995," *Inc.*, December 1995, 54.

Koch and Kallman delivered the bottles J. Koch; Kallman; Jim Koch, interview with the author, July 21, 2011.

Early promotional materials Kallman.

"Straight lager country" and Bell details Yaeger, *Red, White, and Brew*, 48–49.

He asked the usual questions Badgerow.

Might have become a chef CRJ Mellor, "Interview: Larry Bell," *BeerAdvocate*, March 27, 2006, http://beeradvocate.com/articles/661.

already wanted to buy Rick Coates, "Larry Bell: Craft Brew Titan," *Northern Express*, August 23, 2010, www.northernexpress.com/michigan/article-5014-larry-bell-craft-brew-titan.html (accessed June 1, 2016).

rented through trading Ibid.

Could produce in 30 minutes Linda Warren, "Tiny Michigan Brewery Just a Drop in Nation's Beer Bucket," UPI, July 13, 1986.

some iffy batches E-mail from Larry Bell to author's editors at *All About Beer*.

"You can now get more beers" Ibid.

Beer, It's What's with Dinner

When the local wing and Tupper details Bob Tupper, interview with the author, February 2012.

"If we did have to justify our existence" Greg Kitsock, "Dave Alexander on the End of the Brickskeller," *Washington Post's All We Can Eat* (blog), December 17, 2010, http://voices.washingtonpost.com/all-we-can-eat/beer/beer-dave-alexander-on-the-end.html.

Horse Brass, Younger "An Interview with Don Younger," *Seattle Beer News*, January 31, 2011 (a reprint of a 2001 *American Brewer* interview with Younger, who died in 2011), http://seattlebeernews.com/2011/01/an-interview-with-don-younger/ (accessed December 5, 2016).

made Younger nervous Ibid.

Lyon's Brewery depot, Ashworth Author's e-mail exchange with Judy Ashworth, December 2016; Julie Nickels, "The Beginning of a New Beer Renaissance: Remembering Lyons Brewery with Judy Ashworth," VisitTriValley.com, May 25, 2016, http://visit-trivalley.com/the-beginning-of-a-new-beer-renaissance-remembering-lyons-brewery-with-judy-ashworth/ (accessed December 5, 2016).

"There is a new gourmet influence" Carole Lalli, "Beer Is Back," *Tri-City Herald* (Kennewick, WA), August 5, 1984, 4.

"Not for the six-pack drinker" Salmans, "A Local Beer Not for Everyone."

Four Belgian chefs Paddy Gunningham (Michael Jackson's widow), interview with the author, February 2012.

"English beer authority" "Newman's Brews Beer Tasting," *Albany (NY) Times-Union*, October 31, 1986, C8.

"Charlie, the Washington Post" Bradford.

Started by Mike Bosak in 1979 Fred Eckhardt, "The Beer Enthusiast—25 Years," *All About Beer*, March 2005, vol. 26, no. 1.

Robertson background James D. Robertson, *The Great American Beer Book* (Ottawa, Illinois: Caroline House Publishers Inc., 1978), 9–12; e-mail exchange with Julie Johnson Bradford, August 5, 2016. Jackson and Robertson's first *All About Beer* columns both appeared in the November 1984 issue.

"so well made" Robertson, 12.

Readership of 160,000 Barry Witt, *Wall Street Journal*, July 25, 1983, section 1, page 13, column 1.

A weekday circulation of 249,000 "2 Portland Newspapers to Merge Operations," *New York Times*, August 10, 1982.

Would sometimes suggest a particular style Eckhardt.

Ken Grossman's Sierra Nevada; Heat-Moon, Chisolm trip Jonathan Ingram, "'A Glass of Handmade' Revisited," *Beer Connoisseur*, Summer 2011, 48.

Cottone, craft terms Tom Acitelli, "Why Did People Stop Saying 'Microbrew' and Start Calling It 'Craft Beer'?," FoodRepublic.com, April 4, 2016, www.foodrepublic.com/2016/04/04/why-did-people-stop-saying-micro-brew-and-start-calling-it-craft-beer/ (accessed June 2, 2016); Stan Hieronymus, "How Craft Became Craft," *All About Beer*, March 1, 2015, http://allaboutbeer.com/article/how-craft-became-craft/ (accessed June 2, 2016).

As early as 1984 Stan Hieronymus, "Who First Used the Words Craft Beer?," Appellation Beer, July 9, 2010, http://appellationbeer.com/blog/who-first-used-the-words-craft-beer/ (accessed June 2, 2016).

"seemed to fit" Hieronymus, "How Craft Became Craft."

Maybe he had heard it Stan Hieronymus, "Craft Beer: the 1986 Definition," *Forbes*, July 16, 2010, www.forbes.com/sites/booze/2010/07/16/craft-beer-the-1986-definition/#3c7f7f099b9b (accessed June 2, 2016).

Vats and Dogs

The call could not have come Slosberg, *Beer for Pete's Sake*, 71–73.

Bronder-Slosberg friendship Slosberg; Mark Bronder, interview with the author, February 27, 2012.

With 40,000 barrels of six different types David E. Gumpert, "The Joys of Keeping the Company Small," *Harvard Business Review*, July/August 1986, vol. 64, no. 4, 6.

Sierra Nevada was brewing Burton, *Hops and Dreams*, 94.

Was up to 3,000 barrels Davis, "The Best of Brew."

26 craft breweries Bryan Brumley, "The Fizz Factor," Associated Press, September 22, 1985; author's count.

Bronder's father Bronder interview.

They examined the economics Slosberg, *Beer for Pete's Sake*, 66–67.

Two-barrel brewhouse "Reality Check," *Erickson Report*, March 1996, accessed February 21, 2012, www.realbeer.com/redbrickpress/tomb.html.

Initially balked at Slosberg, *Beer for Pete's Sake*, 67.

Slosberg's imitation of Samuel Smith and naming decision Ibid., 70–71; Slosberg.

"The dog's a kick" Bronder.

Beer and pizza powered Slosberg, *Beer for Pete's Sake*, 72–73.

Its executives said it wanted Rogers Worthington, "Giant Miller to Take a Swig Out of Leinenkugel's Stein," *Chicago Tribune*, December 14, 1987, business page 1.

To the Last Frontier and Back

Geoff and Marcy Larson background and startup efforts Geoff and Marcy Larson, interview with the author, February 16, 2012.

Millstream launch, Zuber revelation Tom Acitelli, "Iowa's First Micro-Brewery," *All About Beer*, January 29, 2016, http://allaboutbeer.com/millstream-brewing/ (accessed June 1, 2016).

Cases of their Alaskan Amber "Our History," Alaskan Brewing Company website, accessed February 21, 2012, www.alaskanbeer.com/about-us/our-history.html.

Based on a popular local recipe Larsons interview.

Olde Heurich Brewing Company closed Marc Fisher, "Farewell, Olde Heurich! A Comback Ends," *Washington Post* blog, March 1, 2006, http://blog.washingtonpost.com/rawfisher/2006/03/farewell_olde_heurich_a_comeba.html.

There was one left Melissa Mandell, "Schmidt's Brewery Site (Now the Piazza at Schmidt's)," Historical Society of Pennsylvania, accessed February 22, 2012, www.philaplace.org/story/319/.

Pennsylvania Brewing Company Bob Batz Jr., "Penn Pilsner Beer Is Turning 30," *Pittsburg Post-Gazette*, April 8, 2016.

Dock Street Brewing Tim Blangger, "Tradition Is Brewing," *Morning Call* (Allenton, PA), February 5, 1987; "The Team," Dock Street website,www.dockstreetbeer.com/staff/ (accessed December 27, 2016); "Awards," Dock Street website, www.dockstreetbeer.com/awards/ (accessed December 27, 2016).

Brewing disappeared altogether Rich Doyle and Dan Kenary, interview with the author, February 22, 2012.

Commonwealth Brewing Company and Wort Processors Bob MacDonald, "Boston's Own Brewery-Restaurant Finally Open," *Boston Globe*, August 28, 1986, calendar.

A recession low of 776.92 Jason DeSena Trennert, "Remembering the Reagan Bull Market," *Wall Street Journal*, August 13, 2009.

Rich Doyle, Dan Kenary, and George Ligeti plans and travels Doyle and Kenary interview.

Canada had its own brush "Prohibition," The Canadian Encyclopedia, accessed June 15, 2012, www.thecanadianencyclopedia.com/articles/prohibition.

Horseshoe Bay Brewery & Roller Inn Pub "About Us," Howe Sound Brewing Company website, accessed June 15, 2012, www.howesound.com/aboutus/history.aspx; Papazian, "Trailblazers."

Another creation of Mitchell's Andrew A. Duffy, "A Perfect Pint of Craft Beer Is His Passion," *Victoria (BC) Times Colonist*, June 17, 2009. Mitchell's partners included Paul Hadfield and Raymond Ginnever.

Mass Bay Brewing Company startup; Harpoon Ale Doyle and Kenary interview.

Weeping Radishes, Scottish Lords, and Roller Coasters

Portland Lager "Brewers of Portland Lager Claim Toehold in Maine Beer Market," *Bangor Daily News*, September 3, 1986, 18.

Laird's visit; could not stomach the process David Geary, interview with the author, February 29, 2012.

"After the mash" "History," D. L. Geary Brewing Company website, accessed February 23, 2012, www.gearybrewing.com/history/.

Fundraising and other than the odd bottle of Samuel Adams Geary interview.

He didn't really have, or particularly want Geary interview.

"Ah . . . D.L. Geary's Pale Ale" Alan Pugsley, interview with the author, February 29, 2012.

Its biggest distributive coup Geary interview.

Catamount Brewing Company startup details Marialisa Calta, "Soon, Catamount Amber, a 'British' Pale Ale from Vermont," *New York Times*, December 3, 1986, C18, column 1.

Summit Brewing Company startup details Mark Stutrud, interview by Andy Crouch, *Beverage Magazine*, November 2004, accessed February 26, 2012, www.beerscribe.com/stutrud.html.

Raised $500,000 by selling 30,000 shares "Microbreweries Tap Midwest," *Advertising Age*, August 18, 1986, 58.

James Page Brewing "Beer of the Week (Vol. LV)," May 14, 2010, www.fraterslibertas.com/2010/05/beer-of-week-vol-lv.html.

shuttered in 1967 Randy Harward, "Utah Brewing Timeline," *Salt Lake City Weekly*, August 24, 2011.

Greg Schirf Author's interview with Greg Schirf, August 9, 2016; Dawn House, "Wasatch Beers to Celebrate 25 Years of Fun in Utah," *Salt Lake Tribune*, October 13, 2011; Richard Markosian, "How Beer Saved Park City—Part II," *Utah Stories*, April 2, 2015, www.utahstories.com/2015/04/how-beer-saved-park-city-part-ii/ (accessed August 5, 2016); Gavin Sheehan, "Utah Brewers Cooperative," Salt Lake City Weekly Daily Feed, April 9, 2009, www.cityweekly.net/TheDailyFeed/archives/2009/04/09/utah-brewers-cooperative (accessed August 5, 2016).

still relatively undeveloped Schirf interview; Markosian, "How Beer Saved Park City—Part II."

Seattle trip, meeting with Baune Schirf interview.

Wasatch brewery, brewpub opening; legal change Ibid.; Vanessa Chang, "Brew Pubs Gain an Unlikely Following in Utah," *New York Times*, January 23, 2009; Markosian, "How Beer Saved Park City—Part II"; Sheehan, "Utah Brewers Cooperative."

Bayern launch Author's interview with Jürgen Knöller, August 11, 2016; Kristen Inbody, "Bayern Brewing Is Montana's Oldest," *Great Falls Tribune*," August 1, 2016; Ryan Newhouse, *Montana Beer: A Guide to Breweries in Big Sky Country* (The History Press, July 2013), 53–55; 71. There was only one other brewery in Montana when

Bayern opened—a 1984 resurrection of the Kessler Brewing Co. brand, which had operated in Helena until 1958.

Knöller background, takeover Knöller interview; Newhouse, *Montana Beer,* 53–55; Bayern website, www.bayernbrewery.com/brewcrew.html (accessed August 9, 2016). Bayern was originally part of a brewpub called Iron Horse. Per Newhouse, 56. *"the conservative South"; "Where the summers"* Michael Jackson, *The Simon & Schuster Pocket Guide to Beer, Revised and Expanded* (New York: Simon & Schuster, 1988), 161.

Reinheitsgebot launch, Thompson background Paul Hightower and Brian L. Brown, *North Texas Beer: A Full-Bodied History of Brewing in Dallas, Fort Worth and Beyond* (The History Press, October 2014), 93–94; Bev Blackwood, "Crafty Brewers," Southwest Brewing News, April/May 2010, 6–7; author's e-mail exchange with Mary Thompson, October 2016.

TV segment University of North Texas Digital Library, http://digital.library.unt.edu/ ark:/67531/metadc789222/m1/ (accessed August 9, 2016).

Abita start-up; some of the purest around Abita Brewing Company president David Blossman, interview by Andy Crouch, *The Beer in Me* (blog), September 2009, www. thebeerinme.com/page.php?79; Oliver, *The Brewmaster's Table,* 301.

Uli Bennewitz; Weeping Radish start-up Uli Bennewitz, interview with the author, February 22, 2012.

North Carolina's first commercial brewery Daniel Anthony Hartis, *Charlotte Beer: A History of Brewing in the Queen City* (The History Press, March 2013), 33–35.

"If we had had Budweiser" Bennewitz interview.

Was packed in the summers and produced 400 to 500 barrels Ibid.

Vernon Valley Author's interview with Andy Mulvihill, Gene Mulvihill's son (Gene died in 2012); Tim Donnelly, "The Dangerous Return of the World's Most Insane Theme Park," *New York Post,* June 28, 2014.

Action Park dangers, injuries, deaths Ibid. Also, Gene Mulvihill would face tens of thousands of dollars in fines for insurance fraud, after state officials discovered his Cayman Islands company. Per Donnelly, "The Dangerous Return of the World's Most Insane Theme Park."

"The most uncompromisingly traditional lagers" Jackson, *New World Guide to Beer,* 205-6.

Jackson also cheered Jackson, New World Guide to Beer, 207.

Stoudts, brewery startup Marilyn Marter, "A Brewer's Heady Days," *Philadelphia Inquirer,* November 4, 1990; Timothy Harper, *Doing Good: Inspirational Stories of Everyday Americans at Home and at Work* (iUniverse Star: May 2004), 155-9.

Here, There and Everywhere

He liberally sampled several Bradford.

Defining for the first time Ibid.

Were meant to be exacting and unforgiving Pugsley.

Summit out of St. Paul won the gold Craft beer lovers, or the merely curious, can while away an afternoon searching the Brewers Association's online database of GABF medal winners: Great American Beer Festival website, "GABF Winners," www.greatamericanbeerfestival.com/the-competition/winners/.

Part III

Unhappy Meals

McDonald's protest Mary Davis Suro, "Romans Protest McDonald's," *New York Times*, May 5, 1986, C20.

"We don't want fast food" "Turning the Tables," *Good*, January 7, 2010, www.good.is/posts/turning-the-tables#.

Second Careers

Ed Koch pulled a tap Eleanor Blau and David Bird, "Burgeoning Brewery," *New York Times*, May 14, 1986.

Koch and Potter/Hindy visits Hindy; Reich. Hindy and Reich now both describe themselves as good friends.

Hindy background and standing on a grandstand Hindy; Steve Hindy and Tom Potter, *Beer School: Bottling Success at the Brooklyn Brewery* (Hoboken, NJ: Wiley, 2005), 2.

Sadat assassination William E. Farrell, "Sadat Assassinated at Military Parade," *New York Times*, October 6, 1981, A1.

Hindy said no Hindy and Potter, *Beer School*, 2–3.

Hindy in Brooklyn and Hindy-Anderson Ibid., 5–10.

Davids and Goliaths

Koch wasn't sleeping Kallman.

Samuel Adams distribution PR Newswire, April 25, 1986.

Distributed to the White House, Camp David, and Air Force One J. Koch.

He ordered $2.7 million in equipment Mamis, "Entrepreneur of the Year 1995."

Who by now was running Ibid.

"I'm almost 40" Ibid.

Heineken–Boston Lager contest "Brew Ha-Ha," *MacNeil-Lehrer Newshour*, transcript, August 26, 1986.

500 Miles in a Rented Honda

"You don't have to own your own brewery" Slosberg, *Beer for Pete's Sake*, 67.

They drove 500 miles in a rented Honda Bronder. Pete's would eventually switch to the Minnesota Brewing Company for its contract brewing.

New York Minutes

"Do you know who Milton is?" Hindy and Potter, *Beer School*, 25.

"What makes you think" Ibid., 34.

It would lose more than $1 million Mary Fran Gleason, "Miller, Bud to Boost Production; Matt Hopes to Survive," *Syracuse (NY) Post-Standard*, February 6, 1989.

Matt could not compete Nick Matt, interview with the author, February 23, 2012.

They talked for the next fifteen minutes Hindy and Potter, *Beer School*, 34.

Henry James's novella "F. X. Matt II Dies at 67," *Modern Brewery Age*, January 22, 2001.

Moeller and the recipe for Brooklyn Lager Hindy and Potter, *Beer School*, 27–28.

Raised $300,000 and Hindy returned briefly Ibid., 66–67.

Glaser's design Ibid., 26.

First deliveries and first bottles to Manhattan via water taxi Steve Hindy, "Powered with Pride in Brooklyn," *All About Beer*, November 2007; John E. Pepper, "Upscale Beer Segment Bucking the Trend," *Modern Brewery Age*, July 10, 1989.

On Meserole Street Hindy and Potter, *Beer School*, 79.

15,000 barrels in annual sales and distribution in 22 states Reich.

Reich quotes; scored big on another investment Hindy and Potter, *Beer School*, 158–59, 212.

The Revolution, Televised

Beer Hunter episode "California Pilgrimage," *The Beer Hunter*, August 30, 1990. Accessed on YouTube March 3, 2012, www.youtube.com/watch?v=CtmxXgKU1o0. Anchor Steam was the only American brand in the opening montage.

thirty-eight million households John Burgess, "Offer Made for Discovery Channel," *Washington Post*, February 27, 1989, F5.

One in four beers sold in the country Rich Exner, "Microbreweries Big Products in Small Pubs," UPI, December 25, 1988.

Brewpubs were illegal "Micro Conference Looks into Future," *Modern Brewery Age*, September 18, 1989, 1.

Produced an estimated 120,000 barrels "Local Beers Brewing Popularity," *Chicago Tribune*, January 29, 1989, 11. Readers should realize that production estimates throughout this book are just that. Often they were self-reported figures from individual breweries that were then culled for aggregate numbers.

Pioneering first Tim Blangger, "Tradition Is Brewing," *Allentown (PA) Morning Call*, February 5, 1987; David Enscoe, UPI, December 10, 1989.

Hood River Brewing Jonathan Nicholas, "Ale-ing Economy Gets Set to Take Off," *Oregonian* (Portland), November 9, 1987, B01; Jonathan Nicholas, "New Venture Proceeding at Full Sail," *Oregonian* (Portland), June 27, 1988, C01.

Great Lakes Brewing Janet H. Cho, "Patrick Conway, the Man Behind Great Lakes Brewing and Christmas Ale," *Cleveland Plain Dealer*, July 17, 2011, A1; "Local Beers Brewing Popularity."

Connecticut Brewing Company Vincent M. Valvo, "Hale-Bent to Join Micro-Age (No, We're Not Talking Computers)," *Intercorp*, December 9, 1988, 35.

Deschutes Brewing "Q&A: Gary Fish, Founder and CEO, Deschutes Brewery," *Oregon Business*, October 2008.

Long Trail Brewing Andy Crouch, "Welcome to the Age of Craft Brewery Consolidation," BeerScribe.com, November 24, 2009, www.beerscribe.com/2009/11/24/welcome-to-the-age-of-craft-brewery-consolidation-long-trail-to-buy-otter-creek-brewing/.

Dean Biersch and Dan Gordon Alan Liddle, "Biersch Proves Foam Is Where the Heart Is," *Nation's Restaurant News*, July 17, 1989, 3.

Rogue River Brewing Rogue Ales website, accessed March 5, 2012, www.rogue.com.

Sierra Nevada's East 20th Street expansion and Grossman was especially pleased Ken Grossman, interview with the author, April 26, 2012; Burton, *Hops and Dreams*, 95–99.

Chicago breweries Curtis Hartman, "New Brew," *Inc.*, April 1, 1988, 86; "Brewpubs Foam Up in Chicago," *Nation's Restaurant News*, May 16, 1988, F110.

A Manifesto and Arnold Schwarzenegger

First International Slow Food Congress in its officious tracks Florence Fabricant, "Slow Food Congress Fights for Culinary Culture," *Nation's Restaurant News*, January 14, 1991.

Slow Food manifesto Carlo Petrini, *Slow Food: The Case for Taste* (New York: Columbia University Press, 2001), xxiii–xiv.

New York press conference Florence Fabricant, "A Faintly Amused Answer to Fast Food," *New York Times*, November 18, 1989, C10.

Coming off a decade-long fitness craze Noel Zavoral, "Rating the Exercise Videos: All the Views That Are Fit to Rent," *Minneapolis Star Tribune*, February 23, 1992, 16C.

Home-gym suppliers did tens of thousands Cathy Hindaugh, "Home Bodies Bumping Up Sales of Fitness Equipment Retailers," *Warfield's Business Journal*, January 31, 1992.

An "earlier, slower" time Fabricant, "Slow Food Congress Fights for Culinary Culture."

The Value of Gold

It was a precarious time Gleason, "Miller, Bud to Boost Production"; Matt interview.

Brewery's gold medal and decision to focus on Saranac Matt interview.

"The Tyranny of Fast Growth"

Baghdad bombing details Kim Murphy and David Lauter, "Bush Vow: Wipe Out Missiles," *Los Angeles Times*, January 19, 1991, A1.

Magee background and "I went from earning in the strong six figures" Tony Magee, unpublished, unpaginated memoir manuscript, shared with the author in late 2011; Tony Magee, e-mail message to the author, March 30, 2012.

Marin Brewing Brett Ainsworth, "Marin Brewing Co. Has Anchored Country Mart Through Center's Rough Times," Patch.com, December 28, 2010, http://larkspurcortemadera.patch.com/articles/marin-brewing-co-has-anchored-country-mart-through-centers-rough-times.

"That is not a question" and Magee's big break Magee memoir manuscript.

Grundy tank descriptions Archive Grundy Tank Page website, accessed March 12, 2012, www.soundbrew.com/grundy.html.

Cross-Magee deal and early Lagunitas details Magee memoir manuscript; Magee.

Decision to lead with an I.P.A. Magee memoir manuscript.

"Tyranny of fast growth" Ibid.

Finding Role Models, Defying Labels

Red Bell startup, Bell quotes Marilyn Joyce, "Bond Trader Whets His Appetite with His Own Phila.-based Brew," *Philadelphia Business Journal*, October 29, 1993, 3.

Jumping by double-digit percentages annually Sheryll Poe, "Crowded Market Leaves Some Microbrew Makers Tapped Out," *Austin American-Statesman*, May 30, 2000.

"Heady as prom queens" Julie Flaherty, "Now, the Glass Is Half-Empty," *New York Times*, May 30, 2000, C1, column 2.

Jersey Premium Lager details Donald Janson, "New Beer Makes a Pitch for the Upscale Market," *New York Times*, October 30, 1988, section 12NJ, page 1, column 3.

Had proven extraordinarily popular Kim Tschudy, "Sales Rosy for New Glarus Brewery's Cherry Beer," *Madison (WI) Capital Times*, December 8, 1994, 6B.

Dan and Deb Carey biographies "Brew Crew," New Glarus Brewing Company website, accessed March 14, 2012, www.newglarusbrewing.com/index.cfm/brewery/brewcrew.

"It's like eating fast food" Mike Ivey, "New Glarus Brewmaster a Purist with Credentials," *Madison (WI) Capital Times*, October 6, 1994, B1.

Shipyard start-up details Pugsley; "Our Team," Shipyard website, accessed March 14, 2012, www.shipyard.com/sub/aboutus/team.html.

George Stranahan biography; Flying Dog start-up Roger Fillion, "Rebel with a Cause," *Rocky Mountain News* (Denver), September 22, 2007.

Victory Brewing start-up "About Victory," Victory Brewing Company website, accessed June 16, 2012, www.victorybeer.com/about-victory.

Magic Hat start-up "Vermont's Small Breweries Are Big Business," *Modern Brewery Age*, March 31, 1997.

Kim Jordan was passing her Fridays and $60,000 in start-up costs Kim Jordan, interview with the author, May 17, 2012. New Belgium was incorporated with Colorado on March 11, 1993.

Idea sprang from trips to Belgium Ibid.

New Belgium first sales, initial production Tony Kiss, "From Basement to Big Time: New Belgium Celebrates 25th," *Asheville Citizen-Times*, August 27, 2016.

Odell Brewing; what the Anheuser-Busch plant just north Dick Kreck, "Fort Collins Breweries Friendly Rivals," *Denver Post*, December 21, 1994, E01.

Pregnant with their second child Jordan interview.

Buccaneer Gold Leslie J. Allen, "Brewing the Better Business Plan," *Philadelphia Inquirer*, November 8, 1993.

"If we can get people" Joyce, "Bond Trader Whets His Appetite."

Ghosts Around the Machines

"Center of attention" Douglas Jehl, "President Begins a Lobbying Blitz for Trade Accord," *New York Times*, November 9, 1993, A1.

NAFTA debate "NAFTA: Ross Perot and Al Gore Debate 1993 (1/8)," YouTube video, 9:00, from a televised 1993 CNN debate, posted by "Mike Hansel," November 7, 2008, www.youtube.com/watch?v=5yww5Z3PJIs&list=PL90122AE3819C3C13&index=1&feature=plpp_video.

Manufacturing jobs Barnaby J. Feder, "A Surprise: Blue-Collar Jobs Rebound," *New York Times*, December 6, 1993, D1.

Cherry Brew and Naked Hockey

Calagione background and first homebrew Sam Calagione, *Brewing Up a Business: Adventures in Beer from a Founder of Dogfish Head Craft Brewery* (Hoboken, NJ: Wiley, 2011), 1–10.

His father . . . was not amused Bilger, "A Better Brew."

"The beer was the hit of the party" and beer epiphany Calagione, *Brewing Up a Business*, 10; Sam Calagione, e-mail message to the author, July 2012.

In Prime Time

Pete Slosberg had not counted on the cop Slosberg, *Beer for Pete's Sake*, 135–37.

Commercial details Slosberg 137; "Pete's Wicked Ale -TV Ad For Beer - Pete Signing Autographs, City Cop Asks for Permit," YouTube video, 0:33, posted by "lordielordie," September 15, 2009, www.youtube.com/watch?v=y7yJteNmryU&feature=related.

Aired in 1994 in major markets John Flinn, "Pete's Aims to Be Mega-Microbrewer," *Denver Post*, August 28, 1994, I4.

Sell 2.5 million cases of beer in forty-one states Robert Emproto, "Thumping the Tub for Microbrews, Pete's Ale Grows at Wicked Rates," *Beverage World*, vol. 113, September 30, 1994, 1; "Specialty Beer Market Increases 60 Percent in 1994," *Business Wire*, February 16, 1995.

Were growing exponentially compared to Dick Kreck, "Festival to Pour 1,200 Beers," *Denver Post*, October. 19, 1994, E1; Gene Sloan, "Tapping Micros' Success," *USA Today*, October 21, 1994, A1. The production share is an estimate and comes from the figure 1.67 million barrels for all craft brewers and brewpubs in 1993. Boston Beer's share was 450,000.

"Industry writers can't get"; "It's the judgment of your peers" Kreck, "Festival to Pour 1,200 Beers."

The youthful new president Karen Ball, "Doting Father, Card Player, Crossword Fan—Bill Clinton at Ease," Associated Press, July 8, 1992.

"Skip the fattening deserts" "Valentine's Day Anxiety? A Beer Lover's Survival Guide to February 14," PR Newswire, January 26, 1995.

"I resent it" Bill Atkinson, "Has Spuds Met His Match?," *Business Journal San Jose*, May 11, 1987, 2.

Opened a brewery in early 1989 Bob MacDonald, "Now Brewing in Jamaica Plain," *Boston Globe*, February 23, 1989, 10.

He placed inside the cornerstone J. Koch; Papazian.

Was given to killing cats J. Koch.

The company would talk about plans Charlie McCollum, "Texas Beer Importer Buys Pete's Brewing Co. of Belmont, Calif.," *San Jose Mercury News*, May 3, 1998.

Critical Mass

CD-ROM details "CD-ROM Gives a Taste of Best in Beers," *San Francisco Examiner*, July 17, 1995.

Only four American beers "Picks and Pans Review: *The Gourmet Guide to Beer*," People, April 16, 1984, Vol. 21, No. 15.

Hillman background Hillman, *Gourmet Guide to Beer* (1987 edition).

Julie Johnson became a co-owner of *All About Beer* in an amicable 2008 divorce settlement.

Julie Johnson Julie Johnson, interview with the author, April 7, 2010.

Bradford leaving Association of Brewers; All About Beer acquisition Bradford.

Advice they got from beer writers like Randy Mosher Randy Mosher, interview with the author, September 30, 2011.

He did his research in the pre-Internet way Ibid.

Hieronymus and Labinsky Stan Hieronymus, interview with the author, September 30, 2011.

Brand Kevin Fagan, "Bay Area Reporter Bill Brand Dies," *The San Francisco Chronicle*, February 25, 2009.

Erickson Jack Erickson, "A Writer's Life," accessed March 29, 2012, www.jackerickson. com/Site/Jack_Erickson.html. The *Erickson Report* lasted until 1997.

Don Russell Mark Lisheron, "The Column That Became a Franchise," *American Journalism Review*, February/March 2008.

Worked as a librarian "Lew Bryson," Amazon.com, accessed June 3, 2012, www.amazon. com/Lew-Bryson/e/B001JS7L22.

Only to discover his ignorance Tim Webb, *Good Beer Guide Belgium*, 6th ed. (Saint Albans, UK: Campaign for Real Ale, 2009), 8.

Exercised immense influence Geary interview.

Alan Eames Douglas Martin, "Alan D. Eames, 59, Scholar of Beers Around the World, Dies," *New York Times*, February 27, 2007, section A, 17; "Alan Eames," *Brattleboro Reformer*, February 12–14, 2007, accessed March 28, 2012, www.legacy.com/ obituaries/brattleboro/obituary.aspx?n=alan-eames&pid=86436273&fhid=4763.

New Beer Rules Stan Hieronymus, "New Beer Rules," Appellation Beer website, accessed June 4, 2012, http://appellationbeer.com/.

"Ultimate Beer Run" excerpt and details Don Russell, "Super Suds Put a Head on Sunday's Big Game," *Philadelphia Daily News*, January 26, 1996, 31. Russell eventually turned his column writing for the *Daily News* into a franchise called Joe Sixpack.

Beer magazines Stan Hieronymus, "Beer Magazines Circa 1994," Appellation Beer website, accessed March 27, 2012, http://appellationbeer.com/blog/beer-magazines-circa-1994/.

"Home Brew Digest" Patrick Babcock, e-mail message to the author, March 2012. Babcock and Karl Lutzen acquired the subscription list and Gardener's original programming scripts in 1997.

Digest posts Home Brew Digest archives, accessed March 28, 2012, http://hbd.org/archives. shtml.

The Potato-Chip Epiphany

Charlie Papazian asked the ballroom Greg Koch, interview with the author, September 30, 2011.

When it came to technology "Bill Healy; Built Mount Bachelor Ski Resort," Associated Press, October 29, 1993.

Cameron Healy background Cameron Healy, interview with the author, August 2011.

One of the most successful natural-food brands Suzanne Marta, "Kettle Foods Brings 'Natu-real' Foods to the Mainstream," *Salem (OR) Statesman-Journal*, August 15, 1999, 1E.

The largest potato-chips producer PepsiCo, "Quick Facts," February, 2011, www.pepsico. com/Download/Frito-Lay_Quick_Facts.pdf.

"If I could create a distinctive enough product" Healy.

Revenues beat those of his father Marta, "Kettle Foods Brings 'Natureal' Foods to the Mainstream."

A 1987 trip through northern Europe and Healy started assembling a business plan Healy.

Hawaiian brewing history Robert C. Schmitt, "Hawaii's Beers and Brewers," University of Hawaii at Manoa publication, accessed April 2, 2012, http://evols.library.manoa. hawaii.edu/bitstream/handle/10524/604/JL31149.pdf?sequence=1.

Healy saw opportunity Healy.

The Brewpubs Boom

Launched operations in an old newspaper pressroom "History," Kona Brewing web-site, accessed April 2, 2012, http://konabrewingco.com/wp-content/blogs.dir/2/ files/2011/05/PressKit.pdf.

3,000 barrels produced "Kona Brewing Company President to Keynote Brewbound's Craft Beer Session on December 5, 2011," Kona Brewing website, accessed April 2, 2012, http://konabrewingco.com/wp-content/blogs.dir/5/files/2012/02/Mattson-Davis-to-keynote-Brewbound-session.pdf.

Hawaii charged brewers Paula Gillingham, "Brewers Want State to Let Beer Flow More Freely," Pacific Business News, July 27, 1997, 14.

Brewpub statistics Gerry Khermouch, "Tapping Into the Ethos," *Brandweek*, May 22, 1995, 34.

Legal changes in big states Ron Ruggless, "Texans Jump on the Brewpub Bandwagon," *Nation's Restaurant News*, April 18, 1994, 3.

Triple Rock "Pub," Triple Rock website, accessed April 2, 2012, http://triplerock.com/?page_id=7.

Hickenlooper and Wynkoop start-up William Porter, "LoDo Pioneer John Hickenlooper's Next Challenge May Be a Run for the Mayor's Office," *Denver Post*, July 21, 2002, L01.

Frank Day background and businesses Penny Parker, "Rock Bottom Sees Light of Day," *Denver Post*, September 13, 1999, F01.

Boulder Brewing ownership and name changes Alicia Wallace, "Boulder Beer Co. Brews Up 30 Years of History," *Boulder (CO) Daily Camera*, September 14, 2009.

Quickly became a major hangout Christopher Wood, "Pru Plaza Rejects Some Tenants Despite High Vacancy Rate," *Denver Business Journal*, November 15, 1991, 5.

Red ale was a particular hit Jon Van Housen, "Rock-Bottom Business: Downtown's New Brew Pub Is the Place to See and Be Seen," *Colorado Business*, 44.

New Rock Bottoms Alan Liddle, "Rock Bottom Accelerates 'Brew-n-Chew' Growth," *Nation's Restaurant News*, October 3, 1994.

Heartland Brewery "New Yorkers and Co.," New York Times, January 1, 1995, section 13, page 4.

Hops Bistro & Brewery and Hops Grill & Bar Jack Hayes, "Hops and Harper's Heat Up Casual Dining in Southeast," *Nation's Restaurant News*, May 17, 1993; Khermouch, "Tapping Into the Ethos."

Hickenlooper was said to be involved Khermouch, "Tapping Into the Ethos."

Gordon and Biersch backgrounds "Dan Gordon" and "Dean Biersch," Gordon Biersch website, accessed April 3, 2012, www.gordonbiersch.com/.

With expectations of as much as $7 million Steve Jefferson, "Beer Business Boom Brewing," *Pacific Business News*, November 21, 1994, 1.

Could be made in the back for 20 cents Becky Beyers, "Microbrewer Taps into Beer Market," *USA Today*, March 24, 1995, 3B.

Criticism of brewpub chains Khermouch, "Tapping Into the Ethos."

Suds and the City

And that's what the papers wrote about Bob Liff and Austin Evans Fenner, "Sud Rise a Lift to W'Burg," *New York Daily News*, May 29, 1996, 1. Such articles were indicative of the coverage of Brooklyn Brewery then.

Brewery construction and union sit-down Hindy and Potter, *Beer School*, 164–172.

Attack of the Phantom Crafts

Post-1983 production growth The United States Brewers Association estimated that the nation's breweries turned out more than two hundred million barrels in 1990. Per the Economic History Association's EH.net, https://eh.net/encyclopedia/a-concise-history-of-americas-brewing-industry/ (accessed August 19, 2016).

More than three-fifths Lawrence M. Fisher, "Behind the Bonhomie, the Brewing Industry Gets Tough," *New York Times*, July 21, 1991.

Less than 3 percent of US beer sales Ron Givens, "Big Brewers Notice Success of Small Guys," *New York Daily News*, April 21, 1994, 7A.

"I don't know why the industry doesn't" Peter V. K. Reid, "Fighting the Seventh Beer War," *Modern Brewery Age*, May 20, 1996.

"This one is his" and head-to-head in national advertising campaigns Jim Kirk with Cathy Taylor, "A-B Joins Elks," *Adweek*, March 28, 1994.

"Subtle, sweet taste" "Anheuser-Busch to Introduce Red Beer in Florida," *New York Times*, September 30, 1994, D3.

Even a Rolling Rock Bock Givens, "Big Brewers Notice Success of Small Guys."

Craft brewers' reactions Peter Rowe, "Trouble Brewing: Big Companies Tap Into Craft-Beer Market," *San Diego Union-Tribune*, October 29, 1997.

Blue Moon background Donald Breed, "Blue Moon Brewers Full of Ideas," *Providence (RI) Journal-Bulletin*, December 3, 1997, 3F.

States and virtually overnight "Coors Unveils Microbrews," *Marketing News TM*, October 9, 1995, 14.

Guide notes Seamus Campbell and Robin Goldstein, *The Beer Trials* (New York: Fearless Critic Media, 2010), 91, 125.

"Budhook" and the Bull Beer Market

Redhook IPO background and if it weren't for capacity constraints M. Sharon Baker, "Redhook IPO Won't Slake Anheuser-Busch's Thirst," *Puget Sound Business Journal*, July 14, 1995, 14.

"A screaming winner" Ibid.

Koch's reaction George Gendron, "Brewed Awakening," *Inc.*, October 1, 1994.

Portsmouth Brewery background "A History of Beer, As We See It," Portsmouth Brewery website, accessed April 8, 2012, http://portsmouthbrewery.com/our_beers_brewery/a_history_of_beer_as_we_see.html.

Smuttynose start-up "Peter Egelston," Smuttynose Brewery website, accessed April 8, 2012, http://smuttynose.com/staff/peter_egelston_company_pres.html.

"The future is in your hands" Andrea Foote and Maxim Lenderman, "Of Two Minds," *Beverage World Periscope Edition*, May 31, 1996.

Were starting to question the basic premise Andrew Leckey, "Trendy Suds Could Just Be Duds," *Cleveland Plain Dealer*, February 12, 1996, 2D.

Thomas Kemper-Hart deal "A Little Background About Thomas Kemper Soda Co.," Thomas Kemper website, accessed April 9, 2012,www.tksoda.com/files/press/Company_Background.pdf.

Pyramid IPO "Hart Brewing Co. Joins the IPO Boom," *Modern Brewery Age*, December 25, 1995.

"Primary phase" "Leading Microbrewer Breaks Ground in California," *Business Wire*, January 26, 1996.

Wine IPO "Mondavi Winery Sells 2.5 Million Shares in IPO," Associated Press, June 11, 1993.

Bernau's endgame J. L. Sullivan, "Portland's Bernau to Try His Suds, Stock in OC," *Orange County Business Journal*, September 26, 1994, 12.

To endow a fermentation science "Nor'wester Brewing Co. Endows Fermentation Studies Professorship at OSU," *Modern Brewery Age*, February 26, 1996.

Frederick Brewing start-up details Dan Moreau, "Personal Finances," *Kiplinger's Personal Finance*, February 1994, 140.

Frederick Brewing expansion Dan Moreau, "Microbrewery Is Still Hopping," *Kiplinger's Personal Finance*, August 1996, 10; "A Brewery in Turn-around," *Modern Brewery Age*, September 10, 2001.

Biggest craft brewery by sales Ralph Berrier Jr., "Head Brewer Crafts Ales," *Roanoke (VA) Times*, July 11, 1998, 1.

Pete's Brewing and Boston Beer production numbers "Crowd Hops on IPO Shares of Nation's Top Craft Brewer," *Bloomberg Business News*, November 22, 1995.

Didn't want to leave any heirs Bronder.

An undeclared price war Doyle and Kenary interview. Various media reports at the time tell of price wars, particularly in larger markets like Chicago and New York.

Pete's Brewing as an IPO prospect, including Northern California brewery plans "New Issues—Pete's Brewing Company (WIKD, 25, NASDAQ) Avoid," *Standard & Poor's Emerging & Special Situations*, November 13, 1995.

"At the expense of some of our competitors" Steve Dwyer, "Hail to the Ale," *Prepared Foods*, October 1996, 28.

"63 in '93" Kallman.

Koch arranged for consumers Floyd Norris, "Boston Beer Has an Unusual Public Offering Gimmick," *New York Times*, November 2, 1995, D12.

Boston Beer shares "As IPO Looms, a Look at Boston Beer Company," *Modern Brewery Age*, August 21, 1995.

Koch versus Busch worth James E. Causey, "Brewer Has Intoxicating Rise in Value," *Milwaukee Journal Sentinel*, December 5, 1995, Business, 1.

Trading 37 times higher Andrew Leckey, "Beer Stock Froth Sometimes Chased with Bitter Earnings," *Chicago Tribune*, February 4, 1996, C3.

"Craft beer has become the 'in' thing" "Hart Brewing Co. Joins the IPO Boom."

Last Call for the Old Days

Lindenbusch background Ron Lindenbusch, interview with the author, March 22, 2012.

Vijay Mallya yacht interview Shailaja Neelakantan, "Here Comes the Kingfisher," *Forbes*, July 28, 1997, 50.

Then things went from bad to worse Mike Francis, "Nor'wester Hopes for Best," *Oregonian* (Portland), May 2, 1997, B01.

Brewery in Saratoga Springs Lew Bryson, *New York Breweries* (Mechanicsburg, PA: Stackpole Books, 2003), 114.

Kingfisher ubiquity; owned half of Peter Sinton, "Beer Baron Adds to His Suds Empire," *San Francisco Chronicle*, May 8, 1997, B1.

Controlled the venerable Cliff Feltham, "Mallya Gets Bitter Taste at Wiltshire," *Daily Mail* (UK), April 9, 1994, 69.

Pumped $1.75 million into Humboldt Brewing Sinton, "Beer Baron Adds to His Suds Empire."

UB group was estimated Ibid.

"I'll have a lot more clout" Neelakantan, "Here Comes the Kingfisher."

Ponzi's decision making regarding BridgePort sale "BridgePort Brewery Sold to Gambrinus," *Modern Brewery Age*, October 16, 1995; Ponzi.

BridgePort versus competitors in production Gerry Khermouch, "Microbreweries More Amenable to Majors," *Brandweek*, October 16, 1995, 3.

Embarrassing death Gerry Khermouch, "Miller: Reserves Waning, Micros Ahoy," *Brandweek*, November 13, 1995, 12.

Shipyard-Miller deal and "lifelong wish list" Jeff Smith, "Shipyard Brewery: It's Time for Miller," *Portland (ME) Press Herald*, November 10, 1995, 1A.

Celis stake Ibid.

"I don't think anything" Jeff Smith, "Geary's Not Paling from Shipyard's Big News," *Portland (ME) Press Herald*, November 14, 1995, 2C.

Big Beer's Biggest Weapon

"Each of you [must]" Maxim Lenderman, "Anheuser-Busch Wants Its Wholesalers' Whole Attention," *Beverage World*, September 1, 1996, 70.

"Go home and hug" "Fritz Maytag Addresses National Beer Wholesalers Association Convention," *Modern Brewery Age*, October 12, 1998.

In the early days of their New Belgium Jordan.

Kansas alcohol and Free State Brewery Tom Gress, "If You Want a Beer with Character, Home Brewing Can Give It Your Own," *Kansas City Business Journal*, September 12, 1988, 1.

One skunky batch Jim McDonald, interview with the author, May 22, 2012.

McDonald background and Boulevard Brewery start-up "Cradle of Entrepreneurs Re-Cap: John McDonald of Boulevard Brewing Goes for Regionalism, Sustainability," Kansas City Public Library website, August 4, 2011, www.kclibrary.org/blog/kc -unbound/cradle-entrepreneurs-re-cap-john-mcdonald-boulevard-brewing-goes -regionalism-sustain; "Kansas City Gets First Brewery in 16 Years," *St. Louis Post -Dispatch*, November 10, 1989, 3C; "Our Story," Boulevard Brewing Company website, accessed April 16, 2012, www.boulevard.com/brewery/our-story/.

"Financial incentive is called Budweiser and Bud Light" Max Lenderman, "Mind Games," *Beverage World*, September 1996, 70–74.

Flying Monkey versus Anheuser-Busch Lorene Yue, "King of Beers Tries to Swat Down Flying Monkey, Other Small Brews," *Stuart (FL) News*, September 3, 1996, B6.

Anheuser-Busch sales "Anheuser-Busch Announces Record Sales, Earnings and Beer Volume for the Full Year 1996," *Business Wire*, February 5, 1997.

Considering launching a new ad campaign Gerry Khermouch, "Positioning: A-B to recast Bud as Classic Lager'" Brandweek, March 10, 1997.

150,000 barrels annually Gavin Power, "Brewers Chastise Their Own," *San Francisco Chronicle*, August 16, 1994, B1.

Pacific Ridge marketing, including billboards and locavore pitch Max Lenderman, "In Northern California, A-B Takes on the Locals," *Beverage World Periscope Edition*, January 31, 1997, 1.

The French Lieutenant's Coat

Hindy and Potter, *Beer School*, 196–97; 165.

Hindy-Oliver meeting Ibid., 28–31.

Oliver biography Amy Laskowski, "Changing Lanes: Filmmaker to Beer Brewer," *BU Today*, March 2, 2011; Rachel Wharton, "Garrett Oliver, Brewmaster for Brooklyn Brewery," Edible Manhattan, July 7, 2010.

Everyone again insisted Hindy and Potter, *Beer School*, 30–31.

Oliver joined in 1994 Ibid., 30–31.

List of New York brewpubs Florence Fabricant, "Finally, New York Takes to Brew Pubs," *New York Times*, April 17, 1996, C1.

New York City Brewpub Crawl Marathon Ron Givens, "Relying on Brewed Strength," *New York Daily News*, August 2, 1996, 62.

To the Extreme

Dogfish Head sign incident Calagione, *Brewing Up a Business*, 18.

A clause he sensed the owner Ibid., 12.

Became a bible Ibid., 25.

no longer carried A European Court decision in 1987 that found that the Reinheitsgebot violated the European Union's foundational rules blunted its legal hold on much of West Germany (and, post-reunification, Germany). Breweries thereafter could use formally forbidden ingredients such as malt and hop extracts. Per Tom Acitelli, "The Strange Tale of Roggenbier, the Rye-Based Medieval Beer Style Time Almost Forgot," FoodRepublic.com, November 3, 2016, https://tomacitelli.com/2016/11/03/the-strange-tale-of-roggenbier-the-rye-based-medieval-beer-style-time-almost-forgot/ (accessed December 28, 2016).

Artisan breads and coffees Sam Calagione, interview with the author, April 16, 2012.

"The next food craze" Jack Hayes, "On the Rise: Café-Bakeries," *Nation's Restaurant News*, November 7, 1994, 57.

Even chains . . . and consolidations "Company Overview," Panera Bread website, accessed April 17, 2012, www.panerabread.com/about/company/history.php.

"first brewery to plunk" Hieronymus, "How Craft Became Craft."

Chicory stout ingredients "Chicory Stout," Dogfish Head website, accessed April 17, 2012, www.dogfish.com/brews-spirits/the-brews/seasonal-brews/chicory-stout.htm.

"If you only want to have" "Dogfish Head Chicory Stout," *The Beer Guide*, edited by Josh Oakes (Fort Worth, TX: Savory House Press, 2006).

Beginning in the late 1980s Samuel Adams Double Bock was introduced in 1988, Samuel Adams website, accessed August 31, 2012, www.samueladams.com/enjoy-our-beer/beer-detail.aspx?name=double-bock.

"The world doesn't need" "New Brews on Tap from Sam Adams," *Alameda (CA) Times-Star*, May 21, 2003.

Dogfish Head expansion "Company Profile," Dogfish Head website, accessed April 17, 2012, www.dogfish.com/company/dogfish-way/company-profile.htm.

Calagione hunting for distributors Calagione.

Calagione's Delaware Bay trip Ibid.; "Holy Tort! Rev. Schuller Sued by Flight Attendant," *Philadelphia Inquirer*, August 21, 1997, D02; Melanie Wells, "Entrepreneur as Stunt Man," *Forbes*, November 1, 1999, 228.

The Total Package

Magee's thinking behind labels, including the Oktoberfest excerpt and consumer reaction Magee memoir manuscript.

"In putrid tones" and Lagunitas expansion Ibid.

Magee decided Lagunitas Ibid.

Boos

Geary's comments and crowd reaction Geary; "Craft & Specialty Beer Report: Taking the Pulse of the Specialty Segment at the National Craftbrewers Conference and Trade Show," *Modern Brewery Age*, May 20, 1996, 7.

Boston Beer's contract brewing Michael Saunders, "Brewing Up a Storm," *Boston Globe Magazine*, November 10, 1996, 24.

961,000 barrels and $151.3 million "The Boston Beer Company Inc. Announces Record Results for 1995," PR Newswire, February 26, 1996.

"Ridiculous!" and more boos Geary; "Craft & Specialty Beer Report."

"Contract brewing is the cocaine" Saunders, "Brewing Up a Storm."

"He's just an extremely aggressive salesman" Bill Virgin, "Brewmaster Mixes Personality with Beer," *Seattle Post-Intelligencer*, September 5, 1994, B3.

Oregon brewers' reaction to Oregon Ale Mike Francis, "Brewers Flip Lids at Role of Oregon Ale," *Oregonian* (Portland), April 30, 1995, F01.

Samuel Adams Cranberry Lambic reaction Saunders, "Brewing Up a Storm."

Boston Beer Works dispute Ibid.; Joe Slesar, e-mail exchange with the author, December 19, 2012.

"The Best Beer in America" trademark effort and rejection US Department of Commerce Patent and Trademark Office, "In re Boston Beer Company Limited Partnership," July 31, 1997; US Court of Appeals for the Federal Circuit, 198 F.3d 1370, December 7, 1999.

"The chance of finding a new job" "North Carolina in the Global Economy," Center on Globalization, Governance, and Competitiveness at Duke University, accessed April 24, 2012, www.soc.duke.edu/NC_GlobalEconomy/furniture/workers.shtml.

American manufacturing and went over the cliff Bureau of Labor Statistics, "Employment, Hours and Earnings from the Current Employment Statistics Survey (National)," accessed April 24, 2012, http://data.bls.gov/pdq/SurveyOutputServlet.

As many as 115 craft operations "Specialty Brewers Gather in Atlanta for Annual Conference and Trade Show," *Modern Brewery Age*, April 20, 1998.

"Now we have a category" Geary.

"There is a controversy now" "Craft & Specialty Beer Report."

Medals controversy Ibid.; Geary.

The Movement's Biggest Setback

Around eight million American homes "Weekly Nielsen Ratings," *Stuart (FL) News*, April 28, 1996, 10.

Dateline segment and excerpts "Brew-Haha," *Dateline* transcript, October 13, 1996. The author would like to thank NBC for providing the transcript.

Federal tax credit Ibid.; "Present Law and Historical Overview of the Federal Tax System," report prepared by the Joint Committee on Taxation for the Committee on Ways and Means, January 18, 2011, 38.

Hansen-Fish conversation "Brew-Haha."

Jim Koch watched the episode J. Koch.

175 commercials for the Olympics Andrew Gottesman, "Betting on 5 Golden Rings," *Chicago Tribune*, July 14, 1996, C1.

"It's not going to be malicious" J. Koch.

ATF petitions and reactions Jerry Ackerman, "Brewers Foaming over Labels," *Boston Globe*, January 26, 1996, 38.

Was working on an official definition Lisa Jennings, "'Craft' Beer Craze Crams Store Shelves, Tests Connoisseurs," *Memphis Commercial Appeal*, May 24, 1996, 1C.

Anheuser-Busch launched a television, radio, and print campaign Chris Reidy, "Anheuser-Busch Agrees to Modify Ads Targeting Sam Adams," *Boston Globe*, April 1, 1997, C2.

Miller's response "Miller Brewing Company's Response to Anheuser-Busch's BATF Filing," PR Newswire, January 26, 1996.

Which it introduced in 1984 Scott Hume, "Bud's Spud Plugging Suds," *Advertising Age*, March 6, 1986, 2.

Anheuser-Busch threatened legal action and lured away the ad agency Slosberg, *Beer for Pete's Sake*, 135, 137.

Dan Kenary . . . knew he would never forget Doyle and Kenary interview.

Hickenlooper pulled all Anheuser-Busch brands and "It's been maybe ten years" Don Russell, "No Bud of Mine," *Philadelphia Daily News*, February 14, 1997, 79.

Anheuser-Busch could continue to tell consumers Reidy, "Anheuser-Busch Agrees to Modify Ads."

Lucky Bastards

Greg Koch certainly remembered G. Koch.

Greg Koch background, including frequenting Al's Ibid.; Greg Koch and Steve Wagner with Randy Clemens, *The Craft of Stone Brewing Co.* (Berkeley, CA: Ten Speed Press, 2011), 29–30.

San Diego beer history Ernie Liwag, "Craft Beer in San Diego Society," *Journal of San Diego History*, vol. 53, no. 4 (Fall 2007): 1–5.

Chris Cramer and Matt Rattner background and Karl Strauss start-up "Our Beer" and "Our Namesake," Karl Strauss Brewing Company website, accessed May 4, 2012, www.karlstrauss.com.

Bolt Brewery Gordon Smith, "This Home Beer Maker May Be a Trend," *San Diego Union-Tribune*, December 15, 1987, C1.

Holborn would go on to be Jack Erickson, *California Brewin': The Exciting Story of California's Microbrewing Revolution* (Reston, VA: Red Brick Press, 1993), 124.

Several more entrepreneurs let it be known Greg Johnson, "Brew Pubs Tapping Into Trend of Designer Suds," *Los Angeles Times*, December 10, 1989, B1.

Alpine Village George Hatch, "Torrance Brewery's Cup Runneth Over During Soccer Championship," *Los Angeles Times*, July 8, 1990, 5.

Several operations . . . were firsts Erickson, *California Brewin'*, 109–126.

Angeles Brewing and Richard Belliveau background Ibid., 109; John Medearis, "Tiny Brewery Is Braving Some Stout Competition," *Los Angeles Times*, September 5, 1989, 9A.

Gorky's and Manhattan Beach Erickson, *California Brewin'*, 122, 166.

Koch-Wagner meeting and brewery-location decision G. Koch; Koch and Wagner, *The Craft of Stone Brewing Co.*, 30–32.

Wolfgang Puck quote Richard Martin, "Eureka! Puck Unveils Brewery," *Nation's Restaurant News*, June 11, 1990, 1.

A plan to reopen with Boston Beer and "It just hurts so bad" Kathie Jenkins, "Eureka Won't Be Ale-ing Anymore," *Los Angeles Times*, May 2, 1993, 82.

Koch went to Solana Beach G. Koch.

Stone Brewing start-up G. Koch; Koch and Wagner, *The Craft of Stone Brewing Co.*, 39–41.

This is an aggressive ale Ibid., 44.

The company was losing money; then, March came G. Koch.

A Tale of Two Breweries

Sales-and-marketing operation remained basically a one-man show and left the brewery in frustration Rifka Rosenwein, "Despite Ale's Success, Brewery Loses Out," *Inc.*, October 1, 2000.

Windsor expansion and expenditures Ibid.; "Catamount Looks at Windsor Industrial Park for Expansion," *Modern Brewery Age*, May 13, 1996.

It was all over and "in a state of minor disrepair" "Catamount Closure Leaves Debts, Co-Founder Says Mistakes Were Made," *Modern Brewery Age*, April 24, 2000.

The company's official launch; might go for $5.25 "Mayor Ed Rendell Joins Red Bell Brewing Company at First Annual 'Taste of Philadelphia' Celebration," PR Newswire, January 16, 1995; Frank Dougherty, "At $2.75 Apiece, They're a Strikeout," *Philadelphia Daily News*, April 13, 1999, 7.

Bell told the local press and "If you deliver a good product" Tom Hals, "Red Bell Foams Over with Big Brewing Plans," *Philadelphia Business Journal*, May 10, 1996, 3.

"A sea of first-time buyers" "Top 100 Philadelphia Moments #50 to #26," *Philadelphia* magazine website, www.phillymag.com/home/display/Top_100_Philadelphia_Moments_50_to_26/.

The answers were all yes Jack Curtin, "Stockbrokers Gone Wild," *American Brewer*, Summer 2006.

Red Bell might net Peter Van Allen, "Red Bell's Hangover Continues," *Philadelphia Business Journal*, January 20, 2003, 1.

IPO and stock-price decline Ibid.; "Red Bell Brewing Company Responds to Recent Stock Price Decline," Business Wire, July 9, 2001.

Pennsylvania revoked the company's brewing license Van Allen, "Red Bell's Hangover Continues."

Too broke to go bankrupt Ibid.

The Great Shakeout

Would be the first year Julie Flaherty, "Now, the Glass Is Half Empty; Microbreweries in the Slow Lane," *New York Times*, May 30, 2000, C1.

"Milli Vanilli" entrants, "shitty beer," and "crappy beer" Shared with the author by movement members wishing to remain anonymous.

650 bottles a minute and 200-barrel brewhouse Burton, Hops and Dreams; "Sierra Nevada Installs $2 Million Packaging Plant," *Erickson Report*, March 1996, www.realbeer.com/redbrickpress/erickrpt.html. The brewhouse was installed in 1997.

Sierra Nevada, Brooklyn, New Belgium sales Flaherty, "Now, the Glass Is Half Empty."

number would decline by; over fifteen hundred Author's e-mail exchanges with Bart Watson, chief economist of the Brewers Association, December 2016; Brewers Association, "Number of Breweries," www.brewersassociation.org/statistics/number-of-breweries/ (accessed August 22, 2016). Of the roughly fifteen hundred craft breweries and brewpubs in 2000, about 420 were breweries; the rest brewpubs. The Brewers Association statistics—including the fifteen hundred figure—include only those operations actively selling their beers, not those just with licenses to brew.

Victory Abroad, Defeat at Home

Bozzini change and Production and sales dropped, too "Pete's Announces Year-End Numbers," *Modern Brewery Age*, March 2, 1998.

Lost thirteen cents per share Scott Herhold, "California Microbreweries Are Over a Barrel," *San Jose Mercury News*, March 15, 1998.

Share prices Ibid. Historical perspectives on share prices can also be tracked through Yahoo Finance at finance.yahoo.com.

First real off-year Kallman.

New Frederick Brewing facility and capacity details "1998: Brave New World of Beer," *Modern Brewery Age*, March 22, 1999.

Gordon Biersch deal Kenneth Howe, "Brew Pub Selling Big Stake," *San Francisco Chronicle*, November 21, 1995, B1.

Yakima deal and Grant's quotes Bill Virgin, "International Wine's Latest Vintage: Washington's Oldest Microbrewery," *Seattle Post-Intelligencer*, January 4, 1996, B4.

A particular bugbear of Michael Jackson's Gunningham.

Offered $69 million in cash "Importer Gambrinus to Buy Struggling Pete's Brewing Company," *Bloomberg News*, May 23, 1998.

Two years as pitchman Pete Slosberg, e-mail message to the author, August 18, 2012.

Had taken a lot of fun out Kallman.

Nomura as the biggest owner and fewer than 10 percent Alistair Osborne, "Nomura's £625m Gets Bass Chain of Pubs," *Telegraph* (UK), February 15, 2001; Peter Bartram, *Living It Lager*, Director, April 2001, 48–52.

There were twelve to fourteen examples Nicola Byrne, "Dublin Calls Time on Traditional Irish Pub as Theme Bars Pull in Crowds," *Scotland on Sunday*, April 29, 2001, 22.

Thirty closed in the United Kingdom "Real Ale Campaign in Ferment over Closures," *Western Daily Press* (Bristol, UK), February 27, 2001, 15.

Blind taste test for seventy-five people Dick Kreck, "Micros Hurt by Imports; US Brewers Uniting to Boost Beers," *Denver Post*, October 27, 1999, E04.

Part IV

Plotting a Comeback

Traders literally popped champagne "Dow Jones Reclaims 10,000 Milestone," CBS News, October 15, 2009.

"We're trying not to grow" "Specialty Craft Brewers Gather in Atlanta for Annual Conference and Trade Show," *Modern Brewery Age*, April 20, 1998.

Sales would total $10 million Funding Universe website, accessed May 14, 2012, www.fundinguniverse.com/company-histories/Anchor-Brewing-company-company-History.html.

"Most of the wine in the world" "Specialty Craft Brewers Gather in Atlanta."

To honor the twentieth anniversary "Mendocino Brewing Company Celebrates the 20th Anniversary of New Albion Brewing Company," Business Wire, October 23, 1997.

Tiny Humboldt Brewing Company Ted Appel, "Humboldt Brewing Pulls Out of Chain," *Santa Rosa (CA) Press Democrat*, December 3, 1997, E1.

Shipyard sales growth and "The lesson is" David Sharp, "Specialty Beer Brewers Turn Focus to Local Markets as Boom Goes Flat," *The Chicago Tribune*, May 28, 2000, C7.

Also cut back and happily distributed Flaherty, "Now, the Glass Is Half Empty."

Ommegang Wendy Littlefield, "A Very Long and Boring History of Our Careers in Beer," BelgianExperts.com, May 4, 2011, http://belgianexperts.com/become-a-belgian-expert/1420/a-very-long-and-boring-history-of-our-careers-in-beer/; Ron Givens, "Cooperstown's Future Ale of Fame," *New York Daily News*, August 28, 1998; author's e-mails with Wendy Littlefield, June 2016.

Henry King and excise-tax history Hieronymus, "Henry King."

Often expressed a polite indifference "Our Men in Washington," *Modern Brewery Age*, May 12, 1997.

Vijay Mallya quote Rick Bonino, "Say It Ain't So, Micro-Joe," *Spokane (WA) Spokesman Review*, April 12, 2000, D1.

"McDonald's Versus Fine Food"

World Beer Cup attendance and medals "World Beer Cup 2000," *Modern Brewery Age*, July 10, 2000.

"The natural dynamic is to drink less" Ibid.

Began a decadelong slide Bureau of Labor Statistics.

There were fewer of these as well "What Is the Current State of the American Worker?," *Both Sides with Jesse Jackson*, CNN transcript, September 3, 2000.

Quotes from Hindy, Jackson, Petrini, and Papazian "World Beer Cup 2000."

Craft Beer Logs On

Alstrom backgrounds and BeerAdvocate start-up details Todd and Jason Alstrom, interview with the author, June 2, 2012; "Roots of BeerAdvocate?" April 17, 2012, http://beeradvocate.com/community/threads/roots-of-beeradvocate.12813.

Mark and Darci Silva background and RealBeer start-up details Bernhard Warner, "Insider: The Beer Industry's Silva Bullet," *Adweek*, September 22, 1997; "Welcome to the Executive Offices," Real Beer website, accessed May 21, 2012, www.realbeer.com/rbi/exec.html.

Ale Street News start-up Melissa Brady, "About *Ale Street News*," *Ale Street News* website, accessed May 19, 2012, www.alestreetnews.com/about-us.html; Peter Genovese, "From Stout to Bitter, *Ale Street News* Covers the Industry," *Newark Star- Ledger*, January 19, 2008.

Celebrator start-up, including the Iron Liver Tour "20 Years of Brews News," February/March 2008, Celebrator Beer News website, http://celebrator.com/archives/2008/02/cbn_topstor iessummary.html.

21st Amendment start-up "The 21st Amendment Story," 21st Amendment Brewery website, accessed June 18, 2012, http://21st-amendment.com/company.

RateBeer startup; as Tucker saw it Ken Weaver, "The Quiet Kingmaker," Bohemian.com, May 7, 2012, www.bohemian.com/northbay/the-quiet-kingmaker/Content?oid=2280727; Joe Tucker, e-mail message to the author, May 2012.

At least 1,700 homebrewing clubs Jim Lundstrom, "Homebrewing Enthusiasts Are Branching Out and Making Names for Themselves," *Appleton (WI) Post-Crescent*, May 11, 2002, 1E; Lisa Rauschart, "Bold Brews Go Against Grain of Bland Beers," *Washington Times*, January 25, 2001, M12.

Three thousand judges evaluating 2,668 homebrews Rick Armon, "Beer Competition Coming Here," *Rochester (NY) Chronicle and Democrat*, January 21, 2001, 1B.

"I remember hammering a good guy" Magee memoir manuscript.

Uzbeki Raga Ale episode Magee memoir manuscript. The Oregon Brew Crew confirmed the thread, though the author himself did not see it.

"It's pretty depressing to frequently" Kendall Jones, "Which Breweries Are Overrated?" Washington Beer Blog, January 11, 2012, www.washingtonbeerblog.com/how-does-brewery-become-overrated/.

Motorists lined up more than a mile and a half Webb, *Good Beer Guide Belgium*, 163.

Growing Pains Again

Jeremy Cowan and Shmaltz start-up Jeremy Cowan with James Sullivan, *Craft Beer Bar Mitzvah* (San Francisco: Malt Shop Publishing, 2010), 183–84.

A way to divide up the nation's most competitive Hindy and Potter, *Beer School*, 243–53.

Had taken the brewery as collateral Bryson, 14.

Bodega scene Cowan, *Craft Beer Bar Mitzvah*, 183–84.

Closings and openings "Craft Brew Update: The Craft Brew Segment Basks in Hard-Won Stability," *Modern Brewery Age*, May 13, 2002.

Such as farming walnuts and harvesting wine grapes Burton, *Hops and Dreams*, 105–8.

Rise annually more than 5 percent "The Craft Brew Segment Basks in Hard-Won Stability," *Modern Brewery Age*.

Biggest brewpub chain Greg Kitsock, "Brewpub Chains Merge, But Will It Matter," *Washington Post*, November 22, 2010.

A $2.5 million expansion "Boulevard Brewing Co. Plans Expansion," *Modern Brewery Age*, August 30, 1999, 2.

$2.2 million expansion Jason Stein, "What's Brewing? Specialty Brewers' Cups Runneth Over Thanks to High Demand," *Wisconsin State Journal*, May 15, 2005, C1.

Sierra Nevada's late 1990s expansion Burton, *Hops and Dreams*, 105.

Would eventually produce more than 40 percent Mike Boyer, "Local Brews Still Make Splash with Consumers," *Cincinnati Enquirer*, September 19, 2003, 1D.

Production numbers "The Next Beer War?" Modern Brewery Age, March 25, 2002, 8; Adam Nason, "New Belgium Celebrates 20th Anniversary on June 28th," Beerpulse. com, June 21, 2011, http://beerpulse.com/2011/06/new-belgium-celebrates-20th-anniversary-on-june-28th/.

"For a while" Gerry Khermouch, "Having a Blast During the Great Beer 'Bust,'" *Brandweek*, January 17, 2000, cover story.

David Geary had realized Geary interview.

More modern small breweries "Craft Brew Update: The Craft Brew Segment Basks."

"People ask about" Modern Brewery Age interview with Geoff Larson, 1999 (exact date unknown).

Charlie Papazian put together a slideshow and the movement's professionalization Ibid.

"Queen of Carbs" "Anheuser-Busch Brews Bitter Beer Battle," Associated Press, May 23, 2004.

Jackson excerpt "Miller Merger Could Be a Good Thing," taken from Jackson's speech to the Craft Brewers Conference, Beer Hunter website, June 8, 2002, www.beerhunter. com/documents/19133-001728.html. Used with permission.

Still the Latest Thing

Vinnie Cilurzo background and Blind Pig Vinnie Cilurzo, interview with the author, April 2012.

Worked at his parents' winery "Cilurzo Winery Pursues Fine Wine Crafting in Temecula Valley," *Inland Empire Business Journal*, November 1998, 9.

Electric Dave Tom Miller, "This Brew's for You," *Arizona Trend*, January 1989, 75.

Arizona brewing history Ed Sipos, "A-1: The Western Way to Say Welcome," *American Breweriana Journal*, January/February 1998, accessed May 25, 2012, www.beerhistory. com/library/holdings/arizona-sipos.shtml.

Bandersnatch Kerry Lengel, "Bandersnatch Low-Key and Likes It That Way," *Arizona Republic* (Phoenix), January 29, 2003.

Happily drank at least six bottles' worth Miller, "This Brew's for You."

Arrest for marijuana smuggling and equipment in the hands of other brewers Cilurzo; Kerry Lengel, "Eccentric Electric Bisbee Brewer Content with Small Operation," *The Arizona Republic* (Phoenix), March 27, 2002, 5F.

6 percent alcohol by volume and 92 IBUs in bitterness Cilurzo.

First mainstream-media reference "Coors' Deal with Bass Is Not the Apocalypse," *Alameda (CA) Times-Star*, January 30, 2002.

Vineyards brewing Cilurzo; Tina Caputo, "The B-Word Comes to the Wine Country," *Wines & Vines*, June 1, 1998, 71.

Reopened Russian River as a seven-thousand-square-foot brewpub Bob Norberg, "Downtown Renaissance Continues," *Santa Rosa (CA) Press Democrat*, February 13, 2004, E1.

Bricktown Brewery and quote Tim Goral, "Annual Microbrewery Report," *Modern Brewery Age*, May 10, 1993, S12.

"Huebert Brewery produces" Melissa Marchel, "Oklahoma Couple Poured Their Hearts into a Legal Battle to Open Brewery," *Daily Oklahoman* (Oklahoma City), May 22, 2004.

Saint Arnold Brewing start-up Christopher Helman, "Beer Man: How Brock Wagner Built St. Arnold's Brewing into the Best Microbrewer in Texas," *Forbes*, January 3, 2011.

Texas brewing history "Brewing Industry," Texas State Historical Association website, accessed May 29, 2012, www.tshaonline.org/handbook/online/articles/dib01.

Wagner estimated boosted sales Helman, "Beer Man."

About thirty gallons per Texan per year "Brewing Industry."

Found himself happily planning Helman, "Beer Man."

Moved thirty-one cases of Olde Towne Amber Bill Plott, "Olde Towne's Brewing Ale and Hearty Business," *Birmingham (AL) News*, April 1, 2005, 1B.

Kona Brewing details Aliza Earnshaw, "Kona Brewing Thrives with Portland Connection," *Business Journal*, July 9, 2004.

Maui Brewing start-up details "Ben E. Keith Beverage Distributors Introduces Maui Brewing Co. to Texas," GreatBrewers.com, April 8, 2011, http://greatbrewers.com/story/ben-e-keith-beverage-distributors-introduces-maui-brewing-co-texas.

Rarely miss an opportunity Garrett W. Marrero, "Maui Brewing Company," CraftBeer.com, October 31, 2011, www.craftbeer.com/pages/breweries/featured-brewery/show?title=maui-brewing-company.

Crushing It

Mid-Coast, Chief Oshkosh startup Author's interview with Jeff Fulbright, April 2013; Tom Acitelli, "Canned Mythology," *All About Beer*, August 1, 2013, http://allaboutbeer.com/article/canned-mythology/ (accessed May 31, 2016).

"way under" Author's interview with Fulbright.

Prices starting at around $250,000 Norman Miller, "Can It on the Critique," *MetroWest Daily News* (Framingham, MA), November 24, 2009.

"Dumbest idea" and "nobody will" Alicia Wallace, "Yes, They Can," *Boulder (CO) Daily Camera*, April 18, 2010.

Cask Brewing Systems introduced Greg Kitsock, "Where No Can Has Gone Before . . ." *All About Beer*, July 2009, vol. 30, no. 3.

Dale Katechis background and Oskar Blues start-up Jeremy Henderson, "Give 'Em Ale: Top American Craft Beer Was First Brewed in an Auburn Bathtub," *War Eagle Reader*, November 1, 2011.

Katechis-Lutz Q&A "Oskar Blues Brewery Releases First Colorado Craft Beer in a Can," *Modern Brewery Age*, November 18, 2002.

Found itself with a backlog of orders Joel Johnson, "Canned Beer Is the Future of Good Beer," Gizmodo, August 27, 2010, http://gizmodo.com/5622938/canned-beer-is-the-future-of-good-beer.

Also adopted by Oskar Blues cost about $45,000 "Oskar Blues Cranks Up Canning Capacity," *Modern Brewery Age*, October 11, 2004.

Its distribution wove its way out of Colorado Kitsock, "Where No Can Has Gone Before . . ."; E. J. Schultz, "Dale's Pale Ale," *Ad Age*, November 15, 2010, 22.

Frontier–Dale's Pale Ale deal "Dale's Pale Ale to Take Flight with Frontier," *Modern Brewery Age*, December 23, 2002, 2.

With Gusto

Oliver conversation and book idea Garrett Oliver, interview with the author, May 2012.

"Great beer from around the world" Oliver, *The Brewmaster's Table*, xi.

Oliver learning about Slow Food, trip to Bra, and getting involved Oliver.

Hindy's reaction to Slow Food Hindy and Potter, *Beer School*, 197–98.

"Exactly in step with what" Calagione.

Association of Brewers involvement and Charlie Papazian stepping in Michael Jackson, "Notes from the Road: Turin," Beer Hunter website, December 8, 1998, www.beerhunter.com/documents/19133-000143.html; Charlie Papazian, e-mail message to the author, July 2012.

"Treated like rock stars" Ray Daniels, interview with the author, May 2012.

"Quit chuckling and listen up" Oliver, *The Brewmaster's Table*, 57–58.

"Some American mass-market brewers" Ibid., 353.

"The heady mix of a newly vibrant food culture" Ibid., 287.

Annual revenues of $395,000 Julie Dunn, "Boulder, Colo.-Based Small Brewers Join Forces with North Carolina Association," *Denver Post*, November 2, 2004.

Nerves frayed and other details of the merger "Association of Brewers & BAA to Merge," *Modern Brewery Age*, October 11, 2004; Bradford; Jordan.

A Great Passing

Shelton visit to Jackson "Michael Jackson 'The Beer Hunter'—Interview Preview," YouTube video, 9:52, posted by "SheltonBrothers," September 2, 2007, www.youtube.com/watch?v=DLohwMW7qjU.

A September 14 memorial service in London Carolyn Smagalski, "Michael Jackson—A Final Farewell in London," BellaOnline website, accessed June 4, 2012, www.bellaonline.com/articles/art53112.asp.

"Michael, why don't you ever write about English beers?" "Michael Jackson Toast at Toronado," YouTube video, 4:01, posted by "BeergeekDotCom," October 2, 2007, www.youtube.com/watch?feature=player_embedded&v=OIGftT46bZM#!.

"I think Michael Jackson" Trailer for *The Beer Hunter: The Movie*, accessed June 4, 2012, www.beerhuntermovie.com/.

Beer, Premium

One evening; dialogue with server Daniels.

Daniels background; Cicerone idea Ibid.; Josh Noel, "Beer's Buddy," *Chicago Tribune*, July 11, 2010, 4. Daniels added an "Advanced Cicerone" level in early 2016, between the certified and master levels.

First Cicerone exam details and Van Til quote Josh Noel, "Beer's Buddy"; "First-Ever Master Cicerone Named," *Business Wire*, December 8, 2009.

Oliver at Cheers Beverage Conference; early-morning distributor talks Oliver.

Craft beer sales and production numbers "Brewers Association Announces 2008 Craft Brewer Sales Numbers," Business Wire, February 24, 2009.

"The first time" Marton Dunai, "Craft Brewers Hit Bottleneck," *Contra Costa Times* (Walnut Creek, CA), January 14, 2007.

Greg Koch and Steve Wagner quietly opened J. Harry Jones, "Stone Brewing Quietly Opens Unmarked, High-End Bistro," *San Diego Union-Tribune*, January 6, 2007, NI-1.

Dogfish Head was arriving Bob Townsend, "Rejoice: Dogfish Head Arrives," *Atlanta Journal-Constitution*, March 1, 2007, 6K.

The first twelve-packs of New Belgium's Steve Raabe, "Out of the Bottle," *Denver Post*, May 15, 2008, B5. New Belgium eventually upgraded to a top-of-the-line, seven-million-dollar bottling system, per Jordan.

It cost nearly 40 percent more "Brewers Association Announces 2008 Craft Brewer Sales Numbers."

Hops levels and prices Julie Johnson, "What's Brewing?," *Beverage Dynamics*, September 1, 2008. The author is grateful to various brewers and to writer Stan Hieronymus for explaining the business of hops.

Boston Beer's hops sales Carol Angrisani, "Hip Hops," *Supermarket News*, November 24, 2008, 23.

"Asshole-free" Author attended Philippon's speech.

"They drank wine" "The Classes Drift Apart," *Economist*, February 4, 2012, 36.

Exit the Godfather

Dinner Keith Greggor, interview with the author, March 21, 2012.

Greggor and Tony Foglio experiences in spirits Ibid.; "Our Management Team," Griffin Group website, accessed June 7, 2012, www.tgg.us.com/?p=team.

Few investment bankers Greggor.

Greggor and Foglio bought Greggor; "Keith Greggor and Tony Foglio Invest in BrewDog," BrewDog website, October 21, 2009, www.brewdog.com/blog-article/183.

It was an open secret Greggor; Bronder.

Largest manufacturing business Kate Sofis of SFMade, e-mail message to the author, June 8, 2012. Anchor was biggest by revenue.

"Maytag's departure is a harbinger" Don Russell, "Sale of Industry-Changing Anchor Brewing Triggers a Few Shudders," *Philadelphia Daily News*, May 7, 2010, 53.

Craft Brewers Alliance announcement John Foyston, "Craft Brewers Alliance Inc. to Purchase Kona Brewing for $13.9 Million," *Oregonian* (Portland), August 3, 2010.

Anchor-Griffin deal details Greggor.

"Small is beautiful" "Specialty Brewers Gather in Atlanta."

Reaction to the deal Greggor; Magee; Tom Abate, "Anchor Brewing Co. Sold to Greggor, Foglio," *San Francisco Chronicle*, April 27, 2010, A1.

Big Crowds and the New Small

Pliny the Younger pouring Cilurzo.

"Nary a breeze" "History for Santa Rosa, CA," Wunderground.com, accessed June 9, 2012, www.wunderground.com/history/airport/KSTS/2010/2/10/DailyHistory.html?req_city=Santa+Rosa&req_state=CA&req_statename=California&MR=1.

They forbade growlers the next year and had more staff Cilurzo.

Brew Masters and Eataly details Greg Kitsock, "Beer: Mapping Dogfish Head's 2010 Adventures," *Washington Post All We Can Eat* (blog), January 3, 2011, http://voices.washingtonpost.com/all-we-can-eat/beer/beer-tracking-dogfish.html; the author attended the opening night of Eataly.

GABF details "2011 Great American Beer Festival Winners Announced," Great American Beer Festival website, October 1, 2011, www.greatamericanbeerfestival.com/news/2011-great-american-beer-festival%C2%AE-winners-announced/.

For three years in a row Mike Esterl, "Craft Brewers Tap Big Expansion," *Wall Street Journal*, December 28, 2011, B6.

Craft beer sales and jobs numbers "Facts," Brewers Association website, accessed June 9, 2012, www.brewersassociation.org/pages/business-tools/craft-brewing-statistics/facts.

"The smaller brewers' activity" Esterl, "Craft Brewers Tap Big Expansion."

Definition-change details and "A lot has changed" "Brewers Association Announces Revised Craft Brewer Definition," Brewers Association website, January 3, 2011, www.brewersassociation.org/pages/media/press-releases/show?title=brewers -association-announces-revised-craft-brewer-definition.

Colbert viewer numbers "Jon Stewart's Nielsen Ratings Down 15 Percent; Colbert's Up 11 Percent," *Vulture* (blog), *New York* magazine, January 9, 2008, www.vulture.com /2008/01/stewarts_ratings_down_15_colbe.html.

"This isn't one of those fake holidays" Colbert Nation website video, May 15, 2008, www.colbertnation.com/the-colbert-report-videos/168493/may-15-2008/american -craft-beer-week.

Honey ale at the White House "The Obamas Make History with Homebrewed White House Honey Ale," March 1, 2011, http://obamafoodorama.blogspot.com/2011/03 /obamas-make-history-with-homebrewed.html.

"The Albion Brewery"

Sanguine about the newfound fame McAuliffe, September 30.

Ken & Jack's ale brewery visit details John Holl, "The Rise and Fall of New Albion Brewing Led the Way for the American Craft Beer Revolution," CraftBeer.com, accessed June 11, 2012, www.craftbeer.com/pages/breweries/featured-brewery/show?title=new-albion-brewing.

Scene at Marlowe's The author shared a table with McAuliffe and his daughter, Renee DeLuca.

Forty-Two Hundred and Counting

$20.1 billion deal Michael J. De La Merced and Mark Scott, "Anheuser-Busch InBev Buys Rest of Grupo Modelo, Maker of Corona Beer," *New York Times Dealbook* (blog), June 29, 2012, http://dealbook.nytimes.com/2012/06/29/the-beer-wars-heat -up-with-modelo-deal/.

"On my watch" Tom Daykin, "Anheuser-Busch Gets Buyout Bid," *Milwaukee Journal Sentinel*, June 12, 2008, D1.

"Would have run the risk of becoming the next GM" Theresa Howard, "Beer's Been Going Global for Years," *USA Today*, July 14, 2008, 6B.

Flirting with the milestone Paul Gatza, "US Craft Brewery Count Reaches 2,000," May 23, 2012, Brewers Association website, www.brewersassociation.org/pages /community/ba-blog/show?title=u-s-craft-brewery-count-reaches-2000.

Breezed comfortably "Historic Number of Breweries," Brewers Association website, www.brewersassociation.org/brewers-association/history/history-of-craft-beer/ (accessed June 7, 2016); "The Year in Beer: U.S. Brewery Count Reaches All-Time High of

4,144," Brewers Association website, December 2, 2015, www.brewersassociation. org/press-releases/the-year-in-beer-u-s-brewery-count-reaches-all-time-high-of-4144/ (accessed June 7, 2016); "Number of U.S. Breweries," Brewers Association website, www.brewersassociation.org/statistics/number-of-breweries/, tracks numbers from 1873 to 2012 (accessed June 7, 2016); "Small and Independent Brewers Continue to Grow Double Digits," BA website, March 22, 2016, www.brewersassociation.org/press-releases/small-independent-brewers-continue-grow-double-digits/ (accessed June 7, 2016).

Alabama, Mississippi growth "Map: the State of American Craft Beer—2015," VinePair .com, http://vinepair.com/state-of-craft-beer-map-2015/#chartDescription-3 (accessed June 7, 2016); "Mapping the Rise of Craft Beer," NewYorker.com, http://projects. newyorker.com/story/beer/ (accessed June 7, 2016).

Minnesota change Jim Hammerand, "Twin Cities Brewery Taprooms Boom Five Years After Minnesota Law Change," *Minneapolis-St. Paul Business Journal,* June 2, 2016.

"Drink Socially"

worst possible time; Untappd startup Author's interview with Greg Avola, June 10, 2016; Tom Rotunno, "Two Guys Created Their Dream Jobs, Forged By a Love of Tech and Beer," CNBC.com, April 25, 2016, www.cnbc.com/2016/04/25/two-guys-created-their-dream-jobs-forged-by-a-love-for-tech-and-beer.html (accessed June 8, 2016).

Untappd growth Avola interview.

Guild history, membership Author's emails with Erika Bolden, Jay Brooks, Stan Hieronymus and Lucy Saunders, September 2016.

quickly claimed the biggest share "Cider Production in the U.S.," IBISWorld Industry Report, March 2016.

Craft distillery growth taken from statistics that the American Distilling Institute and the American Craft Spirits Association provided. In another craft beer-craft spirits connection, Bill Owens, who started one of the nation's oldest brewpubs, launched the American Distilling Institute trade group in 2003.

Craft beer demographics "The Demographics of Craft Beer Lovers," Bart Watson, chief economist of the Brewers Association, 2014, www.brewersassociation.org/wp-content/uploads/2014/10/Demographics-of-craft-beer.pdf (accessed June 13, 2016).

Untappd for Business launch Jenny Callison, "Next Glass Subsidiary Untappd Launches Business Feature," WilmingtonBiz.com, May 17, 2016, www.wilmingtonbiz.com/technology/2016/05/17/next_glass_subsidiary_untappd_launches_business_feature/14798 (accessed June 13, 2016).

Craft Beer Turns 185

BA definition change "Brewers Association Board Meeting Produces Strategic Changes," Brewers Association, March 3, 2014; Amy Tindell, "Brewers Association: We Define the 'Craft Brewer,' But Not What It Makes," Kegomatic.com, June 11, 2014, http://kegomatic.com/2014/07/11/brewers-association-we-define-the-craft-brewer-but-not-what-it-makes/ (accessed June 15, 2016).

Dick Yuengling Jr. Author's interview with Dick Yuengling Jr., October 2016; "Dick Yuengling Jr.," D.G. Yuengling & Son website, www.yuengling.com/userfiles/file/15_Yueng_PRKit_Inserts_Biographies-FINAL-web(2).pdf (accessed June 21, 2016); "Dick Yuengling Jr.," Lycoming College "Meet Our Alumni" feature, www.lycoming.edu/profile/alumni/yuneglingDick.aspx (accessed June 21, 2016).

nearly bankrupt Ibid.

one hundred thirty-seven thousand barrels "Dick Yuengling Jr.," D.G. Yuengling & Son website.

falling out; probably doomed Yuengling interview.

Prohibition survival "D.G. Yuengling & Son. Inc.: An American Story," D.G. Yuengling & Son website, www.yuengling.com/userfiles/file/16_Yueng_PRKit-FINAL-web(1).pdf (accessed June 21, 2016). Yuengling by 1900 had several locations operating simultaneously, including in New York City and in British Columbia. All closed except the original brewery in Pottsville. That brewery moved to its present Mahantongo Street location in 1831, after a fire destroyed the first one.

faced a choice Yuengling interview.

best-selling beer on draft Ibid.

Modernization, new beers Ibid.; "Dick Yuengling Jr.," Lycoming College." The light beer that Yuengling introduced in the late 1980s should not be confused with a light lager the company unveiled later.

one hundred, twenty-seven thousand barrels "D.G. Yuengling & Son Inc.: An American Story."

with two things, "don't turn us into IBM," marketing push, turnaround Ibid.

tickled one million barrels Ibid. The brewery would surpass one million barrels annually by 2001.

"We make products" Cristina Rouvalis, "A Head for Business," *Pittsburg Post-Gazette*, January 12, 1997, D5.

continued to price Kyle Parks, "Pa. Brewer to Buy Shut Stroh Plant," *St. Petersburg Times*, April 6, 1999, 1E.

Norbert-Bryson conversation Lew Bryson, "Yuengling: So Much Better Than It Was," *All About Beer*, January 25, 2016.

accounted for about ninety percent Lew Bryson, "That Yuengling Porter News," Seen Through a Glass, November 30, 2009, http://lewbryson.blogspot.com/2009/11/that-yuengling-porter-news.html (accessed June 27, 2016).

closing in on three million Bryson, "Yuengling: So Much Better Than It Was." Pennsylvania's three-tier distribution system may have helped Yuengling's rise by keeping out some competitors who could not find their ways into the state's distribution flow. This aid was a bit ironic, given that smaller breweries often complained about three-tier systems hampering their growth. Per Christopher Lawton, "Quirky Laws Give Yuengling Edge at Home," *Wall Street Journal*, March 23, 2004.

"[T]his medium-bodied beer" "Yuengling Oktoberfest Coming This Fall," Yuengling website, August 11, 2011, www.yuengling.com/news/31/oktoberfest/ (accessed June 27, 2016). *"Bursting with complex hop notes"* Yuengling website, www.yuengling.com/ipl (accessed June 27, 2016).

With this newfangled hybrid Joe Sixpack, "Sixpack of the Week: Yuengling IPL," JoeSix-Pack.net, November 10, 2011, www.joesixpack.net/2015/11/10/sixpack-of-the-week-yuengling-ipl/ (accessed June 27, 2016).

its biggest marketing push ever "Yuengling Launches Largest Campaign in Brewery's History With 'Respect. It's Earned,'" press release via BeerPulse.com, March 24, 2016, http://beerpulse.com/2016/03/yuengling-launches-largest-campaign-in-brewerys-history-4145/ (accessed June 27, 2016).

"As a matter of fact" Dan Adams, "Yuengling Tops Sam Adams Maker as Country's Top Craft Brewery," *Boston Globe*, April 3, 2015.

"I think the Brewers Association" Alistair Bland, "As Craft Beer Starts Gushing, Its Essence Gets Watered Down," NPR, May 9, 2014.

Some pointed out Libby Nelson, "How a Redefinition Made Yuengling the Biggest Craft Brewery in America," Vox.com, April 1, 2015, www.vox.com/2015/4/1/8326509/craft-beer-yuengling (accessed June 27, 2016).

a list of "domestic non-craft brewers" Charlotte Observer website, www.charlottebeer.com/wp-content/uploads/2012/12/Non-craft-brewers.jpg (accessed June 27, 2016). The list proved controversial, so much so that the Brewers Association removed it from its online archives almost immediately. Instead, less than a month after the list's release, the group released a more nuanced statement about craft vs. non-craft: www.brewersassociation.org/press-releases/craft-vs-crafty-a-statement-from-the-brewers-association/ (accessed June 27, 2016).

Newly popular styles; Dogfish Head, Shmaltz releases; GABF style categories Tom Acitelli, "The State of Craft Beer in 2016," Food Republic, January 4, 2016, www.foodrepublic.com/2016/01/04/the-state-of-craft-beer-in-2016/ (accessed June 29, 2016).

Hieronymus article, excerpt Hieronymus, "How Craft Became Craft."

"to change the way"; "whole different" Ibid. The Brewers Association itself emphasized that it was focusing more on ownership and size with its 2014 change. Per Chris Furnari, "Gatza: New Craft Brewer Definition Prioritizes Ownership, Size," March 4, 2014, www.brewbound.com/news/gatza-new-craft-brewer-definition-prioritizes-ownership-size (accessed June 29, 2016).

Conquering Europe

Watt, Dickie; BrewDog startup Jon Henley, "The Aggressive, Outrageous, Infuriating (and Ingenious) Rise of BrewDog," *The Guardian*, March 24, 2016, Life and Style; Kendall Jones, "An Audience With James Watt of Brewdog Brewery," Washington Beer Blog, June 23, 2014, www.washingtonbeerblog.com/audience-james-watt-of-brewdog-brewery/ (accessed July 1, 2016).

"bomb of flavor" Henley, "The Aggressive, Outrageous, Infuriating (and Ingenious) Rise of BrewDog."

Jackson encounter Ibid.

"It was hard" Ibid.

BrewDog releases, controversy Ibid.; "Speedball Beer Facing Sales Ban," BBC News, January 20, 2009; author's interview with Keith Greggor.

"scourge of illegal drugs" "Speedball Beer Facing Sales Ban."

"have surpassed themselves" Roger Protz, "BrewDog Go Bonkers," Beer-Pages, November 30, 2009, www.beer-pages.com/2009/11/brewdog-go-bonkers.html (accessed July 1, 2016).

"a manager at a bar in Northern England" Alex Andrews, "CAMRA, BrewDog, and the Craft Beer Conspiracy," Sabotage Times, September 12, 2012, http://sabotagetimes.com/life/camra-brewdog-and-the-craft-beer-conspiracy (accessed July 1, 2016).

horrible marketing-type suit people Martyn Cornell, "BrewDog Couldn't Be More Wrong in Wanting an 'Official' Definition of Craft Beer," Zythophile, October 21, 2013, https://zythophile.wordpress.com/2013/10/21/brewdog-couldnt-be-more-wrong-in-wanting-an-official-definition-of-craft-beer/ (accessed July 1, 2016).

Tax cut, growth in breweries Tom Acitelli, "The Brits Rip a Beer Tax Page From the Yanks," *All About Beer*, August 15, 2014.

twice ban BrewDog Henley, "The Aggressive, Outrageous, Infuriating (and Ingenious) Rise of BrewDog."

banned the sale; Nanny State release Ibid. It latter emerged that the industry watchdog received only one complaint about BrewDog's Tokyo Imperial Stout—from a Mr. James Watt. That suggested the controversy was more stunt than anything. Per Henley, "The Aggressive, Outrageous, Infuriating (and Ingenious) Rise of BrewDog."

Commercial success, fundraising Ibid.

An increasing number Jenn Garbee, "The American Craft Beer Scene Goes Global," *Los Angeles Times*, February 3, 2011; Alec Luhn, "Russia's Craft Beer Revolution," *The Guardian (U.K.)*, January 17, 2016.

"We really wanted … light years" Garbee, "The American Craft Beer Scene Goes Global."

number of breweries in Europe, leading nations Scheherazade Daneshkhu, "Microbreweries Shake Up Europe's Beer Market," November 28, 2014.

"Up until maybe"; fastest-growing segment Brad Japhe, "How America Is Shaking Up Centuries of German Beer Tradition," Eater.com, February 3, 2016, www.eater.com/drinks/2016/2/3/10904398/america-germany-craft-beer-traditions (accessed July 6, 2016).

"divided into several"; global leader Jackson, New World Guide to Beer, 37.

introduced the first India pale ale "An American Craft Brewer in Norway," CraftCans.com, July 14, 2012, www.craftcans.com/an-american-brewer-in-norwayq-and-a-with-mike-murphybrewmaster-at-lervig-aktiebryggeri (accessed July 8, 2016). Murphy eventually sold the Rome Brewing Co. and eventually moved on to work in the Danish and Norwegian brewing industries. More on the first Americans to start craft breweries in America per Evan Rail, "Europe's 'New' Americans," *Beer Advocate* magazine, July 2015, www.beeradvocate.com/mag/10718/europes-new-americans-beyond-stone-and-brooklyn-american-brewers-are-bringing-new-brews-to-the-old-world/(accessed July 8, 2016).

The author can personally attest, through travels, to the beer-averseness of Italy. Most of the nation's ballyhooed craft breweries are clustered in Italy's north or the Rome region. In the south, they are nearly nonexistent as are craft brands, even ones produced in Northern Italy.

"people literally laughed" Luhn, "Russia's Craft Beer Revolution."

"For the first two years" Paul McMorrow, "Kjetil Jikiun," *BeerAdvocate* magazine, December 2008.

As an example of the volume of European craft beer exports, Nogne O by 2008 was exporting most of its product. Per McMorrow, Kjetil Jikiun.

it would stop reviewing Luhn, "Russia's Craft Beer Revolution."

The Stockholm Affair

Export statistics Brewers Association numbers for 2014 and 2015, www.brewersassociation.org/press-releases/us-craft-beer-exports-top-116-million/ and www.brewersassa`ociation.org/press-releases/us-craft-beer-exports-near-100-million/ (accessed July 5, 2016).

New Carnegie startup Katarina Gustafsson, "A Brooklyn Beer With a Swedish Accent," Bloomberg, October 3, 2013; "Nya Carnegiebryggeriet Open for Beers-ness," Brooklyn Brewery website, May 2, 2014, http://brooklynbrewery.com/blog/international/nya-carnegiebryggeriet-open-for-beers-ness/ (accessed July 6, 2016).

biggest export market; the second-biggest Gustaffson, "A Brooklyn Beer With a Swedish Accent."

Urban Chestnut, including Kuplent career Author's interview with Florian Kuplent, July 8, 2016; "Our Brewmaster," Urban Chestnut website, http://urbanchestnut.com/our-brewmaster/ (accessed July 7, 2016); Evan S. Benn, "Urban Chestnut's Second Location Will Be St. Louis' Largest Craft Brewery," *St. Louis Post-Dispatch*, April 15, 2013.

2012, 2013 production levels E.B. Solomont, "Urban Chestnut to Expand With $10 Million Brewery," *St. Louis Business Journal*, April 16, 2013.

Bavarian brewery launch, beers, export, import Ian Froeb, "Urban Chestnut Begins Brewing in Bavaria," *St. Louis Post-Dispatch*, June 3, 2015; Lisa Brown, "St. Louis Craft Brewer Urban Chestnut Opening Brewery in Germany," *St. Louis Post-Dispatch*, January 9, 2015; Urban Chestnut website, "Urban Chestnut's Hallertauer Brewery Brews First Batches of Bier," http://urbanchestnut.com/press-release-urban-chestnuts-hallertauer-brewery-brews-first-batches-of-bier/ (accessed July 7, 2016).

"It does take…" Froeb, "Urban Chestnut Begins Brewing in Bavaria."

Stone opening Email exchange with Stone representative, June 2016; Neal Ungerleider, "How This Hopped-Up Brewery Is Bringing American Craft Beer to Germany," *Fast Company*, March 25, 2016; Andrew Parks, "American Craft Beer Plans Its German Invasion," *Conde Nast Traveler*, February 5, 2016.

Koch quotations, crushing a palette Ibid.

barely averaged Alexandra Steigrad, "Ratings in for Esquire Network Launch," *Women's Wear Daily*, December 31, 2013. Interestingly, Esquire's viewership would not crest five hundred thousand viewers on average until October 2015, when it aired a Back to the Future marathon. Per Daniel Holloway, "'Back to the Future' Marathon Lifts Esquire Network to Best Ratings Ever," The Wrap, October 22, 2015.

Episodes of the show are available for purchase through YouTube.

"so casual and informational" Carles, "The Modern Male Crisis of Esquire Network," Grantland, October 16, 2013, http://grantland.com/hollywood-prospectus/the-modern-male-crisis-of-esquire-network/ (accessed July 12, 2016).

Canal Winchester plans J.D. Malone, "BrewDog Has Big Plans for Canal Winchester Brewery," *The Columbus Dispatch*, March 15, 2016; "Dog Bless America," Brew Dog website, www.brewdog.com/lowdown/blog/dog-bless-america (accessed July 12, 2016).

"the land that helped" Ibid.

Lessons from Heraclitus

Magee blog post excerpts, feelings about Heineken "The Future Will Not Be Like the Past," Fermenting Ideas of Order (Lagunitas Tumblr), http://lagunitast.tumblr.com/post/128642135601/the-future-will-not-be-like-the-past (accessed July 14, 2016).

Lagunitas expansion, sales volume, capacity Tom Acitelli, "A Guide to Lagunitas, America's Fastest-Growing Craft Brewery," FoodRepublic.com, July 23, 2015, www.foodrepublic.com/2015/07/23/your-guide-to-lagunitas-6-beers-showcasing-the-best-of-americas-fastest-growing-craft-brewery/ (accessed July 14, 2016); "Heineken Enters Into Partnership With Leading U.S. Craft Brewer Lagunitas," HeinekenUSA.com, September 8, 2015, http://heinekenusa.com/2015/09/heineken-enters-into-partnership-with-leading-u-s-craft-brewer-lagunitas/ (accessed July 14, 2016).

Heineken size, reach Heineken, "2016 Fact Sheet: Company Highlights," TheHeinekenCompany.com

rebuffed a takeover bid Patricia Sellers, "The Secretive Heir to the Heineken Dynasty," *Fortune*, September 14, 2016. De Carvalho-Heineken controls the company through control of a holding firm that in turn owns most of Heineken.

Watt tweet Twitter, https://twitter.com/brewdogjames/status/641533939094540288 (accessed July 18, 2016).

some questioned how fresh Jeff Alworth, "We Need to Dial It Back a Notch," *All About Beer*, September 9, 2015, http://allaboutbeer.com/we-need-to-dial-it-back-a-notch/ (accessed July 18, 2016).

"a spectacular Trump-like masterpiece" Ibid.

"There are two ways" Chris Morris, "Shakeup at Craft Beer Giant Stone Brewing," *Forbes*, September 11, 2015, http://fortune.com/2015/09/11/stone-brewing-greg-koch-resign/ (accessed July 18, 2016).

Big Beer Feasts

Goose Island growth, challenges Emily Bryson York and Josh Noel, "Goose Island Sold to Anheuser Busch for $38.8 million," *Chicago Tribune*, March 28, 2011; David Kesmodel, "Behind Anheuser's Goose Island Beer Acquisition," *Wall Street Journal*, March 28, 2011. Goose Island contracted its brewing to the Redhook brewery in Portsmouth, New Hampshire.

"Good beer doesn't..." Don Russell (writing as Joe Sixpack), "Craft Brewers Bothered by Anheuser-Busch Invasion," *Philadelphia Daily News*, June 16, 2006, 61.

The buyer promised York and Noel, "Goose Island Sold to Anheuser Busch for $38.8 Million."

"the honk heard"; reaction anecdotes Paul Schneider, "The Honk Heard Round the World: Goose Island One Year After the Sale," Chicagoist, April 16, 2012, http://chicagoist.com/2012/04/16/the_honk_heard_round_the_world_goos.php (accessed July 20 2016).

one hundred, twenty-seven thousand barrels; majority . . . in Illinois Kesmodel, "Behind Anheuser's Goose Island Beer Acquisition."

"We are market share" Russell, "Craft Brewers Bothered by Anheuser-Busch Invasion."

annual sales doubling Chris Crowell, "Craft Beer Sales to Triple Within 10-Year Period, Says Research Group," Craft Brewing Business, January 24, 2013, www.craftbrewingbusiness.com/news/craft-beer-sales-to-triple-within-10-year-period-says-one-research-group/ (accessed July 20, 2016).

its supposed appeal "Anheuser-Busch to Stop Making Spykes," Associated Press, May 17, 2007.

Goose Island changes Josh Noel, "John Hall to Leave Goose Island as CEO," *Chicago Tribune*, November 16, 2012.

Another change involved Greg Hall, John Hall's son and Goose Island's brewmaster. The younger Hall left the brewery after the Anheuser-Busch sale and started his own cidery in Michigan called Virtue Cider. The cider proved too popular for Greg Hall to keep up with demand—so he sold a controlling interest to Anheuser-Busch. Per Jason Notte, "The Deal That Shook Craft Beer Five Years Ago Is Still Reverberating," Market Watch, April 21, 2016.

its first advertising campaign ever E.J. Schultz, "A-B InBev Proves a Good Home for Goose Island as Big Brewer Helps Cult Craft Rise Brand Readies First Ad Campaign After Three Successful Years Under Wing of Beer Giant," *Advertising Age*, December 16, 2013.

Brewpub sale, closing Ashok Selvam, "Goose Island Finally Relents, Sells Clybourn Brewpub to A-B InBev," Eater Chicago, February 19, 2016, http://chicago.eater.com/2016/2/19/11065454/goose-island-brewpub-sells-annheuser-inbev (accessed July 20, 2016).

Increased sixty-two percent Schultz, "A-B InBev Proves a Good Home for Goose Island as Big Brewer Helps Cult Craft Rise Brand Readies First Ad Campaign After Three Successful Years Under Wing of Beer Giant."

Mergers-and-acquisitions record Manuel Baigorri, "2015 Was Best-Ever Year for M&A; This Year Looks Good Too," Bloomberg News, January 5, 2016.

Acquisitions Acitelli, "The State of Craft Beer in 2016."

would own eight craft breweries Josh Noel, "Anheuser-Busch Buys Devils Backbone, Its 8th Craft Brewery," *Chicago Tribune*, April 13, 2016.

Lagunitas' valuation Peter Frost, "Lagunitas Sells 50 Percent Stake to Heineken," *Crain's Chicago Business*, September 8, 2015.

for twenty-four million dollars Ashlee Kieler, "Here Are the 8 U.S. Craft Breweries Bought By Anheuser-Busch Since 2011," Consumerist, April 13, 2016, https://consumerist.com/2016/04/13/here-are-the-8-u-s-craft-brewers-bought-by-anheuser-busch-since-2011/ (accessed July 22, 2016).

to have cost it thirty-five million Tripp Mickle, "MillerCoors Acquires Craft Brewer Saint Archer," *Wall Street Journal*, September 10, 2015.

Billion-Dollar Worries

he later launched a homebrewing store, Enter Constellation Brands Jennifer Kaplan, "Constellation to Buy Ballast Point Brewing for $1 Billion," Bloomberg, November 16, 2015; Ballast Point website, "How It Began," www.ballastpoint.com/how-it-began/ (accessed July 22, 2016).

Constellation deals Acitelli, *American Wine*, 236; Kaplan, "Constellation to Buy Ballast Point Brewing for $1 Billion."

"We have no interest" Ibid.

Constellation was originally in negotiations with Lagunitas for its first foray into craft beer. Those negotiations fell through amid disagreement over who would control the smaller company post-deal.

Ballast Point expansion Rachel Arthur, "Constellation Brands Outlines Plans for Ballast Point and Overall Beer Business," Beverage Daily, April 7, 2016.

sixteen-billion-dollar takeover Clementine Fletcher and Leslie Patton, "Suntory to Buy Beam in $16 Billion Deal for U.S. Brand," Bloomberg News, January 14, 2014.

biggest craft breweries According to the Brewers Association, the fiftieth biggest craft brewery in 2015 was Revolution Brewing out of Chicago, which was on pace after 2014 to produce three hundred thousand barrels annually. Therefore, the biggest craft breweries were those producing at least a few hundred thousand barrels annually. Per Revolution website, https://revbrew.com/whats-new/detail/revolution-brewing-expands-production-brewery-triples-capacity (accessed July 25, 2016).

produced little surprise; "What he has done" Brendan Coffey, "Sam Adams Creator Becomes Billionaire as Craft Beer Rises," Bloomberg News, September 9, 2013.

"Even though"; "Where else do you see" Brendan Coffey, "Sierra Nevada Founder Grossman Becomes Billionaire on Pale Ales," Bloomberg News, January 20, 2015.

Breweries and private equity deals Jason Notte, "Craft Beer Brewers Learn to Live With, and Love, Private Equity," MarketWatch, March 1, 2016, www.marketwatch.com/story/craft-beer-brewers-learn-to-live-with-and-love-private-equity-2016-03-01 (accessed July 26, 2016).

"Never in my wildest dreams" Jon Chesto, "Firm Joins With Iconic Brewer to Become a Big Player in Craft Beer Business," *Boston Globe*, April 28, 2016.

Victory, Southern Tier partnership Tom Rotunno, "Victory and Southern Tier Brewing Form Alliance," CNBC.com, February 16, 2016, www.cnbc.com/2016/02/16/victory-and-southern-tier-brewing-form-alliance-.html (accessed July 26, 2016).

Anheuser-Busch InBev toyed with James L. Rosica, "Anheuser-Busch Interested in Buying Tampa's Cigar City Brewing," *Tampa Bay Times*, February 8, 2015.

Oskar Blues production Chesto, "Firm Joins With Iconic Brewer to Become a Big Player in Craft Beer Business."

to every state "Oskar Blues Brewery Announces Expansion Into Nine International Markets," *All About Beer* [press release], October 11, 2016.

"liquidity event" Tara Nurin, "The Second Wave Sell-Off: Private Equity in the Craft Beer Market Spells Upheaval Within a Decade," *Forbes*, March 30, 2016.

True Craft "Stone & Greg Koch Announce 'True Craft' As the Answer to Big Beer," BeerAdvocate, May 1, 2016, www.beeradvocate.com/community/threads/stone-greg-koch-announce-true-craft-as-the-answer-to-big-beer.412019/ (accessed July 29, 2016).

"give craft brewers" Mike Snider, "Stone Brewing Co-Founder Announces Craft Beer Angel Investor," *USA Today*, May 2, 2016.

Nearly ninety million Chris Furnari, "SEC Filing Indicates $90 Million VMG Investment in Stone Brewing," Brewbound, July 14, 2016, www.brewbound.com/news/sec-filing-indicates-90-million-vmg-investment-stone-brewing (accessed December 5, 2016).

Koch op-ed Greg Koch, "Stone Brewing Just Says No to 'Big Beer,'" *San Diego Union-Tribune*, February 13, 2016.

"even more power" Bob Pease, "A Big Merger May Flatten America's Beer Market," *New York Times*, June 2, 2016.

AB InBev distribution deals, Justice Department probe, resolution Diane Bartz, "U.S. Probes Allegations AB InBev Seeking to Curbed Craft Beer Distribution," Reuters, October 12, 2015; Tripp Mickle, "Craft Brewers Take Issue With AB InBev Distribution Plan," *Wall Street Journal*, December 7, 2015; U.S. Justice Department release on conditional approval, July 20, 2016, www.justice.gov/opa/pr/justice-department-requires-anheuser-busch-inbev-divest-stake-millercoors-and-alter-beer (accessed July 28, 2016).

would be so small Tripp Mickle and Brent Kendall, "Justice Department Clears AB InBev's Takeover of SABMiller," *Wall Street Journal*, July 2016. The sale of the MillerCoors stake, to Molson Coors, was Anheuser Busch InBev's idea. The sale would instantly make Molson Coors the nation's second-biggest brewer. The AB InBev-SABMiller deal closed in early October 2016.

"In most markets" Steve Hindy, "Don't Let Big Brewers Win Beer Wars," CNN.com, December 12, 2012.

"The Future Will Not Be Like the Past"

The full Super Bowl commercial is widely available on YouTube. The author also saw it during the game.

most watched television show Kevin Patra, "Super Bowl XLIX Is Most-Watched Show in U.S. History," NFL.com, February 2, 2015, www.nfl.com/news/story/0ap3000000467823/article/super-bowl-xlix-is-mostwatched-show-in-us-history (accessed July 29, 2016).

"overwrought pretentiousness" E.J. Schultz, "Bud Is Proudly 'Macro' Amid Micro-Brews in Swagger-Filled Super Bowl Ad," AdAge.com, February 1, 2015, http://adage.com/article/special-report-super-bowl/bud-proudly-macro-swagger-filled-super-bowl-ad/296932/ (accessed July 29, 2016).

"The whole ad" Josh Noel, "Bell's Pumpkin Peach Ale a '(Screw) You' to Anheuser-Busch Ad," *Chicago Tribune*, April 16, 2015. The newspaper substituted "(screw)" for Bell's obvious use of the f-word.

"somewhat odd approach" Jordan Weissmann, "Budweiser's Awful Super Bowl Ad Is a Perfect Illustration of Why Young People Don't Drink It," Slate, February 2, 2016.

"I find it kind of incredible" Josh Noel, "Craft Brewery Co-Founder Not Happy With Super Bowl Ad Snark," *Chicago Tribune*, February 2, 2015.

Yuengling expansion, impact Gary Dzen, "Yuengling Makes Return to a Thirsty Boston Market," *Boston Globe*, April 2, 2014.

Pay-to-play, fine Dan Adams, "State Regulators Investigating Somerville Brewery's Pay-to-Play Allegations," Boston Globe, October 14, 2015; Dan Adams, "Beer Distributor to Pay $2.6 Million Fine in Pay-to-Play Case," *Boston Globe*, March 2, 2016.

Sierra Nevada-Lagunitas dispute Jonathan Kauffman and Steve Rubenstein, "Beer Lovers Torpedo Lagunitas Lawsuit Against Sierra Nevada," SFGate.com, January 14, 2015, www.sfgate.com/news/article/Beer-lovers-torpedo-Lagunitas-IPA-lawsuit-6015913. php (accessed August 1, 2016).

"I went home feeling" Ibid.

Trademark disputes; SweetWater-Lagunitas dispute Alistair Bland, "Craft Brewers Are Running Out of Names and Into Legal Spats," NPR, January 5, 2015.

Tax break background, dispute, compromise Jordan Weissmann, "Why Tax Breaks for Craft Brewers Make No Sense," *The Atlantic*, March 29, 2013; "Craft Beverage Modernization and Tax Reform Act Closes In on 275 Co-Sponsors," Brewers Association website, July 18, 2015, www.brewersassociation.org/current-issues/craft-beverage-modernization-and-tax-reform-act-closes-in-on-275-co-sponsors/ (accessed August 1, 2015); "And Then There Was One—Tax Bill," ProBrewer.com, June 12, 2015, www.probrewer.com/and-then-there-was-one-tax-bill/ (accessed August 1, 2016). The legislation had yet to pass as of February 2017.

"further proliferation" Chris Furnari, "Stone Brewing Restructuring, Laying Off Employees," Brewbound, October 13, 2016, www.brewbound.com/news/stone-brewing-restructur-ing-lays-off-employees. At least one laid-off employee blamed the turn of events on Stone's expansion, including into Berlin. Per Furnari.

"lost his edge"; "mediocre" Crouch, "Wasted."

thoroughly annoyed Author's off-the-record interview with the principal owner of a major craft brewery.

top-selling craft beer style Bart Watson, "Beer Styles: How Preferences Vary By State," Brewers Association website, December 9, 2015, www.brewersassociation.org/insights/beer-styles-by-state/ (accessed August 2, 2016).

Daniel Bradford sold "Rice Named President and Publisher of All About Beer Magazine and World Beer Festivals," *All About Beer* website, September 16, 2014, http://allabout-beer.com/news/rice-named-president-publisher-beer-magazine-world-beer-festivals/ (accessed August 2, 2016).

Charlie Papazian stepped down Tom Acitelli, "Charlie Papazian Discovers Homebrewing and the Rest Is Our History," *All About Beer* website, January 14, 2016, http://all-aboutbeer.com/charlie-papazian-discovers-homebrewing/ (accessed August 2, 2016).

Greg Koch moved on Chris Morris, "Shakeup at Craft Beer Giant Stone Brewing," *Fortune*, September 11, 2015.

Steve Dresler exit "Sierra Nevada Brewmaster Steve Dresler Announces Retirement," BeerAdvocate.com, July 8, 2016, www.beeradvocate.com/community/threads/sierra-nevada%E2%80%99s-brewmaster-steve-dresler-announces-retirement.433413/ (accessed August 2, 2016).

Mitch Steele exit "Stone Brewmaster to Start New Brewery," All About Beer website, June 14, 2016, http://allaboutbeer.com/news/brewmaster-mitch-steele-leaves-stone/ (accessed August 2, 2016).

stepped down as part of a stake sale Jack Newsham, "Harpoon Brewery to Become Employee Owned," *Boston Globe*, July 10, 2014.

Doyle fund, Abita deal Dan Adams, "Former Harpoon CEO Launches New Craft Beer Venture," Boston Globe, April 10, 2015. David Blossman, an early Abita investor, had run the brewery since 1996. Per Abita's website, https://abita.com/news/abita_ in_the_news/amber-dreams (accessed August 2, 2016).

"To not die" Andy Crouch, "Wasted: How the Craft-Beer Movement Abandoned Jim Koch," *Boston Magazine*, January 2015.

Magee excerpt, quotation Magee, "The Future Will Not Be Like the Past."

Epilogue

Statuses taken from brewery websites and press releases, unless otherwise indicated below.

initially scaling back distribution "Thanks for Understanding," an open letter on the Dogfish Head website, accessed August 31, 2012, www.dogfish.com/community /blogfish/ members/sam/thanks-for-understanding.htm.

"I'm still here" J. Koch.

Vanberg & DeWulf sale "Total Beverage Solution Acquires Rights to Vanberg & DeWulf Portfolio," *Brewbound* (press release), March 3, 2014.

Vijay Mallya warrant Amy Kazmin, "Indian Court Issues Arrest Warrant for Vijay Mallya," *Financial Times*, April 18, 2016.

McAuliffe earnings, New Albion trademark Devin Leonard, "Jack McAuliffe, Father of American Craft Brew, Brings Back New Albion Ale," *Bloomberg*, March 29, 2013.

Owades funeral "Visionary Brewer Joe Owades Dies at 86," *Modern Brewery Age*, December 26, 2005.

"Rapidly declining sales" Jay Brooks, "Gambrinus Discontinues Pete's Wicked Ales," *Brookston Beer Bulletin*, February 1, 2011, http://brookstonbeerbulletin.com/gambrinus-discontinues-petes-wicked-ales/.

BIBLIOGRAPHY

The following is not intended to be a complete bibliography. It instead contains books and long articles related to craft beer that might be of interest to the reader, including ones that the author consulted for this book.

Barr, Andrew. *Drink: A Social History of America*. New York: Carroll & Graf, 1999. Baum, Dan. *Citizen Coors: An American Dynasty*. New York: William Morrow, 2000. *The Beer Guide*. Edited by Josh Oakes. Fort Worth: Savory House Press, 2006.

Bernstein, Joshua M. *Brewed Awakening: Behind the Beers and Brewers Leading the World's Craft Brewing Revolution*. New York: Sterling Epicure, 2011.

Bilger, Burkhard. "A Better Brew." *New Yorker*, November 24, 2008, 88.

Burch, Byron. *Brewing Quality Beers: The Home Brewer's Essential Guidebook*. Fulton, CA: Joby Books, 1986.

———. *Brewing Quality Beers: The Home Brewer's Essential Guidebook*. 2nd edition. Fulton, CA: Joby Books, 1993.

Bryson, Lew. *New York Breweries*. Mechanicsburg, PA: Stackpole Books, 2003.

Burton, Rob. *Hops and Dreams: The Story of Sierra Nevada Brewing Company*. Chico, CA: Stansbury Publishing, 2010.

Calagione, Sam. *Brewing Up a Business: Adventures in Beer from the Founder of Dogfish Head Craft Brewery*, 2nd edition. Hoboken, NJ: Wiley, 2011.

Campbell, Seamus, and Robin Goldstein. *The Beer Trials: The Essential Guide to the World's Most Popular Beers*. New York: Fearless Critic Media, 2010.

Cowan, Jeremy, with James Sullivan. *Craft Beer Bar Mitzvah: How It Took 13 Years, Extreme Jewish Brewing, and Circus Sideshow Freaks to Make Shmaltz Brewing Company an International Success*. San Francisco: Malt Shop Publishing, 2010.

Curtis, Wayne. *And a Bottle of Rum: A History of the New World in Ten Cocktails*. New York: Crown Publishers, 2006.

Daniels, Ray. *Designing Great Beers: The Ultimate Guide to Brewing Classic Beer Styles*. Boulder, CO: Brewers Association, 1996.

Eckhardt, Fred. *A Treatise on Lager Beers: A Handbook for Americans and Canadians on Lager Beer*. Portland, OR: Hobby Winemaker, 1970.

Erickson, Jack. *Star Spangled Beer: A Guide to America's New Microbreweries and Brewpubs*. Reston, VA: Red Brick Press, 1987.

———. *Great Cooking with Beer*. Reston, VA: Red Brick Press, 1989.

———. *California Brewin': The Exciting Story of California's Microbrewery Revolution.* Reston, VA: Red Brick Press, 1993.

Grossman, Ken. *Beyond the Pale: The Story of Sierra Nevada Brewing Co.* Hoboken, NJ: Wiley, unpublished first part of manuscript (scheduled publication: April 2013).

Heat-Moon, William Least. "A Glass of Handmade." *Atlantic Monthly*, November 1987.

Hernon, Peter, and Terry Ganey. *Under the Influence: The Unauthorized Story of the Anheuser-Busch Dynasty.* New York: Simon & Schuster, 1991.

Hieronymus, Stan. *Brew Like a Monk: Trappist, Abbey, and Strong Belgian Ales and How to Brew Them.* Boulder, CO: Brewers Publications, 2005.

Hillman, Howard. *The Gourmet Guide to Beer.* New York: Facts on File Publications, 1987.

Hindy, Steve, and Tom Potter. *Beer School: Bottling Success at the Brooklyn Brewery.* Hoboken, NJ: Wiley, 2005.

Holland, Lee W. "The Evolution of the Brewers Association of America," pamphlet, Colorado: Brewers Association of America, 1994.

Jackson, Michael. *The English Pub.* New York: HarperCollins, 1987.

———. *The World Guide to Beer: The Brewing Styles, The Brands, The Countries.* Englewood Cliffs, NJ: Prentice Hall, 1977.

———. *The New World Guide to Beer.* Philadelphia: Running Press, 1988.

———. *Great Beers of Belgium.* 4th edition. London: Prion, 2001.

Koch, Greg, and Steve Wagner with Randy Clemens. *The Craft of Stone Brewing Co.: Liquid Lore, Epic Recipes, and Unabashed Arrogance.* Berkeley, CA: Ten Speed Press, 2011.

Krebs, Peter, *Redhook: A Microbrew Success Story.* New York: Four Walls Eight Windows: 1998.

Lewis, Michael L., and Tom W. Young. *Brewing.* New York: Springer-Verlag, 2001. Line, Dave. *The Big Book of Brewing.* Andover, MA: Amateur Winemaker, 1974.

MacIntosh, Julie. *Dethroning the King: The Hostile Takeover of Anheuser-Busch, an American Icon.* Hoboken, NJ: Wiley, 2011.

Magee, Tony. *So You Want to Start a Brewery?: The Lagunitas Story.* Chicago, IL: Chicago Review Press, 2014.

Mosher, Randy. *Radical Brewing: Recipes, Tales and World-Altering Meditations in a Glass.* Boulder, CO: Brewers Publications, 2004.

———. *Tasting Beer: An Insider's Guide to the World's Greatest Drink.* North Adams, MA: Storey Publishing, 2009.

Ogle, Maureen. *Ambitious Brew: The Story of American Beer.* Orlando, FL: Harcourt, 2006.

Oliver, Garrett. *The Brewmaster's Table: Discovering the Pleasures of Real Beer with Real Food.* New York: HarperCollins, 2003.

Owens, Bill. *How to Build a Small Brewery: Draft Beer in Ten Days.* 3rd edition. Hayward, CA: Bill Owens, 1992.

The Oxford Companion to Beer. Edited by Garrett Oliver. New York: Oxford University Press, 2012.

Papazian, Charlie. *The New Complete Joy of Homebrewing.* 2nd edition. New York: Avon, 1991.

Petrini, Carlo. *Slow Food: The Case for Taste.* New York: Columbia University Press, 2001.

———. *Slow Food Nation: Why Our Food Should Be Good, Clean and Fair.* New York: Rizzoli Ex Libris, 2007.

Sismondo, Christine. *America Walks Into a Bar: A Spirited History of Taverns and Saloons, Speakeasies and Grog Shops.* New York: Oxford University Press, 2011.

Slosberg, Pete. *Beer for Pete's Sake: The Wicked Adventures of a Brewing Maverick.* Boulder, CO: Brewers Publications, 1998.

Smith, Gregg. *Beer in America: The Early Years—1587-1840: Beer's Role in the Settling of America and the Birth of a Nation.* Boulder, CO: Brewers Publication, 1998.

Steele, Mitch. *Brewing Techniques, Recipes and the Evolution of India Pale Ale.* Boulder, CO: Brewers Publications, 2012.

Van Munching, Philip. *Beer Blast: The Inside Story of the Brewing Industry's Bizarre Battles for Your Money.* New York: Times Business, 1997.

Waters, Alice. *The Art of Simple Food: Notes, Lessons, and Recipes from a Delicious Revolution.* New York: Clarkson Potter, 2007.

Yaeger, Brian. *Red, White and Brew: An American Beer Odyssey.* New York: St. Martin's Griffin, 2008.

INDEX

Italicized page references indicate illustrations and footnotes with "n" following the page number.